High Density Living

'Logical urban development can take place only when those responsible for that development are urban-oriented in their philosophy, have a deep and positive attitude toward urban society, and are willing to mould their thinking toward shaping the urban environment to satisfy the needs and desires of an urban society. Cities can be livable; they can be attractive; they can be rebuilt to achieve these desirable goals—and at the same time, they can satisfactorily house many more people than they do now. To achieve this, more public officials, civic leaders and developers, must take a different attitude toward the city, toward housing, toward space, and toward people.'

J. Marshall Miller

High Density Living

Rolf Jensen

Frederick A Praeger
Publishers
New York · Washington

First published 1966

BOOKS THAT MATTER

Published in the United States of America in 1966
by Frederick A. Praeger, Inc., Publishers
111 Fourth Avenue, New York 3, N.Y.

Library of Congress Catalog Card Number: 66 – 12527

Acknowledgements

My grateful thanks are due to:

The Director of Building Research of the Department of Scientific and Industrial Research, Garston, Watford, for permission to quote from the following Crown Copyright Publications:
Craig, C. N.: 'Factors Affecting Economy in Multi-storey Flat Design,' *RIBA Journal*, April and May 1956.
Parkin and Stacy: 'Research on Sound Insulation in Houses and Flats,' *RIBA Journal,* July 1954.
Stone, P. A.: 'Urban Development and Cost Prediction,' *RICS Journal*, October 1959 and January 1960.
Stone, P. A.: 'Economics of Housing and Urban Development,' *The Journa of the Royal Statistical Society,* 1959. Stevens, P. H. M.: 'Densities in Housing Areas,' *HMSO.*

The Chief Architect to the Ministry of Housing and Local Government, London, for permission to refer to the following Crown Copyright Publications:
'Flats and Houses 1958.'
'The Housing Manual 1944.'
'The Housing Manual 1949.'
'The Dudley Report.'
Reiners, W. J.: 'Tender Prices of Flats,' *RICS Journal.*
'Redevelopment of Central Areas.'
'The Density of Residential Areas.'
Lichfield, N.: 'Net Density Cost and Value,' *RICS Journal,* September 1960.

The Architect to the Council, London County Council, for permission to quote from the Publication 'The Planning of a New Town.'

I am also greatly indebted to those architects whose buildings are here illustrated for their kindness and help in supplying photographs, drawings and technical data and for their permission to reproduce these.

Designer

Neville Vine

Printed in Great Britain by The Whitefriars Press Ltd
London and Tonbridge

Bound by The Dorstel Press Ltd
London and Harlow

Contents

List of Tables and Diagrams

Preface

There is no greater or more serious problem confronting the world, and more especially the industrialized, urbanized countries today, than that of how best to deal with the so-called population explosion in a way that will enable people to live in a humane, civilized fashion free from the burdens of modern urban life, where they can both work and play in an equally beneficial environment. This need is no less one of the basic requirements of society today than at any other time in the world's history, but meeting it becomes immensely more difficult. The more industrially progressive and highly organized the community, the more difficult it is; and while the problem of planning for the urban community is one with regional aspects, there are astonishingly close similarities between the tasks confronting the major cities in various parts of the world today, in spite of superficially varying local conditions.

It is because it is felt now, in the light of changes which are taking place, that there is an international basis of common interest in much of the material with which this book attempts to deal, that, contrary to an earlier intention, it is being compiled in a way that makes it more generally applicable, and includes relevant examples from a great many countries.

When the studies on which this book is based were first begun, shortly after the end of the Second World War and in the midst of the practical problem of designing, building and managing homes to meet the appalling post-war shortages in metropolitan London, it was with the object of trying to suggest a solution to the impasse which had then developed in England. Employment prospects in London were increasing rather than decreasing, and the population of London, instead of being diminished by the new towns, was growing steadily. The old problem of journeying to and from work was becoming more acute, and the long lists of unsatisfied bombed-out families and others waiting for housing were growing in an atmosphere of helplessness.

This was due partly to shortages of materials and to technical problems, but much more to the fact that for all too long no government was prepared to admit that decentralization was unworkable. As a first step towards the realization of the need for a practical alternative, the pathetic attempts to apply a garden-city solution to this problem of population expansion on a national scale are well known; and the reluctance to abandon this policy, even when it was manifest that it could no longer be expected to work in the light of events, was unfortunate.

Be that as it may, world opinion is now showing a clear trend in favour of a considerable programme of urban renewal and high urban densities, and the problem now is to ensure that this work is undertaken in the soundest possible way, so as to constitute a real and permanent solution to urban growth and not a first stage in the creation of the slums of the future.

An examination of the impact of this problem, and of programmes of urban renewal in many parts of the world, has clearly shown that the principles which can be applied in the solution are in many cases of global validity.

Hence the decision to extend the scope of this work. With the increasing attention that is being paid to high-density aspects of urb development, schemes for multi-storey flats a proceeding apace. There is no complet comprehensive published work covering t whole field and future potential, although m limited aspects have been dealt with.

This book is not concerned simply with bui ing by government or local government agenci nor solely with one particular type of devel ment—for example, the point block; nor w pictorial data alone, or work in a single count but with all of these and with other equally v subjects, including town-planning conside tions, economics, constructional probler sociological factors, and home ownership, name but a few. It is clear that it is lack of t comprehensiveness which has permitted, regr tably, the piecemeal criticism from the gard city adherents and others to continue.

Although, even as recently as five years a important and valuable work had been done the high-density housing field, more especia in Stockholm, London, and New York, it was s to a very considerable extent passing throug pioneering phase, and a vital battle had still be won. In some parts of the world this is s true today, although to a far more limited exte as can be judged through the wide selection work that is illustrated in this book.

The author was involved in a major *cau célèbre* in trying to gain acceptance of the fi tower blocks in the United Kingdom to exce 100ft in height, with densities for the first ti aimed at a level well above the highest dens zoning postulated by Sir Patrick Abercrom in his proposals. In order to obtain more e nomical use of staircases and lifts, in one the schemes as many as six or eight fl were planned on each typical floor level, w smoke-extract ducts alongside central acc corridors. Open-plan arrangements ins the individual dwellings were also propos to eliminate wasteful internal circulation are as were internal bathrooms and toilets w natural ventilation through shunt flue type du but without mechanical plant. Buildings up to fifteen or twenty storeys in height we to have a single internal staircase, and radi systems of construction involving extensive u of prefabrication in reinforced concrete hand by means of the tower crane were to be us All these techniques were, at that time, entir unknown outside Scandinavia and one or t other Continental countries.

Site coverage by buildings was reduced such a way that seven-eighths of the total a used for the development was available garden and amenity purposes, and only o tenth of the internal floor area represent essential circulation space.

All these advantages, it was shown, were co sistent with excellent planning and structu standards, and had a level of amenity far abo that normally experienced in residential areas our cities. Furthermore, the principles put f ward demonstrated, in what appeared to be t only really practical way, the technique of how reduce or entirely eliminate urban populati overspills and how to facilitate slum-clearar schemes. They also illustrated how to reacco modate people in areas to which they we accustomed and which they preferred, witho all the enormous consequential problems having to move their places of employment a set up anew the whole panoply of local gove

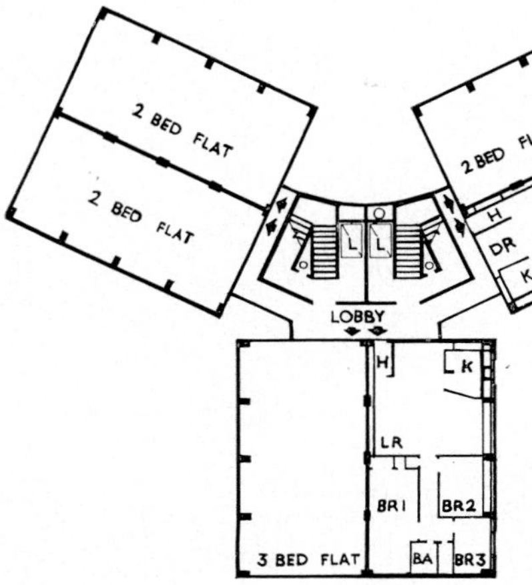

Typical floor plan

roup of fifteen-storey tower blocks designed a West London site, as a part of an urban ewal scheme

‹ins Heights, London, England
hitect: R. Jensen

ment and essential services needed to re-create anything like a balanced community somewhere 'out in the blue'. When all these factors were taken into account, it could be shown that the central area redevelopment was by far the more economical of the various alternatives which had been tried.

Unfortunately, these ideas were largely unacceptable at that stage and met with resistance at both government and local government level, not only as housing, but as town planning proposals. Today, a great many of the principles and proposals put forward are beginning to receive, or have already received, acceptance, albeit in some cases with marked reluctance.

That all this can have happened was possible not only because of the widespread ignorance of the real facts relating to this type of housing and to the town-planning issues and principles involved, but was also due to a considerable lack of knowledge and understanding of the specialized problems associated with planning and the design of housing of this type.

Much of this ignorance still remains today, although there are some indications of an awakening; and it seems even more important that a detailed examination be made now that there is some considerable prospect of an increasing volume of high-density housing in the form of flats and apartments getting under way in many countries. This would ensure that everyone who may be confronted with these problems would have the benefit of the greatest possible range of relevant advice and experience to ensure that such work will form a permanent part in any country's social equipment.

For every one of the schemes which is illustrated in this book, and which has been selected because of its special merits and importance, there are fifty other schemes of very variable quality and, in some cases, some that are outstandingly bad. It is to be hoped, therefore, that this book will achieve a valuable purpose in bringing together necessary data—a task which has taken the best part of ten years to fulfil.

The compilation of technical data from many different parts of the world, the conversion from one set of units of measurement or value to another, and the translation of a great deal of this, have posed considerable practical problems and difficulties. It is hoped, nevertheless, that the data and information given is in all cases accurate and reliable; but some indulgence in these matters, particularly from the authors of the schemes which are illustrated, may, it is hoped, be justified. It is believed that the conclusions which have been drawn from this careful analysis and collation, particularly in the arguments relating to density and cost, are irrefutable and will stand the test of time in a subject which has been one particularly prone to misrepresentation and a great deal of woeful misunderstanding. This cannot be too strongly and emphatically stated.

Of such fallacies none could be more misleading than the suggestion that higher densities necessarily imply slums. The slums of the past were due entirely to bad design, bad planning, bad structural standards, lack of maintenance, and unsatisfactory occupancy—factors which would apply just as readily and as certainly in moderate or low densities, and which are likely in due course to convert many of the present suburban developments to slum areas.

These things have little or nothing in common with the kind of development and planning envisaged in this book. High densities as such are quite certainly not likely alone to produce slum conditions, but rather, in fact, where coupled with good planning and good design, are likely to have quite the reverse effect.

In housing there is no critical mass which, as in the case of atomic physics, is known with mathematical certainty. On the other hand, there is a great deal of empiric data dealing with the problems of large numbers of people living in close proximity. What can be said with complete certainty is that human beings possess a far greater degree of elasticity than would be suggested by the rather over-precise rules of thumb sometimes applied to questions of density and civic space needs. These vary according to circumstances and may lie somewhere between the extremes of 2000 to 3000 persons per acre such as is commonplace in Hong Kong, to the 12 to 15 persons per acre of many of the Australian suburban areas; or, put another way, perhaps somewhere between the extremes of claustrophobia and agoraphobia.

These extremes will be determined in any given set of circumstances by climatic and environmental conditions, the availability of essential services such as water and sewera the accustomed standard of living and habi the occupants, and the typical family's comp tion and needs.

In spite of the ill-informed jibes which sometimes made about the architect seekin build monuments to himself, architect achievement everywhere should be though as a legacy by the artist, as has always been case historically. The architect is no more no less concerned with this in the best w today than at any other time. If he sees in planning of higher-density urban areas important future pattern of living for the milli whose work and daily normal activity necess keeps them in close proximity with the me polis for a considerable part of their lives, only because the architect has, I believe, o those concerned with town planning, sh himself significantly able and anxious to m the sociological needs of the age.

Ultimately, it is believed, every architect have to train as a town planner in order to at a full knowledge of these needs and to ena him to fit his architectural achievements to over-all framework of civic design which fo a natural extension of his activities.

Rolf Jensen Adelaide, 1

'There is some considerable prospect of an increasing volume of high-density housing in the form of flats and apartments getting under way in many countries'

Ocean Park, Santa Monica, California
Architects: Welton Becket and Associates

General Statement and Town-planning Considerations

In earlier days the garden-city idea captured the imagination of many, including architects with world reputations: and in certain circumstances this type of residential environment may provide the best of country and town. In a great many other cases, however, it has been shown as unsuited to meet present-day problems of urban growth, and a totally new answer has had to be found which, while perhaps still retaining some of the virtues of town in country, does so in a very different way from the garden city with its space-consuming propensities.

In those countries such as Britain, Holland and Denmark, in which the density of population is highest, the absorption of food-producing areas by urban expansion is a critical factor. In the not very distant future the United States will be included in this category.

A matter that receives less attention in connection with this absorption of agricultural land and open space is the question of amenity. Towns and cities, particularly in the United States, in Britain, and in many parts of Europe, are now beginning to link up in continuous conurbations. Soon many city dwellers will be entirely remote from the countryside, which they will see only at week-ends or during their annual holidays.

Thus city scatteration becomes a Frankenstein. Quite apart from the psychological effects of mile after mile of unbroken urban development and building, the destruction of trees, plant life, and grass close to city areas is bound to influence climate, increase air pollution, and in time obstruct solar energy and probably diminish rainfall. Also there will be less benefit from precipitation because of the loss of permeable catchment areas.

It seems an intelligent first step, therefore, in programmes of land reform in industrialized countries, to aim at concentrating metropolitan areas as far as is consistent with good living conditions if this can be shown to be a practical proposition; which, it is hoped to show, is the case.

In doing this the inroads into the country can be very considerably reduced, the dead heart of many of our cities revived, and travel between home and work eliminated for many people; for homes are to be brought into close

utchesontown, Gorbals, Glasgow, Scotland
rchitects: Scottish Special Housing Association
mited

proximity to work thus removing the fatigue and expense of daily travel. Some will still be able to live in the suburbs or in the countryside, but these numbers will steadily diminish in the urbanized countries, and the problem will increasingly have to be met in inner urban zones.

In some countries it may be possible and desirable to create new town sites beyond fall-out range from existing centres. The use of solar energy and nuclear energy, with the consequent cheap electric power and ample fresh water, opens up new prospects for this type of development.

This cannot, however, remove the need for urgent programmes of renewal in urban centres.

Costs in multi-storey buildings in urban areas are likely to be higher than cottage construction in rural or suburban areas. The costs of land acquisition are also necessarily much higher, reflecting the element of built-in capital investment in services and facilities which have been provided out of the public purse. To obtain a true comparison in cottage estates the additional costs of creating work places, schools, new streets, electricity, water, gas, telephones, sewerage works, facilities for refuse disposal, street lighting, cultural facilities, and all civic and municipal services, including public libraries, must be taken into account. They very largely exist already in city and urban centres, and this fact puts the question of intensive urban residential development into better perspective.

It is, moreover, socially and economically desirable that city centres should not be allowed to deteriorate further and that the flight of homes from the cities should be reversed and larger numbers of people allowed to live much nearer to their work. If it can be shown that, with good planning, excellent homes can be provided in these circumstances then, even if the cost is high as against some socially less desirable alternative, this would be argued as a rational and a reasonable expenditure of public funds. The provision of sound homes in the right location is a vital part of a healthy society.

Too often has unsatisfactory housing been accepted solely in the light of a limited picture.

City living in the form of flats is nothing new. It was practised by the Romans over 2000 years ago. The policy of concerted flight from the cities, as we know it, probably dates from the Middle Ages, when plague and disease became the inevitable consequences of lack of hygiene and bad living conditions. In spite of this warning the western world, under the impact of the Industrial Revolution, saw the creation of the worst slums in history. This was not because of over-concentration, but as a result of totally inadequate standards of planning and hygiene. The man-created problem of the slums is a recent one, and it is at this obvious ailment that the ineffective remedy of the garden city was aimed.

How true it is, too, that the garden city makes suburbs, for there should be no thought that there is something special and different about this type of low-density development. Just as certainly, suburbs become 'tentacles of the

'Aim at concentrating metropolitan areas'

Hutchesontown, Gorbals, Glasgow, Scotland
Architects: Scottish Special Housing Association Limited

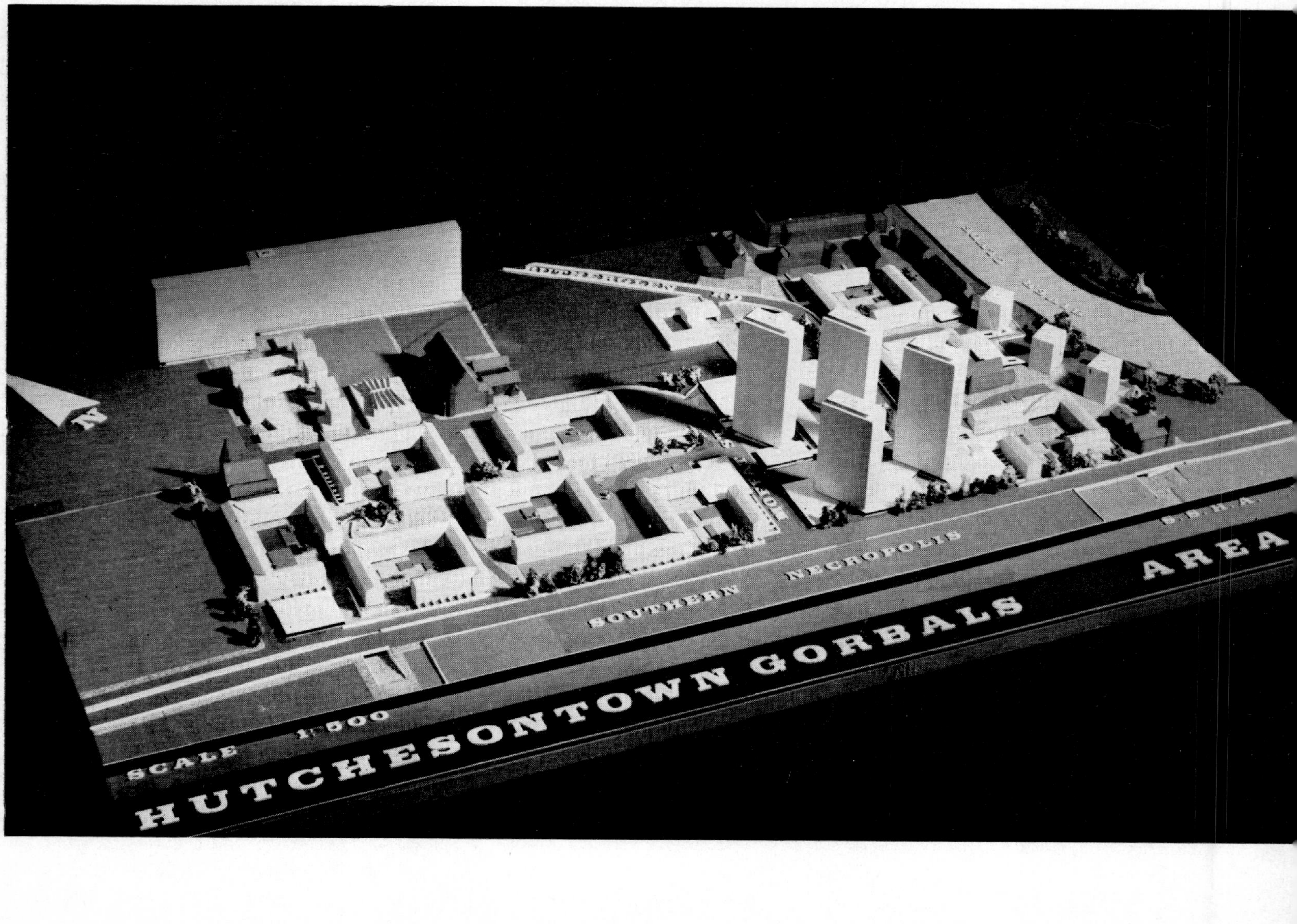

vn' (1). What has also been described else- ere as the 'garden-city will-o'-the-wisp' has ant in practice that nature, instead of being se at hand, has disappeared with the intro- ction of roads and fences, just as seclusion s no longer been attainable with crowded tlement. All we are left with is the pathetic ltiplicity of small 'rich men in their castles', d a city robbed of its essential population.

t is a sobering thought that so much of this blem is not new, and surely in the light of all s experience we can see a better way of nning our homes of the future. How success- y this is achieved is dependent on our en- tenment, knowledge and skill.

t is not intended to suggest a standardized e of dwelling for each and every circumstance. n in intensively-developed residential areas iety is essential, and might be provided, for ample, by the inclusion of a certain number of all patio houses and terraces made possible more compact planning elsewhere.

Sprawl may well absorb much-needed agricul- al or amenity land, but in any event the land and adjoining expanding metropolitan areas he most desirable for any type of development d must be husbanded and used to the best vantage. It is therefore just as important to ply a sound housing and town-planning icy in countries like Australia, where land h an urban potential is strictly limited, as it is Holland, Belgium, the United Kingdom, or the ited States, where the even more urgent nsideration is that of limiting inroads into d-producing and amenity areas.

A further matter which deserves consideration hat of possible future threat of nuclear attack. ile this problem cannot be given the same gree of priority as that of creating a proper ciological framework for normal peacetime ng, it has been argued that this factor tends favour the dispersal of urban areas. However, concentration of urban populations would ow reasonable provision for underground elters on an economic basis, and these could used for storage purposes in peacetime. spersal would make it impossible to do any- ng similar at anywhere near comparable costs with similar facilities and standards of pro- tion.

Alternatively, if we accept a recently expressed viet view that all bomb shelters are useless in esent-day circumstances, then only decentrali- ion, with major urban centres separated to the ent of at least 250 miles, would achieve any gree of protection. In this, Le Corbusier was, so often, well ahead of his time, and over thirty ars ago argued in favour of multi-storey ellings in urban centres as a means of pro- ing the best protection from aerial bombard- nt. At that time the nuclear weapon had not en invented, but the arguments make even tter sense today.

Both long-term sociological considerations in acetime, and conditions during possible war nergency, can be said to confirm the philo- phy which forms the basis of this book.

With the rapid acceleration in scientific ogress, and with what amounts virtually to a ciological revolution in many parts of the rld, it has become increasingly difficult to fore- st developments even ten to fifteen years ead. Yet, in spite of an increasing use of indus- al systems and mechanization in the building lustry, the cost of building increases and the prospects of early amortization of building capital diminish. It is all the more important, therefore, that the homes now being planned and constructed should be equally suited to the changed conditions to be expected in the fore-seeable future. It seems clear that the well-designed and conveniently planned high-density urban residential environment will be far more likely to provide the emancipated existence, free from domestic chores, on which the housewife will increasingly come to insist. Centralized domestic services in the form of garbage disposal, laundries, restaurants, and baby-minding services, with shopping facilities, schools, and children's play areas conveniently close at hand, seem to provide most of the necessary prerequisites for a more ordered, leisurely, existence. To this is added the congenial setting of landscaped gardens, with ample fresh air and sun, away from traffic hazards and near enough to cultural facilities such as community centres, libraries, theatres, and art galleries, and to department stores and group medical clinics. All these will thus be really usable on a large scale for the first time. Surely this is the logical pattern for the future, rather than isolation in the suburban cultural desert in which few of these amenities and facilities are available. In these areas there must be complete dependence on the motor car, and the outlook from the home is too often bounded by the fences, and the frequently untidy yards of adjacent houses with illusions of privacy.

Not only in many ways is it socially undesirable, certainly in many of the Western countries, to house increments of populations in a rural or even suburban setting but it is also physically impracticable. The too-determined hope that this might be achieved, with the correspondingly strict doctrinaire application of arbitrary density limitation in many European cities, has had the effect of condemning many thousands of families to remain in slum dwellings by denying them flats or apartments in a transformed environment; while experience has shown, as might be expected, that, even the most cottage-conscious will come to appreciate and accept these as providing the basis of a full and satisfying life.

In spite of the over-all cost advantages which can be shown in favour of central high-density developments as against the suburban or garden-cities solution, resistance on the score of construction cost, often somewhat higher, continues in many cases, while the importance of the right type of housing in the right place as a social service is too often completely overlooked. It is all the more important, therefore, that glimmerings of light are seen to be appearing. In America efforts are being made to grapple with this most intractable aspect of urban renewal, as well as with the problem of the high cost of central sites, by 'steering Federal subsidies towards cities and away from programmes that produce suburban housing'. It is stressed that 'what is being undertaken is an urban affairs operation in which housing and mortgage finance are largely incidental to the relocation of people and construction of buildings to meet current concepts of urban organization'.

This, with suggestions which have been canvassed of taxation of land values, rather than improvement values, appears to be the most fruitful approach to intensive redevelopment of the areas of badly blighted and obsolete properties found at the core of so many towns and cities, which is where the principal opportunity lies in a massive rehousing operation.

Another point which requires attention in this general survey is the question of traffic generation. Although it is suggested that densities of occupation may in many cases be considerably increased, while maintaining proper design and planning safeguards, the additional population does not imply a proportionate increase in traffic volume, since the major part of shopping and commuting office traffic will be eliminated in direct proportion to the numbers accommodated centrally. Only in the case of service industry and tradesmen's delivery vehicles will there be any increase in volume, but as this will occur at non-peak periods, the effect in most cases will be almost negligible.

While, therefore, in intensive planning, space must be found for the parking and garaging of private cars, local city traffic will not justify any increase in roads. This will only occur as the result of pressure exercised by the suburban and outlying areas.

Any programme for high-density renewal would be incomplete and unbalanced if the same opportunities were not taken to tighten up the planning, on an economical and rational basis, of all the ancillaries to the neighbourhood group. This would include shopping facilities, which can readily be made more compact, and especially schools, which have so often in recent years shown a prodigal waste in dispersed pavilion planning. More workable and compactly planned multi-storey schools, providing an excellent scholastic environment and a worthwhile saving in land, are now being constructed in many places and particularly on urban sites. Formal sports areas of all types are better placed in green-belt locations or in planned green wedges, which has the added virtue of combining utility with amenity in these areas, and of ensuring that there is far less chance of their appearing at some time as possible building sites. As for other open spaces, in the residential areas a substantial proportion of high building will free enough land for local recreational and amenity needs. For these reasons, it can be shown that the arguments based on the so-called 'law of diminishing returns' are quite misleading.

So the future city residential area begins to take shape: a combination of tower blocks of at least fifteen storeys in height, with two- and four-storey garden maisonette blocks, some with their own enclosed patios. The over-all density will be 300 to 400 persons per acre, the buildings taking up no more than twelve to fifteen per cent of the total surface area and the remainder planned as park and recreation area. Complete traffic segregation is a vital part of this comprehensive planning. By this technique cities not only regain life by means of a resident population, but also 'lungs' of open space and badly-needed vegetation. Slum clearance is achieved in the process, existing public services are better applied, and centralized services such as district heating become an economic proposition. The persistent evil of smoke pollution can be virtually eliminated.

All the fatigue of lengthy travel to and from work becomes a thing of the past, and the house or apartment becomes a home in the true sense of the word. Only when these possibilities are understood is it possible to grasp fully the implications of the other alternative: Le Corbusier's

'So the future residential area begins to take shape'

Golden Lane Estate, London, England
Architects: Chamberlin, Powell and Bon

'unrealizable dream' in the suburbs.

The approach to central urban residential development will vary in different parts of the world. In some cases strong prejudices may have to be overcome before the very many advantages of more intensive development can be demonstrated. In others there will be a stronger tradition of city living, and the problem will be one not so much of inculcating the basic principles as of finding the means to carry out programmes of redevelopment to bring existing living areas fully up to contemporary standards.

As the other alternative, the case for intensive urban residential renewal may depend primarily on the better use of valuable city sites, and on providing the other social advantages which have already been referred to, including the elimination of wasteful travel to and from work and the provision of better homes in a more attractive environment. Even where land shortage is not a problem, as for example in Australia, there is an increasing awareness of the importance of urban residential development, which will increasingly be needed as places of employment if industry and commerce continue to expand.

In future the whole onus of responsibility should be shifted in such a way as to make it obligatory for cities to apply density con solely by reference to human needs and to sh that there simply is no alternative to overs programmes, rather than take refuge in the t ready acceptance of the idea that space is limited. Intending developers, also, should be under an obligation to show that proposed s divisions of virgin sites are an unavoidable pa meeting the needs of actual and known prospec home owners for whom there is no other practi alternative. Cities should be required to prod a comprehensive statement of land uses a programmes in metropolitan areas on a lo term forecast before any other ex-urban la is used for residential or other types of devel ment. If all this were done, then there is li doubt that what has too often been though cheap and ready-made solution to metropoli expansion problems would be replaced b realistic policy of concentration with rene and replanning, in which, incidentally, city far more likely to remain city, and country rem country, with untold advantages for all c cerned. The only person who could object such a policy would be the get-rich-qu speculator, who has for far too long had matt all his own way and has imposed scatterat on the country instead of real planning.

Density

This complex question has in recent years received much attention, especially in the European countries in which shortage of land is a most serious problem. In principle the aim has usually been in these cases to ascertain how far densities could be raised in urban areas as a means of saving land elsewhere for agriculture; to what extent such increases in density were likely to result in worthwhile reductions in land used for actual residential development, as well as in urban areas generally, and the likely economic implications of density increases.

It is not solely in the land-hungry countries that the question of density has been examined, for this is clearly always an important criterion in relation to housing.

However, density expressed as intensity of occupation is not by itself the sole qualitative measure of housing development, which also depends greatly on planning and amenity standards, and the livability of homes. There is also the quantitative assessment of density in terms of bulk of buildings, site coverage and any necessary height limitations, as a means of securing balanced open spaces and neighbourliness.

In both respects we have to ensure broadly that families are provided with an optimum total environment in and around the dwelling for both comfort and health, but it is equally necessary to ensure that density of occupation does not overload public services, including water, sanitation, electricity, gas, public transport and roads, after taking into account expansion of these. There are also the closely related services to be considered, including schools, markets, shops, recreation areas, as well as the needs of industries and commerce.

Bad living conditions, it must be emphasized, may derive from lack of light, air, and sunshine; from overcrowding in terms of physical closeness, or from lack of space for cooking and personal hygiene. But they do not necessarily follow from people living at high density in terms of people or dwellings per acre.

Thus it must also be recognized that the slums we know today are almost entirely due to initial bad design, bad layout, poor standards of accommodation and hygiene, and inadequate maintenance. These factors have often been aggravated by lack of proper planning control, which has permitted residential areas to be invaded by squalid industries and by other inappropriate land uses which have led to general deterioration. Significantly, some of the worst slums are not those most intensively occupied.

It is also relevant to understand that a density of 1500 persons per acre may be acceptable in the local circumstances in Hong Kong, whereas in New York 400 persons per acre may be thought somewhat high, and a density of 200 persons per acre looked at askance in London. Local living habits, standards and customs, as well as the services available, have a considerable bearing on this problem.

The unit of measurement of persons or dwellings per acre taken alone can be misleading, and is not necessarily a relevant indication of actual living conditions, residential amenities or overcrowding. It does not reveal the number of persons per dwelling or the number of persons per room, and it cannot therefore indicate the amount of living space per person. This may still be true when total dwelling areas are known. However carefully systems of density control may be devised and applied, a great deal of flexibility will therefore have to be accepted, without attempting to be too precise or arbitrary.

It is evident that there are powerful vested interests in scatteration and sprawl, however sincere the many other believers in the 'small cottage for all in a garden-city setting' may be. The delusion that the populations of the world's cities can continue to be so catered for persists illogically. An alliance of commercialism and social obscurantism has seriously confused a most important issue. It is all the more remarkable that the facts have not long since enforced a more rational policy of urban development, coupled with preservation of the countryside. Instead, the process of urban spread seems to be regarded as inevitable, and in extreme cases conurbations of unprecedented size, 400 to 500 miles in length, are being created, with the complementary neglect of increasingly urgent problems of central urban renewal.

An appreciation of the benefits accruing from higher residential densities, with more enlightened forms of planning and design, can be the principal means of facilitating practical programmes aimed at reviving the dead heart of our cities. It will considerably reduce, or, in many cases, entirely eliminate the need for the spreading rash of suburbia. Le Corbusier fully realized this 30 years ago, as evidenced by his proposals for a 'Radiant City' (1) with residential densities of about 400 persons per acre and only 12 per cent site cover.

It is claimed by those who profess to see in high-density housing the potential slums of the future that such a policy is not only socially undesirable but also uneconomic both in terms of capital expenditure and of alleged limited over-all density gains. The validity of these statements, as well as the arguments that cottage gardens produce more foodstuff than agricultural land, (70) will be examined more fully, especially in the section dealing with economics.

These claims, made in spite of the now mounting evidence of success of the many efforts in mass rehousing and urban renewal through high-density programmes, represent a rearguard action, and are seen reflected in many of decentralization policies such as that of Britain. This aimed at reducing existing urban concentrations of population by persuading industry to move to new and expanded towns, thus diminishing employment opportunities in the cities. This principal objective has not been achieved, as has been officially admitted both by the authors of the plans and by those attempting to implement them.

London, whose population, in spite of a policy of decentralization, has increased since the war, rather than diminished, well exemplifies the problem in its most acute form. Reasons for this include the reuse of industrial sites, even where these have been vacated; the considerable increase in the volume of office accommodation which was forgotten when post-war town-planning controls were first introduced; and, by no means least important, the magnetic influence of the city, not only because of its employment opportunities but also because of the existence of the cultural facilities and amenities which are so often absent for those in the suburbs or the New Town, without lengthy time-wasting and exhausting travel.

It was belatedly discovered by those concerned that only ten per cent of the families being accommodated in the New Towns, which were intended to serve London, for example, had their names on housing waiting lists maintained by the metropolitan boroughs. While this very small trickle of overspill was taking place, the flow from the provinces into London long continued to run at full bore. Thus the prodigious effort and the enormous cost of creating not only new housing but also all the other consequential services as well as roads, factories, and workshops and of acquiring valuable agricultural land, has in an important respect been in vain, and even worse has had the inevitable consequence of heavy commuting and the creation of dormitory suburbs. In many other cities similar problems in various stages can be seen.

In the light of the fundamental failure of so many doctrinaire programmes of dispersal and decentralization, it is disingenuous in the extreme to point to the creation of many undeniably excellent homes in the new suburbs and New Towns, as though this had been the sole original objective. It is very much open to question as to whether or not a great many more families might have been equally well or better provided for with homes, had an entirely different and determined policy of higher-density renewal been vigorously pursued. The hopes for apparently relatively easy and more economical gains resulting from building in outlying areas have in most cases been short-lived and short-sighted.

To revert to the arguments (73) relating to land savings at high densities, one example has been quoted of a theoretical town with a radius of 1·25 miles and a density of 35 persons per acre, housing 60,000 people in the residential areas. This is compared with another town of similar population and radius 0·94 mile and a net residential density of 160 persons per acre. Selection of these densities is arbitrary and not a very real basis of comparison. However, quite apart from the fact that the figures assume quite erroneously that in the case of the higher density this applies only to the residential area, and not to the other ancillary uses, even on this basis, but put another way, there is still a difference at the two density levels suggested of just over two square miles, representing an important saving of valuable urban land, which cannot be minimized by mathematical exercises or otherwise.

It can be shown that, between the more realistic density of about 300 persons per acre net in the residential areas (long ago accepted by Le Corbusier) on the one hand, and the net residential densities of 25 persons per acre recommended by the New Towns Committee on the other hand, there is again a difference in the total land requirements for a town of 60,000 population of 4200 acres minus 1470 acres, that is, 3090 acres or 4·9 square miles (A7).

This of course only represents land that might have been saved had new towns been more intensively developed, consistent with reasonable standards of comfort, convenience and amenity. If, instead of creating new towns or suburban areas, a concentration policy of urban renewal in central areas were accepted as the other desirable alternative, this would have the advantageous result of eradicating blighted areas and slums while incidentally making full use of existing services and facilities and supplementing these where necessary. It would also result in providing excellent homes for large numbers of families close to their places of employment and to all the amenities offered by the metropolis itself, as well as leading to even more valuable savings of land in consequence.

In very many cases the industrial areas, the central business, shopping, civic and cultural areas, educational establishments, transport facilities and so on will, very largely, already exist. It is not unreasonable to suppose that the same assumption can be made about local shops and offices in the neighbourhoods, as well as churches, public buildings, and the necessary service industry and workshops. In all these circumstances, land savings could very well be of the order of six square miles. As this is much more likely to be the type of alternative development policy pursued, it is the possibility of land savings of this order which should be recognized. Stated another way, it could mean one square mile less for every 10,000 people, if we satisfactorily absorb these higher densities in existing urban centres. This should be by no means beyond the bounds of practicality.

Even at more modest net residential densities of about 200 persons per acre, a total saving of 0·9 square mile per 10,000 population might easily be visualized. These are densities which, although perhaps something of a compromise, have already been widely accepted for urban developments.

It must also be clear that it is impossible to draw a graph setting densities against land savings or against costs, and from this make useful comparisons in terms of savings of land or money at different density levels. Such comparisons are unreal, as it is entirely unlikely today, for example, that any urban authority would consider using valuable central sites for two-storey construction, and no graph, however prepared, can take into account the other land uses and facilities which may exist in the urban area but which would have to be created afresh in the new town.

Any effective system of density control must, amongst other things, provide adequate daylighting conditions in all dwellings, not only for the more obvious reasons but because this has also been found a method of satisfying the need for sunlight, space for amenity requirements, access, maintenance of privacy, reduction of airborne noise nuisance, and elimination of fire spread. How well all this is achieved will of course depend on the form of daylighting control used. Most methods have hitherto depended on the use of light angles between blocks, which have entirely disregarded spacing, providing intermittent lighting between buildings, and on rules of thumb for setbacks from site boundaries, which are in most cases vaguely theoretical, and unrelated to actual measurement of daylighting standards.

By far the most satisfactory system is that devized by the British Building Research Station, an explanation of which is given in the handbook 'Redevelopment of Central Areas' (4) where its use was first recommended. The scheme has been referred to as being 'a method for controlling the spacing of residential build-

'An appreciation of the benefits of higher residential densities'

Skyscraper, Milan, Italy
Architects: Soncini and Mattioni

'the greatest possible benefit of uncluttered space round buildings'

Paddington Towers, London, England
Architect: R. Jensen

'there may be arguments for concentrating the maximum of accommodation in high blocks'

Tower Houses, Mittlere Strasse, Basel, Switzerland
Architects: Gfeller and Mahly

gs on a site . . . providing a quick and approximate means of ensuring that buildings are so laced in relation to each other that it would be ossible to attain the daylighting standards ecommended in the British Code of Practice P.3—Chapter 1A provided that in the design of ie dwellings themselves windows should be roperly positioned and of adequate size.'

The system also provides, through the use of ie so-called daylight indicators, a check on the ghting conditions both of surrounding streets nd of neighbouring properties on other plots. he indicators are used as a planning guide at ie stage when the general form of the buildings nd the layout are being worked out, and they e reasonably accurate for this purpose in chieving an approximate five per cent daylight ctor in the habitable rooms of the buildings n the site and on neighbouring sites.

Reference has also been made to the need for ınlighting, and this is of obvious importance in mperate climates, although in other parts of e world the problem may be far more one of iading against excessive solar radiation during any seasons of the year. The British Standard ode of Practice provides that one window in the rincipal living room, and if possible in bedrooms nd kitchens too, should receive sunlight for at ast one hour of the day during not less than n months of the year from February to November; sunlight at an altitude of less than a minium of 5° above the horizon, with an angle to e window of less then 22½° being disregarded r this purpose. There are in current use a ımber of sun and shadow diagrams, sunlight dicators, or solar machines which will provide is information for any given latitude, season, time of day.

Another question must be considered in lation to density control: the economic potenal of the site itself, which may well be of high lue. It is essential that restrictions should not e imposed, unless they are necessary for the aintenance of satisfactory living standards, as herwise the actual development of worthwhile gh-density projects is likely to be jeopardized being rendered unduly costly. Proper design iould aim at striking a satisfactory balance etween achieving the maximum permissible ensity in a given set of conditions to ensure the est possible return economically and in terms families accommodated, while not going eyond the stage at which satisfactory living andards may be guaranteed inside and ıtside the dwellings, while respecting the rights adjoining property owners.

Any system of control attempting to achieve ese ends must desirably be very flexible, so as allow the maximum variety in layout and in the dividual design of particular dwellings, while ing reasonably precise in the conditions which aims to achieve, not only in daylighting but so in the other amenity factors.

In achieving these aims, and particularly that economy, it does not necessarily follow 'that e basic objective in designing mixed layouts to keep down the proportion of dwellings in gh buildings' (74). It may be very desirable deed in certain circumstances to ensure that ere is a reasonable variation in type and size the buildings, and more particularly in their ight. This will not always occur, however, and some cases there may be the strongest arguents for concentrating the maximum amount accommodation into high blocks with a minimum site coverage, in order to get the greatest possible benefit of uncluttered space round buildings.

The stereotyped approach to this problem which says, in effect: 'this development is planned for a zone in which the density has been laid down on a rule of thumb basis and where, therefore, the number of people to be accommodated will be fixed,' finds the answer within this circumscribed condition, which is a quite unrealistic one starting from the wrong premises. Yet this is the basis which is applied in a number of statutory development plans.

On the contrary, the only logical or satisfactory procedure, however development is to be carried out, is to assume that the maximum possible advantage will be taken of density opportunity on any given site. That is to say, achieving satisfactory living standards with the greatest possible economy for the largest number of people; only on this basis can it be expected that the maximum potential of building sites will be realized. Detailed and careful investigation is a part of this process, for which preconceived rules of thumb are no substitute.

In future housing developments of all types, it must be a cardinal point of policy to decide first what is socially desirable, within the over-all town planning framework. Only with this criterion continually in view can developers, or those concerned with the detail design or planning, be expected to interpret intelligently the related problems of economics, density, or housing standards.

Even in those countries where the technique of constructing multi-storey buildings is not yet sufficiently advanced to make these a fully economic proposition, it is arguable that additional cost could in some cases be justified on the basis of the benefits which exist in this type of development as against other alternatives. For far too long have the social costs of housing, a vital basic facility for any civilized society, been begrudged.

The cost arguments, which will be dealt with more fully later, can be totally misleading when related only to capital expenditure on buildings. The alternatives of high-density development and sprawl involve the whole gamut of what have been called 'town-planning costs', in creating places of employment and services which are a consequential and inevitable part of overspill development, but which, to a very considerable extent are already provided in central sites.

Subsequent arguments will show that high-density developments in residential areas need not be more expensive than cottage development, and in some cases may be a good deal cheaper when all factors are taken into account. In no case should there be any temptation to economize by using the cheapest alternative of a number of possible schemes, if this is unlikely to provide the soundest and best of living conditions, or an aesthetically satisfactory environment.

The immediate concern is with densities on expensive central area sites, which will necessarily have to be as high as possible if all the foregoing objectives to which reference has been made are to be satisfied. Selected schemes included here might give some indication of what this maximum might be, but as conditions vary in every instance these are not a complete guide. It is desirable to formulate a more rational approach to this problem, which is what the numerous systems of density control attempt to do. Because of loop-holes or overlapping, evident in almost all those examined, an alternative comprehensive scheme was devised and details of this have been published elsewhere (6). This briefly stipulates minimum room areas, linking building bulk with actual occupation in a way that is neither an encouragement to reduction of accommodation standards below a reasonable level, nor a bar to maximum economy in planning, as all circulation space must be added to the basic formula to give gross floor areas (A4,5) (T3).

Minimum open space for amenity is also stipulated, and related to the number of habitable rooms, and thus directly to the probable numbers of inhabitants in an apartment building. The daylighting code already referred to is a part of the scheme, and was found to be entirely consistent with the 'room space ratio' (A3,4).

Additional space for car parking has to be provided for, and this is necessarily almost entirely underground. Over this, in part at least, garden and amenity areas can be laid out. As a final control, in certain special circumstances only, height limitations may need to be imposed for broad civic design reasons and neighbourliness.

The application of this system is relatively simple in practice and is easily understood. It is capable of giving the most flexible but at the same time a most satisfactory development from all points of view, and on any type of site and in any set of circumstances. It is a complete design guide and tool which makes any other form of control unnecessary and does not impair the economic or housing potential.

It will now be evident that there are no absolute standards in regard to density maxima. The equivalents of 300 to 400 persons per acre have been suggested, and the formula makes provision for density levels such as these to meet the needs of most of the temperate countries. It has to be remembered, however, that in other circumstances, where for example some of the domestic activities are carried out in the open, higher densities have frequently been adopted and are regarded as acceptable (5).

A number of schemes have now been constructed in various parts of the world at a density level of about 300 persons per acre, or over, and the merits of many of these can be judged from illustrations included here. It will be realized that their success still depends very largely on the skill in design, planning and layout, and the extent to which the practical problems of combining a good social environment for the maximum number of people on an economic basis with good aesthetic grouping and civic design have been met.

It is now necessary to consider further the over-all effects of density increases, such as those which have been suggested, when effected over appreciable parts of existing urban areas as a part of intensive renewal or redevelopment schemes. The so-called law of 'diminishing returns' (A2) has already been mentioned as an argument against building high or to high densities, claiming that 'net' density increases are not adequately reflected in corresponding increases in 'gross' or 'town' densities (A1). This has been the subject of a number of studies and is examined in detail in an Appendix (A7–13).

Another British study, argued mainly on a

Central Area, Liverpool, England
Architect: Shankland

'Success depends on skill in design planning and layout'

Lijnbaan Group, Rotterdam, Holland
Architect: Maaskant

basis of economics (11,12), is of special interest in this connection, although it is based on a hypothetical set of conditions and assumptions which would be rather unlikely to occur. Other data worked out at the end of this chapter argues very much the contrary in a more realistic context where, instead of compromise levels of density the maximum potential is taken as the one alternative, as against the normal low suburban densities of the other extreme. The cost comparison must of course also take into account that, in the case of renewal in central urban areas, a high proportion of public services and facilities will already exist. These will only need supplementing to meet increases in population, whereas otherwise new neighbourhoods in an ex-urban setting will require town centres and all the other services and appurtenances. A survey undertaken in Sydney well illustrates this point (75).

There are many other factors which have an inescapable bearing on this problem, such as heavy additional costs for the temporary provision of septic tanks to houses awaiting sewer mains, and the lag in the provision of all other municipal services, including making-up streets and street lighting. Transport becomes entirely uneconomic with the scatteration of residential areas, and the use of the private car is essential, with all the additional cost, frustration and fatigue, and the consequential parking problems. In the case of Sydney (75) (A13) it was estimated that some forty per cent of the total population in the outlying areas was out of reach of any sort of public transport service, and 'that the scattered and low-density pattern of urban development was placing undue strain on the economy and adversely affecting the living standards, health, and well-being of the community'.

In spite of the fact that Australian cities tend to sprawl further for a given population than elsewhere, much the same could be said in relation to a great many of the cities of the western world, where the same advantages and potential exist for an intensification of urban land use.

The degree to which there must be a tightening-up in metropolitan areas can be expressed in another way. If, for this purpose, we consider the case of Great Britain, in which it has been stated that three million people still need to be rehoused; and if the quite modest assumption is made that only half of these are accommodated at densities of about 300 persons per acre, not in any way inconsistent with proper standards of living; then the saving of land as against two-storey development at about 25 persons per acre would be 94sq miles. The true saving would, however, be considerably greater, as this figure only deals with residential areas, and disregards the need to set up municipal services to meet the needs of the overspill programme. The total is much more likely to reach something like 150sq miles for the $1\frac{1}{2}$ million population.

Finally, and perhaps what is really the crux of the whole question of density, is some real measure of the tolerability of living conditions and how far practical experience coincides with theory. This must depend to a very considerable extent on locality, the standard of living of the occupants, and on the detailed design of dwellings, their grouping and relationship to open space and other amenities. It will vary appreciably in every scheme of development, and only through a prolonged and close investigation by sociologists, housing managers, and others concerned can we expect anything like the reliable factual data necessary for the designer to know in advance how to establish conditions which are acceptable to a majority of the future occupants.

Much thought has been given to neighbourhood design at low densities, but a great deal of this is still inconclusive. We have even more to learn about human needs and reactions under conditions of intensive occupation. Theory is no substitute for wide practical observation. What we already know, however, is sufficient to warn us that, whatever the reactions may have been against city life in the past, man's gregarious instincts are still extremely strong and are the means of providing a unique stimulus.

The busy shopping street and the crowded beaches and holiday camps well illustrate this and the urbano-phobia conjured up by some sociological writers and town planners is largely a figment of their imaginations; unlike the very real malady known in Britain as the 'New Town Blues', brought on by loneliness of suburban isolation.

It has been suggested that, if a single density level is maintained over too large an area of development, it may prove to be unduly monotonous. However, at any given density there is a wide range of possible variations in design, grouping, and layout, and in the height of buildings, which, with an ordinary degree of skill on the part of the architects and planners should eliminate any suggestion of monotony. The success with which this has often been achieved can be judged from schemes illustrated here.

On the other hand, sprawling suburbs have shown that too rigid adherence to a single building height will inevitably produce the worst kind of monotony in its visual and psychological impact. This might well also be expected to occur with considerable developments of higher buildings, although few cases exist where this has happened.

Monotony may occur in a too stereotyped architectural treatment repeated over a large area; and, without disturbing the essential basic unity of design, it is equally important that this should be avoided. Landscaping can play a vitally important part in introducing a free and informal variety into large high-density developments, but too much dependence on this alone is insufficient.

LUMIÈRE THEAT
LIJNBAAN
CHARLIE CHAPLIN EN JACKIE COOGAN
IN DE LEGENDARISCHE FILM..
THE KID HET JOCHIE
TOEGANG ELKE LEEFTIJD 2e WEEK

Appendix A

1. *Net density* is the term used to denote the number of persons accommodated on a given site, which will usually include a part of any perimeter roads. *Gross density* is the density of the whole of a neighbourhood area, including, in addition to the housing area, such things as primary schools, local shops, community buildings and churches, service industry and workshops, and provision for local roads and parking areas. *Town density* is arrived at by relating the population of the town to the whole area of the town, including not only the neighbourhood facilities but also the central commercial area, industries, business and shopping zones, educational facilities, open spaces, playing fields, railways and other such establishments.

2. Many years ago, Gropius (2) showed the fallacy in the continually recurring argument that savings of land diminish with higher buildings, as also the use of fixed light angles. He showed that with a 30° angle between adjoining parallel blocks the number of inhabitants could be increased in a typical scheme from 1200 persons in ten three-storey blocks to 1700 in four ten-storey blocks—that is, a 60 per cent increase. Alternatively the same population could be accommodated in eight three-storey blocks or in two ten-storey blocks. In the latter case the angle of light improves from 23°50′ to 17°50′. Planning the higher blocks to the same maximum light angle of 23°50′ on the other hand enables a more compact layout to be achieved with a 40 per cent saving of land or, alternatively, that much more open space for the inhabitants.

3. While the room/area ratio giving amounts of open space per habitable room has been preferred in the density-control formula to other systems such as, for example, floor space index, plot ratio, exploitation coefficient, persons per acre or rooms per acre, these other standards are in fairly widespread use. No single one of these indices can, however, give precise information on the relationship between actual numbers of persons accommodated in a particular building, and the unbuilt-on open space which will be available to them for amenity purposes. The room/area ratio system does this if coupled with a scale of minimum room areas; with the sole proviso of course that occupants are not expected other than in exceptional circumstances to sleep in living rooms, dining rooms, bathrooms or kitchens.

4. As the extent of open space surrounding buildings plays such an important part, not only in maintaining daylighting standards but in meeting all the many other amenity requirements, some explanation of the figures of 130 to 150sq ft per habitable room (in the author's density control system) is desirable. The British Government publication 'Houses and Flats 1958' puts forward a higher figure than this: namely, 170sq ft per habitable room, exclusive of roads. This is, however, an omnibus figure since it makes provision for play spaces, access to dwellings, and vehicle parking—the latter to the extent of 7 to 23 per cent of the total (1 car/5 dwellings or 1 car/1½ dwellings)—according to the number of parking spaces thought necessary. If separate provision is made for parking, as it is suggested it should be, and the corresponding reduction made from the figure of 170sq ft, this leaves a net figure of 130 to 158sq ft per habitable room, depending on the car density.

The density control formula stipulates the provision of 150sq ft per dwelling, which in effect means space for one compact car to each flat or apartment, and it does not seem inconsistent with other recommendations, or at all unreasonable, to make the net open space figure 130 to 150sq ft per habitable room. This should still give conditions equivalent to a typical layout of two-storey high-density terrace houses with individual gardens on which the over-all figure, which is the equivalent of 4 acres per thousand population, is based. It is too true, however, that this is a somewhat pragmatic approach, and it may well be that in practice, after considerable experience, areas of this order will be found over-large in some cases and inhibiting in others. Although the daylighting code would, with certain types of layout, permit a reduction of these standards, it seems reasonable for the moment, in the absence of further confirmatory information, not to go below what is known to provide satisfactory conditions in a moderately closely-developed area.

5. The formula in the system tends to favour densities giving about 250 to 300 persons per acre net, and building blocks of about 15 storeys in height each containing a total of 90 flats of 1000sq ft. A typical example in which each of the six flats to the average floor contained three bedrooms, living room, kitchen, laundry, WC, shower, bathroom and minimal internal corridor, and with an efficiency ratio of 90 per cent, gave a density of between 256 and 320 persons per acre, according to occupation of the flats, which could be either four or five people in each case, and a site coverage of 11 per cent, and plot ratio of 1·64 : 1. In this case it was assumed that 150sq ft per habitable room would be provided and that garages would be underground.

In a similar scheme where garages were placed above-ground, site coverage of building was reduced to 9 per cent, and therefore a site of 1·7 acres was needed for the same total occupation giving a reduced density of 212 to 265 persons per acre, and a plot ratio of 1 : 1·37.

Because of the way in which the controlling formula operates, and in particular the imposition of the 150sq ft per habitable room standard, no great advantages are gained by higher building in this instance. A twenty-storey tower for example, with six flats of 1000sq ft each on the typical floor, gives a density of between 266 and 330 persons per acre with an 8·5 per cent site cover by building, and a plot ratio of 1·7 : 1.

If, on the other hand, as is not unreasonable at these densities, and certainly on larger sites, the open space provision is reduced to 130sq ft per habitable room, then the requirements can be met on a site of total area 1·43 acres giving an over-all net density of 333 to 420 persons per acre. and a 9·6 per cent site coverage.

All of these alternatives easily comply with the daylighting code; and in fact it can be shown (see T2) that on a rectangular site of 12 acres a maximum of eight twenty-storey blocks could be planned in such a way as to satisfy the code. These blocks would each contain 120 flats of 1000sq ft, at an over-all theoretical planned density for the scheme of between 314 and 390 persons per acre. This layout could also in theory be repeated indefinitely in conformity with the code, although for other obvious reasons these are not density levels to be advocated, particularly in the light of the reduction of open spac provision which would be implied.

6. As two of the most frequently used densi criteria are the 'exploitation coefficient' (or i equivalent, the 'plot ratio') and persons p acre, an approximate comparison between thes based on Swedish standards is useful:

Type of Accommodation	Exploitation Coefficient	Persons per Hectare (to be divided by 2·5 to give persons per acre)
Small houses	0·08—0·15	40—80
Row houses	0·25—0·35	100—140
Three-storey houses	0·5—0·6	200—250
High flats	1·54	700 (equivalent to 280 persons per acre)

7. The saving of land in a town with a popul tion of 60,000 can be arrived at in the followin way:

(*a*) Basing calculations on Stone: Ameni land for a neighbourhood of 10,000 would be:

	Acre
Housing	83
Open space	40
Primary schools, including playing fields	17
Soops, offices etc.	5
Community centre and churches	3
Public buildings	2
Service industry and workshops	4
Road and parking	14
	168

Further land will also be required to provid for the town centre facilities in addition to an thing already allowed for in the neighbourhood and for this purpose the following areas ar suggested:

	Acre
Neighbourhood (as above)	168
Industrial areas	56
Business, shopping, civic and cultural	35
Education	32
Open spaces and playing fields	104
Railways, etc.	25
Other large establishments	43
Allotments	50
Total area:	513

The foregoing figures are based on actu surveys of nine major industrial towns, but Ston recommends for preference an average figure c 645 acres, taking into consideration a number c towns of other sizes. From this a total of 388 acres for a town of population of 60,000 is re quired, and this allows for a town density c 15·5 persons per acre and a net density in res dential areas of 39 persons per acre: well abov the recommendations of 12 and 22 persons pe acre respectively made by the New Town Committee in 1946.

(*b*) For comparison with these figures in (a and assuming net residential development a 300 persons per acre and otherwise the hypo thetical creation of entirely new neighbourhood and a town centre with no other increases i densities (such as in fact would clearly b practicable) the following figures might apply:

	Acres	
ousing	33	for population of 10,000
imary schools	4	
en space and playing fields	19	
ops, offices, community ntres. churches, public ildings, service industry and rkshops	18	
ads, parking and allotments	12	
	86	

	Acres	
eighbourhood	86	
dustrial areas in the town ntre	50	
siness, shopping, civic and ltural	35	
ucation	30	
pen spaces and playing fields	Nil	(provision made for this in green belt area)
ailways, etc.	20	
her large establishments	25	
Total area:	246	

ne 246 acres required for the population of ,000 in both neighbourhood areas and in the wn centre is the equivalent of 1470 acres for population of 60,000.

This represents a saving of 2400 acres on (*a*) or per cent—undeniably a very substantial land ving.

Keeble's arguments relating to accessibility ly deal with one rather limited aspect of the hole problem of land use. But accepting the nited line of argument at its face value and comaring (*a*) and (*b*) above, there is even so a reducon in the radius of the town area of over half a ile, or approximately 65 per cent of the total urney from the town centre to the perimeter—by means insignificant. However, the total absorpon of land is in most cases far more important, nd a reduction of 3·75 square miles in land quirements by the adoption of an enlightened olicy of high densities for each town area with a opulation of 60,000 is far from being insignifiant. If, however, the still more rational policy of ban concentration within the existing urban ea is followed, then even greater savings in nd can be made as shown in (c) below. On a mewhat different basis Manthorpe arrives at ery similar potential land savings but using the wer densities of 70 persons per acre net the in sidential areas, and making savings under her headings.

(*c*) If the New Towns Committee's recommenations in Britain are followed this would imply tal land requirements for a population of 60,000 4560 acres. As against this a policy of conentration and urban redevelopment within an xisting metropolitan boundary, assuming the ame population, but catered for by urban reewal at high densities of 300 persons per acre et; and in which number of the existing neighourhood central services and town centre cilities already exist, the following provisions ight have to be made:

	Acres	
ousing (for each unit of),000 population)	33	
eighbourhood, community and entral facilities (assume half ready available and allowing eas on Ministry of Housing urvey figures, UK)	25	
otal for neighbourhoods	58	or say 60 acres each
Town centre facilities including industry, business, shopping, civic, cultural, educational, and open space areas etc. (assume 50% already existing, but open space provision in green belt)	80	
Total provision for 10,000 population	140	or 840 acres for the total town of 60,000 population

The land saving in this case (4560 less 840, or or 3720 acres) means in effect just under six square miles (5·8): probably a far more realistic figure than that shown previously as it relates to a set of circumstances which typifies the alternatives which will frequently exist, and in which the choice is quite simply overspill or not. The many advantages of concentration have already been dealt with, and very considerable land saving is obviously one of these. With the higher density opportunities allowed for with only half of the three million population requiring rehousing in the United Kindom, the resulting saving of 150 square miles must surely convince the most sceptical of the garden-city lovers.

8. A more detailed examination of the net density figures can be informative. Information published in one study relates two-storey development to a density of 124 rooms per acre, ten storeys to 194 rooms per acre, fifteen storeys to 205 rooms per acre, and twenty storeys to only 209 rooms per acre. It is claimed that these figures tend to show the disadvantageous consequences of building high. A more thorough investigation, both of schemes already built, or of planning potentials, would however equate two-storey, moderate-density, terrace development with about 70 rooms per acre equivalent to 70 persons per acre using in this case an occupancy rate of 1. The cases where these densities are exceeded for this type of development will be very rare indeed, and in many cases they will be well below these figures. The suggested density figures for the higher blocks are even less realistic, and all the evidence shows that ten storeys can reasonably be equated with a density potential of approximately 200 persons per acre, fifteen storeys with about 300 persons per acre, and twenty storeys with something like 400 persons per acre.

On the basis of these figures the likely difference between two-storey and twenty-storey development, in terms of density, will therefore be of the order of 330 persons per acre (i.e. 400 minus 70). In other words, raising the building height has increased the accommodation provided by nearly 5 times. If these were the sole land savings to be achieved, which clearly from (*c*) above they are not, then for each population group of 10,000 the high density solution would require 118 acres less (143 less 25 acres) or a reduction of land requirements of 82·5 per cent as against that for typical two-storey development. If the comparison were to be made between cottage development at 25 persons per acre net (much more to the point), the savings are considerably greater.

9. Four-storey building heights are being widely canvassed in Britain at the present time as an economical solution to higher or moderately high density developments (probably the maximum height for walk-ups). The saving of land in this case would be approximately 43 acres or 30 per cent on the two-storey development—still a very well worthwhile economy, although obviously this is not obtaining the maximum return from expensive sites, to the extent that it falls short of a housing potential of 300 habitable rooms or persons to the acre. Instead of being able to accommodate the whole of a population of 10,000 on a 25 acre site, at the higher densities, only one quarter of this number can be accommodated. Therefore the simple and inescapable fact is that four times the total amount of land will be needed for housing alone. These differences in land absorption are meaningful whether or not there is a shortage of areas available for building and for other purposes; or whether simply a matter of safeguarding those uniquely valuable areas immediately adjoining or within metropolitan zones. It may be justified solely as a means of obtaining all the advantages of a more sane and logical distribution of population and more suitable living conditions; and not least preserving and enhancing amenity by eliminating cancerous growths in the cities' lungs while applying therapy to the diseased heart.

10. Quite apart from the obvious fact that with a policy of urban concentration a great many of the community services can be utilized and will only need partially supplementing, there are other reasons why gross density and town density will show appreciable improvement corresponding to net increases in density in the residential areas. It has often been argued that open space, because it is provided on a *per capita* basis, will nullify increases in net densities; but this is only so if we assume that all the playing areas are planned within the neighbourhood. There are strong arguments for not doing this. With towns planned on the green-wedge principle, or with generous green belts, there should be ample areas for recreational purposes in such locations, conveniently placed in relation to neighbourhoods. Such a use of these amenity areas is very much more likely to ensure that they are properly maintained and not at some future date absorbed for other purposes; always a very great temptation to expanding cities. Such a use would not be in any way inconsistent with the preservation of amenity standards as there could still be substantial areas available purely as scenic attraction or nature reserve.

11. The other point which is frequently overlooked is that the swing from the diffuse type of planning once used in a great many residential areas (notably in the new towns in Britain) has been accompanied by similar changes with other building types such as schools. Many of these, after the Second World War, were spread out in the most prodigal fashion in apparent disregard for the extreme administrative inconvenience which resulted from this type of planning, and as though unlimited land were available. Now schools are being planned to higher densities, but again this need be in no way inconsistent with the preservation of reasonable standards. This does not mean however that we should go to the extreme represented by the multi-storey comprehensive school 'factory'.

School needs increase, moreover, only in proportion to the numbers of family flats or apartments planned in a given neighbourhood. Therefore, unless the whole of the populations of cities are to be accommodated at high densities in future (which seems very unlikely for a variety of reasons) and unless (as is also unlikely) the number of families with children provided for, as against non-family dwellings, is in the same ratio as the national division, increases in educational facilities will not correspond to the increases in the total volume of high-density residential accommodation.

12. Another very significant saving in the planning of multi-storey flat blocks, as against more widely dispersed low blocks or houses, is in the road provision. Only in the case of the slab block type of development is there any increase in the length of access roads as the number of dwellings increases, and this will be quite limited, particularly in the more compact forms of planning with relatively high blocks. In the case of the typical point block development, lifts and staircases take the place of access roads and no increase in these latter or in the distribution of services is required, no matter how high the block or how many flats or apartments are planned, over and above what would in any case be required by a single-storey building. This leads not only to considerable savings in cost but also in the greater degree of availability of the space between buildings for recreational and amenity purposes, free from traffic hazards (in this the assumption is still made that parking areas are provided in a way that does not conflict with amenity).

13. In Sydney it was shown that a policy of sprawl would require 152 square miles of land over 20 years; or a 69 per cent increase on the present area of 220 square miles and would, moreover, necessitate expenditure of £54 million on combined works and services and £46 million for land and building over the same period.

Concentration in the central area, on the other hand, could be carried out without absorbing any land. Greatly reduced costs of £8¼ million for combined works and services, and £8 million for land acquisition and building.

While between 25 and 40 per cent of the outlying residential areas were without sewers, the capacity of sewers in the inner suburbs was used only to the extent of 30 to 45 per cent, and there was ample land, even at quite modest density levels, to support an additional population of half a million.

Another interesting fact is that threequarters of the mileage of water mains which serve a population of 8 million in London serve a population of only 2 million in Sydney, and that this in turn inevitably has important repercussions on reservoirs and other capital works associated with water supply and storage. In these same circumstances it is not surprising that it is estimated that £2½ million of capital investment in water mains is inadequately used and could serve an additional population of 200,000 people.

Table 1

Graph showing Relationship of Density with Housing Land Required

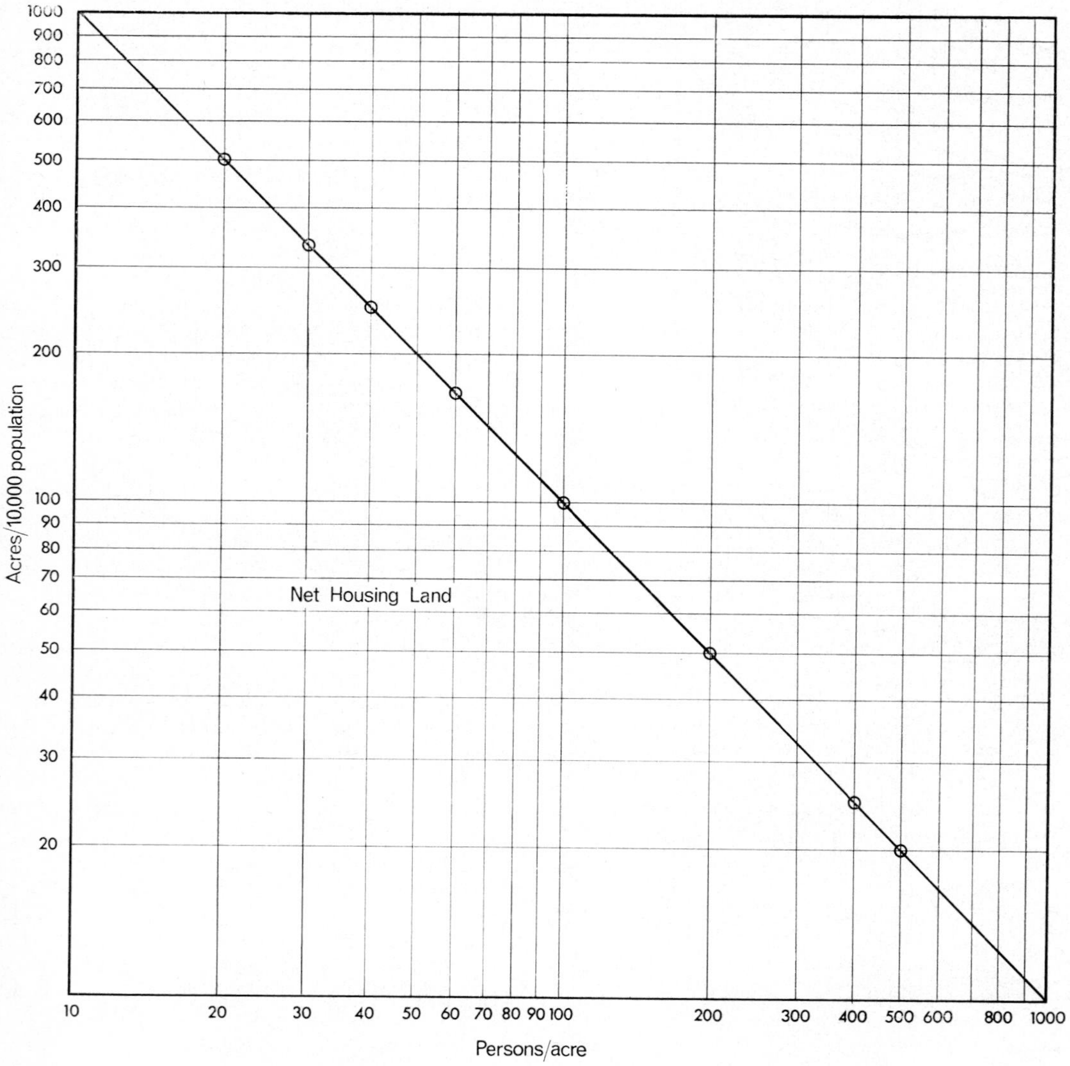

Table 2

Application of B.R.S. Daylight Code

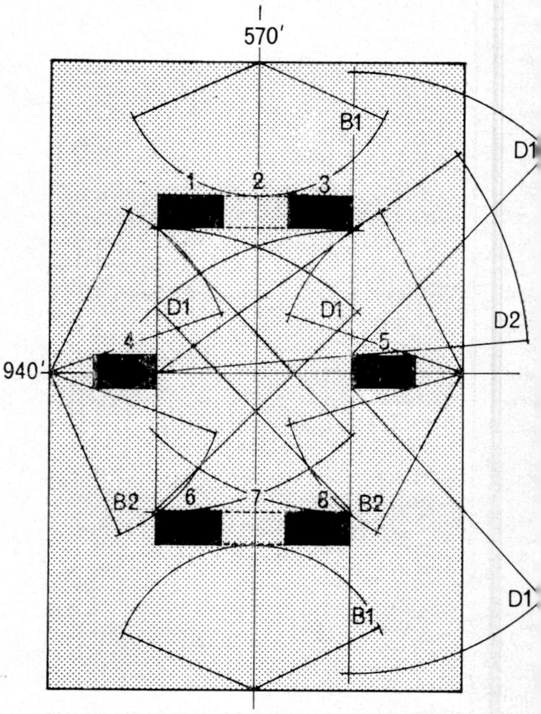

Hypothetical layout of a 12 acre site with 20-stor blocks (each containing 120 flats) and using B.R. Daylight Code Indicators:

(*a*) assuming eight similar blocks with dual aspe planning, a density of between 314 to 390 perso per acre is obtained (according to whether four five persons/flat);

(*b*) if only six blocks are planned, a density of 234–2 p.p.a. is obtained.

In either case good daylight, space betwe buildings, privacy, etc., are seen to be consistent w high densities and the use of the code is not an hibiting factor.

Site coverage for (*a*) 10%, or (*b*) 7·5%.

(excludes access roads and parking areas (assum to be underground)).

Adjoining areas may be similarly developed.

ıble 3

ɔom Area Standards Square Feet (Net)

om	ANZAAS Scheme	NYHA	USA Med. rent	USA High rent	'Housing Manual 1949' (UK)	Dudley Report (UK)	Parker Morris Report (UK)	'Houses & Flats 1958' (UK)	Stuttgart
ing room	170 } 250	150–190	220	295	} 225–270	160		160–180	151
ning room	80 }	30– 80	80–90	110–132		50			
: bedroom	150	125	143	195	135–150	135		135	
her double drooms	120	80–125	110	170	110–120	110		110	75½
ıgle bedrooms	80	80–115	100	132	70– 80	70		70– 80	
:chen	110	45– 70	68–90	88–100	90–110	60–100		85– 90	43– 86
ındry	80				40– 50	35			86–129
throom	60								
ɔ	40								
rridor, etc.	30					35– 40			
lcony	Optional 50		72	90					
. persons									Craig (Av. 76 Schemes)
									sq ft
					300–350		320	300–350	1 rm 350
					500		480	500	2 rm 506
							610		3 rm 709
					700–750		750	700	4 rm 846
					850		850	800	5 rm 1030
					900–950		930		
					1000				
General storage inside							8–15		
Storage outside					50		20		

Table 4

US Schemes (New York)
(Source: NY Housing Authority Publication)

Name	Density	Coverage %	Block heights	No flats
Albany	351	15·05	(6) 14 st.	829
Amsterdam	410·84	22·49	6 & 13 st.	1084
Bronx River	350·29	13·87	(9) 14 st	1246
Brownsville	270·09	22·59	6 & 3 st.	1338
Colonial Park	349	15·07	(8) 14 st.	984
Dyckman	290	13·11	(7) 14 st.	1167
Eastchester	230	17·72	7 & 8 st.	874
East River	322	21·87	6, 10, 11 st.	1170
Elliott	479·4	21·84	11 & 12 st.	608
Farragut	297·84	12·16	(10) 14 st.	1400
1st Houses	273	41·4	4 & 5 st.	123
Fort Greene	315·43	20·07	6, 11, 13 st.	3501
Stephen Foster	378	16·49	13 & 14 st.	1337
Gowanus	355·21	19·29	4, 6, 9, 10, 13, 14 st.	1139
Gunhill	317	15·84	13, 14 st.	733
J. W. Johnson	424·68	18·89	6, 10, 14 st.	1310
A. Lincoln	393·24	19·26	6 & 14 st.	1286
Melrose	326·39	12·71	14 st.	1027
Patterson	406·6	22·4	6 & 13 st.	1791
Jacob Riis	388·62	19·2	6, 13, 14 st.	1768
Governor Smith	399·7	15·55	16 st.	1940
Vladeck	321·67	30·70	6 st.	1771
Lillian Wald	426	18·18	10, 11, 13, 14 st.	1861
Houston	486	18·7	(8) 14 st. 8 flats/floor	844
Lake Meadows	119	9	4, 21 st.	

ıble 5

andards of Space required for a Neighbourhood of 10,000 Population (Alternatives Proposed by Various Sources)
ɘlating Housing Areas to Remaining Areas as a Means of Arriving at Gross Neighbourhood Density, as well as Net Residential Density)

	'Housing Manual 1944' & 'Design of Dwellings 1944' Cent. Normal	(Dudley) Concen. Develt	City of London Plan (interpolated) (a)	City of London Plan (interpolated) (b)	Purdom	Le Corbusier (Contemporary City)	New Towns (UK)	Manthorpe (UK)	Keeble (UK)	Stone	Author	APRR London 'A'	APRR Inner Urban 'B'	'Density of Residential Areas 1952' Table 10	'Density of Residential Areas 1952' Tables 5,6,7
Housing	100	83	100	50	125	25	400	140	285	83	33	100	100	175	105
Primary Schools and Playing Fields	17	17	7		20		50	50		17	4		7	5	13
Open Space	50	40	40	40	30		100	10		40	14	70	40	42	60
Shops and Offices	6	5	6							5	5		6		5
Community Centres, Churches	3	3	6	25	15	40	10	10	233	3		25	40 4	7·9	
Public Bldgs	2	2								2			2		5
Service industry, W/shops	4	4	4		10		100	50		4	18		4	34	4
Main Roads, Parking	17	14	17							14	12 (allot- ments)		17	87	10
							+ 100								
TOTAL	199	168	180	115	200	65	760	260	518	168	86	195	180	351	202
Av. net residl. density p.p.a.	100	120	100	200						(50 ac. for allotments and 300 ac./ 10,000 for Town Centre	300	100	100	57·2	145
Gross n'hood density p.p.a.	50	60	60·6	97·5							116		55		
Addtl. o/s in green belt	20–30 ac.									Town Density:	40·5			30	70

Selected Bibliography and References

1. Le Corbusier. *The Four Routes.* Dennis Dobson Ltd.
2. Gropius, W. *Scope of Total Architecture.* George Allen & Unwin.
3. Ministry of Housing and Local Government. *The Density of Residential Areas.* HMSO, London 1952.
4. Ministry of Town and Country Planning. *The Redevelopment of Central Areas.* HMSO, London 1947.
5. Stevens, P. H. M. *Densities in Housing Areas.* Department of Scientific and Industrial Research, HMSO, London 1960.
6. Jensen, R. A. *Density Control in Australian Cities.* ANZAAS 35th Congress, Brisbane, 1961.
7. Jensen, R. A. High Flats and Higher Densities in Europe and the Metropolis. *J. R. Inst. Brit. Archit.,* March, 1955.
8. Jensen, R. A. A National Planning Enigma. *J. Tn Plann. Inst., Lond.,* January 1953.
9. Stephenson, G. *Perth Metropolitan Plan—Form of Control of Residential Densities.* Government of Western Australia.
10. Manthorpe, W. The Machinery of Sprawl. *Archit. Rev.,* December 1956.
11. Stone, P. A. The Economics of Housing and Urban Development—Part IV. *J. R. Statist. Soc.,* 1959.
12. Stone, P. A. Urban Development and Cost Prediction. *J. R. Instn. Chart. Surv.,* October 1959, January 1960.
13. Lichfield, N. Net Density, Cost and Value in Public Authority Dwellings. *J. R. Instn. Chart. Surv.,* September 1960.
14. Editors of Fortune. *The Exploding Metropolis.* Doubleday.
15. Higbee, E. *The Squeeze.* Cassell.
16. Felt, J. *Zoning New York City.* New York Planning Commission.
17. Bor, W. G. Residential Development Densities. *J. Tn Plann. Inst., Lond.,* January 1961.
18. Abercrombie, P. Where does Planning Stand Today? *J. Tn Plann. Inst., Lond.,* December 1955.
19. Heap, D. Density of Development. *J. Tn Plann. Inst., Lond.,* November 1955.
20. Cullingworth, J. B. *Housing Needs and Planning Policy.* Routledge & Kegan Paul, 1960.
21. Nairn, I. Subtopia. *Archit. Rev.,* June 1955.
22. Lindman, G. *Bostadshöghus.* Stadsingeniörskontotet i Malmö, November 1953.
23. Jensen, R. A. High Density Housing Schemes in Europe. *J. R. Inst. Brit. Archit.,* September–October 1956.
24. Jensen, R. A. High Flats—Lessons from the Continent. *Munic. J.,* February 1955.
25. Jensen, R. A. High Building in West Germany. *Munic. J.,* November 1955.
26. Jensen, R. A. 'High Building in France.' *Municipal Journal,* August 1955.
27. Jensen, R. A. 'Postwar Flat Development in Europe.' *Public Works and Municipal Services Congress* 1956.
28. Jensen, R. A. 'L'habitat à densité élevée en Europe occidentale.' *Architecture D'Aujourd'hui,* AA63, 1955.
29. Jensen, R. A. 'Housing and Town Planning Considerations.' *Symposium, Flats in City Development,*' Adelaide. July 1958.
30. Jensen, R. A. *Expanded Towns or New Cities.* Paper to Berkshire Architectural Society, April 1956.
31. Jensen, R. A. *Perkins Heights.* Reports: October 1953 and March 1954.
32. Jensen, R. A. 'The New Towns Programme.' *Architect & Building News,* April 1950.
33. Jensen, R. A. 'Postwar Flat Development in France.' *Prefabrication,* November 1956.
34. Jensen, R. A. 'New Towns.' *Architects' Journal,* June and July 1950.
35. Jensen, R. A. *The Draft Development Plan (for London).* Report, August 1951.
36. Metropolitan Borough Standing Joint Committee, Works Sub-Committee. *Enquiry Regarding Density Zones.* Report, February 1956.
37. Editorial. 'Higher Densities.' *Architect & Building News,* August, 1960.
38. Editorial. 'Homes in Central London.' *Architect & Building News,* June 1956.
39. Editorial. 'Pros and Cons of High Rise.' *Architect & Building News,* March 1953.
40. Taylor, Eva. 'Are the New Towns in the Wrong Places?' *The Listener,* January 1956.
41. 'Overspill—the need for a unified policy.' *Municipal Journal,* London, August 1955.
42. Gale, Sir Humfrey. 'Overspill and the Aims of Decentralization.' *Municipal Journal,* March 1956.
43. Niering, W. A. 'Conservation to Combat Floods, Water Shortages and Air Pollution.' *Nature in the Metropolis,* New York.
44. Westergaard, John. 'Journeys to Work in London.' *Town Planning Review* (Liverpool), April 1959.
45. Roberts, Sir Howard. 'Problems of Industrial Evacuation.' *Local Government Chronicle (London),* November 1953.
46. Goss, A. 'Paying for Sprawl.' *Architects' Journal,* May 1961.
47. Nelson, G. R. *Freedom and Welfare Housing.* Ministries of Social Affairs, Scandinavia, 1954.
48. Brooke, H. 'The Effect of Housing Subsidies on the Redevelopment of Central Areas.' *Society of Housing Managers Journal,* July 1953.
49. Fraser, R. D. L. 'The Town Planning Problems of Tall Buildings.' *ANZAAS 35th Congress, Brisbane,* 1961.
50. 'Overgang van grond naar niet-agrarische Doelinden.' *Rijksdienst voor het nationale plan* 1954.
51. Chief County Planner, Cumberland County Council, Sydney. *Building Code in Sydney Harbour Foreshore Scenic Protection Areas.* Cumberland County Council.
52. Boeck, R. J. 'Pour ou contre les Appartements Gratte-ciel.' *International Federation for Housing and Planning,* 1961–2.
53. Tatton-Brown, A. 'Report on County of London Plan.' *Architectural Review,* May 1949.
54. Gustavsson, J. 'Housing Policy in Sweden.' Swedish Institute 1949.
55. Mumford, L. and Shankland, G. 'Both Heaven and Hell.' *Town Planning Institute Journal,* November 1961.
56. Editorial. 'The Planning of Dwelling Houses—Collective Services.' *Att. Bo.* 1953.
57. 'Administration, City of London Development Plan 1951.' *LCC London.*
58. Edmonds, R. 'High Building in London.' *Architect & Building News,* May 1956.
59. Jensen, R. A. 'Decentralization.' *Evidence South Australian Industries Special Committee, May* 1962.
60. 'County of London Plan 1943.' *LCC, London*
61. Barry, G. R. 'Agriculture States its Case *Municipal Journal,* November 1952.
62. Boyd, R. *Australia's Home.* Melbourne U 1962.
63. Editorial. 'The Case for Higher Densi Housing.' *House & Home,* April 1962.
64. BBC Discussion. *Skyscraper or Subur* January 1955.
65. Bradbeer, A. 'Overspill and its Attenda Problems.' *Inst. Hsg Conference,* Septemb 1955.
66. Womersley, L. 'Multi-storey Housing Europe.' *Sheffield City Council.*
67. Whyte, William H. *The Organisation Ma* Cape, London 1957.
68. Bradbury, D. 'Multi-storey Housing in t USA.' *Liverpool City Council.*
69. Editorial. 'Loss of Agricultural Land.' *Munic pal Journal,* September 1952.
70. Best, R. H. and Ward, J. T. *The Gard Controversy.* Wye College, London 1956.
71. Fidler, A. G. S. (City Architect, Birminghan 'Housing to High Density.' *Public Works a Municipal Services Congress* 1959.
72. 'Housing Density.' *International Congre for Housing and Town Planning,* Edinbur 1954.
73. Keeble, L. 'Town Planning at the Cro Roads.' *Estates Gazette.*
74. *Ministry of Housing and Local Governme London.* 'Flats and Houses,' 1958, HMSO.
75. Spillman. 'Economics of Urban Expansio *Cumberland County Council,* Decemb 1958.
76. Batholomew Harland. 'Urban land use *Harvard City Planning Studies IV, Cambrid Massachusetts,* 1932.
77. Lovelace, E. 'Urban land use.' *Journ Australian Institute of Planners,* 1942. Vol. X

Economic Factors

Inevitably, in examining town planning and density factors reference has already been made to cost and to social preferences, as it is virtually impossible to consider one aspect of the whole problem of intensive urban renewal entirely *in vacuo* or out of the broad context of comprehensive design for city living.

An especially close link exists between economic and social considerations, since in whatever may be socially desirable cost advantages are likely to have a very considerable bearing on any choices. For example, where there is a strong social tradition of cottage housing, much of the opposition to alternatives has centred on cost arguments.

Contrary to assertions which have been made regarding the cost of high-density developments however, it can be shown that with skilful design and planning there are economic advantages as well as many others.

It is claimed that to adopt higher-density flat construction in Britain, for instance, would cost an extra £200 million a year in providing a programme of 200,000 dwellings on the basis of existing subsidies.

What has been overlooked however is the fact that in the circumstances referred to it would require considerably more than £200 million annually to meet the cost of relocating industry, providing new shopping areas, schools, cinemas, garages, parks and playing fields, as well as libraries, roads, essential services, and all the other adjuncts to the necessary homes and places of work. The cost of very considerable additional overspill land has of course also to be taken into account.

The extent of land absorption in low-density sprawl cannot be denied, although it has seriously been argued that the gardens of cottages erected on what was previously farm-land produce more foodstuff. Full employment, time lost in travelling to and from outlying residential areas, and higher standards of living leading to more food purchased from shops, all contribute to a tendency for garden food-production to dwindle. Even if this were not so, the maximum retail value of produce from farm-land may be as much as six times that of garden food-stuffs.

A most detailed cost examination on a wider basis was undertaken in Britain by the Building Research Station, in which three hypothetical alternatives involving partial urban renewal in conjunction with overspill were examined. One of the important conclusions reached was that in subsidized schemes, losses in exporting urban populations and housing them elsewhere might well outweigh any apparent gains.

Whether or not such arrangements for building in rural areas are made under the aegis of government statutes, such as is suggested in this instance, the conclusion reached is particularly important in judging the economic merits of the two different types of development.

Attempts have also been made to express in monetary terms the enhanced value of city sites due to the high built-in capital investment in the form of services, and the comparable costs which must be expected for the same purposes on apparently cheaper land in outlying areas. Fair comparison is made difficult by the fact that such higher urban values are too often regarded as a legitimate profit element, whereas this is in the main 'betterment' which by right belongs almost entirely to the community, and could justifiably therefore form the basis of a development charge where sites are not used for public purposes such as housing. This would have the additional advantage of permitting this site element to be excluded from the cost equation for purposes of comparison and instead allow a fair evaluation of constructional costs, and planning and design standards.

One approach to this is to be seen in comparative figures established in Sweden, for what are known as 'town-planning costs' required to provide the necessary services, and which partly meets this problem. These are stated as equivalent to from £34 to £43 per room for multi-family dwellings against £137 to £170 per room for small houses; or in other words a cost ratio of about 1 : 4 in favour of multi-storey dwellings. While this may not by any means completely offset differences in land costs, it at least goes part of the way to removing anomalous factors and is, moreover, in reasonably close agreement with the basic £200 to £250 per room underlying the excess of £200 million previously referred to in connection with the housing programme in Britain.

The town-planning, land, and movement costs have been dealt with first as these are likely to have the most decisive effect on policy decisions. In addition, the construction costs and subsequent maintenance, running and management costs have to be taken into account. The initial capital cost of building is affected by a great many different factors including planning efficiency—particularly in reducing non-rentable areas to a minimum consistent with convenience; standards of accommodation provided; standards of fittings and finishes; type of services included; system of construction; the degree of repetition of individual dwellings in a single block, and of the block as a whole; the type of building planned—whether simple in shape and with a low external wall/floor area ratio or the converse; the over-all size of the development, and whether or not complicated subsoil or site conditions lead to abnormal foundation or landscaping costs; and, finally, perhaps as in most types of building, the conditions obtaining in the building industry at the time of tendering, including the extent of work available, the levels of productivity in the various trades, the degree of familiarity with, and efficiency in the type of building being undertaken, and the extent to which any special equipment and experience may be available.

All the foregoing factors constitute normal variables in an extremely complex equation; but in addition every developer at some stage has to strike a balance between the level of initial capital expenditure on his structure and finishes and the long-term maintenance costs. The first of these will always have a very considerable bearing on the second. The total expenditure for maintenance over the life of a residential building is likely to be about eighteen per cent of the initial capital cost. This becomes increasingly heavy, particularly with high buildings, unless every possible opportunity is taken to introduce maintenance-free materials, especially on the exterior of the building, and to install equipment which is as simple and as foolproof as is consistent with proper service, as well as being easily accessible for periodical cleaning and repairs.

A closer analysis of maintenance costs shows

that in relation to initial capital costs, by far the heaviest burdens are likely to be occasioned by any external painting, and in connection with the water service. For these reasons natural cladding materials, such as stone, brick, or concrete panels, and aluminium windows would be good investments for the exterior of the building. So far as the water service is concerned, it is probable that copper tubing would in most cases be a worthwhile economy and in fact does, in any case, show savings on first cost in certain areas.

Heating and lighting equipment and sanitary fittings rank next in order of cost of maintenance, and these also deserve special attention in the initial planning and design.

In no case is it ever possible to make a decision solely on the grounds of economics. Many other factors may have a decisive influence on the choice of equipment and materials: for example, in the case of the external walls, where costs must be considered in relation to durability, weight, strength, fire resistance, weatherproofing, heat-insulation properties, ease of erection, and appearance, as well as the extent of subsequent maintenance.

So far as structure is concerned, one recent survey of a large number of blocks of flats showed a slight cost preference in favour of an orthodox reinforced-concrete column and beam system; probably still the most familiar and widely used system, and one that has competed most favourably with fireproofed structural steel.

Other cost comparisons indicate, however, that of all the structural systems, the flat reinforced-concrete slab with reinforced-concrete columns is the most economical: but as this involves the use of the drop panel its use is scarcely appropriate in anything other than commercial type of building. Very nearly as economical however is the flat 'plate' system with reinforced-concrete floors and columns. Although this has as yet been used to a relatively limited extent, as compared with other systems, it is an almost ideal system for apartments or flats and seems likely to be adopted very much more widely in future, with savings of approximately 30 per cent as against the cost of a steel-skeleton structure. Similar economies are to be anticipated with the use of the lift slab system, which is virtually a type of flat plate construction, but with other special advantages.

Over-all, there are several reasons why the cost of the multi-storey flat building may be higher than that for low building. It must be added, however, that in most European countries, where the multi-storey apartment building has been commonplace for many years, and the techniques of construction are well understood and the industry suitably equipped, costs of high and low buildings are very much on a par.

Details of approximate costs over a wide range of schemes and countries are given in the Appendix (T12–15), and, although there are outstanding exceptions, a single general trend can be discerned. In this connection it should be emphasized that conversions, where made, from one monetary system to another, cannot reflect national differences in costs of living and wage levels. Nevertheless, some generally valid basis of comparison can be made in costs as between different countries and different schemes; certainly in so far as Europe is concerned. In Australia and the United States, on the other hand, high wage levels produce appreciably higher general costs which are not directly comparable.

So far as is possible, costs given are on a common basis relative to flat sizes and types of accommodation. However, materials and construction vary to some extent between one scheme and another. At this stage there is still insufficient data on a precisely similar basis to overcome this problem. Nevertheless, as cost averages, the figures cover a large enough range to give reasonable comparability.

Cost comparisons, or cost indices, between flats in multi-storey blocks and those in low buildings or in single-family houses are also appended. Firm conclusions are, however, in this case difficult to draw. Craig of the British Building Research Station has reported (9), after his most exhaustive investigation of some seventy schemes, that 'there is no systematic relationship between price and the height of the building' (T10). In the cost level figures which are shown in his analysis, two of the schemes of eleven and twelve storeys in height happen to be unduly expensive, and tend to weight the cost comparisons. From a careful examination of the remaining data, however, the difference between blocks of six storeys in height and those of eleven storeys in height is seen to be insignificant. These figures and this conclusion are, however, at variance with much other data, including that from British sources. It may be of great significance that none of the other samples are as large as that taken by Craig, and even those emanating from the Building Research Station over a period of time show inexplicable fluctuations.

The figures due to Triebel (4) and to Lindman (T10) also give a fair representative indication of the trend in most Continental countries in Europe.

Another similar investigation was carried out by the Building Research Institute in Copenhagen (11), and for this purpose a considerable number of projects in which those of three, five or ten storeys in height predominated, were examined. In this case precise comparability was specifically assured by selecting cases with uniform constructional systems, materials, and equipment, and similar planning. The conclusions were that 'variations in building price are so small and so influenced by many variable assumptions that the question of high or middle-high dwellings cannot be decided on the basis of economic calculations alone. The number of storeys changes both directly the use-value of the dwelling and the conditions governing the choice of building form, construction, and type of flat planned. These matters appeared to have greater importance than the actual economics of a varying number of storeys.'

While comparisons may be somewhat indecisive on the evidence given, it does not seem unreasonable to expect that there will in many cases be some increases in cost as between the walk-up type of dwelling, the cottage, and dwellings in higher blocks of say four, five or more storeys in height, in which lifts are required. The extent of such increase will depend on planning efficiency and the degree to which the lift is shared by dwellings.

The fact that the costs of a normal lift installation in an apartment building will be equivalent to about five or six per cent of the over-all cost of the building or indicates the need to ensure that it is used in the most economical way from a planning point of view.

Much the same can be said about the st case, and of the advantages which exist wher duplication is not stipulated by Building Re lations.

From the figures which are available it a appears reasonable to conclude that there i general levelling out of costs at about eight or storeys, particularly where there is floor-to-fl repetition, and there are therefore probably v good grounds indeed for accepting the view Stone, already quoted.

A wide concensus of information now av able appears to suggest that, in spite of need for heavier foundations and a speci designed structural system, and for equipm which is not normal in low buildings, such refuse disposal facilities, lifts, and fire hydrar and in some cases mechanical ventilation equ ment, the economies which result from verti repetition, particularly in the higher buildin and from more efficient techniques, will off these extra costs to a very large extent so tl they are no longer a decisive element.

Further economies are made likely by t selection of the right type of layout and by t correct proportion of high and low buildin Standardization of building elements and equ ment, and the adoption of modular coordinati can play a considerable part in effecting wor while economies, as can also prefabricati techniques and the elimination of obsolete a wasteful building processes, many of which ha widespread repercussions extending into number of other trades.

In this type of building particularly, good orga ization and preplanning at the design stage vital. This means better and earlier collaborati with the building contractor, with specialis and consultants. There is evidently still sco for further economies in a number of directior as well as for improvements in efficiency, whi spell economy in upkeep and maintenance.

Evidence once again appears to suggest th maintenance costs will be higher on the t building, in view of the necessary upkeep by t landlord of large communal garden areas, t maintenance and repair of lifts, central heatir mechanical ventilation, vacuum cleaning syste and possible refuse disposal and laund equipment, and the cleaning of the comm parts of the building. Many of these items are course met by individual property owners other cases, and cannot be regarded as extra However, a small additional capital outlay m result in very considerable savings in respect external painting, by the use of self-cleani materials for the cladding, and windows d signed to be reglazed or cleaned from with the building.

Management and administration costs w vary greatly according to the type of schem being lower in the better standard home owne ship type of dwellings than in an econon rental scheme. Even the system of home owne ship can have a considerable bearing on th problem, and it is difficult to draw any gener conclusions or valid comparison. Clearl however, the most significant way in whic appreciable savings can be made in maint nance and management costs and other ou goings is by economy and compactness in th initial design, and by striking a rational balanc between initial capital outlay and reduction depreciation.

at reinforced concrete slabs with reinforced ncrete columns'

ur Violiet, Angers, France
chitect: I. Schein

Appendix B

1. 'The value of rate (tax) income from a block of housing may exceed the marginal saving resulting from exporting the occupants, especially when the associated government grants are considered. Again the loss of a block of housing may result in a loss of a part, or all, of any rate deficiency grants. (This refers to British government subsidies.) Thus, the net effect of exporting a block of low-cost housing may be a loss of revenue far exceeding the saving in expenses. This loss may be increased if the exporting authority has to pay the receiving authority an annual contribution on dwellings built for population exported under an agreed overspill scheme. The value of these net losses may offset the cost of retaining the population and providing rate subsidies to house them in high blocks of flatted dwellings.'

2. In this same study, many of the cost implications of spilling population into rural areas and decentralizing their places of employment, as against those of constructing new homes in the form of flats in central areas close to existing places of employment, are examined. It was estimated that the costs of removal alone, including industrial premises, would amount to some £3½ million for the 60,000 population of a new town. This compares with the £4½ million excess cost for a similar population of 60,000 given for Sydney's projected overspill.

3. Far greater savings could have been shown in the Building Research Station's study had there been a more realistic acceptance of readily attainable high densities, and had it followed the Department's view that 'once committed to high building, say ten storeys and above, it costs little more per dwelling to build really high, and it may be possible to double the height without incurring much extra cost.'

Had advantage really been taken of the full high-density potential in this otherwise most interesting analysis it could readily be shown, on the basis of figures already quoted in the previous chapter and on the assumption that half of the neighbourhood, community and town centre facilities already exist and will be supplemented, that these, together with the displaced population, can be reaccommodated within the central urban zone without creating any overspill whatever, and without exceeding net densities of 300 persons per acre: a policy which is desirable from economic as well as other points of view.

4. Since a payment of £1 per annum pays the interest on, or is equivalent to the capital value of £16·2 at 6 per cent, extra capital expenditure to the amount of £16,200 might well be justified in order to save a cost of £1000 per annum on the running or maintenance bill, other things being equal. This argument might well apply in relation to a choice of either materials or equipment and could, for example, in certain instances be equivalent to the saving of the cost of one employee.

5. An interesting practical illustration of economic feasibility is to be seen in a recent development carried out near Melbourne, Australia. This development, which was located in what had been a run-down area covered with slum shacks, only a mile and a half away from the city centre, provides 198 new buildings where 80 slum dwellings existed previously. The site, which was just over three acres in net area, not including peripheral roads, was built on to the extent of only 24 per cent site coverage at a density of 155 persons per acre approximately—and the remaining three quarters of the area landscaped and laid out as garden, with minimum access roads.

The total cost of the site was A£152,000. On the basis of standards laid down in local building acts, only 18 standard houses could have been built on this site, which would have meant a land cost of £8400 per dwelling. In the case of the scheme carried out, however, the land cost averaged only £745 per dwelling; and this is land which is already fully serviced with all the necessary drainage, sewerage, water, electric power, and gas supplies, as well as bitumen-paved carriageways and paved footpaths.

Construction costs were £3400 for each of the 90 two-bedroom flats, and £3200 for each of the 30 one-bedroom flats, or rents of £5/15/6 or £5/9/– a week respectively—both of these figures including part capital cost and interest as well as sinking fund, maintenance, garden upkeep, lift maintenance and operation, rates, insurance, caretaker and administration.

6. It has already been argued that there is considerable capital investment in the services which exist in central urban areas, and, as has been shown quite conclusively in more than one place, these are often far from being fully utilized. There is an economic measure which reflects this use and this is the extent to which rates produce a full yield on these services. The rates paid prior to redevelopment in this same scheme to the local government authority were £872 per annum. After redevelopment the total rate amounted to £9990 per annum: figures which also indicate capital appreciation in the form of buildings and the extent to which the governing authority's budgetary position stands to with all-round benefit.

The foregoing figures relate mainly to r footpaths, drainage and water services, bu electricity and gas organizations also rec considerably higher revenues as the res better use of existing services.

Where in the same city suburban dweller faced with charges of at least 25/– a wee travel to and from their homes and plac work, they now pay at most about 4/– a wee travel over the very much shorter distance

The costs of construction of this scheme the rents which are being charged cl approximate to those for other types of dwell but the overall economic advantages appreciable, quite apart from the social ac tages, which do not need repetition. This sch is only one of a number which have alr shown a clear path to the solution of the p lems of urban renewal, slum clearance, revitalizing the dead heart of our cities.

7. It was recently estimated in London over a million people undertake exce journeys to and from work daily, at an an cost of £21½ million. These journeys repres lengthening of the working day of almost fifth and were equivalent to the loss of a la force of 220,000 people.

In the same survey it was found that there 556 jobs for every 100 resident workers in ce London, whereas in the remainder of the la administrative county there were about 87 for every 100 resident workers. Outside county, in the provincial areas, there were 73 jobs for 100 resident workers: figures w show very clearly indeed the serious imbal between jobs and homes in the central Lor area.

Table 6

Extract from 'The Planning of a New Town', LCC 1961

Housing Costs, Subsidies and Rents at year 15

	11-storey	4-storey	2-storey
1. Room average	2·25	3·4	4·72
2. No. of dwellings	414	6193	11,296
3. Average cap. cost/ dwelling[1]	£2400	£2140	£2010
4. Average land cost/ dwelling (% £600/ac.)	£8	£28	£43
5. Average develt. cost/ dwelling[2]	£99	£213	£296
6. Total cost/dwelling (*3* + *4* + *5*)	£2507	£2381	£2349
7. O'spill subsidy rate/dw./ annum	£12	£12	£12
8. Normal subsidy rate/ dwelling[3]	£63	£36	£28
9. Total subsidy amt/ dwelling/annum (*7* + *8*)	£75	£48	£40
10. Annual debt charge/dw. @ 5% int. over 60 years (*6* × 5·283%)	£132	£126	£124
11. Management costs/ dwelling	£44	£33	£33
12. Gross annual outgoing/ dwelling (*10* + *11*)	£176	£159	£157
13. Net outgoings/dwelling (*12* — *9*)	£101	£111	£117
14. Weekly rent/dwelling (*13* ÷ 52)	38/11	42/8	45/–
15. Weekly rent on 6⅛%	48/10	51/11	53/10

[1] Includes superstructure, foundations, drains, all outside works, contingencies, etc.

[2] Includes residential roads, amenity open space, playgrounds, play space and club rooms.

[3] As in Housing Bill 1961 (UK).

Table 7

Comparative Costs: Dwellings in London and at Hook

Height of building and dwelling size	London £	Reduction %	
2-storey, 4-room	2440	21·7	
4-storey, 3-room	2365	13·3	
11-storey, 2·1	2310	0	
2·25	2400		

ble 8

nual Costs/Dwelling £ (1961 Subsidies)

5% int.	2 Major roads, bridges, and p.u. services (no subs.)	3 Garaging	4 Land	5 Building Costs in Year 15	6 Minor roads, amen., open space etc.	7 Mant. Charges	8 Total outgoings (4,5,6,7)	9 Subsidy	Weekly rent 10 Ec. rent less subsidy (8–9)
: sity .a.									
	22·40	15·95	1·06	122·93	8·29	37	169·28	56	43/7
	28·37	7·82	2·69	100·90	19·39	33	155·98	41	44/3
⅛% int.									
	26·71	18·90	1·26	146·60	9·89	37	194·75	56	53/4
	33·83	9·32	3·21	120·53	23·12	33	179·66	41	53/4

le 9

nparative Costs, etc. 11-Storey Tower Blocks: Different Plan Types

rce: "Houses and Flats" 1958 (London)

type (cent. htd)	A Gross flr area av./dwg fs	B Net floor area av./dwg fs	A–B Common access space as % flr area	C Hab. flr area av./dwg fs	A–C Common access space + circn and service space % gross flr area	D External wall area av./dwg fs	Gross floor area to extl wall area ratio	Estd cost/dwg (bldgs only) S£	Habitable flr area to extl wall area ratio	
' Block stair lifts flats/flr	704	582	17·3	462	34·4	660	1·07	2040	·70	
ectangular Block lifts stairs flats/flr										
) alternative	713	591	17·1	445	37·6	527	1·35	2110	·84	
) alternative	695	567	18·4	450	35·3	527	1·32	2100	·86	
ouble Rectangle stairs lifts flats/flr cent. corridor)	731	586	19·8	439	40·0	446	1·64	1920	·98	Most economical arrangements
hort Slab stairs lifts flats/flr cent. corridor)	691	571	17·4	437	36·8	442	1·56	1900	·99	
urbine stairs lifts flats/flr	830	592	28·7	457	44·9	737	1·13	2360	·62	Least satisfactory

(excludes site works costs and abnormals)

le 11

ation of Cost with Height for Flats

of storeys	2	3	4	5	6	7	8	9	10	11	12	13	14	15	16	17
/square metre	366	328	308	300	327	323	320	421	417	413	455	452	449	446	444	442
over 5 storeys %/m²	22	9	3	0	9	8	7	40	39	38	52	51	50	49	48	47

K. Enderlein (Zentral Institut für Städtebau, Berlin)

Table 12 Indicative Gross Cost and Density Data (as available)

Scheme	Cost	Density
Sweden		
Reimersholm		·93 FSI 180 p.p.a.
Vällingby HSB (569 flats)	595 kr/m² (63/–/f²) S£2230/flat	
S. Hammarby (548 flats)	£2275/flat	110 p.p.a.
S. Guldheden (9 blocks of 38 flats)	£2700/flat	
Västertorp (90 flats)	4/10/f³	
Malmö (432 flats)	(60/–/f²)	
Generally 1954	3 flrs– (62/–/f²) 12 flrs– (56/6/f²)	300 p.p.a. (inner city)
United Kingdom		
Hallfield II (1949)	60/9/f² £1838/av. flat £689/av. hab. rm	176 p.p.a.
Eastbourne Terrace (1951)	54/–/f² £1935/av. flat	200 p.p.a.
Adpar Street (1956) (2 11-storey towers)	65/–/f² £2340/av. flat	158 p.p.a.
Loughborough Road (1958)	65/3/f² £2196/flat	
Roehampton (1958)	68/2/f² £2386/flat	
Bentham Road (1958)	66/–/f² £2254/flat	
Picton Street (1958)	61/3½/f² £2140/flat	
Perkins Heights	£1680/av. flat	315 p.p.a.
London generally (1960) (16–20 storey block)	£2750/flat 1, 2, 3 bedrooms	
BRS target (Craig) (1956)	48/–/f² £1630/av. flat £540/hab. rm	
Min. Housing UK (1958) 'T' block	£2040/flat	
Rectangular block	£2110/flat	
Double rectangle block	£1920/flat	
Slab block	£1900/flat	
Turbine block	£2360/flat	
Park Hill (1959) (5–14 storeys)	53/7/f² £1969/flat	192 p.p.a.
USA		
Bronx, New York (1957) (11–12 storeys)	$10·08/f² $10,700/flat	219 p.p.a.
Germany		
Kassel (1951) (50 flats)	68 DM/m³	
Grindelberg (204 flats)		250 p.p.a.
Holland		
Zuidplein	Fl.90/m³ Fl.17,200/flat	
Australia		
Sydney (1960)	£3250–6950/flat av.	
Torbreck (1960)	820/–1420/–f² £8600/av. flat	3·56 FSI
Domino (1960)	107/–/f² £3543–7086/flat	200 p.p.a.
Kingston Terrace (1960) (14-storey)	83/–/80/6/f² £5600/flat	
South Melbourne (120 flats)	£2705/flat	155 p.p.a.
France		
Sotteville	41/–/f²	250 p.p.a.
Villeneuve		250 p.p.a.
Pantin	41/6/f²	200 p.p.a.
Asnières		
Sèvres		250 p.p.a.
Chambéry		280 p.p.a.
Brest	49/–/f²	100 p.p.a.
Generally	£1600/av. flat	
Switzerland		
Malagnou	46/–/f²	180 p.p.a.
Letzigraben (1951)	47/–/f²	150 p.p.a.
Mittlerstrasse	53/–f²	350 p.p.a.
Denmark		
Bellahøj	£1500/av. flat	140 p.p.a.
Søndermarken	34/–/f² £2650/av. flat	250 p p.a.
Sorgenfri	38/6/f²	215 p.p.a.
Generally	39/–/f² £1400/flat	350 p.p.a. (inner city)
Italy		
Tuscalano		200 p.p.a.
St Paolo		250 p.p.a.
Generally	£1250/av. flat	
Norway		
The Hoff	47/6/f² £1500/flat	

Table 13
London Flat Costs on Room Basis (1951)

	£
LCC Scheme 1	577
2	661
3	707
Winchelsea House	684
Kelfield Ct	530
Wimbledon LCC	699
London LCC Av.	640
Fleming Ct	640
Queens Park Ct	740
Hallfield I	775
II	689
J. Aird Ct	718
Eastbourne Tce	651
Lancefield Ct	793
Tavistock Ct	716
St Philips	679
Gilbert Sheldon House	685
Church St	667

Table 14
Hansa Quarter, Berlin (1956) Flat Costs

No.	DM/m²	Storeys	% inc. of 5 storeys
5 Gottwald	390	4	30
9 Luckhardt	467	4	56
26 Taut	462	4	54
28 Senn	424	4	41
14 Niemeyer	558	7	86
16 Aalto	430	8	43
8 Vago	463	8	54
7 Gropius	460	9	53
15 Jolenecke–Samuelson	454	10	51
18 Hassenpflug	470	16	57
19 Schwippert	573	16	90
Le Corbusier	475	17	58
1 Muller–Rehm	443	17	48
20 Lopez–Beaudouin	554	14	85

(300 DM/m² normal)

Table 10
Costs related to Storey Heigh

STOREYS:

Reference
(1) *Institute of Bldg Research, Hanover*
(Dr Triebel)
(*a*) Cost of constn/flat 1 lift
(*b*) Cost of constn/flat 2 lift
(4 flats/floor)
(*c*) Alternative plan
(*d*) Alternative plan and 2 flats/floor no lift

(2) *City Engineer Malmö, Sweden*
(G. Lindmann)
Scandinavia
Cost/m² living area
(1953)

(3) *Belgium*
(Bldg Society)
Antwerp
Brussels
(1954)

(4) Denmark (1951)
(Min. of Hsg)
Costs/m²

(5) Cost Research Panel
RICS (UK)
(1954) analysis

(6) Ditto March 1958

(7) Ditto July 1958

(8) Ditto 1960

Case Study 18 Schemes
Costs/ft² gross
2·10 st. acc. balcony incl. in (
4·10 st. stair acc. incl. in (*a*)

(9) Bldg Res. Stn London
(Craig) 72
(April 1956) Schemes
(*a*) 700 ft² } survey
(*b*) 900 ft² }
(*c*) Target 680 ft²

(10) Min. of Hsg London
(Publn. *Houses & Flats* 1958)
Cost/dw. Excl. of access are
(*a*) 4 pers: 720 ft²
(*b*) 6 pers: 910 ft²
Additional to block for acces
for lifts (8 pers)

	2	3	4	5	6	7	8	9	10	11	12	13	15	20	Remarks
															Cost in D-Marks
		9833		8962		8851		8768							10·8% *reduction* 3 to 9 st.
		10610		9542		9303		9155							13·7% *reduction* 3 to 9 st.
	9642	9056		8982		9303		9155							16·0% *reduction* 1 to 9 st.
	no lift			1 lift			2 lifts								
	9642	8989	8655	8486											20·9% *reduction* 1 to 5 st.
															In Swedish Kroner (and sterling)
		482·2	454·2		452·9		439·5		436·9		441·1				9·4% *reduction* 3 to 10 st.
		(= 62/ft²)									(56/6 ft²)				·85% 10 to 12 st. increase
															Index figures
			100			119									21·4% increase 2 to 13 st.
			100			126									61·5% increase 2 to 13 st.
															Costs in Danish Kroner 14% increase
		422													
							40/6								Costs in sterling 42% inc. houses to. flats (cent. heating=£100—250/dw.)
	134										199				*Index figures* 48½% inc. houses—flats stair access (balc. access no economy)
/.		33–46/– (43/– av.) £1480/dw.			53–69/– ft² (54/– av.)		54–58/– ft² (54/– av.) £1910/dw.								29% inc. 3 to 8 st.
>			680 ft²					690 ft²							
2		47·97/– ft²					51·85		54·91/–						74% inc. 2 to 12-st. houses—flats or
/.		£1845/dw.					£2334/dw.		£2342/dw.						14·5% 3 to 13-st. flats
									£2230/dw. (59/– ft²gross £2628/dw. (63·55 gross			61·27/– av.)			18 schemes only and sample 6 to 13 st
									£1938/dw. (48·39/– gross £1972/dw. (47·08/– gross £2642/dw. (62·18/– gross £2319/dw. (52·93/– gross			52·64/– av. ft² gr.)			1/3 shows 50–60/– 1/3 40–50/– 6% only in 30–40/– and only 30% in 60–70/– av. shown are therefore misleading
					58/–	62/–	61/–	61/–	59/–	67/–	67/–	ft² net			
)					45/3 to 71/3	51/8 to 74/9	51/9 to 73/8	50/6 to 68/1	49/– to 69/3	51/7 to 89/2	62/8 to 73/9	Say 61/- genl av.			Insignificant difference 6 to 11 st. Samples show wide varieties of all levels. Av. indecisive
		size of sample			18	4	16	7	10	15	2				
							60/– ft²								
							53/– 48/– (£1630/dw.)								
															These are estimates not actual
		£1380/dw.		1530			1745				1845				33·7% inc. 3 to 12 st.
		1620		1790			2050				2170				34·0% inc. 3 to 12 st.
		1000		1850			3300				5150				Deduct £150 for each lift stop omitted
		2700		3300			4200				5100				

Table 15

Summarized National Comparative Flat Costs (Crude Averages)

UK:	S£1838	(1949)
	1935	(1951)
	2340	(1956)
	2196	(1958)
	2386	(1958)
	2254	(1958)
	2140	(1958)
	1969	(1959)
(Target)	1630	(1956)
	2040	(1958)
	2110	(1958)
	1920	(1958)
	1900	(1958)
	2360	(1958)
	2750	(1960)
	1680	(1954)
Australia:	A£2705	
	8600	
	3543–7086	
	5600	
	3250–6950	

US:	$10,700	1958
Sweden:	S£2275	
	2700	
	2230	
	av.1400	1954
Germany:	S£1165 av.	
Denmark:	S£1400 av.	
Switzerland:	S£1750 av.	
Italy:	S£1250	1954
Norway:	S£1500	
France:	S£1600	
Holland:	S£800	

Table 16

Cost Comparison Low and High Blocks Summarized

(Based on rates per sq ft)

(1) *Triebel* (Germany)	*16% redn.*	1–9 st.
(2) *Sweden*	*9·4% redn.*	3–10 st.
(3) *Britain* *Houses & Flats—1958*		
(*a*) (Theoretical example)	*34% inc.*	3–12 st.
(*b*) Lichfield: (Theoretical analysis)	*27·7% inc.*	2–12 st.
(*c*) CRP 1954	*42% inc.*	Houses to high flats
(*d*) CRP 1958	*29% inc.*	3–8 st.
(*e*) CRP 1960	*14·5% inc.*	3–13 st.
(*f*) *J. R. Instn Chart. Surv.* March 1958	*48½% inc.*	2–12 st.
(*g*) Reiners	*25% inc.*	3–12 st.
(*h*) Stone BRS	*85% inc.*	2–12 st.
(*i*) Craig BRS 1956	level	6–12 st.
(*j*) Min. Housing 1958	*29½% inc.*	3–12 st.

Table 17

Effect of Access Systems on Cost

Source	Balcony Access	Staircase Access
Craig BRS	60/–/f²	64/–/f²
Living in Flats—UK	—	b.a. + £320/flat
RICS Cost Research Panel 1958	index 247 equiv. to £2120	250 (12-storey blocks £2142
Houses & Flats—1958	£2120	£2280 (12-storey blocks)
RICS 1960 Survey	£1938–2642/flat (48.39/– to 62.18/–/f²) 61.27/– av.	£2230–2628/flat (59/– to 63.55/–/f²) 62.64/– av.
RICS March 1958	Shows graphically no detectable difference in cost at 3, 5 or 12 storeys (appr.) 160	170 (8 storeys)

Table 18

Analysis of Cost Proportions of Main Elements in 90 Schemes (in UK)

(Source: RICS, CRP 1960, and BRS Craig)

Cost distribution	BRS Craig 72 schemes	%	CRP 18 schemes	%
Substructure	4/0/f²	8	4/11/f²	9
Superstructure	19/0/f²	38	18/5/f²	37
Fittings and finishes	17/0/f²	35	17/5/f²	35
Heating and plumbing	£290/dwelling	14	£261/dwelling	13
Lifts	£110/dwelling	5	£115/dwelling	6

Table 19

Cost of Lift as Proportion of Whole Building Cost (and Other Service Rates)

Source	% Building cost	
RICS CRP 1960 6–13 storeys	7·4% *av.*	(*a*) *RICS Cost Research Panel* 1960 states: lift cost about £375–400/storey rise if 7–8 flats/floor; or £56 dwelling (2–3 flats/floor = £177/dwelling)
Staircase access 10 storeys	5·38 of 59/– : 9·1% 5·61 of 63·5/– : 8·85%	
Balcony access 10 storeys	2·94.48·39 : 6·1% 1·27.47·08 : 2·7% 2·95.62·18 : 4·7% 4·20.52·93 : 7·95%	(*b*) Refuse chute £9–30/dwelling av. (Garchey system £96–137/ dwelling av.)
LCC Fitzhugh	9·1%	(*c*) Plumbing £160/dwelling av.
Ackroydon	10·3%	
Sheffield Parke Hill	1·03.38·61 : 3·7%	(*d*) Electrical installation £100/ dwelling av.
Craig BRS av. 72 cases	5%	(*e*) Central Heating £100–250/ dwelling av.

Table 10—*continued.*

(11) Bldg Res. Stn London (Stone) (1959)
(*a*) Index for Inner London (*J. R. Instn Chart. Surv.*)
(*b*) 770 ft²
(*c*) 910 ft²
(*d*) 2 bedroom
(*e*) 3 bedroom

(12) Ditto (*J. R. Statist. Soc.*)
(*a*) Constn.
(*b*) Site works and services
(*c*) Estate running costs

(13) Reiners (*J. R. Instn Chart. Su*
(August 1958)
Adj. to 680 ft²

(14) Cumberland CC
Sydney (1958)

(15) Min. of Hsg London [
(Lichfield) p
£/person/annum equivalent
(*a*) Constn.
(*b*) Running Costs
(*c*) Total cost incl. land (w/o subsidy)

STOREYS

														Irregularity not explained
100	130	133	138	133	140	138	140	138	150					50% inc.
£1400/dw.										2700				Alternative 92%
1600										3000				figures 87% inc.
1230								2202	2275					85% inc. 2 to 11 st.
1470								2631	2720					
81	97	110	120	127	133	137	142	145		150				Annual costs £/dw.
17	15	14	13	12	12	12	12	12		12				85% inc. 2 to 12 st.
33	33	33	45	45	45	45	44	44		44				
	50/6	53/5	56/1		60/6				63/1					25% inc. 3 to 12 st.
	1·1						1·4–1·5							Index figures (estimates only)
														Assumes annual equivalents on 60 yr
			80	100	120		140	160	180	200	220	240	300	term repayment of cap. @ 5%
18				18			20			23	24	24		W.land @ £40,000/acre
5				5	5		5	5	6·1/2	8	8	8		@ 200 p.p.a. land = 20% total cost
26					25						24	24		@ 70 p.p.a. land = 54·5% total cost
														27·7% inc. 2 to 12 st.
2	3	4	5	6	7	8	9	10	11	12	13	15	20	Remarks

Selected Bibliography and References

Economics

1. Spillman, G.: 'Economics of Urban Expansion.' *Cumberland County Council*, December 1958.
2. 'The Economics of the Council House.' *PEP Broadsheet*, January 1950.
3. Reiners, W. J.: 'The Tender Prices of Local Authority Flats.' *R. Instn Chart. Surv. Journal*, August 1958.
4. Triebel, W.: 'Technical Progress of the Reduction of Constructional Costs in Dwellings.' *Institut für Bauforschung, Hanover.*
5. Priddle, R. A.: 'Building Economics.' *Architectural Science Review.*
6. Editorial: 'Report on Moray Court, South Melbourne.' *Foundations* 1960 (6).
7. Lichfield, N.: 'Economics of Planned Development.' *Estates Gaz.*, 1956.
8. Wibberly, G. P.: *Agriculture and Urban Growth.* Joseph 1959.
9. Craig, C. N.: 'Factors Affecting Economy in Multi-storey Flat Design.' *J. R. Inst. Brit. Archit.*, April and May 1956.
10. *Pratt Institute, Brooklyn, NY*: 'Methods of Reducing the Cost of Public Housing.' Dow Chemical Co.
11. Madsen, A. and Heiberg, E.: 'Hojt eller halvhojt boligbyggeri.' *Byggeforsknings institut, Copenhagen.*
12. Editorial: 'Cost Analysis—Flats.' *Archit. (Build.) J.*, April and July 1955.
13. Cost Research Panel: 'Factors Affecting Relative Costs of Multi-storey Housing.' *RICS Journal*, March 1958.
14. Cost Research Panel: 'The Cost and Design of High Flats.' *RICS Journal*, May 1961.
15. Cost Research Panel: 'Report on the Cost of Flats and Houses.' *RICS Journal*, July 1958.
16. Cost Research Panel: 'The Cost and Design of Low Flats.' *RICS Journal*, June 1960.
17. Cost Research Panel: 'Planning the Cost.' *RICS London*, May 1958.
18. Cost Research Committee: 'Cost Control at the Design Stage.' *J. R. Instn Brit. Archit.*, September 1958.
19. Metropolitan Boroughs: 'Variations in Cost of Repairs to Council Flats.' *Metropolitan Boroughs Standing Joint Committee*, January 1952, London.
20. Stone, P. A.: 'The Economics of Housing and Urban Development—Part IV.' *Royal Statistical Society Journal* 1959.
21. Stone, P. A.: 'Urban Development and Cost Prediction.' *RICS Journal*, October 1959, January 1960.
22. Lichfield, N.: 'Net Density, Cost and Value in Public Authority Dwellings.' *RICS Journal*, September 1960.
23. *New York City Housing Authority:* 'Construction Cost Analysis.' (1945).
24. Colean, M. L. and Davis, A. P.: 'Cost Measurements in Urban Redevelopment.' *National Committee on Housing*, New York, 1945.
25. Ludlow, W. H.: 'Land Values and Density Standards in Urban Redevelopment.' *J. Amer. Inst. Plann.*, October–December 1945.
26. McHugh, F. D.: 'Cost of Public Services in Residential Areas.' *Trans. Amer. Soc. Civ. Engrs*, CVII, 1942.

Social Factors

In a general way many of the arguments already put forward on town-planning grounds in support of high-density urban developments as against other alternatives, are based indirectly on considerations of social policy.

However, it is necessary to examine more fully the social aspects of this question in view of their importance in relation to environment and because this too has perhaps been the area of greatest criticism, especially from the orthodox 'garden-city' school.

With a regrettable tendency to ignore the evidence to the contrary, especially in countries such as Sweden, Switzerland, France and Denmark, objections are still focussed on family aspects of flat life. It is argued that communal playing and recreation areas are no substitute for individual gardens, where, it is suggested, some degree of privacy exists.

How far this may constitute a real deprivation for children in flats, needing correction in some other way, as with balcony gardens, or whether this is an assumption resting on one or more fallacies is a question that deserves some consideration. The theoretical assumption which is fundamental to so much traditional planning, particularly in relation to the neighbourhood idea, is that the garden is an indispensable part of the single-family house in order to ensure the proper physical and mental development of the child. It provides, also, for other things such as parental relaxation, and, somewhat paradoxically, gardening and fruit and vegetable production—all of which are anything but relaxing.

The truth is, however, that no suburban development affords outdoor privacy, but merely establishes clearly defined boundaries to properties serving only to prevent physical intrusion (which would be no less true of a private balcony to a flat). It permits free rein for individual ideas in garden layout; and helps perpetuate the idea, steeped in antiquity, of the rich man in his castle. It also creates however, an area of increased responsibility for maintenance and upkeep, additional to that of the dwelling itself.

Visual intrusion is usually impossible to prevent, but in practice this real loss of privacy does not seem to be resented by the majority of suburban dwellers.

Noise is transmitted from one garden to another and from each dwelling to its neighbours, so as to defy any hope of the aural privacy which is readily available in any reasonably designed apartment building. Why then the fiction of suburban seclusion, which must surely in any case be at variance with the ideas of neighbourliness which we are currently asked to accept?

Another basic fallacy is the one which says, by implication, that as the child must have its own play-patch it should not have to play in company with others. On the contrary, it is essential for the development of social conscience and awareness that children of all ages should frequently meet others with different viewpoints and interests, both in their work and their play. It is surely obvious that the child denied these opportunities is the one to be pitied and it is perhaps one of the most serious indictments of the typical suburb that so many of these have made little or no provision for collective play areas with the necessary safe access.

The Radburn idea attempted to meet just th need, but its practical application has be all too rare. However, in a number of rece examples of suburban and new-town develo ment, the individual garden or patio attached the dwelling is greatly reduced in size, a compensation is found in community playi areas similar to those associated with flat li Where these occur in the dispersed suburb layout, they have to be linked together wi pedestrian parkways, which have relative limited amenity value and use up large areas valuable land in total, and which would be much greater benefit combined together communal parks and recreation areas.

The fact is that while clearly 'it has been tacit assumption in much housing and to planning during the present century that t ideal house for the young family with childr is a cottage or a villa, or a semi-detached hou with a garden,' it is increasingly evident that garden can be the most controversial place earth' (11). As civilized communities devel truly cultural interests, and with the increasi pressure on time, particularly in the suburb where commuting may absorb anything up to sixth of the life span of the bread-winner, the is no longer the same opportunity nor often t inclination to do more than the essential mi mum of gardening. Beyond this, the limited ti available for leisure pursuits can be spent in many more rewarding or, if need be, more laxing ways. The evidence of this can be se in the labour-saving garden, or in the number neglected gardens in those neighbourhoo where it is merely a consequential burden whi arises from the economic necessity of finding dwelling in an outlying area where land co are lower.

The economic necessity, rather than fr choice, underlies the acceptance of the sub ban dwelling in a great many cases and further evidenced by the fact that it operates spite of the heavy drain on the family budg both in terms of money, time and energy, creat by travel. The fatigue part of this equation, r though it is, cannot readily be evaluated. Ma are spending 3 to 4 hours daily, travelling in a out of cities, and this travel may cost as much twelve times that for city journeying.

While all this commuting takes place there in most regions an undue concentration employment in urban centres with a diminishi volume of housing. No doubt can remain as the remedy, when we are reminded that ' greater the spread the more attractive the cent area is for employment that cannot be decent lized', and that 'although the ideological ar ments about decentralization and about hous and gardens will no doubt continue, the soc statistics prove that already the facts have ov taken us' (11). In other words there can now no escaping the urgent need for more hous near to work in metropolitan areas. As has n become clear, a great deal of employment is mobile, either because it is unable or l amenable to functioning outside the 'cent business district'.

No-one appears to dispute that the flat apartment can be eminently suitable for young couple. There is seldom adequ realization, however, that in most of the west countries at least, due primarily to a lon expectation of life, there is increasing incider of an ageing population, and in the majority these cases the large family dwelling with the burden of the upkeep of a garden is an anachronism. The labour-saving flat on the other hand, all on one level and equipped with modern conveniences including lifts, refuse chutes, and a private balcony, and with the companionship of families and children nearby, is in many ways the ideal remedy for melancholia or boredom. Near at hand is the garden, not a demanding 'patch' surrounded by fences and needing constant attention, but a large, spacious and well-maintained park-like area giving a unique sense of freedom.

It has sometimes been suggested that, although there may be advantages in the provision of communal play areas for children living in flats, these are unsuitable for the very young, and that, because of the distance from domestic supervision, this results in these children being kept indoors as a precaution. Enquiries, and actual observation and experience in a large number of cases, indicates that the contrary is true. The domestic duties are reorganized in such a way as to allow more time for individual supervision of children's play out of doors, or alternatively mothers look after groups of children on a roster system. In many European schemes trained supervisors are employed.

On the other hand, some of the reasons given by families interviewed in flats in London as advantages of living high are revealing. The majority cited better air and healthier conditions; and many, the quiet, the good view, the daylight and sun, the feeling of not being enclosed, and

ıe labour saving flat with modern conveniences ɖ a private balcony'

ıligfeld Development, Zurich, Switzerland
:hitect: Steiner

th these areas are
ociated children's
houses'

Terrasse, Oslo, Norway
hitects: Torp and Torp

the sense of privacy. It will be apparent, ironically enough, that many of these have been argued previously as theoretical defects.

Some familiar disadvantages of living high were also referred to in the survey, such as lift breakdowns and vertigo, but most can readily be overcome by care in planning, or by reasonable parental precautions. It is most desirable that the communal recreation areas should if possible segregate children into age-groups, in order to avoid injury to the young by the older and more boisterous children, and in order to ensure in each case provision of the most suitable equipment and activities. One of the suggestions for this grouping has been that quite small areas should be provided for children of two to five years old, as near as possible to the entrances of each flat block, as has been done in many Scandinavian developments, and containing sandpits, play sculpture or equipment and a safe unclimbable fence surround. With these are associated frequently the 'playhouses', particularly for use in bad weather. This may be the best location for necessary toilet provision, especially for the very young children, if dwellings are some distance away.

The National Playing Fields Association in Britain (5) has recommended that each child in this group should be given an area of about 4 square yards and that each of the playgrounds should accommodate not more than 37 children: standards which appear to be reasonable, and in conformity with practice in a number of countries.

The five- to ten-year-olds can use more centralized facilities, although these should still be conveniently located in relation to apartment access. In this case 10 square yards per child is recommended with a maximum of 40 children to each playground. Simple foolproof equipment only is recommended, but unless there is supervision no equipment at all would be a safe rule to follow. Some paved all-weather surface may also be desirable; but the main emphasis should be on usable grass areas with trees and shrubs, play sculpture, climbing frames, and mock-ups of vehicles linked by stepping-stone paths which blend in sympathetically.

The senior group of nine- to fifteen-year-olds, in which there should be 15 square yards per child, with a total of just over 50 children in each area, can be completely centralized, and located up to a quarter of a mile from dwellings for preference, in order to avoid noise nuisance. These areas will need a still higher proportion of all-weather paving suitable for the very much harder wear they are likely to receive. Formal equipment is less appropriate, as it is important to allow maximum space and scope for free activities: ball games with suitable enclosures, and camping areas, with space too for 'junk' playground activity with building materials, and a lock-up tool shed. Larger numbers of children must have covered facilities for use during bad weather and at other times, for plays, dancing, modelling, painting, and perhaps also a library.

There may be some untidiness associated more especially with the junk playground, but this seems a necessary safety-valve for children who must otherwise respect the amenities of flat and garden alike. A great deal can be done to mask and give a greater degree of privacy to all the free-activity play areas, by the judicious use of shrubs, rock walls, and landscaping with flower beds.

Provision for all these areas, together with that needed for adults, can readily be met from the 150 sq ft per habitable room which has already been recommended. Of the total area available about a quarter of an acre is suggested for playgrounds for every 100 to 130 children, although this cannot be regarded as a hard and fast figure. It is assumed moreover that children older than those specifically provided for will, by cycling or walking, be able to reach major open spaces for more formal games and sports.

Not strictly as a part of the children's play area, but associated with it, there might well be accommodation of very simple type for a limited number of pets. In redevelopment areas the abandonment of pets can often form a very real deprivation, particularly for children, and may be psychologically so serious as to nullify completely all the other advantages which flat life, with its community play facilities can have. Many types of pets could be accommodated in an annex to the children's playhouse, or in something akin to the box-room or store-room—a vitally necessary space for every apartment building. These could also be used for dogs and cats if it were impossible to accommodate them in the flat without causing a nuisance. The cost involved in this would be extremely small as compared with the whole development, and could be the means of meeting a difficult family problem or eliminating a potent cause of friction between landlord, tenant and neighbour.

There is much to be said for setting aside space in the garden as quiet secluded areas, sheltered by trees and shrubs, and provided with comfortable seats where elderly people can sit and enjoy the sunshine in peace. For preference these should be located quite close to the children's play areas since there seems to be a bond of sympathetic interest between the young and the old, which greatly benefits both.

There is no need for amenity garden areas to be hedged in with restrictions and prohibitions if planned intelligently, although some temporary restrictions may be necessary in the early period of growth of grass, shrubs and trees. These, however, should not be permanent, but planting should be in the form of the most durable materials and the least susceptible to damage, accidental or deliberate. The grouping and arrangement of the planting should be free and informal rather than formal and 'municipal'. Only in this way can an uninhibited and homely quality be achieved.

There is little merit however in attempting to divide up garden areas into individual plots with the idea of creating pride of ownership. This arrangement fritters away valuable garden space without producing correspondingly worthwhile benefits, and experience has shown that the plots are not really wanted, and quickly become neglected and untidy.

Clothes should, wherever possible be dried in the open air. It is obviously impracticable to do this in garden areas adjoining multi-storey blocks of flats without creating an unsightly nuisance, but provision can often be made for this purpose on a flat roof, or alternatively sometimes a complete floor of the apartment block is set aside for both drying and laundry facilities. The communal laundry which has often been used for reasons of economy is inevitably seldom popular with flat dwellers, and is now tending to be replaced wherever possible by laundries to individual dwellings or small groups of dwell-

re is little merit in attempting to divide up len areas'

enveronikan, Göteborg, Sweden
nitects: Brolid and Wallinder

need for amenity garden areas to be hedged in
n restrictions'

on Estate East, Wandsworth, London, England

ings. This is also better from a management point of view.

Included in these independent arrangements will also be drying facilities, which can be in the form of a heated cupboard, or better still a louvred or screened enclosure adjoining the flat balcony.

So often in the suburban house the garage becomes the repository of surplus junk, and often a baggage, furniture, pram or bicycle store for which no space exists inside the home. It is essential that equivalent storage accommodation exists for every flat, but this can usually be away from the flat itself without causing undue inconvenience.

Another use of the suburban garage is as a workshop, and equivalent communal space is very desirable indeed in every flat development of any size. This may also be associated with a room for meetings, dances, amateur theatricals and other social gatherings. Experience suggests however that these facilities may well be delayed until there is spontaneous demand for them on a wide enough scale; although the initial planning should provide space for the purpose.

Particularly in those cases where flats accommodate a substantial proportion of young or elderly couples, a restaurant in or near the premises, and with full service facilities, may be well justified. The use of the facilities by outside patrons also can often create a lively atmosphere; but may in some types of scheme be regarded as intrusive.

Two other factors with an important bearing on the social aspects of high-density urban development are, first, the form of access, with the effect it has on privacy and the exposure of tenants and visitors to noise, traffic disturbance and weather, as with the access balcony; and second, the arrangement of similar rooms where dwellings adjoin, as a means of reducing noise nuisance, as, too, the location of lifts and refuse chutes.

These will be examined in more detail in a subsequent section devoted to the detailed planning of the building.

The need for specific areas for car parking or garaging has already been commented on. In order to obviate infringement of amenity these should, wherever practicable on grounds of economy, be placed underground, since this will remove the cars from sight while often providing roof areas which can be planted suitably as additional garden space. One car space per family will generally suffice, although this will obviously differ with the circumstances and the location of the scheme. In the not too distant future, certainly in America and Australia, two cars per family will be the rule rather than the exception. Then parking space will have to be entirely underground, if amenity space is to remain, or the economics of the scheme not seriously jeopardized.

It is implicit in all the foregoing that whenever high-density development takes place this should form a part of a fully comprehensive pattern of planning, linked with all the necessary facilities, including shops, schools, places of employment, and cultural facilities. It is especially important too that crèches and nursery schools should be located within convenient walking range of every flat in which there are likely to be small children. All of these factors taken together should then add up to an ideal total environment from a sociological as well as other points of view.

'High density development should form part of a comprehensive pattern of planning'

Kärrtorp, Stockholm, Sweden
Architect: Klemming

Selected Bibliography and References

Social

1. Brooke Committee. 'Living in Flats.' *HMSO,* 1952.
2. Willis, M. 'Living in High Blocks of Flats.' *Hous. Cent. Rev.,* January 1954.
3. Jensen, R. A. *Social Needs of Families in Flats.* Report, London, November 1950.
4. Willis, M. 'Play Areas on Housing Estates.' *Hous. Cent. Rev.,* November 1953.
5. *National Playing Fields Association.* 'Playgrounds for Blocks of Flats.' December 1953.
6. Gooch, R. B. 'Selection and Layout of Land for Playing Fields and Playgrounds.' *National Playing Fields Association.*
7. Lederman, A. and Trachsel, A. *Playgrounds and Recreation Spaces.* Architectural Press, 1955.
8. *Deutschen Gesellschaft fur Gartenku und Landschaftspflege:* 'Kinderspielplät Callwey, 1957.
9. Lindquist, N. and Odquist-Bark, E. 'Bå familier i höghus och trevaningh *Byggmästaeren A2*, 1958.
10. Logie, G. 'Playgrounds.' *Architect,* Lonc June 1954.
11. Symposium. 'Family Life in High-Den Housing.' *RIBA*, May 1957.
12. Grove, A. B. and Chadwick, G. F. 'A F Area in High-Density Development.' *Ho Cent. Rev.,* November 1953.
13. Sudell, R. 'Development of Children's P grounds.' *Munic. J.,* London, May 1954.
14. Wilson, J. C. 'An Inquiry into Commu Laundry Facilities.' *HMSO*, London, 194
15. *Metropolitan Association Chief Hous Officers.* 'Questionnaire on Laundri London, June 1953.

Grouping, Layout and Detail Planning

It is hoped that it may be agreed that whatever the dimensions of an urban housing project it is a part of the civic design mosaic, and this implies recognition at the outset that grouping, planning and design cannot be carried out solely on an introspective basis, but in relation to neighbouring developments, existing or proposed. These relationships must be considered as part of a long-term comprehensive plan, even if in some cases it creates slight temporary inconvenience.

High buildings will obviously form an important element in most high-density housing developments, and in view of their prominence it is all the more important that they are grouped and located satisfactorily and that the highest standards of architectural quality are attained, even if, as seems inevitable, this necessitates aesthetic and town-planning control by a co-ordinating authority. Precisely how this form of control is applied is always a vexed question, and will depend very much on the circumstances of the case. It is clear that these matters cannot be handled beneficially for the community solely by those responsible for individual schemes, since in these cases there cannot possibly be the knowledge of long-term intentions or proposals in adjoining areas necessary to achieving compatibility. Only through such a coordinating authority can major or minor developments be designed to fit appropriately into the town-planning framework.

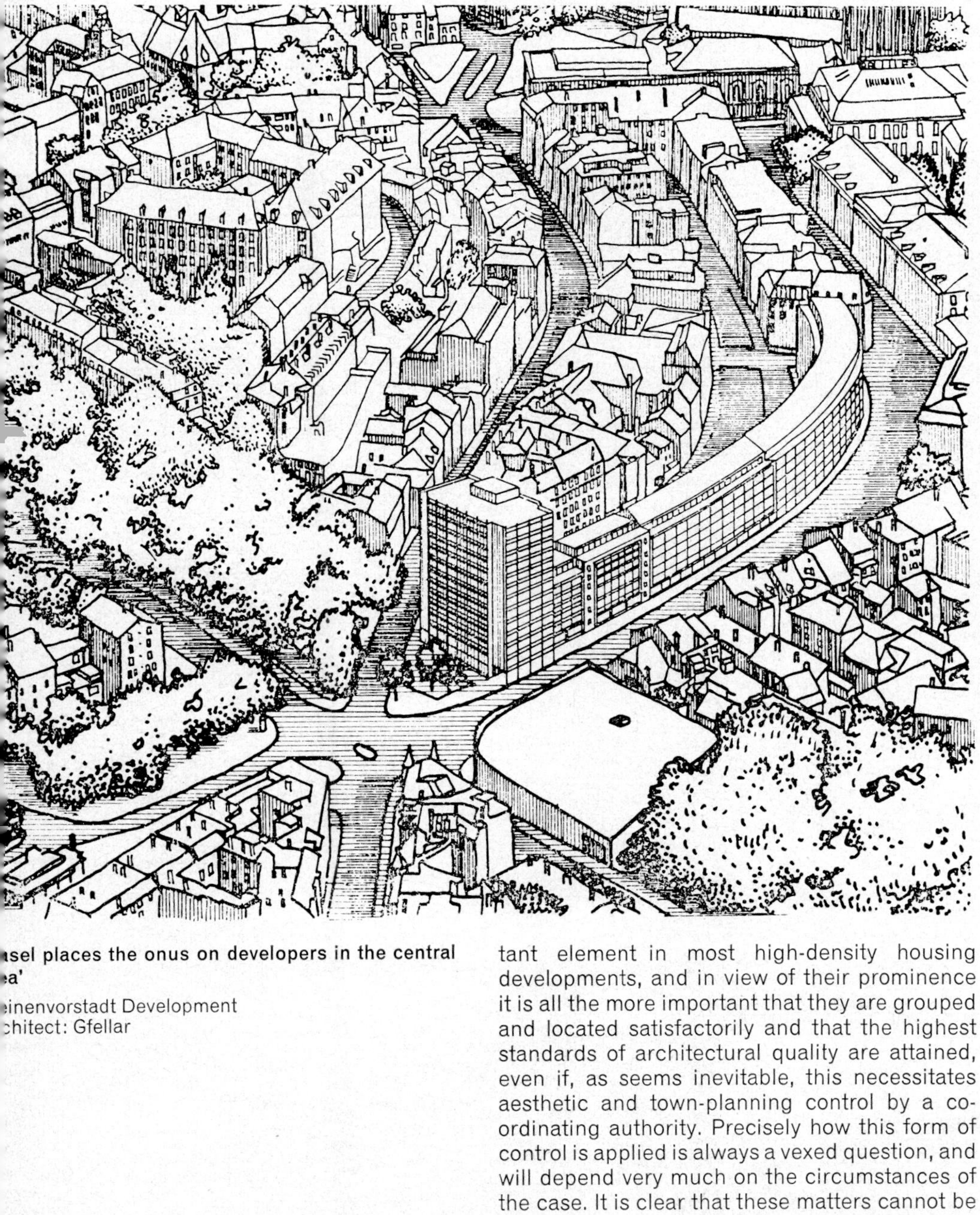

asel places the onus on developers in the central ea'

einenvorstadt Development
chitect: Gfellar

The London County Council thought it worthwhile to produce a set of guiding rules which were used in conjunction with their statutory town-planning powers as a means of dealing with this problem. Another civic planning authority, in Basel, Switzerland, places the entire onus on the developers in a central urban area, who have to show that their proposals are not likely to be objectionable either aesthetically or in relation to civic design. The technique used in this usually involves making a number of photomontages and perspective drawings of the project in its intended setting, as seen from key points.

As a means of ensuring adequate natural lighting in streets and for neighbouring properties, especially where high buildings are involved, too many of the systems are based on arbitrary rules of thumb, which are of questionable efficiency and tend to produce stereotyped building forms and layouts.

A most satisfactory way of dealing with this problem lies in the use of the daylighting code referred to earlier. This provides the necessary flexible form of control, ensuring reasonable daylighting conditions in the development and for neighbouring properties and streets. It also serves as a valuable planning tool with which grouping of buildings can be tested at an early stage to meet both aesthetic and functional requirements. The use of this system could, amongst others, logically entirely supplant the existing statutory safeguards given in many cases to owners adjoining development areas.

Another basic and indisputable need, if this type of development is to achieve a human quality, is that of variety, without detracting from an equally desirable unity. There are, however, too numerous cases in which 'lamella' blocks have been repeated or extended over large areas with little or no change in orientation. It may often be very much better to accept quite frankly some imperfections in aspect and sunlighting in order to ensure that variety and the total environment do not suffer.

Overshadowing may be a part of this problem and here there is a question of judgement. It may seem desirable from one view point to plan for internal courts and amenity garden areas so as to provide some privacy. On the other hand, one of the great advantages of the 'point block' is in the creation of park areas surrounding buildings with an absence of any sense of enclosure or restriction. What is needed is perhaps a nice balance between privacy and space.

Too extensive a use of the point block in large groups, without contrasting buildings of other types, is also unsatisfactory and can lead to a 'candlestick' effect which may be just as monotonous as repetitive slab layouts. A judicious balance of different building types in which high buildings are interspersed with and linked to low flat or maisonette blocks or terrace houses, is likely to produce the best results and will provide the necessary visual contrasts and establish a transition in scale from the more massive buildings and larger spaces to human dimensions.

Large unbroken oceans of lawn lapping at the foot of high cliffs of building can often be rather unrealistic in terms of practical use and may entirely deprive an urban area of the essential quality of townscape, which must be re-created in a contemporary idiom.

A great many different plan arrangements and building types have now been devised to suit high-density conditions; so that there is no longer the simple distinction between the basic types of slab and point block. There are now many combinations of these, with some using less orthodox forms of access such as the central corridor or 'skip-stop'.

Because the point block is not limited to the earlier characteristic four flats per typical floor, it often becomes in effect a short slab block. The slab block, on the other hand, very often uses the type of access normally associated with the point block. For convenience, however, these terms will be retained, as they are generally understood, and in spite of the merging of types, can still be identified with a special characteristic, which in the case of the point block is very low site coverage; and in the case of the slab block normally a predominantly horizontal treatment.

It is desirable to consider some of these typ more fully, particularly in relation to the acce systems, and to distinguish the princip characteristics, the advantages and the di advantages. The four main types of slab blo arrangement are:

(*a*) Direct staircase access (with either tw three or four flats per floor per staircase
(*b*) Balcony access;
(*c*) Central corridor access (including 'triple and other skip-stop arrangements);
(*d*) Maisonette (or 'duplex', including gard flats).

Of these the most frequently used is the dire staircase access with two flats on the typic floor to each staircase, and to a single lift. As th type of planning rarely makes provision f interchange as between one staircase and and another, these elements serve a relative limited number of dwellings, and provide

'Planning arrangements of maisonettes'

Churchill Gardens, Pimlico, London, England
Architects: Powell and Moya

ernative lift service in the event of break-wns. The arrangement is not an economical e, but it has the great advantage that all ellings may have dual aspect, and if needed, ough ventilation.

The balcony access system, often claimed to more economical, can no longer be justified these grounds. It can only be associated at satisfactorily with small dwellings in which re becomes no question of passing habitable oms. Traffic will, however, probably have to ss both kitchens, bathrooms and entrance lls, all of which will have to have window enings on that side of the building. This is refore not an arrangement likely to achieve vacy, and is one that creates a difficult sthetic problem in the dominating horizontal ect of the balconies, which building regula-ns normally require to be unglazed and screened.

Access balconies also create a serious poten-l risk to children, of vertigo to the elderly or the nsitive, and invoive certain exposure to the ments. They overshadow the rooms on that le of the building, and are frequently noisy. me have seen them as meeting grounds and means of fostering neighbourliness, but perience shows that a great majority of tenants slike them.

A preferable system, and one which makes aximum use of stairs and lifts, is that based on central corridor access. If this is to function fely in an emergency such as a fire, however, is essential that there should be no 'dead ds' but that staircases be located in the ngs, rather than in the centre of the block, as so often the case. There is, however, no objec-n to lifts being placed centrally.

The simplest form of corridor access is that th single aspect flats on a wide frontage on th sides of the corridor at every floor level. other versions the corridor occurs on every cond or third floor, and from this access is tained either to flats on the same level, or up down to maisonettes of the 'scissors' or oss-over' type. Another similar system is the ndwich'. All the variations on this theme have en devised with the main idea of reducing the mber of lift stops and thus obtaining econo-es in lift gear and openings. In some instances ey also provide dwellings with dual aspect, t at the cost of additional internal staircases d inconvenient changes in level.

Good standards of insulation are of course al to the corridor walls with this system. rforations should also be reduced to the nimum, and this renders cross-ventilation practicable to any but the corner dwellings—great disadvantage, in warmer climates pecially, unless air-conditioning can be onomically justified.

The fourth planning arrangement associated th the slab block is that in which all the dwell-gs are 'maisonettes' planned on two levels. se of this system appears to suggest certain ssible economies, in that an access balcony necessary only at alternate floor levels, and in any cases timber intermediate floors within e dwellings are permissible, since these do not nstitute party structures separating different cupations. Fire-escape needs, however, make second balcony at bedroom level practically sential, and although this can be made lighter construction and smaller than the normal cess balcony the economy achieved is slight.

Extra expense is also involved in individual staircases to each dwelling in addition to the main access staircase, which must still run the full height of the building. The lifts may stop at alternate floor levels, with some saving on switch gear and landing gates, but total savings in cost are outweighed by extras, and the advantage of dual aspect by the inconvenience of dual levels and the need for an access gallery.

Typically this form of planning results in a site coverage of about twenty-five to thirty per cent. There is some tolerance in orientation in the dual aspect system, but much less so with the single-aspect flat using balcony access. This will have a bearing on and must be related to grouping and enclosure.

The planning of blocks round a central internal court—encountered in Italy and Spain, is a lesser variant. In other cases too, slabs have, as an elaboration, been linked in long curved ribands or labyrinthine forms or in segmental patterns, but with no difference in basic charac-teristics.

The earliest point blocks were planned with four or five flats to the typical floor, and in the majority of cases direct access was provided from a core staircase and lift. They were essen-tially a development of the direct staircase access system which has already been considered in relation to the slab block. In an effort to intro-duce greater economies, consistent with privacy and convenience, a considerable number of variations on this original theme have been devised. In some cases the staircase lobby may link with as many as eight flats direct. In other cases short internal spur corridors link the lobby with even iarger numbers of flats and thus make for a more economical use of the lifts and stairs.

In some schemes short access balconies are used instead of corridors—a much less satis-factory system. Using one of these basic methods or combinations of these, some of the resulting planning forms are:

(*a*) The square or rectangular plan, with either one or two staircases planned internally or on outside walls according to local building acts, and providing access to from four to eight flats to the typical floor with direct access, or up to a maxi-mum of twelve to sixteen flats per floor with central corridor access links;
(*b*) The double linked rectangle;
(*c*) The 'Y' or 'T', normally with three flats to the typical floor (one per wing), but six or more flats have also been planned on the 'back-to-back' system;
(*d*) The cross, normally with four flats to the typical floor;
(*e*) The windmill or multi-wing system, with wings planned as in (*c*).

In addition there are the swastika, the polygon, the triangle, the 'H', the linked double cross, the circle, the cluster or butterfly plan, and other free forms.

With a multiplicity of plan arrangements such as these it is only possible to evaluate them in general terms alongside a common set of criteria. Generally speaking, the simplest plan shape will be the most economical, both from a structural point of view and in reducing the extent of external wall. The plans based on the rectangle are simpler and speedier to construct using standard systems. The reduction of peri-

'The square or rectangular plan'

Stieracker, Birsfelden, Switzerland
Architects: Gass and Associates

Lillo Terrasse, Oslo, Norway
Architects: Christiansen and Roslend

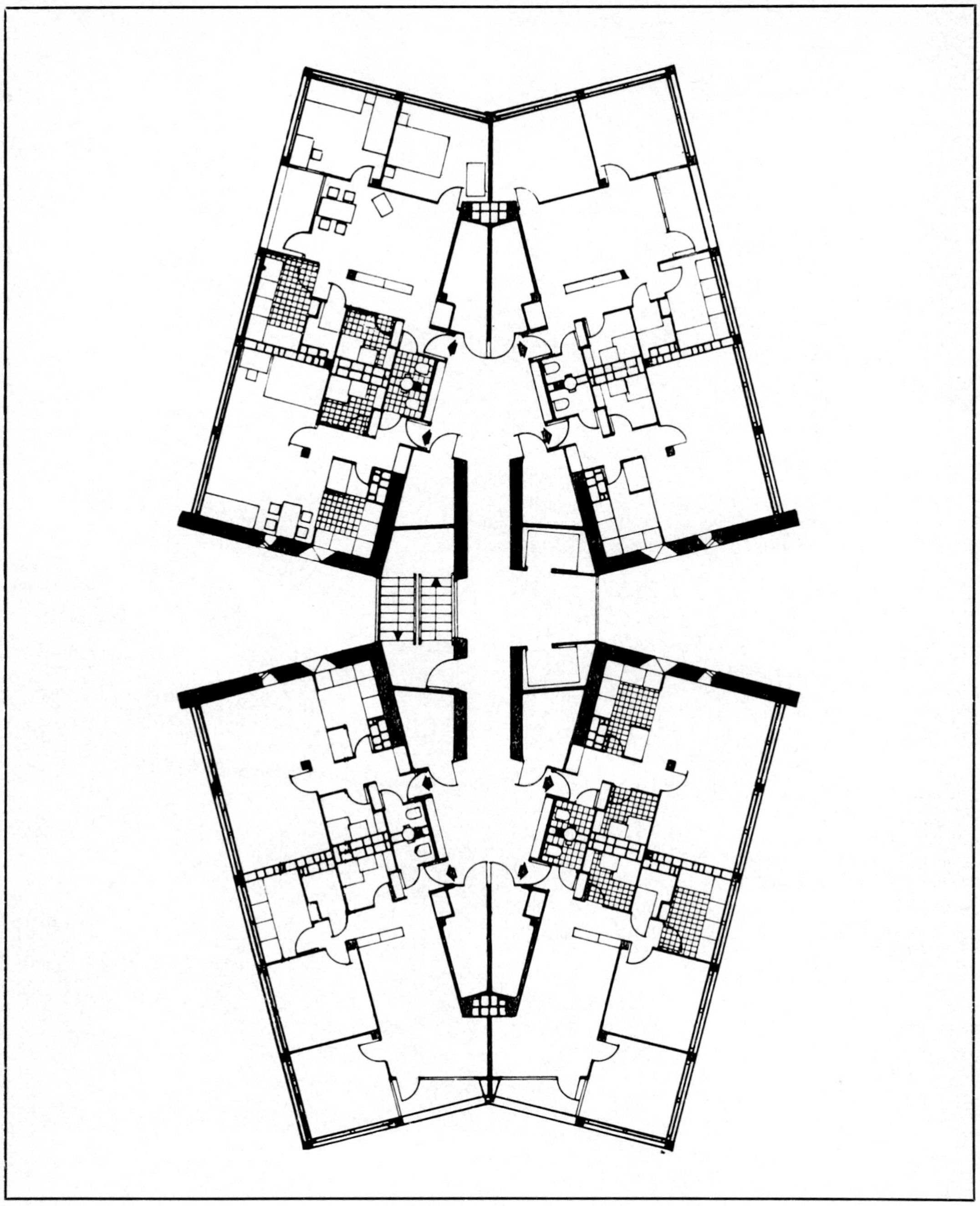

'There is a multiplicity of plan shapes'

Firminy-Vert, France
Architects: A. Sive, N. Rour, Delfante and J. King

'Planning footpaths away from the building'

Tuscolano Estate, Rome, Italy
Architects: M. Renzi and S. Muratori

meter wall also has the advantage of not only reducing initial capital cost, but limiting surface area through which heat transfer can take place between the inside and the outside of the building. The circular plan presents the smallest possible perimeter wall as a ratio of the enclosed floor area, but there are obvious planning difficulties. The square plan is more practical and nearly as efficient.

These simpler shapes have been used a great deal, but even with superficial variations possibilities of aesthetic variety are limited—a matter of special importance in larger schemes. They do, however, confer the boon of greater privacy to the individual dwelling and freedom from overlooking and noise transmission between neighbours. These become increasingly difficult with more complex shapes; as does achieving ideal aspect, orientation, insolation and daylight, and freedom from overshadowing.

If a point block is to contain a wide range of flat sizes, including family flats, it becomes increasingly difficult to use simpler plan shapes or the more compact forms, and internal spur access corridors as well as back-to-back arrangements become inevitable. There is no reason, however, why this type of planning should not be perfectly satisfactory if pass doors are provided between terminal flats to obviate the risk of these tenants being cut off by a fire within the dwelling. In order to avoid their being cut off by a corridor fire, two flats to the wing should be the norm, unless some other secondary escape can be provided.

This limitation will also ensure two outside walls and therefore dual aspect and view for each dwelling, as well as cross angle ventilation and good daylighting and insulation.

So far as internal planning is concerned it is essential that advantage be taken of the possibilities of vertical repetition and standardization. The location of service runs will encourage this, as well as probable over-all economies in structure and equipment.

Some flexibility will, within limits, still possible, but it is seldom possible to desig dwellings specifically to the needs of the indi dual client. Nevertheless within the prescrib limitations of structure and services a congen environment for the large majority of famili must be the aim, with the maximum degree adaptability.

In temperate climates the sizes and aspec of windows should be dictated primarily natural lighting needs and requisite sunlig even if this should involve double glazing reduce heat losses during the winter. In warm climates, however, it will be necessary to restri window areas as a means of reducing s glare and heat absorption from solar radiatio In satisfying daylighting and insolation howev overlooking and view must also be considered.

The importance of privacy in relation to acce systems has already been stressed, but it equally important inside the dwelling. F example, bathrooms and W.C.'s should not

nned adjoining and in full view of callers at front door, and with cross traffic from bed-ms across the entrance hall. It is equally satisfactory to force visitors to a flat to pass et facilities and bedrooms on the way to ng areas. All these objections can be over-ne by planning with well-defined day and ht zones, in all but the very small units, as uld be normal in house planning.

The day area, consisting of living room, ing room, kitchen and laundry, should be ar the entrance to the dwelling. There may o be a separate tradesmen's entrance in this ea. The night zone should be self-contained h bathrooms and toilets *en suite* with the drooms.

n some cases building regulations permit en planning' where the living room becomes circulation centre, leading to other rooms; in ers it is not permissible and it is necessary provide an internal hall or corridor connecting habitable rooms to the entrance hall. This stipulation is intended to obviate risk of those in rooms remote from the entrance being cut off by a fire in the day rooms. This appears to be a remote possibility and has the great disadvantage of enforcing the introduction of wasteful internal circulation areas as a heavy non-productive on-cost, nor are these entirely free from theoretical risk.

It is, however, certainly not a desirable solution to this difficulty to plan bedrooms near the flat entrances; rather should greater reliance be placed on contemporary structural standards and heating installations.

It is most desirable that the dwelling should be self-contained so far as is practicable, and while some storage accommodation may have to be provided in a basement, other facilities, including laundry and drying area, should preferably be within the dwelling itself. Another way too of ensuring privacy is to make all the main plumbing stacks, as well as gas and electricity and other services such as central heating and piped radio or television, accessible from public hallways, so that it is unnecessary to enter flats for maintenance or inspection, except of branch services.

Other ways in which privacy of the individual dwelling can be assured or greatly added to are in structural insulation standards both to party walls and floors; these have a vital bearing on privacy and this will be discussed in a later section. Airborne sound is a more intractable problem: not so much from adjoining buildings, however, as from one flat to another vertically within the same block, particularly in those seasons when most of the windows are likely to be open. Projecting balconies may somewhat minimize this possibility, but with the consequential disadvantages of cost and overshadowing. A better system is one in which windows are staggered from one floor to the next to provide maximum separation.

Unless planned with considerable care balconies may actually result in a loss of privacy.

It is also very questionable, strictly on grounds of utility, whether in many climates the limited degree of their use warrants the additional cost involved, whether they are designed to project from the main face of the structure, or recessed at the expense of one of the main rooms. To be of practical value they must be at least 6ft in clear depth and 12 to 15ft in width. This means an addition of about 10 per cent to, or a reduction from, the total area of the flat; in neither case very good economics.

Similar benefits can be obtained by including full-height windows with balustrades to the living rooms. When opened these convert the area of the adjoining room to usable space equivalent to the balcony, at all seasons, and without reduction of essential living space.

The location of lifts and refuse chutes requires serious consideration, as nuisance can be caused if these adjoin habitable rooms. Instead, the lift shaft should form a self-contained core structure isolated from the remainder of the building; and refuse chutes planned remote from bedrooms or living rooms but as close as possible to kitchens. This will mean, very often, the sharing of this facility by four to six flats on each floor. There are exceptions where every flat is served independently, as, for example with the Garchey system, but this is rarely adopted for reasons of cost.

Privacy in the building as a whole, by discouraging those who are neither residents nor legitimate visitors is very desirable. In some cases it has been thought sufficient to provide an enclosed entrance lobby where are located tradesmen's and postmen's delivery boxes, under supervision of a caretaker. Elsewhere it has sometimes been considered necessary to install telephone communication between flats and the main entrance. The entrance door is then normally locked, and access to the building is either by key or by the remote electrical release of the lock by a tenant after telephone communication. This is an excellent but somewhat expensive system widely used in Europe.

The staircase in a high building is an important and costly element in the design, and it is essential that within reason it should give access to the maximum number of flats at each floor, and that it should not be duplicated. While certain building regulations at present insist on two staircases, despite the limited separation in point blocks having only four flats to typical floor, this ruling is based on a mista concept of security which it rarely guarantee

As an alternative arrangement in cert circumstances building regulations in Lonc require natural cross-ventilation to the st case lobby, which nullifies one of the gr advantages of the point block, namely enclosed lobby, by turning this into a w tunnel. This seems a most unsatisfactory w of removing smoke in the event of fire. Much be preferred is the arrangement widely used Scandinavia in which a roof ventilator, which c be opened from the ground floor, is located o the staircase well.

The stair well should not immediately adj habitable rooms but should be planned as a s contained part of the central service core. T is the arrangement which has been adopted the majority of Scandinavian point blo schemes. It has the virtue of eliminating sou transmission into the dwelling. The cent location also obviates the need for natural lig ing, which can constitute a practical a aesthetic problem. It must, however, be assum for this purpose that artificial light will alwa

be available at key points from a fully protected emergency installation.

In apartment blocks privacy for ground floor tenants is always difficult to achieve. Planning footpaths away from the building is only a partial solution. Omitting living accommodation at ground floor level, and allowing a free flow of space underneath the building except where the entrance hall and staircases occur, is one alternative, and using the whole of the ground floor for common facilities such as tenants' storage areas, restaurants or shops is another.

There are differences of opinion as to the introduction of shops and restaurants in residential buildings, but with careful design and management they may stimulate a lively atmosphere without creating harmful results. They should, however, have independent entrances located as far away as possible from that used by the apartment residents.

The planning efficiency of the individual flat will depend on a number of factors, many of which are common to all dwellings. The interrelationship of the various areas has already been touched on. Movement of heavy furniture in and out of a multi-storey building causes special problems in spite of lifts, and therefore wherever possible there should be adequate built-in cupboards throughout. Recommended areas for the individual rooms should be exclusive of these cupboarding requirements.

It is a golden rule in any domestic planning, and no less so in flat design, that a theoretical furnishing scheme should be applied in order to test the validity of the room areas and shapes.

While it is necessary, except in the small efficiency flat, to allow for easy service between the kitchen and the dining space, it is essential that this working area is fully partitioned off from the remainder of the dwelling to restrict the passage of fumes and smell, in addition to efficient exhaust devices being fitted over cookers. In this way too the untidiness of cooking and washing-up can be confined. The kitchen should also have its own independent natural light and ventilation, and wherever possible, in the family flat at least, a view. The use of modern labour-saving equipment and orderly arrangement are otherwise not enough in this very important part of the dwelling.

In any event with correct night and day zoning in larger flats it is almost impossible to arrange

e introduction of shops with careful design may mulate a lively atmosphere'

iligfeld Development, Zurich, Switzerland.
chitect: Steiner

dding to privacy by omitting living accommo- ation at ground floor level and providing restau- nts'

evelopment for Adelaide, S. Australia
rchitect: R. Jensen

that bathrooms and kitchens are located together in the same flat. While such an arrangement, leading to the grouping of plumbing, may be very desirable in single-family houses, this is much less important in multi-storey flat buildings. The addition of a plumbing riser is likely to be a reasonably economical provision since it will couple a number of flats, and is far less objectionable than would be unsatisfactory use-zoning.

Bathrooms, toilets and laundries can be satisfactorily and more economically planned in entirely internal locations, thus reserving external wall areas and natural light for those rooms where these are essential. Duct ventilation works efficiently with or without mechanical extraction fans.

Ideally the kitchen should be planned immediately adjoining the living room and should never necessitate service across a hallway or corridor. If planned for example with two-way cupboards and drawers into the dining space, as well as a hatch, greater convenience will result, and space for informal meals with a fold-away table is also a boon.

Open planning of the dwelling has many advantages, particularly in the elimination of internal corridors or lobbies, which are often difficult to light and ventilate satisfactorily, and which looked at one way represent a possible loss of additional habitable space. Elimination of these, quite apart from the slight possible additional fire risk which does not seem really significant, does however mean—which is more important—that the main living area becomes also a traffic and communication centre. This can be expected to work reasonably well with a small dwelling designed primarily for adults. Where there are young children, however, the noise, traffic and lack of privacy in the living room can be serious under normal circumstances, and make entertaining guests difficult if not impossible. In such circumstances internal corridors may have to be accepted, but it is important that they should be reduced to the absolute minimum in area—which implies skilful planning.

Much has been said recently of the need for flexible planning, although little significant progress has been made with this in flat design. First, many of our outdated building methods must be replaced. This whole question is closely linked with that of the adoption of a greater degree of standardization, with modular co-ordination and prefabrication techniques. These must gain wider acceptance if flexibility, economy and speed of construction are to be achieved. The need is especially urgent in most multi-storey building where, within the fixed frame of reference of the structure and the sanitary core, these methods would enable changing family needs and individual requirements to be better met.

With regard to sanitary arrangements it seems desirable that, in any dwelling containing more than one bedroom, toilets should be separated from bathing areas. In larger family flats, these should in time also be planned with shower and bath separated, wherever possible, in independent cubicles, in order to prevent the bathroom becoming a domestic 'bottleneck'. Traditionally, wash-basins are installed in bathrooms, but they are increasingly being located as 'vanity-basins' in dressing rooms or bedrooms: all these arrangements give greater privacy and avert the 8 a.m. family competition.

In a larger type of flat a separate cloakroom and toilet may very well be justified, in addition to the other sanitary facilities. This can be the means of avoiding cross traffic from the day areas into the night zone, which can thus be kept as a self-contained area. The type of service for cooking, the availability of electric power-points, the use of flushing valves to toilets and choices of materials are all matters common to the design of any type of dwelling.

In the temperate climates, and certainly in larger schemes, it is likely that hot water will be provided from a centralized plant. With these the tendency is to introduce metering devices, which is a more equitable arrangement than payment of a flat charge. Such a centralized system will always be more economical than local hot-water heaters, either gas or electric fired. In warmer climates, however, it is more likely that there will be local forms of water-heating, and space may have to be found for either gas water-heaters or electric-storage heaters somewhere in or adjoining the kitchen. Very compact electric or gas units are widely obtainable now in a form that can readily be accommodated underneath the sink. Another type of gas water-heater, also in general use, has a very simple outlet of the 'balanced flue' type which barely protrudes outside the building.

Central heating is particularly suited to high-density housing developments, whether or not they are part of a district heating scheme. It is labour-saving, especially where using gas or oil fuels, and economical. With these systems skirting or baseboard radiators are a particularly neat arrangement, or alternatively standard radiators under windows are entirely satisfacory and in no way impair the flexibility of the flat layout.

The room air-conditioner seems likely to be used increasingly in higher-income flats, and if these are of the reverse-cycle type they can meet quite widely varied climatic conditions. Their use, although not economical, has a great many other advantages in practice, particularly that of cleanliness. Even if not installed initially, in those schemes which depend otherwise on electric radiators for local heating, space where units may be neatly installed later should be specifically reserved in the outside wall.

In climates with a reasonable seasonal stability electric floor heating has a great deal to commend it. It permits the fullest degree of flexibility in planning by eliminating radiators and pipe runs, and it is silent and clean in operation.

The windows, as all other parts of the building exterior, must be selected so as to minimize maintenance and cleaning problems. Aluminium sections are an even better long-term investment than galvanized steel, timber, concrete, or any other material, except plastic coated steel or wood, which seem promising. For normal windows a bascule-pattern frame swinging through 180° readily facilitates cleaning or re-glazing, but causes some problems with curtains. Alternatively, the casement-type window with extended cleaning hinges is excellent from all points of view, but the double-hung sash or horizontal sliding casement are least satisfactory from the point of view of cleaning, re-glazing or area of ventilation. Where balconies are planned the use of concertina-type doors serves to give the effect of an extension to the living area.

'The adoption of a degree of standardization an modular co-ordination'

Marselis Boulevard, Aarhus, Denmark
Architects: K. Friis and E. M. Nielsen

Double glazing has so many advantages in most climates that, being usually well justified economically, it must become the standard. In colder climates it permits the use of relatively large areas of glass for effective daylighting without serious heat losses. In warmer climates, if the external glass is ventilated top and bottom, it can be the means of considerably reducing solar radiation intake, and this can be made still more effective with venetian blinds in the space between the two sheets of glazing.

Adequate structural standards are especially important as the best means of stopping both fire spread and noise transmission. With the concentration of use of the common staircase and lifts, and with flats closely adjoining one another, it is essential that fire and smoke spread should be prevented between dwellings and the common access lobby, as well as between one dwelling and another. Even more vital is it that fire should not be able to reach the lift or staircase. Thus, at least a two-hour fire rating for all the main structural party walls and floors, as well as for staircase and lift enclosures, should be regarded as the minimum. Entrance doors to flats, lift enclosure doors and staircase doors for the same reason must be self-closing and smoke sealed.

The foregoing measures are also the most important contribution to minimizing impact and structure-borne noise, especially if used in conjunction with glass silk quilts under floor screeds, vermiculite spray to soffites, and soft floor finishes.

As a further means of obviating fire and smoke spread, ventilation and plumbing ducts should be designed with flame-baffled registers and fire-proof access doors. This will then make unnecessary the solid seal at each floor level insisted on in some cases for plumbing ducts—a precaution which can make access for maintenance extremely difficult. The use of the 'shunt flue' system is an added safeguard and also gives high immunity from sound transmission.

As a yardstick of good planning the efficiency ratio of net usable area to gross area should be between 85 and 90 per cent, although 93 per cent has been achieved. This will depend not only on design skill but also on the type of planning arrangement adopted. Less favourable ratios will point to unnecessarily high flat costs. It is one of the several important advantages of the point block that it tends towards good efficiency ratios. The maisonette type of planning, assuming secondary escape balconies at bedroom levels is, however, extravagant in circulation areas, with an efficiency ratio of about 80 per cent.

A further criterion is the external wall-to-floor ratio. This will depend mainly on three factors: the over-all size of the building, its shape, and the floor-to-ceiling heights. The last, being a matter for building regulations, can be varied only within narrow limits.

Although a circular plan may be the most efficient, it is more likely to be expensive structurally, less conducive to planning with room shapes which can be readily furnished, particularly difficult in climates where sunshading is required, and has considerable aesthetic limitations. Even the square plan, which may be next in efficiency, is not aesthetically ideal, and a balance between the various design factors must therefore be struck.

ꞁppendix C

o illustrate these differences numerically, and ɔr purposes of direct comparison, a hypo- ɪetical case may be taken of a building circular ɪ plan with a radius of 35ft. This, with a 9ft floor- ɪ-floor height, gives an external wall-to-floor ɪtio of 1 : 1·93; or, expressed another way, the ⨯ternal wall area is equivalent to 51·75 per cent ᶠ the enclosed floor area. A square building ?ft on the side would be almost exactly equiva- ·nt in area, and with the same floor-to-floor eight would have a ratio of 1 : 1·75, or external all equivalent to just over 58 per cent of the ·tal enclosed floor area. This difference of 25 per cent gives a useful picture of the rela- ʋe efficiencies of one aspect of the design, with ɪportant cost implications.

With a still larger enclosed floor area even etter results are obtained. The 'Domino' plan ith its double-linked rectangle, for example, as a gross typical floor area of 5952sq ft with ɪ efficiency ratio of 87·75 per cent and a floor-to- all ratio of 1 : 1·67. If it had been possible to an this building in a circular shape with the ɪme enclosed floor area, this would mean a ameter of 87ft and a floor/wall ratio of 1 : 2·2 or ɪ per cent. Assuming instead a square building the same area, 77ft on the side, this would ve the almost identical result of a floor/wall tio of 1 : 2·15 or 46·5 per cent. Craig was able show in his survey of a large number of hemes that the range in this respect was de, varying between 1 : 0·7 to 1 : 1·58. These jures suggested averages of 1 : 1·2 for rec- ɪngular slab blocks and 1 : 1·2 for the remaining hemes investigated. It was concluded that a asonable figure for a square point block would ɜ a ratio of 1 : 1·4, but as can be seen this jure would be appreciably improved upon th a larger number of dwellings to the typical ɔor and therefore with a larger gross floor area.

The 'Chequers' scheme is a further example the benefit to be expected by an increase the gross floor area, in this case giving a ɔor-to-wall ratio of 1 : 2·05 or 48 per cent. From ese figures, it would therefore seem not un- asonable to suggest that a target wall-to-floor tio of 1 : 2, or 50 per cent, should be aimed although it is again stressed that this must ·pend to some extent on the variable factors ·eady referred to.

The comparative efficiency-ratio figure for the hequers' scheme is 89·86 per cent, and for the aig survey an average of 84 per cent for six- eleven-storey blocks covering a range of tween 81 per cent and 89 per cent in the ajority of cases. The over-all range was, how- er, a great deal wider, being as low as 71·3 per nt in one balcony access scheme and as high 90·9 per cent in the case of another such heme. The averages for balcony access were wever lower than those for staircase access hemes. These were 83 per cent and 84·6 per nt respectively. The wide variations are a finite measure of the extent to which planning ll has been brought to bear, but these figures ɜ also to some extent influenced by the total mber of flats on the typical floor and the type flats, therefore also the gross floor area. It is early impossible, even in the most economically anned scheme, to reduce the space require- ents of the staircase, lifts, and entrance lobbies low a certain minimum figure. Therefore, to obtain a high proportion of usable area apart from circulation areas, and so that the cost of staircases and lifts should not be high in relation to the cost of actual dwellings, the larger the number of flats it is possible to plan reasonably on a given typical floor level, the better.

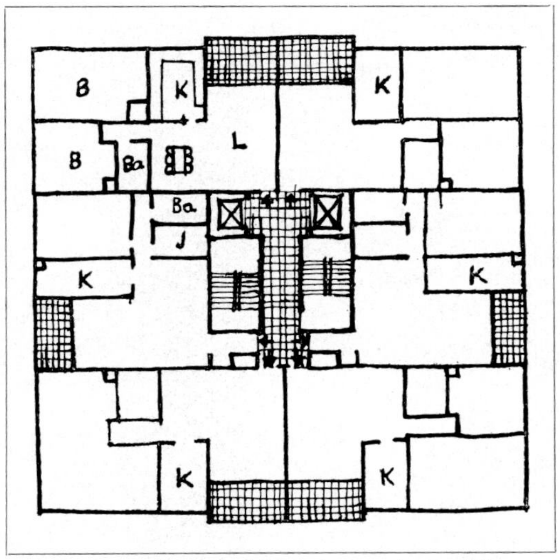

Planning of tower block to meet conditions stipulating twin staircases; with six flats/floor. Circulation area 9·2% $\left(\frac{590}{6400}\right)$

Selected Bibliography and References

Detail Planning Section

1. Ministry of Housing and Local Government. *Flats and Houses 1958*, HMSO, London,
2. Cleeve Barr, A. W. *Public Authority Housing.* Batsford, London, 1958.
3. Peters, P. *Wohnhochhäuser.* Callwey, Munich, 1958.
4. AIA, New York Chapter—Committee on Housing 1949–50. *Rental Housing under FHA–608*, AIA, 1950.
5. Yorke, F. R. S. and Gibberd, F. *Modern Flats.* Architectural Press, London, 1958.
6. Lindquist, N. Bostadshöghus. *Byggmästeren,* 1958 (A7).
7. Jensfeldt, S. Höghus. *Byggmästeren,* 1957 (A4).
8. IUA. *Habitation.* Elsevier.
9. Cleeve Barr, A. W. Housing in the 1950s. *J. R. Inst. Brit. Archit.,* April 1962.
10. Bruckman, H. M. and Lewis, D. L. *New Housing in Great Britain.* Tiranti, London, 1960.
11. Ministry of Housing and Local Government. *Housing Manual 1949.* HMSO, London.
12. Ministry of Housing and Local Government. *Design of Dwellings.* HMSO, London.
13. Ministry of Works and Ministry of Health. *Housing Manual 1944.* HMSO, London.
14. Armstrong, P. Housing—Planning for Amenity. *J. R. Inst. Brit. Archit.,* March 1947.
15. Rasmussen, A. D. and Vedel-Petersen, F. *Nyers Etageboligplaner.* Statens Byggeforskningsinstitut, Copenhagen, 1956.
16. Schule, W. *Die Zweckmässe Wohnung.* Inst. für Technische Physik, Stuttgart, 1953.
17. Graham, N. and Woodcock, R. Economics and Design of Multi-storey Flats. *Munic. J., Lond.,* October 1955.
18. Tijen, W. van. Het Woongebouw aan het Zuidplein te Rotterdam. *Bouw,* 1949 (4).
19. Korenkov, V. O tipe zhilogo doma dlya yuzhneykh raionov strany. *Arkhitektura, Moscow,* 1956 (5).
20. Lindquist, N. Brandskydd i Hoga Bostadshus. *Byggmästeren,* 1956 (B9).
21. Kristensen, E. Faelles Nordiske Regler for Hojhuse? *Byggeindustrien,* 1956 (7).
22. Editorial. The Fire Protection of Buildings, *Instn. Heat. Vent. Engrs. J.,* February and March 1961.
23. *Means of Escape in Case of Fire.* LCC, 1954.
24. Eastwick-Field, J. and Stillman, J. Flats in Berlin 1958. *Archit. (Build.) J.,* October 1958.
25. ECA. *Neuer Wohnbau.* Otto Maier, Ravensburg.
26. Codes of Practice Committee. *Daylight BSCP3 IA* (1948). British Standards Institute.
27. Editorial. *The Lighting of Buildings (Post-war Building Study No 11).* HMSO, London.
28. Hopkinson, R. G. Daylighting. *Byggmästeren,* 1955 (A4).
29. Delve, F. W. (Chief Officer, London Fire Brigade). High Buildings—Fire Precaution and Fire Fighting Arrangements. *Off. Archit.,* July 1959.
30. Editorial. Hide Place Development, Westminster. *Archit. (Build.) J.,* June 1960 and March 1961.
31. Editorial. Kitchens in Low-rental Flats. *Wirtsch. Bauen,* 1951 (3).
32. Jensen, R. A. Vällingby. *Architect, Lond.,* July 1955.
33. Editorial. Perkins Heights. *Architect, Lond.,* February 1954.
34. Editorial. Gilbert Sheldon House. *Architect, Lond.,* February 1954.
35. Editorial and Jensen, R. A. Perkins Heights Multi-storey Flats. *Builder, Lond.,* August 1954.
36. Editorial. Paddington Borough Housing. *Architect, Lond.,* April 1953.
37. Editorial. Hallfield Estate. *Architect, Lond.,* November 1954.
38. Editorial. Fulham Place Housing Scheme. *Architect, Lond.,* January 1949.
39. Editorial. Project for Connaught Mews. *Architect, Lond.,* February 1948.
40. Editorial. Paddington Towers. *Architect, Lond.,* November 1956.
41. Rosner, R. Housing Problems Pre-war and Post-war. *Architect, Lond.,* December 1952.
42. Editorial. Design for Fire Safety. *Archit. Engng.,* March 1956.
43. Awe, E. Höghusens Brandskyddsproblem. *Brandskydd,* 1957 (7).
44. Rigby Childs, D. and Whittle, J. Space and Housing. *Archit. (Build.) J.,* September 1960.
45. Pound, G. T. Planning for Daylight. *J. Tn. Plann. Inst., Lond.,* May 1947.
46. Smith, G. E. K. *Sweden Builds.* Reinhold, 1950.
47. *Trees in Town and City.* HMSO, London, 1958.

Structure

While it is intended in this section to deal only with those structural problems and techniques which have special relevance to the multi-storey residential flat building—a field of activity which has been particularly fruitful in regard to structural development—a number of these are also applicable to other multi-storey buildings. Some of the systems or techniques have in fact been first developed in relation to other building types as, for example, the office block. The term structure is used in its comprehensive sense and for convenience the section is divided into six sub-sections as follows:

(1) Foundations.
(2) Superstructure.
(3) Cladding.
(4) Internal partitions.
(5) Stairs and lift enclosures.
(6) Party walls and floors.

(1) *FOUNDATIONS*

The provision of satisfactory foundations was for long thought to be a controlling factor in the design of multi-storey buildings of any type. This, it has now been realized, is seldom if ever the case and reference to a number of the multi-storey constructions in Mexico City and Sao Paolo, for example, show that even in the most unlikely conditions foundation problems can be solved in a way that allows, within reason, almost unrestricted heights.

The strip or pad foundation in reinforced concrete, with or without steel grillages, is still the most economical form of foundation (or 'footing' as it is sometimes erroneously termed), and on the assumption of bearing pressures not exceeding about three tons per square foot, as for example with good quality clay, this would certainly be the first alternative to be considered. As the strips or pads increase in superficial area they will approach the point at which it is just as economical to link them up into the form of a continuous reinforced-concrete raft. If this occurs it is important, however, to ensure that there is equalization of bearing pressures in order to avoid differential settlements and therefore cracking. This can usually be achieved by the careful design and distribution of loading points from the superstructure, and to some extent through the reinforcement of the concrete itself. If, however, doubt exists, it is far better to design separate pads. Even in this event any appreciable differences in bearing pressures must be avoided, if foundation heave (7) is to be eliminated (particularly where pads are in close proximity one to another). The buoyant caisson, a development of the concrete raft, provides a monolithic structure of raft and retaining walls, with the floor above and a series of internal load-bearing division walls (5). This may be the equivalent of one or more floors in depth. The advantage of this system is the bonus in the form of building loading which can be applied to the subsoil equivalent to the volume of earth excavated. Only when this load is exceeded is it necessary to supplement the foundations with piling, for example.

In an apartment building it is unlikely that basements of more than a single floor in depth would normally be required, although this may change as car-parking provision has increasingly to be created underneath the building as the most economical space solution. Where subsoil conditions are suitable, and other things being equal, a basement ten feet deep will reduce the net pressure under the foundations significantly to the extent of about half a ton a square foot, or equivalent to the loading of a four- to five-storey building.

Piling will normally be adopted in cases where unsatisfactory subsoil conditions exist, and there is little need to discuss most of these systems in detail as they are of general application. However, there are a number of advantages, including economy in the use of proprietary systems based on a composite unit and reinforced-concrete shells (6).

The alternative, the precast pile, frequently involves cutting and waste before capping; but practical loadings closely correspond with theoretical deductions: which is not always the case with *in situ* piling (4).

When rock underlies poor subsoil the most economical system may still be that of steel piling, although reinforced concrete is being used more widely even in this type of situation.

(2) *SUPERSTRUCTURE*

Although in the superstructure traditional load-bearing masonry has largely been replaced by the structural frame, there are recent examples of engineered brickwork, both in Switzerland and Britain, and up to eleven storeys in height; using bricks with a high crushing strength and not exceeding approximately eleven inches in thickness in the lower floors. There are good reasons, however, for regarding these examples as exceptions to present trends; more especially as they perpetuate the laborious system of laying bricks individually.

Frame systems, either in steel or reinforced concrete, are still the most widely used and have many advantages such as flexibility and standardization. The steel-frame building is in most cases somewhat dearer than reinforced concrete, even where the concrete casing is fully stressed. Economies are further achieved if the concrete casing is replaced by asbestos or vermiculite spray, which is simpler to apply and produces appreciable reductions in foundation loading (9,10).

The reinforced-concrete frame may achieve savings equivalent to twenty-five per cent of the cost of the structure, compared with steel; but the main disadvantage lies in the large sectional areas of the beams and columns, which even more than with steel may constitute a restriction on internal planning flexibility if allowed to intrude into the dwelling areas. Currently a number of precast concrete systems are being widely used, some being developments of the basic column and beam. These in many cases allow much speedier construction and the almost complete elimination of site formwork; but have seldom proved to be quite as economical as the more orthodox systems, except with large-scale mass-production. Residual problems invariably occur with whatever advantages there may be, and these are achieving continuity at the connections, and a sound bond between the precast and the *in situ* concrete. For these connections special shuttering has been used in some systems but in other cases the connection is a mechanical one, either through bolting or welding.

Chemical bonding agents are solving the other part of the problem and this makes the 'shell'

e reinforced concrete frame may achieve ings'

ensborg, Malmö, Sweden
:hitects: Thorsten Roos and B. Thornberg

system all the more useful. This system, devised by the author, appears to overcome most of these shuttering and casting difficulties, and provides for full continuity between column, beam and slab: the slab being either in the form of precast concrete filler beams and tiles; prestressed planks with concrete topping, or hollow concrete beam infill units. In neither case is any form of shuttering required; but alternatively, any form of *in situ* concrete flooring could be used with temporary telescopic centering members resting on the beam shells.

The 'flat plate' system (18) with an entirely flat soffit, and thus such advantages as considerable savings in the cost of shuttering, elimination of false ceilings; greater simplicity and speed of erection, and flexibility of internal planning, no longer governed by projecting beam positions, is the most significant of all structural developments; and is now covered by standard codes in Britain and the United States.

With this system an economical range of spans is 21 to 25ft, and a 7in slab will reduce deflections to a negligible quantity with high quality concrete. Steel columns have the advantage of smaller dimensions but involve erection problems. Concrete columns, while larger in size, can usually be masked in walls or partitions, and give full structural continuity.

The lift slab system is in effect a special form of flat plate system, but the fact that the slabs are cast at ground level, thus eliminating all but the edge shuttering, greatly simplifies construction, and in cases where the planning is in simple forms suited to the system, it is one which can offer still further advantages and economies.

Variations and modifications of the basic system have been used with, for example, a waffle type slab, for weight reduction; or circular steel columns or rectangular reinforced concrete columns as alternatives to the more usual square steel columns. These have, however, usually been used in non-domestic types of building.

An advanced development of lift slab has been used in Russia, where not only the floors but also the cladding, with windows, and the internal partitions complete with doors are erectec their entirety before being raised into posi by the jacks.

Another similar technique of ensuring that major part of construction work in flat buildin carried out under cover at or near ground l is the 'jack-block' system recently develo in London (21,D1). As the name sugge in this case the floors are jacked up from be rather than lifted.

Some of the structural systems recently be used in multi-storey apartment building sho tendency to revert to the load-bearing princi One of the more interesting—the 'climb shuttering' system (D2)—used with hydra jacking gear, offers many advantages c *in situ* reinforced concrete work with ortho shuttering but also presents problems wh used for external walls. Its most appropr use seems to be that of forming the lift staircase core walls.

Another form of load-bearing wall syst which has been widely used in Scandinavia Britain is the so-called box-frame system,

'The climbing shuttering system as used in Denmark with hydraulic gear'

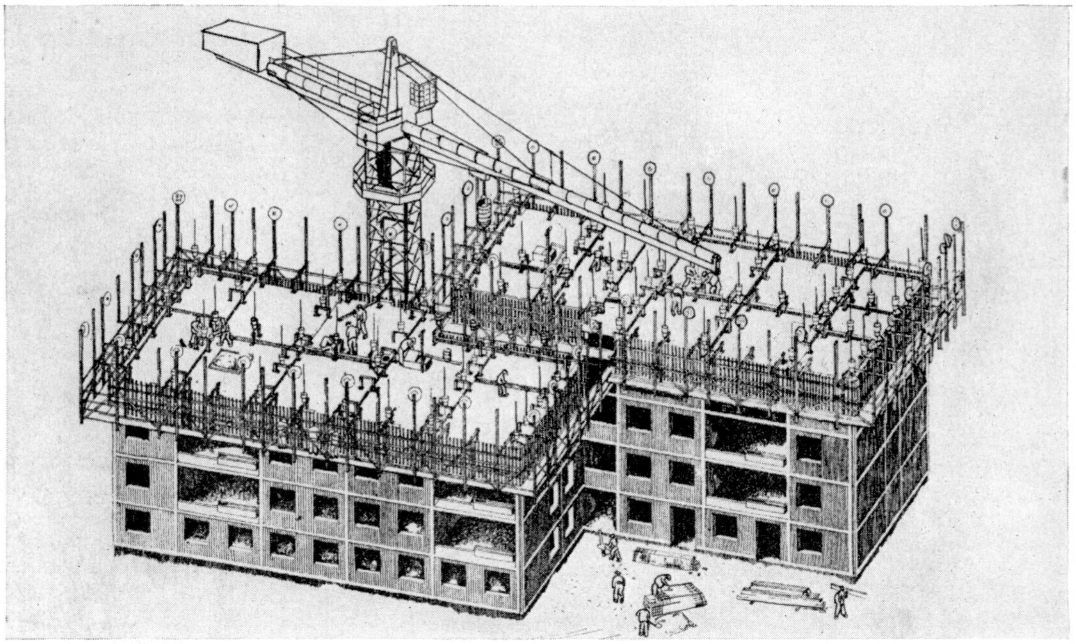

ame systems have many advantages including xibility'

genfrivang II, Copenhagen, Denmark
chitects: Stephenson and Associates

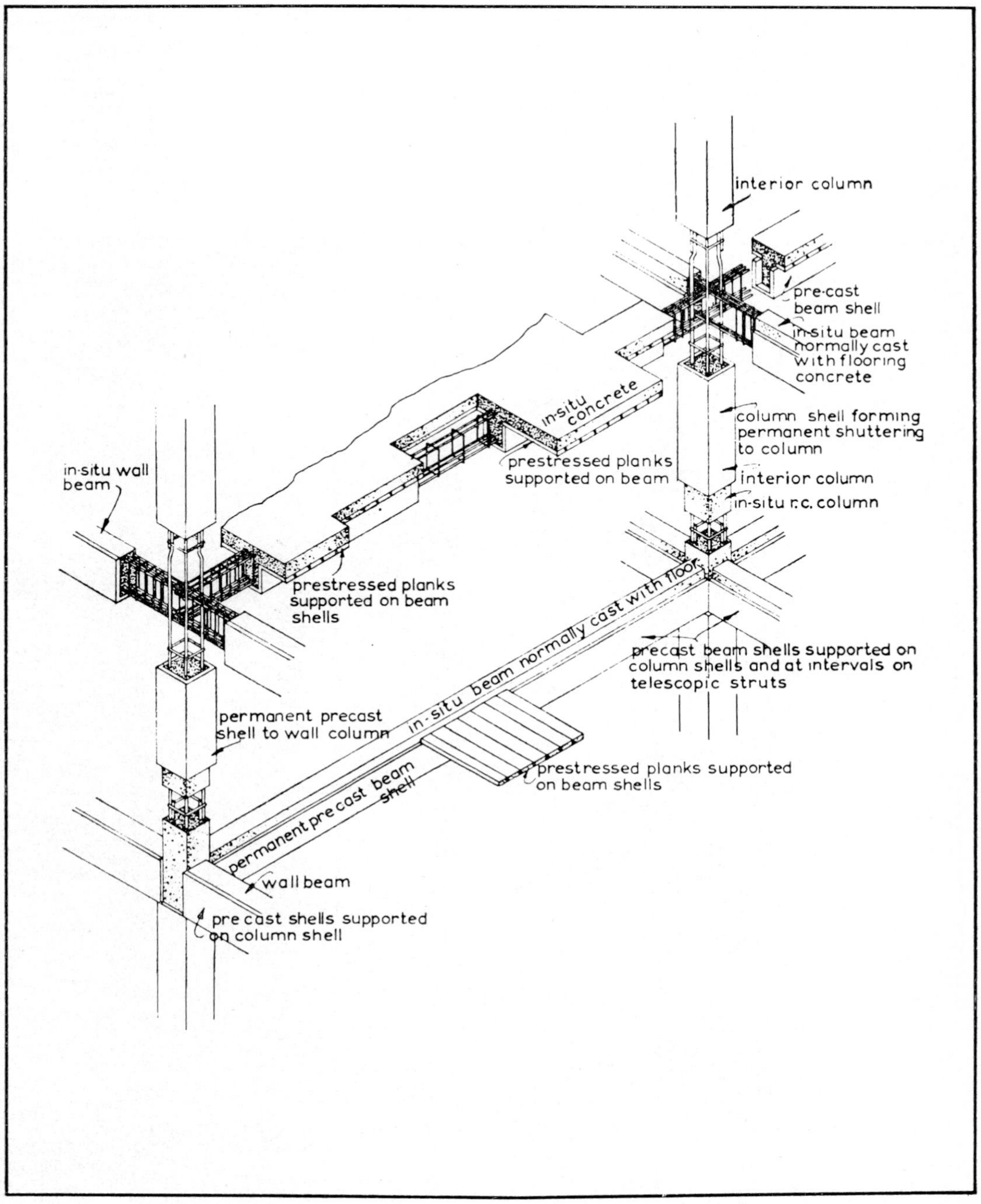

The R.J. precast shell reinforced concrete frame system overcomes many site casting difficulties

cellular cross-wall system, in which the walls forming the party division to the flats run transversely across the building and are the vertical load-bearing elements. These may be constructed either in reinforced concrete; plain concrete, or in 'designed' brickwork. The system is one which tends to restrict flat planning within the framework of the standardized structural grid, although the walls can be perforated to a limited extent. The exterior cladding then becomes a non-load-bearing weather screen. In this case, however, many building regulations require a sill-height fire-resisting back-up wall, or a slab-projection at every floor level to prevent vertical fire spread.

(3) *CLADDING*

Still more recently, a number of schemes using heavy precast concrete external wall, floor and partition units have gone into production in Europe. Many of these have produced significant economies and offer prospects of a much-needed rationalization of multi-storey construction techniques. The Ohlsson and Skarne, and the Sundh systems from Sweden, the Camus and the Coignet systems from France, the Reema system from Britain, and the Bigontina from Italy are all variations on the same basic principles.

Windows and doors are cast into panels which are complete with finishes; which for external walls may consist, for example, of a hard impermeable cement or exposed aggregate layer outside, a core of 3in to 4in of aerated concrete or 'leca' concrete, and an internal plaster lining. For internal walls there will either be a plas finish or a special concrete finish ready painting or papering. Floor slabs can be c structed ready to receive screed or finish material, or in the case of kitchens or bathroo can have tiles already cast on. The system been highly mechanized in Russia, with ur factory-produced on a moving belt system, wh after curing in autoclaves, and in the stack yard, are then transported on special vehic to the building site.

Handling these panels, which weigh as mu as five tons (D3), necessitates the use of a tov crane or gantry. Assembly usually invol welding of reinforcement at the connections bolting units together through gusset plat and then grouting with *in situ* concrete. In so cases prestressed ribs are formed in the joi between panels. Precast stair flights are r almost commonplace and greatly simplify s work. Precast balcony units have also been us and complete bathroom units, with all fittin plumbing, and floor and other finishes have be factory produced, and are still capable or be transported and handled by cranes.

The Lugatenko system (D4), which is typi of a number of experiments being made Russia with the object of increasing the rate productivity and construction, shows a comp hensive use of prefabrication and preassem techniques. It is based on a 'box unit' system a embodies five completely fabricated stand units. These are (*a*) a stair unit, (*b*) sanitary with living kitchen complete, bathroom a

'Freedom of window pattern'

Bogenhausen, Munich, Germany
Architects: Ludwig and Ruf

oilet, (*c*) combined smaller sanitary unit, (*d*) the oom and alcove unit, and (*e*) the living room ınit.

In order to obtain dividends from the use of ıny of the prefabrication systems, standardiza-ion, both of the units, in the planning of the ndividual flats or apartments, and of the ɔuilding block as a whole is essential, and, noreover, they are only practicable if a fairly arge number of similar blocks is repeated, in ɔrder to justify the necessary factory tooling, and he manufacture of moulds and special fittings. 'hese factors have tended, in practice, to pro-luce a visual monotony in architectural treat-nent, layout and grouping which many will con-ider entirely justifies any slight additional costs nplied by less repetitive, less mechanized ystems where variety and aesthetic quality can e more readily achieved.

Cladding as an element of the structure can-ıot really be separated from the remaining tructural elements, as traditionally and in some f the recent developments it forms one of the nore important parts of the structure itself. In ither case little in the way of variety of treat-nent is possible other than through a frank xpression of the material itself or necessarily vith some materials a plaster rendering. The rchitectural expression will also largely be mited as traditionally by inelastic ratios of solid ɔ void.

In the case, however, of frame construction or ross-wall construction the external wall can e designed with weather, heat and sound ısulation as the main considerations and when elieved of its load-bearing function, there is n almost complete degree of freedom in window attern and in the sizes of openings. Consistent vith the over-all requirements of insulation and eduction of loading on the structure, a wide ariety of materials is now available, used alone r in combination in a way that is not only fficient functionally but which also provides a reat many possible alternative forms of archi-ectural expression and treatment, and uses of olours and textures.

Logically, this may seem to suggest a form of urtain-wall (D5) treatment such as is being sed in so many present-day commercial uildings. The curtain wall can, however, only e designed in a limited number of ways and e possibilities of relief in the form of depth, ght, shade, changes of texture and the surface uality of materials tends to be somewhat mited. That the curtain wall is in reality nothing ore than a veneer is patent, and to this extent tends to deprive a building of one of its more nportant qualities, solidity.

Reinforced concrete has also been used in a umber of cases for the external non-load-earing cladding, usually in two distinct and 11) different ways. The first method consists floor-to-ceiling height slabs or floor-to-sill eight slabs 1ft 6in to 2ft in width, which are ced on site into a perimeter beam system, as an ıter non-waterproof skin to a cavity wall, the ner leaf of which can be built in a variety of aterials. Windows, doors and balcony elements e then fixed subsequently.

Provided that suitable mechanical handling uipment is available on the site, a much etter system, however, appears to be the one sed in a number of European projects in which e whole panel from floor to ceiling, filling a ructural bay, is cast in one operation, with windows, doors and any other fittings already in position; very much as in the load-bearing systems.

Panels of this type are normally cast in the factory and subsequently (16) transported to the site and placed in position with the help of a tower crane. However, in some cases the slabs have been cast on the floor adjacent to the openings that they will ultimately fill, and when suitably cured, are then tilted up into position with the help of a special winch.

These slabs will also in this instance be of composite material as in the heavy precast techniques.

All the veneer and panel treatments suggested are ideal in eliminating maintenance problems and in providing colour and textural interest (D6,33,34). Their use also has the very distinct advantage of reducing site work to the minimum and in speeding up assembly; and this is usually done, moreover, without the need for scaffolding; although proper mobile handling equipment is indispensable.

In comparing the load-bearing wall, and the non-load-bearing systems, it is becoming evident that the reinforced prefabricated panel which has such a wide variety of possible applications has with very little increase in weight and thickness an ample load-bearing potential, and its use in this more fully developed form is tending to supplant the non-load-bearing (19) panel associated with frame construction. The advantages inherent in the older traditional system of construction in which support and weather screen were embodied in a single element are thus revived in a way which allows for speedy and economical site assembly, full use of standardization and repetition, considerable reduction in weight on foundations, minimum internal loss of space due to wall thickness, and maximum performance on heat, weather and sound insulation.

(4) *INTERNAL PARTITIONS*

The tendency in the more rational forms of contemporary construction is to avoid wet finishes wherever this is practicable. This has been one of the reasons, in commercial building, for the almost universal use of moveable partitions of various types (D7). This trend has not been followed to the same extent in domestic work, although the advantages would be many. With flat plate construction a de-mountable type of partition can facilitate variations in the internal layout of a dwelling to meet the varying needs of different families.

(5) *STAIRS AND LIFT ENCLOSURES*

It was emphasized earlier (D8) that enclosing walls to lifts and staircases, as well as party walls and floors, has not only a structural function but also one of sound insulation. For staircase and lift walls 7in of solid concrete or 9in of brickwork are a reasonably satisfactory solution for both purposes, and difficult to better either in terms of economy or speed of construction. Modular concrete blocks have also been used for this purpose very satisfactorily, particularly where combined with an orthodox reinforced concrete frame system. Precasting techniques, on the other hand, have rarely been used in these locations, and perhaps the main reason for this is that these walls are nearly always used as an important part of the structure and designed to meet wind stresses. This therefore implies fully monolithic construction and is one of the reasons why the climbing form system has proved to be so eminently suitable for this part of the building.

(6) *PARTY WALLS AND FLOORS*

For party walls between flats or apartments 7in of solid reinforced concrete or 9in of brickwork are required for acoustic reasons, and these should therefore be made to play their part as structural members, as they are capable of doing. Precast blocks or prefabricated slabs may form an alternative but in these cases, as also with brickwork or concrete, plastering will be unavoidable in order to ensure an imperforate membrane.

The floor will, in the majority of cases, be more than just a structural element but will also be a party division between two apartments. Five inches of reinforced concrete has been found to provide reasonably satisfactory sound insulation for both airborne and impact noise, provided that an absorbent finish is laid on the top. A considerable improvement, however, is achieved by what has now become the widely-accepted standard practice of adding a sound-absorbing quilt of glass wool or other such material on top of the structural slab with a 2in screed or floor finish on top of this. Ideally the finish should then be in the form of wood parquet or block, rubber or soft vinyl tiling. Carpets, where these are economically feasible, provide considerable additional immunity from impact noises, although a great deal of the benefit goes to the neighbour. In central corridor access planning an absorbent finish is essential, although wear-resistance and economy will probably dictate rubber tiling for this purpose, as too in access lobbies.

Most of the recently developed structural systems have not only technical but also cost implications, both of which are of vital importance. Cost differences as between multi-storey building and low building have frequently been exaggerated, but there are undoubtedly special problems in constructing multi-storey buildings in that organization, skill, preplanning and above all adequate equipment are essential if work is to be carried out efficiently from both a time and a cost point of view. In many cases cost disadvantages which have been alleged in the case of multi-storey buildings have been entirely due to inadequate knowledge and experience, and to the use of obsolete methods and equipment, which have a critical effect not applicable in other types of building.

Proof of this is to be found in a number of the Continental countries, where competence in multi-storey construction of dwellings and other buildings has followed in the train of lengthy experience in this specialized field, with corresponding cost advantages. In countries where a small cottage tradition has long persisted, adaptation to multi-storey forms of construction has been slower and much more painful, and costs for this type of work are by comparison still high.

The importance therefore of considering structural techniques and problems in the early design stage cannot be too much stressed, both as an essential factor in the architectural problem, but much more today because of its decisive economic effect. If multi-storey buildings, as part of high-density residential urban renewal schemes, are to play their part in the future, the need to think in terms of valid and progressive structural techniques cannot be exaggerated.

Appendix D

1. A prototype block has been designed, 17 floors high and containing six flats on each typical floor, of which two are bedsitters and four one-bedroom flats. The building is 60ft square over-all and designed round a 30ft hollow square core. This core, which is intended to house lifts, staircase and services, will be constructed of concrete blocks supported on forty 220-ton hydraulic jacks. Alternate jacks will raise the blocks $7\frac{5}{8}$in at a time at a speed of 1in every three minutes, and these blocks will then subsequently be bonded together with *in situ* concrete and reinforcement. Floor slabs will be cantilevered out 15ft from the core on all four sides, with four cross-over pre-tensioned concrete beams and a system of secondary infill beams providing the supporting system.

All the work, including partitions and finishing, will be carried out at ground or first floor level, and with excellent weather protection in the form of temporary screens, until the cladding is in position. External walls will be all of the metal curtain type in order to reduce weight on the slab edge to the minimum. This most interesting proposal, in which the average flat cost is estimated to be only £2770, is claimed to ensure cheaper and speedier construction. It appears to have many of the advantages, in fact, of the lift slab system, particularly in some of its latest forms, but in this case planning would have to be very carefully integrated with the structural system, and a similar number of large flats could not in any event be accommodated at each floor level without the cantilevered slab becoming structurally uneconomic.

2. In the climbing shuttering system the double skin shuttering to the walls is fixed through a series of steel yokes to hydraulic jacks which are supported on the steel reinforcement. These jacks, operated through hydraulically controlled double actuating clutches, climb up the reinforcement bars as the concrete sets. The jacks are co-ordinated through a central control panel, but if necessary can be master-controlled manually in order to correct any slight errors of alignment.

The system has been used to a considerable extent in Scandinavia and Germany, and is one which, if used in the right way and in the right type of building (of simple shape), can show many advantages, particularly in simplifying the normal procedure of erecting and stripping necessary in orthodox types of shuttering. With this system, once the shuttering has been erected, it remains assembled in position until the whole height of the building has been completed. If it is used to form the perimeter walls, then pockets must be left in the wall in which to insert the floor slabs as the climbing formwork descends a floor at a time. This problem, and that of forming window openings, is a complication which has tended to limit the use of the system (which was originally devised for constructing silos) merely to the service-core walls, or ducts for plumbing and services.

No matter how carefully this work is carried out, the concrete surface does not form a suitable finish, and this has led to precast concrete blocks of various types being placed in many cases inside the moving shuttering to form an external skin to the perimeter walls. In other cases the walls are rendered on the outside in cement and sand, and plastered on the inside. These wet finishes are, however, not themselves really satisfactory either for the exterior of a multi-storey building, because of subsequent maintenance, or for the interior, because of delays to other trades.

This system has been used with normal reinforced concrete, with no-fines concrete or 'leca' concrete, all of which require wet finishing coats.

3. In all heavy pre-casting techniques lifting eyes or threaded lifting bolts are cast into position as well as the necessary continuity bars and fishplates. Electric conduits are cast into the middle of floor slab units as are any hot or cold water pipes; all of which can subsequently be coupled up before grouting at joints with *in situ* concrete is carried out. Roof slabs, instead of being finished with tiles or vinyl squares, have polystyrene or other suitable insulating material fixed on the upper surface ready for screeding or covering with asphalt or roofing felt. Speed and simplicity have been assured with this system, and the resulting economies can be gauged from the extraordinarily low cost given for a three-room flat of 520sq ft, erected on the Camus system (which is typical), of £1070 including central heating, hot water and floor finishes. These systems clearly call for a number of prerequisities: first of all, elaborate and accurate preplanning, including the greatest possible degree of modular coordination and standardization, also excellent factory and site planning for both the manufacture and handling of prefabricated units; and adequate mechanical equipment.

4. The Lugatenko system was devised to be applied normally to five-storey blocks but can readily be extended to eight storeys if need be. The block itself is also standardized to contain 14 single-room flats of 320sq ft each, 22 two-room flats of 445sq ft each, 20 three-room flats of 580sq ft each, and 10 four-room flats at 700sq ft each. One of these blocks can be erected in 30 days from a total of 250 standard units, and with the assistance of a five ton crane. The units are all constructed on a solid concrete slab base with concrete ribs and asbestolite linings. Solid reinforced concrete corner posts are poured *in situ* after the units have been placed, and in conjunction with the concrete grouting between the adjoining slab units. This both ties the whole construction together and provides the necessary stiffness.

5. As a slight variation from the normal curtain wall treatment, floor to ceiling height panels fitted in between structural bays are another alternative. Provided the edges of the slabs and the outer face of the cross walls or structural columns are suitably covered and protected, this method has the considerable advantage of limiting the panel sizes to units which are readily handled on the site. Aesthetically it gives greater prominence to structural expression, breaks up into recognizable units what can otherwise be large unbroken surface areas of wall, and does so in a way that confers a feeling of scale which is directly related to the size of the dwelling or the room and therefore has a direct visual significance.

If in a multi-storey building windows occur in one floor immediately over the windows below many building regulations insist that there should be a fire back-up wall up to window-sill height in order to prevent the spread of fire fr one floor to the next. This still however leave number of possible alternative materials whi may be used to form the outside panel skin the spandrils. This can be either in simple sh materials such as porcelain enamel on steel, aluminium in plain sheets or textured pane coloured asbestolite or fibrolite, plain sar blasted or coloured glass panels, faience tiles, or even timber panels. The main factors be borne in mind are lightness in weight, fr dom from maintenance problems and, as far possible, a self-cleaning finish. In some cas these materials can be used in composite for with a sandwich of insulating material such foamed polystyrene with a cavity separating t panel from the back-up wall. Otherwise t cavity itself can be filled with insulating mater either in the form of quilts, or pumped in plastic form. Ideally the panel filling the wh of one structural bay will be factory prefab cated, including windows, french doors, b conies (if any), and all finishing materials a insulation. Site assembly is then a relativ quick and simple undertaking.

6. The external finish to concrete panels c be textured in a variety of ways such as w board shuttering (33,34); rubber, plaster or cc crete moulds; sandblasting; bush-hammerir scrubbing, or spraying to expose the aggrega The aggregates may be ordinary sands a gravels or, alternatively, may include crush bricks of various colours and sizes, or ev broken glass. Some excellent effects have be obtained, notably in Norway, with the use metal stencils and sandblasting, which not o expose the colour of the aggregate, in contra to the surface protected by the stencil which then often highly polished, but do so in the fo of a definite pattern. Another possibility is apply to the concrete a veneer of marble, tile faience.

7. Prefabricated cellular double-skin plast board panels are one solution to the problem providing movable partitions, and these can jointed up after assembly and subsequen papered or painted direct without the need any wet plastering. They provide a homogeneo finish which is clean and solid in appearan In this and other systems electric wiring ru can be taken behind the skirting.

Other systems are floor-to-ceiling heig prefabricated gypsum cellular panels; doub skin fibrous plaster panels, wood chip-boa composition panels with plywood facing, laminated celotex panels. All of these are easy erect or dismantle, are light in weight, do r require drying-out time during construction, a provide an excellent finish. It is unfortunat true, however, that in many cases two-cc plastered finishes on wood wool, clay block, brick partitions are cheaper in first cost due the conservative tendencies of the buildi industry to price out what are sometim obviously labour-saving innovations; but in t course of time the speedier and simpler erecti techniques associated with the dry syste must prove more economical as well as prov ing the additional advantages of weight-savi and flexibility, which appear to be of just as gr importance as in the modern office building the family home in future is to meet its contir ally changing needs.

8. The staircase can be most conveniently onsidered as a structural element entirely in- ependent from the surrounding walls which are ere not only to provide sound insulation and ructural stiffening but also fire isolation. eated as a separate element the staircase can constructed in a number of different ways. ne flights may be pre-cast with the landings esigned to receive end support only, or, alter- atively, half-landings can be formed of pre-cast nits let into pockets left in the enclosing wall. upported on this and on the floor slab above d below, are pre-cast concrete stringers or rriages, which are themselves grooved to ceive pre-cast treads and risers.

While the second of these alternatives pre- nts a broken soffit, this is not really serious, d the system has a very considerable advan- ge over complete pre-cast flight and half- nding in the ease of site handling. The units n readily be placed in position by two men thout the assistance of any mechanical uipment, and in the one or two cases in which has been used the speed and simplicity of ection have been noteworthy. As the staircase reinforced-concrete construction has so often oved to be a bottleneck, this economy and nplification can have implications far beyond actual cost of the staircase itself, in speeding the whole construction programme.

Selected Bibliography and References

Structure Section

1. *London Building (Constructional) By-Laws 1952.* LCC, London.
2. *Buildings of Excess Height under Section 20 of the London Building Act.* LCC, London.
3. Civil Engineering Codes of Practice Joint Committee. *Site Investigations.* Institute of Civil Engineers.
4. Meyershof, G. G. *The Ultimate Bearing Capacity of Foundations.* Geotechnique, December 1951.
5. Williams, G. Foundations for Tall Buildings. *Archit. (Build.) J.,* November 1959.
6. *West's Piling System.* West's Piling & Construction Co., London.
7. McClelland, D. Foundation Heave and Multi-storey Building. *Progr. Archit.,* June 1961.
8. Diamant, R. M. E. Precast Concrete Systems for Flats. *Architect, Lond.,* October, December 1961; March, April, August, September 1962 *et seq.*
9. Creasy. Costs of Steel and Reinforced Concrete Frames. *Inst. Civ. Engrs. J.,* December 1959.
10. Dunican, P. Economics of Multi-storey Flats (Construction). *Archit. (Build.) J.,* January 1954.
11. Editorial. Sundh System of Reinforced Concrete Construction. *Archit. (Build.) J.,* April 1953.
12. Hiort, E. Kallton-Systemet. *Arkitekten,* January 1950 (3).
13. Deininger, K. Hochhaus in Béton aus Wurttemberg. *Bau u. Bauindustrie,* 1954 (8).
14. Editorial. Lightweight Concrete Load Bearing Construction. *Archit. (Build.) J.,* March 1961.
15. Dunican, P. Structural Steelwork and Reinforced Concrete for Framed Buildings. *J. R. Instn. Chart. Surv.,* August 1960.
16. Editorial. New Flats in Leeds. *Off. Archit.,* 1960.
17. Schultz, K. Die Entwicklung der Plattenbauweise. *Bauplan. u. Bautech.,* 1954 (8).
18. The Plate Floor System. *Truscon Rev.* 1956 (12 & 15).
19. Bigontina, G. and G. La Prima Construzione Industrializza. *Ediliz. Mod.,* 1953 (No 51).
20. Trippe, P. A New Production Line Technique in Building. *Architect, Lond.,* July 1961.
21. Editorial. Jackblock Construction. *Architect, Lond.* February 1962.
22. *No Fines Concrete—Multi-storey Housing.* G. Wimpey & Co. Ltd., London.
23. Chapman, R. F. Structural Concrete with Special Reference to Multi-storey Concrete Frame Buildings. *Constr. Rev.,* November 1958.
24. Campbell, B. LCC Housing. *Concr. Quart.,* January–March 1956 (28).
25. Jensen, R. A. Traditional Systems Laborious. *Prefabrication,* July 1956.
26. Editorial. Tangye Climbing Jack System. *Architect, Lond.,* November 1954.
27. Rostron, M. Cladding Heat Transmission. *Archit. (Build.) J.,* February 1960.
28. Hardy, A. Thermal Comfort and Building Structure. *Archit. Rev.*
29. Schneider, P. Bauakustik auf der Interbau Berlin. *Schalltechnik,* September 1957.
30. Henkl, M. and Westphal, H. Untersuchung über die Schallangsleitung in Hochhausen. *Schalltechnik,* September 1957.
31. Parkin, E. H. and Stacy, E. F. Recent Research on Sound Insulation in Houses and Flats. *J. R. Inst. Brit. Archit.,* July 1954.
32. Brandt, O. and Dalen, I. Ar Ljüdisoleringen i vara bostadshus tillfredsstallande. *Byggmästeren* 1952 (31).
33. Wilson, J. G. *Concrete Facing Slabs.* Cement and Concrete Association, October 1954.
34. Wilson, J. G. Architectural Treatment of Concrete Surfaces. *Building Materials Digest,* March 1955.

Services

The range of services to which reference needs to be made as involving special problems in high flat buildings are:

(1) Lifts
(2) Heating and hot-water installations, including district heating and air-conditioning
(3) Sanitation, plumbing, and water
(4) Electrical installation
(5) Refuse-disposal systems
(6) Telephones, radio and TV installations
(7) Fire protection
(8) Miscellaneous services, including ventilation ducts, lightning conductors, vacuumation systems, and rain water disposal.

(1) *LIFTS*

Of all the equipment which must be regarded as an indispensable adjunct of high building, the lift is in many ways paramount and has in fact played a vital role in the development of multistorey construction. For elderly people and the very young in high-rise buildings the lift is the sole means of communication with the ground and the outside world. It is therefore important that this link should always be there functioning effectively, so as to be almost taken for granted, and that in no circumstances should there be a sensation of separation from easy contact with the surrounding garden. Only in this way can the full benefits of flat life be experienced.

The completely reliable lift still appears to be some way off, but even when this is ultimately achieved, there will always be the need for periodical maintenance work to be undertaken, when the lift will be out of operation. In spite of the considerable cost of this piece of equipment duplication seems almost unavoidable, and it is therefore all the more important that the planning is so devised as to ensure the largest number of flats being served by the installation. Only in this way can the cost of this equipment, which is likely to be between five and ten per cent of the total cost of the building, and an extra with which lower buildings are not encumbered, be spread so as to keep the oncost on the dwellings within reason.

Seen in this light the characteristic point block with four flats to the typical floor is likely to be expensive in lift provision even if only one lift is installed. With two lifts this type of building should have at least six to eight flats to the typical floor and be not less than fifteen storeys in height, but for preference thirty, in order to arrive at a reasonable cost distribution for this service. In the direct staircase access type of planning at least three flats should be planned to each staircase lift tower, and, preferably four, with interchange facilities for emergencies.

Obviously economic use of the lift installations need be no problem in the case of access balcony and central corridor access schemes. Even so, as has been inferred elsewhere, this advantage has to be balanced against other objections in both of these systems.

Assuming that lifts are grouped in pairs, one lift with an eight-person car can be a moderate speed installation of 100 to 150ft per minute; bearing in mind that the much better service provided by a 350ft per minute installation would very nearly double total cost. The slower sp creates no undue inconvenience except poss in an emergency, such as fire. Even in th circumstances, the difference in speed anc clearing capacity would not be serious, in v of the fact that, with modern forms of constr tion, only one or two floors in the building likely to be affected at any given time.

The eight-person car will take a load of 12((7) which is adequate for all normal purpo such as a perambulator or furniture as wel for emergency fire equipment. The second of the pair (also moderate speed) should h ever be large enough to take a stretcher (c coffin) and this will mean a narrow twelve-per car. In spite of the appreciably higher cost volved this is nevertheless a problem which to be met.

While in buildings up to about 12 storeys height, speeds of 100ft per minute will prov reasonable service and economy in opera because of the simpler electrical gear, 15 tc storey buildings require lift speeds of 20(350ft per minute wherever economically feasi as a means of reducing longer waiting tir which would otherwise occur with the grea distances travelled.

It is of course important that the electr installation should be suitably located a protected, so that it will remain in opera during a fire or other foreseeable emerger Not only will the lift be needed to help evacu the building occupants in the case of a fire, also to bring members of the fire-fighting cr up to the scene of the outbreak with their eq ment. It seems logical to consider the lift insta tion as an auxiliary means of escape in the c of a fire, and that so far as practicable th installations should be planned independe of staircases, so that they effectively constitu real alternative which is unlikely to be affec by smoke or fire simultaneously with the st cases.

The emergency lift should be fitted wit fireman's key switch at ground level so tha can be taken out of normal service during a and quickly brought down to ground level this way the car also remains under local c trol as long as it is in use by the Fire Brigad

British standards aim at a maximum of dwellings served by each lift with a maxim walking distance from the lift to the flat entra of 150ft. One lift only is tolerated for up to storeys in height but above this level two are regarded as mandatory. Even up to storeys a single lift is of questionable va particularly for elderly people and mothers w small children, and only in the large-scale m rehousing problems such as faced Britain a the second world war or in similar conditi elsewhere could this degree of austerity justified, in the certain knowledge that occasions the single lift will be out of operat It would be very much better, for example austerity in standards is rigidly imposed to m economies in the lift installation by planning pairs stopping at alternate floor levels, a sys which halves the number of landing doors, never involves residents in more inconvenie than the descent from one floor to the next.

Another possible economy lies in the omiss of lift car doors, but although enquiries have elicited information of any accident in Continental countries where this is custom it does imply obvious risks, especially to child

The more widely accepted practice of instal-
ɡ self-closing car and landing doors appears
eferable and, in order to eliminate possible
ks, all doors should be fitted with sensitive
ges which immediately respond to any obstruc-
n in the opening and prevent the door from
sing until this is removed.

Another safety measure concerns the location
landing call-buttons, and there is much to be
d for placing these out of the reach of very
all children. The alarm button however must
within their reach, as they may otherwise, in
te of all safeguards, find themselves trapped
a defective lift and unable to give an alarm
nal. Small children should not be encouraged
travel alone; they should in any case be super-
ed while playing, and have toilet accommo-
tion and shelter at garden level.

n these days the lift is a complex piece of
uipment and if it is to carry out its functions
ciently it is essential that it is used solely as a
ant facility. The installation of tradesmen's
ivery boxes and postal boxes for every dwell-
, at ground level, is a valuable means of
viating lift journeys by tradesmen, and through
s any consequential abuse of equipment and
quent breakdowns.

Abuse of lifts can still further be reduced by
suring that access to the building at ground
el can only be obtained by those having
itimate business there.

Typical installations in flat blocks suggest
t the over-all cost of the lift installation in
h buildings of between ten and twenty
reys will vary between five and ten per cent of
total building cost, or between £150 and £250
flat. The number of dwellings served by
h lift will have a dominant effect on the cost,
so will the type of control system used and
height of the building. It is estimated that
ut half of any increases in cost are due to the
a height of the building and half to the
rease in speed and the system of control.

HEATING AND HOT WATER

n those climates in which space heating is
uired for at least a part of the year district
ting (13) appeared at one stage to show great
mise, and although installations of this type
e been in use for a great many years in a
nber of cities in the United States, and more
ently in Russia, Germany and other European
ntries, they have not been very numerous.

he greatest potential of the system lies
oubtedly in the reduction in manual labour
erwise rendered necessary with small solid
installations, and in the centralization of
trol and supervision. The larger the installa-
, however, and the more buildings served,
more complex the equipment tends to
ome and the more vital is skilled engineering
ervision. Where the caretaker/handyman was
ally perfectly competent to supervise the
l domestic central heating and hot-water
t and also carry out the limited amount of
ing, this is no longer feasible with a district
ting installation or with a centralized plant.
multiplicity of complex equipment, a break-
n or malfunction in any part of which may
n depriving a large number of buildings of
r essential space-heating and hot-water
uirements, necessitates full-time qualified
ineering supervision.

ispersal too usually simplifies concealment
moke stacks within buildings, and these can thus be conveniently combined with incinerators.

Cost advantages were often claimed for the centralized or district systems but these comparisons were seldom entirely conclusive; they varied very much from scheme to scheme, and in some cases depended on the availability of a supply of surplus heat from an existing generating station or similar source. Now that gas or oil fuels are so widely used the problems of stoking and supervision are very greatly simplified and there is no longer even a slender case for centralization on this score, whatever the extent of a development.

The added practical complications of running district heating mains through existing streets and a network of existing services is also one which must weigh heavily against this system in any redevelopment scheme.

There is too the general question as to whether central heating plants of this type can long continue in use in face of cleaner, less restrictive, more readily installed and pleasant alternatives, except where there are especially abundant supplies of natural oil, coal, or gaseous fuels.

Even in such circumstances it is arguable that the fuels are better used in electricity generating stations, which have to be provided as an indispensable part of the equipment of any civilized community and which are increasingly likely to be supplemented through nuclear energy, solar energy and cheap water power. Moreover they are operated much more efficiently. For most types of buildings, where there is even a reasonable degree of climatic stability, central heating can, as has already been suggested, be obtained more comfortably, more conveniently and with lower initial capital and running costs (20) through floor radiant panels (23) than in any other way.

Another alternative system also depending on electric power is the room air-conditioning unit, which if correctly installed provides an efficient year-round service. It is not however at present as economical as other systems.

Yet another system depending on electric power, the practical application of which may not be far off, is the thermo-electric system of heating and cooling through panels of bimetal construction which, with a reversal of direct current, will give either heating or cooling, as appropriate. The great advantages of such a system when it comes into practical operation, as it is hoped it will, is the manner in which the panels can be recessed into the structural walls, thereby leaving floor areas completely unimpeded, and in providing a clean comfortable form of both heating and cooling without noise, ductwork or pipework. This could very well develop into the most logical use of electric power in the creation of an ideal human environment.

For the time being is seems inevitable that many of the more orthodox central heating installations (19) will be installed, so long as fuel and equipment for the purpose are readily available, as well as techniques of design and installation. So far as flat developments are concerned, with this type of installation the baseboard type of heater or a low under-sill radiator are most satisfactory in supplying heat near the window, where it is most needed, and where the unit is least likely to create an obstruction. Experience tends to indicate that hot-water systems, even with the need for booster pumps, have many advantages over steam, which is frequently noisy and likely to cause scorching of atmospheric dust particles. Surveys over a wide range of schemes have also shown that hot water is the more economical.

Another system which even further improves the distribution of heating is one in which the heat battery coils (26) are supplemented by an electrically-powered fan which is mounted vertically and blows the warm air from the radiator cabinet through a series of grilles, and if need be ducts, into the various rooms.

Provision of domestic hot-water supplies can be made in a wide variety of ways in the multi-storey flat block. The local boiler plant or the centralized or district heating system can be the source of the supply through local calorifiers or central calorifiers: the former having the advantage that the consumption can be more readily controlled or metered. Both of these require of course considerable lengths of lagged plumbing and the necessary ducting. If, however, suitable fuels are obtainable economically and this type of system is run in conjunction with a similar central heating system there may be justification for obtaining hot water in this way.

The alternatives are, however, the use of electric immersion heaters of the storage type which in some cases can be supplied at off-peak periods with low-tariff electricity. Alternatively, there are the gas-operated circulation heaters, or the instantaneous geyser type of heater. The use of either of these would, however, depend on the gas installation being available, which would seem unlikely unless this were also to be used for cooking purposes. Otherwise the installation of a gas service would hardly be economic as an alternative option or merely for this single limited function. Certainly producer water gas from coal fuel must ultimately, as a source of domestic energy, for cooking, heating or other purposes, have a doubtful future as compared with other sources of supply which are very more readily distributed, and which do not depend on fugitive fuels.

The electrically-powered domestic heat pump is a further system which appears to have many potential advantages and is already in limited commercial production in Britain, providing both domestic hot water and larder cooling.

Solar heating for hot water as well as refrigeration has also greater possibilities for many parts of the world than has so far been realized. Where climatic conditions are suitable—and this does not necessarily imply tropical or arid countries—the installation is comparatively simple and can produce considerable economies when coupled with an alternative booster. Where roof spaces are not required for other purposes the collector panels can be located there quite unobtrusively. The sole practical disadvantage of this type of installation is that circulation pumps have to be provided. This may limit its effectiveness in high buildings.

(3) *WATER SUPPLY, SANITATION AND PLUMBING*

It can be assumed that the water services to most high-rise buildings will have to be boosted by duplicated pumps, in extreme cases, through intermediate stages at about every tenth floor, to roof tanks supplying water for all normal domestic purposes and through sealed tanks filtered at inlets and outlets for drinking-water supplies. In those cases where an independent fire-hydrant service is required inside the building, a boosted service to a third set of roof tanks will be needed.

A typical installation for a building accommodating 80 flats would be about 6500 gallons storage for normal domestic and drinking-water services and, if local building or water-supply regulations require it, about another 3500 gallons for emergency fire-fighting purposes.

It is of course essential that the electrical installation to the pumps, as elsewhere, is fully protected so as to guarantee continued service in spite of fire in any part of the building. While it is desirable that there should be independent fire-fighting facilities supplied from roof water storage and with a distribution system to hose reels and hydrants at every floor level, there should also be a dry or wet riser coupling accessible at each landing, to which the fire-brigade pumping appliances at street level can connect and thus provide water at high pressures to the inside of the building.

Apart from the main distribution service, which will probably have to be purpose-made, prefabrication should be used as far as possible for both cold- and hot-water services as well as for wastes to bathrooms and kitchens. These can be in the form of completely pre-assembled units, manufactured in the factory on jigs from a prototype, thus saving considerably on skilled site labour. Copper has shown itself to be the ideal material for this purpose, and it is being widely adopted, not merely for luxury work, but where the initial cost, which is slightly higher than that of other systems such as galvanized barrel, is very largely offset by the ease of fabrication and its ultimate durability.

It still appears likely that plastic tubing, with its great advantage of permanence, will, with well-designed junctions and pressure valves, have a potential for domestic plumbing of all kinds in due course, even in quite high buildings.

In sanitary plumbing generally efforts have been made in a number of countries, particularly in the last ten to fifteen years, to simplify systems without detriment to performance and hygiene, in a way that would receive the necessary support of sanitary authorities. One most important development has been the 'single stack' system (28), which is a considerable advance on earlier systems and appears likely to have an application in high buildings in the near future.

Another interesting development has been the use of pitch fibre in recent years, not only for main drainage services outside the building, where the material has considerable advantages over the older salt-glazed stoneware or even over iron pipe, but also inside the building for the vertical stacks, as a substitute for the customary cast-iron or copper piping. Pitch fibre is considerably more economical than other material, is comparatively easy to work, is flexible, and is particularly durable.

(4) *ELECTRICAL INSTALLATION*

It is remarkable that in this field, where there have been so many advances unrelated to building, more advantage has not been taken of this experience to produce preassembled systems of the type used in motor-car and aircraft production (36). One such system, the 'Octopus', appeared briefly but was relatively short lived. Today the major part of the internal wiring to the dwelling is purpose-made. Yet because of the repetitive factor standardization would suggest itself as an obvious means of obtaining speedier and simpler installation, and appreciable economies.

The ring-main system (35) also suggests a means of applying much-needed rationalization in this relatively unexplored field.

Space will have to be found for one or more electrical substations in any development of size. Since these are space consuming if an adequate service is to be assured they may be located in basement areas. In this case, however, independent access and forced ventilation will be required, as well as provision for trapping oil from transformers should these be fractured. For these and other reasons they are better placed not underneath buildings but under adjoining garden areas, which are more easily accessible when transformers have to be moved.

Road, foot-path and garden lighting must be planned with the same care as the installations within the buildings. A number of attractive but unobtrusive fittings, which will blend well with the garden landscaping, can now be obtained. Well-designed and efficient lighting of the garden areas not only makes them usable for longer periods but is a very desirable safeguard even in the more law-abiding cities. For this same reason the fittings should be properly protected against vandalism and should be time-switched as a labour-saving measure.

(5) *REFUSE-DISPOSAL SYSTEMS*

Only in very low blocks is the ordinary bin system tolerable. Even then the collection of receptacles can prove an unsightly nuisance. Tenants used to have 'binettes' in their own kitchens, but the capacity of these is small and the need for frequent emptying involves regular journeys up and down the public staircase or in the lift—both of which are equally objectionable.

The alternatives to the bin system are first the electrically-operated sink disposal unit, which, however effective, is subject to severe limitations in the type of material it will tackle, and which does not eliminate a container for bottles and tins, needed in every flat. In some cases these units are not sanctioned by the local sanitary authority as they involve increased use of water and a complication with sewerage-disposal plants. There are moreover obvious objections to anything other than clean food refuse being put down a sink, which is used for so many other purposes.

There is also the Garchey system (32), a water-borne system which operates through a separate sink and hopper unit and will accept a wider range of domestic waste. It involves however quite elaborate mechanical equipment and special plumbing, and an extra cost of at least £100 per dwelling.

By far the most popular system, because of its relative simplicity and economy, and one for which a British Standard exists, is the dry chute (33) system discharging either into Standard removable bins at ground level or into an incinerator. One chute is considered adequate to serve a total of about 20 flats, using a $1\frac{1}{4}$ cu yd container emptied twice or three times weekly. This may serve two, four or even six flats at each landing level. Although self-sealing hoppers are normal the chutes should be located away from the staircase, preferably in a lobby in order not to create a route for fire or smoke spread, which could seriously jeopardize the use of a vi means of escape.

In buildings of more than four storeys in heig using the dry chute system it is essential ensure that the largest number of flats sha each chute. In order to increase the over- capacity of the chute rather than duplicate it, i then desirable to arrange a battery of containe which are moved periodically as each is fill assuming the frequency of clearance is at le twice or three times a week. The 'Paladin' is c such piece of equipment. Good vehicular acce to the container housing is essential and the ho ing should normally be kept locked and must as far as possible airtight. These facilities sho moreover be planned without impairing privacy of flats or without detriment to the use the gardens.

As it is very undesirable that the contai housing should be accessible to tenants, w the possible risk that it may be left open convenient arrangement for tenants on lowest floor, which obviates bins, is that having a special chute with access near to first half landing to the staircase.

Refuse chutes, as has already been poin out, are a potential source of noise nuisance, a it is essential that they are located in a serv core and away from habitable rooms in the fl Moreover they should be installed in such a w as to isolate them, with acoustic material, f the remainder of the structure, by using wroug iron straps as fixing points at floor levels intermediate levels with suitable packing tween the strap and the pipe itself, the p being in reinforced concrete or salt-gla stoneware.

If no collection service exists, or if this infrequent, the incinerator system would hav be adopted. This means providing space not for the chute itself but also for the flue. Ag this is a standardized piece of equipm available in a number of countries and one works very effectively, except for the residu incombustible material such as bottle and which still have to be disposed of separately

(6) *TELEPHONES, RADIO, TELEVISION INSTALLATIONS*

The most important general point to st with all these services is that provision be m so far as is practicable at the time of const tion for installations in every dwelling, as ot wise unsightly surface wiring may be unav able. Even if, as is sometimes the case, the vice company or authority is unwilling to the actual wiring or branch service tenants have signed individual agreeme sleeves can usually be located at suitable po in cavity walls or ducts in order to minir surface wiring runs (37).

In many urban areas radio rediffusion serv exist, which obviate the need for indivi receivers and which give tenants a choic high quality reception from a number of diffe stations. The rental charge is usually low, there is much to be said for the system w frees tenants from the responsibility of ec ment ownership and obsolescence, and is popular.

In many cases, the rediffusion companies up with the telephone system, and will instal services within the building at no cost to developer, or in some cases paying a re charge for their right to install.

Television is also installed on a similar rediffu-on network in many areas and with a choice of ›rfect reception from a number of 'channels'. s with radio-diffusion the service only necessi-tes the addition of the switch panel in a parti-ılar flat if and when a tenant decides to accept e service. A simple form of receiver can then › connected and is maintained as part of the reement with the rediffusion company. Its ain advantage, however, is in the elimination of arger number of unsightly antennae, many of nich will, in any event, in multi-storey frame ildings, probably be ineffective.

For this reason, even if a full rediffusion stem is not required by tenants, it is essential have a central common aerial system as the ly means of obtaining reasonable reception the television signals, and to enforce a ban private outdoor antennae.

With any of these systems local amplifier uipment will almost certainly be required for ch of the main dwelling blocks. This can ually be conveniently located in or alongside › lift-motor room housing on the roof, where › central antenna can also be installed. The ace required at this point, as well as in riser cts, is very small.

FIRE PROTECTION

Since in the multi-storey building means of cape in case of fire cannot be as readily hieved as in a single-storey building, in which merous doors or windows can be used, much eater care in planning and more stringent ecautions in the provision of fire-fighting uipment and in structural fire-resistance ndards must be aimed at in order to provide requisite degree of protection for the resi-nts. That occupants will be sleeping during a bstantial part of the time in which the building n normal use makes this all the more impor-t; and because in any case buildings are reasingly planned to heights beyond those at ich it is possible to depend on fire brigade pliances (4–7) for alternative means of escape.

t has been emphasized that one of the funda-ntal considerations in planning dwellings d their means of access should be that if the ed to escape from the location of a fire arises re will be no possibility, so far as can be eseen, of any occupant of the building being off. How this problem is met, and the degree seriousness with which it is viewed varies atly in different parts of the world. The long eriences of fires in cities such as London and w York bears closely on this; and the codes in these cases very precise.

Although in some cases a four-hour period of resistance is specified for the main structural rs and party walls this seems a little unreali- since most fires which can be confined to locality of the original outbreak for a period half an hour to an hour are likely by then to e been extinguished as the result of efforts of brigades. This period will vary in different es with the geographical location of the build- s and the distance from the Fire Brigade adquarters, as also to some extent with the ree of efficiency of the alarm system and the ade. It does not seem unreasonable, how-r, even in the most extreme cases, to consider period of more than an hour for the fire rating he principal structural elements as something he nature of an insurance policy rather than oved need.

It is fortunate that the structural standards which are required to meet other conditions—namely, the stability of the building and freedom from noise transmission—will also in the main secure a requisite fire grading. This is true with regard to all party walls and floors as well as to service ducts. In order that the latter should not be a weak link in the fire isolation system, it is of course important that the enclosure to the duct should be of the appropriate fire grading, including any necessary access doors. In some instances, as has been remarked elsewhere, building regulations require that such ducts should be sealed off by a continuation of structural floor slabs at every floor level. This system, however, reduces the value of the duct and convenience of access to the services, and the alternative is therefore preferable.

As an additional worthwhile precaution, fusible link dampers are often installed at a number of points in vertical rises in order to reduce the risk of fire spread, particularly into branch ducts.

A further potential weakness in the structural system, so far as fire spread is concerned, lies in window and door openings. Reference has already been made to the need to protect these from vertical spread.

Because with access balconies some risk of flame spread and cut-off of escape still exists, it is highly desirable that windows adjoining should be at transome level only, and that escape stairs should be placed at both ends of the balconies.

If the doors giving access to the flats from the lobby or entrance hall are to be effective in preventing fire and smoke spread, the doors themselves as well as the frames must be fire-resistant and they should be fitted with reliable self-closing mechanisms and desirably with a threshold.

In order to prevent both smoke and fire spread self-closing fire-resistant doors are also vital to the staircase and lift enclosures. London building regulations also require, not very appropriately, that, in circumstances where a second escape staircase is not provided in buildings exceeding the height at which external portable escapes can be used, landing lobbies at each floor level should be provided with a specified area of (often chilly) cross-ventilation.

Alternatively the practice in a number of cities is to require ventilation at the top of staircase towers and lift wells. This may come into operation automatically in the case of a fire, as a means of preventing smoke logging. A vertical smoke extract duct with fans at roof level and high level louvred grilles at each landing level adjoining lobbies would seem an even better solution—if the need is thought to exist for these admittedly rather stringent precautions.

Another method of dealing with this problem is to pressurize entrance lobbies and staircases in order further to discourage possible smoke penetration, although it is impossible at this juncture to say that fire-resistant self-closing doors alone may not be adequate.

As a means of inhibiting fire spread 'fire loading' should be reduced: and partition materials should, for example, be based on gypsum, wood wool, clinker block or clay block, all of which have a comparatively high fire rating. The use of softwood on the other hand should be limited to skirting, and possibly floor finishes. Where timber is required for door linings and frames, and preferably also for floor finishes, hardwoods should be used. It is equally important that incombustible finishes to walls and ceilings should be chosen wherever possible. This would suggest plastic emulsion, rather than natural oil-based enamels or paints.

Any type of central heating has much to contribute in minimizing potential fire risks. On the other hand, any form of portable heating equipment, particularly those depending on the use of oil fuel or gas, and to a rather lesser extent on electricity, imply some degree of risk and are to be discouraged, particularly in living rooms or circulation areas. These are the areas in which, together with the kitchen, the greatest degree of risk is likely to be.

In the case of the typical point block form of planning, building regulations may stipulate that flats should be 'one in line' from the staircase: or, in other words, that there should be direct route from the entrance door of each flat to the staircase lobby. If, however, self-closing fire-resistant entrance doors are fitted to all apartments there seems to be no valid reason why an escape route should not pass the entrance doors to other neighbouring flats. Such an arrangement is still very much to be preferred to the access balcony system, even where staircases are located at both ends of the balcony. While there may be less risk of the balconies becoming smoke-logged, the possibility of flame spreading through adjoining windows as, for example, from bathrooms and kitchens, cannot be ruled out, whereas with the point block planning there will be no openings on to the central access lobby other than the entrance doors to flats, which can be made adequately smoke and fire-resistant within the fire rating period of the materials.

In central corridor access planning staircases must be located at the ends of the corridor within fully protected fire enclosures. Secondary means of escape from flats located in the middle of the block can if necessary be gained through one of the bedrooms, which will then have a fire-resistant, self-closing door similar to the entrance door of the flat. The corridor should be fitted at a central point with a pair of self-closing smoke cut-off doors, and secondary means of escape may be provided to the end flats through a fire-resistant hatch on to the staircase half-landing. Alternatively, this can be achieved by the use of a fire-resistant pass door into an adjoining flat, operated by a sealed key.

In the case of normal staircase access planning the position is very much akin to that in the point block. It is only in the very unlikely contingency of a fire occurring in the access lobby that escape is likely to be difficult. With adequate structural standards of fire-resistance, however, it would be preferable in these circumstances for occupants to remain within their own flats.

In maisonette planning, particularly where the intermediate floors are constructed in timber, the risk of a rapid spread of fire throughout the whole of an individual apartment may be considerable, and this is another argument which tends to militate against this type of planning. In practice a secondary means of escape is frequently provided by means of a continuous balcony at bedroom level, but this in no way answers the problem of rapid fire spread within the dwelling itself, and, what is more important, into sleeping areas.

Some of the most important differences in practice occur in relation to staircase and lift installations. These arise in part from the fact that, quite illogically in many cases, the lift is not regarded as a secondary means of escape from the building. Unless an outbreak of fire occurs in the lift or entrance lobby, in which case it would be impossible for it to be used by any of the occupants at that floor level, the lift, in spite of slight delays in responding to calls and its limited car capacity, will form a valuable contributory means of assisting in the evacuation of the building. This is in spite of the fact that it may not be possible or usual to provide for the exit from the lift at ground floor level direct to the open air: a matter of concern only in the rare event of a second outbreak of fire occurring at this point. If adequate steps are therefore taken to ensure that the whole of the electrical installation providing power to the lifts is fully fire-protected, then, with the comparatively small population at any given floor level in multi-storey residential buildings, the lift can and should be regarded as a useful means of escape, should the necessity arise.

As it appears logical to regard the considerable investment in the lift installation not only as a means of providing normal access but at other times as an insurance policy, escape staircases may be thought of as a second line of defence—albeit a very important one. In this light, the single staircase which is widely accepted now in many countries in point block planning and for blocks of unlimited height, appears to be entirely adequate. In fact, in this type of planning, the introduction of a second staircase rarely achieves any worthwhile gain, since the distance separating the two gives no assurance that where access to one is affected by smoke or flame the other would not also be involved. In the case, however, of other forms of access duplication of staircases may frequently be unavoidable.

Opinions also vary on the suitable location of such staircases as are installed or required. Location on an outside wall is still sometimes insisted upon on the assumption that this will more readily remove any possible smoke penetration and may also provide natural lighting. If, however, the planning of the staircase is as a fully fire-protected enclosure with self-closing fire-resistant access doors, and no other possible means of smoke penetration into the staircase well, the only other possible source of risk could be an outbreak of fire within the staircase itself. This, however, appears so unlikely with the lack of combustible material and the high fire grading of the staircase structure as to be almost ruled out. In the unlikely event of their being some slight smoke penetration from fires in other parts of the building, in spite of the precautions which are now almost the invariable practice, an automatic or manually-operated smoke vent at the head of the staircase well will allow this to escape with or without the use of fans.

As for lighting, the windows may be of benefit during the daytime; but on the other hand the cost of providing a protected artificial lighting system and keeping it in operation is likely to be very small. An internal staircase frees the use of the outside walls for that part of the accommodation which must necessarily depend on natural light and ventilation and leads to much more economical and compact planning. In all the circumstances there is little justification for insisting on external staircases; a practice in some building regulations which has not moved with the times.

In some cases, too, building regulations require that escape staircases should debouch direct into the open air. This is a complication in the planning which, if it were to be accepted, would necessarily enforce the placing of the staircase on the outside wall, and the provision of the exit with special self-closing doors, internally operated. The logic of this is impossible to see when looked at in the light of present-day conditions.

Practice varies somewhat in the use of sprinkler installations. These are generally thought of as a means of localizing outbreaks of fire at a very early stage, and where conditions may otherwise be conducive to rapid and extensive spread. This would be particularly the case in warehouses or garages where it is rarely possible to subdivide the space into fire-isolated units without impairing convenience in use. The fire loading in residential apartments cannot, however, be regarded as constituting a high risk and localization will be achieved as the result of compartmentalization of the floor space into dwelling units. As sprinklers are unsightly and necessarily imply an appreciable degree of water damage, their use, other than in circumstances in which there is no other satisfactory remedy, is unwarranted.

If, however, basement garaging is planned then sprinklers should certainly be used, as also in basement transformer stations and boiler rooms; and in these cases should be in the form of foam outlets. Otherwise automatic carbon-dioxide dispensers should be installed, and such areas should always be planned with independent and direct means of escape to the open air.

The addition of an automatic electric-alarm system may sometimes be justified, particularly at key points such as staircase lobbies and entrance halls to flats. With well-organized fire services, this system has most of the advantages in a central locality of the sprinkler system in calling early attention to the outbreak of any fire, without consequential water damage.

There are many current fallacies regarding high residential buildings, and not the least of these relates to the alleged fire risk. This problem, and suggested safeguards, has been dealt with at length as it plays a prominent part in most building regulations, and in the minds of many who would argue this as another compelling reason for not putting families high above the ground.

That safeguards are necessary is undeniable; for although there is no record as yet of any serious incident due to fire in a high residential building, there may always be a first time. More than normal precautions may very well be justified, if only for psychological reasons. A balance must, however, always be struck where these appear to go beyond ordinary logic and reason, and therefore become economically unjustifiable.

This is one direction in which we have still much to learn, and where clearly many of the building regulations err on the side of extreme caution in the absence of more specific information or experience. The suggestions which are made here as to standards constitute what, from a present consensus of specialized knowledge, seem to afford reasonable safety as set against likely risk.

(8) *MISCELLANEOUS SERVICES*

Ventilation Ducts. With the increasing use internal bathrooms and toilets it is desirable make some specific reference to the means ventilating these. Ideally a fresh-air inlet as v as an air extract should be provided to ea compartment, which in effect implies a separ duct to each running in the ordinary course events, the full height of the building. The spa required to do this would however be qu prohibitive, and fortunately the 'shunt fl system has provided the solution.

It was usual, where this system was origin used with open fires or stoves, to limit the nu ber of these discharging into the main bra to a total of five. Where, however, the shunt du are used for ventilation to bathrooms and toil a larger number than this can, if need be, allowed to discharge into the main duct. For purpose the branch ducts are about 7in by and the main duct about 12in by 8in, cl internal dimensions. The open ends of the bra ducts inside the flats are covered with adju able grilles which are pre-set by the installat engineers, before flat occupation, to equa the air flow.

If fresh-air ventilation is then required exactly similar system in reverse is instal with an inlet into the stack usually brough horizontally to the underside of the first fl slab.

The European practice is simply terminate the main ducts at roof level v a specially designed louvred cowl. W experience shows that this provides perfe satisfactory conditions, even in quite h buildings, for any of the internal bathroc and toilets. Practice elsewhere has howe been to insist on fans in duplicate at level, thus considerably adding to initial ca and running costs. Recent reports by British Building Research Station have ten to reinforce the views and experience of Co nental countries that natural ventilated du properly designed can provide an effective satisfactory form of ventilation, fully up accepted normal standards. The system has added advantage moreover of never break down, and is quieter.

Acceptance of these views should go a l way to reducing considerably the cost, wh hitherto has averaged between £15 to £24 flat, including the installation of mechan extract ventilation, builders' work and ductin a wide range of high flat schemes in the Lon region.

Lightning Protection must not be overloo as a necessary safeguard in all classes of h buildings. While the extent of the risk va according to local climatic conditions, installation of this type appears to be well wo while as an additional precaution, with psyc logical as well as material advantages.

Although it is desirable that the most di route is planned for the conductor tapes the some degree of flexibility in their routing. If have to be placed externally, coloured PVC tapes are now available to assist in concealm These should, however, be planned at the liest stage, when it is usually possible to p them in reasonably unobtrusive positions. this in mind internal locations may be s factory provided that a direct link with an exte earth termination can be achieved wit structural difficulties.

ıese installations are frequently undertaken pecialists, and it is important that they should ny event be planned in accordance with epted standards. An example of this is the sh Code of Practice 326.101 (38) which down fairly precisely effective means of iding this form of protection.

in-Water Disposal. A properly designed rain-r disposal system will of course be re-ed, not only for hard standings, paved and areas at ground level but also to the build-itself (39). Roof areas can generally be ned in such a way as to drain to outlets h discharge to down pipes taken in plumb-ducts, but it is also equally important to re that any balconies are adequately ned, and this cannot always be achieved ugh such ducts.

oviding special ducts for this purpose can somewhat extravagant solution and may e maintenance and inspection of the pipes cult. On the other hand a reasonably neat tion may be achieved by using a down-pipe em with an open socket and spigot joint a perforated collar grating, coinciding with loor level of the balcony. This stack runs the height of the building without swan-neck ections and can be tucked into a back er of the balcony where it is scarcely visible, easily inspected and maintained.

cuumation System. The central vacuuma-system is still regarded as something of a ry but is commonplace in a number of pean high-density schemes, particularly Sweden. Obviously, if conditions in flat ks are to compare with those in the normal te house, public entrance halls and lobbies ot be forgotten. And yet frequently these areas of cold austerity with no shred of fort. They have the forbidding look of an nanted no-man's-land and their mainte-ce and upkeep all too often appears to be ıer the responsibility of the management f individual tenants. It is equally noteworthy in the better developments these are given attention with attractive decorations and coverings.

a valuable means of maintaining these s, the piped vacuum system, especially in high buildings, may well be economically iable.

Appendix E

1. With alternate floor opening the economy, which varies between £150 to £250 a storey, goes beyond the immediate saving in landing doors, for with this arrangement the two lifts cannot be interconnected and there is also a saving in electronic equipment. All this of course implies some reduction in the standard of service but if economies must be effected it seems less serious to have slight delays through waiting for the lift to arrive rather than that on occasion there should be no lift at all available. Full collective calling appears unwarranted in residential building in spite of the saving in current and waiting time, as the additional capital cost is heavy, bearing in mind particularly the volume of traffic involved. On the other hand installation of the down collective system may very well be justified at a cost of £25 per lift per floor additional, and this ensures that the descending car responds to landing calls as they are received in sequence.

The full collective system which handles all calls would add a further £25 per lift per floor. If the pair of lifts are interconnected so that the landing call is answered by the nearest lift travelling in the required direction approximately another £100 is added to the cost of the installation for each building storey height. Savings in time as well as in current consumption are involved in the use of both of these systems and these partly offset the additional capital cost, but bearing in mind the volume of traffic the down collective system may be justified where the full collective system would seldom be so, except in a luxury scheme.

2. In many cases floor-heating installations are specially favoured in using low tariff electricity at off-peak periods during the night time; with the floor slabs then retaining enough heat to provide comfortable conditions for the following day; with possibly a short top-up period during the late afternoon. This kind of installation allows for flexible planning and movement of partitions to meet changing family needs, and has none of the unpleasant effects of dust scorching associated with other forms of central heating. The heat coils do not create obstructions, do not scorch the decorations, and yet provide an evenly distributed comfortable heat. This is achieved completely silently and in a way that entirely eliminates local sources of smoke pollution; transferring this problem to the well-organized power station, which, even if it uses oil fuel or coal, will almost certainly these days have the necessary precipitation plant and washing plant to prevent atmospheric pollution. Transfer later to nuclear power or solar energy will also be relatively simple.

The saving in capital cost of boiler houses, mains, ducts both outside and inside the buildings, as well as in all the ironmongery and hardware, is likely to be considerable, but has so far received no more than a limited amount of attention. A Building Research Station Report published in London concludes however that on running costs the electric floor-warming system is the cheapest as against the other alternatives of orthodox central heating, gas fires or local electric fires. A survey which formed the basis of this report also showed, as might be expected, that this type of heating gave the most evenly distributed temperatures and that it was very much liked by tenants.

One of the other advantages that has not been listed but is far from being unimportant is the ease with which this type of heating can be metered so that payment is in proportion to use. This, however, is much more difficult and expensive in the case of other more orthodox forms of central heating.

It must be recognized of course that this system is not one to be used in very changeable climatic conditions, but only where cold conditions are likely to persist for fairly predictable periods. In more changeable conditions quicker and more flexible forms of heating are needed and these in any event can only be provided locally in the form, for example, of electric radiators, which should be available also in cases where floor warming is installed, for use during the equinoxes.

3. In spite of the fact that with the reverse cycle air-conditioning unit there is a gain of heat over and above that normally provided through electric radiators due to the latent heat and compression system, these installations, whether in the form of local room units or centralized units require power for the compressor and the fan, and are of course designed to give cooling as well as heating. For all of these reasons they are more expensive in installation and running costs than the floor coils, but it must be borne in mind that they provide an all-year-round service in a wide variety of different climatic conditions. As standards of living rise in so many of the cities of the world, and certainly in those climates where there is excessive humidity and summer heat, air conditioning is coming to be thought of more and more as an essential. It is probably therefore a matter of economics to decide whether or not an installation of this type is justified, whether it be considered in terms of a cottage or a flat. The sole possible difference in the latter case is the possibility that the installation may be centralized, but the conditions in which this is likely to occur in high-density flat developments, or even to be advisable bearing in mind the complications and the inhibiting influence of duct networks, must be very limited indeed.

There are numerous objections to duct systems, particularly the difficulty in residential buildings of achieving concealment consistent with distribution of the conditioned air, and in setting up potential sound and fire transmission routes. Even the local room air-conditioning units at their most efficient can never be entirely free from noise in operation, and therefore cannot compete as a source of room heat energy with floor coils.

4. Two alternative systems are adopted for the normal domestic supply; one with a break tank from the main from which the water is subsequently pumped through a special recoil valve to the high level tanks, which in turn supply the service drops. Even if only five floors are supplied from each tank, orifice breaks or pressure-reducing valves are needed in these service drops in order to keep the pressure constant at the outlets. If the pumping is staged, then a second pair of booster pumps draws from the high level tanks supplied from basement level and in turn pumps to roof level. Each intermediate tank must be supplied with a regulating valve in order to ensure the equalization of pumped pressures at all outlets including ball valves.

As a second alternative to this system the pair of supply pumps at ground or basement l may draw direct from the main and supplen existing mains pressure. Of the two alternati the first, involving space for a two to t thousand gallon reserve tank or even larger r in the event of a mains breakage or supp being temporarily discontinued, be a precaution to take. Some reserve will of co also be held in the higher level tanks but may prove to be inadequate if the mains su is cut for more than a few hours.

The separate drinking-water service sh be taken normally by a second set of boo pumps direct from the main without any in mediate tank which could otherwise b possible source of contamination, even if it v sealed. Filtration of the supply can then place as the water is pumped into the tank higher level, and as the water is drawn off in down service further filtration can be affec This pumping may also as with the princ service be carried out in stages and the s valving will be needed in order to equa pressures both on supply valves and draw points.

5. Research undertaken by Wise and Cro the British Building Research Station has le the 'single stack' plumbing system. This, it be noted, is distinct from the one-pipe sys which, while taking wastes and soil connect into a single stack, has vents to all fittings a separate vent stack. The single stack system the other hand omits all vents up to and incluc five storeys in height and by careful desig junctions takes all wastes and soil pipes in single 4in soil and waste stack. The ground fittings are for preference connected direct the sewer with this system, which has been clusively shown to be free from anti-siphon and the other troubles which sanitary engin so long feared would occur once vents v eliminated.

Further investigation is being undertaker the single stack system and it has already b applied, with vents to WC's only, in an eight storey flat block. Even this suggests a worthwhile economy and simplification. thought that over twenty-five storeys in he the 4in stack may prove inadequate, but u that height, depending of course on the num of fittings discharging into it, research sh that it appears to function perfectly well.

6. The rising mains to the tenants' meters be standardized to a limited degree but from meter the whole of the remaining installa could very well consist of a series of stand ized pre-assembled sections or groups cables in 'looms'. If in addition the 'ring-m system set out in the British Code of Prac were to be adopted, and the main part of installation carried behind skirting boards, would greatly simplify the installation and layout.

The ring-main system has a number of o advantages, one being the extent to w flexibility in the use of individually fused fitt may be obtained, on the single 30 amp n fuse. The main, taken round the perimeter of flat, can leave the whole of the internal partit unobstructed, and yet allow for good distribu of power points and lighting points wher needed. Spurs can be taken off the ring n for the purpose of providing bracket wall fitt or ceiling fittings, but these can very ofter dispensed with altogether in favour of l gs supplied by the skirting board sockets. large dwelling of more than about 1000sq ft area two separate ring mains may be ired. It is always desirable that an adequate ber of lighting and power points are in-ed at the outset, but additional points can be ed relatively easily and cheaply to this em.

off-peak current is used either for floor ing or for domestic hot-water supply these gs, as well as electric cookers, will of course netered separately. All the meters should ccessible from outside the flat.

Most of this equipment has been standard- in Britain and a number of European ntries with provision for rodding and ventila- at roof level and with air-tight self-sealing per doors which automatically prevent a ibility of refuse from a higher level being ted at an intermediate floor level. The best ese designs are in stainless steel and fitted a rubber gasket. It is found in practice er not to provide water points for hosing down nside of the chute but to keep it as dry as sible. There should, however, be provision nosing down the container housing in the of a bib tap and floor gulley.

Dry or wet risers (practice in this regard es in different cities) are vitally necessary in igh buildings, to avoid hoses being dragged hrough staircases from the Fire Brigade's ps at ground level; a procedure which in-ably creates a considerable degree of un-essary water damage. In some cases wet s are used in preference, at whatever the ding height. The normal British practice, ne other hand, in part due to possible freez- risk with the wet riser, is that dry risers are ys used for preference up to a height of t. This would be the preferable arrangement ny cold climate. Above the 200ft level wet s are customary as these will then have to be ed from intermediate-level storage tanks ch will be serviced with the normal booster ps to the building at basement level—which t be in duplicate and suitably protected to-er with electrical services to obviate any sibility of their being put out of action during mergency. The whole installation will be so gned as to give pressures of not less than to the square inch at the highest floor, or nimum flow of 200 gallons per minute. Where k-tanks are installed between the normal ns supply and the booster pumps it is essen-hat these should have sufficient capacity to v for a reserve being available during fire-ting operations when the Fire Brigade may be wing from this source.

ser coupling boxes at ground floor level and each landing level should be secured by s which will be operated by the fireman's also used in taking over control of the lift. ccess roads to these points, as well as hard dings for Fire Brigade equipment, are ential but can usually be combined with ice access roads used by tradesmen and se collectors. Wherever possible these uld be planned as cul-de-sacs in order to d the temptation to other vehicles to use n as through-routes, thereby impairing the ty and convenience of users of the garden s. In buildings up to a maximum of 80ft er in some cities) regulations often insist on ess for mobile escape vehicles to all sides he building on which habitable rooms are located. It is to be hoped that views will undergo a change in regard to the very limited value which can be placed on mobile escape from the exterior of the building in the case of a fire, which at best must be regarded as extremely hazardous and dangerous, and for the elderly and very young probably quite impracticable. With adequate fire construction standards and proper planning precautions this piece of equipment may before long find a use solely as a means of giving the Fire Brigade itself access with its hoses to parts of high buildings which for some reason or other are otherwise inaccessible.

In the event of such a stipulation for access by escape ladders this can frequently be done by introducing removable chains or barriers to the hard standings which makes them inaccessible to normal traffic. Instead of these areas being in the form of paved road an attractive alternative more in keeping with the amenities is that of the use, for example, of hollow concrete blocks set into lawn.

9. The space required for the vacuumation plant is limited and could easily be placed in the equivalent of one of the typical tenant's store-rooms at basement level. The suction main can be accommodated either in the lift well or in a duct alongside the fire hydrant main. The operating equipment consisting of a hose and cleaning tools is detachable from a very neat connection at floor level which is normally covered by a surface plate. Space would generally be found for the equipment in a similar cupboard to that used by the fire hose reel let in flush with the wall adjoining the access lobby.

Selected Bibliography and References

Services Section

1. Hampton, R. F. 'Boosted Water Supplies for Multi-storey Buildings.' *IHVE Journal,* October 1961.
2. Editorial. 'Services for Tall Buildings—Symposium.' *Architects' Journal,* December 1959.
3. Anderson, M. B. V. 'Mechanical Services in High Buildings.' *ANZAAS* 35th *Congress.*
4. 'New Housing Estates and Blocks of Flats.' *Advice as to Provision of Fire Fighting Facilities—LCC.*
5. Editorial. 'Reduced Fire Risk of Tall Buildings.' *Official Architecture and Planning,* April 1954.
6. Delves, F. W. 'Fire Precautions in Buildings.' *RICS Journal,* February 1961.
7. 'Precautions against Fire,' CP3 Chapter IV (62). *Council for Codes of Practice, British Standards Institute.*
8. Loader, P. F. and Milray, E. A. 'Space and Water Heating in Local Authority Flats.' *Architects' Journal,* June 1961.
9. BRS London. 'Heating in Local Authority Flats.' *HMSO* London 1961.
10. Adamson, B. *Fordelingmatning for varme och varmvatten.* Teknisk Tidskrift 1956–86.
11. Egerton Committee. 'Heating and Ventilating of Dwellings.' *Post-war Building Study No.* 19. *HMSO* 1945.
12. *Heating and Ventilating Reconstruction Committee, DSIR.* 'District Heating Post-war Building Studies Nos. 31, 32.' *HMSO* 1953.
13. Mission to US 1947. 'District Heating in American Building.' *National Building Studies No.* 7. *HMSO* 1949.
14. *British Coal Utilization Research Association.* 'Solid Fuel Installations Post-war Building Study No. 10.' *HMSO* 1944
15. Weston, J. C. 'Domestic Water Heating.' *IHVE Journal,* February 1950.
16. *DSIR.* 'Domestic Heating in America.' *HMSO* 1946.
17. Parry, N. 'Domestic Heating.' *Building Digest,* July 1952.
18. Margolis. 'Pimlico District Heating System.' *Architects' Journal,* December 1950.
19. *Building Research Station, National Building Studies Research Paper* 34, April 1961. 'A Study of Space and Water Heating in Local Authority Flats.'
20. *Heating and Ventilating Research Association, Report* May 1951. 'The Heating of Buildings by Off-peak Electrical Supplies.'
21. Bruce, H. H. 'Off-peak Floor Heating.' *JIHVE* August 1952.
22. 'Wire Fabric Heating.' *Progressive Architecture,* March 1961.
23. Moule, J. W. 'Electrical Floor Warming.' *National Smoke Abatement Society,* London 1955.
24. Engebretson, C. D. and Ashan, N. G. 'Progress in Space Heating with Solar Energy.' *IHVE Journal,* May 1961.
25. Mase, R. N. 'Radiant Cooling.' *ANZAAS* 1961.
26. LCC. 'Warm Air Heating at LCC Brandon Estate.' *IHVE Journal,* March 1961.
27. BRS London. 'One Pipe—Single Stack Plumbing.' *Digest No.* 48, November 1952 and No. 49, December 1952.
28. Wise, A. F. E. and Croft, J. 'Investigation of Single-stack Drainage for Multi-storey Flats.' RSHJ, January 1952.
29. Editorial. 'American Experiments. The National Plumbing Code.' *Architects' Journal,* April 1952.
30. Editorial. 'US Plumbing Codes.' *Architectural Forum,* December 1950.
31. Barrow, F. L. 'Sanitary Services: their effects on the planning and design of buildings.' *RIBA Journal,* December 1950.
32. *The Garchey System of Domestic Refuse Disposal.*' Matthew Hall, London.
33. Allen, P. G. and Miller, A. 'Refuse Disposal in Blocks of Flats.' *Housing Rev,* London, March–April 1960.
34. Goldsmith, H. J. 'Thermoelectric Cooling.' *IHVE Journal,* September 1960.
35. Editorial. 'Ring Main Electrical System.' *RIBA Journal,* January 1953.
36. Gilbert, T. C. 'Electrical Installations—Post-war Practice.' *Architect & Building News.* September 1955.
37. Wright, L. M. *Facilities in Buildings for Telephone Service.*' Paper 1961.
38. Codes of Practice Committee. 'Lightning Protection CP326.101 (48).' *Codes of Practice Committee, HMSO.*
39. Tanner, G. C. A. 'The Disposal of Rainwater.' *Architectural Review.*

Tenancy and Ownership

It has been implicit in all that has been written so far that whenever the expression 'tenant' has been used this implies occupancy of a flat or apartment either by paying rent or as a home owner.

Home ownership is so firmly held to as a tradition in some countries, that although many of the convincing arguments for more and better central urban residential development are viewed sympathetically, the principle of the flat or the apartment tends to be accepted somewhat reluctantly unless linked with home ownership.

In Britain, however, partly due to lack of choice in the acute housing shortage after the second world war, there has been a very much more complete swing over to the idea of renting flats; and the bulk of such building carried out since 1946 has been through the agency of local governing authorities with the help of financial subsidies from both these sources and central government.

Whatever may be the prospects of improvement in construction costs of the flat, with increases in efficiency in building and planning techniques, the problem of the high cost of land in the central urban areas on which most renewal and many of the high-density residential developments will be located, is one that cannot easily be met with normal financing—which often means rents or costs being too high to meet the needs of the many families this kind of development should be catering for. Subsidies have been found unavoidable by those cities which have been most progressive in mass housing of the best type.

Such subsidies applied to the purchase and clearance of land have normally been linked with private-enterprise developments of flats for selling or letting, in the United States; in England, however, a very extensive system of subsidies not only to cover land purchase but also any higher costs of construction has been in operation for some years.

In some cases indirect forms of subsidy have been extended to housing associations in Britain—these being formed as voluntary bodies with very much the same financing facilities as local government housing agencies. A substantial contribution to the total housing provision has also been made through the new towns corporations grants, the major part of which however relate unfortunately to low-density suburban development.

In most of the European Continental countries financing is undertaken through three main channels: central government agencies, local government, and housing associations, societies, or cooperatives. In many cases schemes will be financed by all three of these bodies, in varying proportions of responsibility, but the private-enterprise financed scheme is extremely rare. This too is a system which had to be devised specifically to meet a massive programme of flat and other home construction made necessary in most cases as the result of war damage and the need to redress practically ten years of lag in building operations, as well as that of meeting normal population increase.

It seems inescapable that if the necessary programmes of flat development as a part of central urban renewal are to be carried out to
the extent needed to meet the requiremen
families at all income levels, legal powers
be needed to acquire sites in these locatio
existing use value, rather than at specula
values artificially inflated in consequenc
surrounding community development activi
Some form of subsidy may otherwise be
voidable.

Only in these ways is there likely to be s
cient encouragement to the authorities
cerned and property owners to undertake
necessary rehabilitation of so many ce
sites which are at present lying derelict or b
inadequately used. Certainly slum-cleara
schemes are unlikely to make headway wit
appreciable financial stimulus, and if this
to be provided from government or local gov
ment sources, it is likely to create obv
difficulties for home-ownership schemes,
few could theoretically, and probably in prac
benefit at the expense of the majority of
payers in obtaining a home in a favour
location at much less than prevailing ma
costs, and the benefit too of a realizable ca
asset.

It is obviously unlikely that there would
much public support for such a scheme
which the control of the investment passed
of the hands of the constructing or financ
authority. For these reasons it is unlikely
that there will be a serious impact on the w
programme of urban renewal, slum cleara
and urban residential development in those ca
where housing has been mainly concerned w
private enterprise and home ownership u
there is a greater degree of government in
vention in the financing, and a wider accepta
of the principle, of rented accommodation.

This is far from suggesting, however, that
privately-financed scheme has not an impor
part to play in providing much-needed ur
living for a significant sector of the econom
is obviously highly desirable that this sho
continue alongside other forms of developm
to meet the needs, wherever it is practicabl
do so, of those who prefer to invest in a hom
their own. It may well be that in many instan
this will involve the borrowing of money
mortgages, as is the case in other types
property. But, where a clear title to land
normally be used as an important part of
security collateral in cases of single owners
this is obviously impossible in the case of m
tiple ownership such as in a block of flats.

Two alternative systems have been adop
to meet this difficulty: the first of these is
'company' system in which individuals who r
each wish to own a flat combine together int
group and, either from their own resources
from borrowing, or both, promote a compa
which undertakes construction, and in wh
each of the participants takes one or more sha
As a part of the shareholding, accommodat
will be held by the participants, who will a
combine together to accept financial respo
bility for the maintenance and upkeep of
building, which would usually be done throu
a manager and a small maintenance compan

Because of difficulties experienced in borro
ing on the basis of a share in a company
second alternative scheme has been devis
and is in operation in at least one State in A
tralia, namely, the 'stratum titles' system. T
system purports to give a full certificate of ti
for the flat including parts of the party walls a

ɔors; and a share in the common access and ɛrvices. As it is vitally important that the possi-ɫity of flat purchase may be extended to those ho do not necessarily possess ready capital r outright purchase in these schemes, this stem, which has been worked out by govern-ent legal officials and given statutory sanc-ɔn, appears to be an ingenious solution. ırticularly is this so when it is borne in mind at in the company system, when one of the iginal shareholders finds it necessary to sell s flat, he must either continue his share of sponsibility for the maintenance of the com-on parts and the administration of the block as whole, or appoint a responsible agent or anagement company to do this on his behalf. the case of the stratum title a clear equity ists which can be wholly transferred when ɛsired to some other individual.

ɛlected Bibliography and References

ɿancy Section

George and Piercy, E. F.: 'The Sale of Flats.' Sweet & Maxwell.

Editorial: 'Financing of the Promontory.' *Archit. Forum,* January 1950.

Conclusions

It is perhaps not too optimistic a hope that what goes before will show convincingly that there are in general no insoluble practical problems impeding the undertaking of many more, vitally needed, urban renewal residential developments—although there are sadly, still many cases of lack of knowledge or under-standing or of plain old-fashioned prejudice.

For those who are in search of a viable solution to one of the most critical social problems of the day it is believed there are clear indications of the right course, as well as encouragement from what has already been achieved.

Within the compass of this book it is only possible to place emphasis on the more impor-tant factors and to draw together some of the many threads. Many important contributions have been made collaterally to one or other aspect of the whole range of understanding of high-density residential development and these must be given their due weight and attention if the subject is to be fully comprehended.

Illustrated are examples of some of the best schemes undertaken in recent years in a number of countries, including North and South America, Austria, Australia, Belgium, Canada, Denmark, England, France, Finland, Germany, Holland, Italy, Norway, Sweden, and Switzerland. For the sake of convenience the countries have been arranged in alphabetical order, and the various schemes illustrated have been grouped together within the respective countries.

Needless to say, the list of countries in which important and significant work in the field of high flat development has been carried out is not by any means necessarily complete. Within the limitations of what it has been possible to include in the scope of this work, however, the examples have been chosen both from an architectural point of view and because of the significance of their contribution to the problem of town planning.

The schemes have also been selected with a view to illustrating the diversity in planning and in design generally which has resulted from the enormous amount of research and thought which has gone into this type of development all over the world, particularly in the last fifteen or twenty years.

Australia

1 Blue's Point, Sydney

Architect: H. Seidler

This 23-storey tower block of 168 flats is one of the first of its kind in Australia, and is intended as the first stage of a very much larger central area slum clearance and redevelopment scheme. The design is such, with a very low site coverage, that construction of this block on a restricted cleared site was a means of assisting subsequent decanting in the surrounding area.

The design is similar to a number of European schemes but local conditions necessitate duplicating the staircase and planning for three lifts, so that even with six flats to the typical floor the planning is not nearly as economical as would be the case with more liberal building bye-laws.

The typical floor arrangement provides for six two-bedroom units but as an alternative in some cases four bedsitters replace the two centre two-bedroom units. Originally internal bathrooms and kitchens were provided to all flats subsequently the kitchens were transferre the outside wall with natural light and ventil in all the larger flats.

An alternating pattern of inset balconies been used which gives interest to and av monotony on the exterior but results ir appreciable loss of space in the habitable a

The planning is ingenious and fits well int simple overall form of the building with veniently arranged dwellings.

Construction is in reinforced concrete l bearing walls and frame and reinforced conc floors on a piled foundation. Precast conc blocks are used for most of the external clad within the exposed concrete frame.

A parking area and garage is associated this building for a total of 132 cars, 40 per ce which are under cover. There are also comm laundries equipped with automatic machine well as tenants' storage lockers.

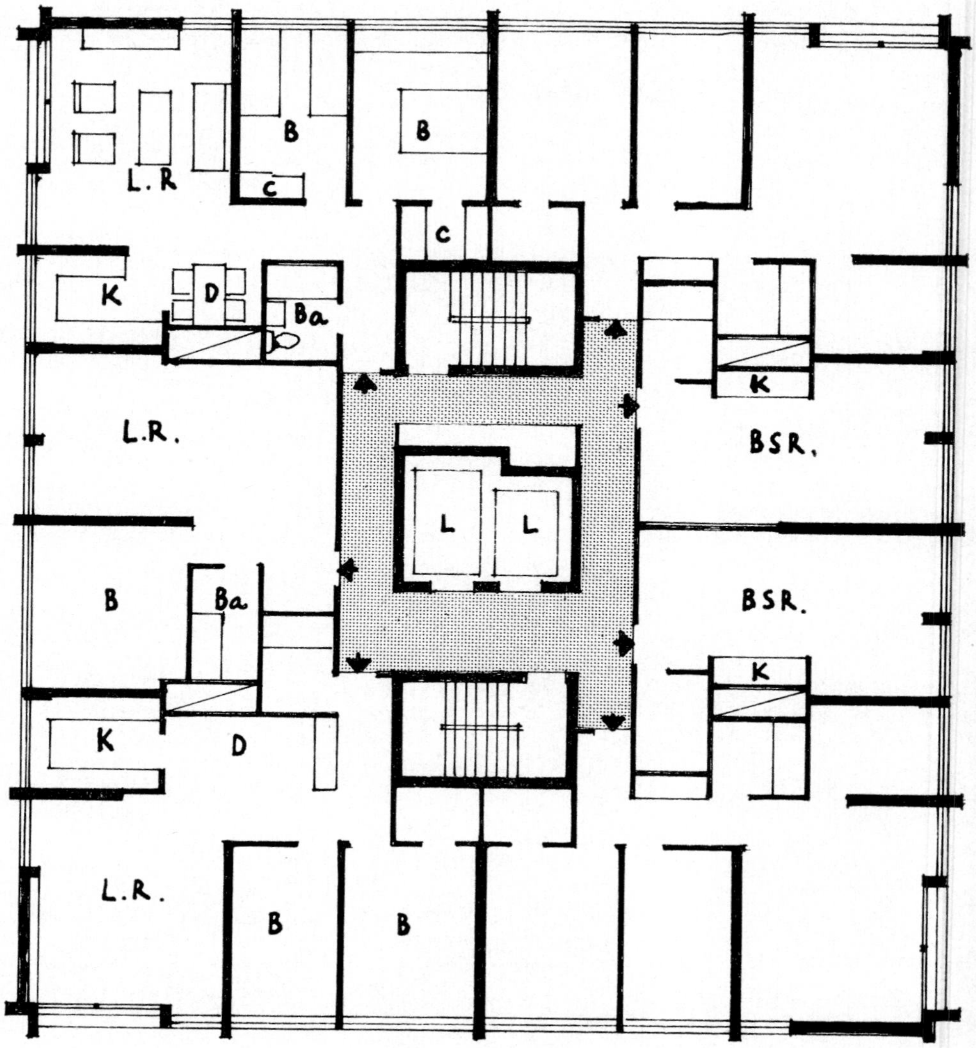

Typical Floor Plan

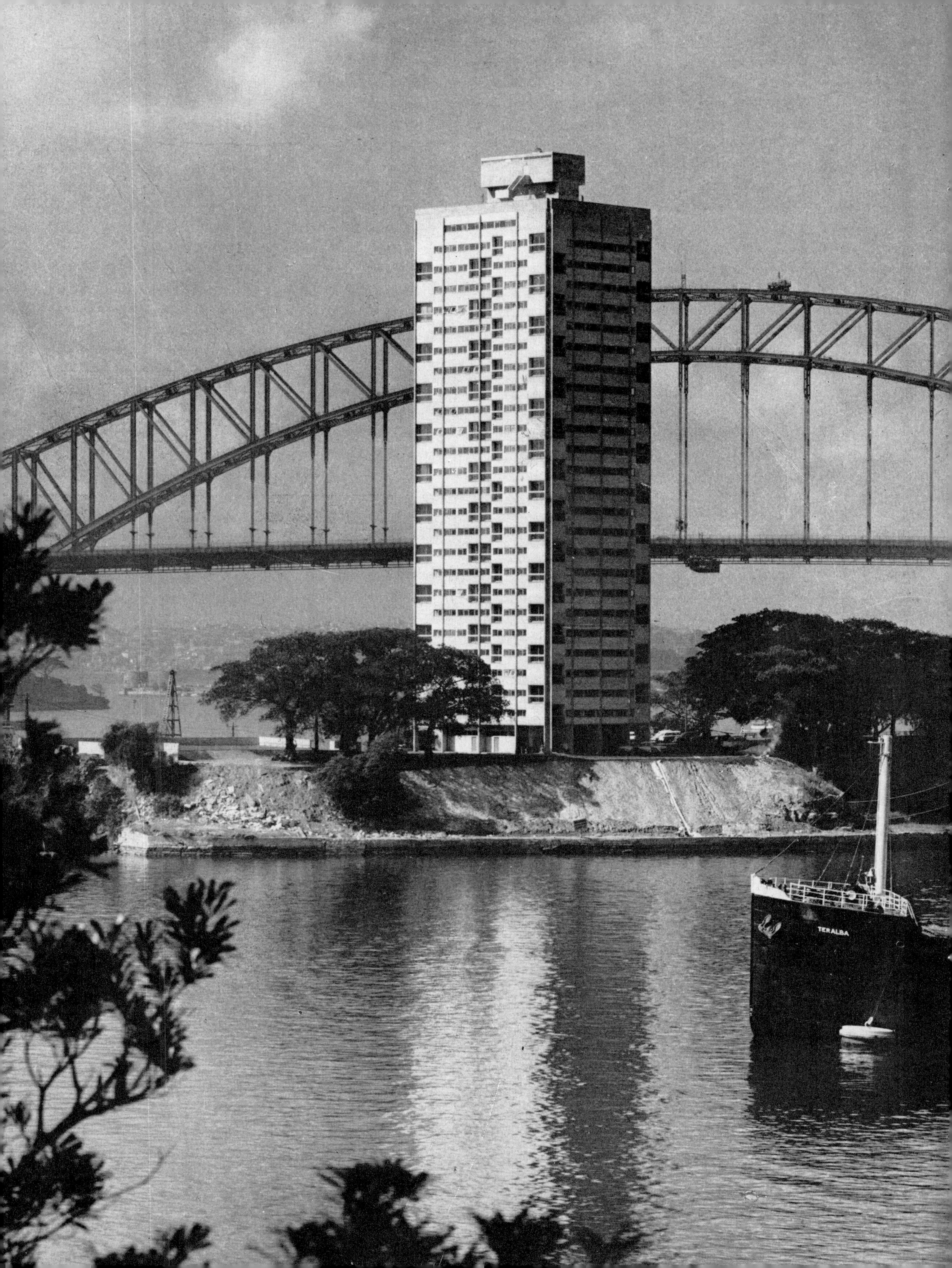
TERALBA

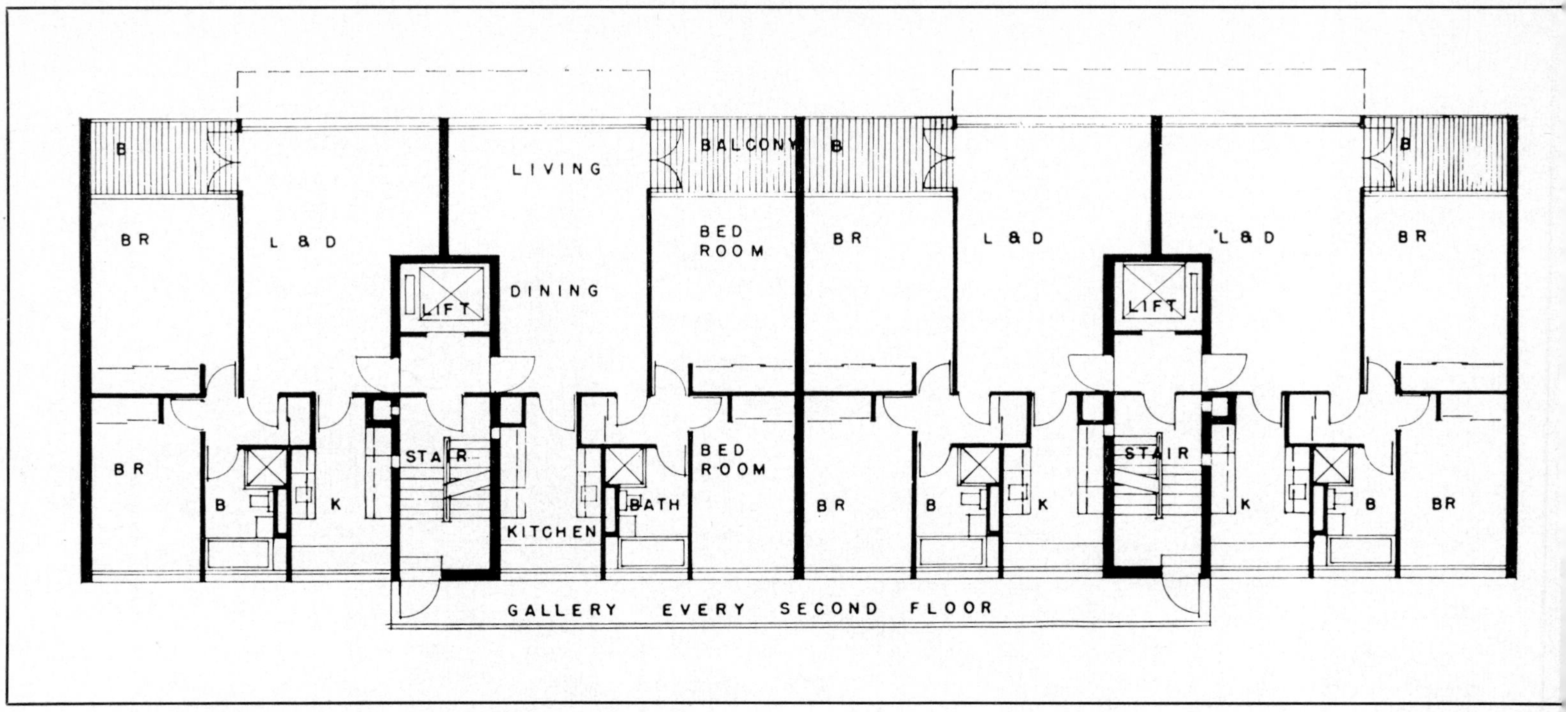

2 Ithaca Gardens, Sydney

Architect: H. Seidler

A slab block of 40 flats overlooking the harbour, erected on a half acre site. All of these are two-bedroom units with kitchens and bathrooms located externally and normal staircase and lift access—but with provision for emergency interchange by means of galleries at the rear of the building.

These have been depressed in order to avoid nuisance from traffic passing bedrooms.

Two communal laundries are located at roof level. Covered car parking is provided under the building.

Construction is in reinforced concrete with $9\frac{1}{2}$in flat plate floors and columns contained within wall thicknesses.

Camperdown, Sydney

rchitect: H. Seidler

 low cost scheme for Sydney City Council ontaining 141 flats with skip stop access. This rrangement reduces circulation areas and yet rovides alternative forms of exit in emergency s required by building regulations. Lifts are in ee standing towers and give access at half anding levels. This may mean a maximum of alf flights and a length of corridor to traverse to each a flat, which though normally not excep- onable could be difficult with stretcher cases.

Construction is in flat slab reinforced concrete ith off-form exterior concrete.

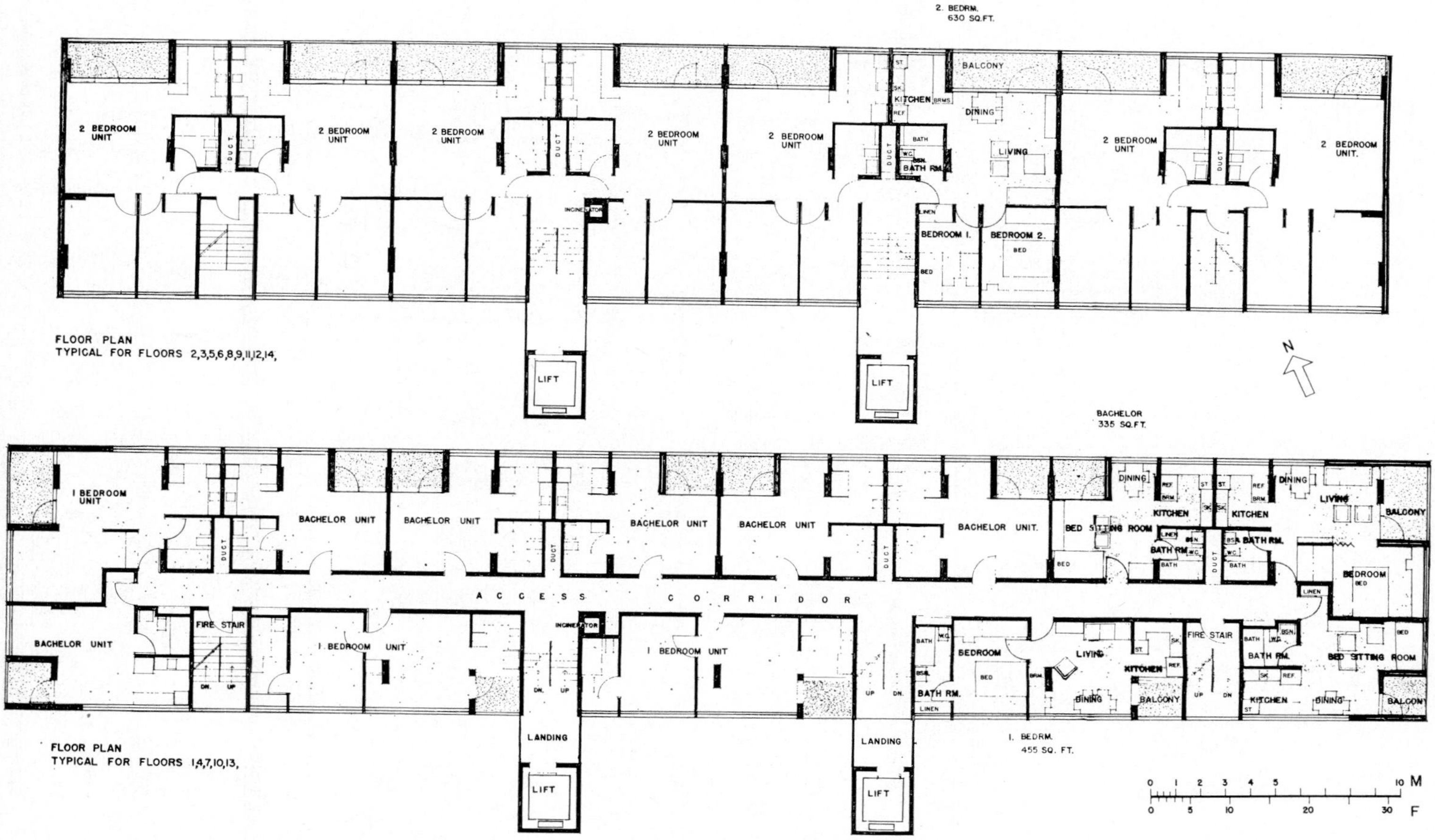

4 'Fairlie', Melbourne

Architects: Yuncken, Freeman and Associates

This nine-storey block, planned on luxury standards, reflects a European influence. There are two large flats only to the typical floor with two staircases, but rather surprisingly only one lift.

One of the flats has three bedrooms and a large living/dining area, and the other two bedrooms. Kitchens and bathrooms are both on external walls, but one of the flats has an internal shower and W.C., and both internal cloakrooms.

A large balcony terrace runs the whole length of one side of the square building, and each flat has a triple aspect.

At roof level there is a single large penthouse apartment containing three bedrooms, living room, dining room and kitchen with roof terrace on all sides.

Electric floor heating and hot water are provided throughout, and there is a refuse chute, as well as sink disposal units, as also tenants' telephone communication with the entrance hall.

At ground floor level there is a drive-in portico and entrance hall as well as garages at the rear.

The system of construction is reinforc concrete frame with membrane walls in the cc and reinforced concrete floors. A continuc pattern of concrete mullions is taken all rou the building including the west side where forms the balcony front in conjunction with i balustrades. Heavier reinforced concrete pilc at ground floor level are used to form the portic

Sun control is assisted by the use of balconies on the west elevation and blinds installed also.

The site area is just over quarter-acre extent and density approximately 210 pers per acre. The cost of the building was £200, in 1961.

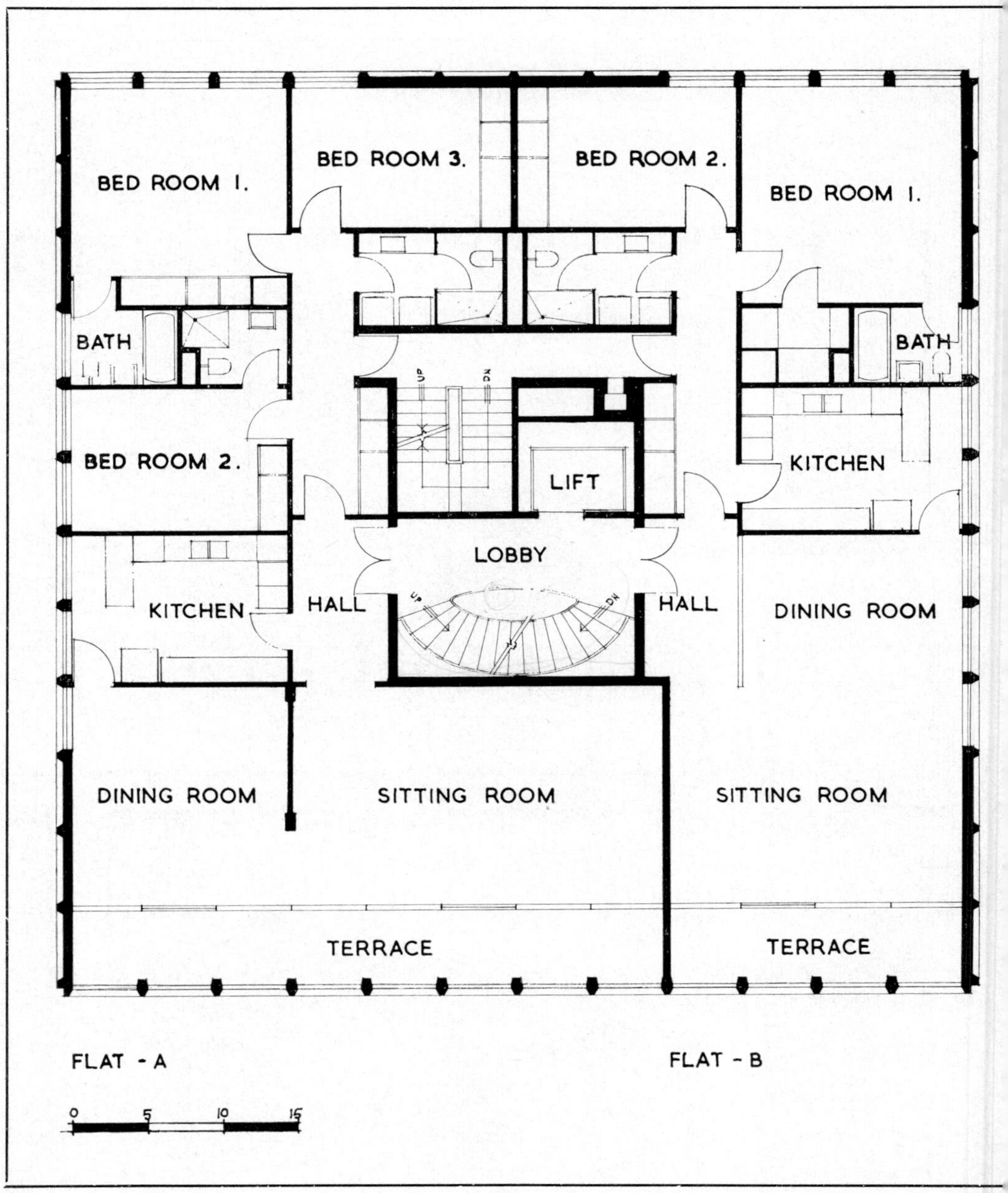

5 Edgewater Towers, Melbourne

Architect: Benshemesh

A 13-storey slab block containing 100 flats ingeniously planned on the central corridor access principle with two stairs and two lifts giving access to eight flats on the typical floor, four of which have two bedrooms, and four one bedroom. All the flats are planned with combined kitchen/dining areas and internal, mechanically ventilated bathrooms. There are extensive balcony areas to all the flats, but paradoxically the smaller flats having these to the bedrooms as well as to the living rooms.

The ground floor is planned with an entrance foyer, two one-bedroom flats, and four two-bedroom flats. Carports are also provided on the basis of one per flat.

The construction is reinforced concrete frame with precast concrete external cladding.

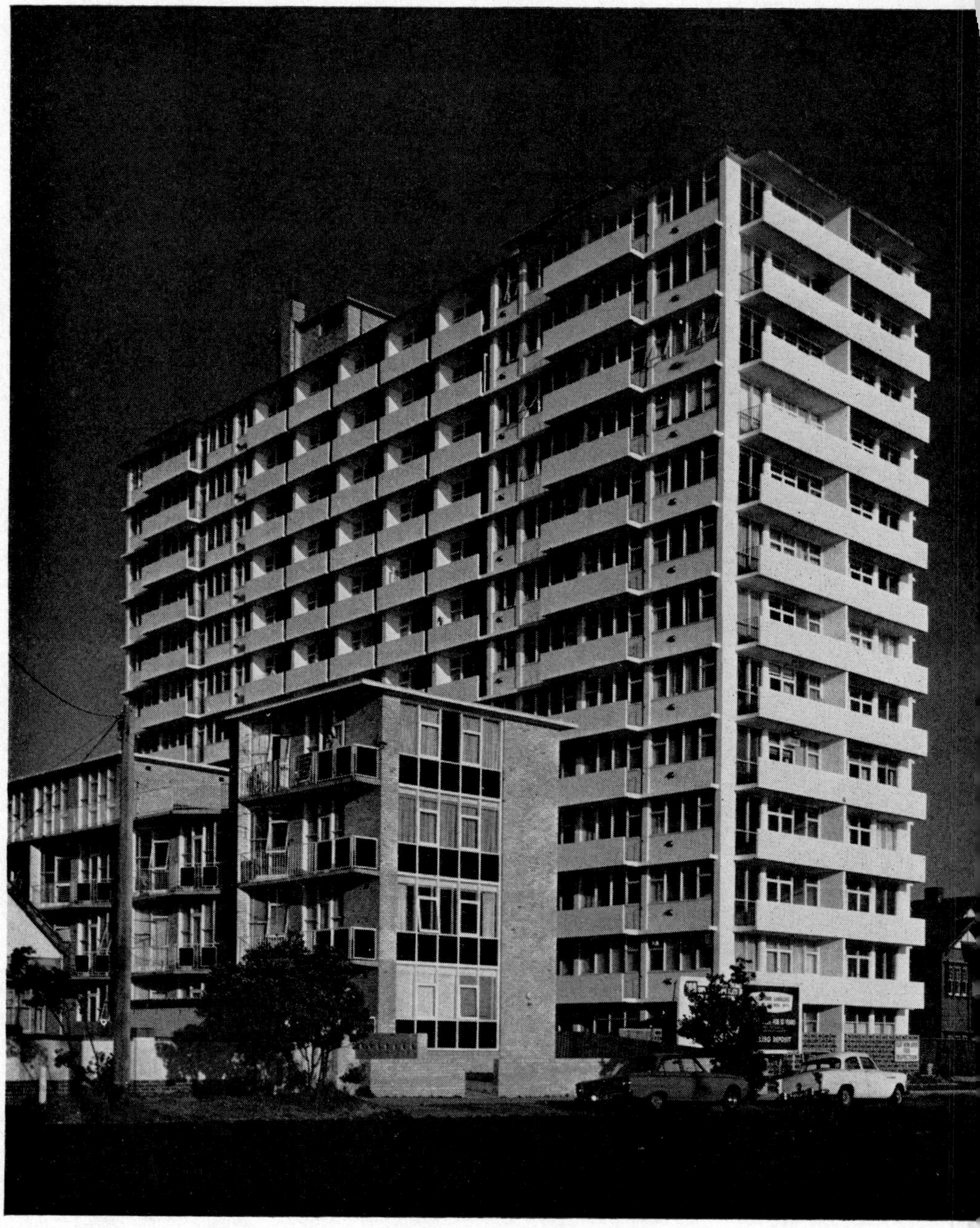

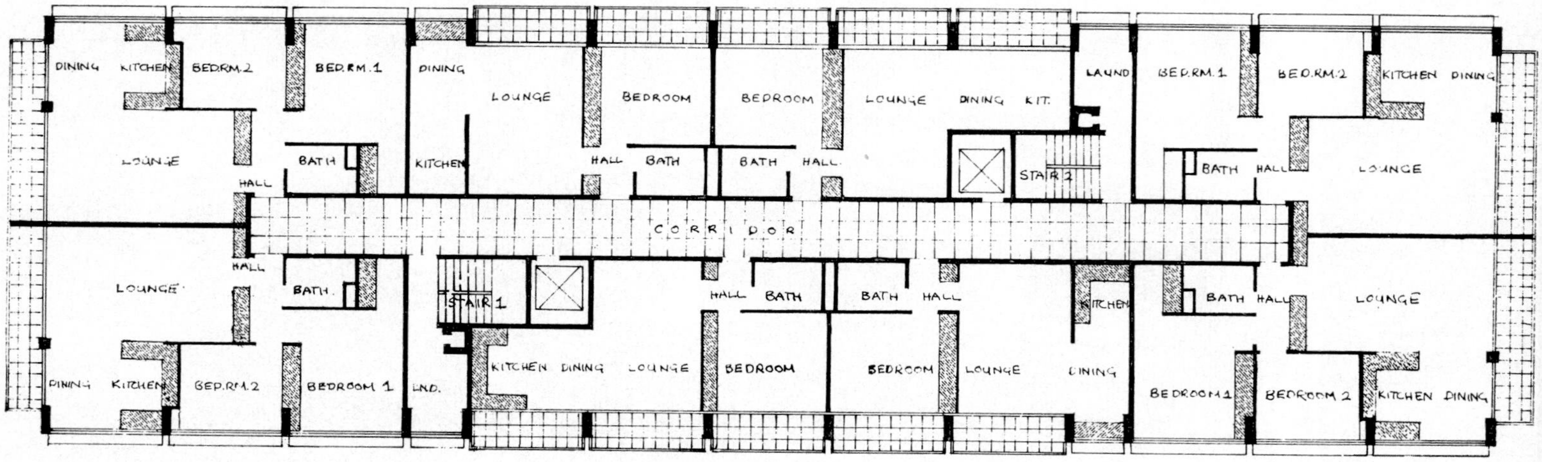

Emerald Hill Court, Melbourne

chitect: B. Evans and Partners

development on an inner urban site of just over ee acres in extent, including a 16-storey tower ock with 90 two-bedroom flats, and 30 one-droom flats; three four-storey slab blocks oviding 50 three-bedroom maisonettes; one ee/four-storey slab block containing 16 three-droom maisonettes and 12 bedsitters.

The density of development is 155 persons per re, and site coverage 24 per cent. Parking ace is provided in the development for a total 48 cars only.

The planning of the tower block, which is of e double rectangle central corridor access oe, is an ingenious arrangement and similar to e British Ministry of Housing 11-storey double wer block prototype. It provides for the use of o staircases on external walls, and two lifts ving access to a total of eight flats on the oical floor.

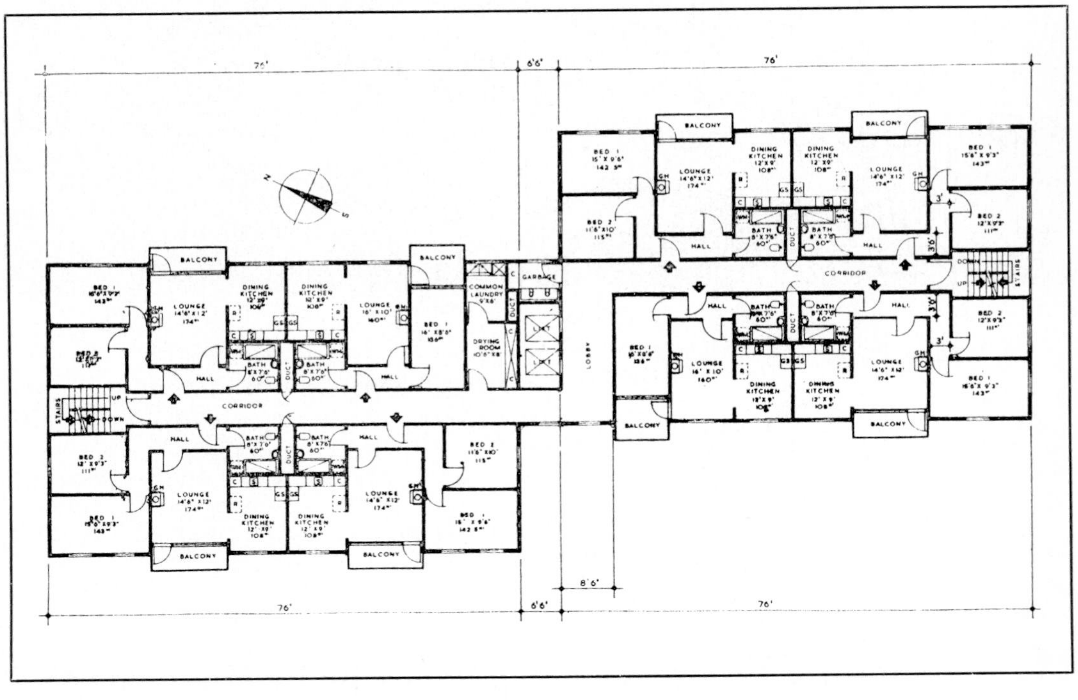

7 Colebrook, Sydney

Architects: Peddle, Thorp and Walker

One of Sydney's largest apartment blocks with 108 dwellings in a 17-storey tower, planned on a compact but well landscaped site overlooking Double Bay, and adjoining a local shopping centre.

The typical floor contains eight ingeniously arranged flats, five of which have two bedrooms, one is a bedsitter and two one bedroom. All except the bedsitter have large private balconies.

Kitchens are unfortunately planned in interi location, on the American pattern.

Alongside the scissor type stairs and tw lifts are ventilation and light wells—a somewh unusual feature currently.

A garage is placed under the paved terrac A swimming pool is also included in the schem

Construction is in reinforced concrete fran and flat plate with reinforced concrete membrai walls.

Total cost: £950,0(

'Torbreck', Brisbane

hitects: A. H. Job and R. P. Froud

s building was completed at the end of 1960—reinforced concrete frame generally—the den Block being 'lift slab' construction with lt-up structural steel columns—the Tower ck monolithic reinforced concrete but with t plate' construction of the floors.

'he Garden Block is of eight storeys, ground or being for parking and caretaker's unit—en flats on each of the next six floors—four flats on the top floor—single lift to all floors.

The Tower Block is of 20 storeys (13 of flats—ground floor shops and restaurant, three semi-basement parking, two semi-basement store, one lower entrance floor), plus tank room, lift machine room and observation room—23 floor levels.

Thirteen of these floors were designed to have seven flats each—but some variations have placed eight on one floor, five on one floor and four on top floor. Originally designed for 150 dwellings the block now has 135, due to some of these being combined together.

Cost of erection of the building: approximately one million pounds.

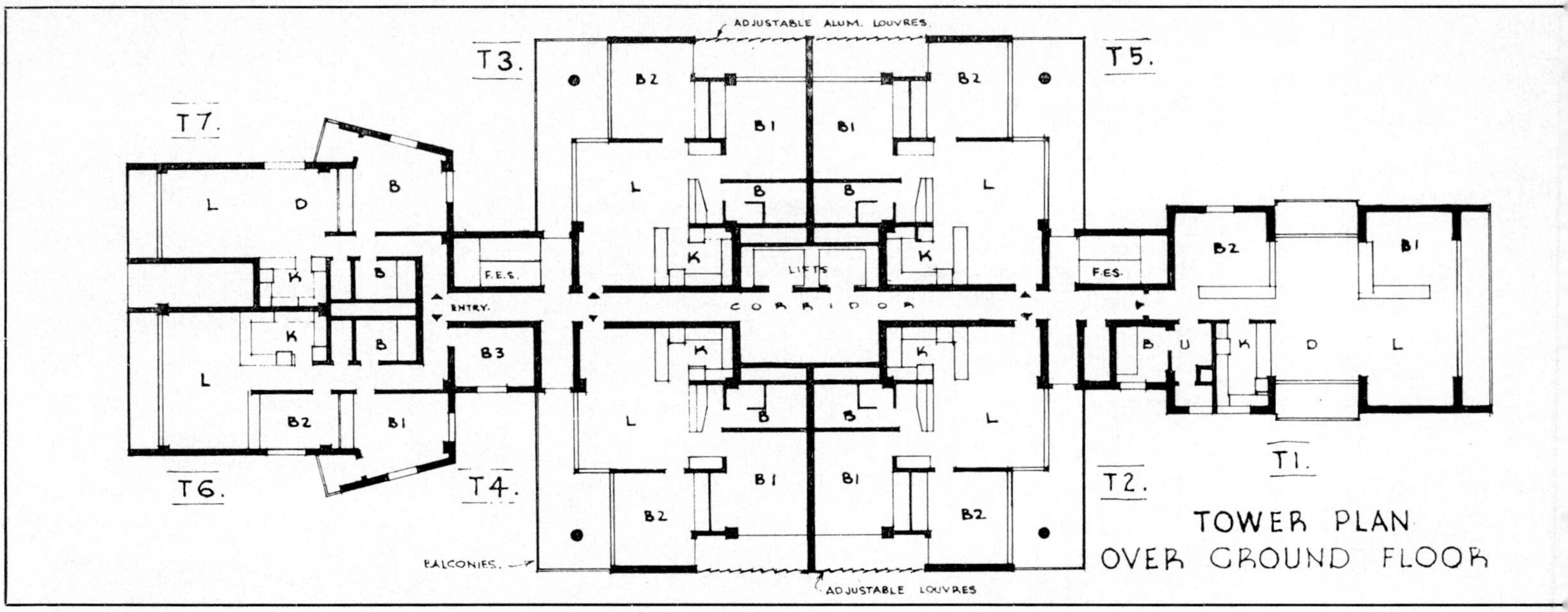
ADJUSTABLE ALUM. LOUVRES.
T3.
T5.
T7.
B2
B1
B
L
D
K
F.E.S.
LIFTS
ENTRY.
CORRIDOR
B3
U
T6.
T4.
T2.
T1.
BALCONIES.
ADJUSTABLE LOUVRES
TOWER PLAN
OVER GROUND FLOOR

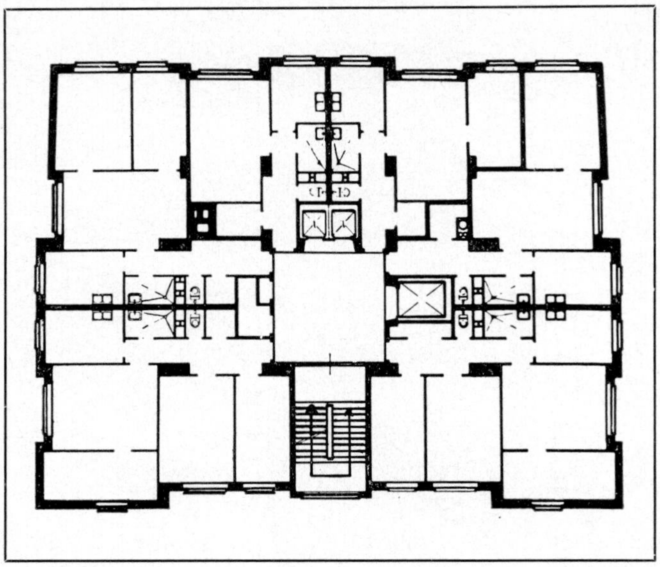

Austria

1 Matzleinsdorfplatz, Vienna

Architects: Schlauss and Hruske

This development is for a single tower block c confined site in an inner urban area. As will seen it provides for 18 typical floors with six f per floor, together with ground floor and pe house as well as basement. The ground fl contains three shops, pram shelters, machine rooms; the roof, a covered terr space, a restaurant, and the usual access rooms and equipment space, and the basem containing boiler house as well as fuel stora rentable cellar space and laundry.

A typical floor contains two one-room fl one two-room, one three-room and two fo room units, accessible from three lifts an single staircase.

The system of construction is in reinfor concrete frame and reinforced concrete sl external walls being in 15 in. hollow brick c struction and the foundation in the form c heavy concrete raft.

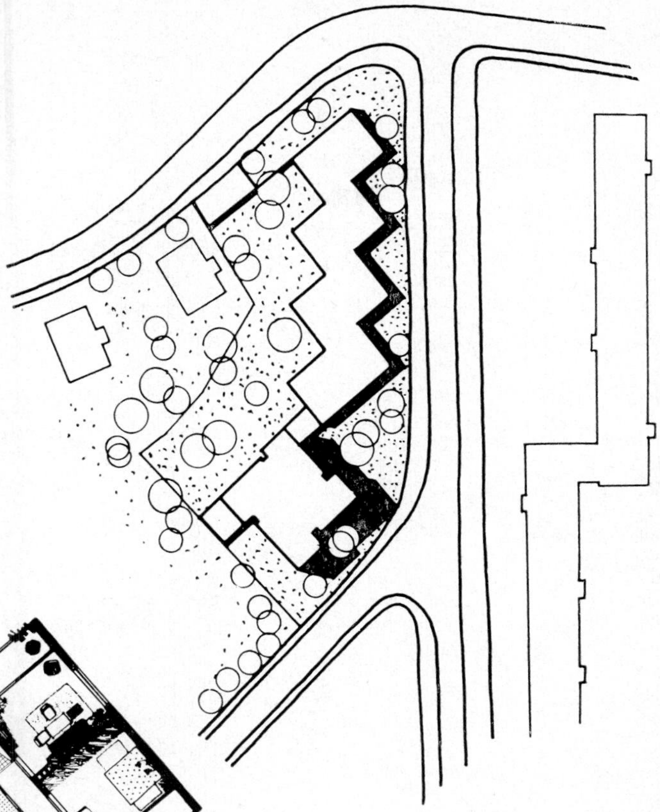

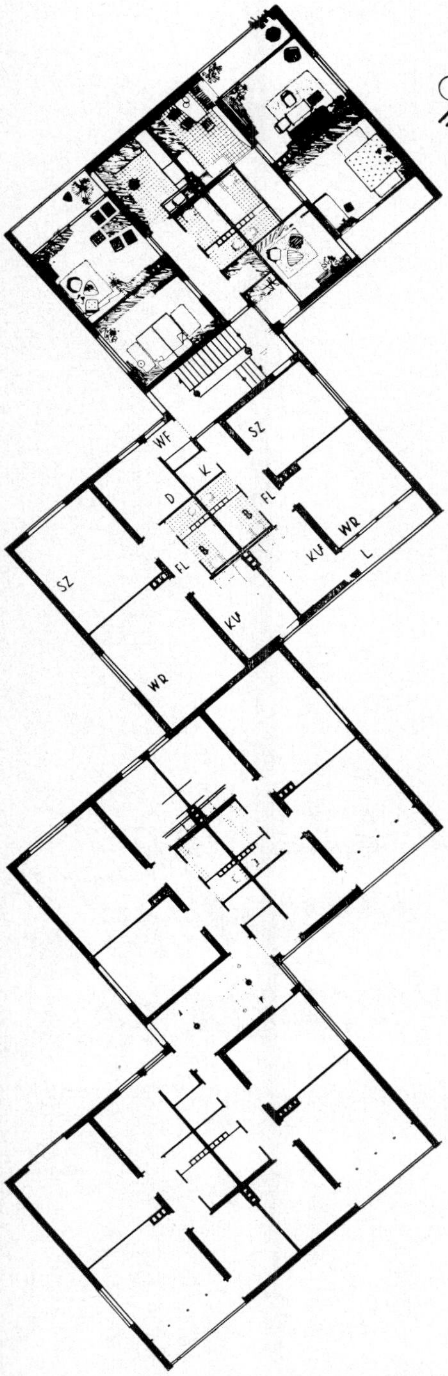

2 Am Froschberg, Linz

Architect: A. Perotti

The development includes a 14-storey tower block and a serpentine three-storey block, which are linked together to form a single unit. The tower block is of particular interest in the form of planning adopted which is a variant of the swastika type of arrangement, on split levels.

The tower is planned mainly for single people and all the accommodation therefore is in the form of bedsittingrooms with their own bathrooms and kitchens adjoining. A single staircase and twin lifts provide the vertical access, horizontal access being by means of naturally ventilated short branch corridors.

The system of construction is reinforced concrete with load bearing walls. A typical floor contains eight units, giving a total of 104 flats. The ground floor contains a shop, an espresso bar, motor cycle garage, ski storage and studio space. Each flat has its own private balcony running the full width of the living room, thereby providing a useful additional extension to the interior living space, giving the whole scheme a simple and clean appearance.

See also page 81.

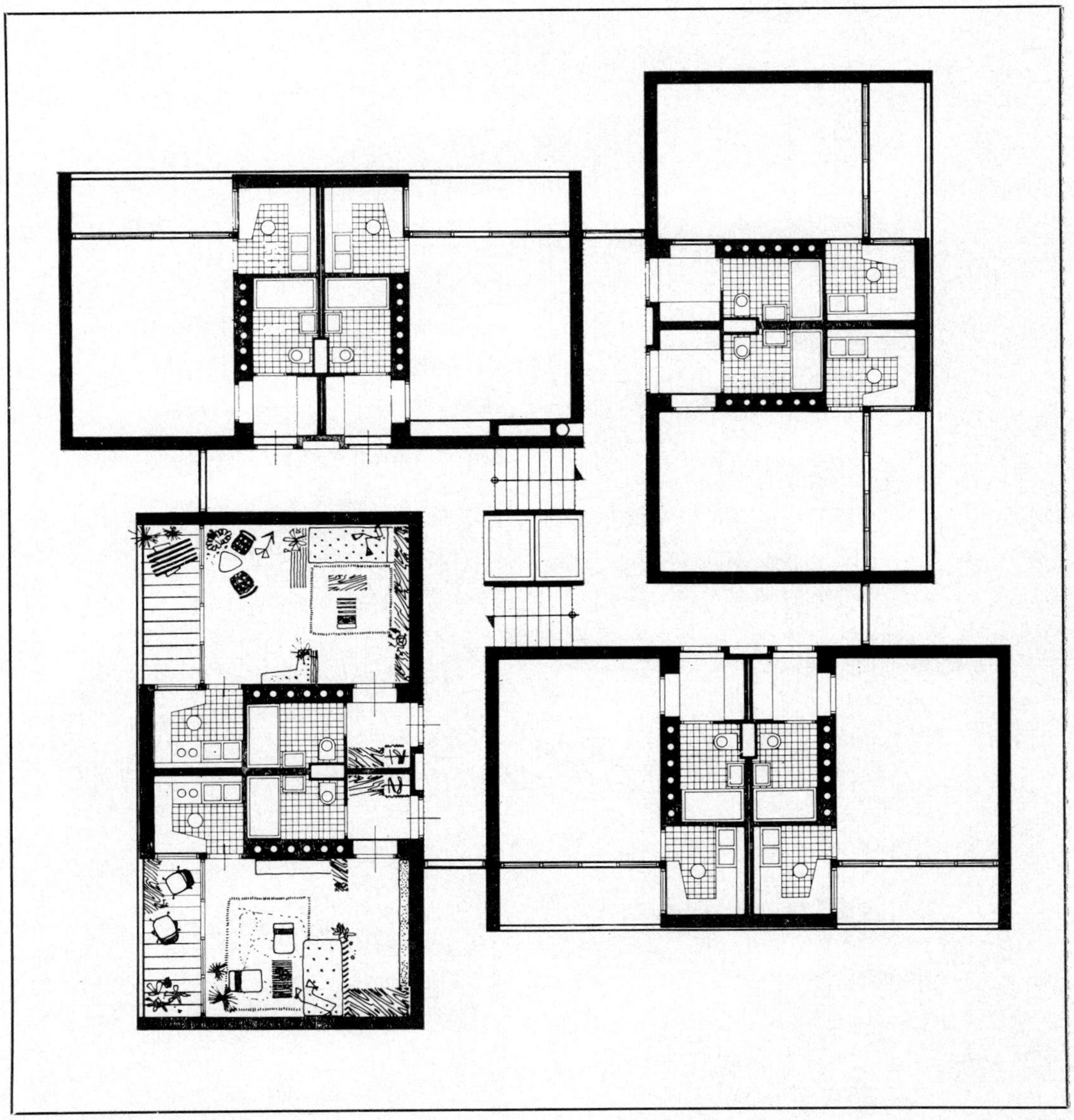

lgium

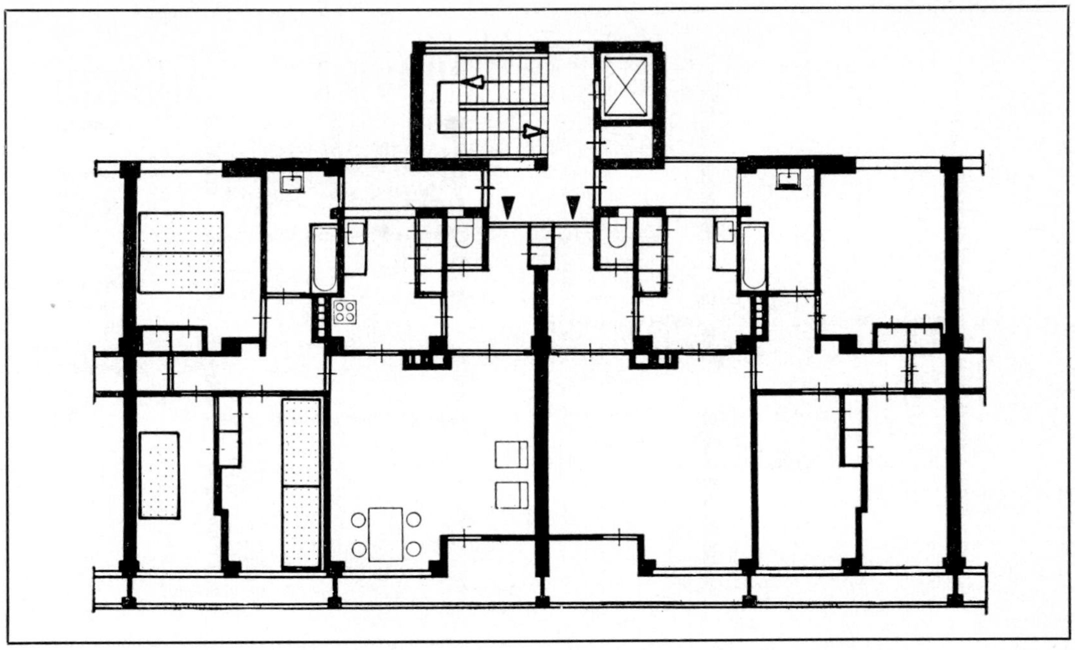

.ngleur

'tects: Group Egau

velopment on a site of just under one acre isting of three slab blocks of three, eight thirteen storeys in height. The lower group iildings contains 50 dwellings with shops, dry and creche. Most of the flats on the :-storey building, are served by orthodox stair and lift access with short access onies.

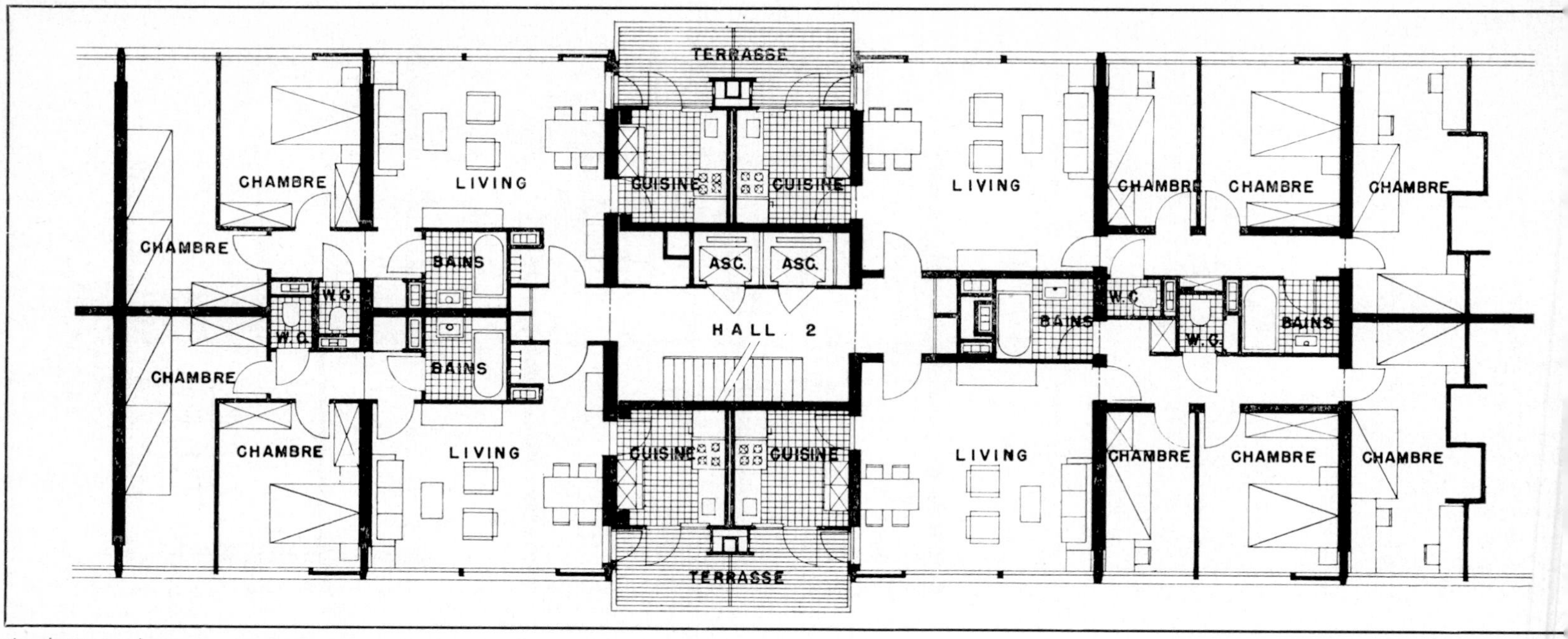

Angleur, cont.

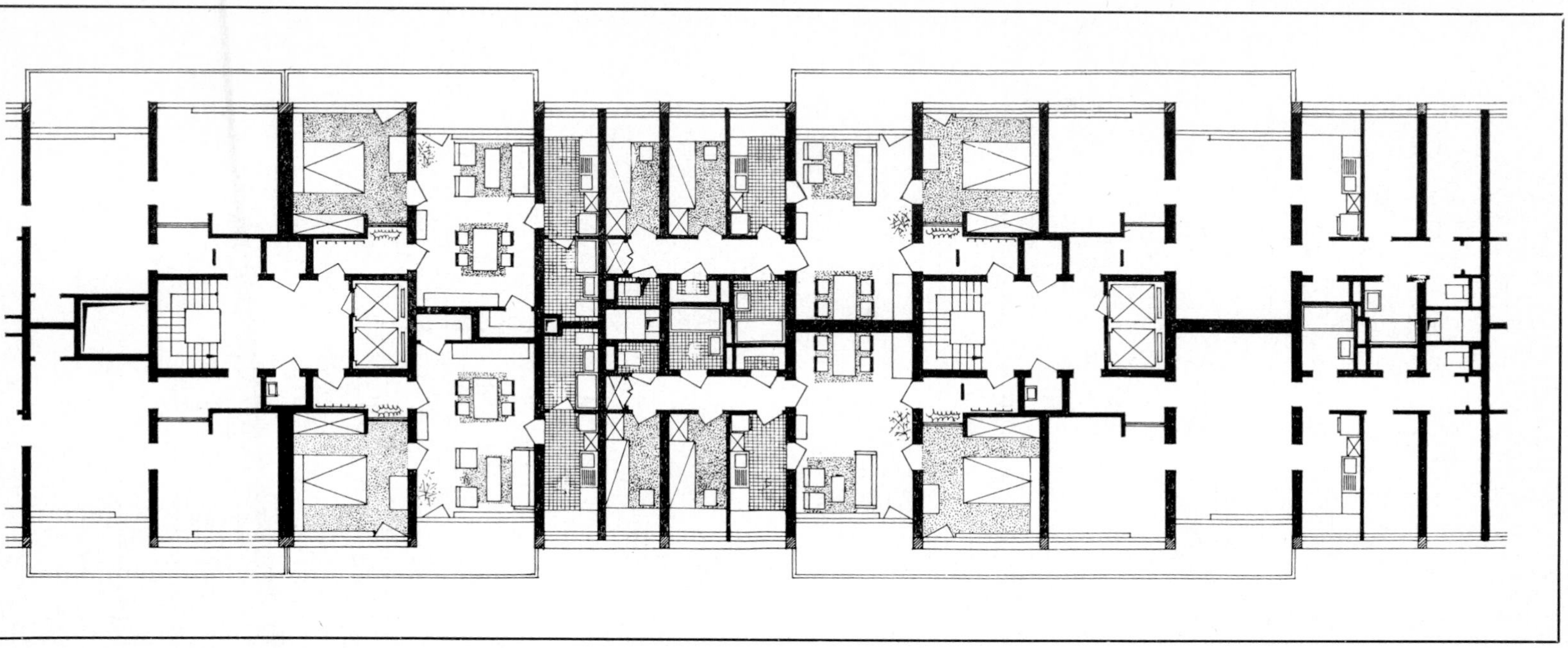

La Maison Liégoise, Champ-des-Manoeuvres, Liége

hitects: Group Egau

area of nearly 45 acres with a magnificent ıtage to the River Meuse accommodating) people in 1746 flats at a density of 150 per-s per acre and with a building coverage of roximately 25 per cent; with about half the developed as park and the remainder as car k and roads.

Most of the development is in the form of storey blocks but there are also five-storey cks for larger families linking the tall build-s.

typical arrangement in the short slab block sists of five flats on the typical floor, two of ch are of the three-bedroom type, two have bedrooms and one one bedroom.

the larger flats the bedrooms are split, thus olving traffic from one of the bedrooms at st crossing the living room to and from the hroom.

hree lifts and two staircases are used to ve these flats—a not especially economical ingement. The larger blocks have 20 on the cal floor—four per stair and pair of lifts.

djoining the site there are children's play-unds, and schools and shopping centre are nned, as well as a library, swimming pool, cert hall and community centre, health tre, creches, and a church.

he ground floor to the blocks, which are tly arcaded with wish-bone type pilotis, tain caretaker's accommodation, space for ms, tenants' delivery boxes, refuse con-ers, and a mortuary room. The basements he blocks contain pram and bicycle parking central heating plant.

onstruction is reinforced concrete frame for ement and ground floor on piled foundations load bearing walls of precast concrete cks in the upper storeys. The exterior of the ding is largely faced with ceramic tiles and , together with the well integrated pattern of e balconies and fenestration has helped to duce an impressive overall architectural lity.

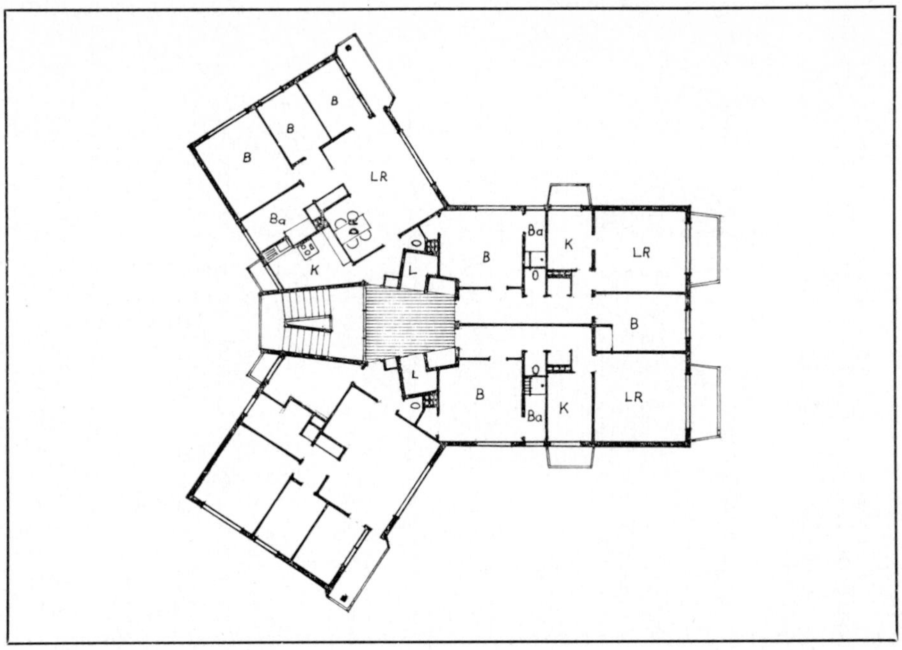

3 Star Flats, Ghent

Architect: Coppieters

A 13/14-storey Y plan or star type plan containing a total of 70 flats with four flats to the typical floor including two in one wing and on a back to back system. Two-thirds of the flats are of three-bedroom type and the remainder evenly divided between two-bedroom and one-bedroom.

Access is by means of a single staircase and two lifts and these have been very neatly placed at the intersection of the wings so as to waste little or no space.

Most of the flats are planned with separate day and night areas with the bathrooms en suite with the bedrooms, and the kitchen placed immediately adjoining the living room/dining room.

Each of the flats has ample private balcony space adjoining the living room, as well as a secondary balcony adjoining the kitchen.

The system of construction is steel columns encased in reinforced concrete and the external cladding mainly in brick work.

ɩnada

Maclean Park, Vancouver

ɿitect: McClennan

omprehensive 'Superblock' development to vide 423 flats in the whole scheme of which occur in the first stage. The total planned ulation will ultimately be just over 1200 on a area of 12 acres, the design density being persons per acre gross.

ne majority of the flats provided are small s averaging between 1·4 and 1·8 bedrooms flat. A parking space has been planned on basis of approximately one car per two flats.

his is a mixed development containing slab :ks of varying heights and contains two torey tower blocks and two-storey row houses three- and four-storey maisonettes forming main portion of the scheme. Fire resisting struction is used throughout with a rein- ed concrete frame for the tower blocks. All dwellings in the lower blocks are designed to e their own gardens, and provision is also ɪe for adequate children's play areas.

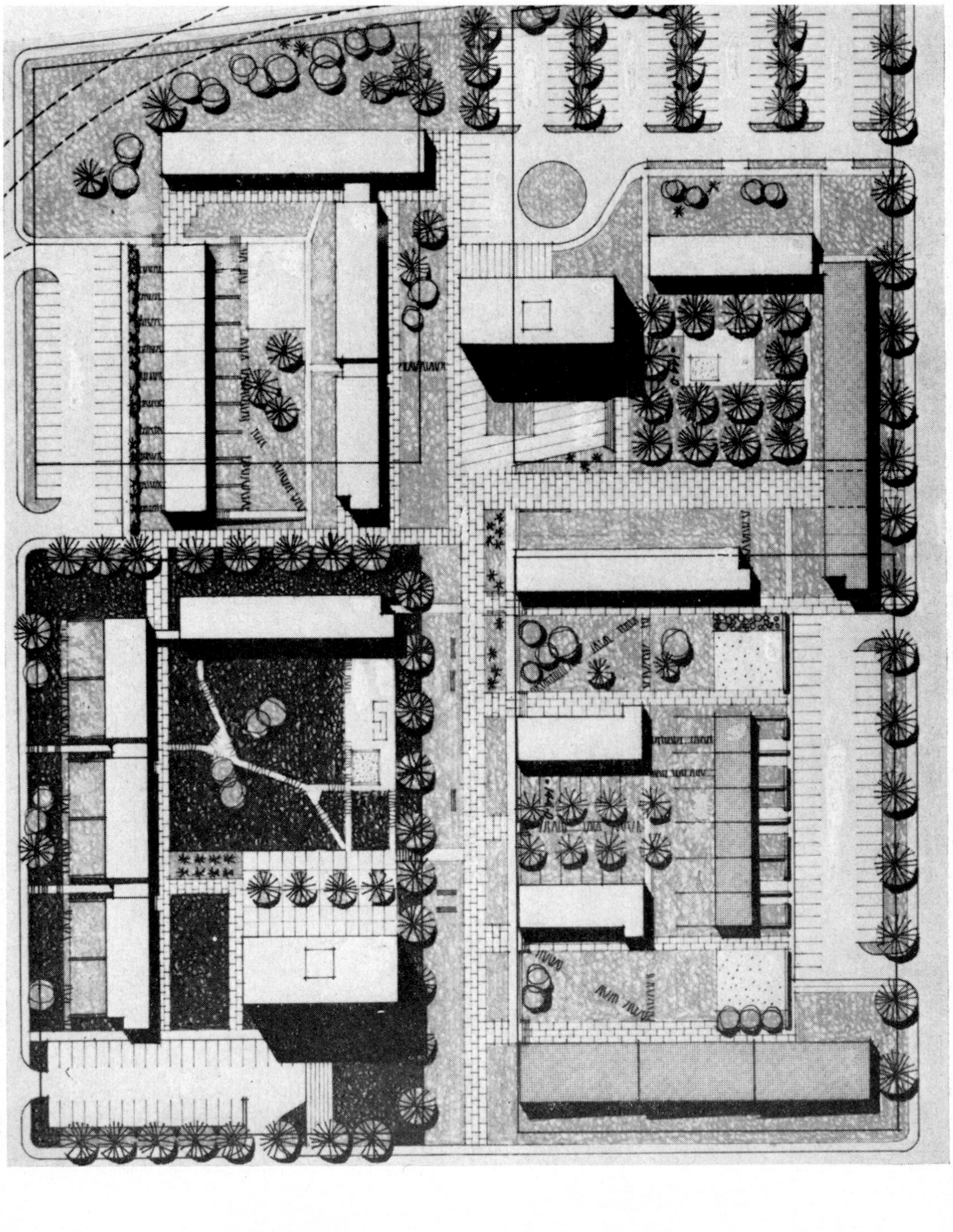

Denmark

1 Collective House, Aalborg

Architects: Poulsen and Blegvad

A 13-storey slab block containing 44 one-bedroom flats together with two large penthouses and shops and garages in the lower two floors. This block depends for its compact planning on the use of the internal staircase and lift with each staircase serving two similar units at half landing level and two at full landing level, planned on a back-to-back arrangement.

The system of construction is reinforced concrete frame and slab together with the extensive use of concrete panels to the external walls and spandrels, used with the characteristic good proportions and discipline to be found in most Scandinavian work.

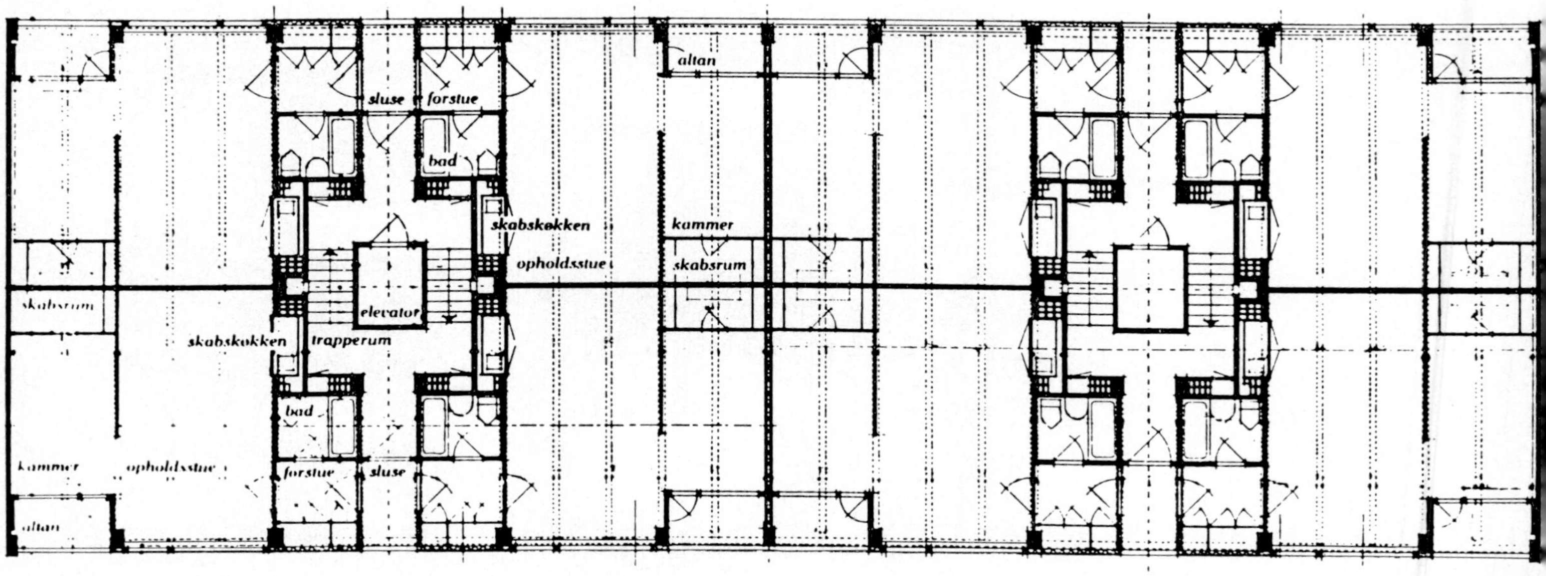

Bellahøj, Copenhagen

chitect: Dan Fink and Associates

large area in the inner part of Copenhagen mprehensively developed and providing in multi-storey blocks ranging from eight to storeys in height, a total of 1297 flats. In addi- n local shopping, centralized laundries, a hool, open air theatre, district heating station, staurant, youth hostel, children's centre luding creche, kindergarten and recreation a, and underground garages are included.

The whole area has been excellently land- aped, including a park-like area in the centre the development itself adjoining a picturesque e. The overall density is approximately 140 rsons per acre gross, but within the residen- zones proper, the density is appreciably her. The average cost works out at approxi- tely £1500 per average flat, these varying from e-, to three-bedroom types.

The typical plan arrangement in the individual cks of linked rectangles each with two flats, s the common staircase and lift tower as the king element and this provides access to one r of flats in one block at full landing level. s arrangement is extremely economical d gives unusual and visually interesting hitectural forms with the practical advantage t each flat, with three outside walls, has ellent cross ventilation and natural lighting; hough with the disadvantage that this tends newhat to inflate the cost with the higher o of external wall to floor area, and to increase problems of heat and cold insulation.

he planning arrangement allows for all hrooms and kitchens to have natural light and tilation, and all flats have their own private conies.

he system of construction is reinforced con- te treated in a number of different ways; in earlier stages having been very largely cast, except for floor slab infills, but in later ges almost entirely cast *in situ* with the use of nbing shuttering. All the blocks depend to a siderable extent on the use of precast crete multi-core facing blocks or slabs: in case of the blocks constructed with climb- shuttering these slabs were incorporated in the shuttering as construction proceeded. s in the case of so many of the large resi- tial development schemes in European ntries this was carried out by a large building ety in conjunction with the city authority.

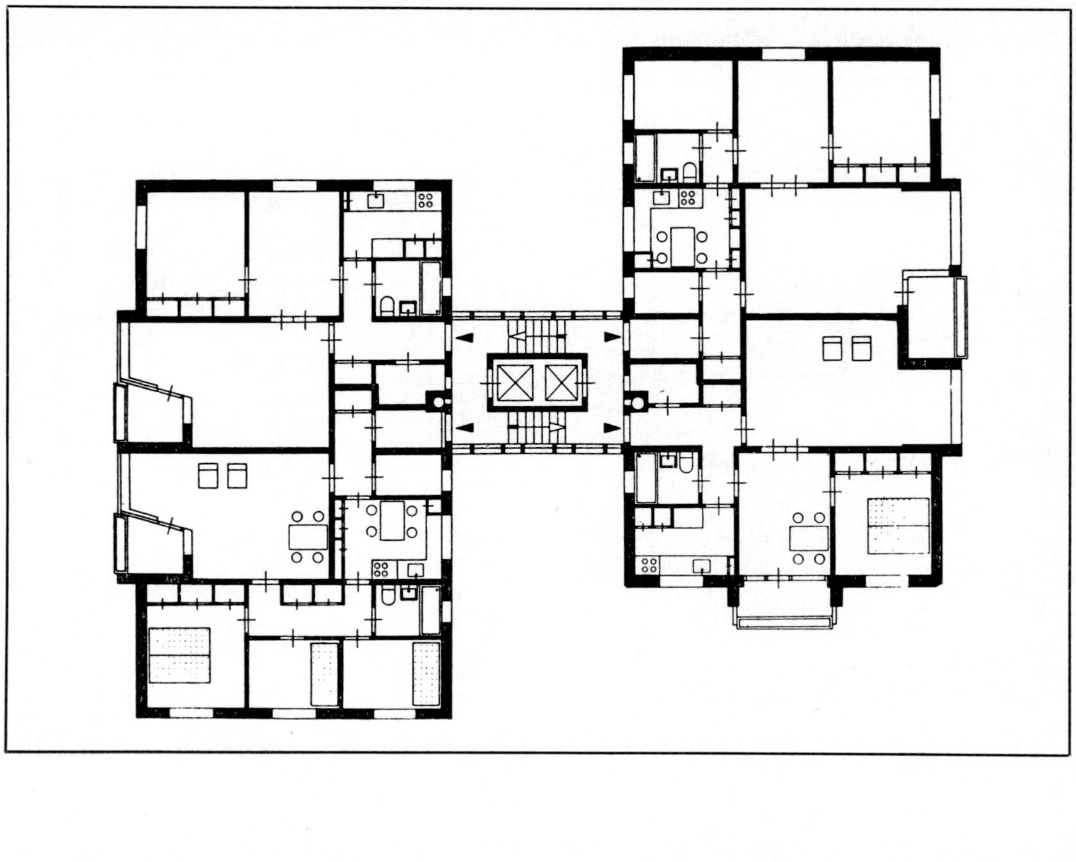

3 Søndermarken, Copenhagen

Architect: E. Kristensen

A development consisting of five 16-storey poi blocks of the linked rectangle or domino type, a slightly different pattern however from th adopted at Bellahøj.

The scheme also includes a children's centr a library, shops, garaging and a central heatir station. Garaging is for 50 cars and the heatir station adjoins one of the point blocks by whic means it is possible to mask the chimney stac

The whole scheme includes 430 flats of whic 280 are three-room, 140 four-room, and th remainder penthouse units with terraces. Th form of planning adopted has allowed for acce to six flats per floor from the single staircase ar twin lifts, one of the lifts being located in eac block and the staircase forming the linking un an extremely economical arrangement and on that allows for alternative forms of egress in th event of fire, rather than having all of the concentrated at one point.

The system of construction is reinforced co crete with precast concrete facing slabs, erecte with the sliding form system.

Communal laundries with drying facilities a provided in each of the blocks at ground flo level.

The net density of development of this scher is approximately 250 persons per acre but ev so adequate landscape and garden areas a available adjoining the blocks.

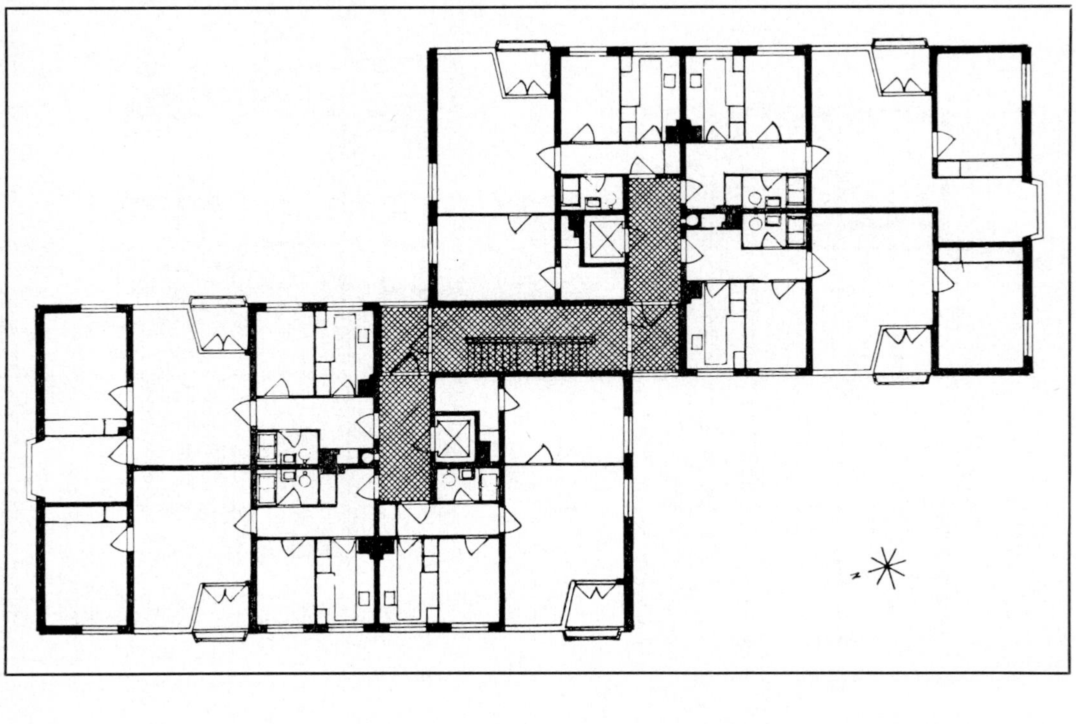

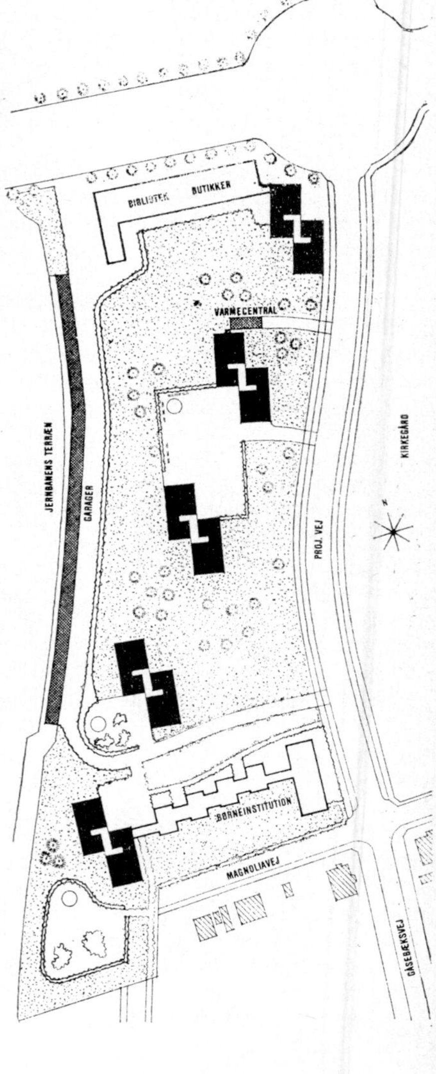

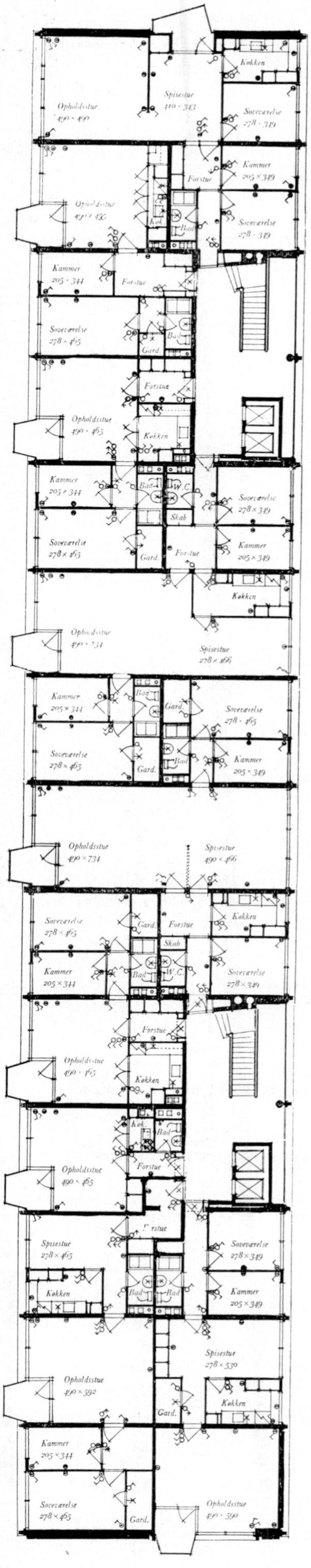

4 Sorgenfrivang II

Architects: Stephensen and Associates

A mixed development including 56 row houses, three large 15-storey slab blocks containing 430 flats, 12 shops, 108 garages, a restaurant, a cinema, offices, and clinic as well as ample parking space for the ubiquitous Danish bicycle. The site is eight miles from the centre of Copenhagen near an S-Station.

The buildings are partly in prefabricated concrete construction. Certain elements, however, such as the supporting partitions are cast *in situ*. The dwelling types vary; there being 84 flats of 130 square metres (four rooms and two small rooms) and 22 quite small flats (26 square metres). In addition the ground floor contains 12 old-age pensioner's and three invalid pensioner's flats.

The collective institutions comprise machine laundry for small laundering, restaurant, entertainment room, hobby room and kindergarten (80 children), housework assistance centre, and a reception with internal telephone to all flats.

An extension of the shopping centre is projected south of the S-station, including post-office, bank, public library, and hotel, thus securing all the functions needed in a limited urban community. The total cost of the scheme is 29½ million kroner: density of development 250 persons per acre.

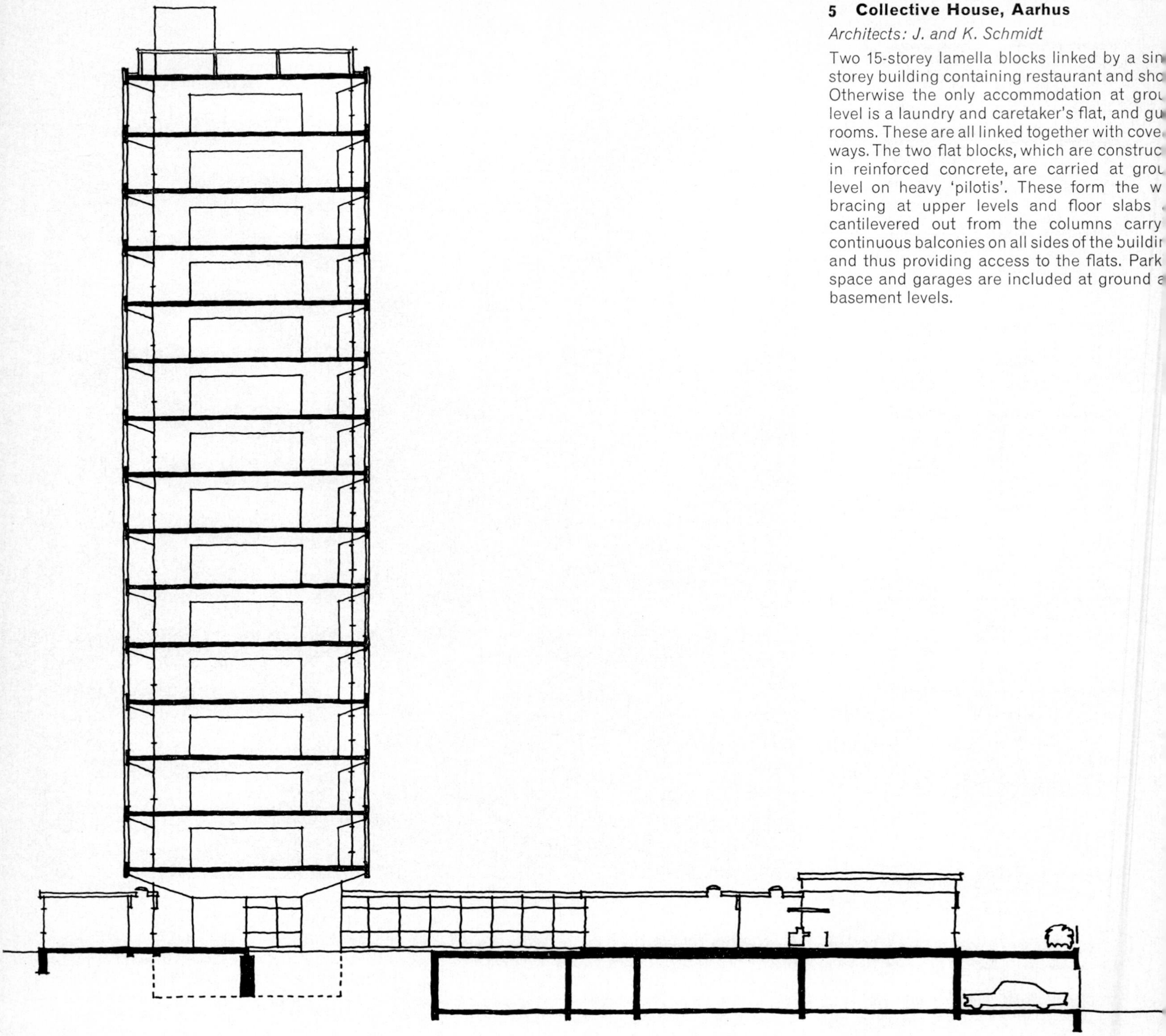

5 Collective House, Aarhus

Architects: J. and K. Schmidt

Two 15-storey lamella blocks linked by a sin
storey building containing restaurant and sho
Otherwise the only accommodation at grou
level is a laundry and caretaker's flat, and gu
rooms. These are all linked together with cove
ways. The two flat blocks, which are construc
in reinforced concrete, are carried at grou
level on heavy 'pilotis'. These form the w
bracing at upper levels and floor slabs
cantilevered out from the columns carry
continuous balconies on all sides of the buildi
and thus providing access to the flats. Park
space and garages are included at ground
basement levels.

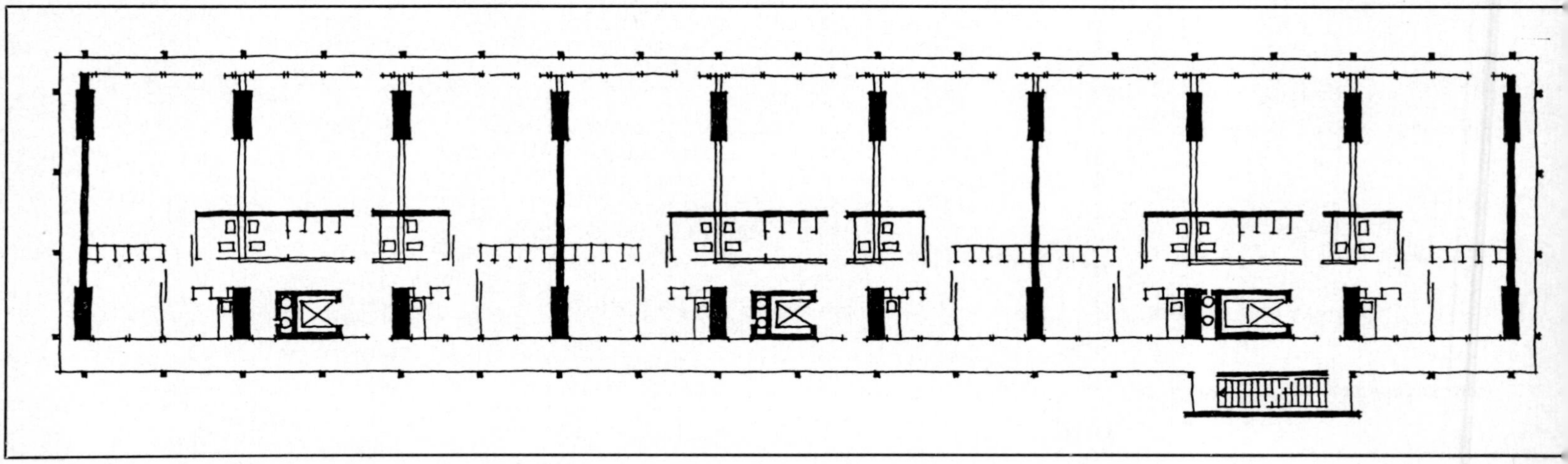

6 Marselis Boulevard, Aarhus

Architects: K. Friis and E. M. Nielsen

Five similar blocks on a narrow site alongside Marselis Boulevard and planned with the balcony access system; and yet aesthetically pleasing. The 14-storey blocks have six flats to the typical floor served by a single stair and twin lifts. Flats vary from three-bedroom to two-bedroom, and some of the larger units have a bedroom adjoining the access balcony. Most bathrooms are planned internally. There is ample balcony space to every flat. Underground garages and bicycle sheds are provided to alternate blocks as well as surface parking areas.

Construction is in reinforced concrete—with the end walls in prefabricated units.

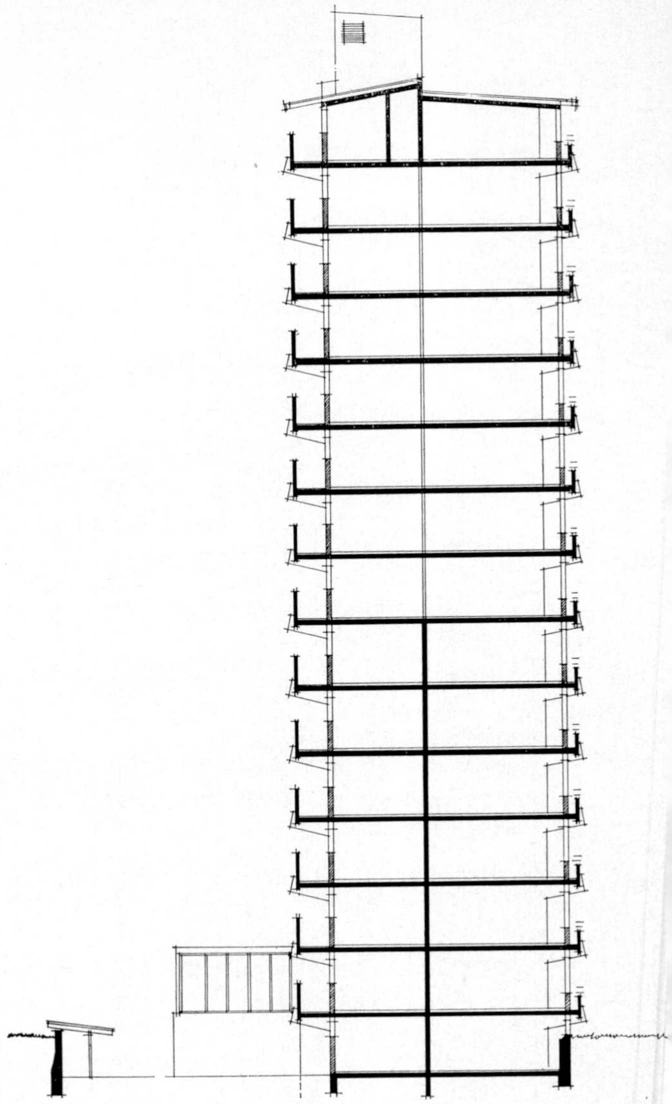

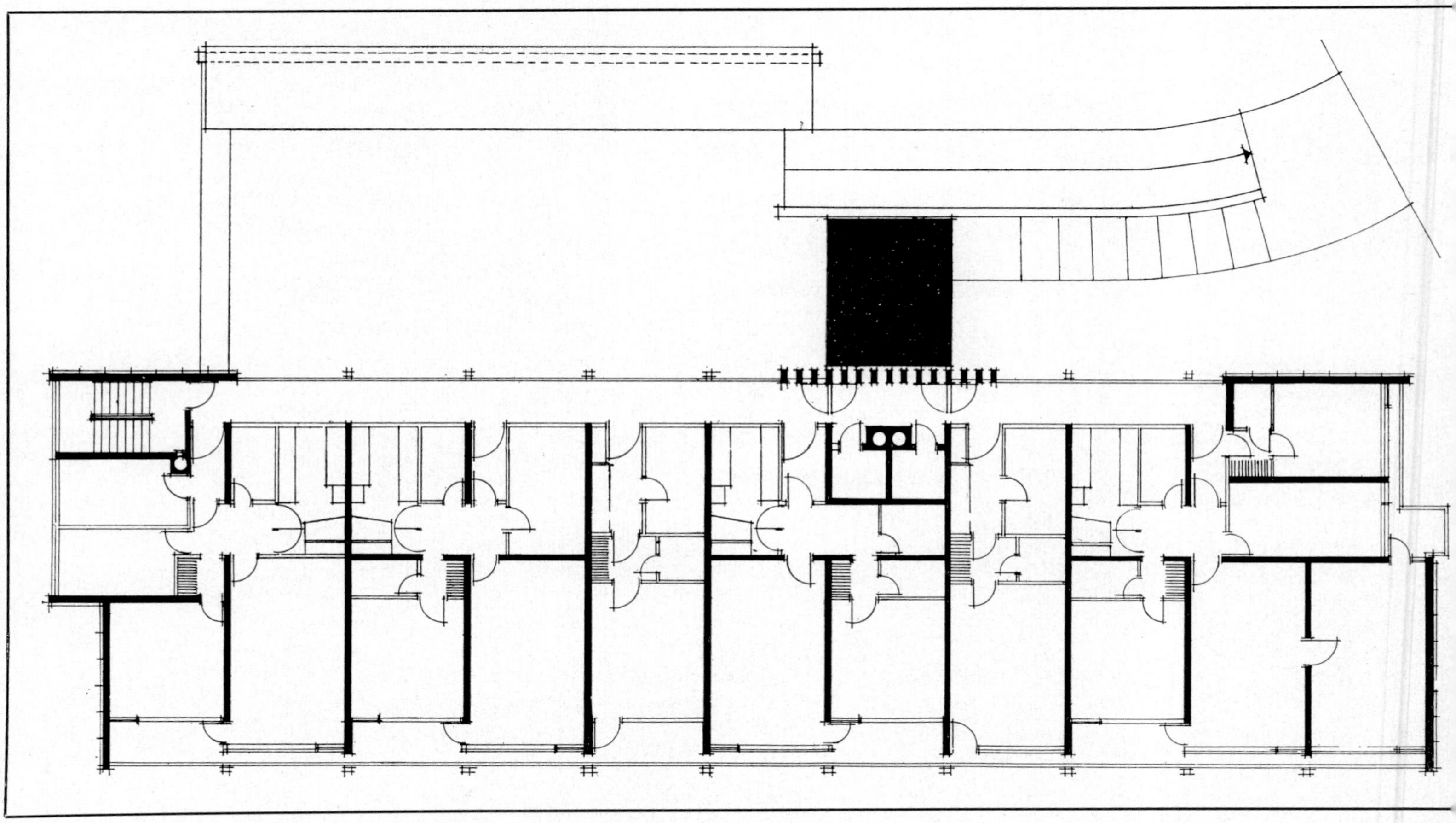

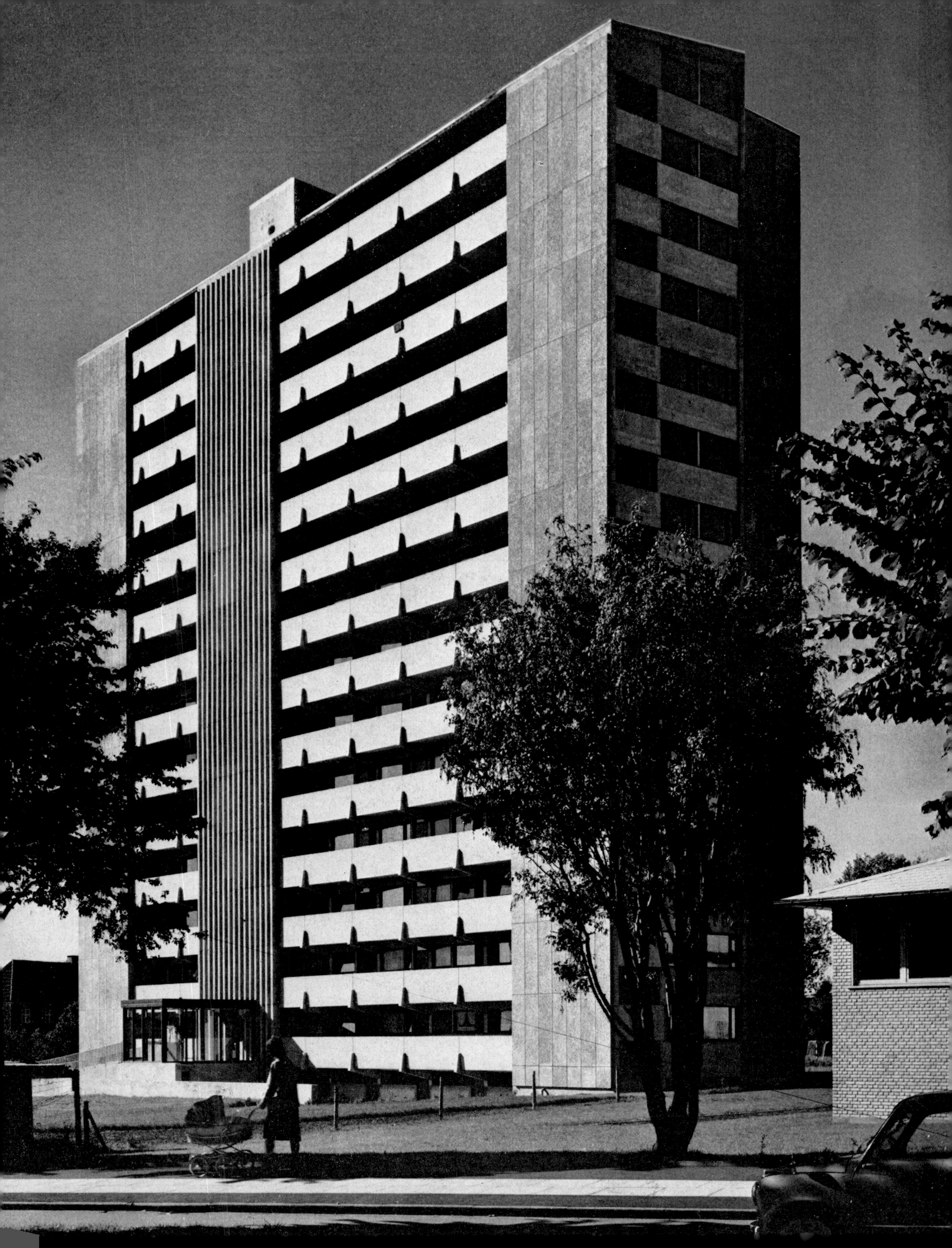

Finland

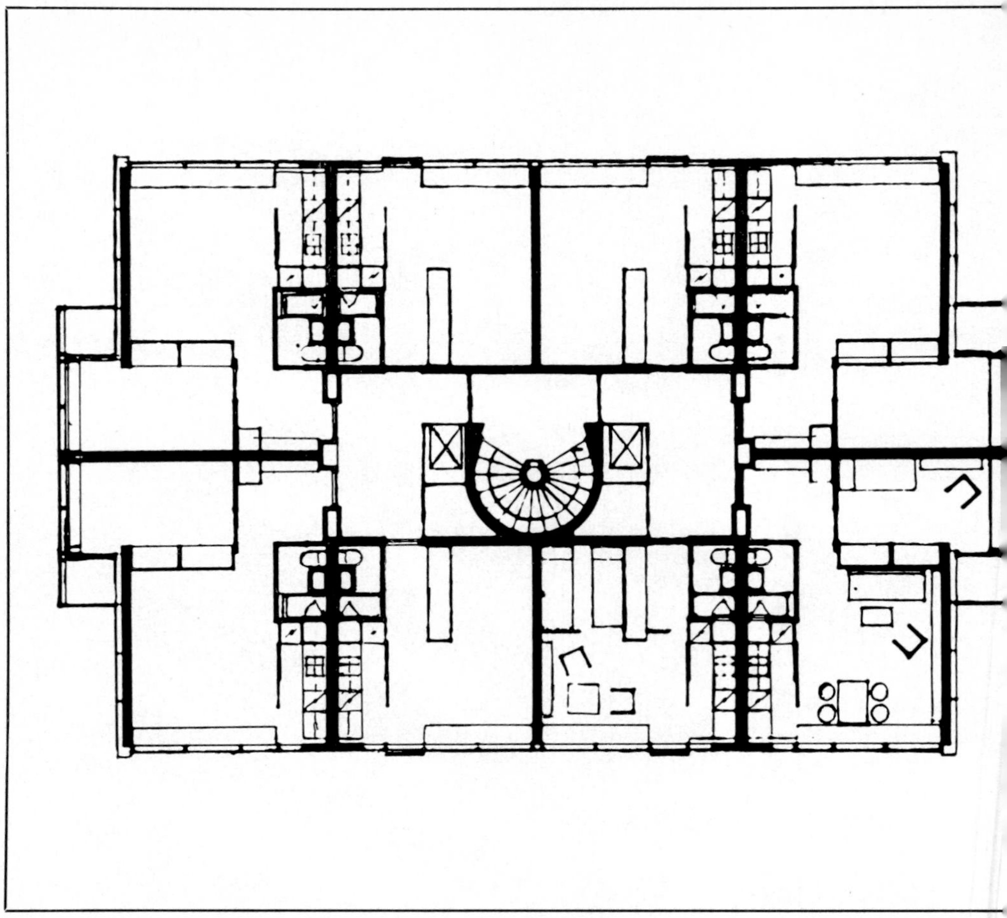

1 Otsontormit, Tapiola

Architect: V. Rewell

A single nine-storey tower block designed as a collective house, and part of the larger Tapiola New Town development.

This block contains an equal number of bedsitter flats and of one-bedroom units. It is designed round a reinforced concrete cross wall system of construction on a standard structural grid with four of the bachelor flats in the centre of the block, and the four corners containing the single-bedroom units. Bathrooms and kitchens have been very economically grouped together with the kitchens receiving natural light.

The vertical access is by the medium of an internal circular stair similar in design to a great many of the Swedish examples, and also from the two lifts—an economical and compact arrangement.

Instead of reducing the living room areas at the expense of inset balconies or, alternatively, instead of the additional cost of projecting balconies, these living rooms all have the French window with the external balustrade which gives most of the advantages of the balcony without sterilizing valuable space for this purpose. They also provide a very effective punctuation in the external architectural expression of the building which is otherwise extremely well proportioned, simply conceived with strip windows, and with an interesting variation in texture in the spandrel panels.

The two lower floors are devoted to central heating, tenants' storage and central laundries as well as refuse containers.

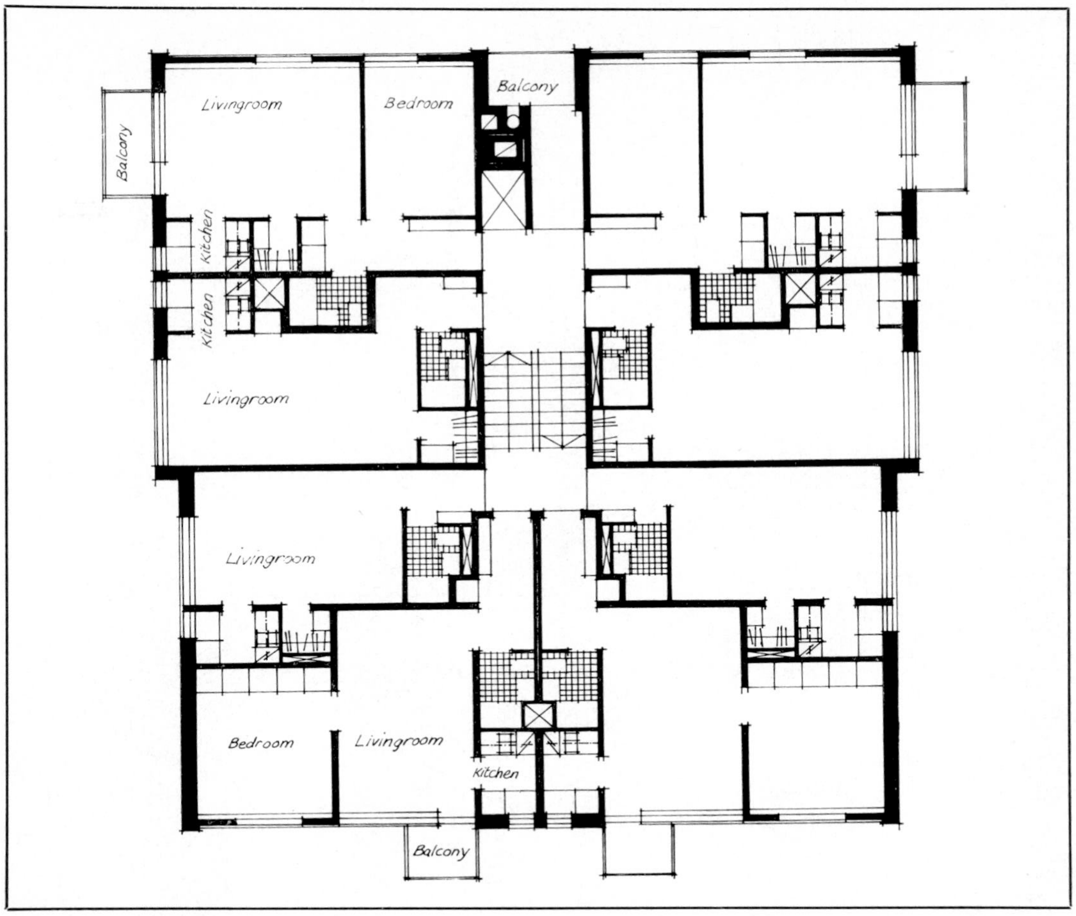

Tower Block, Oulu

hitects: T. Salo and M. Karkulahti (1959)

:ompact and neatly planned site block of storeys in height designed in conjunction a three-storey slab block for a central town .

he four one-bedroom and four bedsitter flats each typical floor are accessible from single rcase and lift—half at full landing levels and at intermediate levels. There are tenants' es and service plant at semi-basement level. h flat has an internal bathroom and naturally kitchenette. Construction is in load-bearing sonry.

France

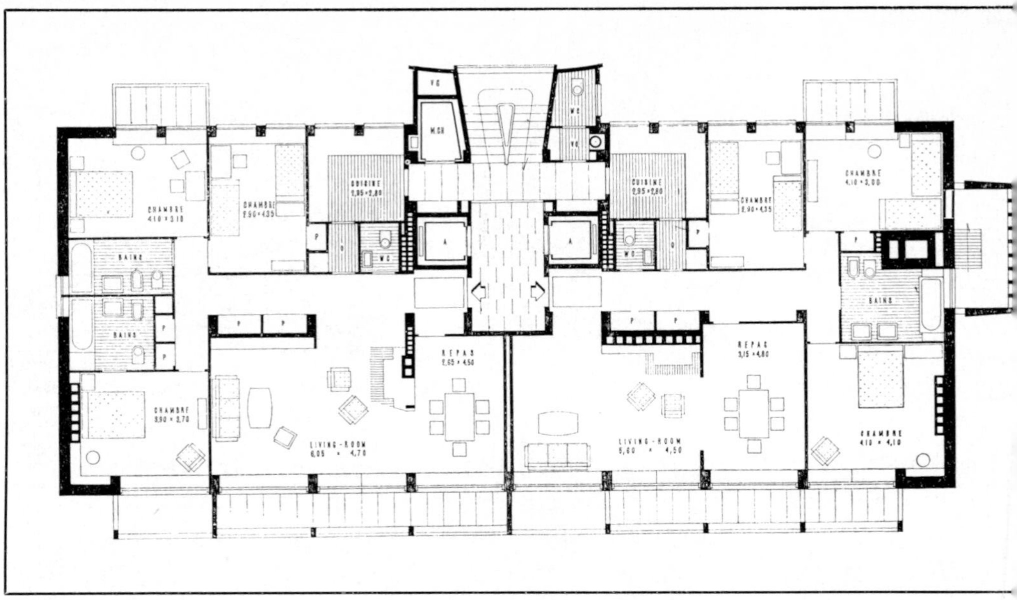

1 Rue de Docteur Blanche, Paris

Architects: Massé and Ginsberg

A single luxury block in the centre of the city closely hemmed in by neighbouring buildings, but nevertheless with excellent garden and landscaping; the block being raised on pillars at ground floor level in order to give this garden continuity and maximum effectiveness.

The block is 12 storeys in height of which 10 are taken up with dwelling units up to sixth floor level, three flats to the floor—two with three bedrooms and one with one bedroom—and above this level two flats to the floor of the three-bedroom type. These are served by a single staircase and three lifts of which one is a goods lift. Roof level is taken up by mechanical equipment and roof terraces and there is a basement containing garages.

Four-storey wings also containing flats complete the development, these being mainly in the form of duplex or studio flats and service dwellings.

The construction is *in situ* reinforced concrete frame.

Pantin, Paris

hitect: D. Honegger

large area redevelopment in a run-down ›urb to provide a total of 2000 dwellings, ether with a commercial centre, a cultural ıtre, bus terminal, and garage for 500 vehicles.

˜he first stage of this development, contains a al of 811 dwellings. In the completed scheme per cent of the flats will be of the bedsitter e, 15 per cent will have one bedroom, 50 per ıt two bedrooms, and 15 per cent three ɟrooms and 10 per cent large family flats with r bedrooms. Density is 347 persons per ctare.

\ large central pedestrian area has been nned with four 20-storey tower blocks adjoin-. There are also a number of 14-storey cks and some five storeys in height; these of the slab type.

˜he 20-storey blocks are planned with central ridor access, single staircase and pair of lifts, ɟ eight flats on the typical floor of which two bedsitters, two one-bedroom, and four two-ɟroom type units. The flats are compactly and ›nomically planned on the back-to-back basis h naturally lit and ventilated kitchens and ernal bathrooms.

˜he 14-storey blocks are of two different types, ch however served by single staircase and r of lifts. One of these, Type B, has however ɜ flats to the typical floor of which two are)-bedroom, two one-bedroom and one bed-er type: the other, Type C has four flats to the ical floor, one of which is a three-bedroom t and the remaining three two-bedroom units. nternal corridor circulation rather than open nning is used in all of these units.

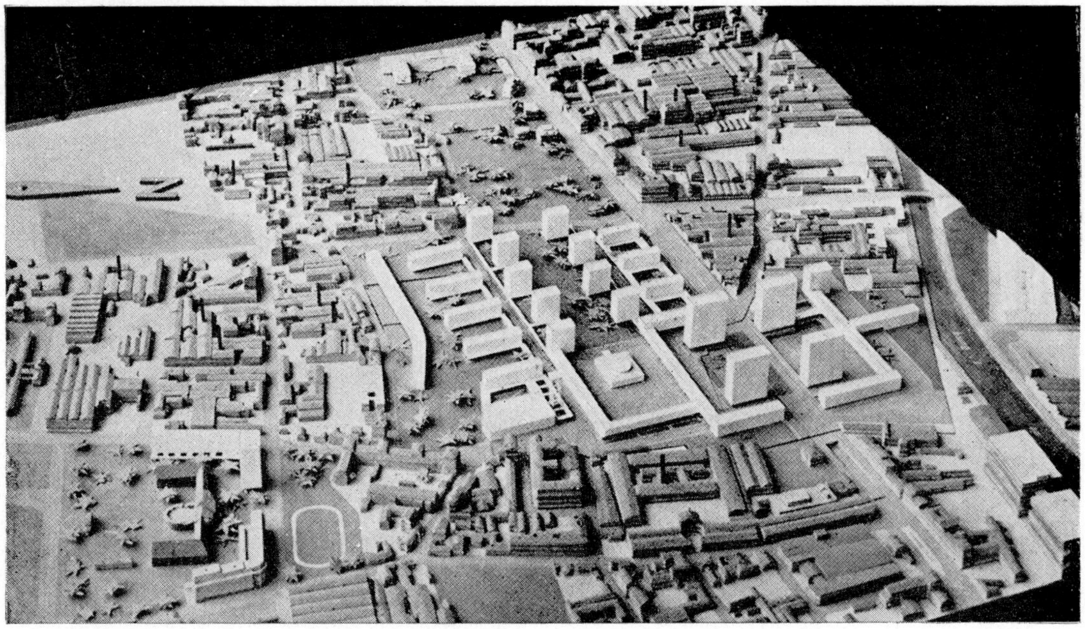

System of construction is reinforced concrete frame with an extensive use of precast reinforced concrete elements both in the floors and the external walls.

3 Front de Mer Sud, Le Havre

Architect: P. E. Lambert

This forms an important part of the massive reconstruction scheme of the war damaged city and port which involves amongst other things a total of 5000 flats being constructed and a large team of architects under the general supervision of Perret. This has produced an excellent example of comprehensive master planning with a fine conception of three-dimensional civic design.

The harbour front area was for obvious reasons of high priority and formed an important first

stage. It consists basically of a linked system of four-storey blocks with two 13-storey blocks interposed. In this part of the scheme 12 different flat types have been used varying in size from bachelor flatlets to five-bedroom type, with a total in all of 1200 units.

Exposed structural reinforced concrete has been used throughout with precast wall elements jacked into position from adjoining floors.

The tower blocks are served by single internal staircase and two lifts with five flats to the typical floor—one bedsitter, three with two bedrooms, and one with three bedrooms. Bathrooms are all planned internally; the kitchens to the larger flats all on external walls. Internal flat planning tends to suffer, however, to some degree from cross traffic.

The typical four-storey block has four flats to the typical floor with direct access from a single staircase, and no lift; two of these flats having two to three bedrooms, one one bedroom, and one being a bedsitter, again with internal bathrooms but external kitchens.

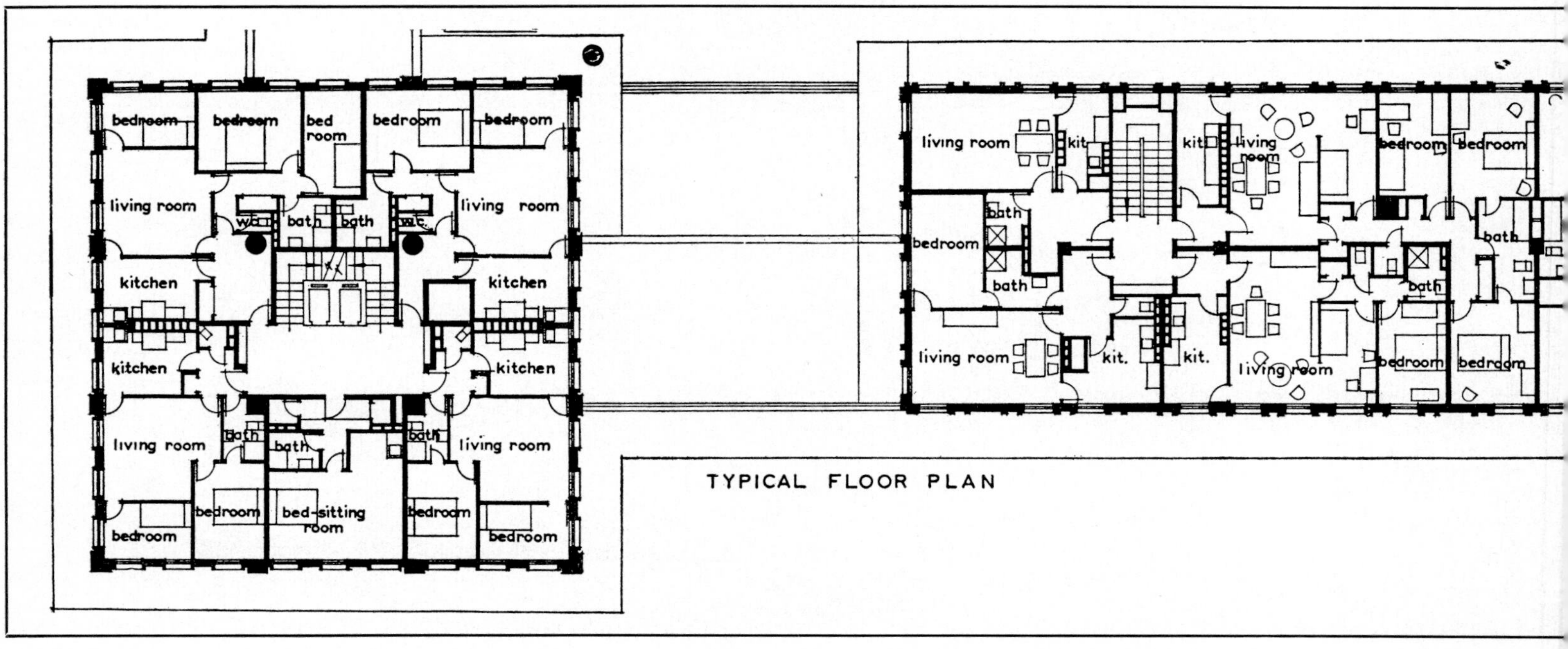

TYPICAL FLOOR PLAN

Tour du Stade, Chambery

chitects: L. Chappis, R. Berthe, and M. Fournier

two blocks included in this scheme one is a ir-storey block of the slab type with direct cess of orthodox pattern, with two flats to the ical floor; and the whole block contains similar units.

The dominant element in the development, nsists of a 'T' shape tower block 16 storeys in ight containing 60 flats served by two stair-ses and three lifts. Four flats are accessible at ch floor level, two of which have two bedrooms, d two one bedroom, each flat with its own vate balcony.

The ground floor level is partly open, with otis, and partly occupied by shops. There are o two basement floors containing central ating and services, and tenants' storage ace.

The site area is approximately $1\frac{1}{2}$ acres in tent and the density of development at proximately 230 persons per acre, site cover-e being approximately 15 per cent.

System of construction is *in situ* reinforced ncrete frame with reinforced concrete floors.

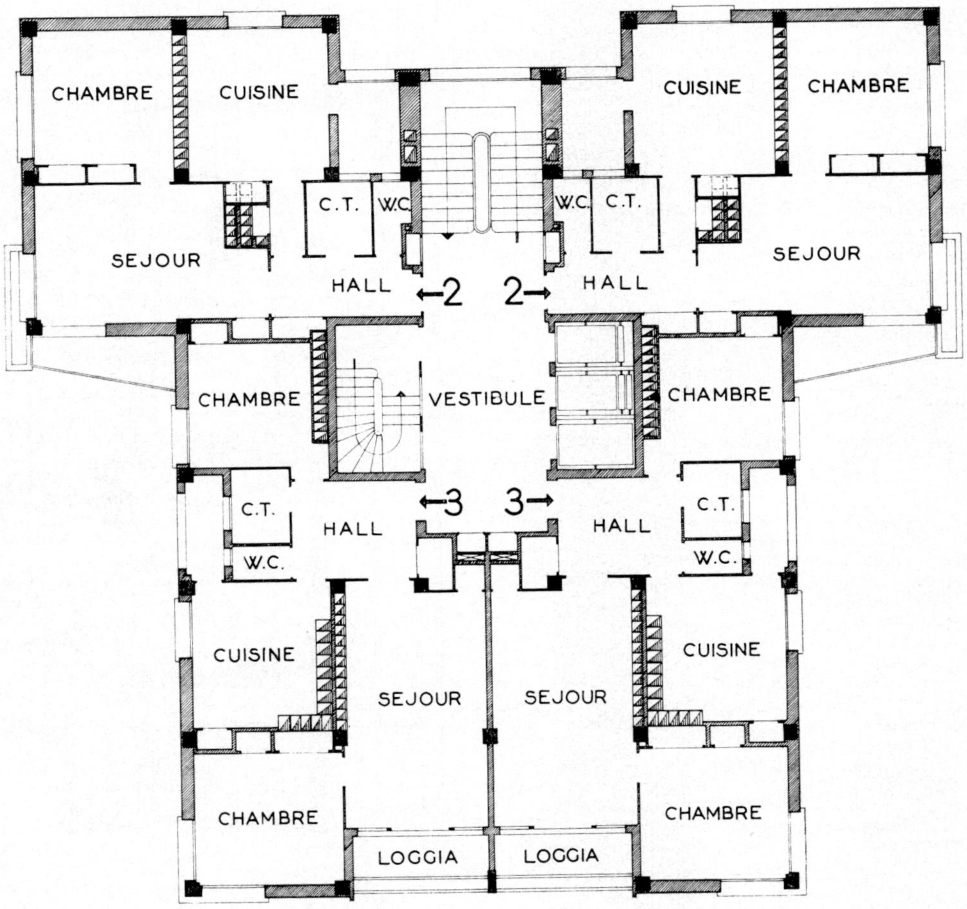

5 Ville Neuve St. Georges

Architect: Solotareff

The part of this development which is of special interest are the four tower blocks of similar design, although the whole scheme provides accommodation for 5000 inhabitants, the remainder being in low slab blocks designed by other architects and of orthodox direct staircase access type.

The development also includes a school, kindergarten, market, cultural centre, bus station and parking areas, in addition to generous park and garden areas.

The tower blocks are planned in the form of a T and each is served by a single staircase and pair of lifts with four flats on the typical floor; two of these having two bedrooms and two three bedrooms, with all kitchens planned on external walls and all bathrooms internally. A refuse chute is provided to each individual flat at each floor level.

Of the 15 storeys 12 are used for living accommodation and are similar in layout. The entrance level is devoted to tenants' storage accommodation, postman's and tradesmen's boxes, and in one block a caretaker's flat. The two upper floors contain tenants' drying cupboards, communal rooms and hot and cold water storage.

The system of construction is *in situ* load-bearing reinforced concrete walls internally with precast reinforced concrete mullions externally, and concrete slab infill panels. No balconies are provided to the individual flats and while this may in many ways be entirely logical economically and from climate point of view, there is a lack of relief to the fenestration pattern which is made up of a single standardized unit, and to the whole extent of the building.

The overall density of development is comparatively low, being approximately 65 persons to the acre with only $2\frac{1}{2}$ per cent of the ground covered by building. The density, however, in the area occupied by flats is considerably higher. In this regard the whole scheme could well be compared with English new towns.

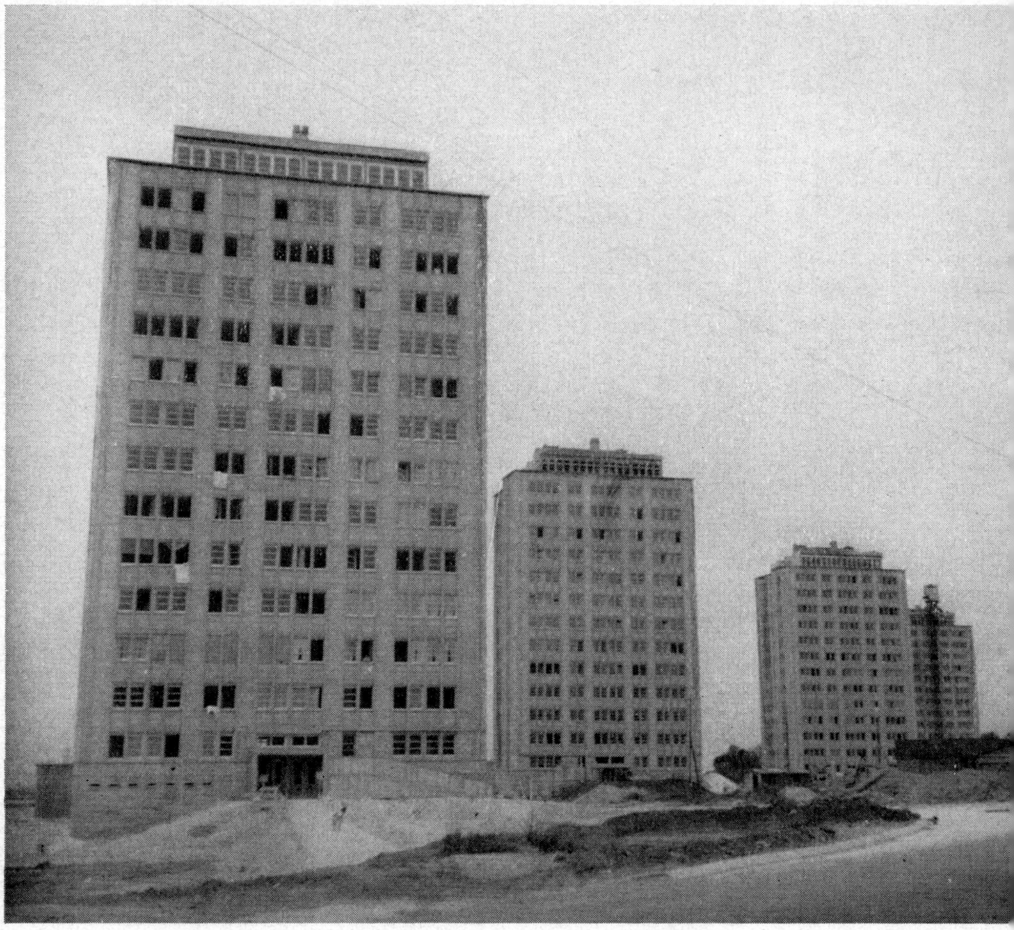

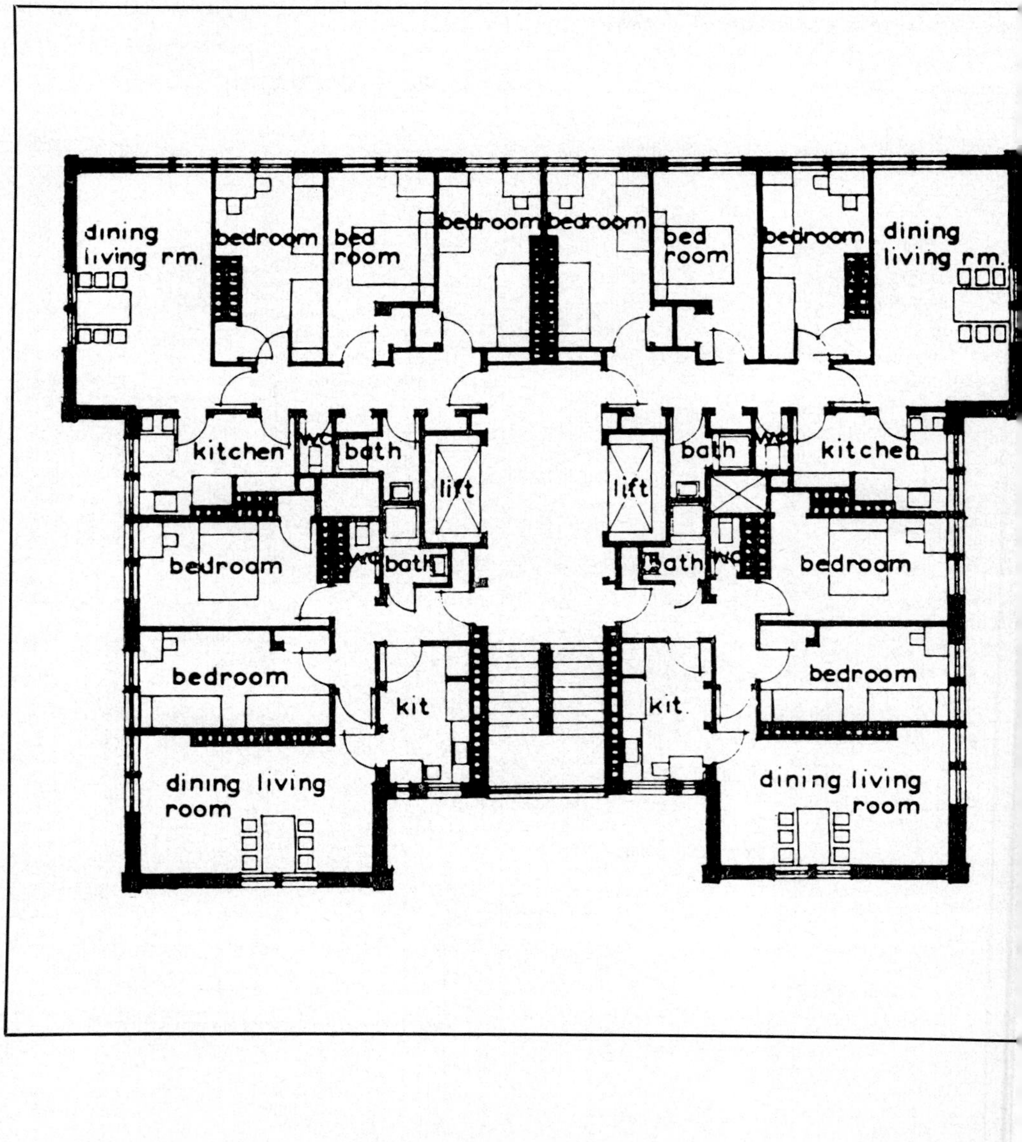

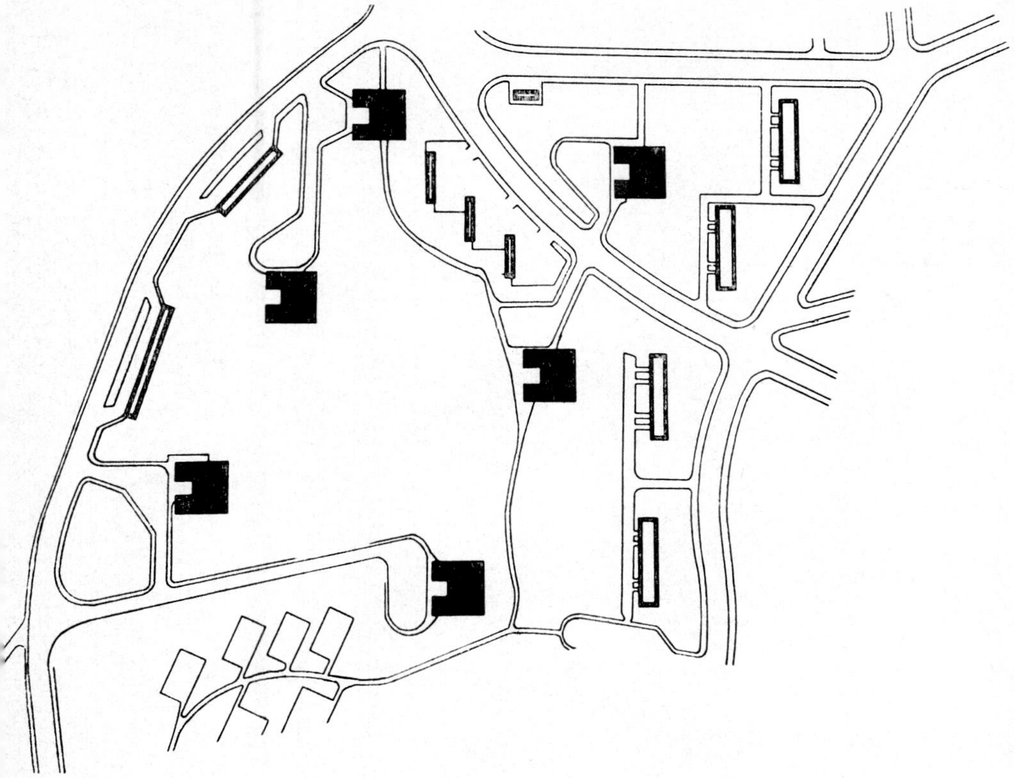

Group Queliverzan, Brest

:hitects: Gravereaux and Lopez

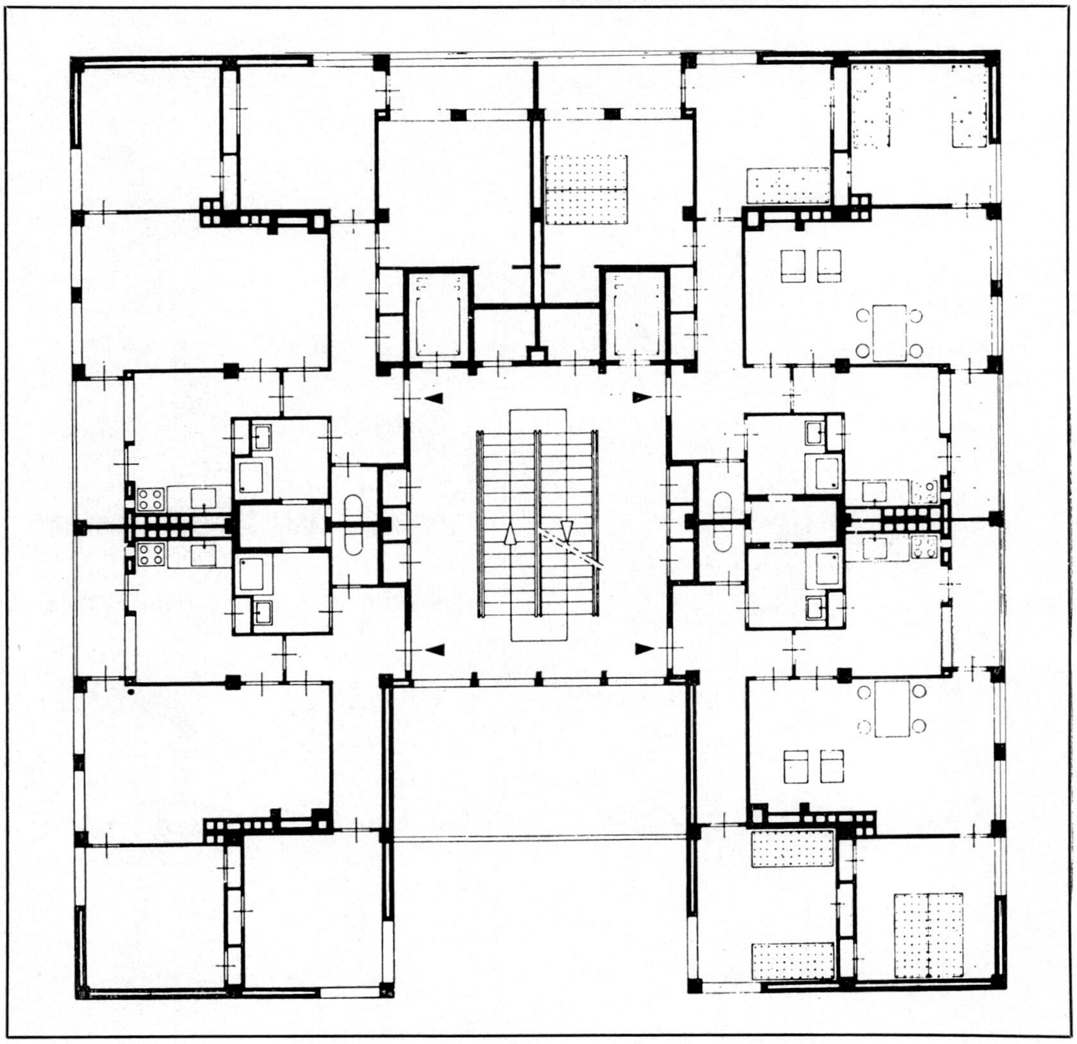

›art of the post-war reconstruction programme an area that suffered serious war damage. e scheme consists of six tower blocks as the ncipal elements, three of which in the first ge were 12 storeys in height and containing ›tal of 48 flats each; four to the typical floor, of ich two are the two-bedroom type, and two ee-bedroom type. These are served by twin s and twin staircases of the scissors type.

˜he final three blocks are of a slightly different :tern and contain 72 flats each, 48 of which are the two-bedroom type and 24 with one bed-m, the extra space being found for these in hollow U, thus producing an even more ˜active looking building architecturally with-: the re-entrant court.

:ach flat, even in the later blocks, has at least al aspect. Each flat has a private balcony and s adjoins both living room and kitchen. throoms are, however, remote from the bed-m zone and involve internal cross traffic. Two refuse chutes are provided at main landing el.

\s in all the more intelligently designed point cks of this type meters for the services can be d from landing level without the necessity for ering flats.

˜he ground floor level is largely open, being ried on a system of V shaped piloti. These, as ll as the frame to the superstructure, being ıstructed in reinforced concrete. External dding is also in the form of precast concrete bs with an internal skin of wood wool.

\ warm air system is provided to all the flats.

7 Firminy-Vert.

Architects: A. Sive, M. Roux, Delfante and J. Kling.

A tower block used as an element in a very much larger development in order to reduce the built-on area in a locality subject to coal mining subsidence.

The design of the tower block is unusual and could perhaps be best described as a broken rectangle since it is basically a refinement of the more orthodox point block planning, but in this case with the introduction of V-shaped incisions to break up the solidity of the long side of the building.

A very economical arrangement of eight flats to the floor is provided, accessible from a single staircase and pair of lifts. Four of these at each floor level are of the two-bedroom type, and four are bedsitters, the larger flats having balconies, and in all cases kitchens planned externally although those to the bedsitters are provided with very limited natural light and ventilation from squint type windows. Bathrooms are planned in the larger flats remote from the bedrooms and close to front entrance doors.

Four large tenants' storage rooms are provided at each floor level.

The architectural expression is interesting in its alternation of balcony and window element, and an overall form which has succeeded in giving a sympathetic treatment to a large building mass. The whole block contains a total of 136 flats in the 17 floors above a ground level which is largely occupied by tenants' storage and access to stair and lifts.

System of construction is reinforced concrete frame and floors with reinforced concrete membrane walls in the centre of the block adjoining staircase and lifts.

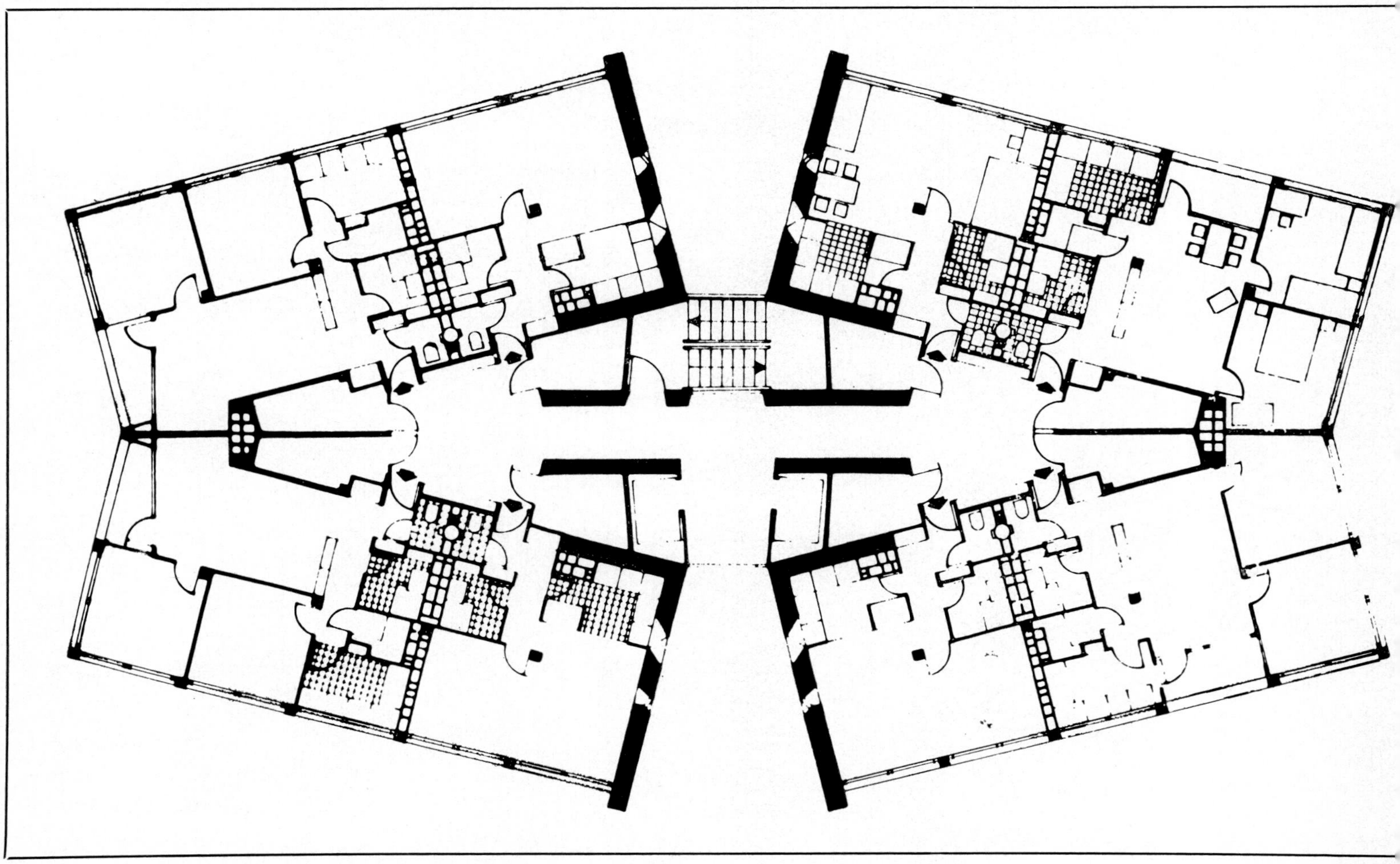

8 Fontainebleau Tower

Architects: J. Warnery, J. Saubot and J. Pierchon

A boldly conceived yet simply and cleanly designed 19-storey tower block forming a part of a large development. The use of recessed balconies is in this case well justified in order to break up the solidity of the building, and this, together with the staggered pattern of french window type balconies, provides the necessary architectural interest.

Planning of the block is extremely economical and compact with a single core staircase of the Scandinavian type and twin lifts. Eight flats are planned at each typical floor, four of which are of the two-bedroom type and four one-bedroom, all kitchens being planned on external walls and bathrooms internally although somewhat remote from bedroom zones.

System of construction is reinforced concrete *in situ* cross walls with reinforced concrete floors and raft, external cladding being in pumice concrete rendered externally.

As in so many of the schemes in European countries ventilation shafts are on the shunt system. Central heating is provided throughout.

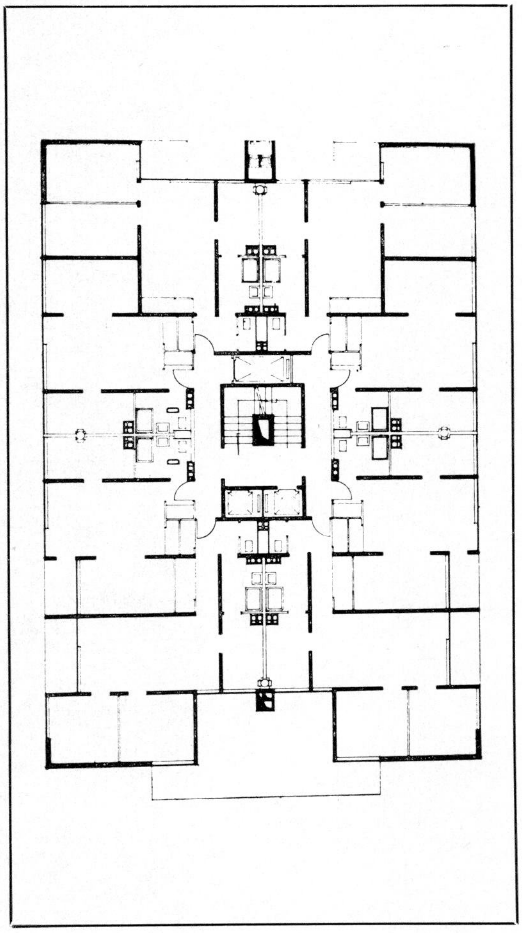

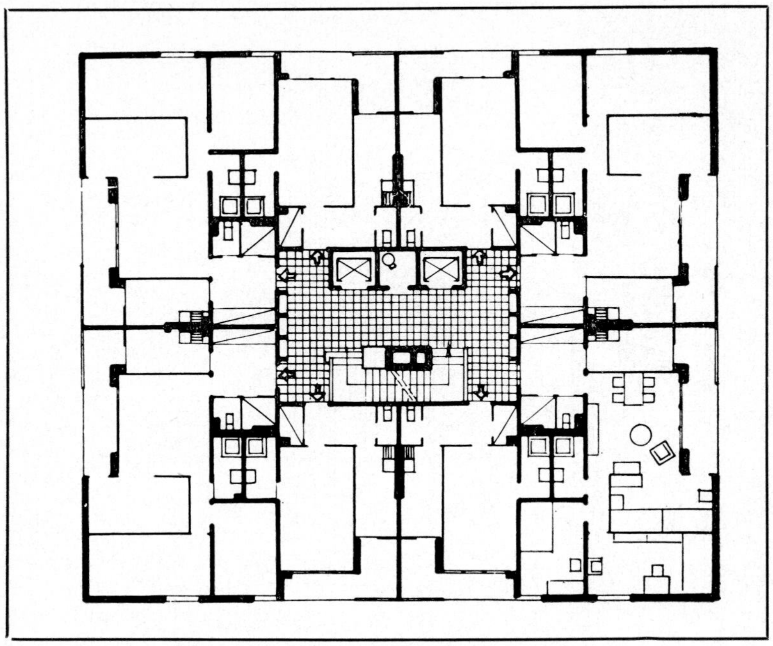

9 Saint-Dizier Tower

Architects: J. Warnery and J. Saubot

Another extremely successful and economic planned point block of the Scandinavian t with access to eight flats on the typical fl from a pair of lifts and a single staircase. Fou these flats in the angle of the building are of three-bedroom type and four bedsitters located in the centre, all dwellings hav extensive private balconies recessed within lines of the main structure. Use zoning particularly well organized in this case with bedrooms in close proximity to bathrooms the kitchen conveniently placed by the entra hall and adjoining the living/dining area, sharing the private balcony.

Refuse chutes accessible from landing le are also provided. Central heating is included and shunt flues for the ventilatior bathrooms.

Reinforced concrete load-bearing constr tion is used with masonry infill to the exter walls and wood wool internal lining.

In this 18 storey block there is a total of flats.

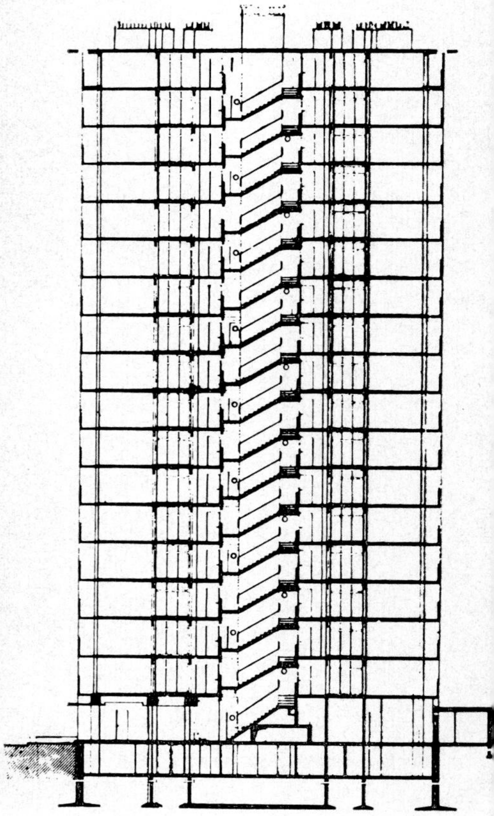

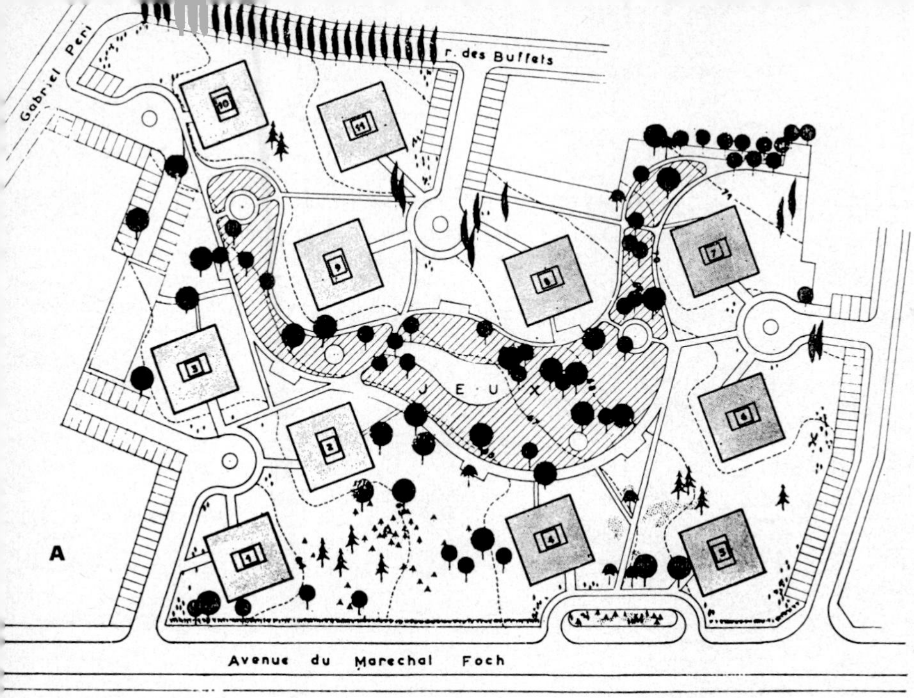

A

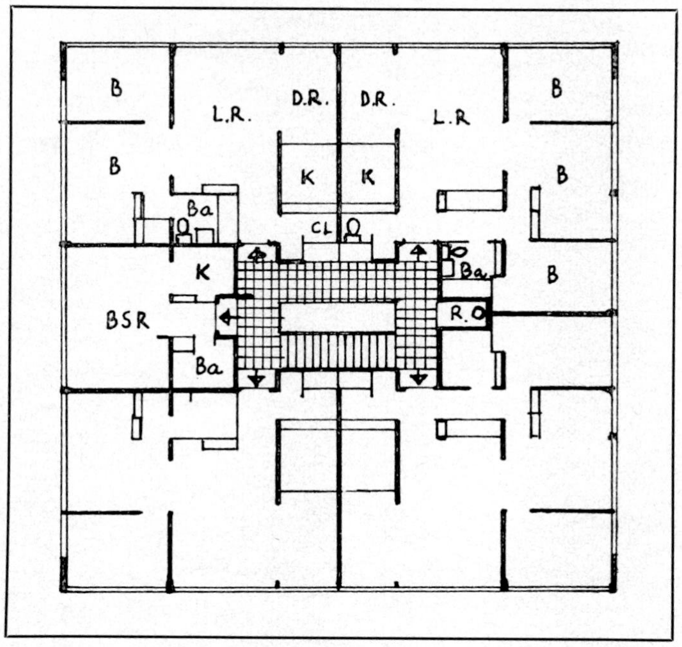

Les Buffetts, Fontenay-aux-Roses

rchitects: Lagneau and Associates

he central section of a major development :heme in the Greater Paris region which cludes, in total, 1800 flats of which some 500 are accommodated in six-storey slab ocks of orthodox design.

This group contains 260 flats, however, in identical blocks which are given considerable ariety in their treatment by an intelligent use of xisting site levels and excellent landscaping. 'hile these blocks are not multi-storey buildings the true sense of the word, the system of anning is identical with many of the point ocks. In this case, because the buildings are ıly five storeys in height, they are regarded as alk-up dwellings and no lifts are included but ace could readily be found for this and the entical planning would then be ideal for uildings of 12 or 15 storeys in height.

The arrangement of the individual flats is tremely good with proper functional use nning and elimination of all wasteful internal rculation areas; a compact service core with ngle staircase providing entry to five flats on e typical floor. Two of these are of the three- edroom type, two have two bedrooms, and one a bedsitter.

What is particularly noteworthy is the archi- ctural treatment which does not depend on lconies but solely on the delicacy of the well oportioned fenestration and the effect of a ht panel infill within the structural members ıt without the disadvantages of many curtain all treatments. The structure is clearly ex- essed and there are interesting contrasts in the e of materials.

The ground floor is in part carried on pilotis d the remainder of the space taken up with trance hall and tenants' storage. The whole pearance is one possessing a floating quality th a particularly clean overall form without necessary excrescences.

11 Maisons-Alfort

Architects: Heaume and Persitz

A 21-storey tower block containing 120 flats and designed in conjunction with a large 10-storey slab block. The tower is one of the tallest blocks in Europe, utilizing heavy reinforced concrete prefabrication applied to both cross walls anc floors. Vertical access is by means of two stair cases and two lifts stopping at alternate floo levels.

The ground floor to the block is taken up wit tenants' storage, services and caretaker's flat This and the basement extend beyond the perimeter of the superstructure and reinforcec concrete counterforts extend on the two mair frontages, thus transferring vertical and winc load to the basement which also accommodates tenants' storage and services.

Twelve upper floors are similar in thei planning and contain six flats, at each level o which the two smallest have a dining/kitchen living room and one bedroom, and the other fou a dining/living area, kitchen, three bedrooms an bathroom with reasonably satisfactory us zoning.

The structural grid is standardized to th extent that all bedroom spaces are similar; th living rooms are also similar to one another, an a third structural element is used for the bath room and kitchen areas to the larger flats.

All flats have private balconies set in from th exterior face of the building and these, togethe with the alternating pattern of fenestration an spandrel panel, as well as the variation in colour used, go a long way to produce a workabl but attractive building.

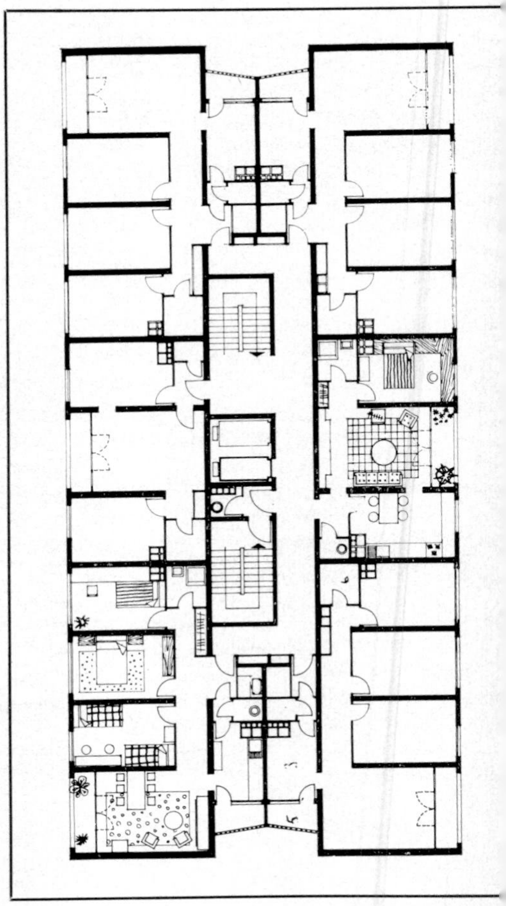

12 Tour Viollet, Angers

Architect: I. Schein.

A 15-storey tower block in a town reconstruction area with a small four-storey block of flats adjoining as well as children's play areas, parking space and a small block of offices. The site area is small, being only half an acre in extent and on this a total of 56 flats are accommodated in the tower; 28 with three bedrooms and 28 with two bedrooms, in addition to the caretaker's flat, thus giving a density of about 400 persons per acre.

Access is by means of a main staircase and a single lift, but a secondary escape staircase is also provided.

On the ground floor, apart from the entrance hall and the caretaker's flat, there are club rooms, play spaces and service areas, and the typical floor linked with the staircase through a somewhat congested central corridor access has four flats—two two-bedroom and two three-bedroom type.

Bathrooms are planned internally with mechanical extraction, and this is also provided to kitchens although these are on external walls. Each flat has its private balcony.

The system of construction is reinforced concrete cross wall and frame and reinforced concrete gable walls. Otherwise external treatment consists entirely of metal windows and metal spandrel panels.

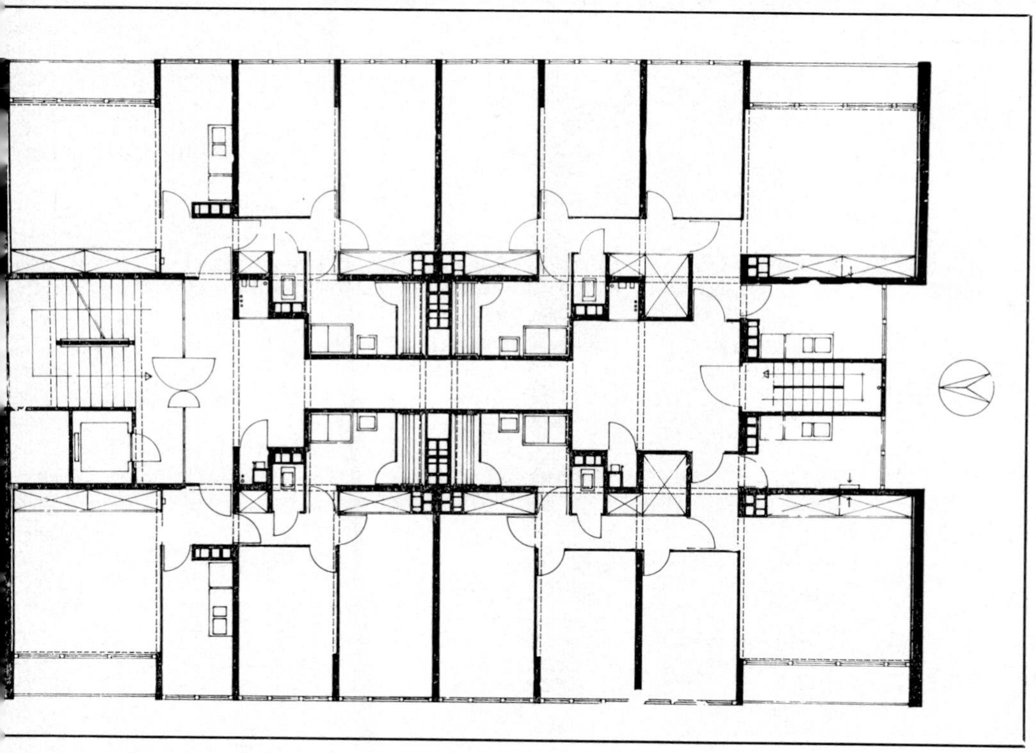

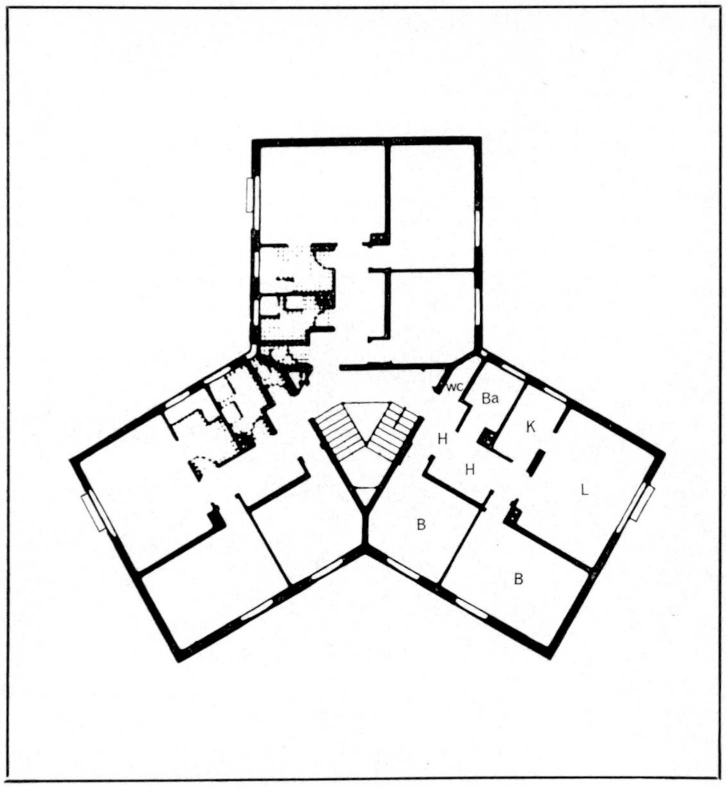

13 Les Courtillières, Pantin

Architects: Aillard and Vedres

A further section of a large slum redevelopm area north of Paris, and in this case the wl scheme containing a total of 1223 dwelling ur The scheme is particularly noteworthy, m perhaps for the six-storey serpentine blo than for the 13-storey tower blocks, and extent to which these are integrated one v the other or with the intervening open space open to question. Aspect, moreover, particul in the serpentine blocks, becomes a matte mere chance. Some relief from the dea monotony of the enormously long slab blo characteristic of so many of the recent hous schemes in France is welcome, but whether solution is a practical or a desirable one rema to be seen.

A somewhat similar development has a been carried out at Bobigny with a total 1500 flats.

At Pantin the star or Y plan blocks are interest although two staircases and two lifts used for only three flats on the typical floor, th all being two-bedroom units. No day and ni zones are allowed for. Bathrooms and kitch are grouped together.

The ground floor to the blocks contain flats together with tenants' storage and entra hall.

The other noteworthy feature of this schem the rather unusual rhythmic pattern created the window and french door unit, a fenestrat pattern used throughout in the tower bloc This is relieved only by the expression of structural grid and the somewhat wayw treatment of the balconies to certain of the fl

The Camus system of construction was us

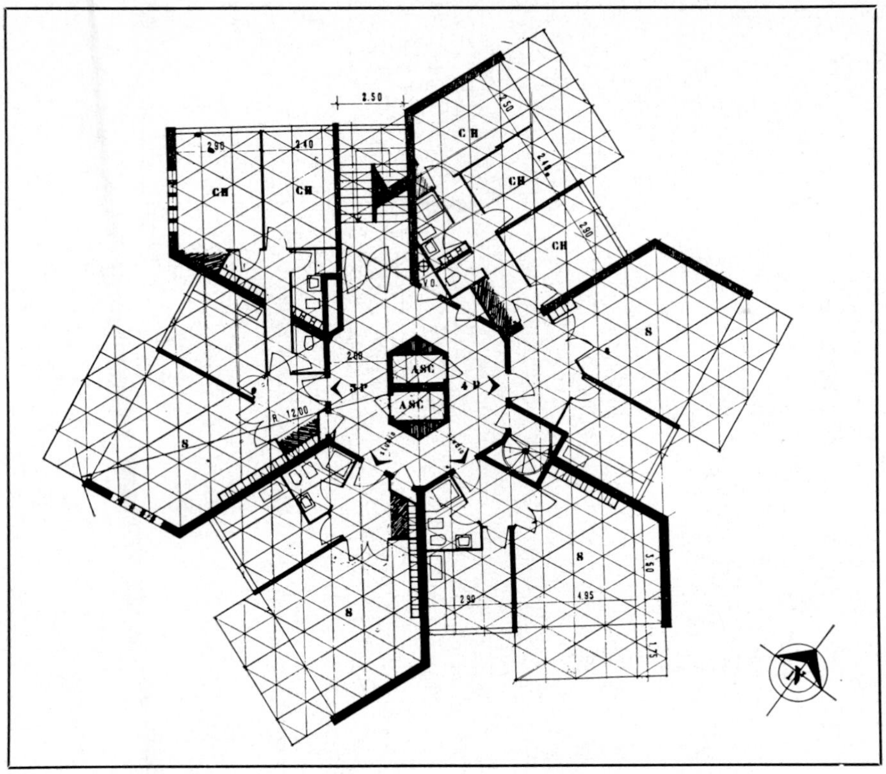

14 Valras-Plage Les Elysees

Architects: P. Jaulmes and J. C. Deshons

A site with beach and mountain views has inspired this imaginative scheme which comprises in houses, low and high blocks of flats some 360 dwellings with the hexagonal block as the focus.

Shops and restaurant occupy most of the ground floor space. The 14 upper floors are each planned with four dwellings; two bedsitter, one with two bedrooms and one with three. Access is via two lifts and main stair—with a secondary emergency stair. Each flat has a generous private balcony which also forms a part of the sun control system.

Construction is in load-bearing reinforced concrete walls and slab.

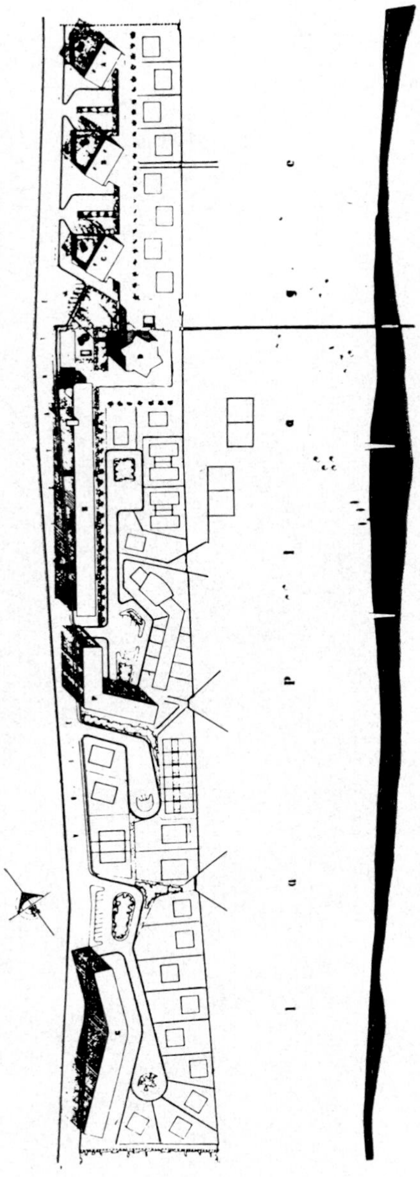

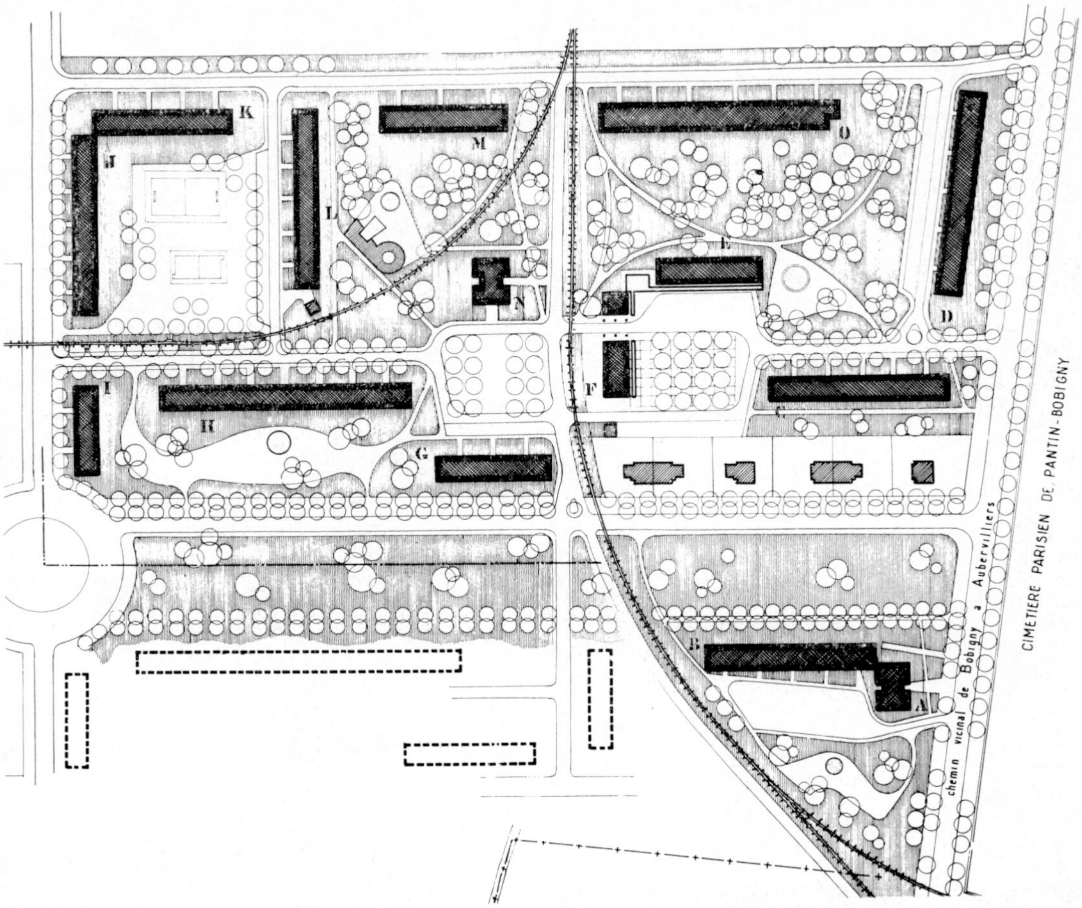

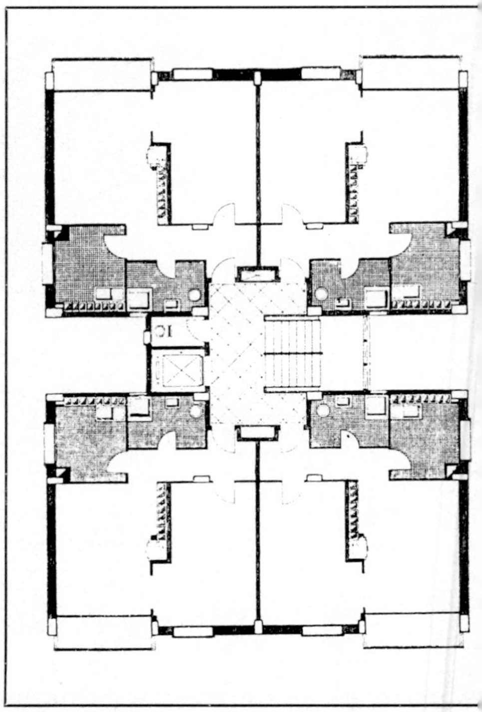

15 Bobigny, Paris

Architects: A. G. Heaume and A. Persitz

This area North of Paris is being transformed by the complete rebuilding and expansion in progress towards a programme of 3000 dwellings and services.

The scheme illustrated occupies a site of nearly nine hectares and will provide about 600 dwellings at a density of about 160 persons per hectare, in the form of five-storey s blocks and eight- and ten-storey tower bloc In the low blocks are three-, four- and five-ro dwellings whereas all dwellings in the to blocks are identical with two rooms. Th latter are served by a single stair and lift, a each flat has a full width balcony. Standa zation has been applied to planning and c struction which is based on a load-bearing v system of masonry and reinforced concrete.

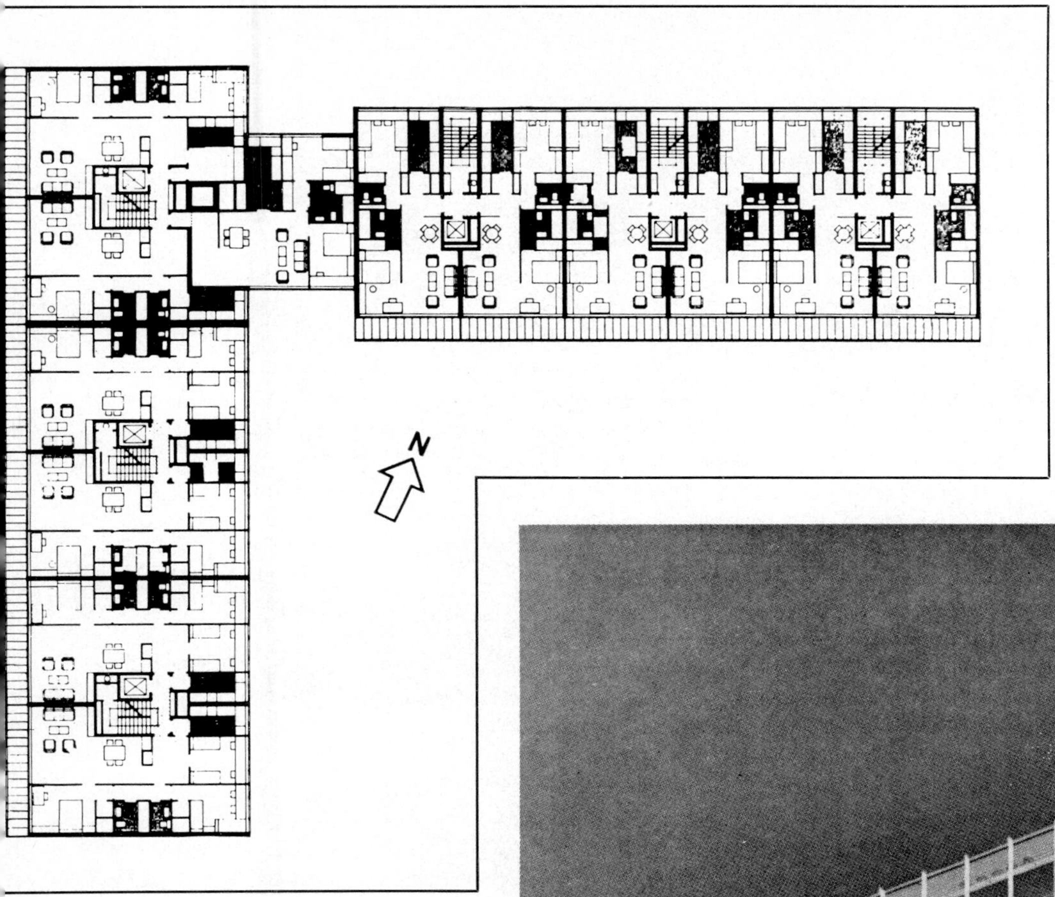

Quai de Boulogne, Paris

hitect: J. Ginsberg

-ee blocks of twelve, eight and three storeys a riparian site adjoining the Seine; and built over a two-storey podium containing parking ages and services; and with a roof terrace. particularly clean and well proportioned hitectural conception both in massing and in ail with very satisfying proportions, and edom from the current idiom of the bizarre. vantage has been taken of the riverside ation by introducing a promenade, accessible all flats at first floor level. From this level cess to flats is by means of single staircase l lift to pairs of dwellings.

'he flats are planned with dual aspect between d-bearing cross walls, and all have con-uous balconies on one facade.

17 Maine Montparnasse, Paris

Architects: Equipe A.O.M., E. Beaudouin etc., and J. Dubuisson

A massive renewal operation over the main line terminal at Montparnasse in the centre of the City, embodying both offices and flats of a variety of sizes and types in a 50-storey and 18-storey block.

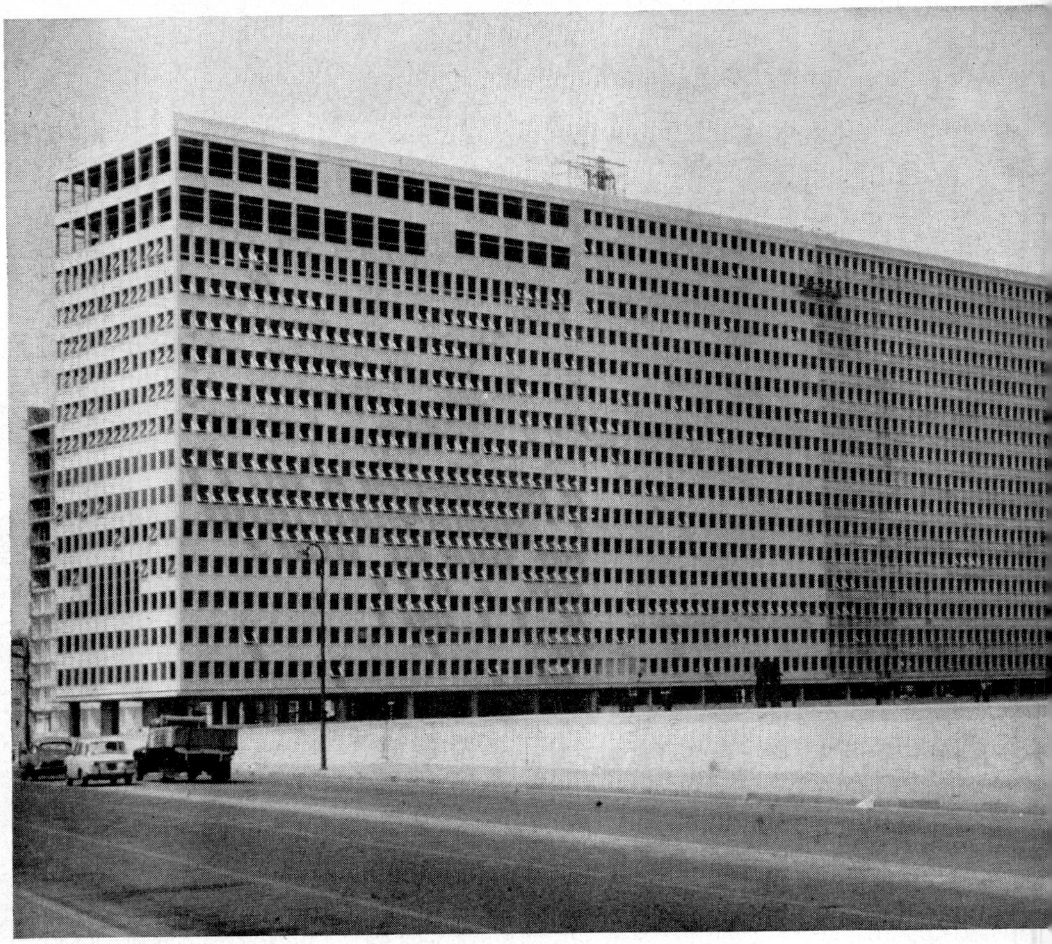

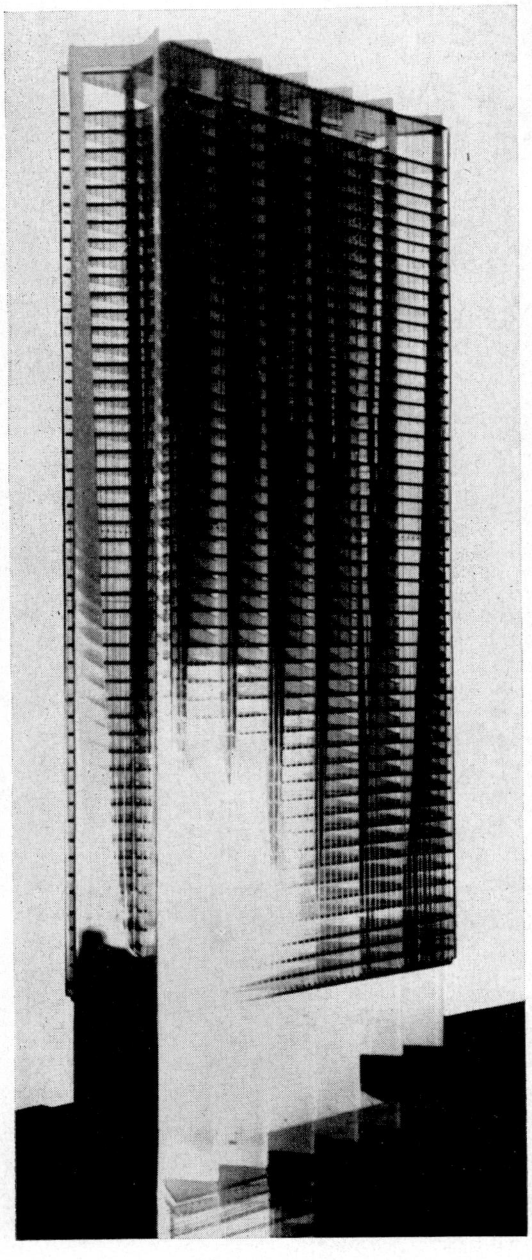

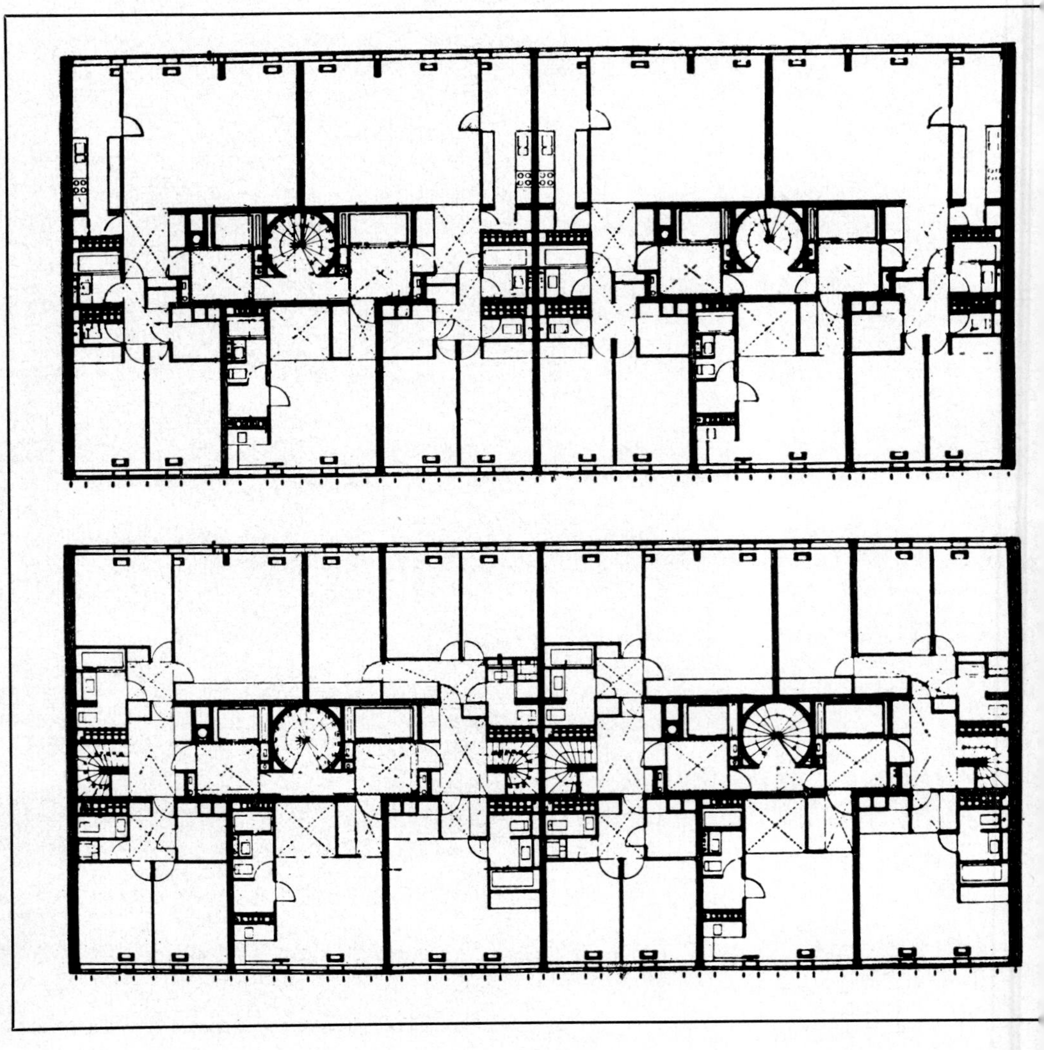

Cité de L'Abreuvoir, Bobigny

hitects: Aillaud and Vedres

e thousand five hundred flats disposed in tower blocks, three cylindrical and three with 'Y' plan, 11 storeys in height; and in lower serpentine blocks predominantly four storeys in height. This arrangement has produced advantages of spaciousness with low building coverage, but also of some screening from the clutter of adjoining suburban building. The circular plan results in somewhat awkward segmental shaped rooms and internal kitchens, as well as bathrooms. The blocks appear to finish off at roof level rather abruptly.

The 'Y' blocks are better, giving three similar two-bedroom units at each typical floor with a very economical service core. Construction makes extensive use of prefabrication techniques on the Camus system.

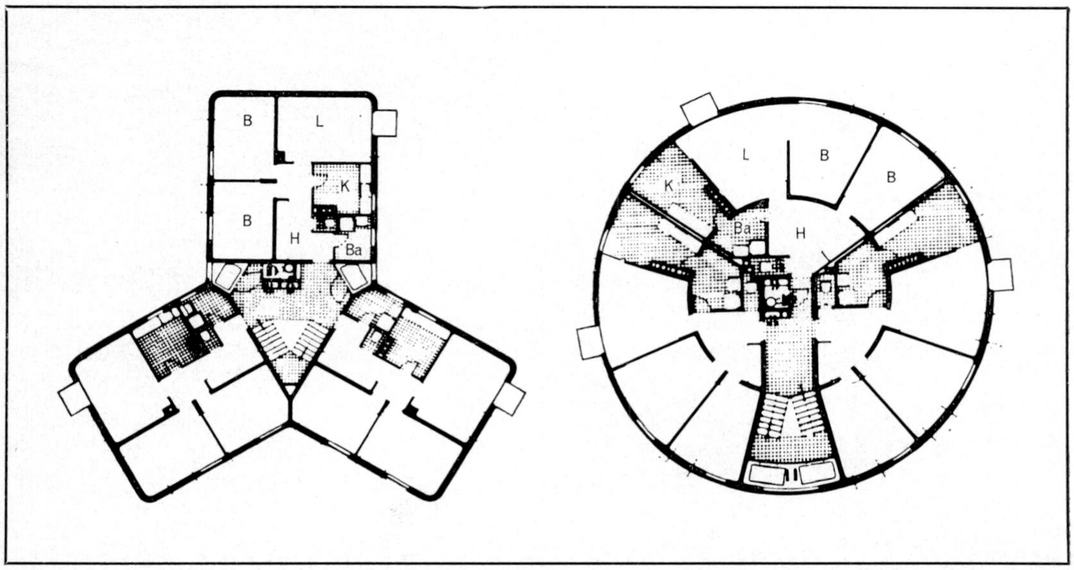

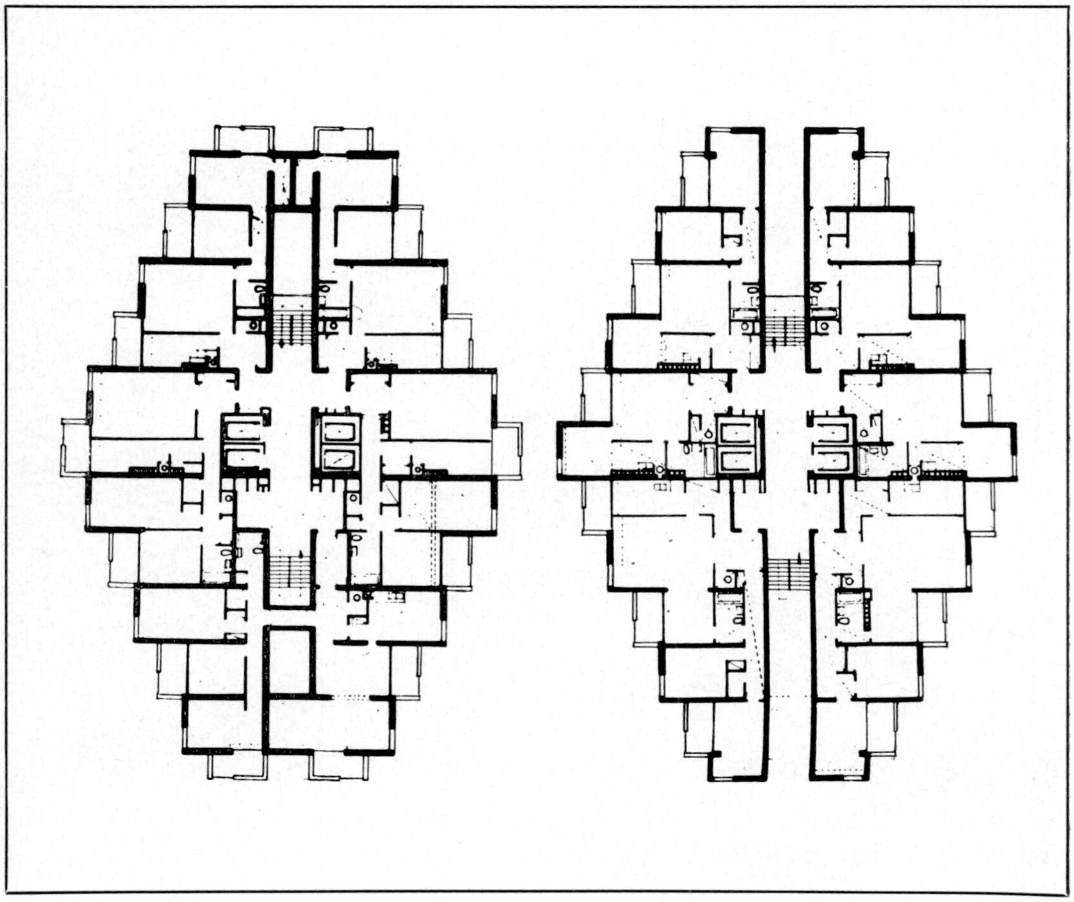

Germany

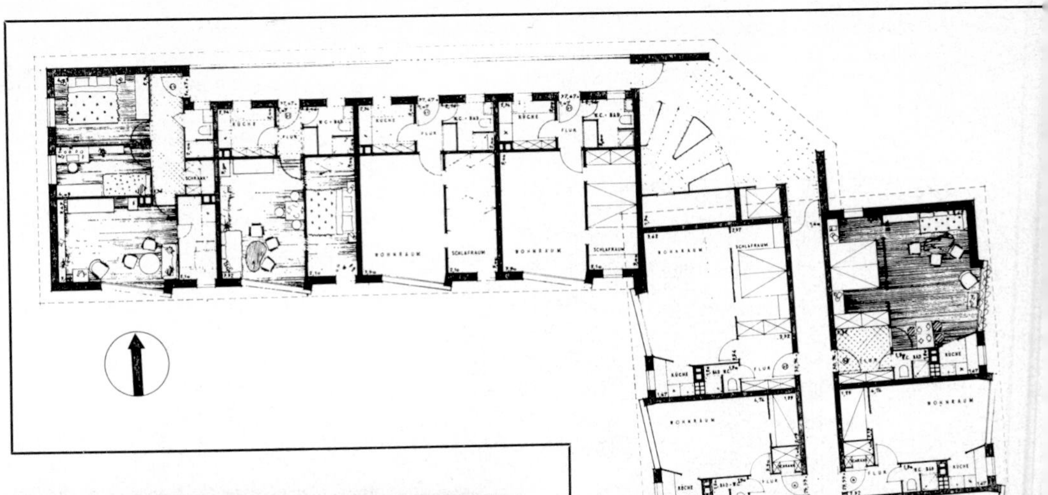

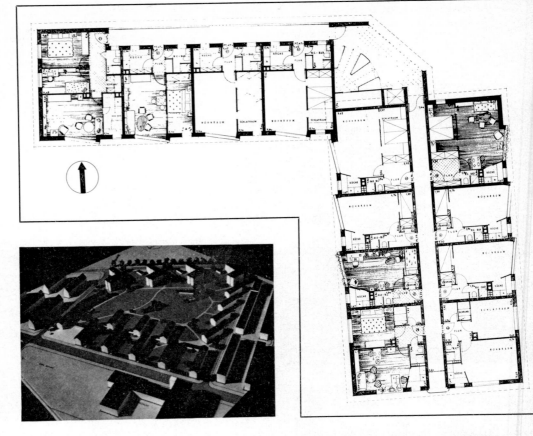

1 Alter Teichweg, Hamburg

Architects: Sprotte, Neve, Tinneberg and Van Berg

A large and well-landscaped housing development containing 496 flats, eight shops and a restaurant in the northern part of the city with accommodation provided in a number of parallel slab blocks and in four similar interesting L-shape blocks which combine balcony access in one of the wings with central corridor access in the other, accessible from a single central staircase and lift.

Each typical floor to the block contains 12 units all of which are either of the one-bedroom or the bedsitter type.

The blocks which are six storeys in height are of load-bearing masonry construction. Density overall is 350 persons per hectare.

Cost: 51.75 *DM per cubic metre*

Grindelberg Estate, Hamburg

hitects: Hermkes, Jager and Associates

comprehensive development consisting of 15-storey blocks, six ten-storey blocks, and 13-storey block with a particularly high ndard of architectural design to the individual cks and of landscaping to the area as a whole, ch was fortunate in retaining the benefit of a siderable number of mature forest type trees.

ne of the unusual features of the scheme is t of combining municipal district offices in centre block with a proportion of one-room s, the offices occupying roughly one-third of whole block and incidentally utilizing the ernoster system of vertical circulation; the s throughout being served, however, by lifts ch stop at neither first nor top floors; an nomical arrangement which also has the antage of eliminating unsightly penthouses.

he planning of the individual blocks varies siderably. Block 1 consists entirely of bed-ngroom units, and the single staircase and of lifts by means of central corridor access e 12 units to each typical floor. Block 4 on other hand, one of the other 15-storey blocks, a staircase and pair of lifts serving three to each typical floor of which the majority single bedroom units. In this case two out of e of the flats have dual aspect whereas in k 1 all the flats are single aspect.

both blocks shops and offices occupy the ower floors, and there are large studio flats, sun terraces accessible to all tenants at roof . The clean way in which these are finished projecting roof canopy is noteworthy.

Block 5, also 15 storeys in height, is planned with a single staircase and lift serving 11 units with single bedroom or bedsitters by means of central corridor access.

Block 12, 10 storeys in height, has eight flats of varying sizes to the typical floor served by means of central corridor by a single staircase and lift.

Block 11, one of the 10-storey blocks, is of the orthodox standard direct staircase access type with two two-bedroom flats to the typical floor.

All blocks are planned on a north-south axis and therefore have east and/or west aspect. District central heating is provided throughout and this is independently controlled on the two main building frontages. A large two-decker underground car park is also provided in the centre of the area.

In the earlier stages the structural system was steel skeleton with brick and pumice block cavity wall infill. Subsequently reinforced concrete frame was substituted for the steel.

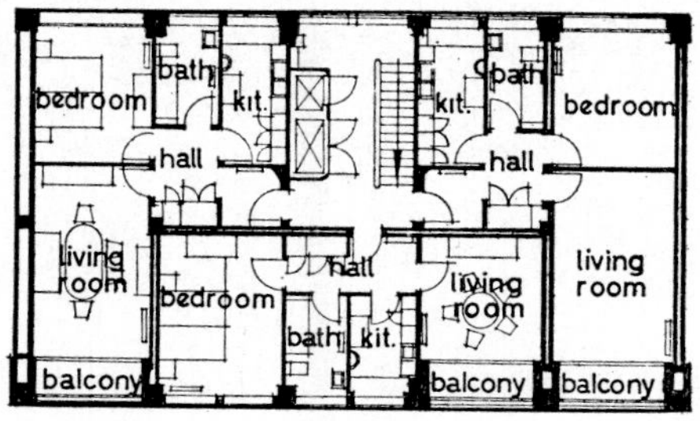

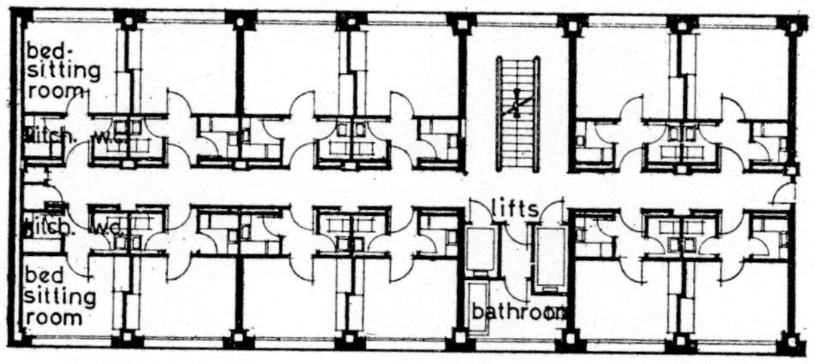

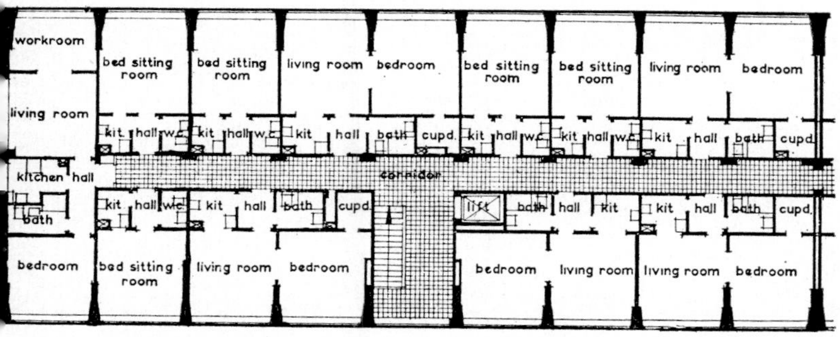

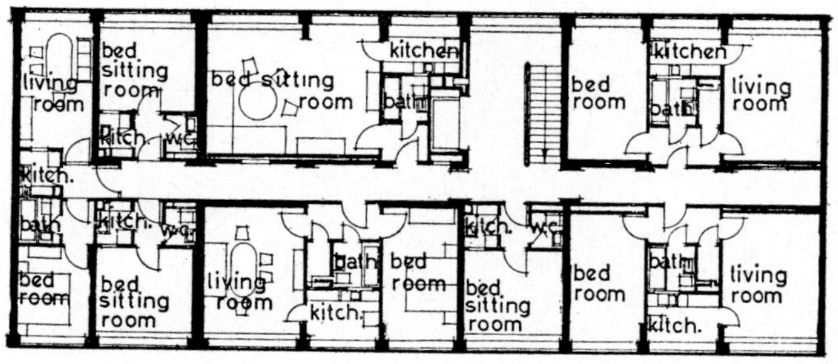

3 Hansa Project 7, Berlin

Architects: 'The Architects Collaborative'
Partner in Charge: Walter Gropius
Architectural Consultant: Wils Ebert

To quote the author of this scheme:

'This nine-storey flat building is part of a lar development of a bombed-out area—the Har District in the centre of Berlin, Germany. T apartment block has been designed for middle-income class—64 three-bedroom ur and two larger penthouse apartments. slightly curving the south elevation, the buildi makes an inviting gesture. Three differ textures of white—smooth white stucco agai rough white stucco, and white enamel balcony railings combined with the sky-b soffits of the balconies gives a serene impressi Part of the first floor is open for children's pl

The structure is a reinforced concrete skele with wall fillings of blocks made from bo rubble. The foundations stand on a bed of sa ten feet thick for better load distribution rather porous soil.

The plan of the apartments has delibera not been made an open one, but each room separately accessible from a hall. Since apartments are to be rented by families varying sizes and habits, this type of plan is m flexible than an open one, giving greater priv to the individual of any age. It adapts bette the varying stages of the family life—you couple, babies, adolescents, old people. In so cases the living room and the adjacent bedro have been separated only by a curtain o folding door instead of by a wall, allowing a la space for social gatherings.'

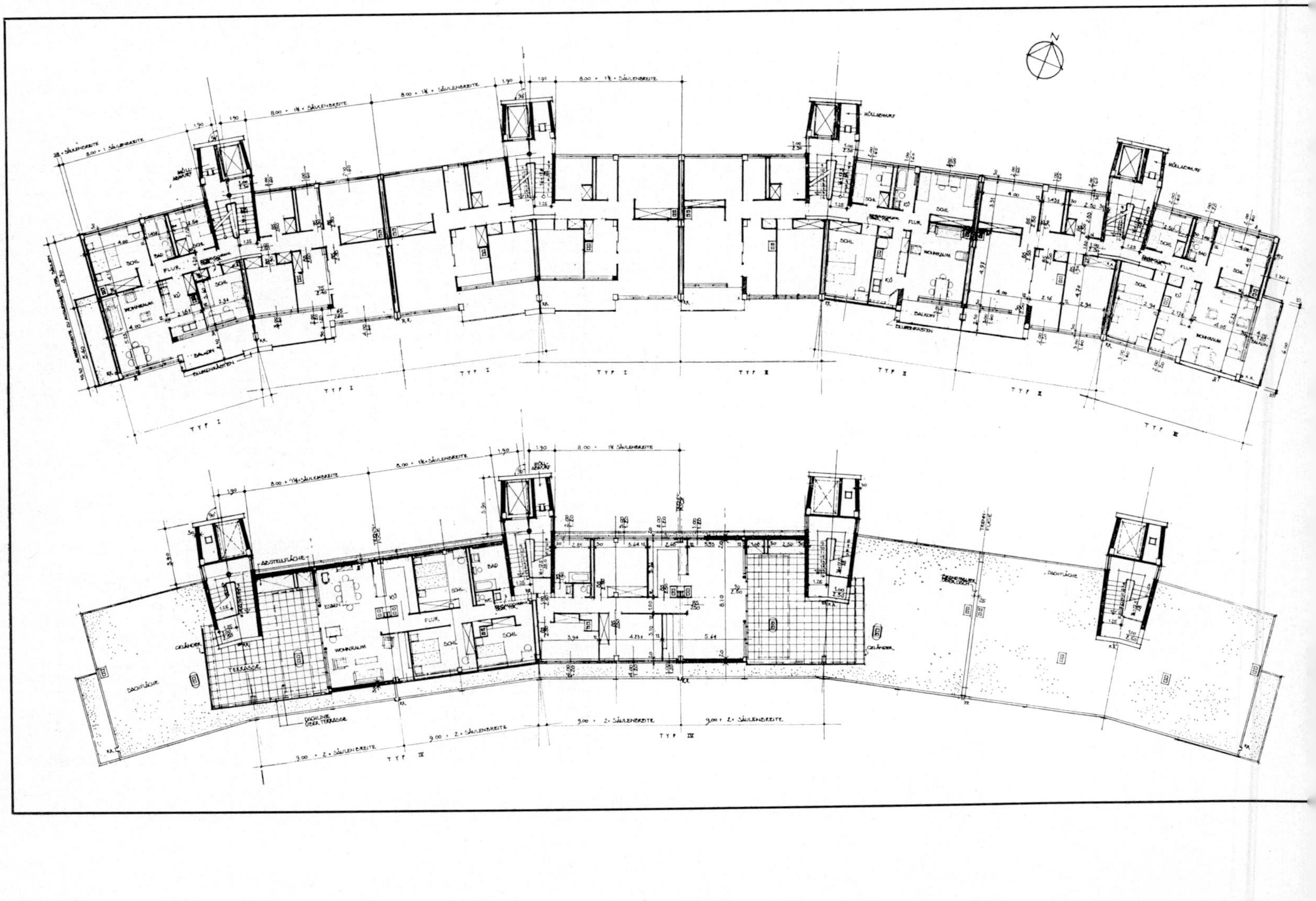

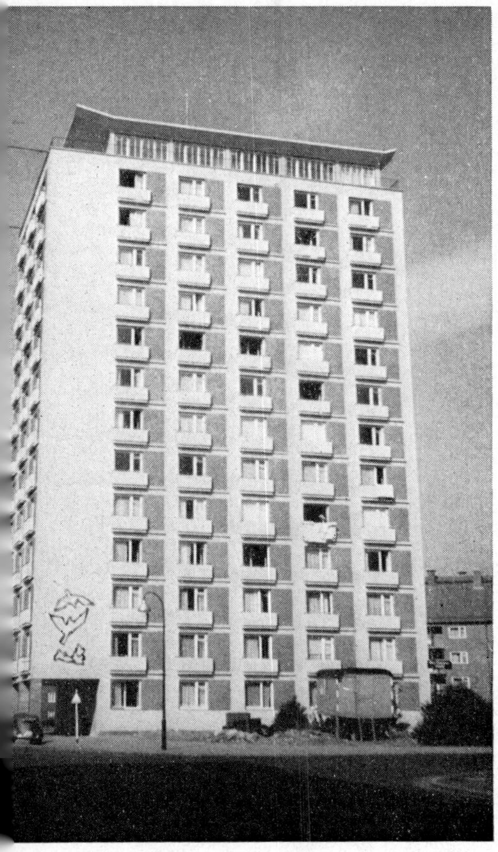

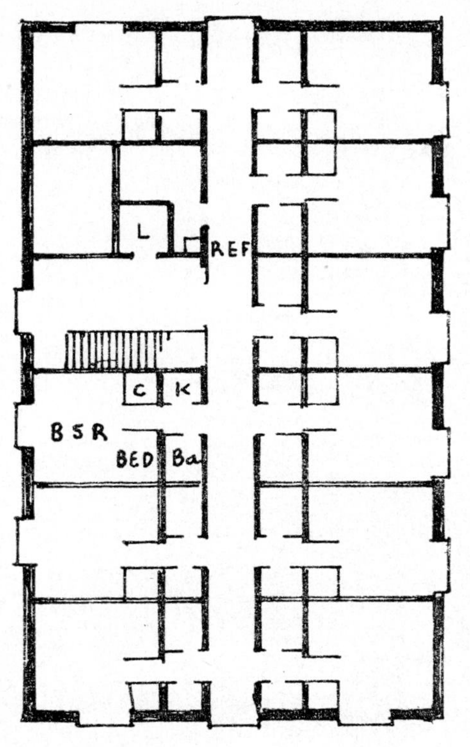

4 Habichtsplatz, Hamburg

Architect: Knerlich

A 14-storey tower block associated with three- and four-storey slab blocks in a very much larger development of which the tower block forms the focus.

The block contains 118 one-room flats and 10 two-room flats with the typical floor planned to accommodate 10 identical bedsitter units, accessible from single staircase and lift and central corridor. A secondary escape staircase is provided from ninth to fourteenth floor and at the roof level, which is finished with a neatly cantilevered slab, is the lift motor room, air conditioning machinery, restaurant and other public rooms.

A basement with communal services is also provided.

The ground floor is planned with a recessed arcade on one frontage and there are therefore only eight bedsitter units on this floor.

The form of construction was climbing shuttering with *in situ* reinforced concrete, this part of the building being completed in 14 days and with 10 per cent economy being claimed on the whole cost of construction. Brick infill panels partly cement rendered have been used for the exterior treatment, and each flat has a simulated balcony with french door.

Overall density of development is approximately 180 persons per acre.

Tower Flats, Bad Godesberg

:hitects: Appel, Letocha and Associates

Government sponsored development to house ›ployees of an international organization in an ractive rural setting. The development con- ts of 152 one-room, 128 two-room, 100 three- m, and 40 four-room flats with a 12-storey ver block containing 72 single-room flatlets nned eight to the typical floor, accessible m the central core unit, containing single ircase and lift.

The two lower floors of the 12-storey block ntain shops, a medical centre and administra- e offices.

The roof contains lift machinery, tank rooms, d there are in addition two basement floors h tenants' storage and communal services.

Construction of this block is in reinforced ıcrete frame with masonry infill.

An identical development to this has also been rried out in Bonn.

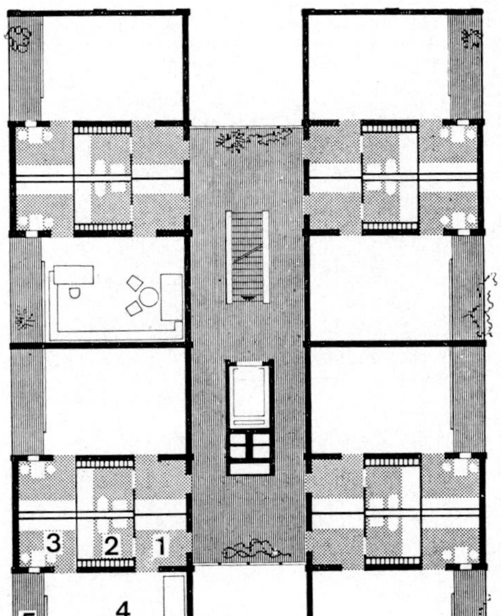

1 Cloakroom
2 Bath
3 Kitchenette
4 Living-cum-dining room
5 Terrace

6 Am Roseneck, Berlin

Architects: Lobotka and Associates

A single 16-storey star or Y block with six flats to the typical floor, two of these having three bedrooms, two two bedrooms, and two being bedsitters, the larger flats only having private balconies, but all with south aspect. Vertical access is by means of a single staircase and two lifts with a secondary staircase for emergency use only.

All kitchens have natural light and ventilation as well as the bathrooms to the larger flats.

An extremely economical piece of planning in spite of the internal access corridors, giving direct approach from front door to each of the habitable rooms, unlike most Continental flat plans.

Advantage has been taken of an inherently stable structure with considerable use of unreinforced designed mass concrete load-bearing walls; a system, however, which tends to reduce the internal flexibility in planning.

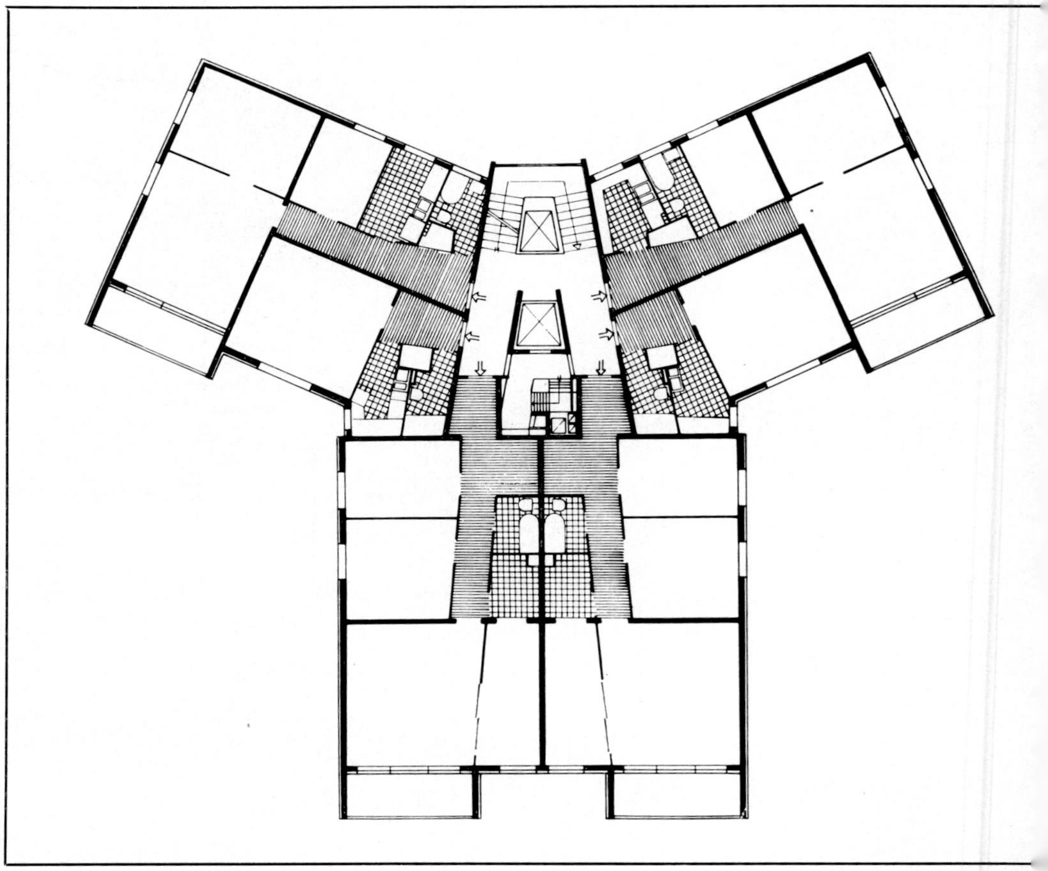

Project 18, Hansa District, Berlin

chitect: G. Hassenpflug

nother noteworthy contribution to the Interbau ousing Exhibition. In this case a 14-storey ctangular point block with five flats to the floor rved by a single staircase and pair of lifts, care ing taken to isolate the staircase within its own e protected enclosure and to provide a natur- y ventilated circulation area to the flats.

The typical floor contains five units, four of ich are in the normal plan of identical type nsisting of two bedrooms with bathroom *en ite*, living room, kitchen, small hallway and akroom, both kitchens and bathrooms being anned on outside walls. The fifth unit on the ical floor consists of a single bedroom flat th its own kitchenette and bathroom, in this se both planned internally and mechanically ntilated.

The structure has been ingeniously arranged th with the use of reinforced concrete cross lls and stiffening membrane walls, together th a modulated system of precast concrete llions on the exterior to give the maximum ssibility of flexible sub-division of each of the t units around its own service core. This has the architect to suggest a number of other ernative ways of planning the typical flat.

An extremely economical and well-planned d designed scheme which takes full advantage research into problems of high density living d into recent structural developments, the uctural system being simply expressed in e external architectural treatment which shows the advantages of prefabrication and ndardization together with the intelligent use a simple system of fenestration and materials ich are maintenance free.

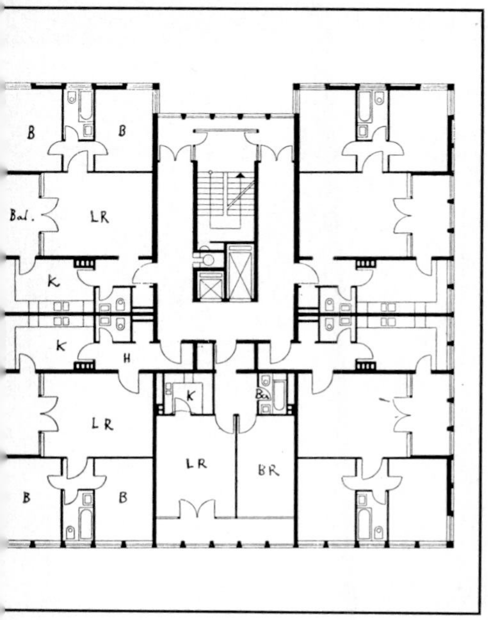

8 Project 1, Hansa Area, Berlin

Architects: Muller-Rehm and Siegmann

A set piece 17-storey tower block of bachelor flats, which was one of the contributions helping to set the very high standard of the Interbau Exhibition. The planning shows a considerable advance on earlier high density housing, although this scheme includes no family units.

Each of the bedsitter flats, however, has a kitchenette adjoining its own window and this, with the alternating pattern of balconies to each of the living rooms, and with the intelligent use of materials to the exterior of the building particularly, establishes an attractive rhythmic architectural quality, taking full advantage of the significant third dimension.

A single staircase is also used in this block together with twin lifts both of which gives access on to an open ventilated gallery at each floor level. A dry dust chute is also included in the central circulation core.

Shops are included at the ground floor on one side of the building and parking spaces on the other, together with caretaker's flat containing three rooms.

The balconies are of minimum area and are intended to form an extension of the living room with the french windows rather than a sitting-out place.

The roof, with its neat cantilevered slab, contains laundries, drying and ironing rooms, storage space, and window cleaning and maintenance gear.

The basement provides central heating plant and other mechanical equipment together with tenants' storage.

Structural system is reinforced concrete load-bearing walls and slabs, the walls faced on the outside with storey-high precast concrete panels backed with insulation.

The whole effect of this scheme is very greatly enhanced by the fine planting and landscaping surrounding it.

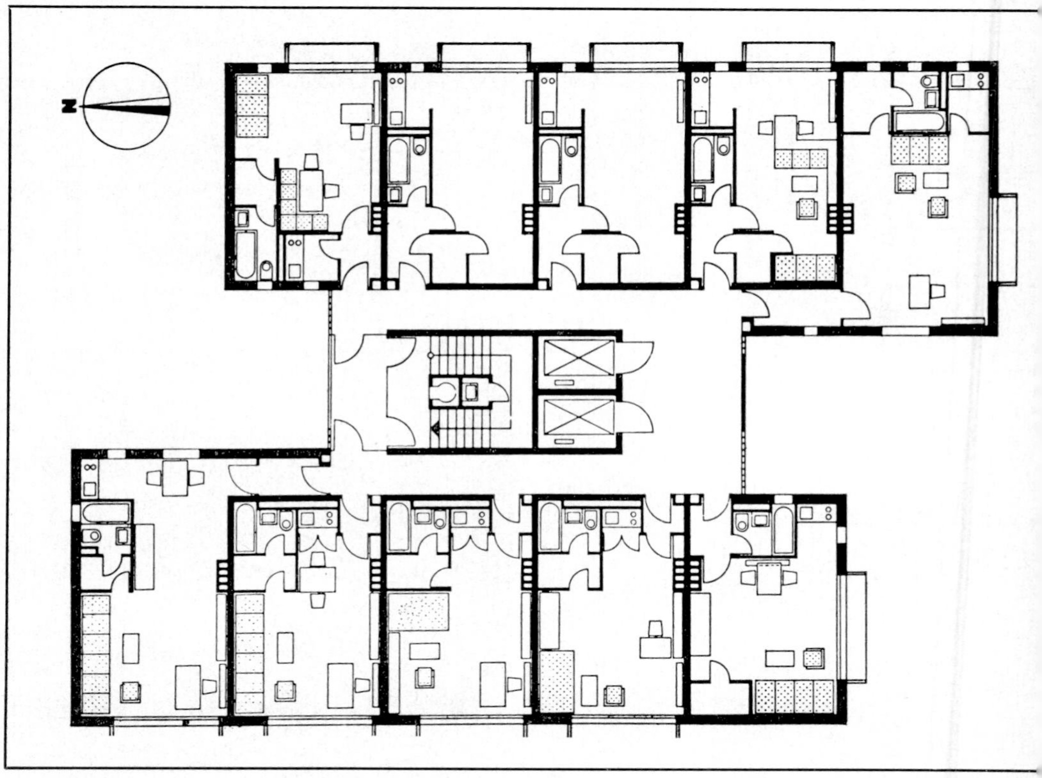

ʻroject 12, Hansa Area, Berlin

itect: Baldessari

ıfinement of the normal rectangular plan t block with its two bowed facades but :h nevertheless has not entirely succeeded eaking the monotony of a rather featureless stration pattern.

ıe system of planning is similar in principle ıat of other Interbau projects with a single case central access core and cross ven- ıd galleries. These serve eight flats to the :al floor four of which are two-bedroom and bedsitters. These latter have balconies ining the living room; the larger flats a ȷe type balcony only adjacent to the second oom, the value of which seems doubtful.

ılf the building at ground floor level contains taker's flat, and two other flats, and the other a bank. The roof is entirely taken up by an ı terrace, and the basement occupied by a .r for tenants' storage, laundry, mechanical pment, and a bank strongroom.

ınstruction is *in situ* load-bearing reinforced :rete walls.

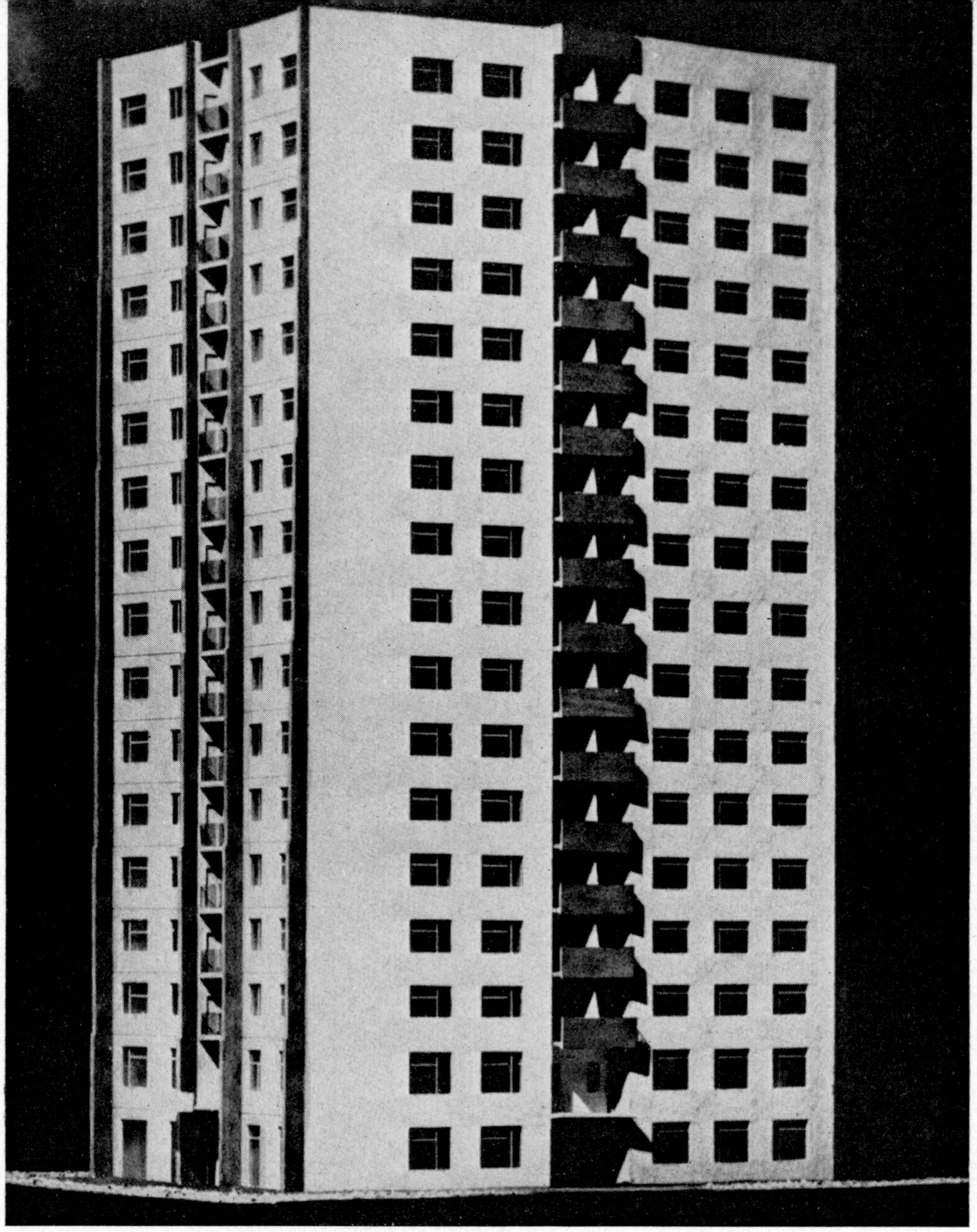

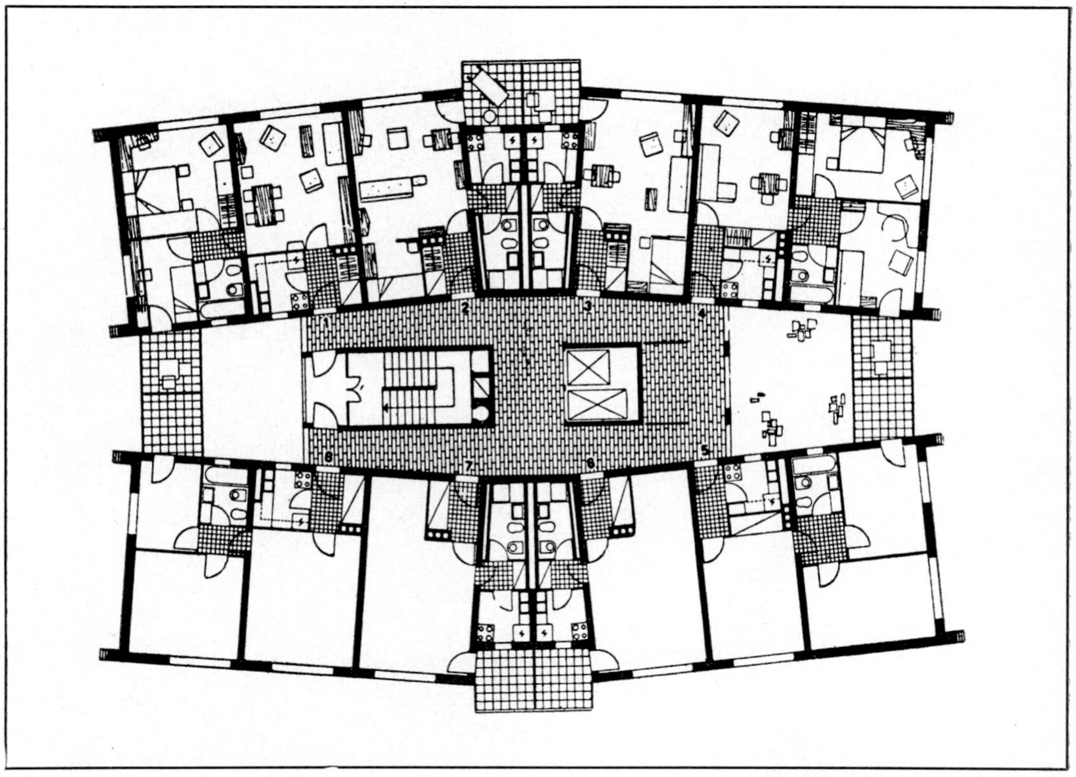

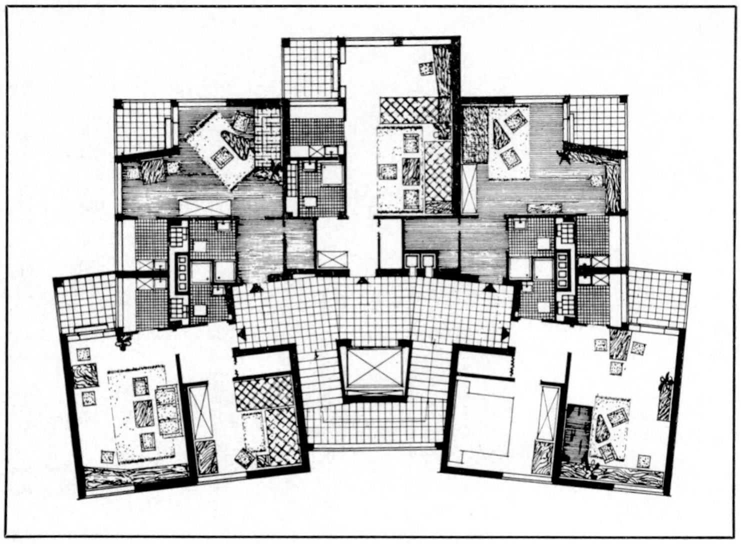

10 Sophienstrasse, Kassel

Architect: P. Bode (1952)

A block with a total of 50 flats 10 storeys in height with three bachelor flatlets and two one-bedroom flats to the typical floor, and five bachelor flatlets and two shops at ground floor level and with cafe and open terrace at roof level.

Direct access is obtained from single lift and staircase. A refuse chute is also included in the service core. Central heating equipment, tenants' storage and laundries are accommodated in the semi-basement.

Construction is reinforced concrete frame and floors with masonry infill.

Total cost 525,000 *D. Marks.*

Esslingen, Stuttgart

itect: H. Herkommer

development consisting of four identical ks 10 storeys in height each with a total of ats, as well as garage blocks and spacious scaped park areas.

slightly unorthodox building plan with its flats to the typical floor provides for a ety of aspects and depends for access on a le staircase and a single lift only. Refuse tes and central heating are provided.

ne typical arrangement at each floor level sists of three single bedroom units and one bedroom flat with bathrooms and kitchens ped round separate ducts, and some in- al cross traffic to and from these facilities.

undries and drying rooms are planned at level and there are two basement floors with ertible cellars and central heating equip- t in one of the blocks.

ternative systems of construction have been l in the different blocks, including both *tu* load-bearing concrete for both internal external walls with brick facing, and load- ing brickwork throughout.

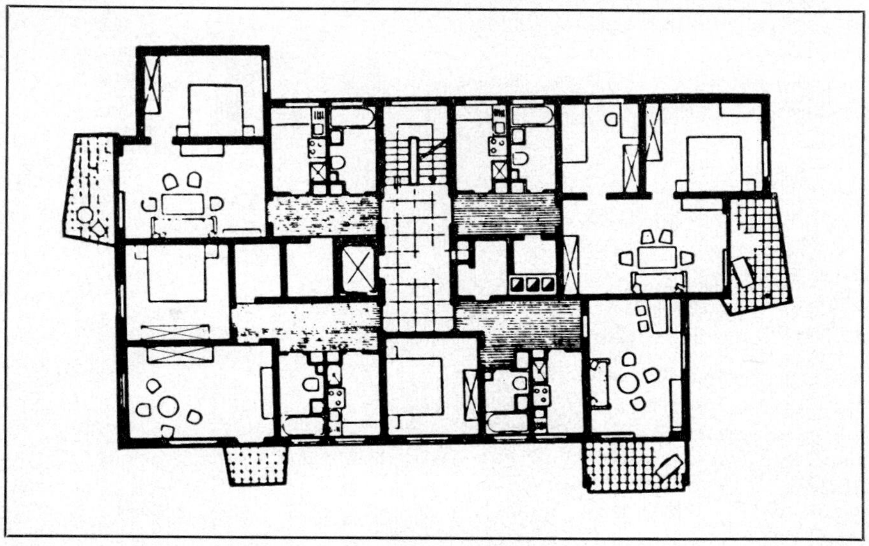

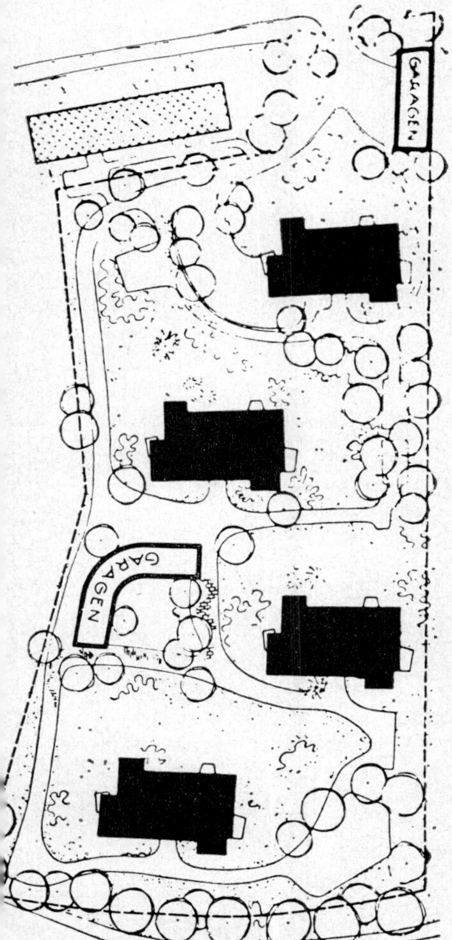

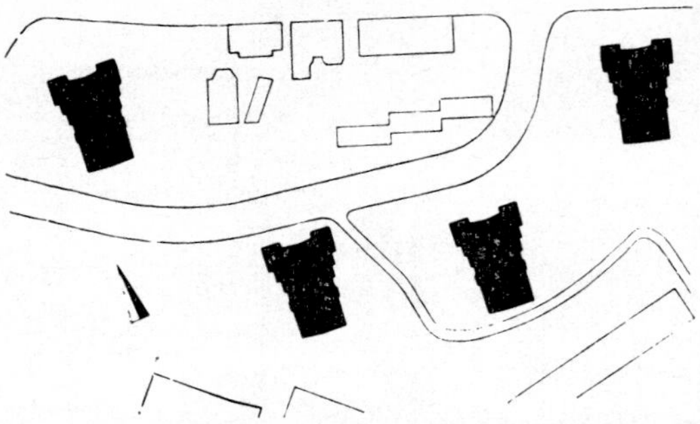

12 Mönchstrasse, Stuttgart

Architect: H. Conradi

Four identical 14 to 15-storey blocks are included in this development. A 'telescope' type of plan is used for these blocks in which each flat has a balcony with direct south aspect. These are planned in an alternating pattern so that every other flat has a second balcony in addition, either adjoining the main bedroom or the kitchen at the rear part of the block.

Two staircases and two lifts provide vertical access. Central heating flues and refuse chutes form a core around which a double corridor form of access is planned; the whole arrangement of the six flats to the typical floor not being the most economical in circulation areas.

The typical arrangement of flats consists of four one-bedroom units and two two-bedroom units with bathrooms planned away from bedrooms a scheme which involves cross traffic and some inconvenience.

Two shops are planned at ground floor level together with two bedsitter and two two-bedroom flats.

Construction is in reinforced concrete load-bearing walls with reinforced concrete floors; using the Feidner system.

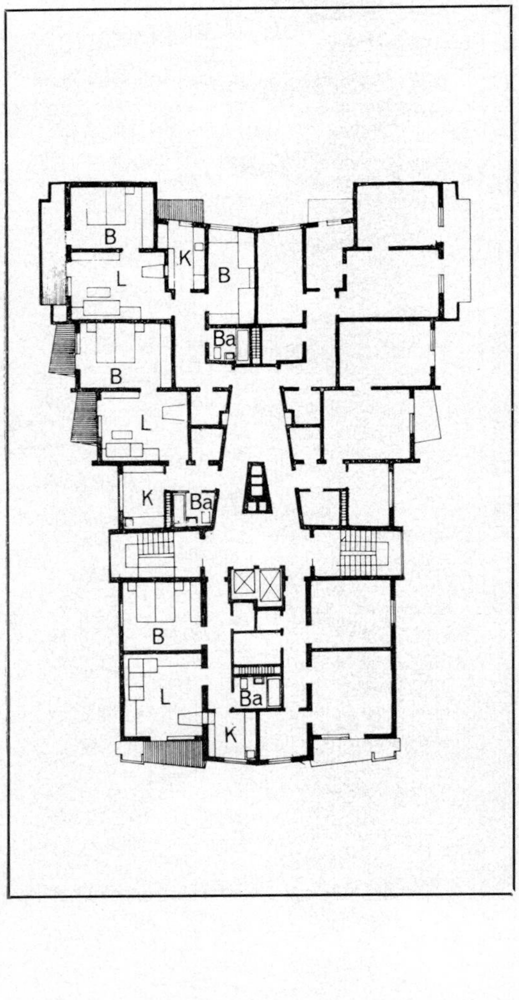

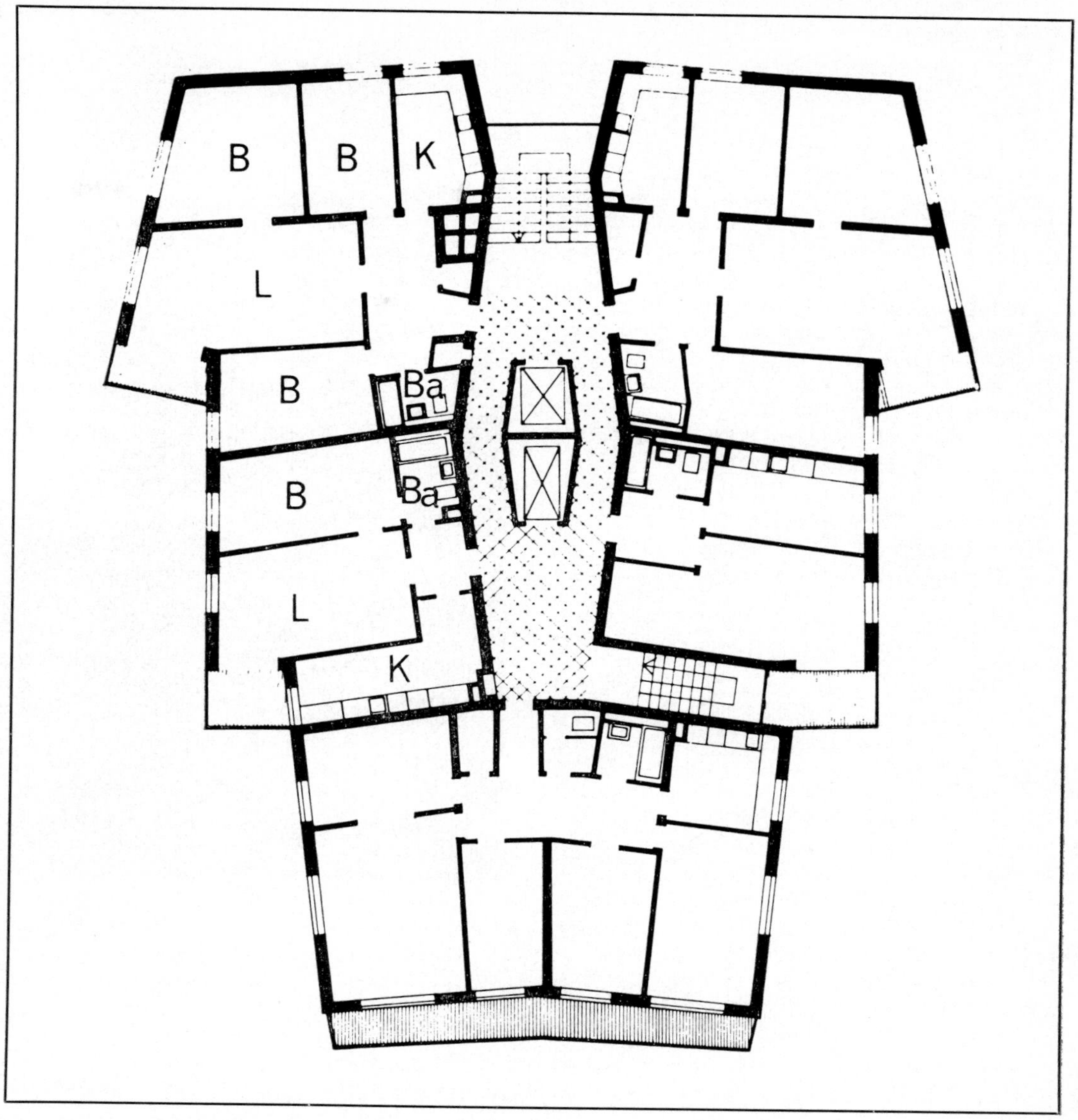

Unterer Eselsberg, Ulm

rchitect: A. Wilhelm

hree 16-storey blocks of the taper or 'telescope' an with six flats to the typical floor, two of hich have three bedrooms, three one bedroom id the remaining flat being a bedsitter. An ternative arrangement to this, however, ovides for five flats on the typical floor of hich two would be three-bedroom type, one a ur-bedroom unit, one with one bedroom and e a bedsitter. All living rooms have large ivate balconies adjoining with southern aspect. ccess is via central core with two lifts and a ngle staircase. Refuse chute and central ating are provided.

The roof, which is finished with a charac-istic cantilevered slab, contains laundries and tdoor terraces for tenants.

There are two basement floors to the blocks ed for tenants' storage, prams and bicycles.

Construction is in reinforced concrete load-aring walls exterior and interior and concrete ors. Infill walls are of sandwich construction astered on the outside and with plasterboard the inside.

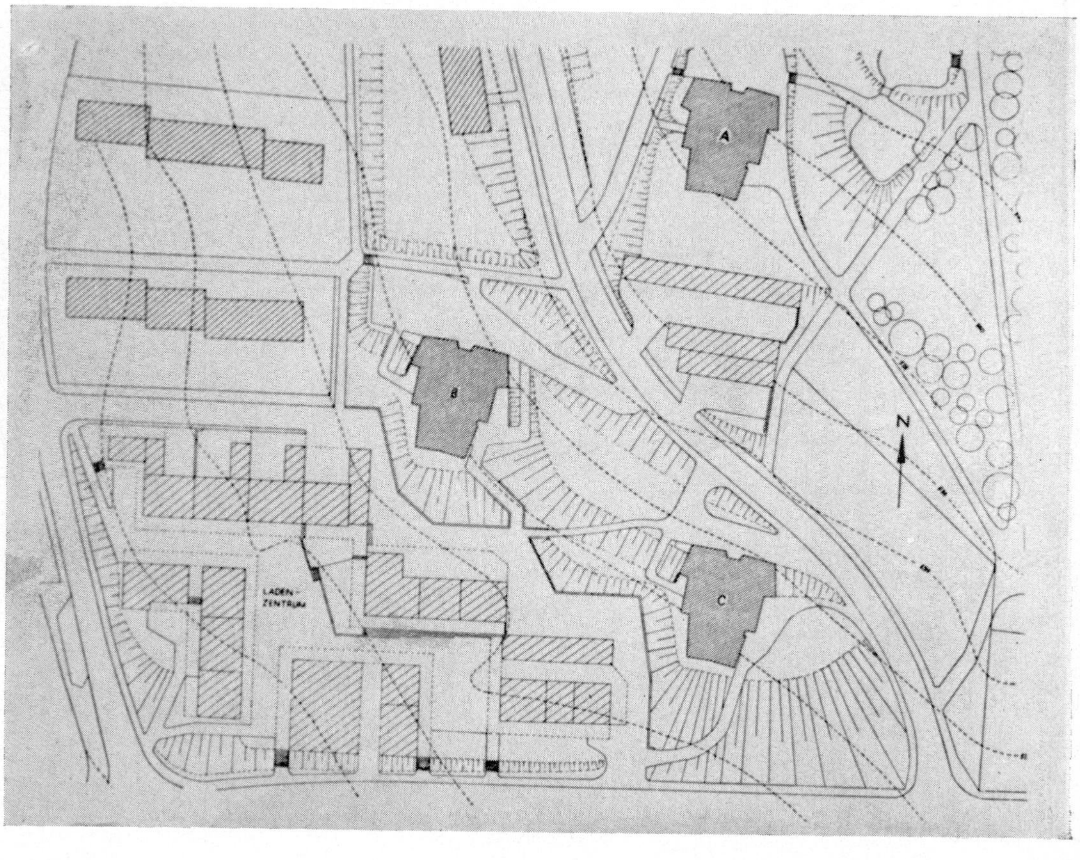

14 Bogenhausen. Munich

Architects: Ludwig and Ruf

Two similar T shape point blocks forming a part of a larger development including two-storey terraces. Each of the point blocks, 15-storeys in height has an arrangement of seven flats of varying sizes on each typical floor accessible from a single staircase and pair of lifts in the access core with the lifts stopping at alternate floor levels.

Two of these units are similar bedsitters, one flat has one bedroom, and there are in addition four two-bedroom flats.

In spite of the fact that living rooms are used as circulation areas two of these units have rather lengthy internal corridors and bathrooms located away from the bedrooms. Each flat has its own private balcony, including the single bedroom unit which occurs in the centre of the main block and which results in a rather odd asymmetrical treatment. Otherwise the *in situ* load-bearing reinforced concrete structural system is well expressed in the exterior with a pleasing alternation of brickwork infill and rendered gable end walls.

The fenestration units, although standardized, give a very satisfactory overall architectural effect with the alternating bays containing the private balconies.

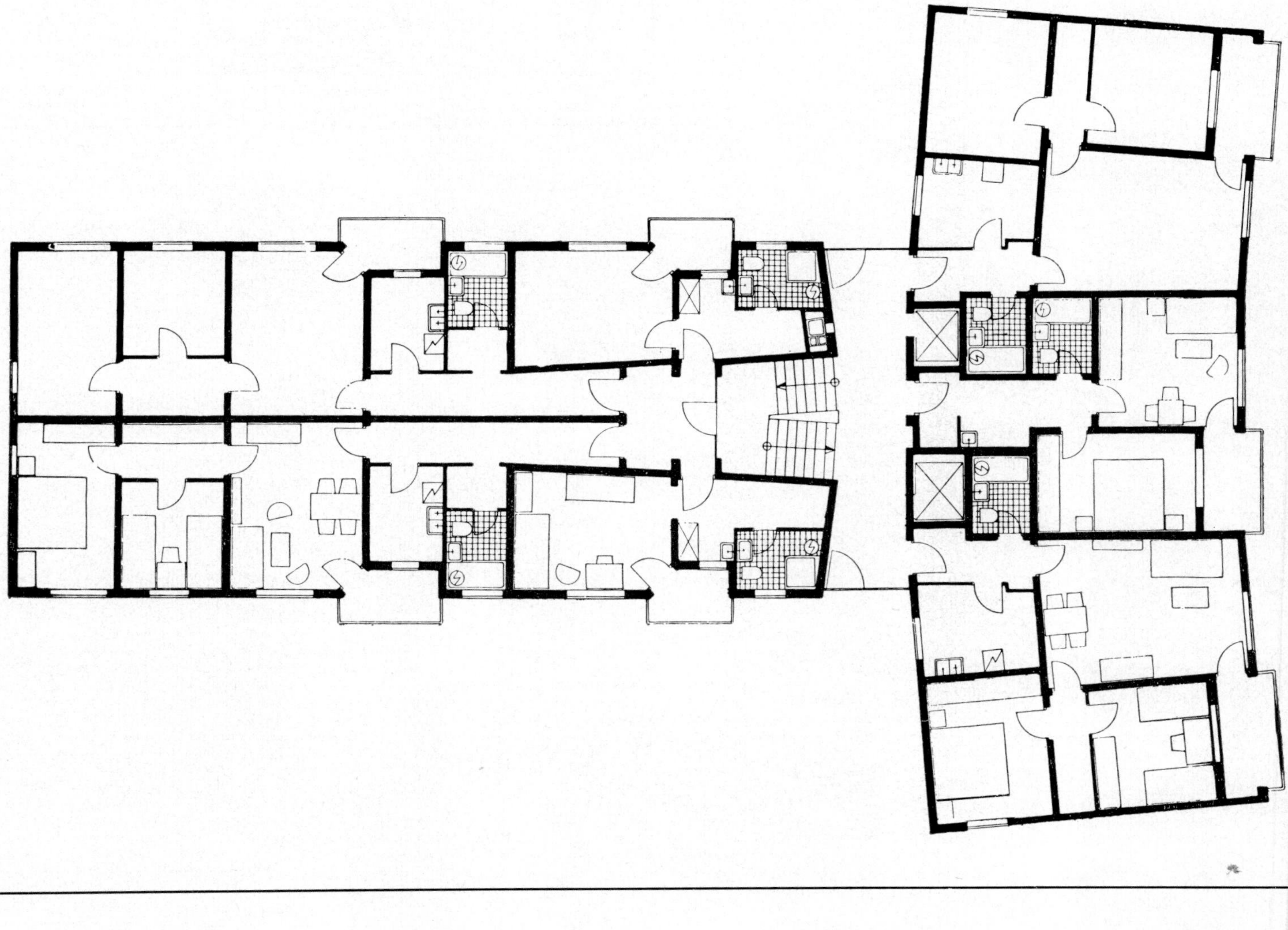

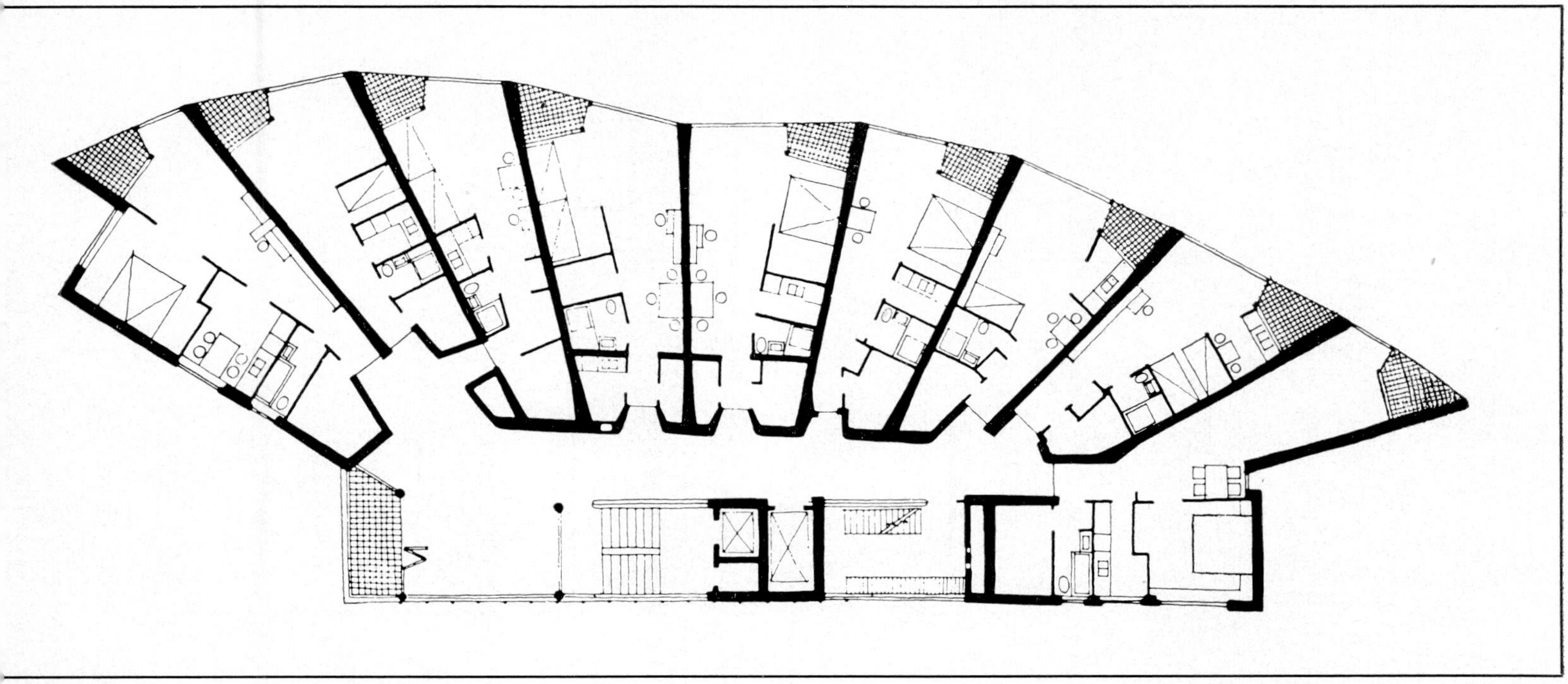

High House, Bremen

ritect: A. Aalto

oject which has with some justification been cribed as startling and which, because of its sual character, justified its inclusion here. nning, with the characteristic Aalto unduog form, is reminiscent of a fan or pack of ds.

he effort to fit in accommodation to the preceived unusual external form, even with the ll one-bedroom and bedsitter units, leads to umber of rooms of rather odd shape much likely when allowing the internal planning function to condition the external shape and n.

he intention of this building is that it should ommodate single office workers in the main, a compact unit has therefore been aimed at. lifts are provided together with one main rcase and one for emergency use only. The give access at half landing level. There is an door garden terrace at each typical floor, ring each group of nine flatlet units, each of ch has, however, a private balcony.

he Feidner constructional system has been d with thermally insulated structural concrete s, and solid concrete floors. All kitchens er than those to the end dwellings, as well as nrooms, are located internally.

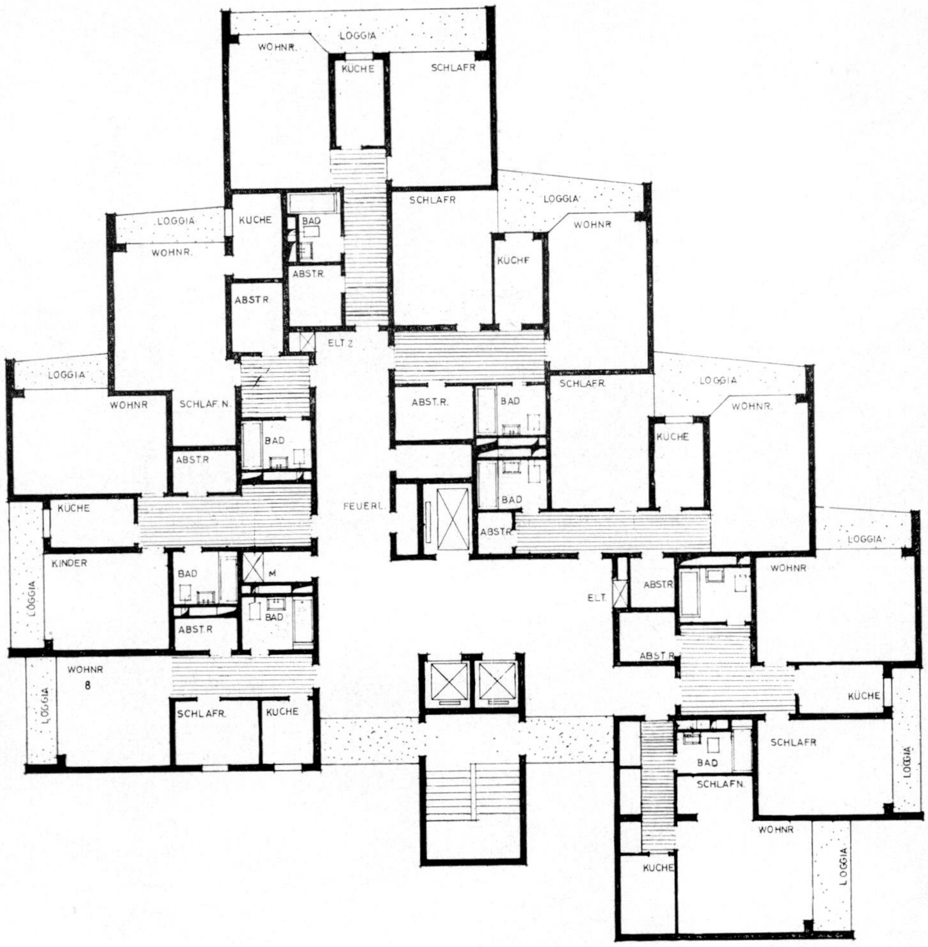

16 Edigheim, Mannheim

Architects: W. Tiedje and J. Lehmbrock

Fringe area mixed development at moderately high overall density of 180 persons per hectare but with a high density zone of multi-storey tower blocks. Part of an industrial settlement on a site of nearly 17 hectares forming the first stage of a much larger scheme.

The present stage contains 688 dwellings to accommodate some 2000 people.

The 21-storey tower block contains small units with six one-bedroom dwellings and two bed-sitters to the typical floor served by a single stair and three lifts, via lobby, corridor.

All bathrooms are mechanically ventilated but kitchens located on outside walls. Every flat has a large balcony which is a feature of the external architectural treatment.

The layout and design which also includes kindergartens, church, playgrounds, community centre, heating plant and laundries was varied at a late stage to place a larger proportion of dwellings in the lower blocks and single family houses. Unfortunately in this process some of the earlier merit in architectural quality and grouping has been lost.

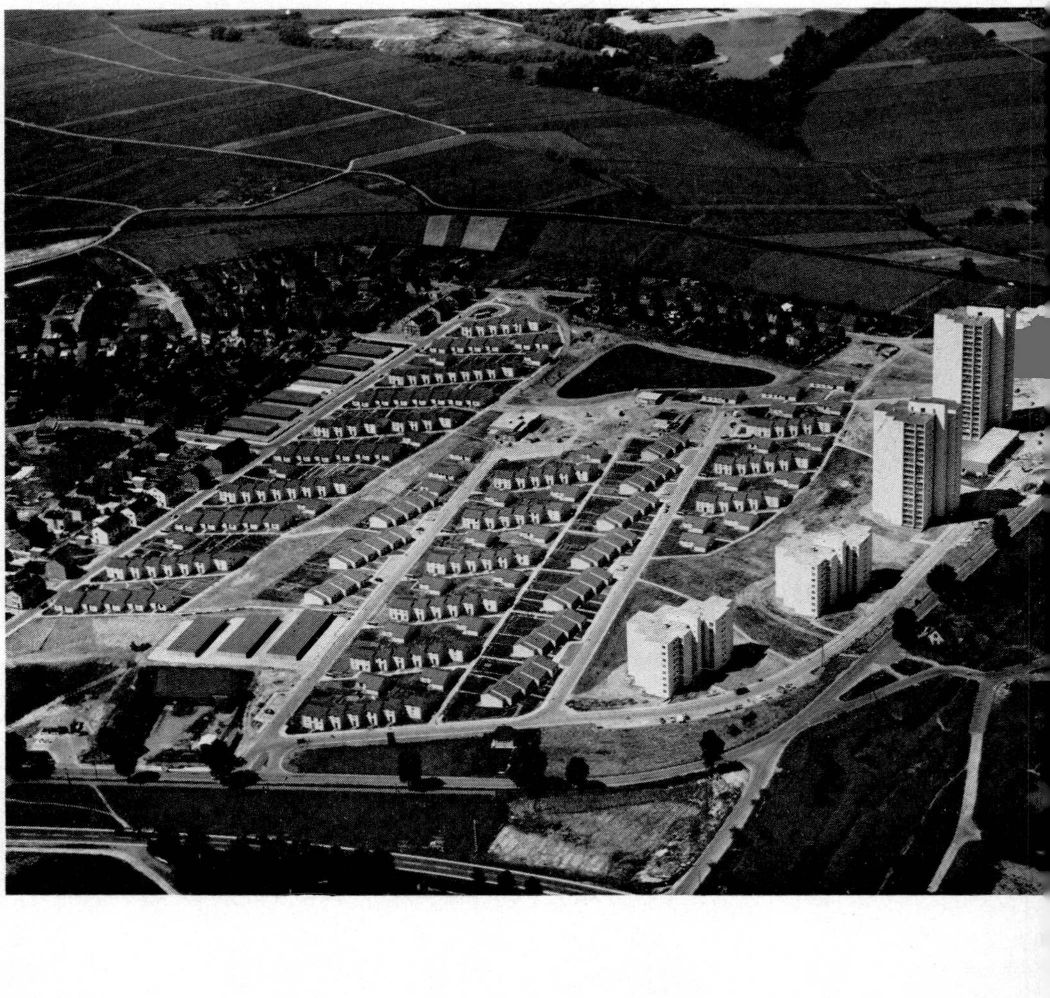

Star Flats, Nijmegen

itect: Nefkens

roject which will ultimately consist of five tical blocks of which two have been con- cted in the first stage. These blocks are oreys in height and although described as flats are unique in the very neat planning ngement of the individual flats and their ionship one with another. Privacy and dom from overlooking has clearly been an ortant consideration in the planning and has been achieved to a considerable degree. ne ground floor to the blocks contain tenants' es and eight garages per block in a ratio of less than one garage per four flats. The typical floor contains four flats accessible from a single staircase and pair of lifts, planned extremely compactly and with a minimum of circulation space. In one wing which is tapered in shape two two-bedroom flats are planned on a back-to-back basis with kitchens and bathrooms adjoining and with therefore a rationalization of the plumbing layout which makes for economy.

Similar economies have been achieved with the other two flats planned one in each wing, both of these being three-bedroom units. The individual flats also in this case have an ample sized balcony adjoining the living room, as well as a secondary balcony which in the case of the two-bedroom flats adjoins the larger bedroom, and in the case of the three-bedroom flats adjoins the kitchen.

Form of construction is reinforced concrete frame and this has been well expressed in the external architectural treatment which is extremely pleasing and well proportioned and free from any unnecessary superfluous elements.

The layout and general arrangement of the blocks has also been intelligently conceived in a way that permits only the minimum of interference of the garden and landscaped areas by access roads, and which therefore gains maximum advantage from the use of the point block type of planning.

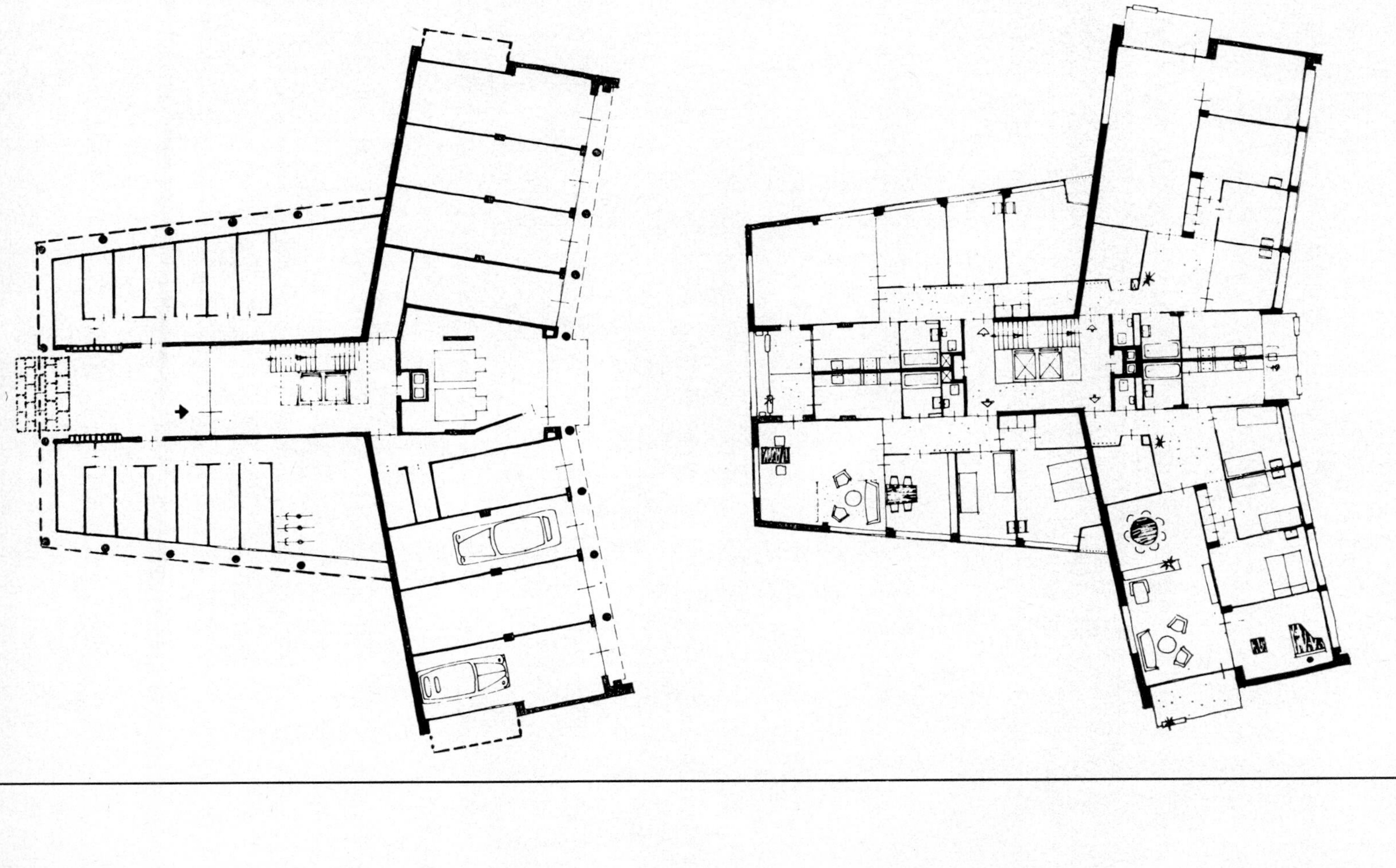

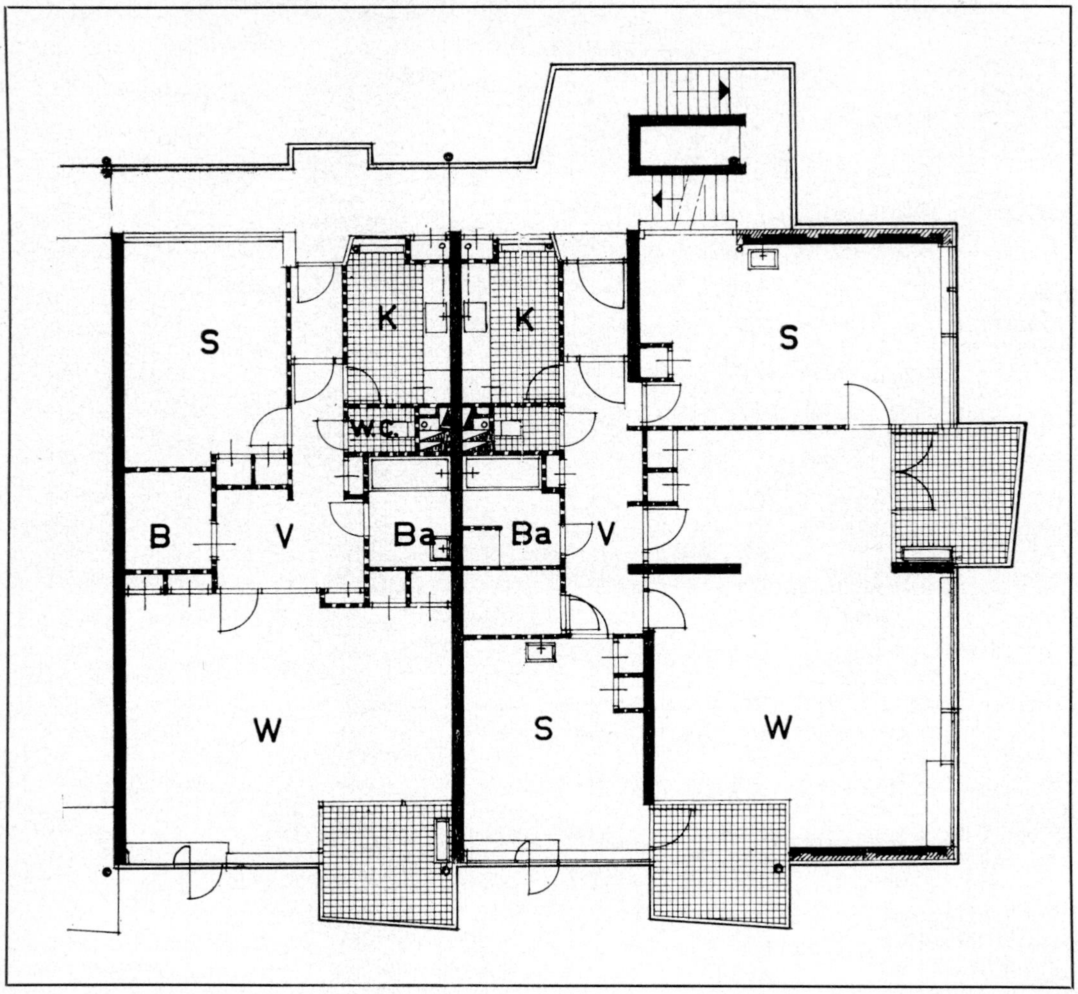

2 Lijnbaan Group, Rotterdam

Architect: Maaskant

Part of the reconstruction of the central are Rotterdam and adjoining the well kn Lijnbaan shopping centre, which has made important contribution to the philosophy of design of shopping centres, restricted enti to pedestrian access.

This group makes a noteworthy addition to whole of what is likely to become one of leading cities in Europe. It contains a tota 630 flats distributed in three 13-storey blocks, two nine-storey blocks and three th storey blocks, as well as providing 81 gara and 65 shops.

All the flats are orientated on a north-sc axis.

The high blocks are all planned on the acc gallery principle and contain a majority one-bedroom units planned between a reg system of load bearing cross walls. Two-bedr units are planned at the ends of the high bl the kitchens adjoin the access balconies, bathrooms and W.C.s planned internally ventilated and lit artificially.

The whole system of planning follows much what has become accepted Du practice during the last 15 or 20 years in m storey blocks; and evidently no undue conc is felt about the proximity of bedrooms to acc balconies with the possibilities of loss of priv and noise transmission which occur.

A private balcony has been provided for e flat and it is this element in the design gives the block most of its character as we the carefully studied proportions of the fenes tion. While the balconies are in this case la enough to contain table and chairs the jus cation for their use and their cost is still ope debate, particularly in European climatic c ditions and the possible risk that may be volved, particularly in high blocks. Even tho the majority of the flat units are small in size possibility that children may be accommoda cannot be ruled out even in this instance.

The external cladding to the building is ma in the characteristic yellow Dutch brick, attractive in appearance. This, together with planning and relationship of the various bl of different heights, forms a most impres development, and one of especial importanc view of the substantial number of dwelli being created right in the heart of the city.

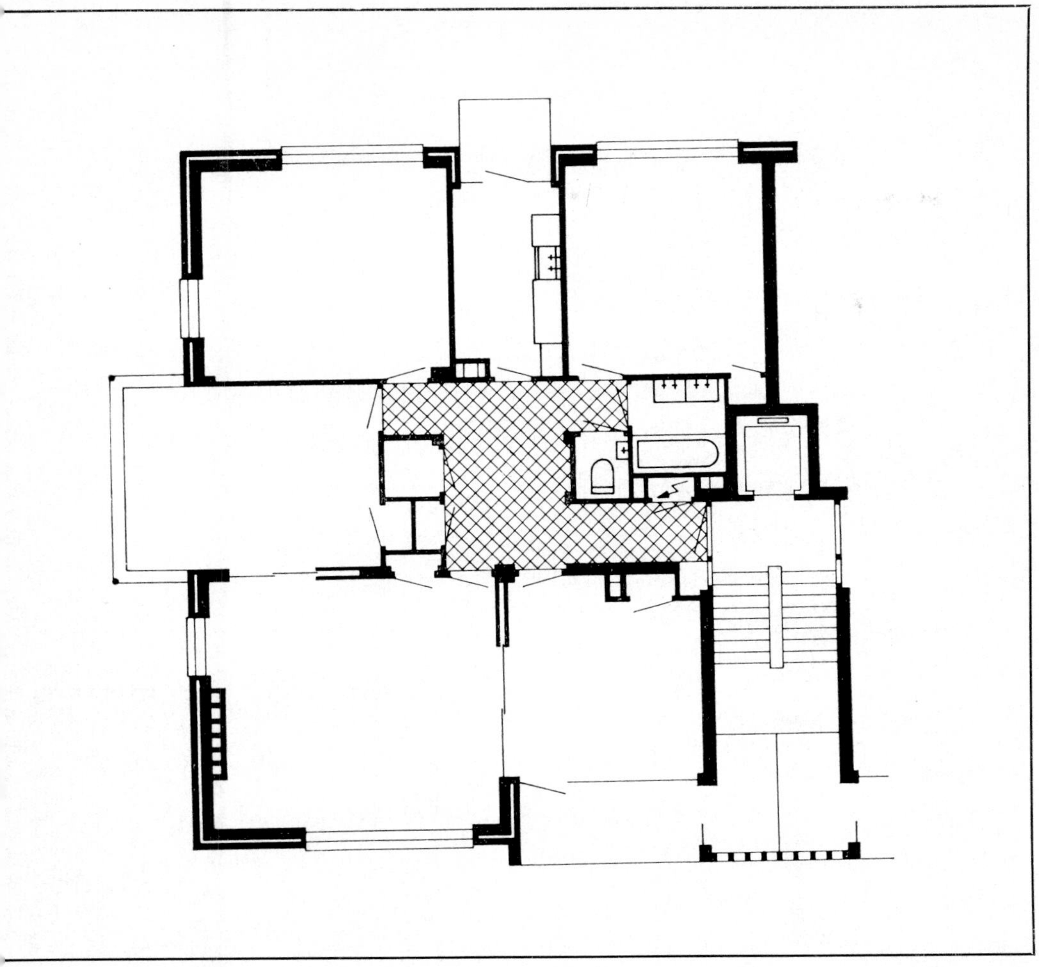

3 Duttendel, The Hague

Architect: P. Zanstra

A total of 168 flats in what is a quite characteristic Dutch layout of four similar parallel blocks; each seven storeys in height; and with normal staircase access and either six or eight flats to the typical floor. The intermediate flats in the block are similar to the end flat shown in plan but with two bedrooms instead of three.

The third balcony bedroom is a feature of the end flats; and all flats have drying areas at half landing level masked by a concrete screen wall on the outside.

Construction is in brick load-bearing wall and facing, with reinforced concrete columns at ground level forming an undercroft.

Underground garages ensure the maximum amount of garden and site amenity development.

Italy

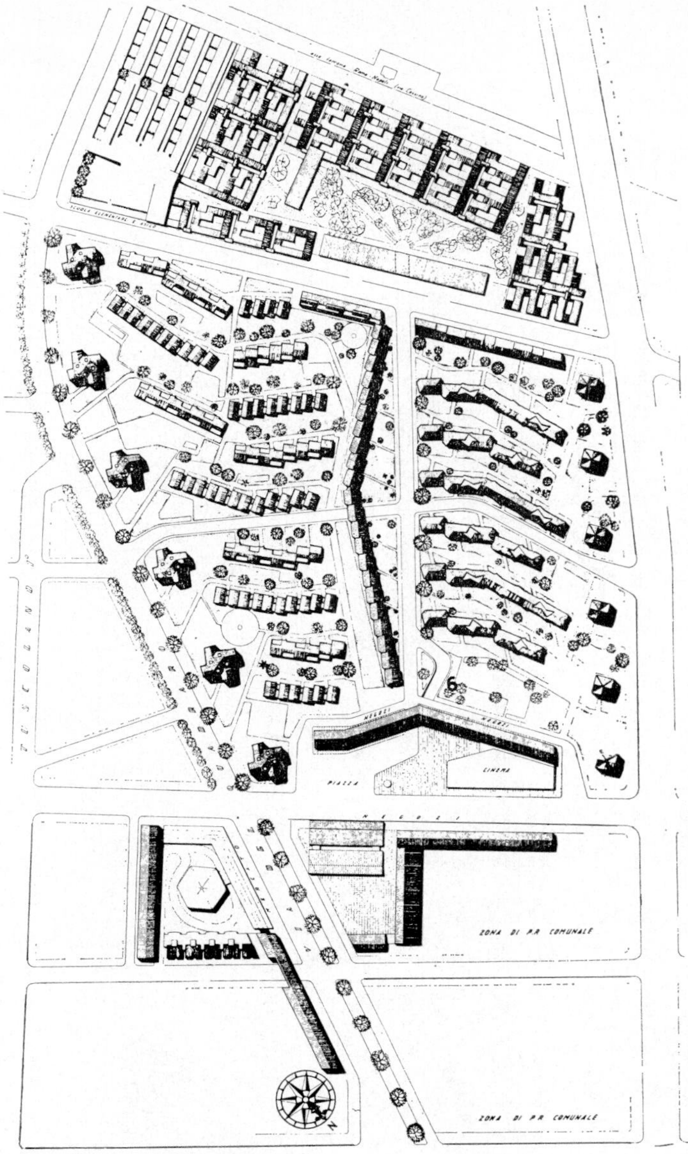

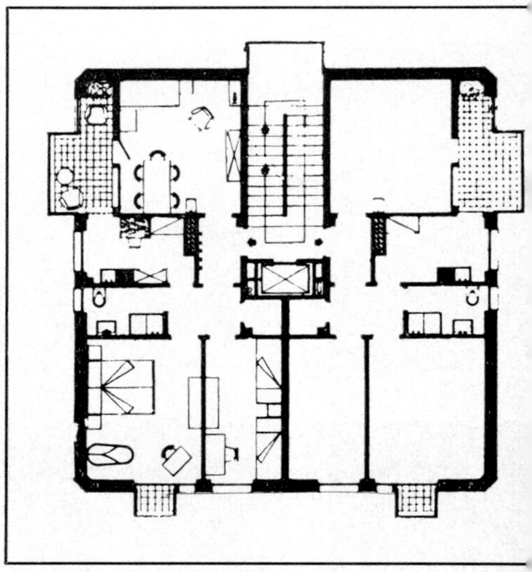

1 Tuscolano Estate, Rome

Architects: M. Renzi and S. Muratori

A 40 hectare comprehensive development a gross density of 200 persons per acre. Not c have the developers succeeded in housin population of 20,000 people in this large devel ment, but they have done so in a variety different environments in which various part the comprehensively planned scheme poss a distinct individuality without sacrificing overall cohesion.

One main centre and four subsidiary cent are the basis of the planning and these cont apart from the housing units, market, sho cinema, stores, administrative buildings, underground garage, school, ample play fields and children's play areas. Particu attention has been paid to the landscaping a this is of an unusually high quality, add very greatly to the appearance of the estate a whole, with which clean white rendering to building blocks with their attractively colou sunblinds and balcony patterns, as in so man the schemes in Italy, form such an effec counterpart.

Two distinct types of tower block dese particular comment: the first of these o swastika type plan is 10 storeys in height a

:ains four flats on the typical floor, each of :h is identical in plan and contains the usual bined living room/dining room, kitchen and bedrooms and bathroom. Separating each of wings is a loggia forming an extension to, accessible from each of the kitchens. Living ns each have their own private balconies in tion.

ie main central staircase is ingeniously nged so that access is obtained to one of the at each quarter landing level. A single lift is ided to each of the blocks.

ie tapered shape of each of the wings forms leasing refinement visually and does not imentally affect the internal planning.

ie system of construction is reinforced crete frame with masonry infill and rough finish externally.

x of these blocks are included in the scheme contain a total of 240 flats. There are also eight-storey blocks planned with only two to the floor with a simple staircase access. block is square in plan and the flats, which all identical, are of the two-bedroom type ther with living/dining area, kitchen and iroom. As in most of these schemes a base- t is also provided containing laundries and able storage space.

ow pitched roofs are used on all of these :ks, very much as was the case in some of the ier Scandinavian examples. Proportion, use aterial, the effect of scale in these buildings, r relationship with the lower blocks are ormly good, as also the fenestration pattern the use of the balcony punctuation.

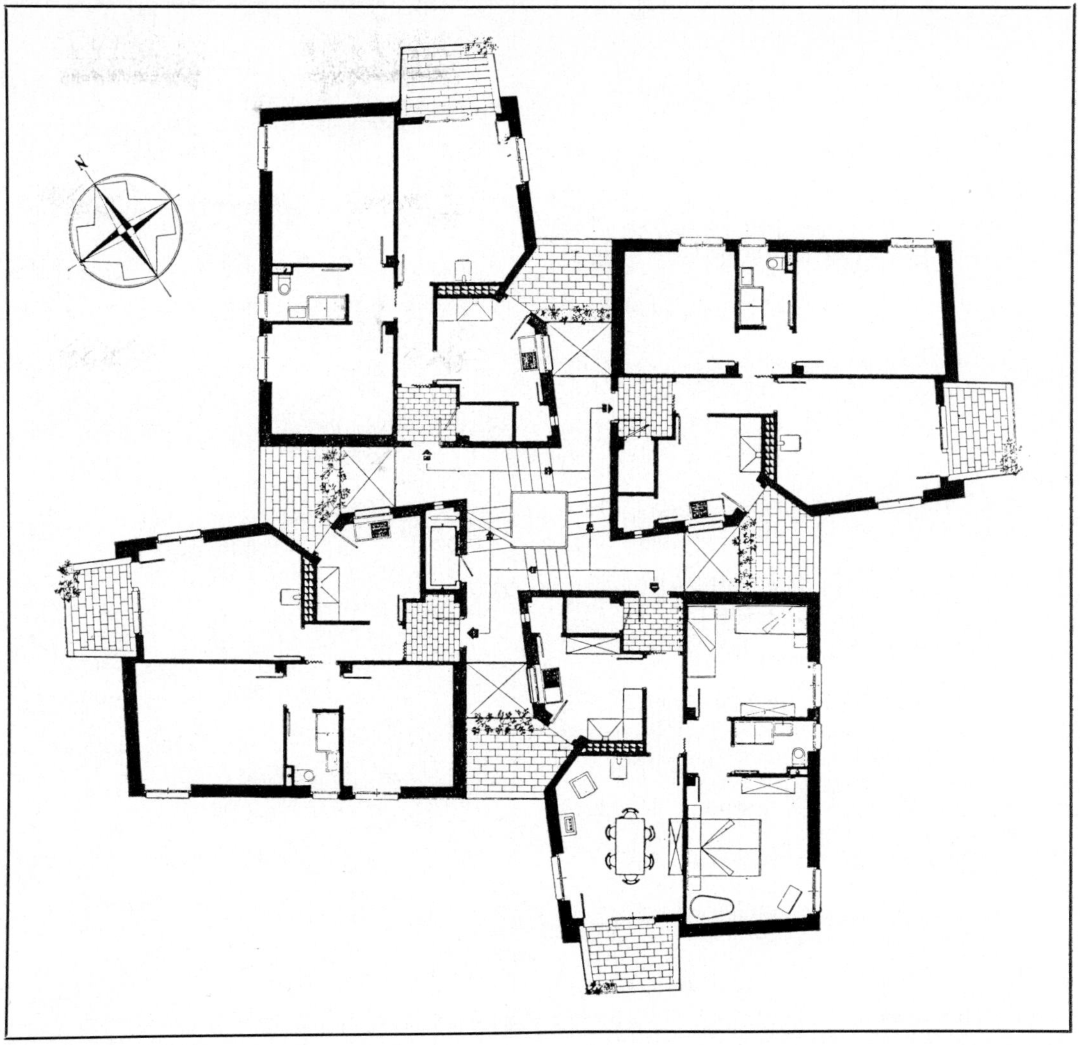

'The Skyscraper', Milan

itects: Soncini and Mattioni

building, planned as a 29-storey tower, is a :tical attempt to show how to utilize valuable in inner urban areas both for commercial residential purposes; the two uses being irded as mutually supporting. It was for a time claimed to be the tallest reinforced crete building in Europe.

ie building occupies the whole of its own area and is planned in close conjunction neighbouring buildings only approximately t in height. The height contrast is in no way armonious however, and is to some extent sted by the large landscaped square imme- ely adjoining the building.

ie lower part of the block above street level up to the 30 meter level has been planned to ude offices, a post office, cable office, bank, ist department, a safe deposit, a creche and room for children, a swimming pool and a Above the 30 meter level the accommoda- consists entirely of luxury flats with two e flats to the typical floor. The building also udes an underground garage for tenants has its own electrical generators and diesel ors for emergency electricity supply. As the ding also has its own well it can be said to stitute an almost entirely self-contained city iiniature.

Four lifts have been planned specifically to serve the offices and business accommodation and four solely to serve the flats. There are also two service lifts and two staircases which are used for emergency purposes only.

The reinforced concrete frame to the building was poured *in situ* and includes massive membrane walls alongside the lift and staircase wells for stiffening.

The flats contain a very large living/dining room area together with three bedrooms and bathrooms *en suite*, a fourth guest bedroom and accommodation for servants. The service gallery at the rear of the building can also be used in cases of emergency as a secondary means of escape, communicating as it does with service lifts and staircases.

A well integrated architectural composition combining the different uses effectively within a single treatment.

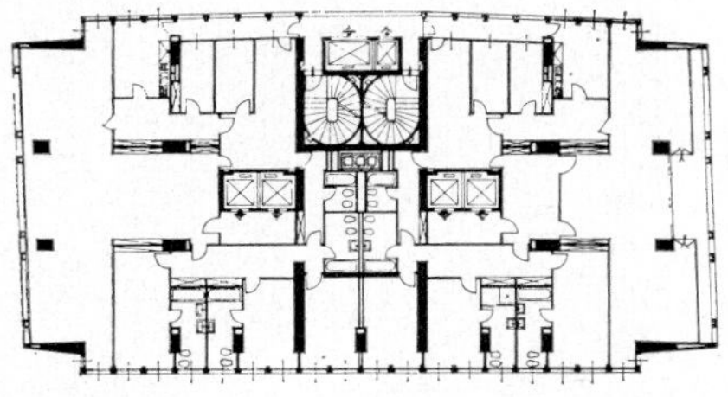

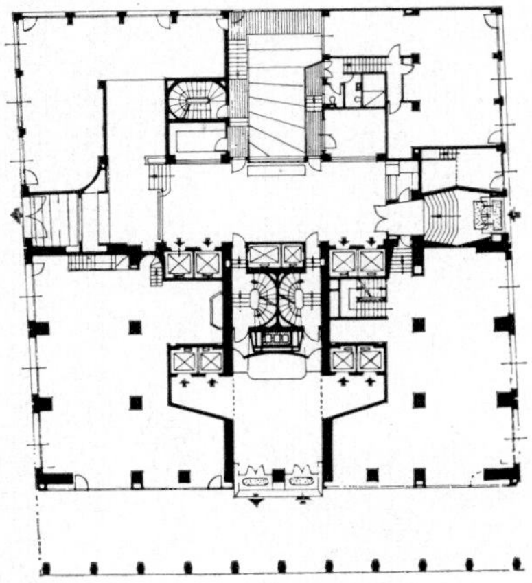

Norway

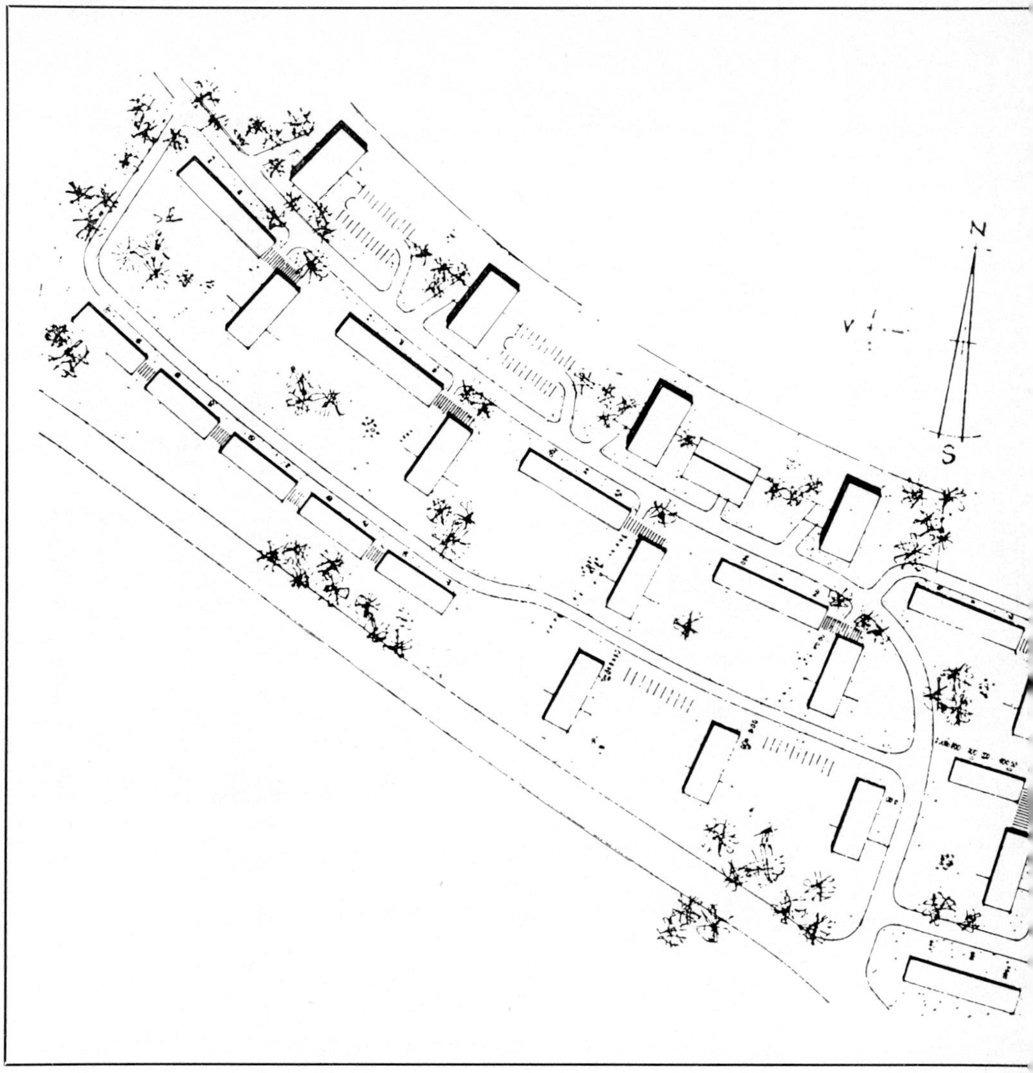

1 Lillo Terrasse, Oslo

Architects: Christiansen and Roslend (1960)

An extensive development on the fringe of and overlooking the city of Oslo containing in all 600 flats of which 264 are in the four 11-storey short slab blocks, and the remainder in three-storey slab blocks.

The ground floor to the 11-storey blocks contain communal services, and the typical floors four two-bedroom flats and two one-bedroom flats. The form of access is by means of a central corridor which is served by staircases at either end and a single lift.

The individual flats are extremely pleasantly planned on a generous basis without in any way being wasteful. Dining rooms are easily served from kitchens but can be readily cut off from the living area should this be desired. Bathrooms and kitchens in each case form a compact core with a common plumbing stack. The main bedroom is spacious enough to provide an area

ıitable for a dressing room adjoining but the ·lationship of this bedroom to the bathroom is ıch that traffic must pass either through the ning room and living room or, alternatively, rough the kitchen to reach it, neither of which ems a particularly good arrangement.

Balconies are provided to each of the living oms but these are hardly large enough for tting out on: they do however help to punctuate ıd break up what could otherwise be a rather onotonous elevational treatment.

Much more attractive for their architectural ıality are the three-storey blocks with a clear rizontal emphasis and windows effectively ouped together with an excellent feeling of ale and proportion. These flats are all of the o-bedroom type together with living room ıd dining area and a bathroom/kitchen core at is similar to that in the 11-storey block. They e arranged four flats to the floor on the typical or, accessible from two staircases in an thodox manner.

The form of construction is reinforced concrete ad-bearing walls together with concrete lumns and floors.

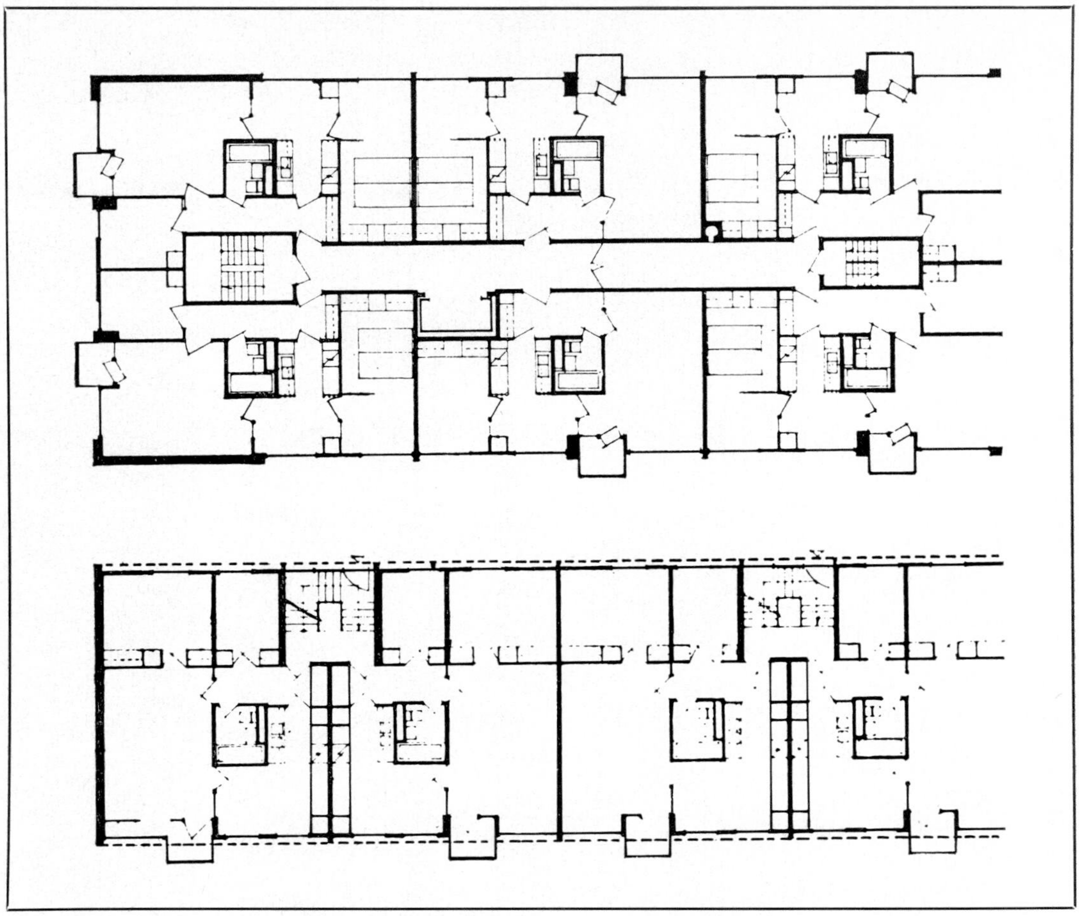

Hoff Terrasse, Oslo

chitects: Torp and Torp

is interesting scheme includes one 14-storey wer block, a number of four-storey slab ocks, a children's farm, and a shopping centre. ne of the main reasons underlying the use of 14-storey block was that it enabled the veloper to restrict the height of the remaining ocks to four storeys which in Norway are garded as walk-up flats, and which therefore minated the need for lifts.

The planning of the 14-storey block follows a newhat unusual pattern inasmuch as the ts are arranged in a stepped pattern in order give each tenant a view over Oslo Fjord and a are of the southern aspect, and insolation.

The block contains a total of 76 flats with the ntral heating and other communal services on lowest floor. A typical floor contains six units, r of which are one-bedroom and two two-droom at each floor level.

Access is by a short central corridor, duplicate ircases and lifts.

The planning in many respects follows ropean and particularly Scandinavian trends d has produced an interesting result in regard the tower block particularly, both functionally d visually. The great defect, however, seems be the inconvenient location of bathrooms in relation to bedrooms, due no doubt to too much emphasis being placed on linking these bathrooms with the kitchens—a policy which has less advantages in a multi-storey block such as this than would be the case in lower buildings, and certainly not to be recommended if it introduces other planning defects.

A concession has been made to tradition in the design of the roof which is of a pitched type, a feature to be seen also in some of the earliest Swedish point blocks. In this particular instance this may have been justified to some extent in view of the close proximity to the other lower blocks which have pitched roofs.

A happier arrangement of the whole would, however, appear to be that of designing all the blocks with flat roofs as certainly being much more appropriate in the multi-storey block which is the main feature of this scheme.

The children's farm deserves particular comment and this is a feature also found in a number of other German and Scandinavian schemes. It is a means of providing children with organized recreational areas where they can use their imagination and where they can play during inclement weather under cover. The importance of this factor in the design of family flats in high density areas cannot be overstated and the solution of it in this particular development is an infinitely better one, it would appear, than that of merely providing hard play areas with formalized types of equipment which are often dangerous to children without the necessary supervision being available.

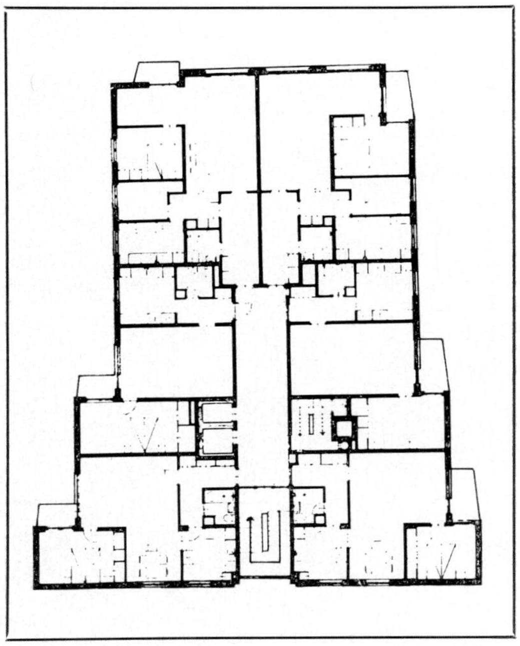

. Manglerud, Oslo

rchitect: J. Engh

ɔur similar 13-storey tower blocks which are the ain elements of a central group, which together ith a small shopping centre adjoin the subur- an Station of Manglerud. The whole develop- ent also includes a number of four-storey rrace blocks. The tower blocks have six flats to e typical floor served by two lifts, and a main ıd a secondary staircase. Four of the flats ɔntain one bedroom and two are bedsitters. aundries and tenants' storage are provided at ound level.

Construction is in reinforced concrete partly *situ* and part precast.

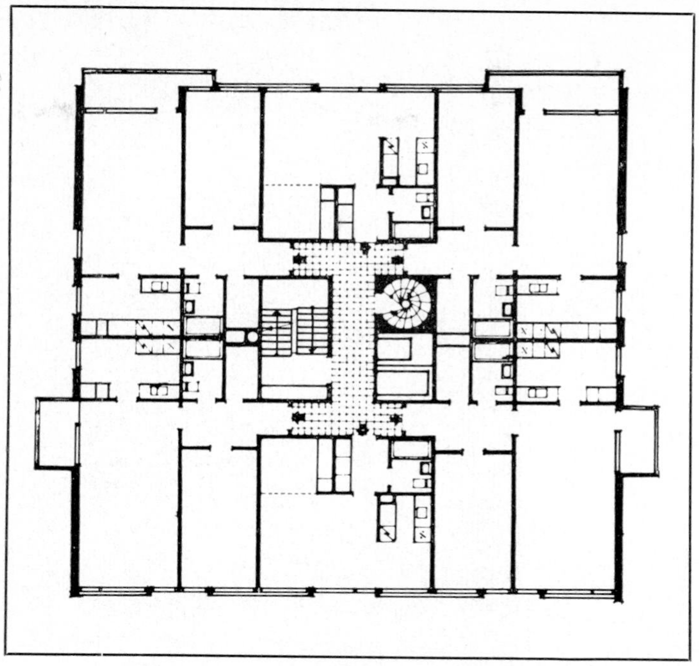

South Africa

1 Grootdrakenstein, Johannesburg

Architects—Le Roith & Partners

An urban development on an extremely re-tricted site, providing accommodation entirely in the form of small flatlets of which there are ten on the typical floor served on the access balcony principle by two staircases and two lifts. There is a total of 122 flats in the scheme and the block, 13 storeys high, covers approximately 60 per cent of the site area with most of the flats having north and west aspect.

Lock-up garages and servants' quarters are provided at ground floor level, and there is a roof garden and storage space in the upper part of the building. Central heating and hot water are provided.

Reinforced concrete frame construction is used with cavity brick infill externally, and hollow block partitions internally with hollow block concrete floors. The structure is expressed externally and painted on rendering; with rendering to the parapet walls.

2 **Von Brandis Heights, Johannesburg**

Architects—Le Roith & Partners

A single 13 storey block planned in a pattern to accommodate 20 one-bedroom fl and 112 bedsitters, accessible from the sin free-standing staircase and lift tower.

Refuse chutes are provided as well as t large box rooms for storage at ground fl level, a restaurant and garages, but no garc work as such. Central heating is also provide

Construction is reinforced concrete fra with 9in hollow block floors and walls betwe the flats, and brick infill walls. Balcony fro are in asbestos cement panel.

BRANDIS
LOUREN

South America

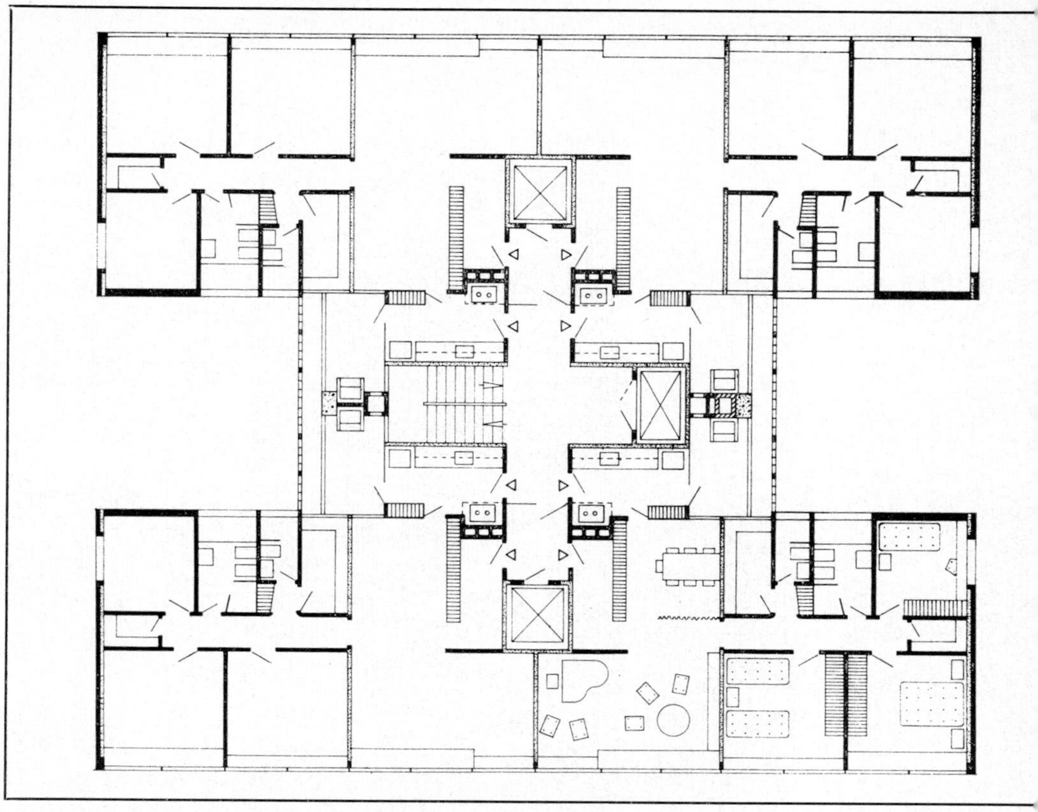

1 Seguradora Brasileira Building, Sao Paulo, Brazil

Architects: Rino Levi and R. C. Cezar

A single tower block of H plan of special interest because of the fenestration pattern, influenced to a very great extent by the use of shutters to control solar radiation. This 18-storey block has 14 storeys of flats with ground floor raised on pilotis with shops as well as entrance hall and communal facilities and contains four flats on a typical floor accessible from a single staircase and three lifts: obviously not intended as a low cost scheme. A basement garage is provided.

The flats are all identical, being large three bedroom units with both kitchens and bathrooms naturally lit and ventilated. Each flat has a separate service entrance and a kitchen access via a private balcony to refuse chutes. Day and night zoning works well. Circulation space is reduced to an absolute minimum, although as in Continental schemes the living room is used as part of the circulation medium. Sun shading has been given special attention in the form of balconies.

The system of construction is reinforced concrete with load bearing membrane walls brought down on to the concrete pilotis at ground floor level.

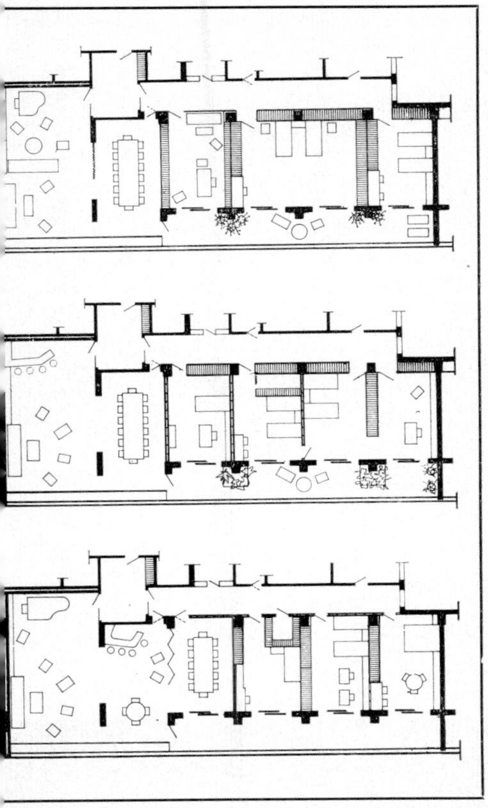

'Prudencia' Building, Sao Paulo

:hitects: Rino Levi and R. C. Cezar

is is frankly a luxury building but nevertheless interest. It is built on an extremely confined e in the best part of the City and almost actly one acre in extent. There are nine floors ntaining flats with four flats to each typical or, each 4300 square feet in extent. In addition ere are two penthouses on the top floor of 50 square feet each, a total of 38 dwellings.

Each bank of flats has a separate lift to serve as well as sharing a service lift with one joining flat only. A single staircase serves ch pair of flats to each floor.

With the frame construction which has been ed a number of possible permutations in ernal room subdivision is possible and some these are shown. The block occupies approxi-ately 50 per cent of the total site area and is ilt very close to the street frontage but with an ractive garden forecourt. The ground floor vel is also raised above street level and this ows for a very simple arrangement of an derground garage for 40 cars without deep cavation. At the same time easy ramped trances do not in any way inconvenience nant access to the building.

The ground floor which is built up on pilotis entirely open except for the lift and staircase ells, the remainder of the site being suitably ndscaped. In keeping with the luxury standards this building complete air-conditioning is ovided as well as high performance sound sulation.

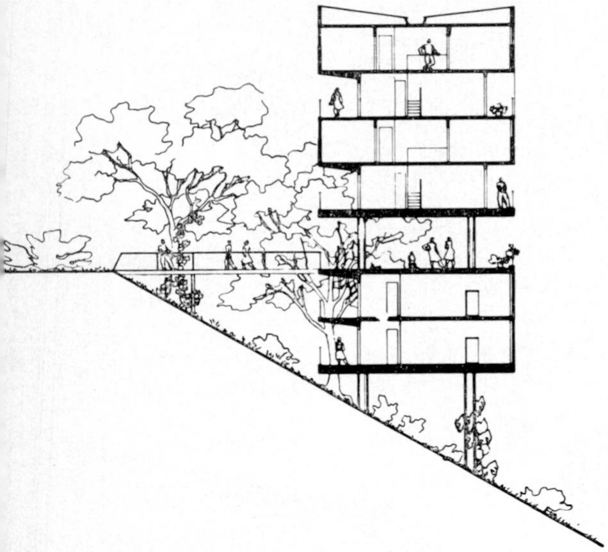

3 Pedregulho Development, Rio de Janeiro

Architect: A. Reidy

This unusual development consists primarily of one single serpentine block 850 ft in length following the winding contours of the hillside on which it is constructed, although there are a number of other ancillary buildings forming a part of the development including, a children's primary school, gymnasium, swimming pool, playing areas, health centre, creche, market, laundry and nursery schools.

The main block is seven storeys in height and is built up on concrete pillars free of the sloping ground on which its stands. The two lowest floors contain entirely one-room apartments; the third floor is to a substantial extent left open to form a covered playground for children; also to accommodate administrative offices, social services, nursery and kindergarten, while the upper four floors provide for two layers of duplex apartments all of which contain two bedrooms.

No lifts are provided in the scheme, access being entirely by means of four main stairca
located at nodal points. Each staircase provi
access to approximately 16 of the one-ro
apartments at each floor level, or eight of
duplex apartments. In so far as the one-ro
apartments are concerned the access balc
principle can be accepted as an economical
practical solution. With the duplex apartme
the upper level or access gallery unfortuna
passes over the top of bedrooms to the lo
level duplex flats, which is not an enti
desirable arrangement. The galleries in
scheme are enclosed which reduces cr
ventilation and is not always acceptable un
building regulations.

Architecturally this is an extremely interes
scheme and one which well expresses the r
forced concrete construction which is us
Whether it is socially desirable to house a c
plete community of this magnitude as it w
under one roof may be somewhat doubtful.

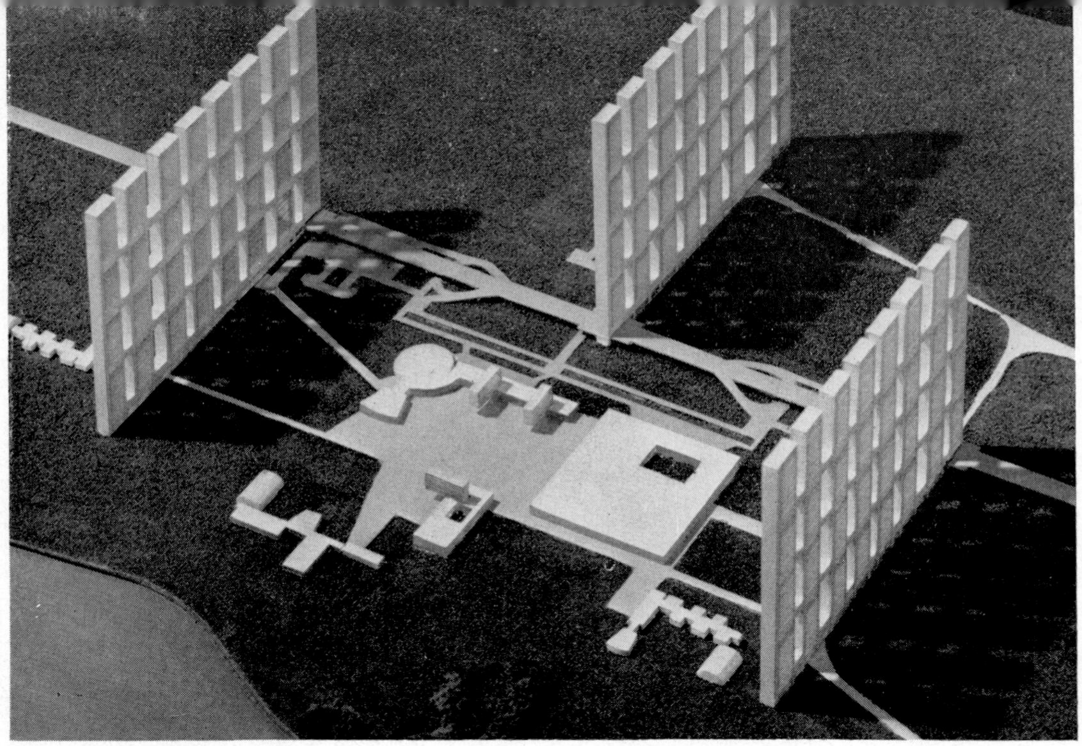

3rasilia Superblock

ıitects: Rino Levi, R. C. Cezar and L. R. Franco

trated are three blocks forming a district :re and a detail of one of these blocks which ı a part of a 'grand design' for a section of)0 inhabitants in Brasilia, of a most imagina- type. These 70-storey blocks each to accom- ate 16,000 people in four linked units are)ably scarcely within the present bounds of :ticability. Nevertheless this comprehen- y worked out town planning project with its -contained units with shops, kindergartens, th centres and recreation areas as well as munal facilities on a district and town basis)hasizes the compromises which all too often t the possibilities of many urban renewal emes.

5 Antonio Ceppas Building, Rio de Janeiro

A single block constructed on a somewhat restricted city site but with an intelligent use of the ground area by the expedient of raising the building on concrete pilotis: a system particularly favoured in Brazil by local building regulations. Apart from landscaping work at ground level a single flat only occupies a part of the undercroft, together with entrance hall staircase and lift lobbies.

The six upper floors contain four flats each accessible from the single staircase and the twin lifts, and in spite of the limitations of the site all the main habitable rooms have excellent views.

The slopes to the site have been utilized to provide underground car parking space.

The system of construction is reinforced concrete and a great deal of use has been made in the external architectural treatment of louvres and lattice grilles, the concrete being faced externally very largely with mosaic. In the Spanish tradition use is made in the planning of two internal light courts or areas as a means of providing natural light and ventilation to the service areas of the flats.

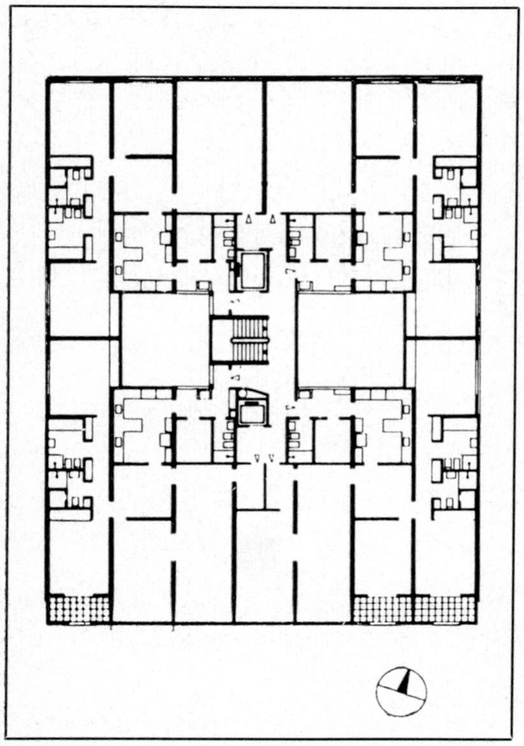

Cerro Grande, Caracas

hitect: G. Bermudez

nost distinctive scheme consisting of one e block of the Unité type, built on a pre-tous slope which accounts for the fact that only is the lowest floor at ground level raised concrete pilotis, but the fourth floor is also very ely open and treated in the same manner ce at this level bridges are taken across to upper part of the sloping ground behind the ding in order to provide secondary access.

f the 15 storeys 13 are occupied by flats, lex and simplex flats being at alternating els with the access level coinciding with the er level of the duplex flats in each case. Access is by means of two detached elevator and staircase towers linked by bridges to access galleries.

The flat arrangement provides extremely workable individual units together with interesting variations in the overall pattern which do much to break down the rather massive and monumental scale of the block as a whole and bring it back more to the domestic scale.

The building is rather attractively severe in its simplicity, extremely well proportioned and with just the relief needed at roof level, in the form of a concrete canopy with its series of linked barrels enclosing tank and lift machine rooms as as well as a youth club.

There is a total of 156 flats in the block as a whole, including 96 of the duplex type with three bedrooms, combined living room/dining room, and kitchen and bathroom; and 60 of the simplex type with four bedrooms, living room/dining room, kitchen and bathroom.

The system of construction is in reinforced concrete frame with reinforced concrete floors. To complete the scheme a supermarket adjoins on the same site and with its shell roof is an interesting foil to the architectural treatment of the flat block.

7 Presidente Juarez Centre, Mexico City

Architect: M. Pani (1952)

This large development on a 62-acre site provides housing accommodation for 3000 people, a school and children's garden, a medical centre, shops, and also parking space for 100 cars. The blocks of flats are all of the slab type of four, eight, and eleven storeys in height, with accommodation varying from one room up to family flats all with bathrooms and kitchens and served by lifts. The blocks have been carefully planned on the site to avoid overshadowing one another and to give individual flats both an east and west aspect.

Particular attention has been paid to landscaping, especially in the children's areas. Included in the scheme is a creche for 450 children.

The eight-storey blocks are planned on the normal access gallery principles with access, however, at alternate floor levels serving three banks of duplex flats and with the typical floor containing 12 units of either the three-bedroom or the four-bedroom type. Each block has twin staircases and twin lifts, with the flats adjoining the staircase lift tower having private balconies at both dining room and bedroom level.

The 11-storey blocks are planned on the access gallery principle and contain a majority of one-bedroom units, with two free standing staircase towers to each block with staircases enclosed only by an open metal balustrade and pairs of lifts adjoining which serve alternate floor levels.

The scheme also contains a number of blocks with walk-up flats and these are planned on the staircase access principle with either four flats to each landing level in a back-to-back arrangement with an equal number of either one-bedroom or two-bedroom units, or, alternatively, with two flats to each landing level, each unit being of the two-bedroom variety, and in these cases the bedroom elevation being treated with somewhat unusual saw-tooth arrangement with rather restricted window areas.

The system of construction is in reinforced concrete frame and the external treatment is mainly in brick infill but extensive use is made of coloured concrete panels, and in a number of cases mosaic panels with Mexican motifs.

This scheme has been erected primarily for government employees and occupies an excellent site near to the centre of the city adjoining a large tree-shaded park.

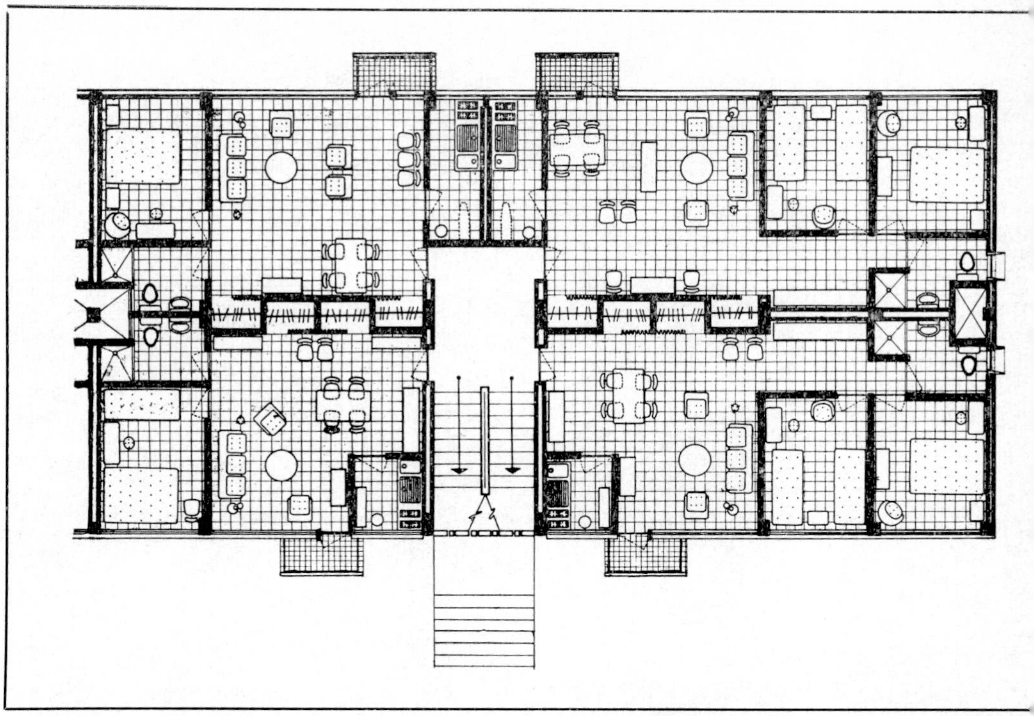

Araoz and Salguero Building, Buenos Aires

hitects: A. and L. Morea

ifficult urban site planned to take best advan-e of local building regulations; and subse-ntly reduced from the 25 floors intended to loors.

f these, 12 floors have two flats per floor each n three bedrooms. There is a basement age connected by ramps, expressed on the erior, at three levels. Tenants storage is also vided for in the basement.

ertical access is by one of three lifts or stair-e, and the remainder of the planning is on somewhat luxurious basis.

tructure is in reinforced concrete, on a dular grid.

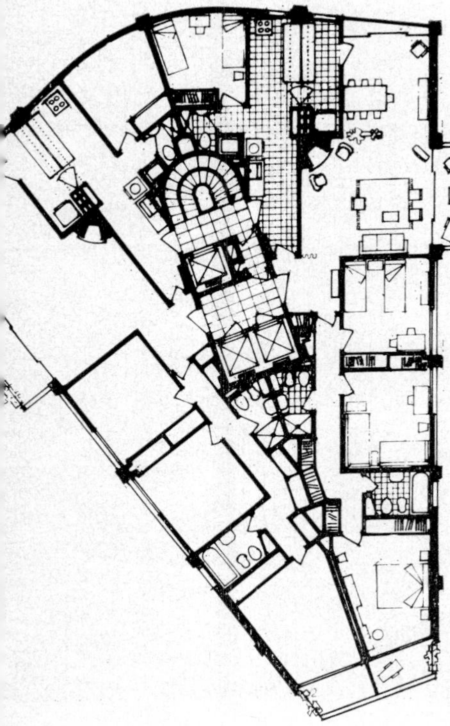

Sweden

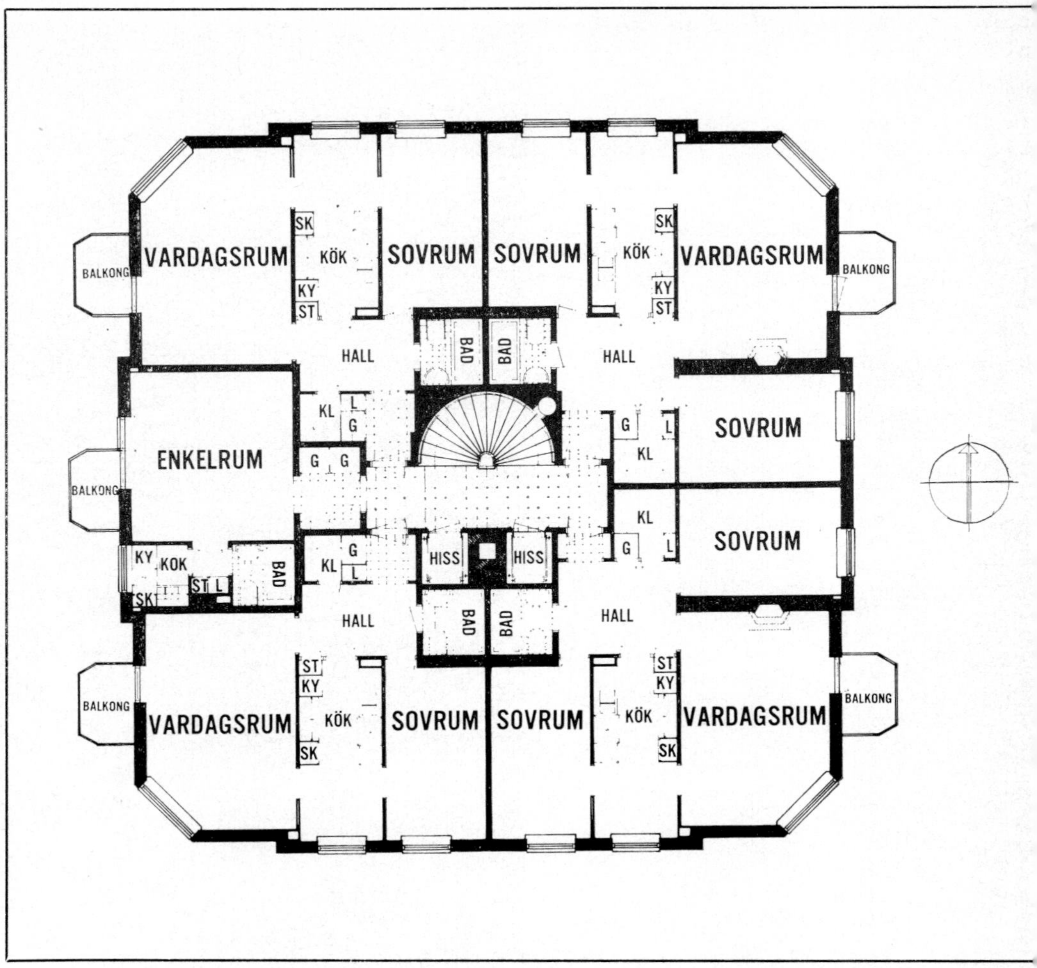

1 Danviksklippan, Stockholm

Architects: Backstrom and Reinius

A self-contained scheme of nine point blocks eight to ten storeys in height on a prominent site near the centre of the city, and one that is amongst the pioneering schemes having had a tremendous influence on similar developments in both Scandinavia and other countries.

It was constructed during the Second World War and takes the compact and economical planning system evidenced in Drancy a stage further than hitherto. The then innovation of the ubiquitous internal spiral staircase to be found in so many Scandinavian point blocks was one of the most important contributory factors. By this means public circulation space has been cut to a negligible minimum.

The planning at the typical floor level varies considerably and it is one of the advantages of this scheme that it possesses this degree of flexibility. One arrangement has a large living and dining area adjoining kitchen and maid's bedroom, together with three bedrooms *en suite* with bathroom, two such units occupying the whole of the floor space at one level. A more usual arrangement is that, however, with four or five units to the typical floor. With the four flats to the floor three have one bedroom and the remaining one a large studio flat with two

ooms, study, kitchen and bathroom. With flats to the floor two have two bedrooms, one bedroom and one is a bedsitter.

hile zoning in the internal planning works in the smaller units, the larger flats involve e cross traffic from one of the bedrooms :h is separated from the remainder and the room.

ojecting balconies are provided to all the g rooms and in some cases also to main ooms in order to maintain a continuity of rnal treatment.

iere is a total of 391 flats in the whole elopment, and the heights of the blocks are sted to suit site levels and to maintain the e roof level throughout.

me of the blocks are provided with two lifts a single staircase, and others with only one. e is a dry refuse chute in each block and ral heating to all accommodation. In addi- in some of the dwellings, there are open laces.

stem of construction is one which is emely popular, particularly in Sweden, that *situ* poured reinforced concrete forming the nal lining of the external walls with pumice crete blocks on the exterior, and internal -bearing walls and reinforced concrete s. A pitched roof is used as in the case of a ber of other Scandinavian schemes, largely onsequence of climatic conditions, particu- snow.

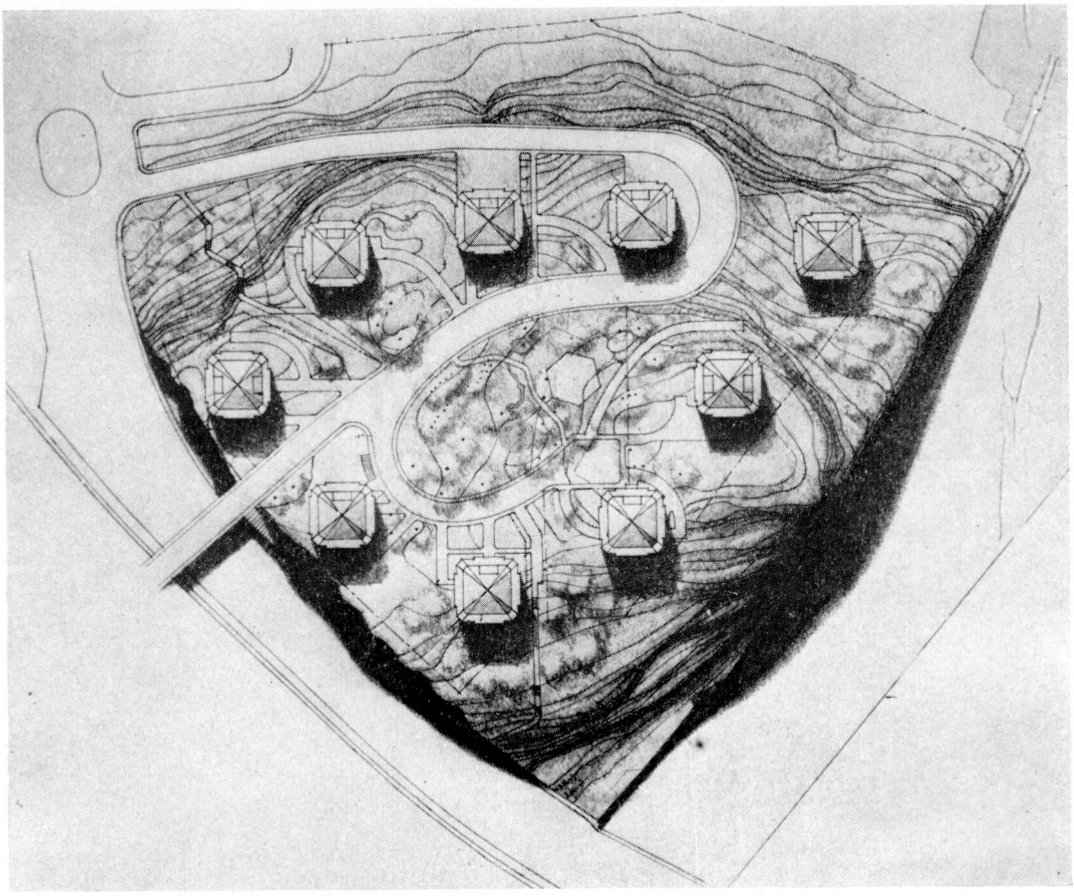

Rosta Estate, Orebro

itects: Backstrom and Reinius

estate development noteworthy for the pro- n of some 1500 flats in three-storey blocks he linked star type and a single 11-storey er block containing a total of 64 flats built in junction with a restaurant and shops which the focus of the scheme.

he completion of what consists of a neigh- rhood development is achieved by the vision of an assembly room, theatre, nursery ool, primary school, garages, and laundry.

the tower block the basement is planned as nants' workshop; the ground floor contains bedsitter units, and the upper floors six of type of unit accessible from a single free nding spiral staircase and single lift. The pped arrangement is also used in the planning e to provide individual private balconies to h flat.

onstruction is reinforced concrete for walls, lightweight concrete insulation and cement dering externally, and reinforced concrete rs. Central heating and hot water are pro- ed from a single boiler house serving the ole estate. This also serves the communal ndry and steam baths. A refuse chute is also vided.

mple enclosed areas and landscaped den providing children's playgrounds and enity space are included in this scheme.

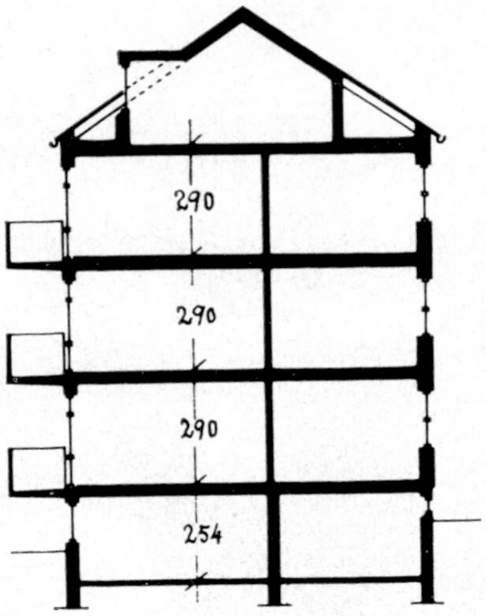
290
290
290
254

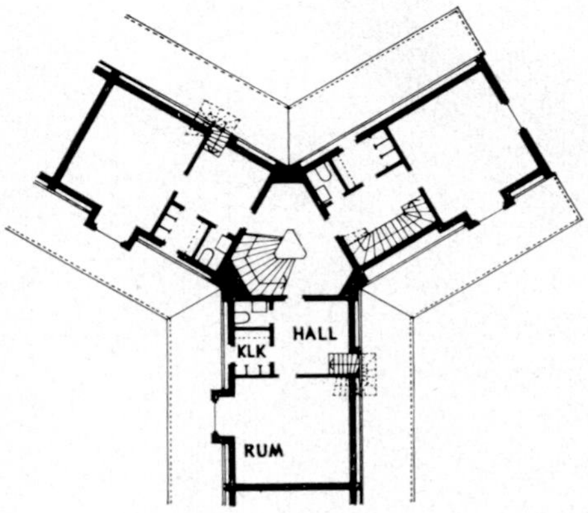
KLK
HALL
RUM

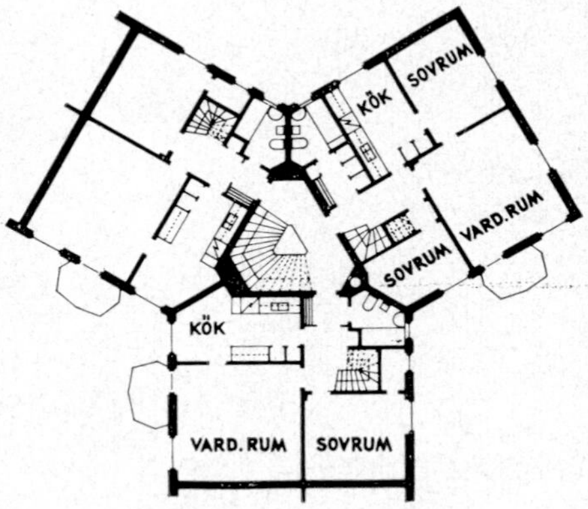
KÖK
SOVRUM
VARD.RUM
SOVRUM
KÖK
VARD.RUM
SOVRUM

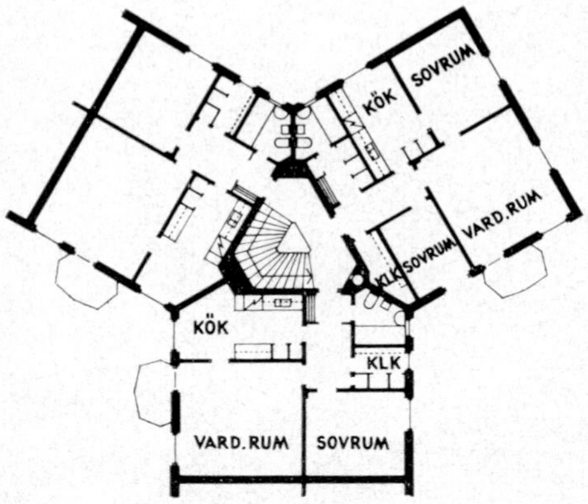
KÖK
SOVRUM
VARD.RUM
KLK
SOVRUM
KÖK
KLK
VARD.RUM
SOVRUM

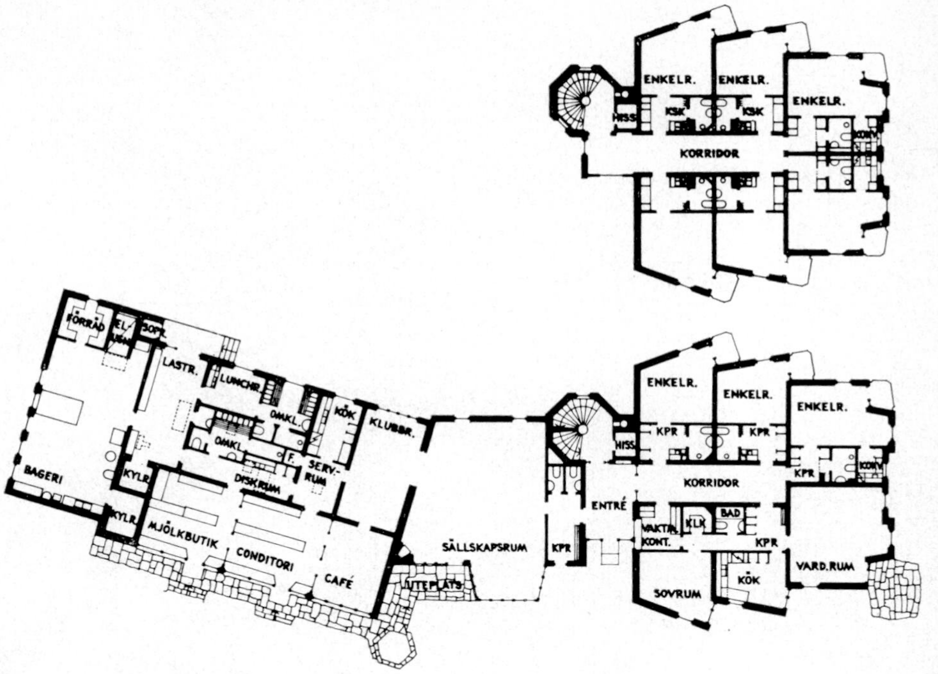
ENKELR.
ENKELR.
ENKELR.
HISS
KORRIDOR
FÖRRÅD
LASTR.
LUNCHR.
KÖK
KLUBBR.
BAGERI
KYLR.
DISKRUM
SERV-RUM
MJÖLKBUTIK
CONDITORI
CAFÉ
SÄLLSKAPSRUM
UTEPLATS
KPR
ENTRÉ
ENKELR.
ENKELR.
ENKELR.
HISS
KPR
KORRIDOR
BAD
KLK
KONT.
SOVRUM
KÖK
VARD.RUM

Kärrtorp, Stockholm

hitect: Klemming

ne example of the free form of development zing low, continuous linked serpentine :ks punctuated at intervals by point blocks with a very high standard of landscaping in intervening areas, which is in many cases in form of enclosed courts, although in no case ne back of the building of less importance in development than the front.

he terrace blocks normally contain three full rs of flats with a half basement containing ants' storage. Orthodox direct staircase ess is the basis of the planning and every has its own private balcony.

he point blocks are seven storeys and eight eys in height, and four of the seven-storey :ks are linked together with shops on the und floor. The eight-storey blocks form sidiary neighbourhood centres.

he main focus to the whole scheme is a storey tower block. In all there are some 870 s accommodating approximately 4000 inhabi- ts in dwellings which vary in size from lsitters to four-bedroom family flats.

'he low blocks are in masonry load-bearing nstruction; the seven- and eight-storey point cks in monolithic concrete faced with pumice ck and rendered; and the 12-storey block is *in situ* reinforced concrete cross wall con- ıction.

'he seven-storey block is planned with a ıtral spiral staircase with lift located in the ldle of this, both serving two flats at half ding level, and two at full landing level, all hese units being identical one-bedroom type.

'he 12-storey block contains eight flats on the ical floor accessible from single staircase and r of lifts. Four of these units are bedsitters, l four the two-bedroom type.

ι more detailed description is given under the lingby scheme where a similar block was also nstructed.

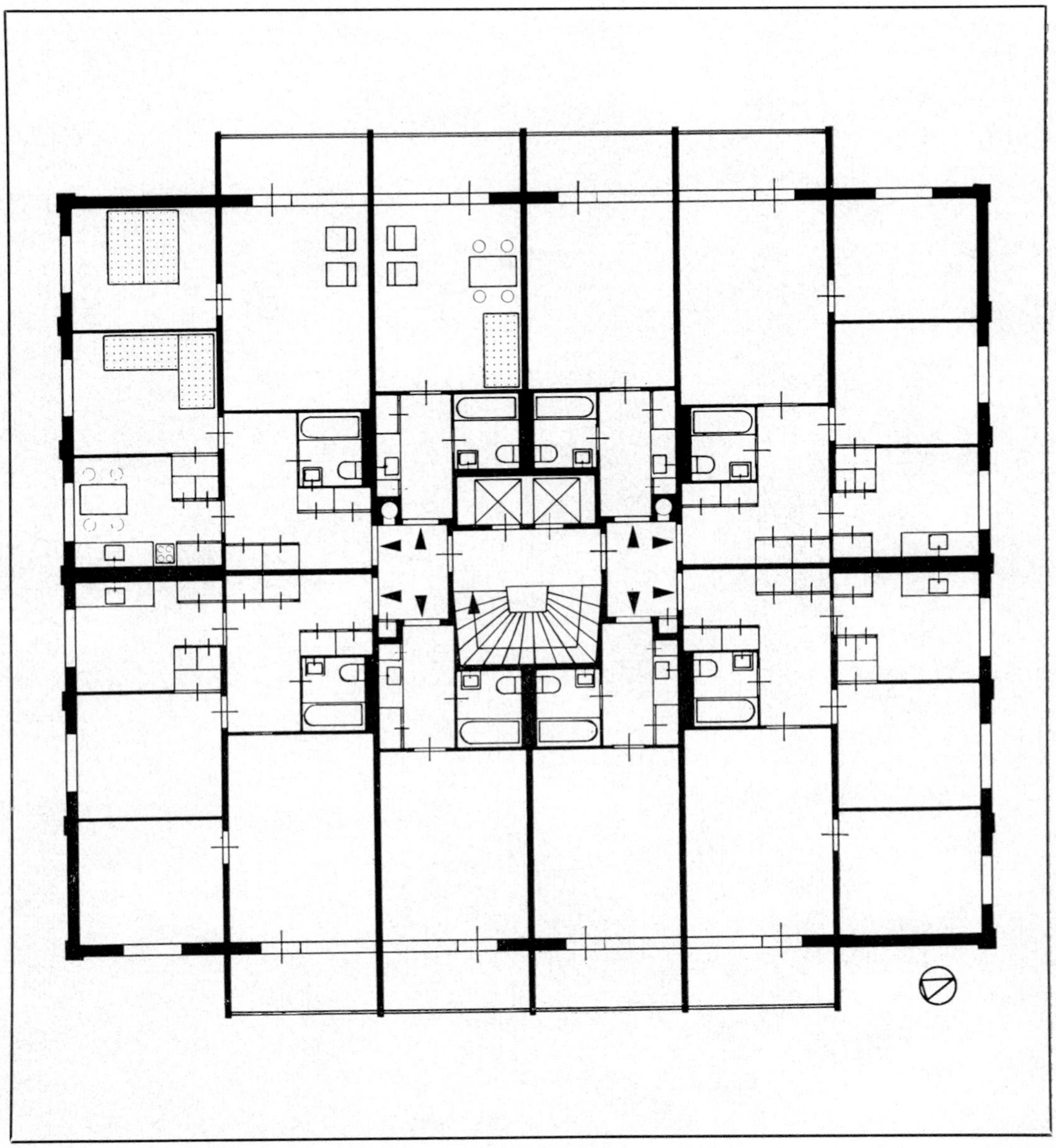

4 Vällingby, Stockholm

An outstanding comprehensive development which is in effect a new town to take a population of 60,000 people.

The overall master plan was prepared by Markelius, including carefully studied three-dimensional models. A number of architects subsequently contributed the designs for detail sections of the development. (Overall plan and aerial views show the general layout.)

The first of these sections which is of particular interest is a group of four swastika plan point blocks adjoining the centrum and designed by *Klemming.* These are planned in close proximity to three and four storey continuous terrace development and owe a considerable degree of their effect to the way in which the grouping has been studied.

A single spiral staircase core with central lift is the basis of the planning of those tower blocks which have five flats to the typical floor; three with one bedroom and two bedsitters, each flat with its private projecting balcony. Monolithic

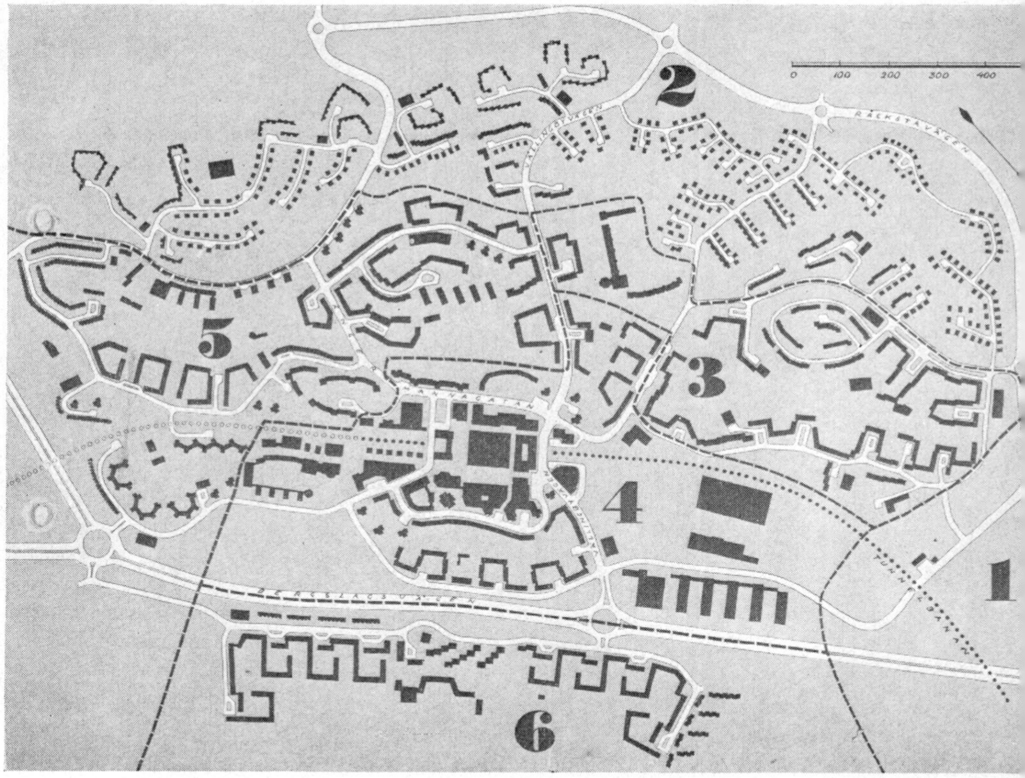

poured concrete for external walls and floors is the system of construction, with aerated concrete blocks forming the outside skin subsequently rendered.

The whole design is extremely clean and simple in its conception with no unwanted excrescences particularly at roof level where the flat roof has by now been accepted as suited to climatic conditions. A refuse chute is also included in the central core, and at roof level an automatic smoke escape device which ventilates the staircase in the event of fire, a system which is mandatory with the internal staircases in Sweden.

As with the majority of Swedish point blocks, the choice of which was greatly influenced by the need to limit excavation in solid rock, a basement floor is provided which is used for tenants' storage or can be adapted as an air raid shelter.

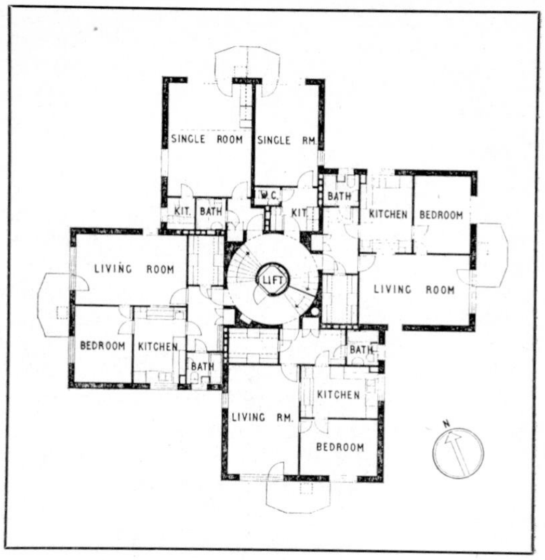

Another group of three tower blocks also signed by *Klemming* and also 11 storeys in ight is located in the south-west corner of the ntral area.

The planning of these is practically a prototype, nost square in shape with a circular staircase d lift in the core—a shape, incidentally, which by far the most economical in cost of external lling in relation to a given floor area, and a st efficient one from the heat loss point of w.

The typical floor to these blocks contain six ts, two of which have one bedroom and four dsitters of different sizes, again with the vision of private balconies constructed as a e standing element. A basement floor ants' storage cum air raid shelter is also vided.

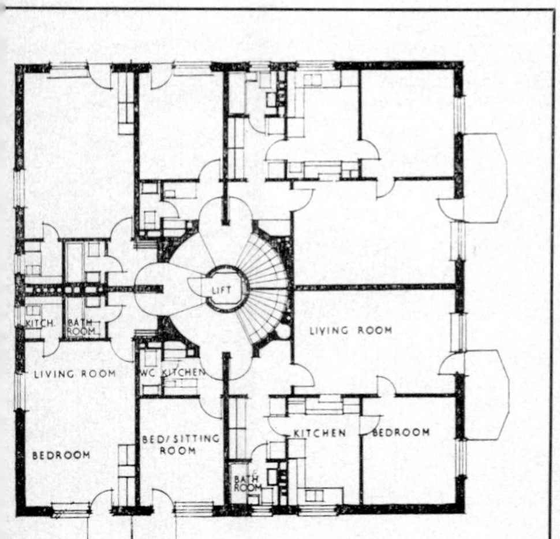

6 A still further group of four point blocks linked by a single-storey office and shop block, and designed by *J. Bjurstrom*, is located on the north side of the shopping piazza. This is known as Ritstiftet.

The point blocks, which are planned to an irregular shape, are also a maximum of 11 storeys in height including ground floor level which partly oversails the business and shopping block, and partly accommodates caretakers and tenants' storage. Above this level a single staircase and pair of lifts gives access to two bedsitters, two one-bedroom flats, and two two-bedroom flats.

The system of construction is similar to that of the other Vällingby point blocks. Refuse chutes and central heating are also provided, as well as a central refrigeration plant to serve individual kitchen units.

This whole group is a particularly effective part of the central development of Vällingby, and one that is a well integrated combination of buildings of different heights.

A podium contributes a transition between the formality of the piazza and the freer development of the residential area signified by the point blocks themselves.

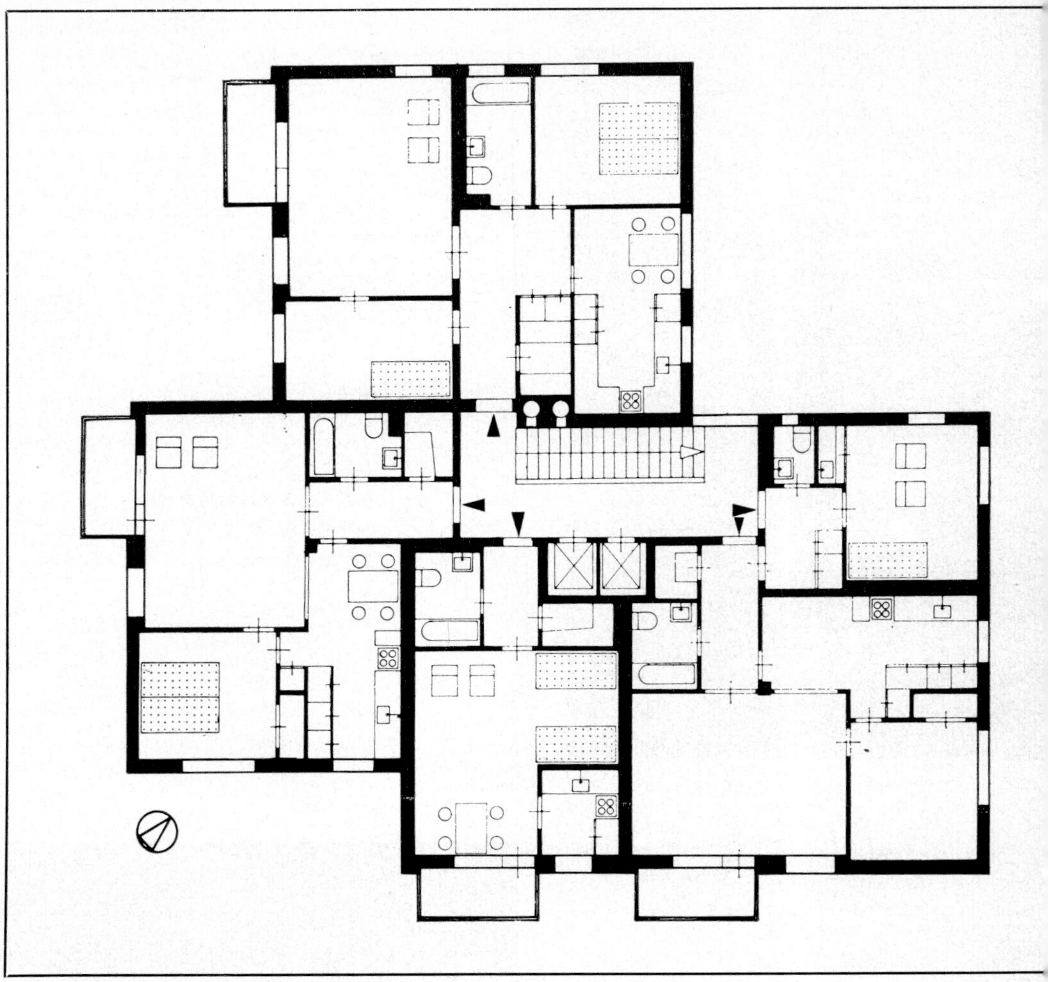

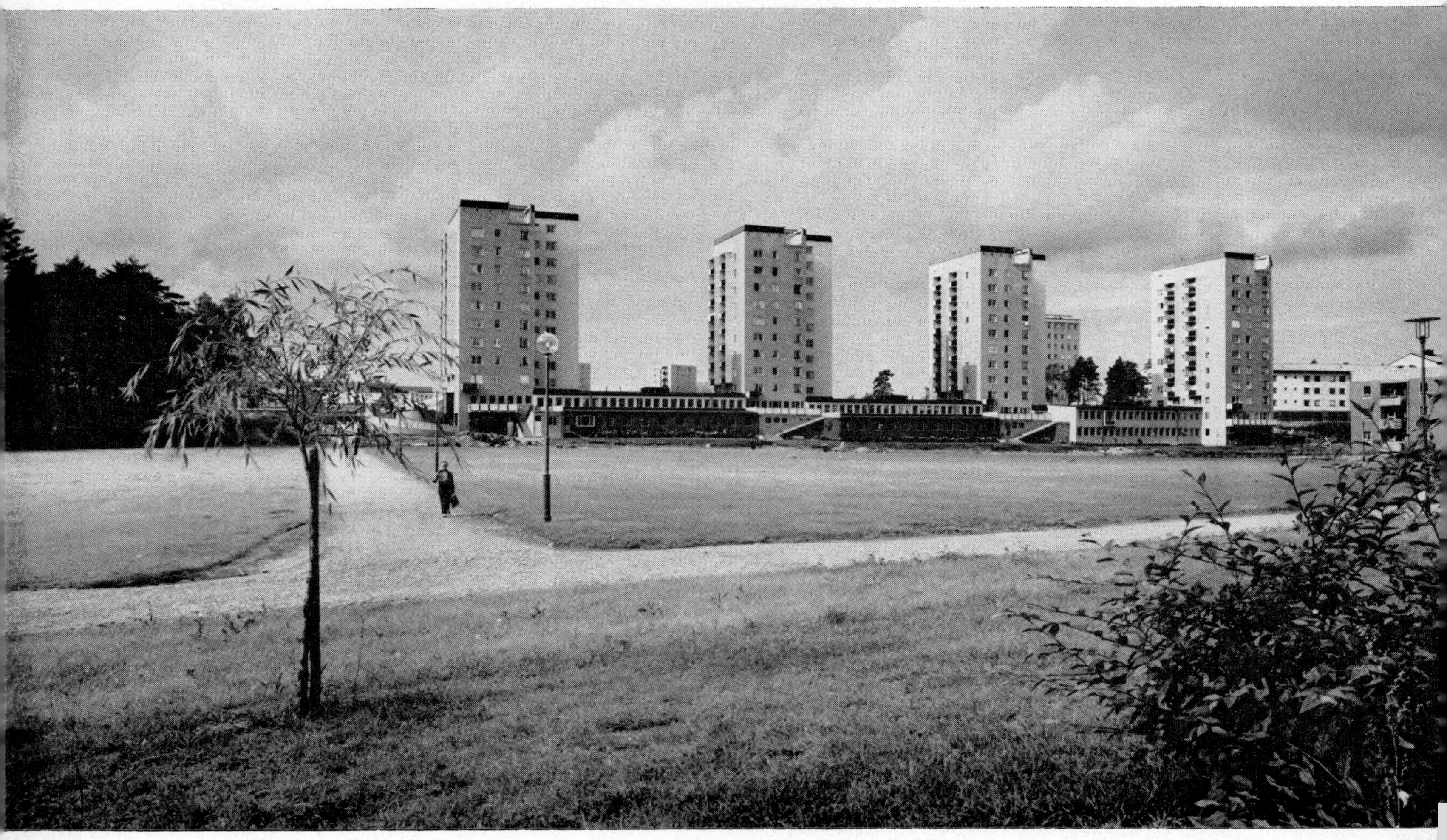

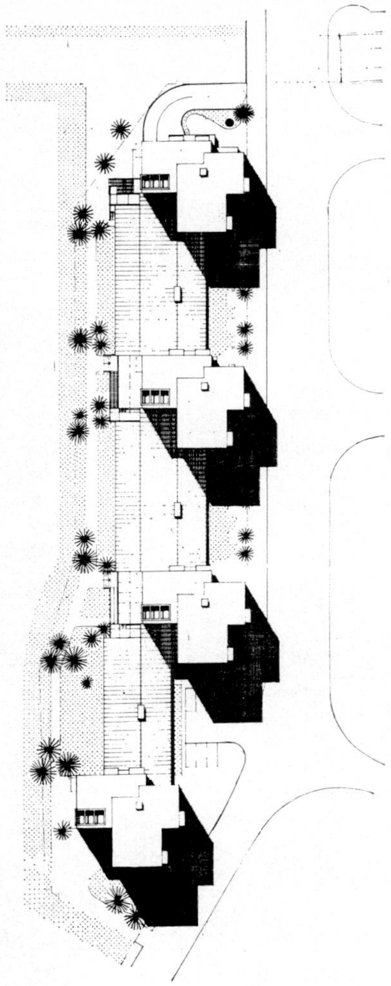

win point blocks of a slightly different design n are located to the north-east of the central ɔping area and these are designed by ker and Gate. They are also 11 storeys in ht and more or less square in plan with a ral spiral staircase and circular lift core. In case four flats to the floor are served—two full landing level, and two at half-landing —all of the flats being one-bedroom units inset private balconies which serve both g rooms and kitchens and allow natural and ventilation to bathrooms.

ne system of construction is monolithic rein-ed concrete faced with aerated concrete ks and rendering.

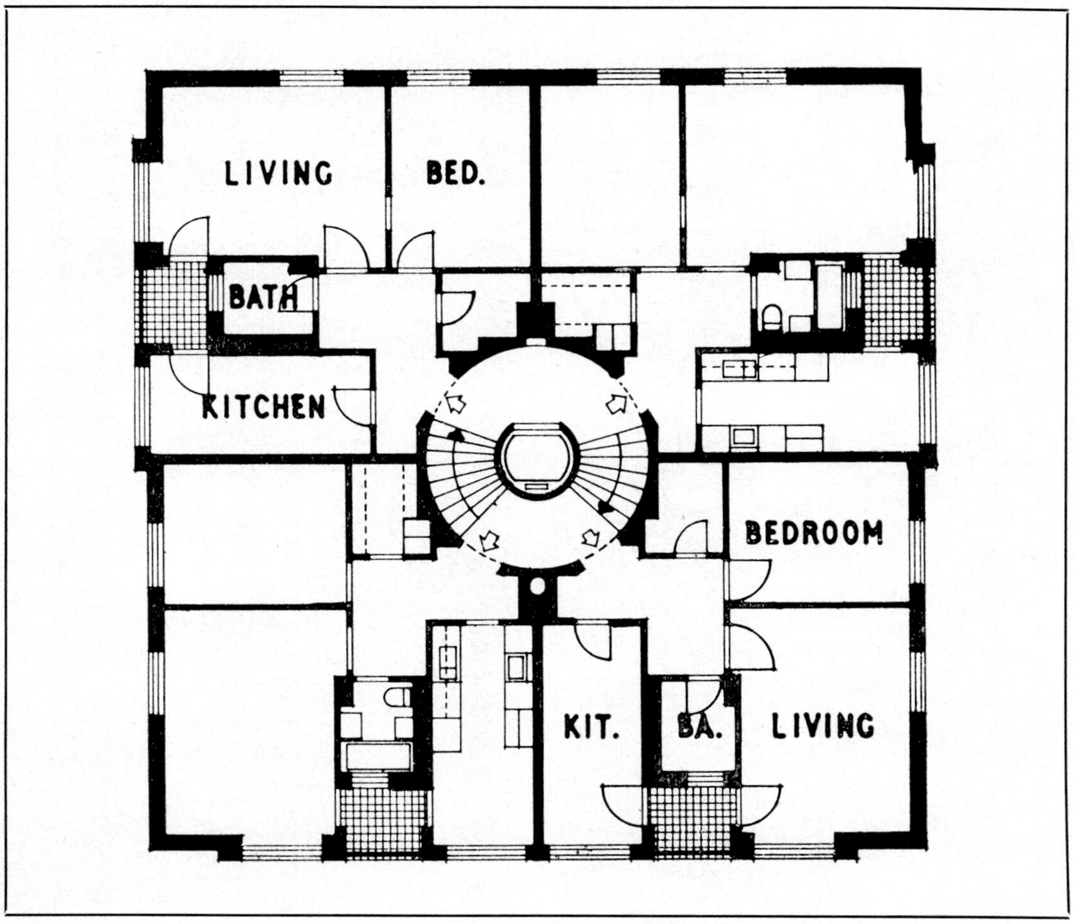

8 To the south-east of Vällingby in a suburb *Blackeberg* a group of three point blocks designed by *Laudon and Persson* have been erected with the stepped type plan and a rectangular internal staircase giving access to two flats at half landing level, and four flats at full landing level. The planning arrangement in this case enables each flat to have its own private balcony with south aspect. At each typical floor the flats are two one-bedroom, two two-bedroom, and two bedsitter units; all with naturally lit and ventilated kitchens and with internal bathrooms.

A single lift serves the whole block which is also provided with refuse chute and central heating.

Load-bearing monolithic concrete construction is used with an external skin of aerated concrete blocks rendered. These blocks are nine to ten storeys in height with a basement level containing tenants' services and storage.

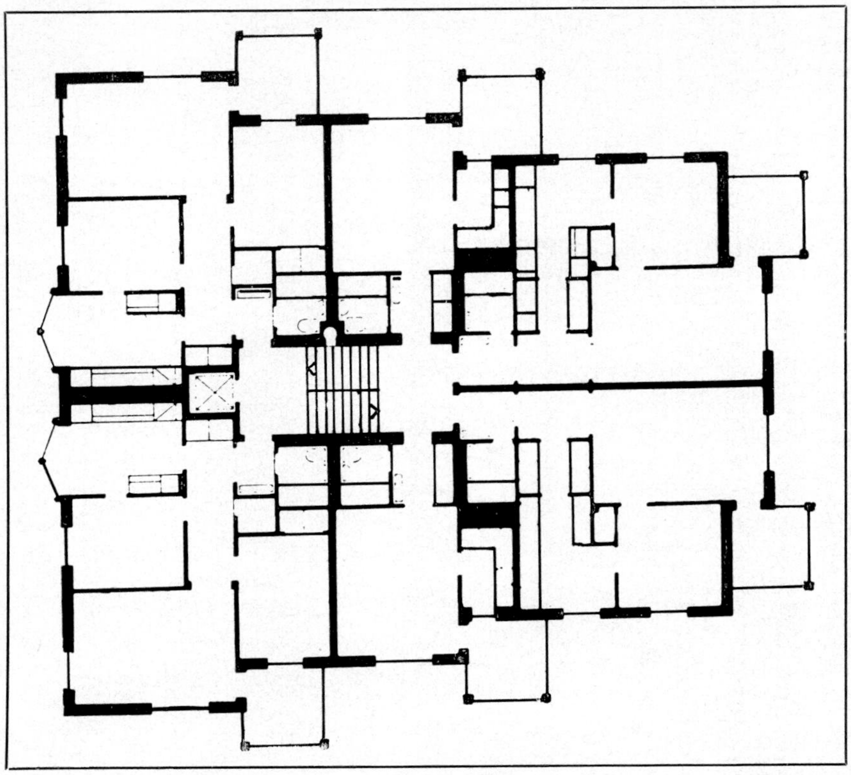

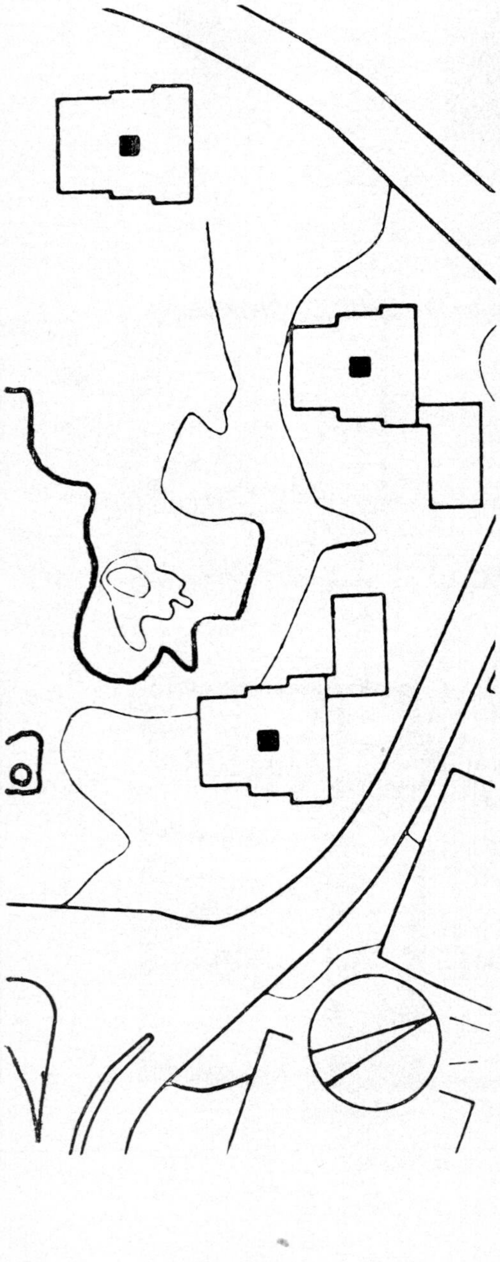

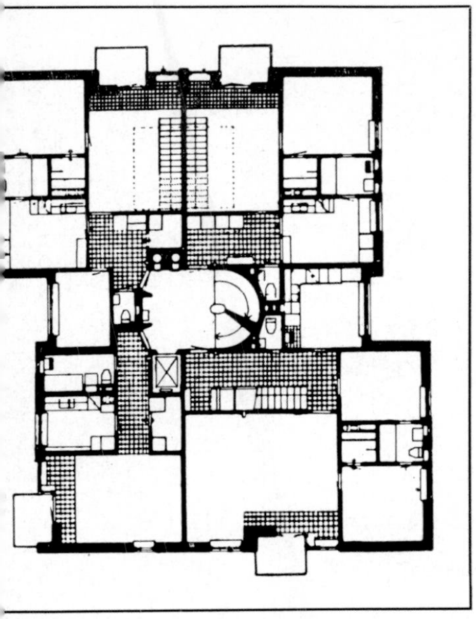

9 Forming a part of the South Spanga development and adjoining Vällingby on the south-west at *Hässelby* is the so-called '*Family Hotel*' designed by *Carl-Axel Acking.* This consists of four tower blocks linked together by a sub-structure of lower buildings of various types and enclosing a series of courts and garden areas.

The towers are all similar in pattern with a circular staircase core and a single lift providing vertical access. There are four flats on the typical floor fitting in to a staggered rectangle shape. The two upper floors contain maisonettes with roof garden.

The ground floor is an entrance hall, porter's lodge, shops, restaurant, kindergarten, and a garage and servicing station link and interpenetrate at this level.

The blocks have nine floors above ground floor level including roof level, and while they form a well-integrated group the individual blocks suffer from a rather awkward space frame at roof level and other excrescences. They are constructed with a reinforced concrete frame with walls of thermally insulated concrete. Both brick and rendered block are used for external cladding.

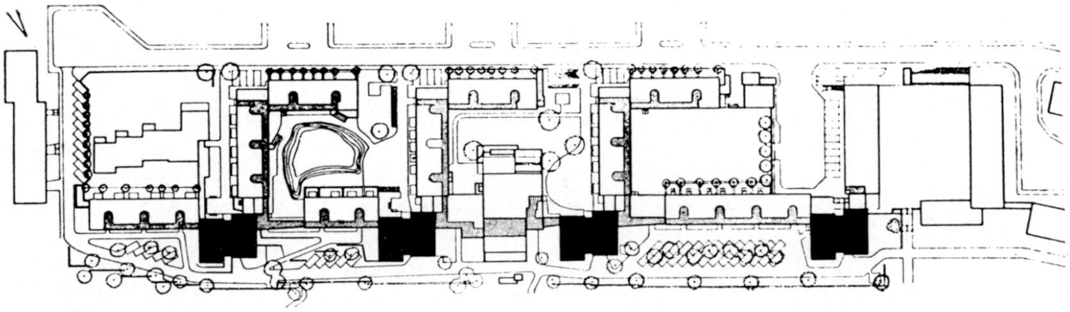

10 In the *Grimstå* area of Vällingby is located a 14-storey tower block designed by *Klemming,* a development somewhat similar to the block built at Kärrtorp. This block also has eight flats served by a single staircase and pair of lifts at the typical floor with practically no circulation area or corridor apart from the lobby adjoining the lifts. This extremely economical planning is associated with a very high standard of architectural design with a pleasing contrast in the colour of the structural frame which is expressed on the exterior of the building and the dark infill panels. An interesting balcony pattern is also achieved with an alternation of solid and grille.

System of construction was reinforced concrete cross wall, all the main walls and partitions being load bearing. Two refuse chutes are provided, and central heating throughout, equipment for this being accommodated in basement and this in turn is served by the dis heating system.

The two upper floors of the block are plan as maisonettes, or duplex flats, and the lift m room is also accommodated at this level wi avoids projecting penthouse, and contrib greatly to the clean roof line.

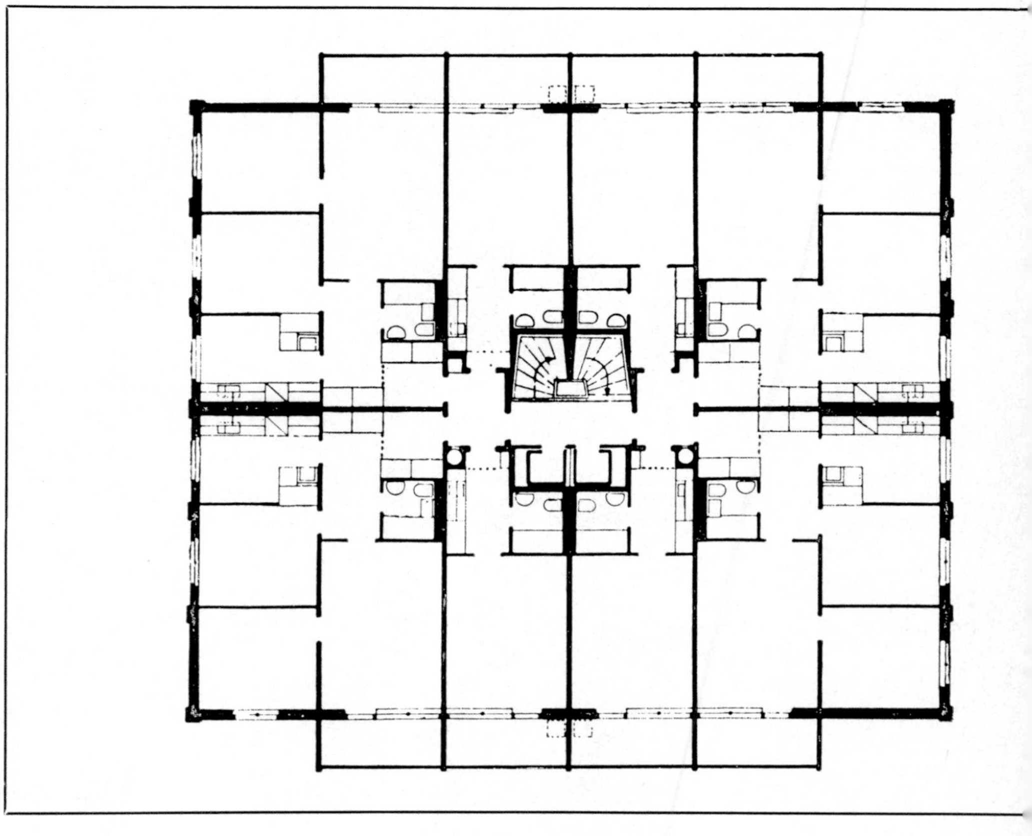

nd **12** Two of the most recent additions to Vällingby Scheme are four nine-storey point ks in the *Grimstå* area, with a most attractive side setting which remains relatively un-ırbed as the result of concentrated building. ıese blocks which are all identical have four bedroom dwellings to the typical floor metrically disposed round a semicircular and single lift core. The linking balconies ılso an emergency escape route. The second ıese recent developments is an equally well ceived and designed group of 490 dwellings *ässelby Strand* known as *Väggfaltet:* by the ıitect *J. Bjurström* for H.S.B. Building Society. group includes three-storey and eight-ey slab blocks arranged round a central focus our similar point blocks. Shops are also ıded in the area.

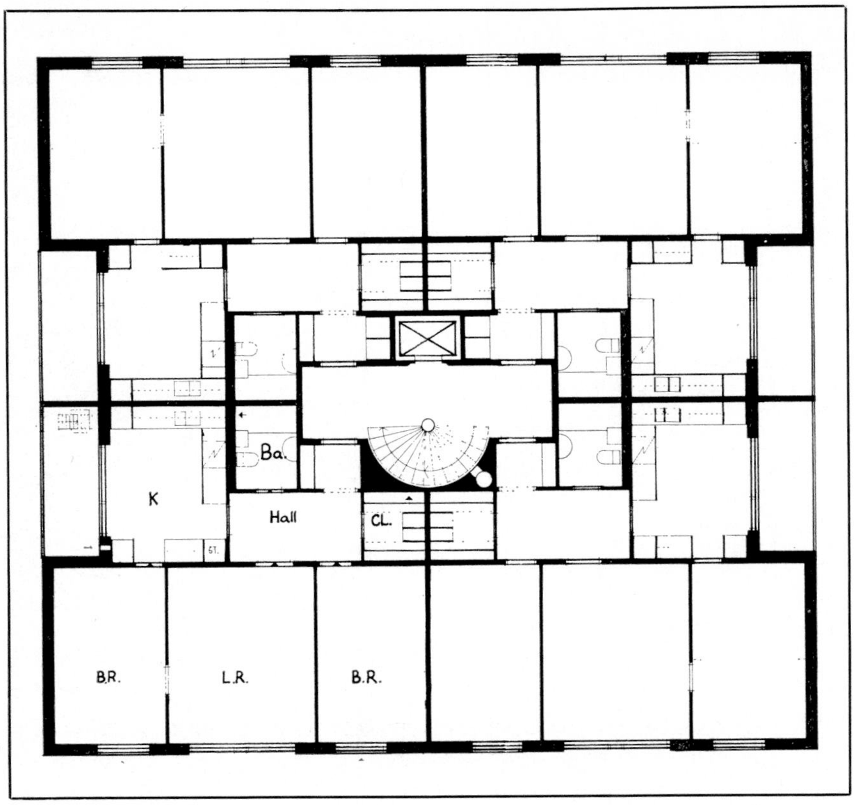

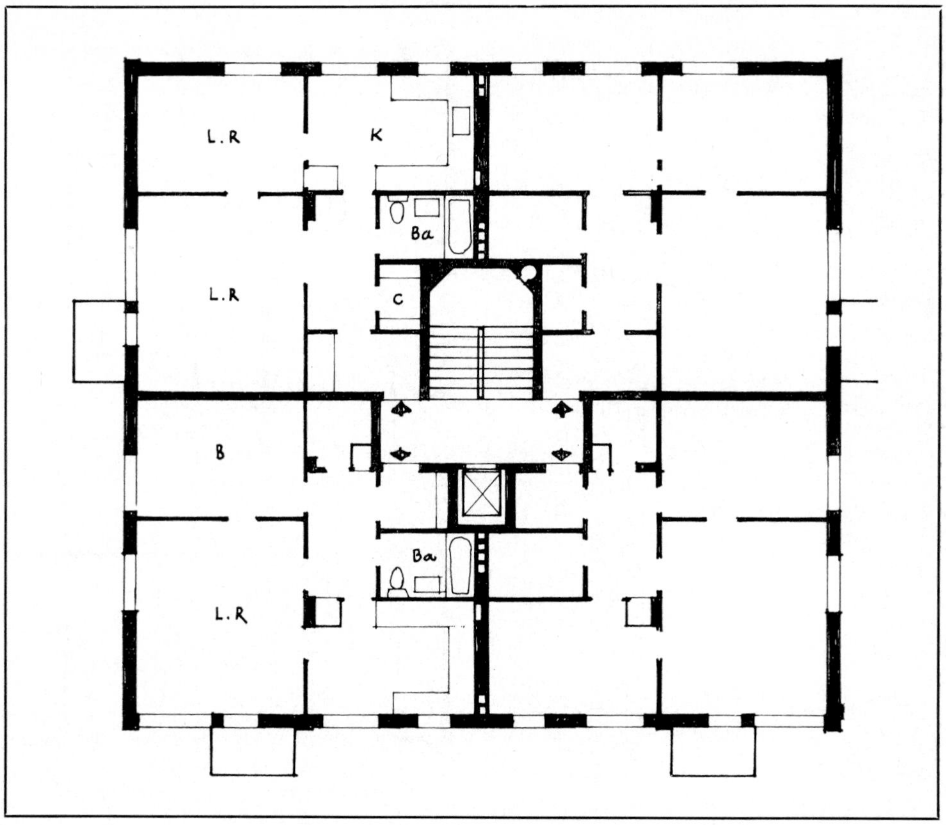
L.R
K
Ba
L.R
C
B
Ba
L.R

Sörgenfri, Malmö

itects: Jaenecke and Samuelson

te of approximately half an acre in extent eloped with three L-shaped four-storey ks, and three eight-storey 'domino' blocks, point blocks being planned on the south meter of the site in order not to overshadow enclosed garden areas or other flats.

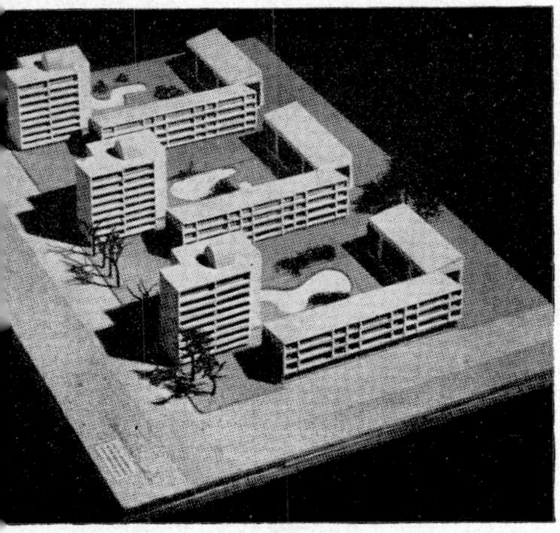

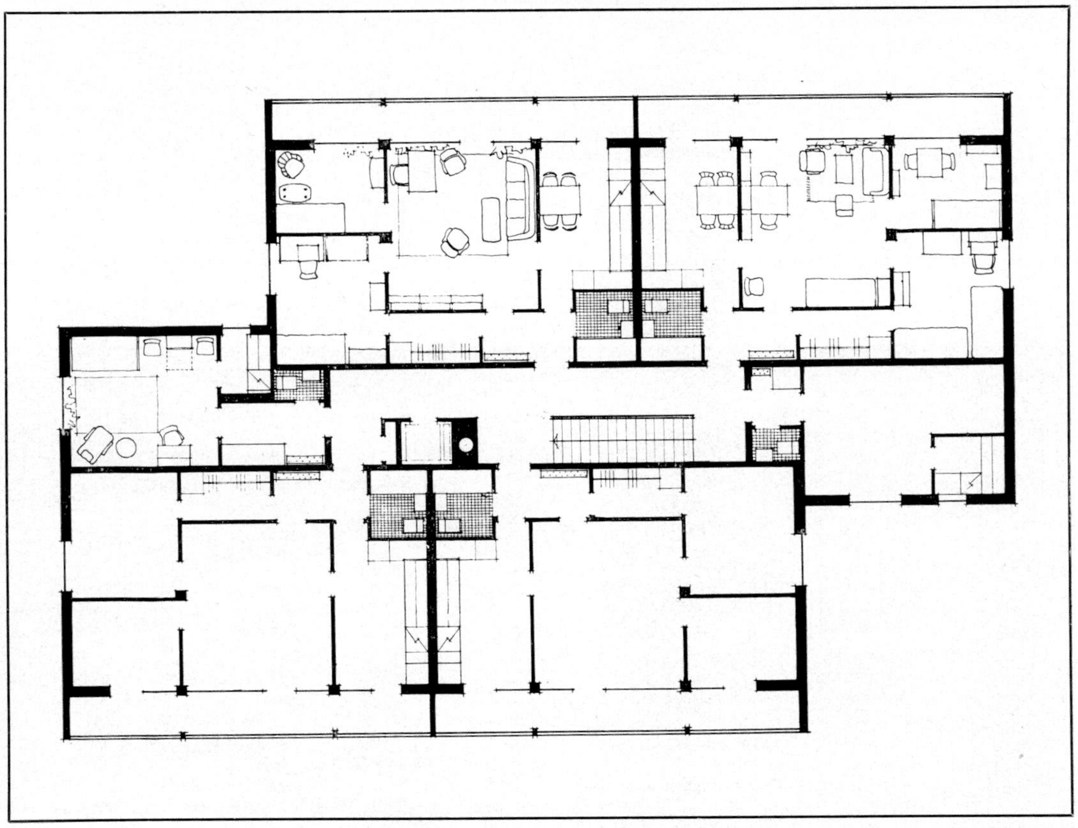

The low blocks are of direct staircase access with three flats to the staircase on each typical floor, each of the one-bedroom type. The construction of these is in brick and block load-bearing cross wall but with balconies in reinforced concrete. Floors and roof are also in reinforced concrete, and a half basement is provided for tenants' storage.

The tower blocks are planned with a central circulation core containing a single staircase and lift and refuse chute, and these give access to the typical floor level to four identical two-bedroom units and two bedsitters. The two upper floors, however, accommodate maisonettes each with four bedrooms, living room and kitchen. The system of construction in this case, however, is in reinforced concrete frame with brickwork and block infill.

A continuous balcony has been provided along the main front of all the buildings in the group. Shops are also included at ground floor leve one of the four-storey blocks.

A scheme with a clean architectural qua with the structure well expressed, even allov for the weakness of the butterfly roof on multi-storey tower blocks, and the lean-to roof the battered face of the four-storey slab bloc features which seem to be out of keeping v the straightforward approach otherwise sh in the planning and the design.

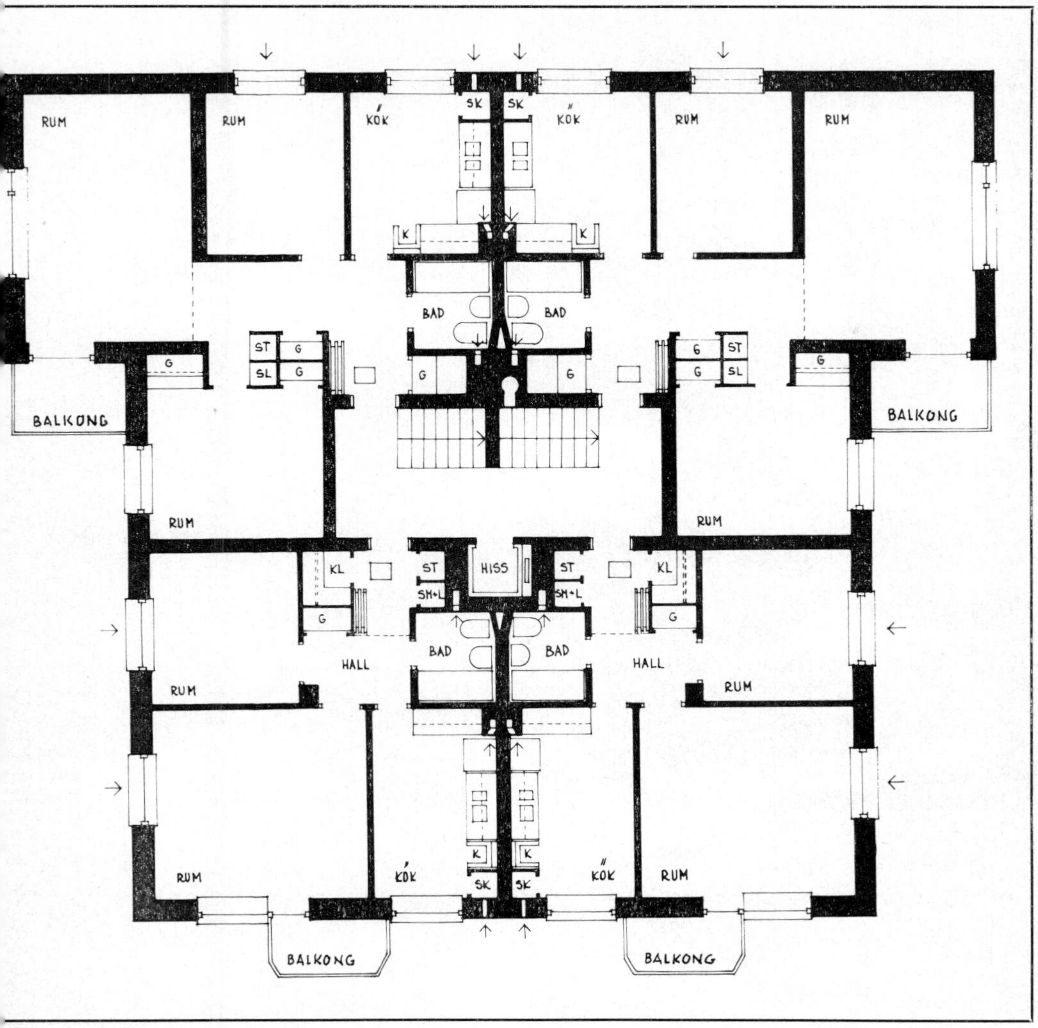

14 Södrahammarby, Stockholm

Architect: Sandberg

A group of similar T-plan point houses six storeys in height in a Stockholm suburb. These are planned with four flats to the typical floor accessible from the single staircase and lift—two one-bedroom and two two-bedroom units, each with private balcony and south aspect. Bathrooms are linked with kitchens and are therefore not zoned.

The more traditional pitched roof has been retained in these examples, and part of the roof space used for a penthouse flat. Refuse chute is provided and there is basement storage accommodation.

System of construction: load-bearing brick walls with concrete floors.

Vattenveronikan, Göteborg

·hitects: Brolid and Wallinder

art of the Guldhelden development, a suburb ·öteborg, master planned and then handled ·etail by a number of different architects.

wo types of nine-storey point block form the n element of this particular group, both ·ewhat unusual in planning and elevational ·tment. The planning system is similar in ·tment to that used at Bellahøj in Copenhagen ·, in effect, two rectangular blocks each ommodating two flats at the typical floor ·l with a staircase forming a link and neces-ting access to two of the flats at full landing ·l, and two at half landing level. The main erence between the two types of block used ·his group is in the proportions of rectangle in ·and the flat composition; in one case there ·g one three-bedroom unit, two two-bedroom, one one-bedroom flat; and the other case two-bedroom units are placed side by side ·he same block, and the other part contains three-bedroom unit and one one-bedroom ·.

seful partly inset, partly projecting balconies provided for every flat.

he zoning of bathrooms, particularly to the ·er flats, is, however, not entirely satisfactory,

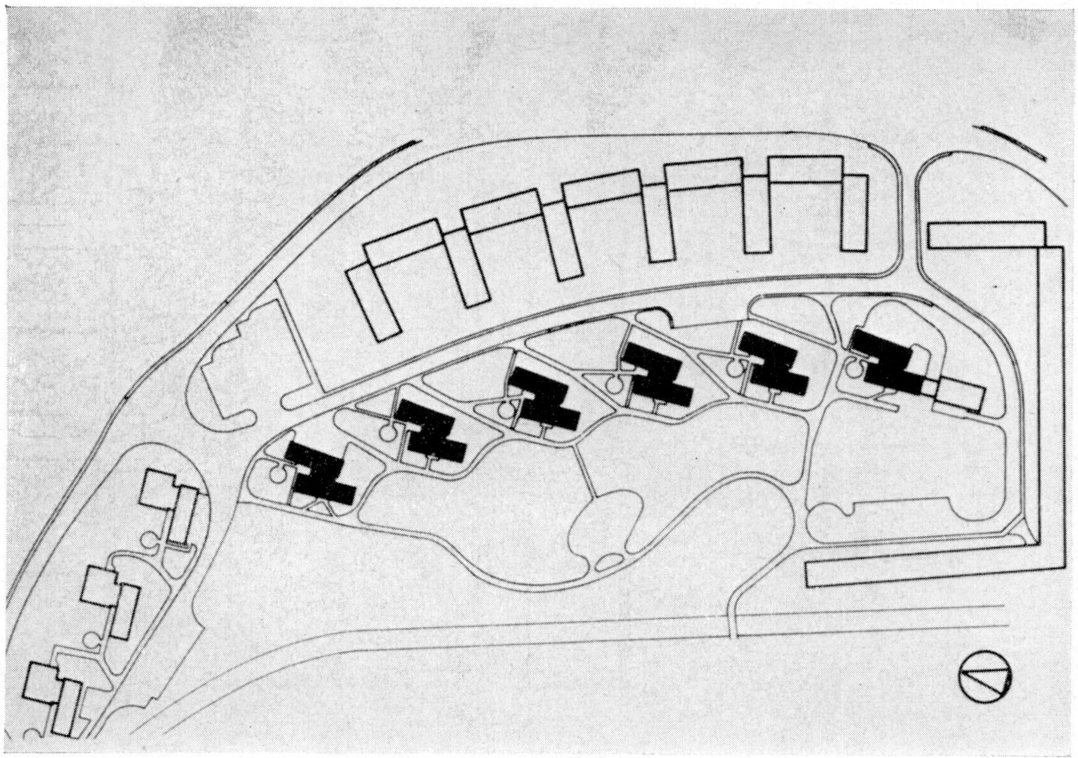

although in other respects the design is plea
and the changes in level well handled wi
successful compromise between tradition
contemporary in the low-pitched roof line.

Shops are also included in this developr
as a part of low three-storey terrace blocks,
whole scheme excellently landscaped wi
minimum of interference from traffic roads.

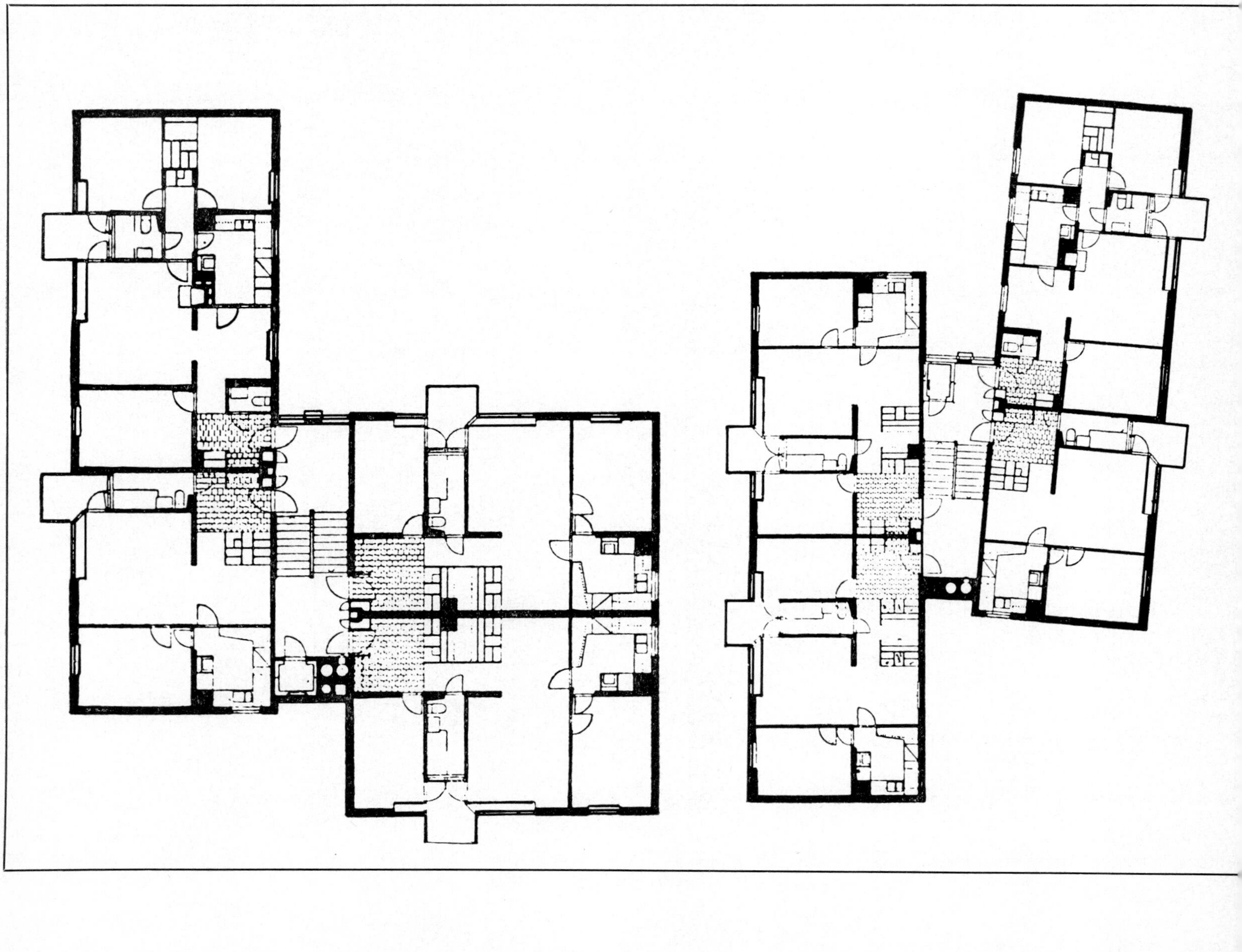

Nytorp Quarter, Malmö

:hitects: Jaenecke and Samuelson

group of four nine- and sixteen-storey slab •cks forming a part of a larger development of)0 flats in an inner urban locality adjoining lmö Stadium.

'he scheme provides for low site coverage d ample park and garden areas adjoining, ether with garages and vehicle parking, ces, restaurant, filling station, and theatre. e whole development is heated from a central tion and laundry and drying facilities are luded in the blocks.

3oth the nine-storey and the 16-storey blocks planned similarly with internal staircases :h of which, together with the single lift, ves on the typical floor five flats of which two three-bedroom, and three one-bedroom ts, the larger flats having dual aspect. irouping of bathrooms and kitchens has been en precedence over function zoning. Other- e this is a neat planning arrangement with ry flat having extensive private balcony vision.

ystem of construction is reinforced concrete ss wall and floor with reinforced concrete ne to the balconies.

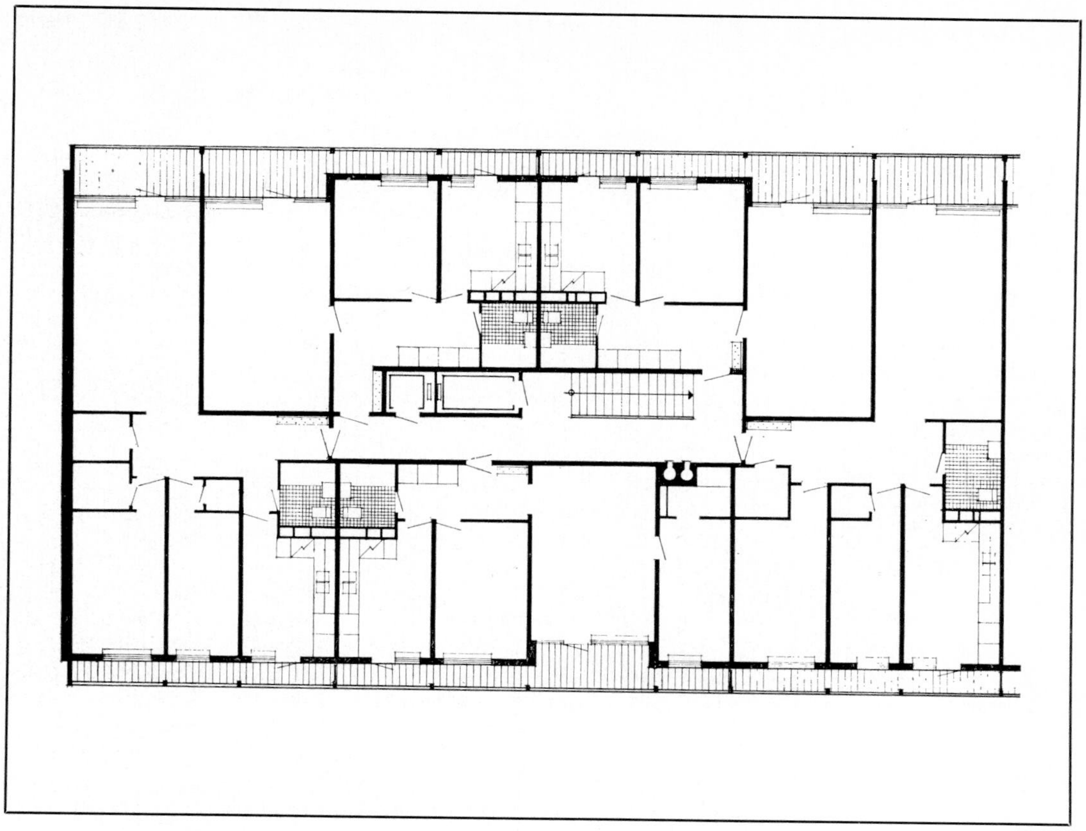

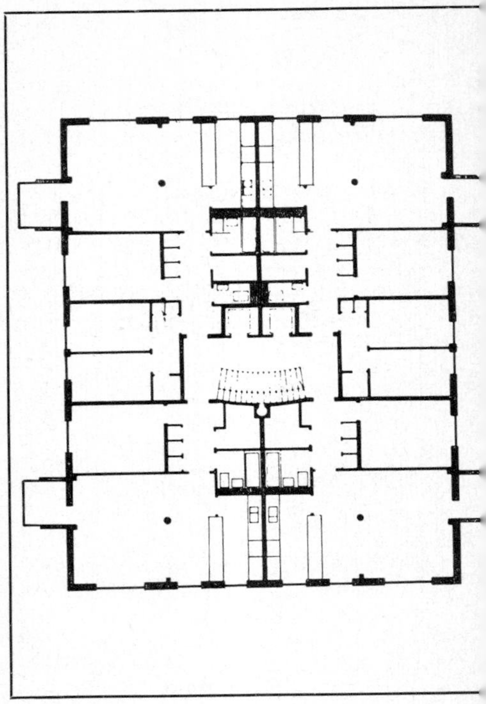

17 Skärmväggen, Högdalen, Stockholm

Architect: H.S.B.

A series of 11-storey tower blocks designed and built for the building society H.S.B. and forming part of a larger development of 490 dwellings. Three-storey slab blocks are also included.

The tower blocks have an economical circulation core with internal staircase and a pair of lifts is used to give access to four flats on the typical floor; two of these have a large living/dining area opening on to the kitchen, and three bedrooms, and the other two living and dining room plus one bedroom with a reasonable compromise between use zoning and grou of plumbing.

A refuse chute and central heating are provi

The larger flats, in addition to the inte bathroom with W.C., have an additional W.C. cloak room.

At basement level there are shops and tena storage areas, but as will be seen from illustration there is a deficiency of enclo parking area.

Construction is in monolithic reinfor concrete with external aerated concrete b rendered. Internal partitions are also in pre aerated concrete slabs.

18 Kortedala, Göteborg

Architects: S. Brolid and J. Wallinder

A comprehensive town development to accommodate in all 25,000 inhabitants, and divided into a number of areas for implementation. An imaginative scheme is illustrated for one section which forms the extreme south-west corner of the area and which includes long curving terrace blocks of flats and a group of five prismatic shape point blocks, community halls, libraries, restaurants, a cinema, and a church.

The point blocks, apart from the rather irregularly shaped living rooms, are ingeniously planned around a triangular circulation core with single staircase and lift. There are three flats to the typical floor, one of which is accessible from half landing level and the other two at full landing level, by which means a sloping roof has been introduced to a very flat pitch corresponding with the half storey height difference.

The block is 11 storeys in height and all of the flats are of the two-bedroom type with naturally lit kitchens and bathrooms which are grouped together rather than being zoned.

The overall form of the plan is preserved by the use of triangular balconies at the extremities of the building, but in spite of the interesting form that results from this aesthetically, the shape may not be the most useful in practice.

The terrace blocks are three to four storeys in height and mainly direct staircase access.

This scheme also has four flats to the typical floor and the blocks are nine storeys in height.

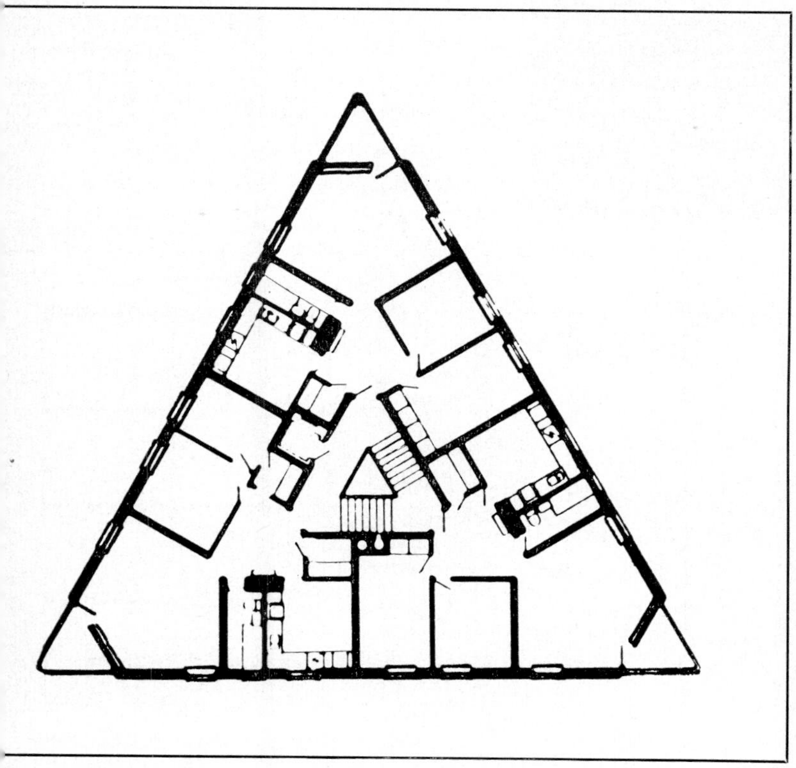

19 Oxnö, Fårsta, Stockholm

Architect: Lönroth

A single 11-storey slab block designed in cc junction with a small block of shops on a r stricted central site, containing a total of 60 fla Garages, cycle and tenants' storage are provid in the lower floors. Each of the upper floc contains six flats served by two internal ser circular staircases and two pairs of lifts. T two flats in the centre of the block have thr bedrooms each as well as a large dual aspe living/dining area, two of the bedrooms bei *en suite* with internal bathroom, the thi bedroom being provided as a maid's room.

At the extremities of the building are fo similar units, with somewhat inconvenien placed bathrooms and rather large internal h areas which also serve as dining rooms.

This is reasonably economical planning the large flats involved, and the inset balconi are a valuable extension to the internal habitat areas.

The exterior is clean and efficient withc being monotonous. The construction is *in s* concrete cross wall with sandwich concre external cladding.

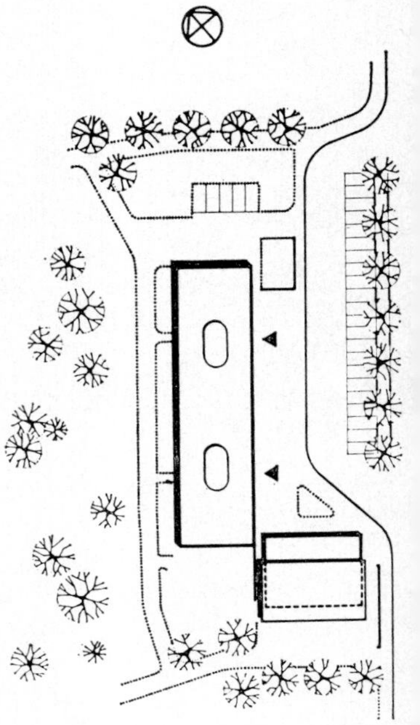

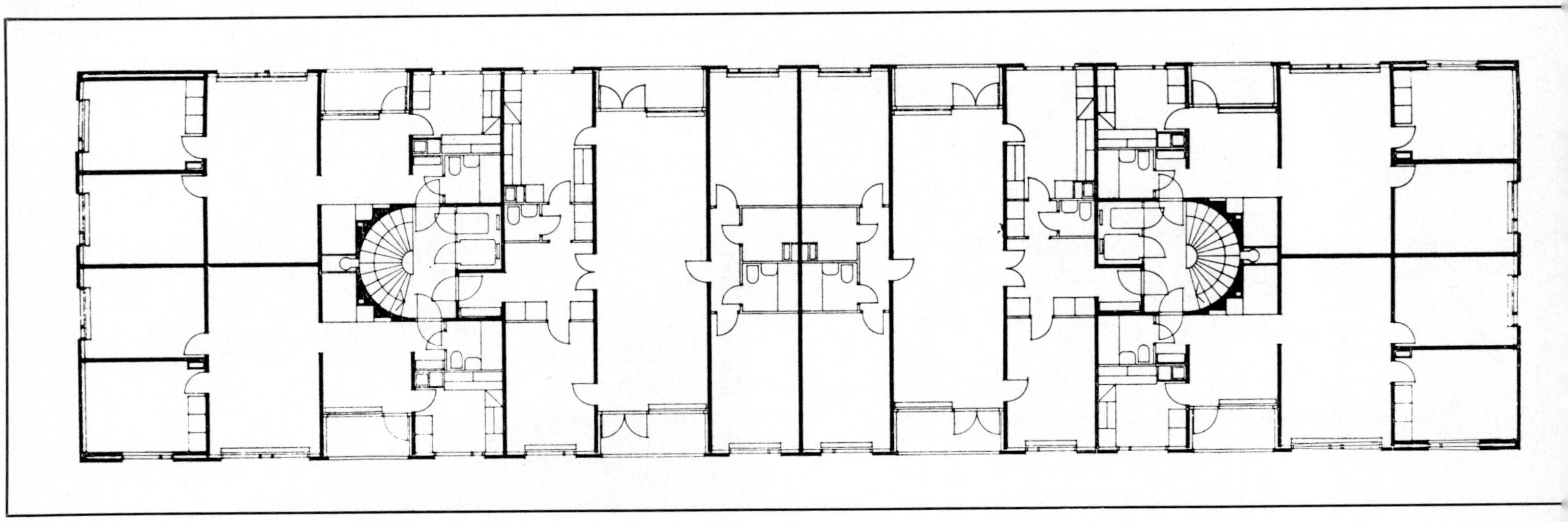

20 Lörensbörg, Malmö

Architects: Thorsten Roos and B. Thornberg

An impressive development consisting of a 16-storey and a nine-storey slab block with linking single storey shops. In the higher block of the two the system of continuous balconies on both sides of the building, popular in south Sweden, has been used although access is by means of two internal core staircases and four lifts. The balconies, with their reinforced concrete supporting framing, and in contrast with the well detailed gable end walls, help to confer an attractive architectural quality on the building, and they are of value from a maintenance point of view. Their practicability, however, in the climate seems open to question.

The 16-storey block has 10 flats at each typical floor level accessible from two staircases and four lifts. These are four two-bedroom units. four with one bedroom, and two bedsitters, with in all cases internal bathrooms planned however away from the bedroom zone.

The nine-storey block follows a similar planning principle with an internal staircase and single lift serving four flats at each typical floor level—two two-bedroom and two one-bedroom units. In this case inset balconies are provided to living rooms only.

Construction is in both cases reinforced concrete frame with precast concrete slab and tile external cladding.

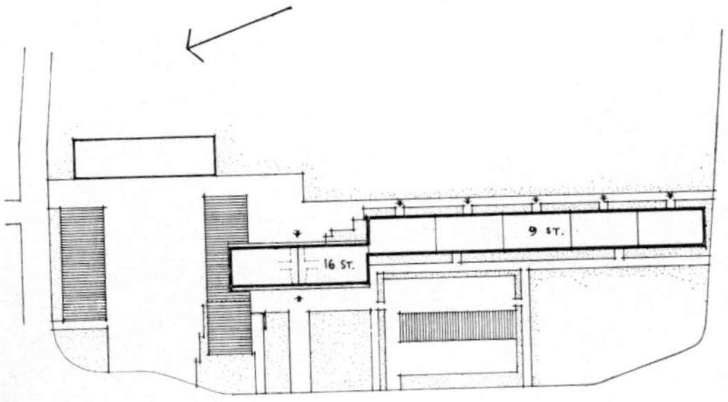

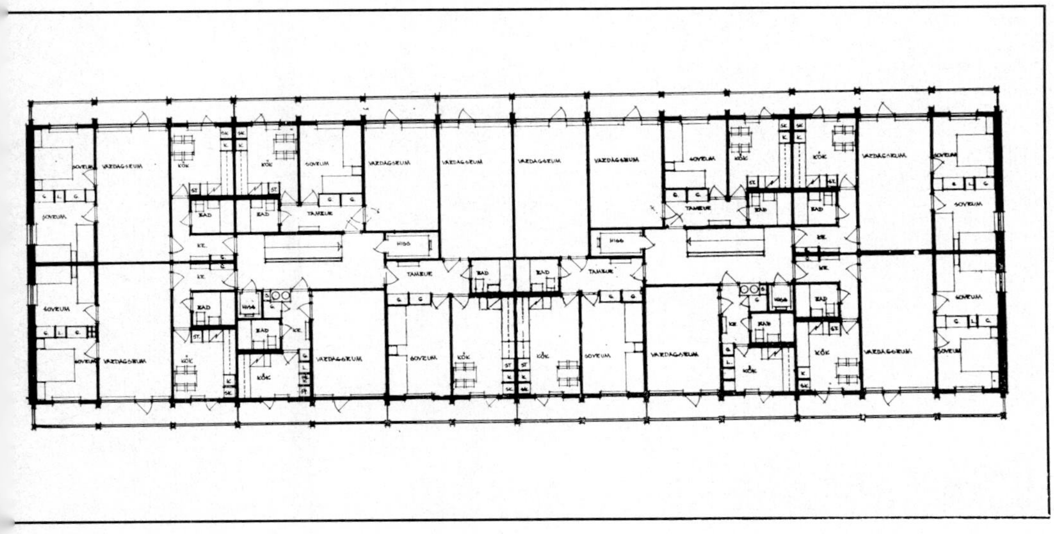

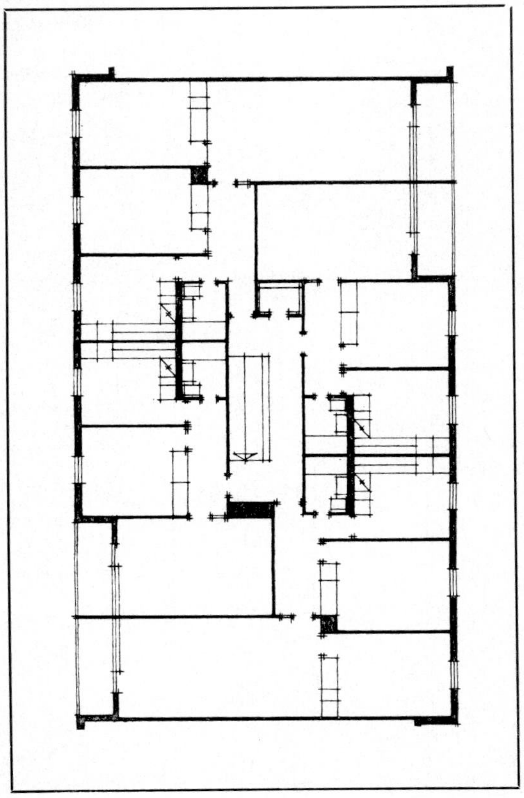

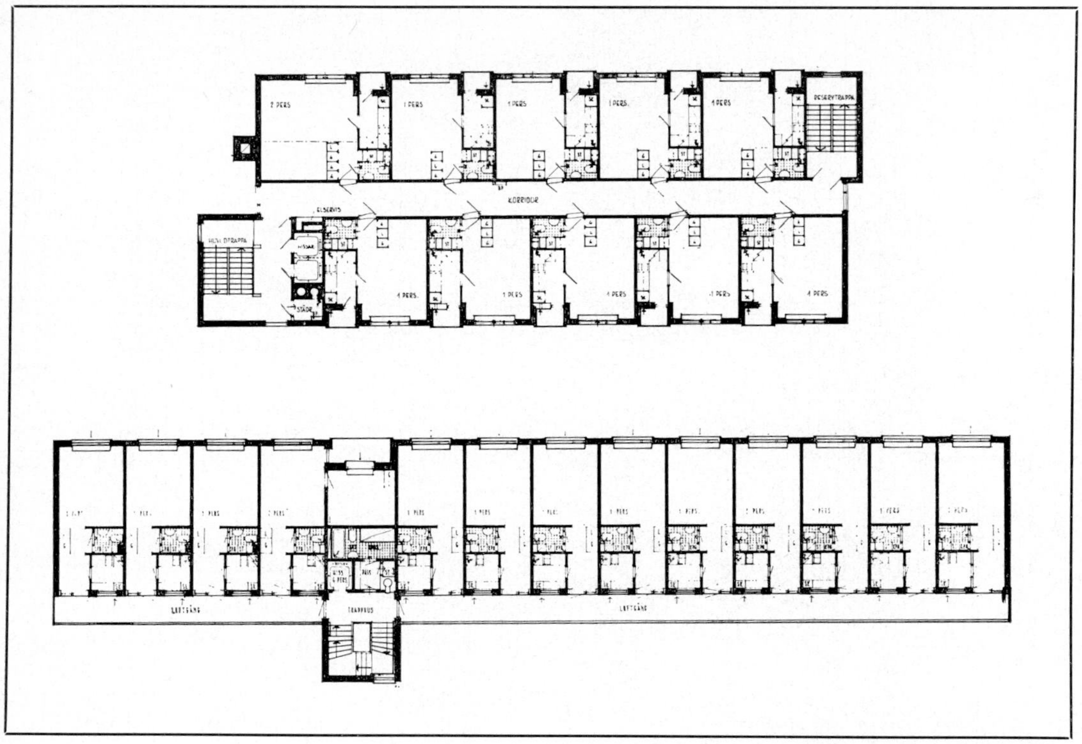

21 Pensioners' Home, Enskede, Stock holm

Architects: C. and H. Åkerblad

The pensioners' home has been erected for th Stockholm Public Assistance Authority an contains 99 one-person flats and 11 two-persor flats in a 13-storey building and 40 dwellings in four-storey one with access galleries. The ide of this form of planning was to test the suitabili of a pensioners' home located in a tall, slend building with the advantages afforded by sho connections and easy access to lifts. The low floors have been provided with space for joinery and engineering shop and a weavin room in which are conducted experiment courses, designed to give employment to th pensioners. There are also certain small room which can be used by the pensioners as ten porary work rooms. There is also a laund equipped with washing machines, and a servic kitchen. The building is of off-form concrete ar all the equipment in the flats is designed f factory manufacture and assembly on the site

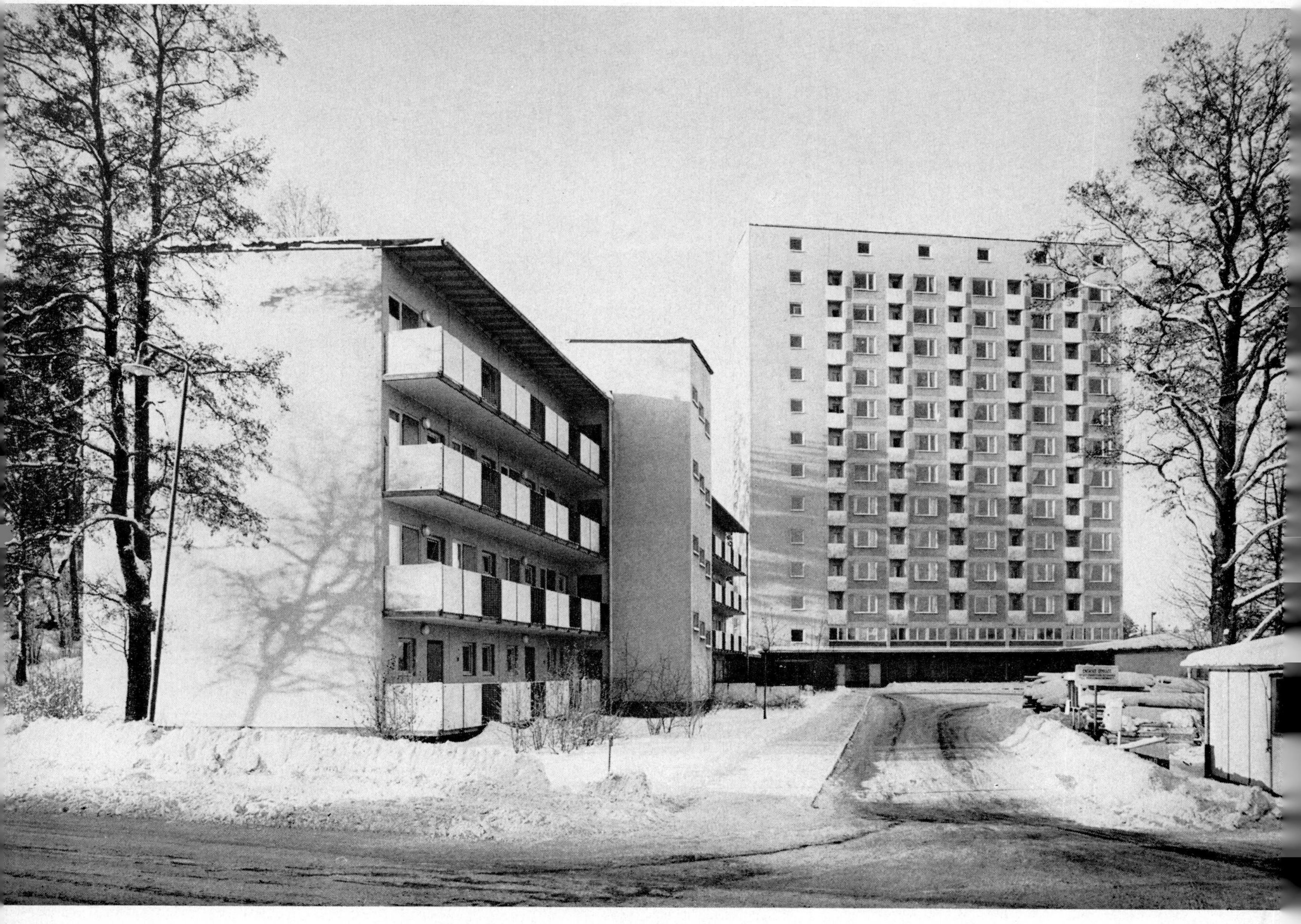

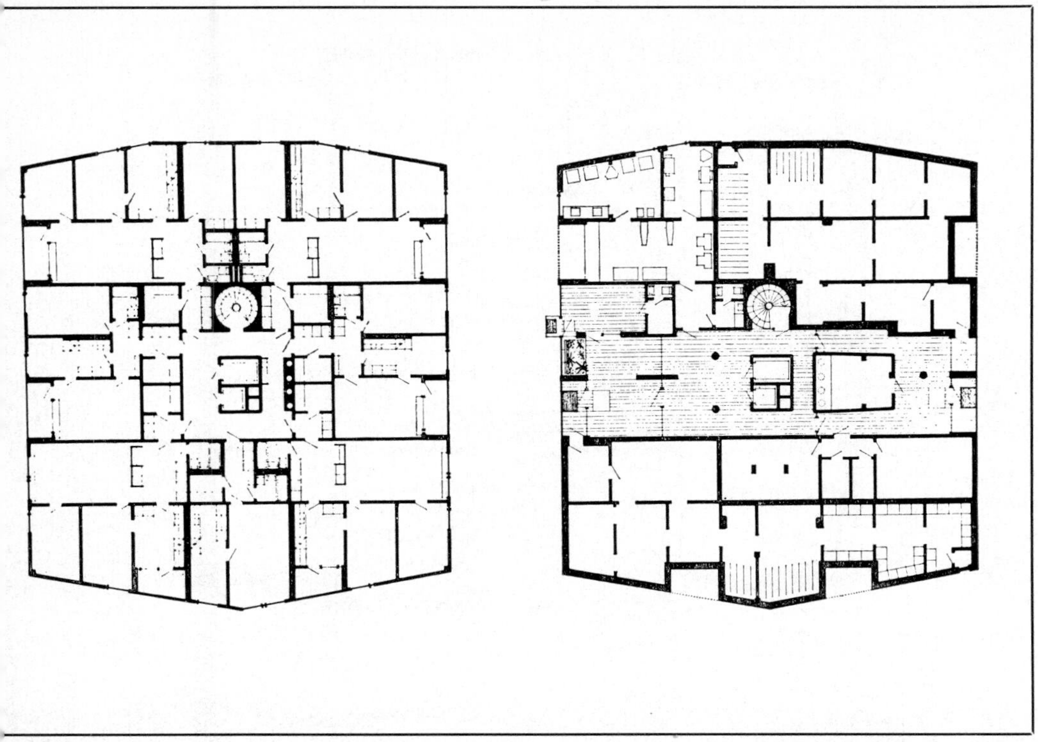

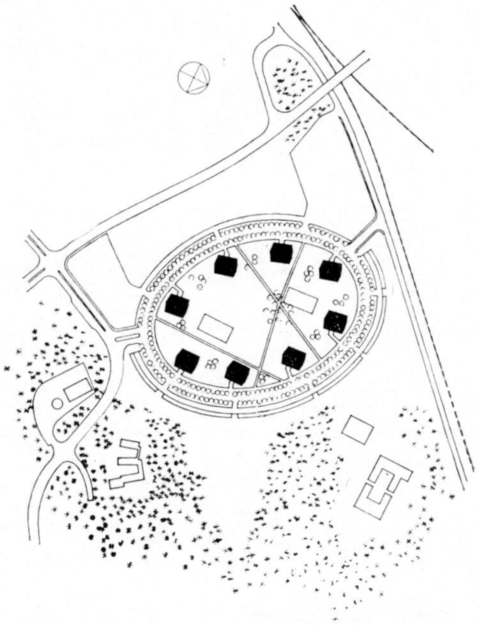

22 Täby

Architects: S. Lindström and Associates

A group of eight 17-storey point blocks arranged in a formal elliptical pattern and slightly reminiscent of candles on a birthday cake. Immediately adjoining the site provision has also been made for car parking, a central boiler house, an infants' school and an elementary school.

At entrance level each block contains shops, laundry, air raid shelters, heating distribution equipment, and refuse containers. Floors 1–14 inclusive are planned similarly with seven units to the floor accessible from a central lobby served by a spiral staircase and two lifts. These are one bedsitter, two two-bedroom units, two three-bedroom units, and two one-bedroom units—an economical, ingenious, and compact piece of planning.

The top two floors are planned as maisonettes, four of these being provided in the angles of the block in addition to two one-bedroom and one bedsitter flat units at each of the top levels.

A patented system of construction was used in this scheme involving *in situ* poured concrete with climbing formwork for the lift well which was erected first and used as the basis of subsequent construction of the remainder of each of the blocks which are in reinforced concrete load-bearing cross wall and reinforced concrete floors.

Although bathroom zoning is not ideal in any of the flats this scheme has considerable architectural merit both in its planning and external treatment, although the too formal arrangement of the group and the much too close spacing of the blocks, having regard to their height and overshadowing, is unfortunate. A proportion of lower linking blocks would have also assisted very greatly in overcoming what is almost a height monotony of a new type.

Switzerland

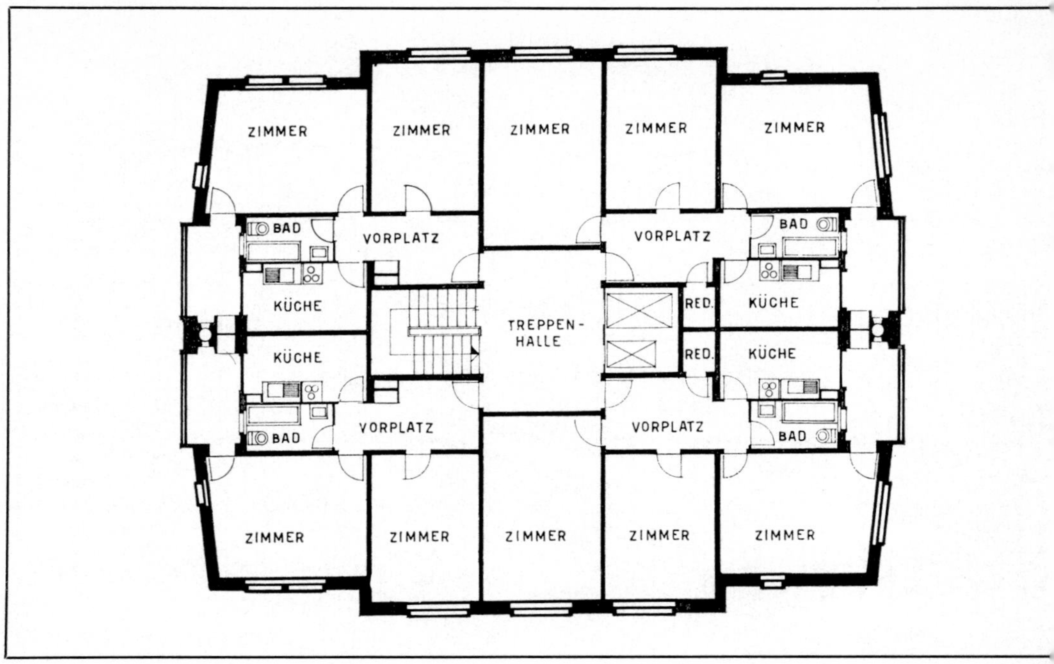

1 Tower Houses, Mittlere Strasse, Basel

Architects: Gfeller and Mahly

Urban replanning in the high density field with a total of 150 flats in three tower buildings, in a key location close to the heart of the city.

Each block, which is planned with a single internal staircase and two lifts contains 50 flats, 24 three-room and 26 two-room units two of each type on the typical floor. Direct access to the habitable rooms in each of the flats is obtained from an entrance hall, and both bathrooms and kitchens have natural light and ventilation. Private balconies adjoin the kitchens and living rooms and these also give access to the refuse chutes.

Although the staircase is planned internally it receives a certain amount of borrowed light through the kitchens.

The ground floor contains two two-room flats as well as the entrance hall, two laundries and two drying rooms. The entrance hall is planned as vestibule with tenants' lockers for postal and other tradesmen's deliveries; the inner doors are kept locked to ensure privacy of the block. The lock is operated by the tenants by remote control for visitors who use a telephone intercommunication system.

A basement is also provided to each of the blocks containing tenants' storage rooms.

The system of construction is brick load-bearing walls throughout, with reinforced concrete floors, the brickwork having a maximum thickness of 15½in for external walls. Basement and ground floors are, however, in monolithic concrete construction.

Heiligfeld Development, Zurich

hitect: Steiner

splendid comprehensive town planning and sing development undertaken by the Zurich Council. The housing, which has been nned round the fringe of a large central park a, is in the form of three-, four-, and eight-storey slab blocks, and two 11- and 12-storey tower blocks. Garages, restaurant, kindergarten school, church, and excellent children's play areas all form a part of the scheme, and a fine open air swimming pool is located nearby on the other side of Letzigraben which forms the northern boundary of the scheme proper.

There are four of the three-storey blocks and these are of the normal staircase access walk-up type and call for no special comment.

Four- and eight-storey blocks, however, have been combined together in three well composed groups with each of the main units planned on a chevron system. The eight-storey block is designed on the access gallery principle with six flats to the typical floor, and the four-storey block with four flats to the floor are accessible from two staircases. A single lift is provided in the eight-storey blocks.

Four-storey and eight-storey blocks are linked by means of a garage and store block which helps to provide a well integrated arrangement, and also to control the penetration of vehicular traffic into the site so that the major area is accessible only for pedestrian traffic through a series of well laid out pedestrian parkways and paths.

The focus of the scheme is provided by the two Y-shaped towers each containing 44 flats with four flats to the typical floor. Two of these at each floor level contain one bedroom and two are of the large bedsitter type with naturally ventilated kitchens and bathrooms.

Another variant of the typical floor arrangement provides for two one-bedroom units and two two-bedroom units with smaller living areas.

The ground floor contains entrance hall, staircase and lift access, bicycle sheds and pram sheds as well as tenants' storage and laundries. The basement floor provided includes further tenants' storage space as well as central heating and other services.

The blocks are constructed with a concrete *in situ* frame and infill panels in masonry finished in white Tyrolean cement with the structural members exposed. The cantilevered roof deck and the floors are also all in reinforced concrete.

The density of development of the whole area is approximately 150 persons per acre.

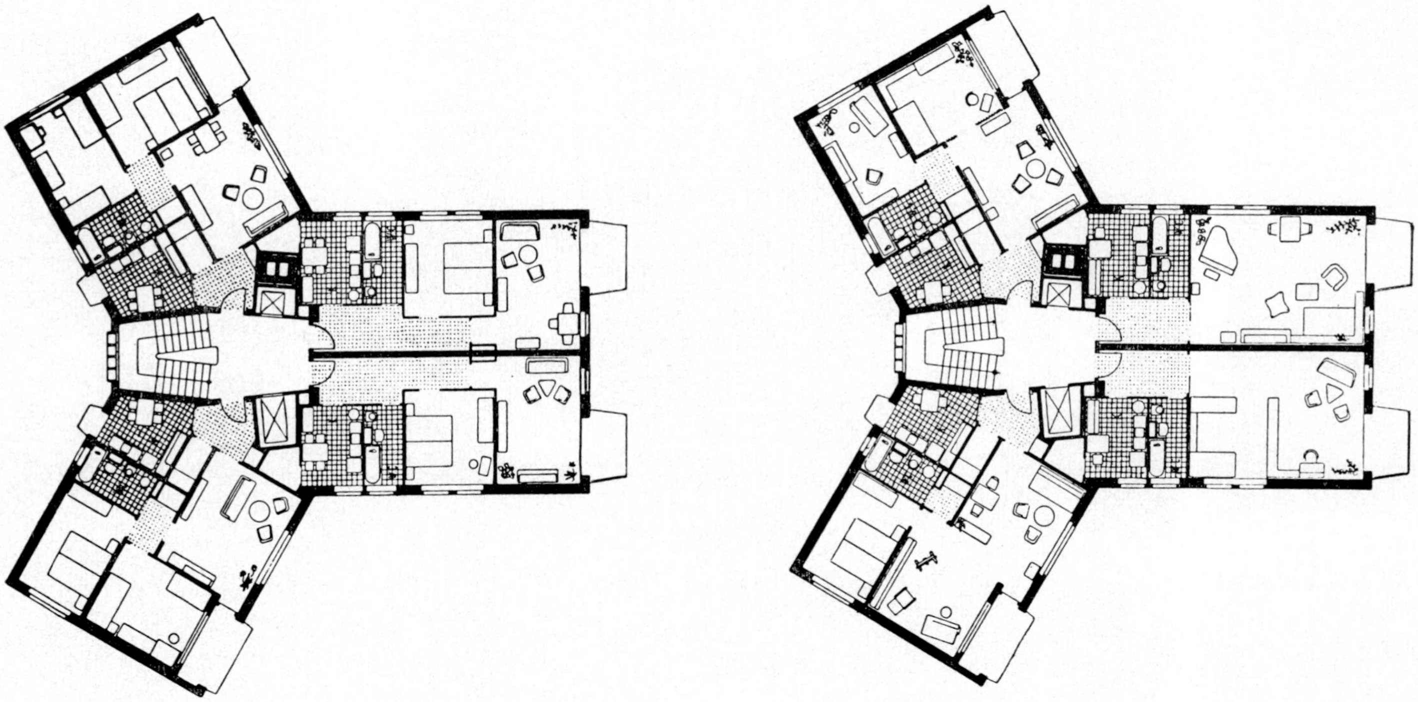

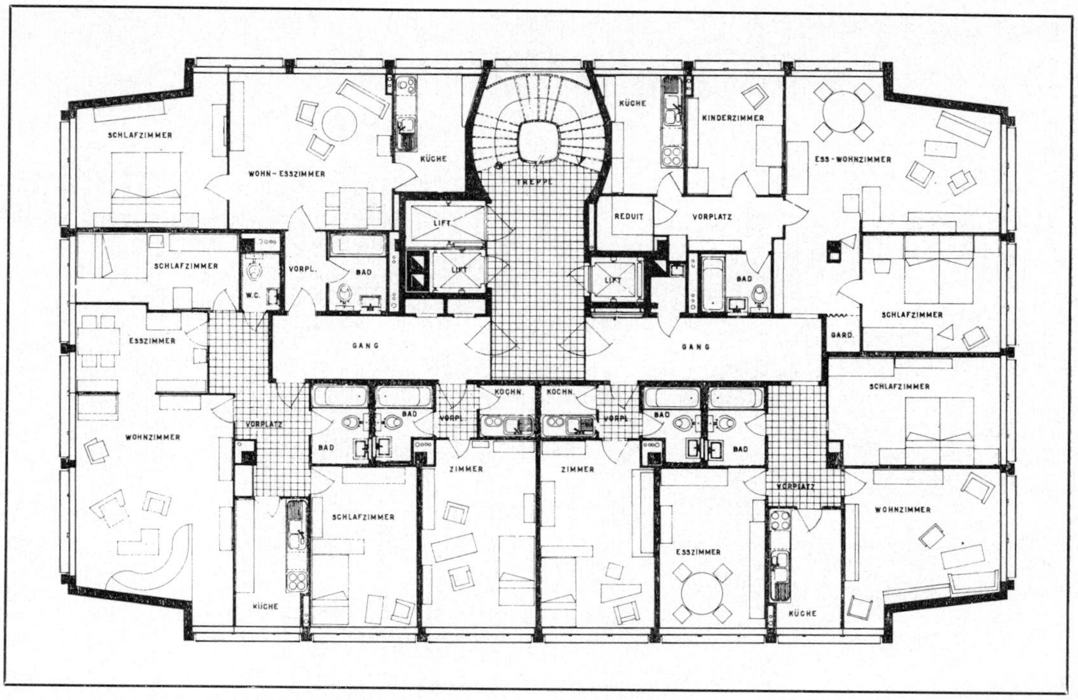

Steinenvorstadt, Basel

rchitect: Gfeller

ᐱn inner city zone development forming an ntegrated part of a larger town planning econstruction scheme with the intention of etaining some of the residential properties raditionally forming an important part of the entral area. The principal focus of this develop-nent is formed by a 13-storey block containing hops, business and other commercial proper-es in the lower four floors, and in the upper oors a series of flats. Access to these is by the ingle staircase and three lifts and a short entral corridor.

The typical floor contains five units of which wo are bedsittingroom units, one a one-bed-oom unit with living room, kitchen and bath-oom, and the other two two-bedroom units vhich also include living room and study, itchen and bathroom. Bath and W.C.s are all rtificially lit and ventilated, and kitchens aturally lit.

The system of construction is reinforced oncrete frame with reinforced concrete panel nfill.

4 Malagnou-Parc, Geneva

Architect: M. Saugey

A single H-shaped block containing accommodation for 450 people in 175 flats on a site of approximately $2\frac{1}{2}$ acres at a density of 180 persons to the acre.

The typical floor contains 24 flats of varying sizes—four bedsitters, eight one-bedroom, four two-bedroom, and four five-bedroom units. Access to these is via a staircase located at the intersection of the arms of the H and four lifts at each of these points.

The ground floor contains, apart from the entrance hall, shops, kindergarten, cloak room and play room, cleaner's room and a post office, as well as servants' room and a petrol filling station. Ten of the flats are also located at this level including six of the one-bedroom type and four bedsitters.

The centre section of the block is carried one floor higher than the remainder and this contains eight flats.

The system of construction is in reinforced concrete utilizing precast concrete columns and cast *in situ* floors and beams. External infill consists of hollow terra cotta blocks bonded and faced on the outside with artificial stone and on the inside with plaster.

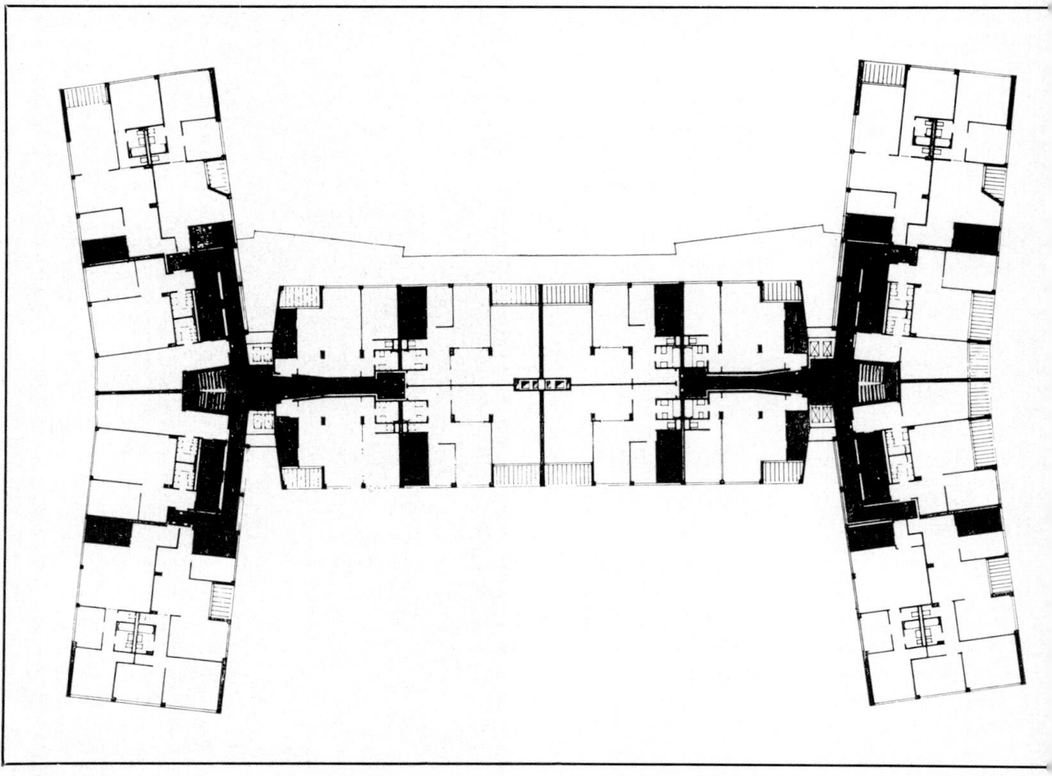

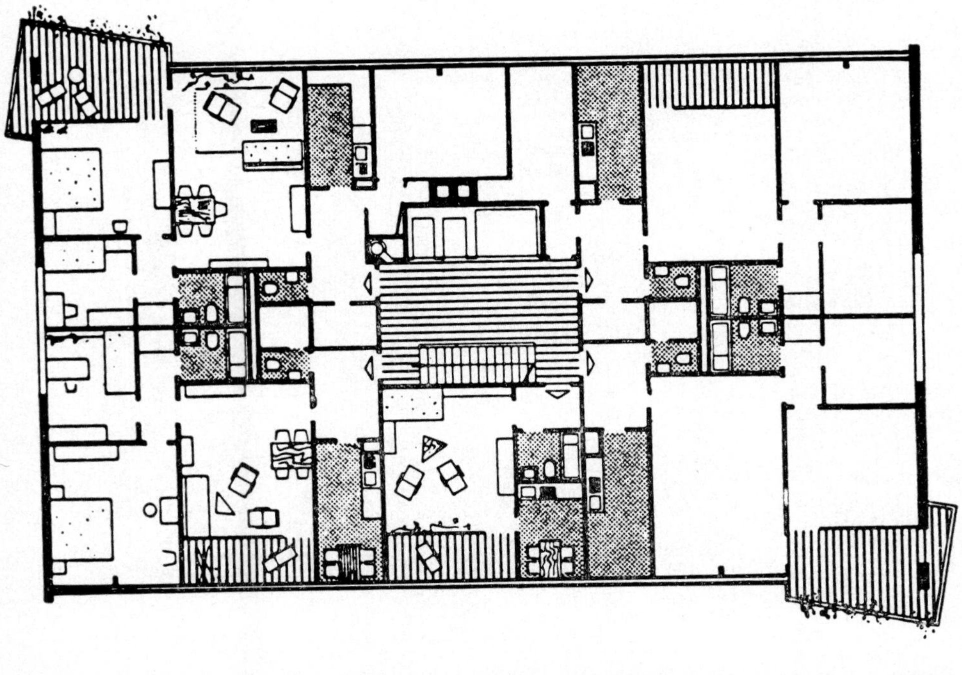

5 Stieracker, Birsfelden

Architects: Gass and Associates

Three similar 17-storey point blocks of Scandinavian type with five flats to the typical floor accessible from a single staircase and three lifts.

The normal arrangement of the typical floor provides for two three-bedroom flats, two two-bedroom units, and one bedsitter, each of the flats having a private balcony, kitchen on the external wall and internal bathrooms and W.C.s sharing common ducts. The roof space is taken up by one large studio flat with living room/dining space, kitchen, study, three bedrooms and bathroom.

Ground floor level is entirely open except for the entrance hall and access to lifts, being raised on pilotis. The basement provides space for 25 cars, bicycles, four laundries, rentable cellar space, and heating installation.

The system of construction is mixed, having steel frame at ground floor and basement level, and the upper floors with interior walls of brick and the narrow end walls and balustrades of reinforced concrete with steel stiffeners to the window walls.

United Kingdom

1 Churchill Gardens, Pimlico, Westminster

Architects: Powell and Moya.

A derelict and bomb-damaged inner urban area of some 33 acres comprehensively redeveloped following an architectural competition immediately after the Second World War. Because of the problems of decanting, development phased in four distinct stages, the whole scheme providing 634 dwellings with 73 per cent in 9-, 10- and 11-storey blocks, 8 per cent in 7-storey, and 19 per cent in 3- and 4-storey blocks at an overall density of 59 dwellings or 200 persons per acre.

Generally, in the first stage, the maison
principle has been used for the lower blocks,
staircase access system in the high blo
Initially monolithic reinforced concrete walls
floors formed the basis of the structural sys
with brick outer cladding and wood wool inte
lining. In later stages this was changed to a n
orthodox system of reinforced concrete fl
carrying 11in cavity wall brickwork for
external walls with concrete columns
stiffening membrane walls.

The first stage nine-storey blocks are plan
with projecting staircase towers and a sir
lift adjoining serving two flats at each floor le
the majority of these being of the three-bedr

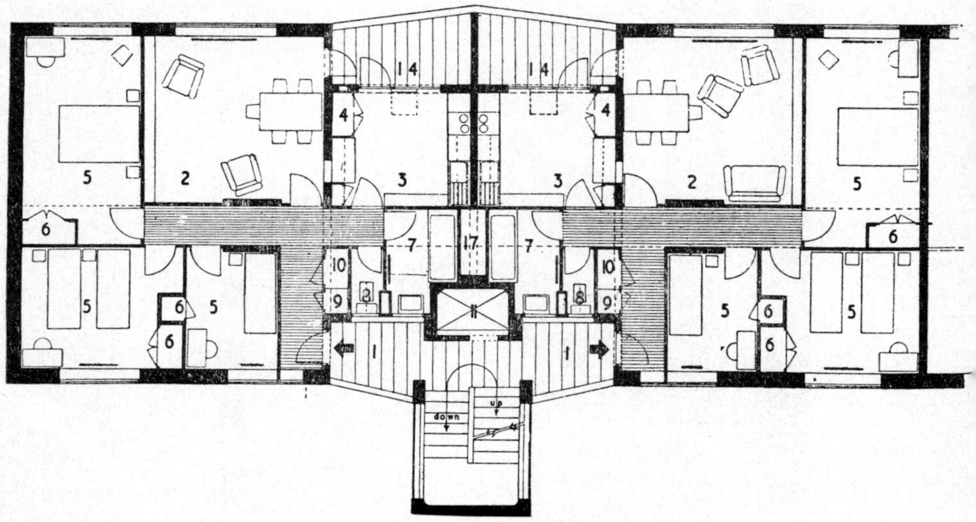

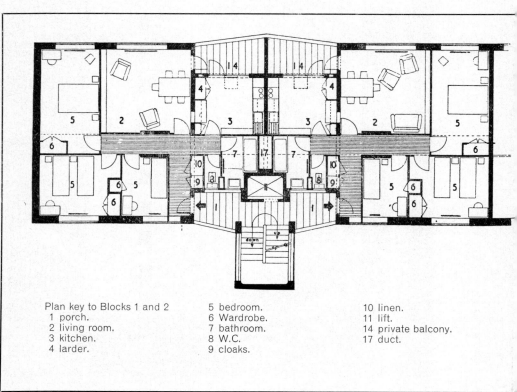

Plan key to Blocks 1 and 2
1 porch.
2 living room.
3 kitchen.
4 larder.
5 bedroom.
6 Wardrobe.
7 bathroom.
8 W.C.
9 cloaks.
10 linen.
11 lift.
14 private balcony.
17 duct.

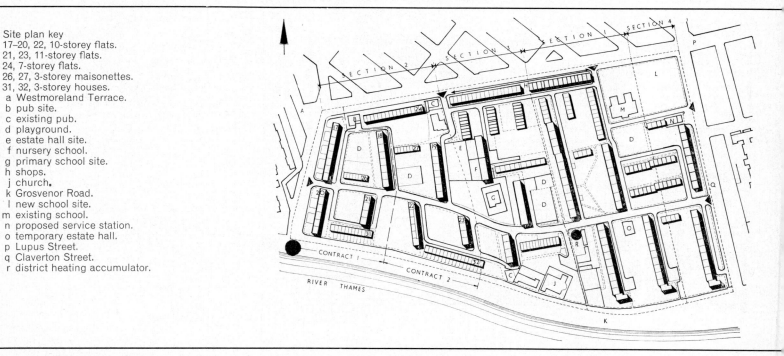

Site plan key
17–20, 22, 10-storey flats.
21, 23, 11-storey flats.
24, 7-storey flats.
26, 27, 3-storey maisonettes.
31, 32, 3-storey houses.
a Westmoreland Terrace.
b pub site.
c existing pub.
d playground.
e estate hall site.
f nursery school.
g primary school site.
h shops.
j church.
k Grosvenor Road.
l new school site.
m existing school.
n proposed service station.
o temporary estate hall.
p Lupus Street.
q Claverton Street.
r district heating accumulator.

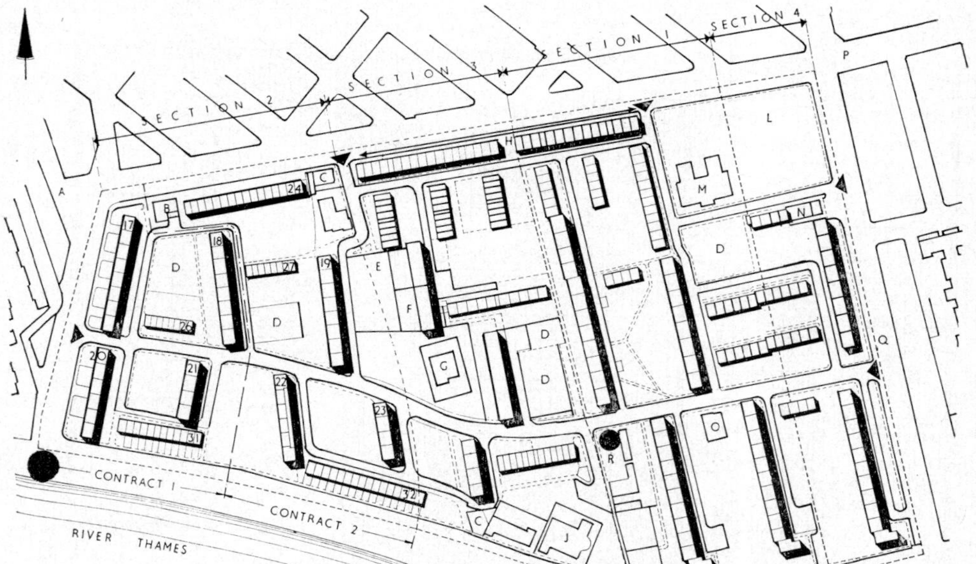

e and unusual only in so far as the kitchen is nned adjoining the balcony which is also essible from the living room, and the bath-m closely adjoining the short access balcony l the front door.

'he private balconies to the flats have a ved front which has allowed space for a ondary spiral staircase from the sixth floor to the top of the building to allow secondary escape across the roof terrace in accordance h the requirements, at that time, of the lding Act authority.

'anks and lift motors have been neatly uped together in a distinct'.:e series of drums 'oof level.

In the early blocks no dust chutes were provided but these were added in subsequent stages. All the high blocks have basements containing communal laundries, drying rooms, and tenants' storage areas.

Schools, a community centre, a church, a hall, very adequate children's play areas, and garaging are included in the scheme as well as a number of shops which occupy the ground floor space in the seven-storey blocks facing Lupus Street.

It is claimed that, to meet the economic problems confronting the developer, the access system was changed in the later part of the scheme as well as the height of the tall blocks which was increased by one floor to ten storeys. A continuous access balcony was provided in these blocks with three staircases to the typical floor containing six flats of which the majority were of the two-bedroom type, as well as by two lifts—the economy being chiefly in the reduction of the total number of lifts by one, and the elimination of the secondary spiral escape staircases between sixth floor and roof level, a development which improves in quality in the later stages, particularly in the treatment of space in between buildings and the relation-ship of blocks of different heights. Overall density 201 persons per acre.

2 Gilbert Sheldon House, Paddington, London

Architect: R. Jensen

An eight- and a four-storey slab block forming part of a redevelopment scheme intended to accommodate at this stage 40 families—30 in two-bedroom flats and two in one-bedroom flats in the eight-storey block, and eight families in three-bedroom maisonettes in the four-storey block at an overall density of approximately 136 persons per acre.

The typical floor to the high block contains four flats with two staircases and two lifts. While kitchens and bathrooms are grouped together for convenience in dealing with plumbing, in this instance traffic between bedrooms and bathrooms has been confined to a night area and away from the front entrance door, although escape requirements still necessitate a short internal circulation corridor to allow direct access from each habitable room to the front door.

At ground floor level two of the flats are of the two-bedroom type and two of one-bedroom but with larger dining/kitchens. Standard dry refuse chutes are planned to each of the staircase wells.

Economics and tradition decided jointly that open fires were to be provided to each flat and this has also necessitated fuel storage, the fuel being delivered by lift.

Each kitchen which is naturally lit and ventilated has its own clothes drying facilities.

From fifth floor upward in the eight-storey block linking balconies have been used as the most economical means of providing secondary escape in case of fire.

The system of construction is *in situ* reinforced concrete frame and slab with piled foundations to the eight-storey block. The external cladding is mainly brickwork; the end walls to the eight-storey block are in reinforced concrete gunite sprayed.

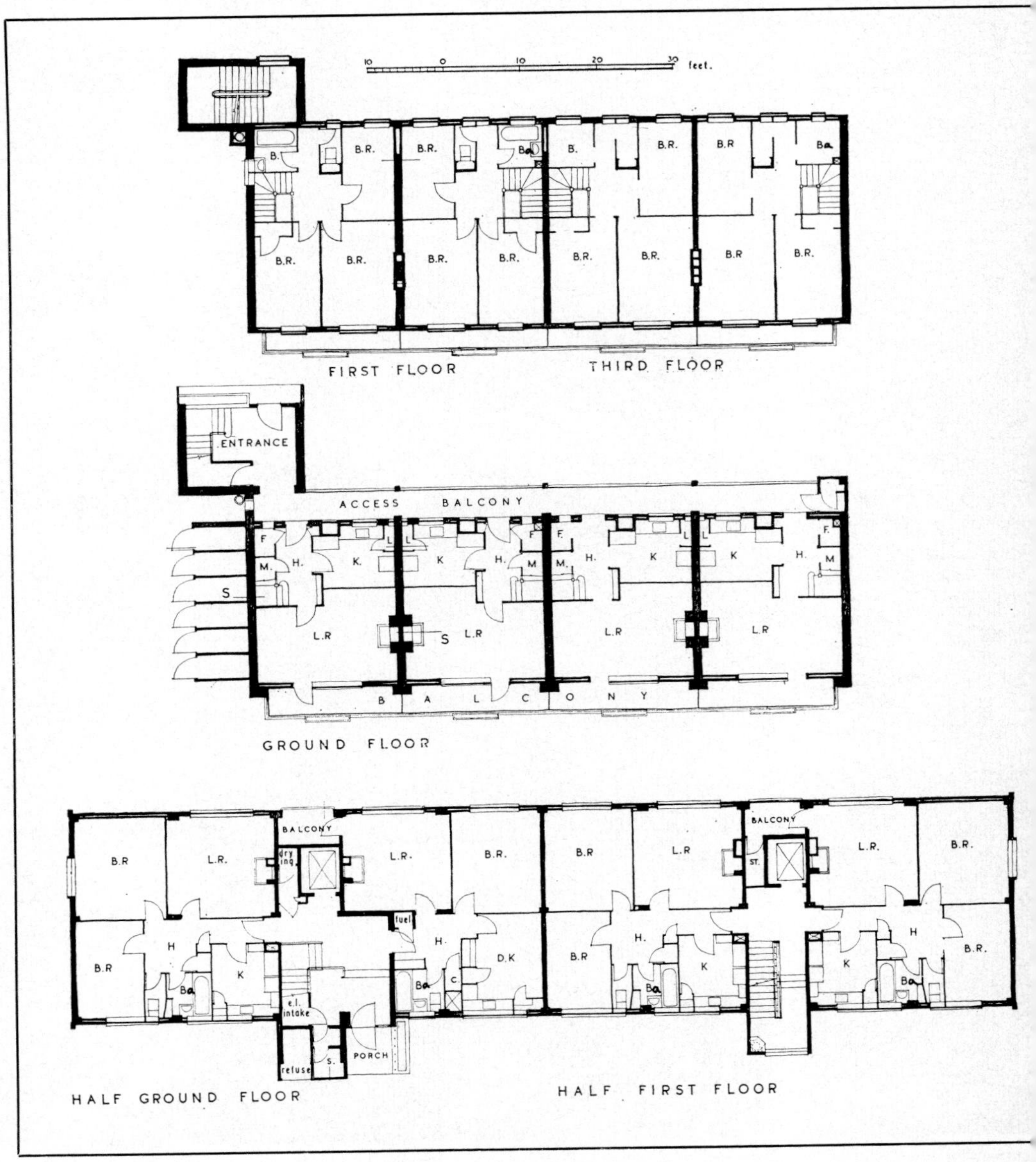

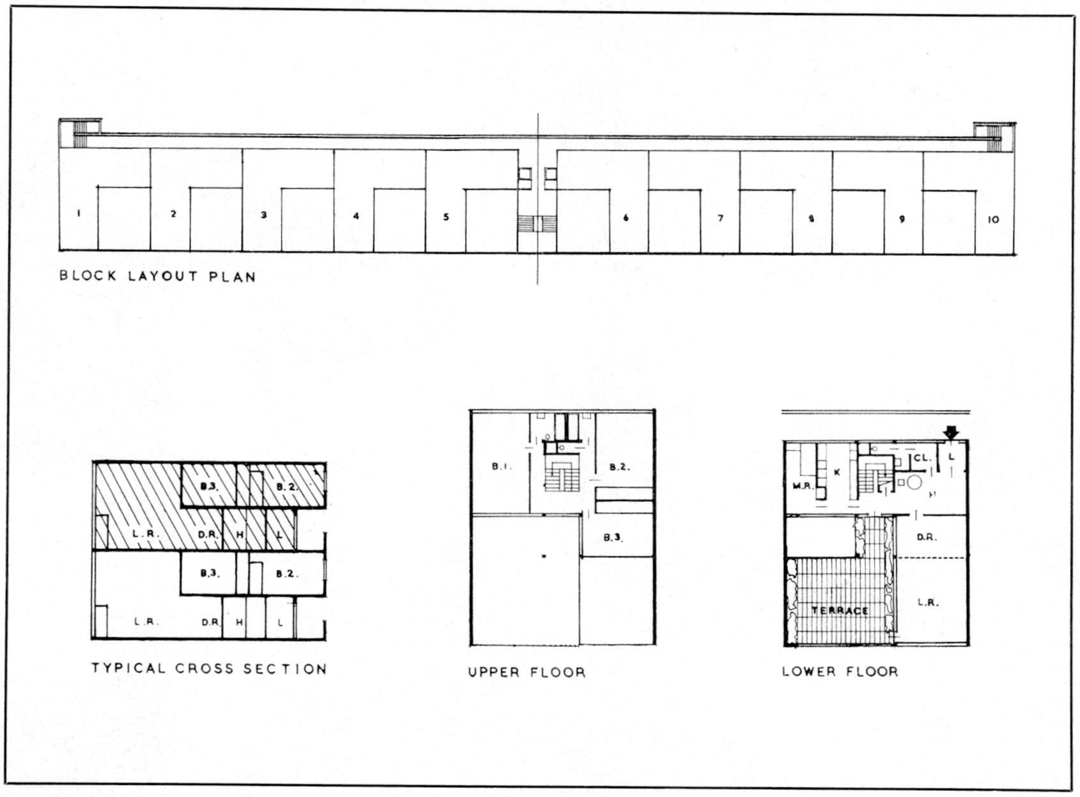

Connaught Mews, Paddington, London

rchitect: R. Jensen

scheme for the development of a four acre site djoining Marble Arch and overlooking Hyde ark with a concert hall to house 2000 people as ell as a branch public library, reading room, formation and welfare centre and offices, and ten-storey block of maisonettes including ops, restaurant and roof garden. Because of e considerable concentration of traffic, partly a result of building a concert hall on this site, e Marble Arch traffic system was also re-signed as a corollary to this scheme.

The ground and first floor to the ten-storey ock are entirely occupied by shops and staurant with an open air terrace at first floor vel overlooking Hyde Park. Above this there e four layers of maisonettes with ten units in ch layer. Each maisonette contains living om/dining room at the lower level together th kitchen and maid's room and large open ivate garden terrace. Both the living room and e terrace are double volume areas and extend through the two floors occupied by the aisonette. In addition, at the upper floor level, e three bedrooms and two bathrooms.

These self-contained garden flats are of the xury type and therefore seem to justify their n private built-in gardens.

Access to the units is by means of central aircase and twin lifts via access balconies on e north side of the block. These, however, do t pass any of the habitable rooms. Secondary aircases are also placed at the ends of the ocks.

The system of construction is monolithic *situ* reinforced concrete.

Four large penthouse units with their own vate garden terraces are planned at roof level.

4 Golden Lane, City of London

Architects: Chamberlin, Powell and Bon

One of the first developments of residential accommodation to be erected right in the heart of the City of London for many years, and on a total site area of just over seven acres 562 dwellings have been provided at a density of 200 persons per acre.

The dwellings which are 17 per cent bedsitting-room, 48 per cent one-bedroom, 28 per cent two-bedroom, and 7 per cent three-bedroom units are planned in one high 16-storey which forms the main focus, and in a series of seven-, six- and four-storey blocks grouped around intervening playground areas, paved areas, bowling green and community centre. A public house, restaurant, 20 shops, a badminton court and swimming pool are also included as well as a boiler house to supply the whole scheme in the basement of the 16-storey block.

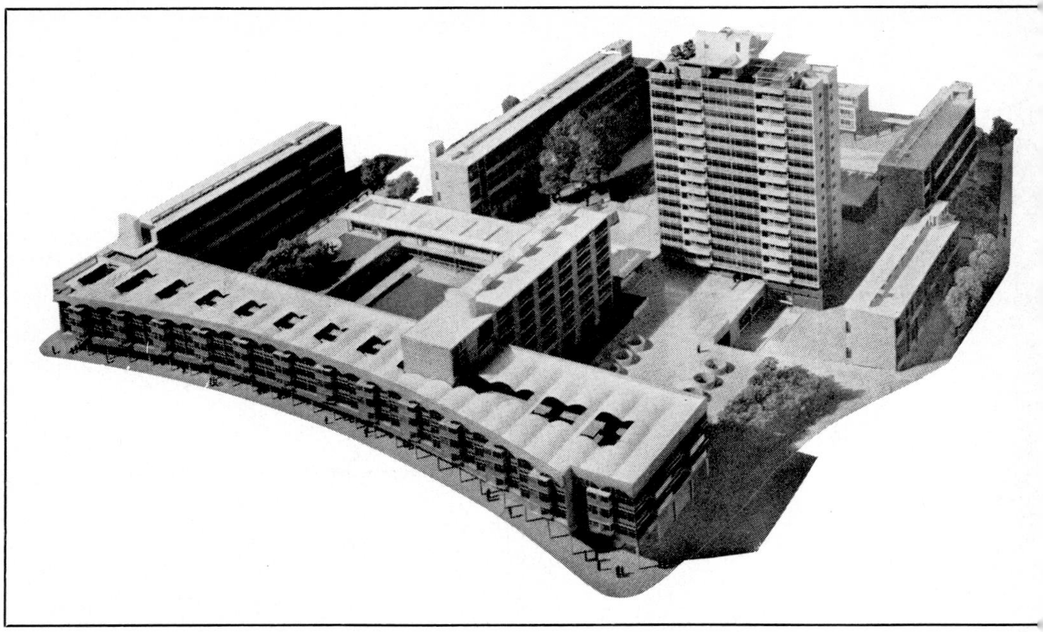

he six-storey blocks consist of three layers naisonettes all either of the two-bedroom or three-bedroom type. These are compactly nned and with an interesting architectural lity which lacks a certain unity with the focal t of the scheme, the multi-storey block. This torey block is one of the few English examples entral corridor access. It is served by two and two staircases, and the typical floor tains eight identical one-bedroom units.

onsiderable ingenuity has been used in viding secondary escape which is provided neans of a door in each of the bedrooms. In end flats this involves the use of cat ladders n to the half landing level.

he 16-storey block has a reinforced concrete ne and floors and the lower blocks brick load ring walls with reinforced concrete main rs and basement and timber intermediate rs, suspended from the reinforced concrete rs by steel hangers which are concealed in partitions.

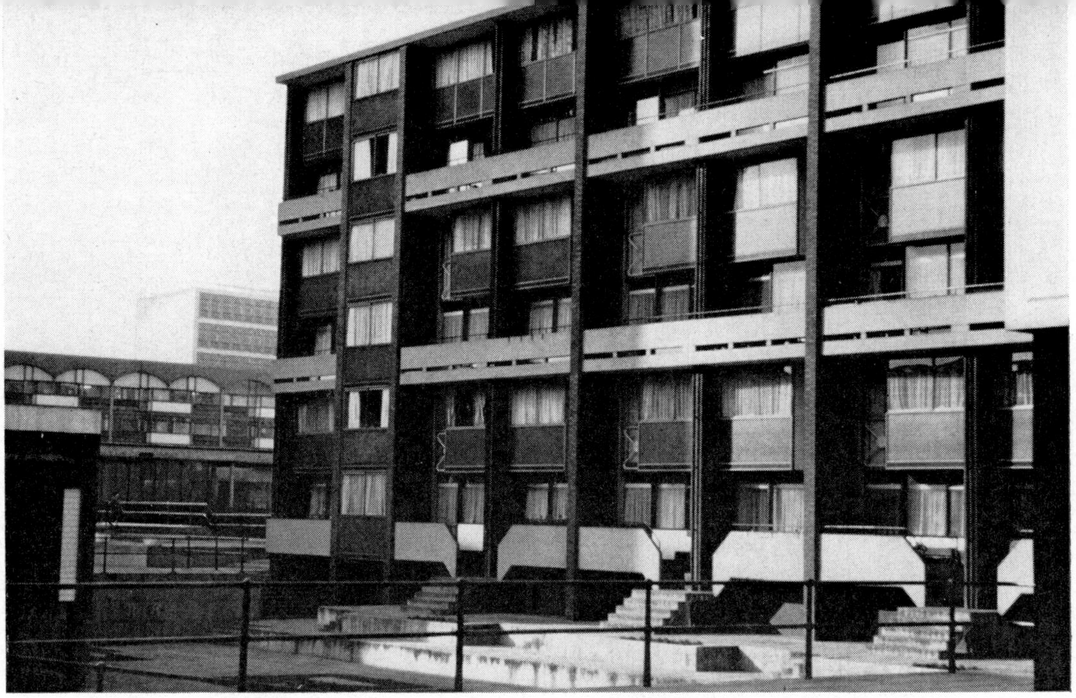

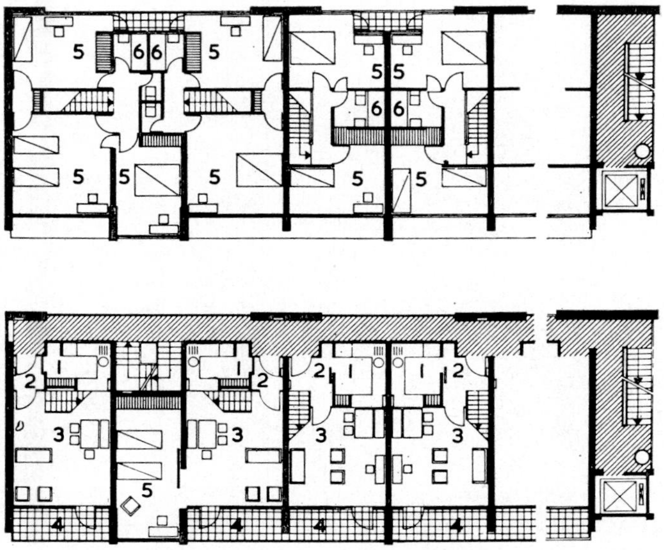

Typical maisonette plans on 4th and 5th floors

Typical maisonette plans on 1st, 2nd and 3rd floors

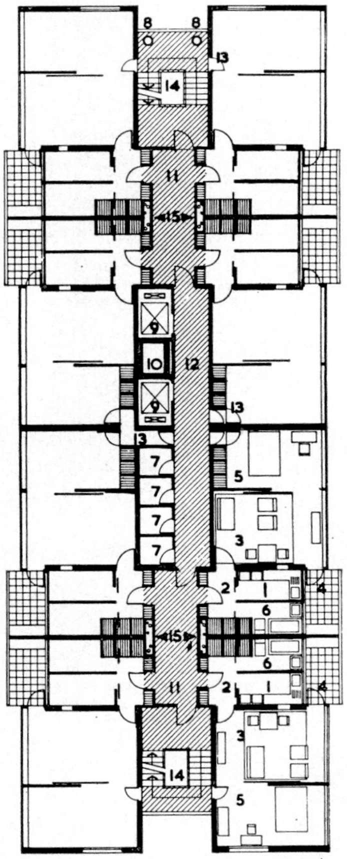

1 kitchen.
2 entrance lobby.
3 living room.
4 private balcony.
5 bedroom.
6 bath and W.C.
7 tenants' store.
8 refuse chute.
9 lift.
10 boiler flue.
11 common lobby.
12 lift lobby.
13 escape door.
14 public stairs.

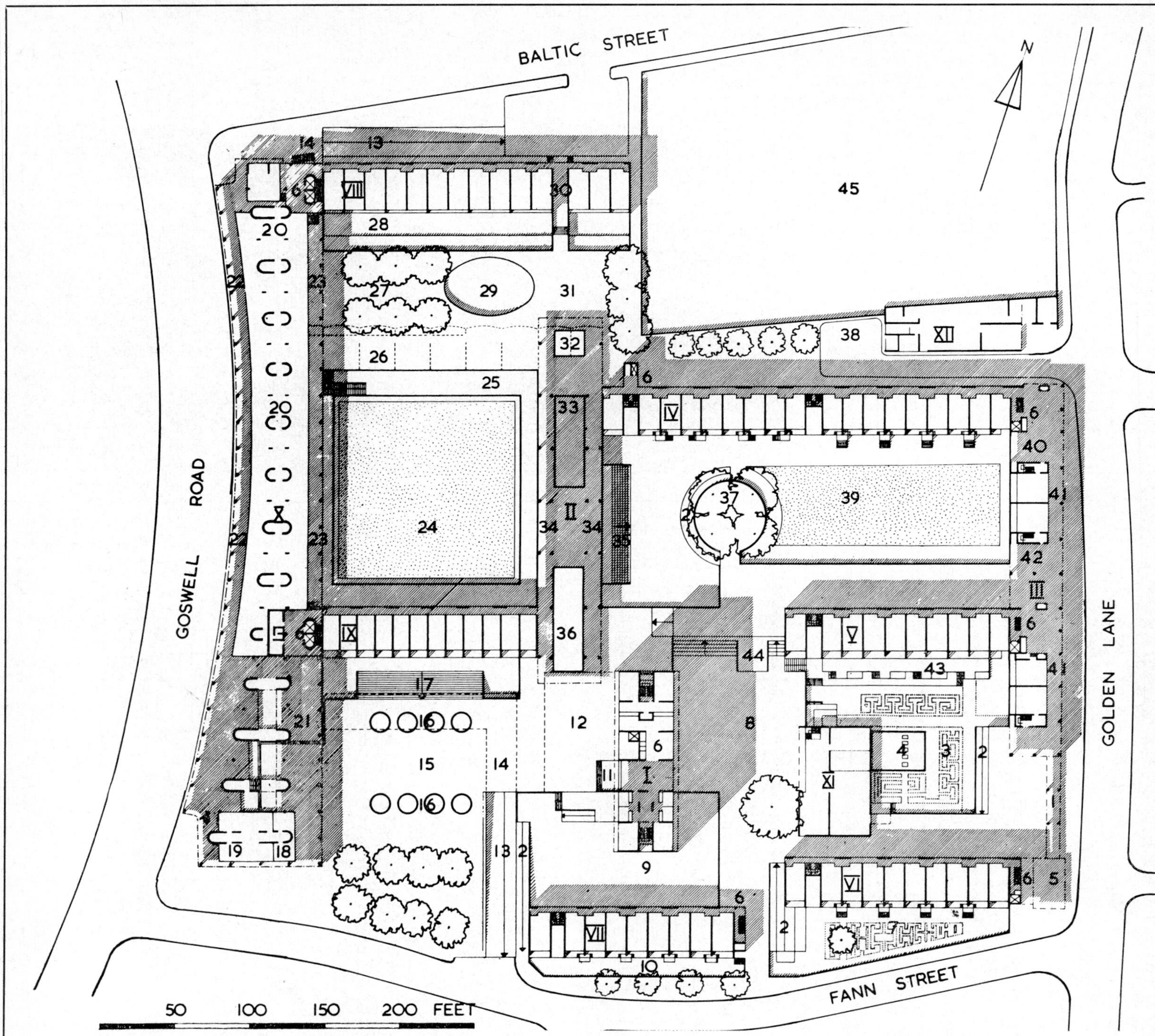

I *Great Arthur House:* 16 storeys; 120 flats of 2 rooms on 15 floors; estate office; laundries, etc., at ground level, stores in basement.
II *Recreation Building:* (to be built); badminton court, swimming pool, etc.
III *Stanley Cohen House:* 4 storeys, 32 flats of 1, 2, 3, & 4 rooms.
IV *Basterfield House:* 6 storeys; 54 maisonettes of 3 & 4 rooms.
V *Bayer House:* 6 storeys; 30 maisonettes of 3 & 4 rooms.
VI *Bowater House:* 6 storeys; 30 maisonettes of 3 & 4 rooms.
VII *Cuthbert Harrowing House:* 4 storeys; 18 maisonettes of 3 & 4 rooms.
VIII *Block at Baltic Street:* (to be built); 6 storeys; 42 maisonettes of 3 & 4 rooms, with additional low level floor of 14 one-room flats.
IX *Block at Bowling Green:* (to be built); 6 storeys; 72 one-room flats.
X *Block at Goswell Road:* (to be built); 4 storeys; 147 flats, mostly of 2 and some of 3 rooms, with 6 guest rooms, on 3 floors above shops, etc.
XI *Community Building:* hall at ground level, club rooms at lower level.
XII *Estate Workshops:* serving all Corporation's housing estates.

1 Pedestrian approach to site under strip canopy.
2 Pedestrian ramp to low court and tenants stores in basement.
3 Low level court with formal garden layout.
4 Pool.
5 Canopy.
6 Entrance lobbies to blocks of flats.
7 Low level court with grass and paving.
8 Main pedestrian piazza.
9 Low level court south of boiler house, paved.
10 Low level court south of Cuthbert Harrowing House.
11 Open way through under Great Arthur House.
12 Boiler house below ground level.
13 Ramp down to underground service road.
14 Service road below ground.
15 Pedestrian forecourt at ground level with garages under.
16 Vents to garages.
17 Steps down to low level court and open way through under Block IX.
18 Restaurant.
19 Public house.
20 Shops.
21 Open way through under Block X.
22 Covered colonnade over pavement.
23 Covered colonnade under Block X.
24 Low level court with bowling green.
25 Terrace to Residents Club.
26 Residents Club at lower level.
27 Playground for older children.
28 Low level private terraces to one-room flats in Block VIII.
29 Sunken pit for ball games.
30 Way through under Block VIII.
31 Playground for younger children.
32 Nursery room.
33 Swimming pool.
34 Pedestrian bridge.
35 Steps between low courts and open way through under Recreation Building.
36 Enclosed badminton court and gymnasium.
37 Bastion containing trees.
38 Service road to workshops.
39 Low level court with lawn and decorative paving.
40 Open space under Stanley Cohen House.
41 Covered colonnade under Stanley Cohen House.
42 Open way through under Stanley Cohen House.
43 Stepped terraces south of Bayer House.
44 Plinth for sculpture.
45 Site for future L.C.C. Primary School.

Lincoln Estate, Tidey Street, Stepney, London

:hitects: J. L. Martin, H. Bennett and W. Lewis etc. (L.C.C.)

development including 99 three-room maison-es in a single tall block, 282 four-room maison-es, and 41 small three-storey flats, and terrace houses, at a density of 38 dwellings or) persons per acre.

By the use of the 19-storey block 45 per cent of the other dwellings have private gardens.

The multi-storey block contains cross-over type maisonettes orientated with all living rooms and dining/kitchens with south aspect. Internal corridor access occurs at alternate floors and is serviced by twin lifts and a single staircase. In this arrangement half of the tenants go upstairs to bed in the English tradition, but the other half reverse the process and go downstairs to the bedrooms. The structure is reinforced concrete box frame.

The block contains 11 identical two-bedroom units at each floor level with the staircase and lift well arranged asymmetrically. The architectural expression with the delineation of each floor level rather than the skip floor treatment usual with maisonette planning gives very much better sense of scale, and the direct reflection of the structural system employed.

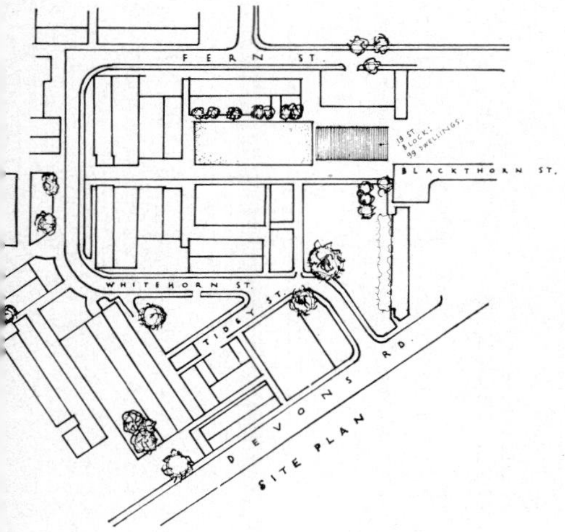

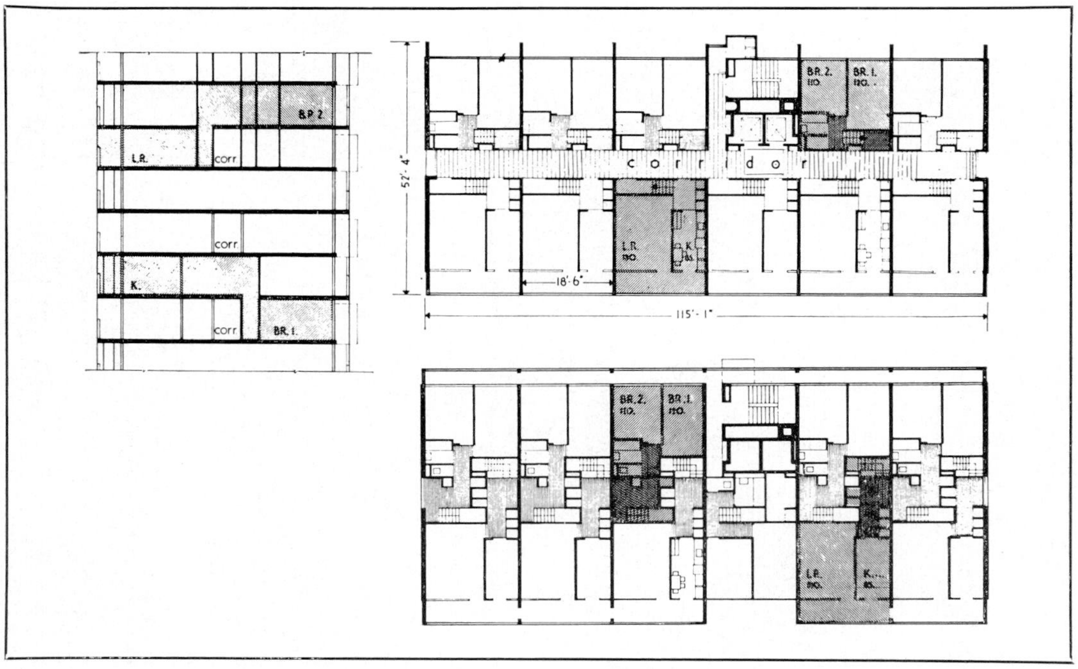

6 Park Hill, Sheffield

Architect: L. Womersley

An ambitious and original project involving demolishing 800 slum dwellings and replacing them with 2000 flats and maisonettes of which this first stage provides 994 dwellings giving a density of 200 persons per acre plus a shopping centre, public houses, laundries and other amenities.

While in some respects the scheme is reminiscent of Beaudouin's Cité Rotterdam at Strasbourg in its serpentine quality, and also somewhat akin to the triplex planning system, the scheme in its execution is entirely unique.

The method of circulation is by the use of wide access galleries at every third floor level. These have been called access streets in this scheme. They are conceived not only as the means of providing access to the accommodation but also as a meeting ground where neighbours may talk and children may play—an entirely contrary policy to that of securing the greatest degree of privacy which has usually been regarded as a fundamental part of the planning of high density flat developments.

Noise transmission is also a problem with the system of planning adopted since the streets run over and under bedrooms as well as other rooms. Internal dog-leg staircases have been linked in an interesting way with the structural system being carried in back-to-back pairs in an H shaped reinforced concrete load bearing wall which helps to stiffen the whole structure. Otherwise the structural system consists of reinforced concrete frame and floors which allows the greatest possible flexibility in planning.

The considerable slope in the site has been used to give access to certain of the galleries additional to that provided by staircases and lifts at frequent intervals. Continuous circulation is thereby obtained to any part of any building entirely under cover. A single roof level is maintained throughout the scheme with addi-

ıl storeys being added to the buildings as slope permits, and this applies not only to ›strians with perambulators but also to the trolley and other small service vehicles.

›nerally, the arrangement of the units is that are placed below the deck level of the ›nal streets, maisonettes facing on to the ›t and at the next highest level.

ıe internal spaces between the groups of ›lings have been imaginatively treated and ›ase in scale and size as the height of the ›ling increases at the lower parts of the slope.

ıere is a total of 13 passenger and three ›s lifts to the whole scheme giving an ›mely economical average of 62 dwellings lift. A considerable degree of standardiza- has been adopted in the reinforced concrete ›tural units, balconies, internal stairs, ser- installations.

ıe whole scheme is centrally heated and a ›hey refuse disposal system is provided as as mechanical ventilation to internal rooms. All kitchens are naturally lit and ›lated.

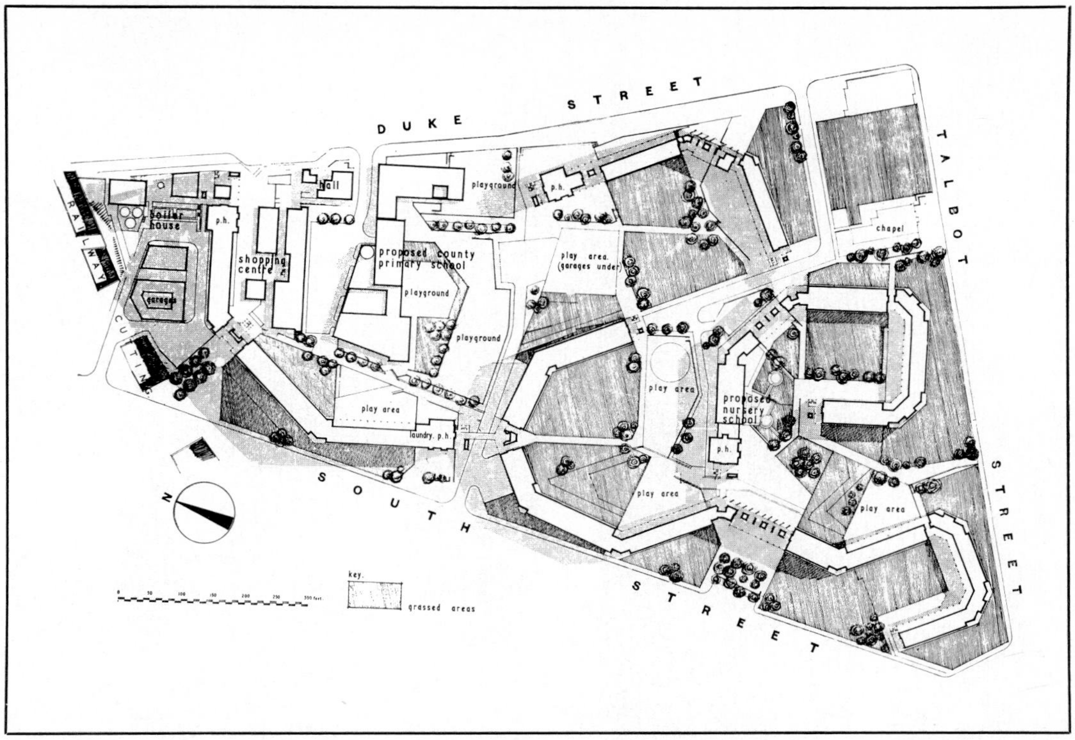

›lmington Estate, Picton Street, Cam- ›erwell, London

›itect: J. L. Martin and others (L.C.C.)

›ther scattered slum clearance development ›terest principally however in the design of 11-storey and four-storey blocks which form ›main components to the scheme. The whole ›lopment includes 682 dwellings at a density ›3 persons per acre.

ıe 11-storey blocks are planned to accom- ›ate maisonette units of the narrow frontage first made familiar in Corbusier's Marseilles ›me, although in this case the dwellings › dual aspect. All are of the two-bedroom with combined living room/dining room kitchen at access level.

›ntinuous balcony treatment has been ›ted for both main facades of the building, not only allowing for access, but large ›ate balconies to the flats at alternate floor ›s, and narrow escape balconies have also › provided linking the bedrooms.

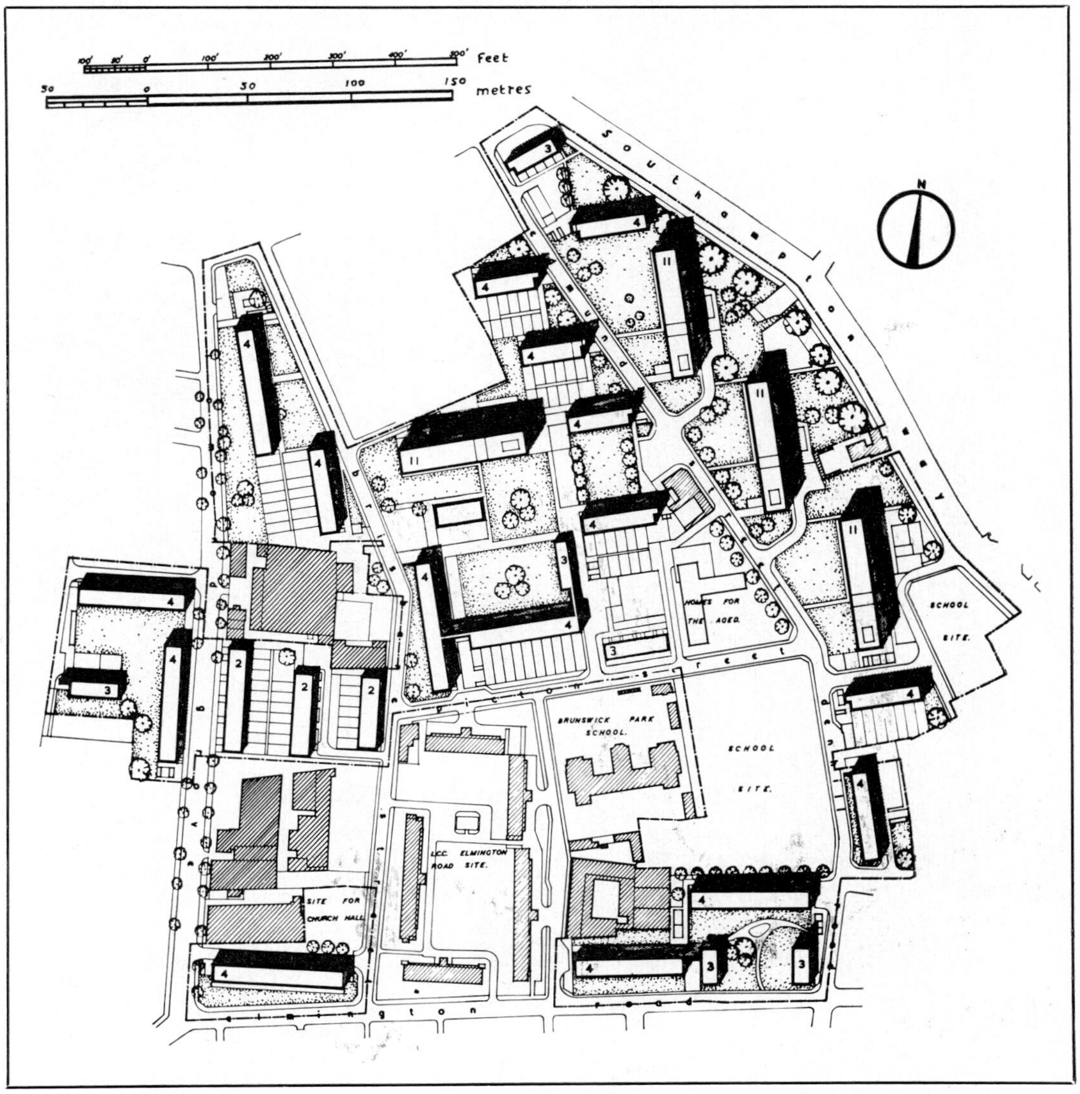

˜he structural system consists of 7in rein-
:ced concrete cross walls with alternate walls
˜einforced, precast main floors, prefabricated
ber intermediate floors, and prefabricated
ber external walls and partitions. Gable walls,
wever, are of precast concrete granite faced
bs with a cavity and insulating block interior
ng. Balcony fronts and dividing screens are
aluminium. Space heating is by means of
w combustion stoves with flues carried in the
ckness of the party walls. A standard type of
chute is used for refuse disposal and there is
drying cabinet in each of the dwellings for
ants' laundry.
:ach typical floor contains 15 of the standard
ts served by two lifts and a single staircase
ced asymmetrically in the block.
˜he four-storey blocks contain two layers of
isonettes, one group accessible from ground
or level, and the other from an access balcony
d staircases located at the ends of the block.
e units are in this case of the three-bedroom
e, and the living rooms have an internal
cony.
˜he ground floor to the 11-storey block includes
umber of two-room flats as well as tenants'
rage.

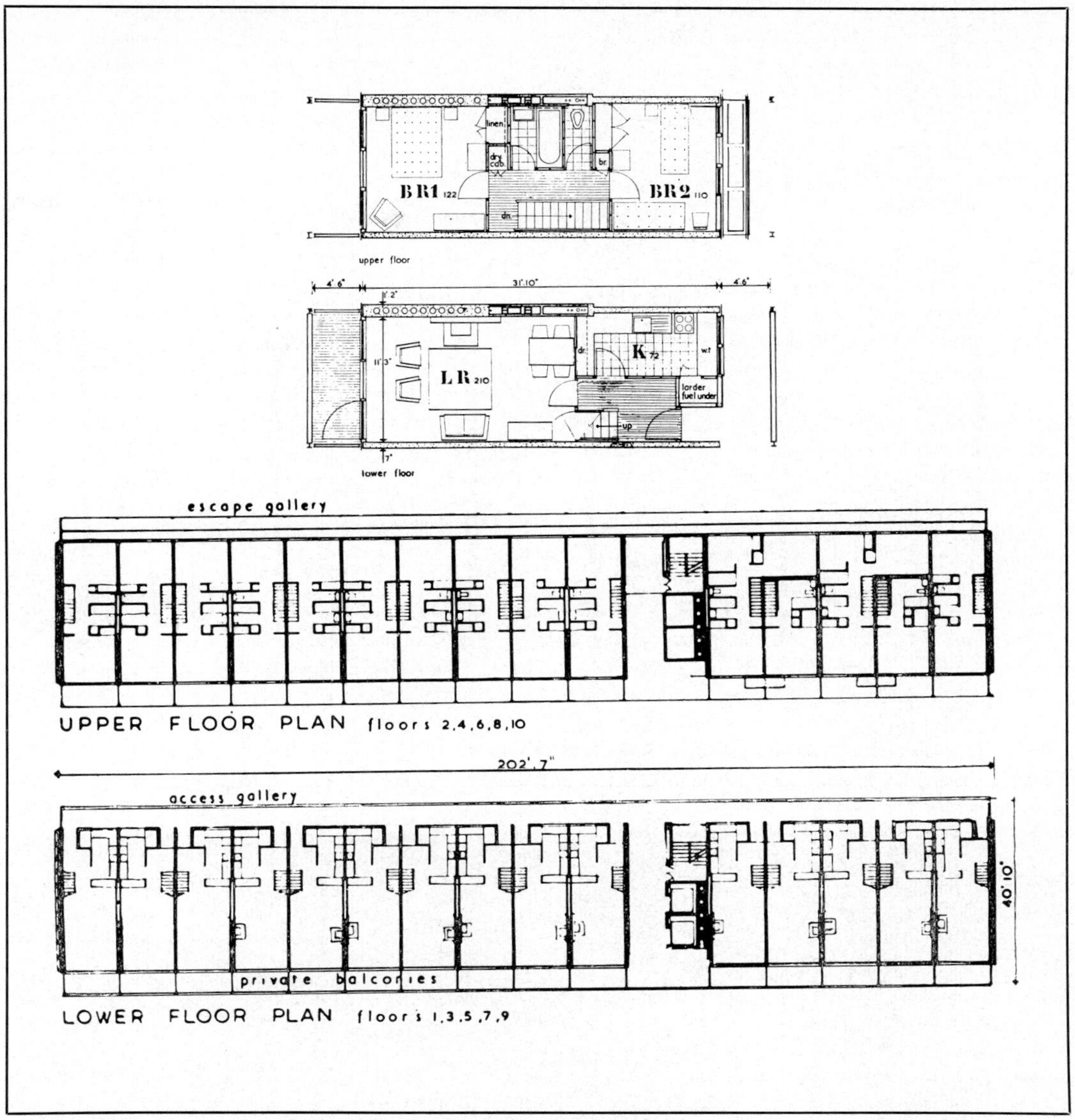

Lamble Street, St. Pancras, London

:hitects: Powell and Moya

site of 3·6 acres developed at a density of
) persons to the acre and including one
storey slab block containing 50 flats and
four-room houses.
The typical floor to the ten-storey block con-
ns five units of which three are of the two-
droom type, one a bedsitter, and one one-
droom. These are served by two lifts and a
gle staircase via access gallery. A basement
also provided with tenants' storage space,
ndries and caretaker's workshop.
The scheme is characterized by its bold yet
tinctive architectural treatment emphasizing
reinforced concrete frame structure which
nsists of 6in party walls, intermediate frames
d 6in precast prestressed floor beams. External
ill is in the form of glazing or 4½in brickwork
th 3in clinker-blocks internally.

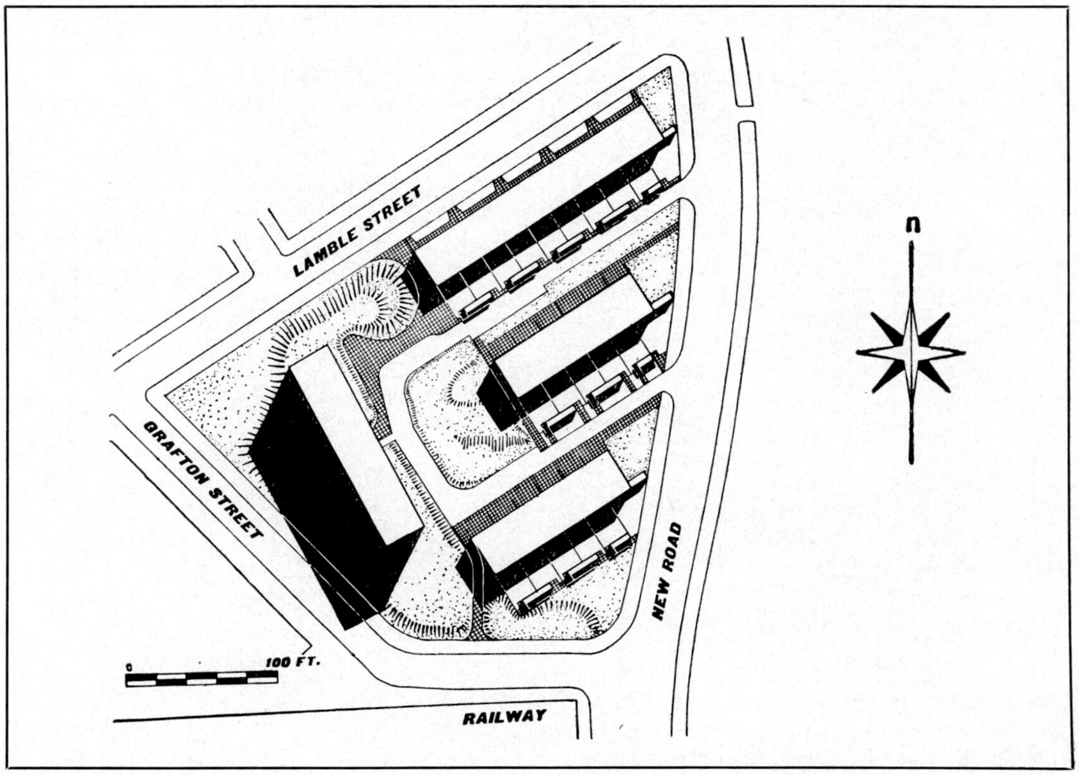

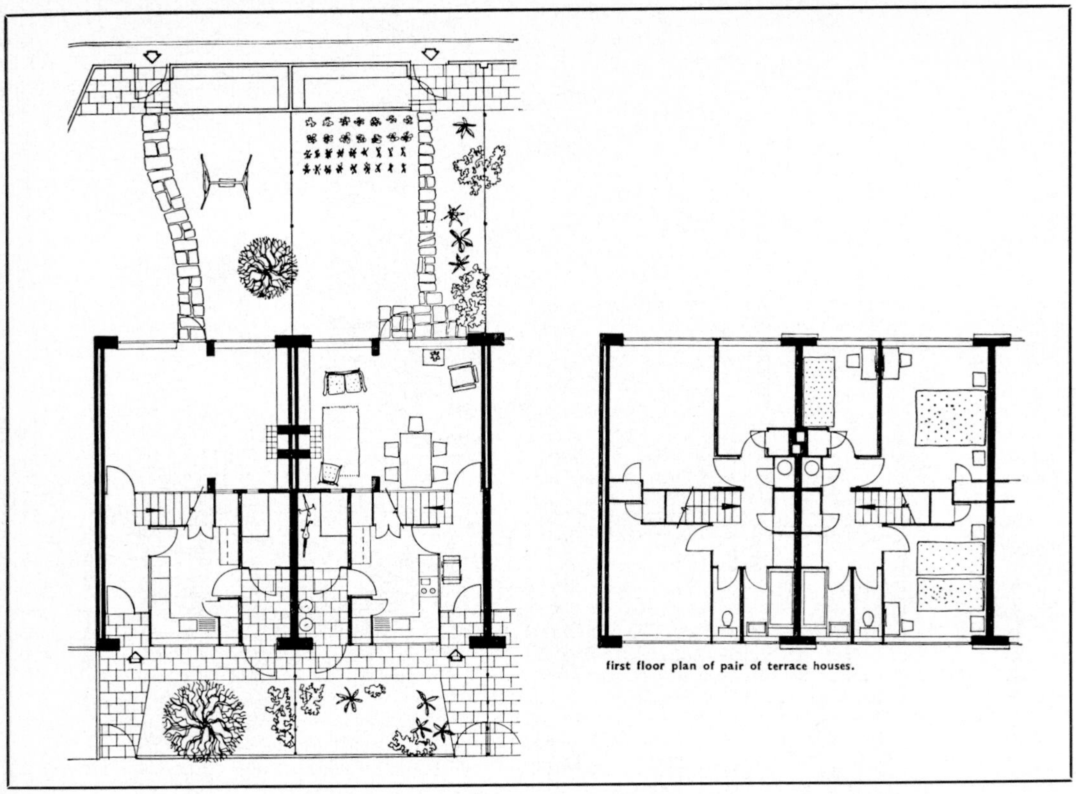

first floor plan of pair of terrace houses.

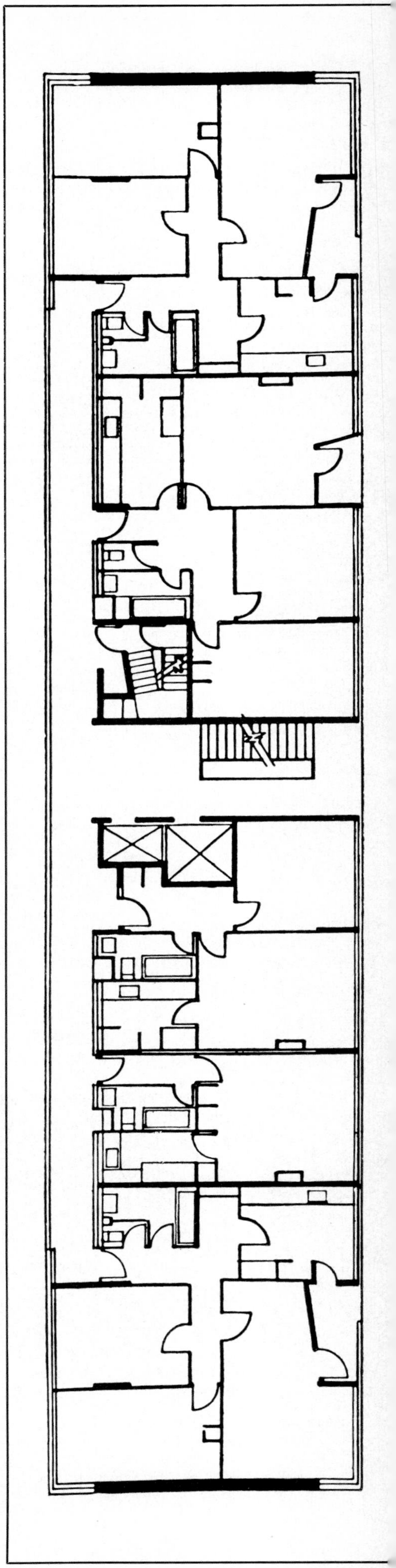

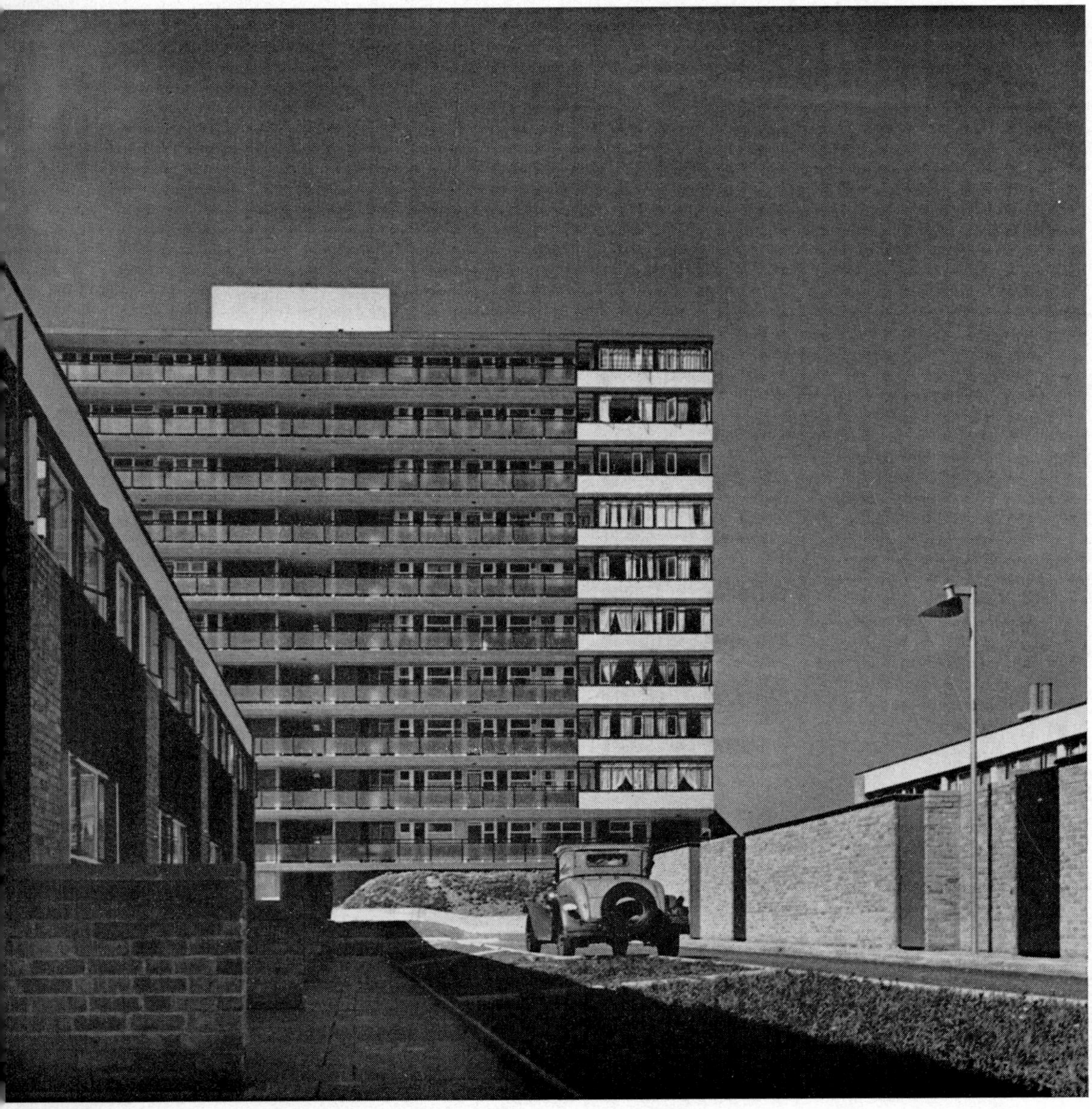

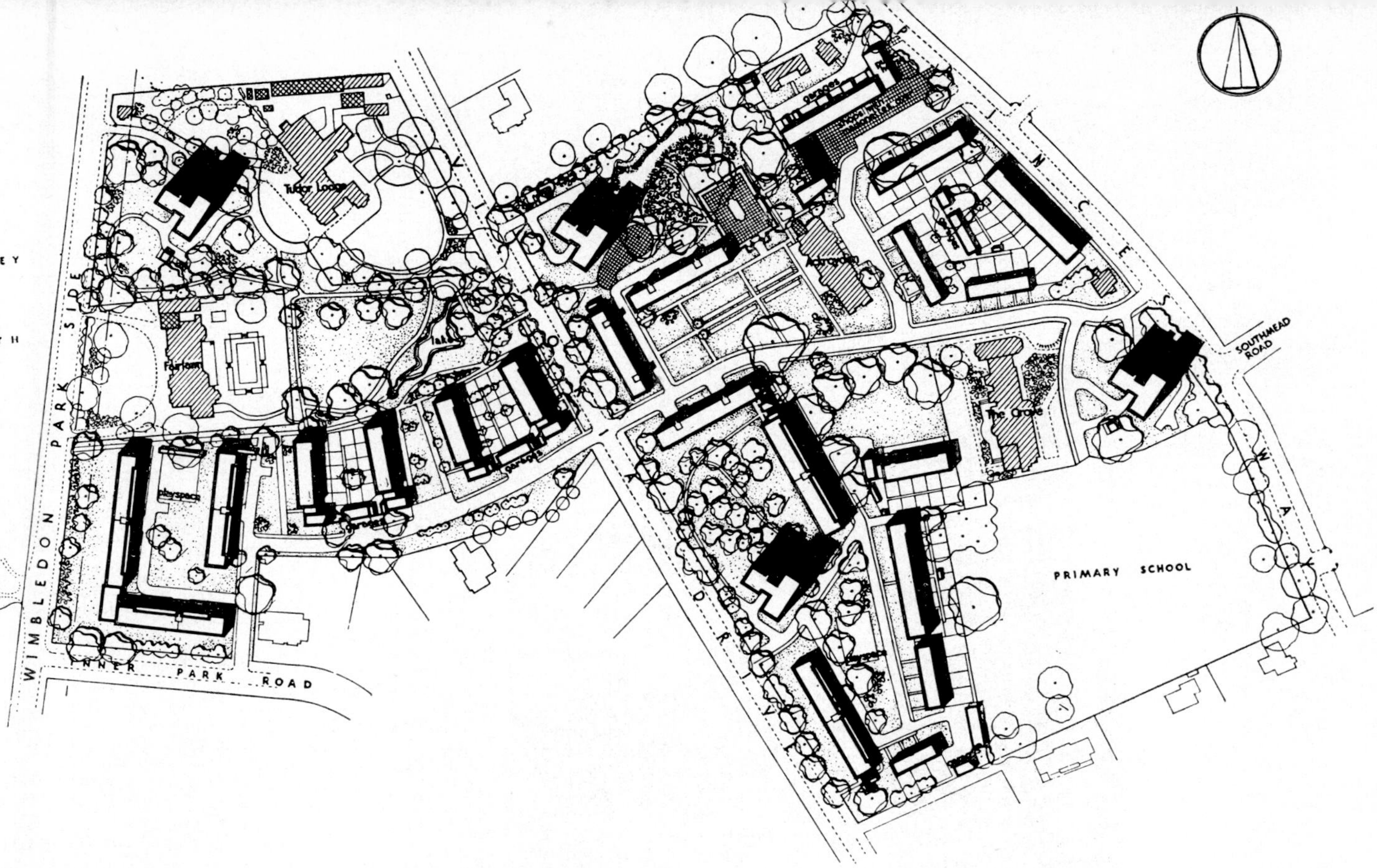

Ackroydon Estate, London

rchitect to the Council (L.C.C.)

ɔur hundred and forty-six dwellings planned in ı area originally consisting of large gardens to ːctorian mansions with many full grown trees hich have been made the basis of a fine ndscaping scheme.

About one-quarter of the accommodation is in ɹe form of four-storey blocks containing aisonettes. There is also a small proportion of rrace houses and about half the accom-odation is in three- and five-storey balcony ccess blocks. Just over a quarter of the total ccommodation is in the form of two-bedroom ats in T shape point blocks—an early example the use of this type of planning in England.

The overall density of the scheme is the modest gure of 96 persons per acre.

There are three of these point blocks of which ʌo are 11 storeys in height and the third eight oreys. They are in reinforced concrete frame onstruction with pad foundations and brick avity walls.

The typical floor provides three units all of the ʌo-bedroom type served by twin lifts and twin aircases from an open access landing. Bath-oms and kitchens are all naturally lit and ntilated.

The ground floors to the blocks contain two ʌo-bedroom units, a laundry and a toddlers' om. Club rooms, shops, tenants' stores, and ay spaces for children as well as a small oportion of garages are also included in the evelopment.

The design and layout of the whole scheme is pecially well conceived with well designed arden spaces and landscaping. The archi-ctural treatment of the individual blocks is roughout of a very high order with a close milarity to some of the best Scandinavian hemes.

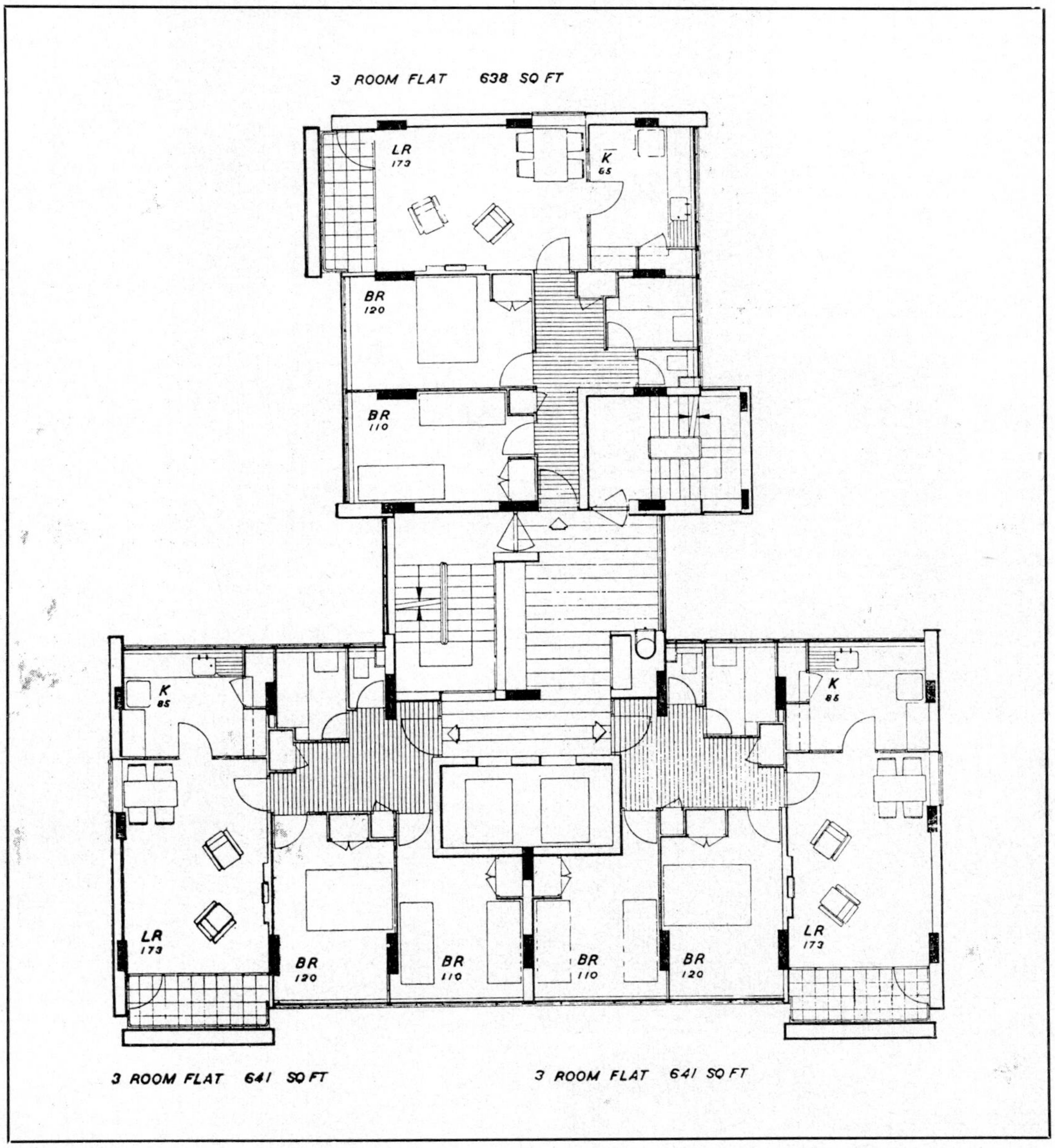

Perkins Heights, Paddington, London

itect: R. Jensen

; scheme which was designed in 1952/53 was of the earliest which attempted fully to apply economics and the planning principles of Scandinavian point block in England. For the time a nett density of over 300 persons per e was shown to be practicable by means of then unprecedented use of 15-storey blocks a unique Y plan and six flats to the typical r, accessible from a single staircase and a of lifts.

ne whole scheme provided for a total of flats with 90 in each block. Initially, twin rcases were included on the insistence of Building Act authority, but under pressure single staircase principle was subsequently epted under certain conditions. Proposals to the living room of the flat as a circulation dium were not acceptable and internal, rather teful communicating corridors were insisted n by the Building Act authority for each flat.

wo-thirds of the total number of flats were of two-bedroom type and one-third three-room units.

he system of construction is reinforced crete frame allowing the maximum flexibility he flat planning, and reinforced concrete rs and concrete piles for the foundations.

he planning of the individual flat unit has n based on the conception of a day area and elf-contained night area in which the bath-n is arranged *en suite* and close to the bed-ns without involving the need for cross traffic.

his scheme which would have housed 2 persons in the three point blocks was igned in conjunction with, and to link up with adjoining housing development. Due to a e number of innovations which have since ome acceptable the scheme was rejected subsequently replanned in another form of ather more orthodox but architecturally less enturous type.

aretaker's accommodation, tenants' storage, ps were also included as a part of the overall elopment. A very low site coverage of just r 13 per cent was attained which allowed for dscaping and garden work on a generous le with adequate childrens' play areas. vacy as between tenants was an important sideration in the design of the point blocks, particularly freedom from the possibility of rlooking, consistent with a high average of olation to the flats.

he space between the buildings was decided careful analysis of seasonal overshadowing.

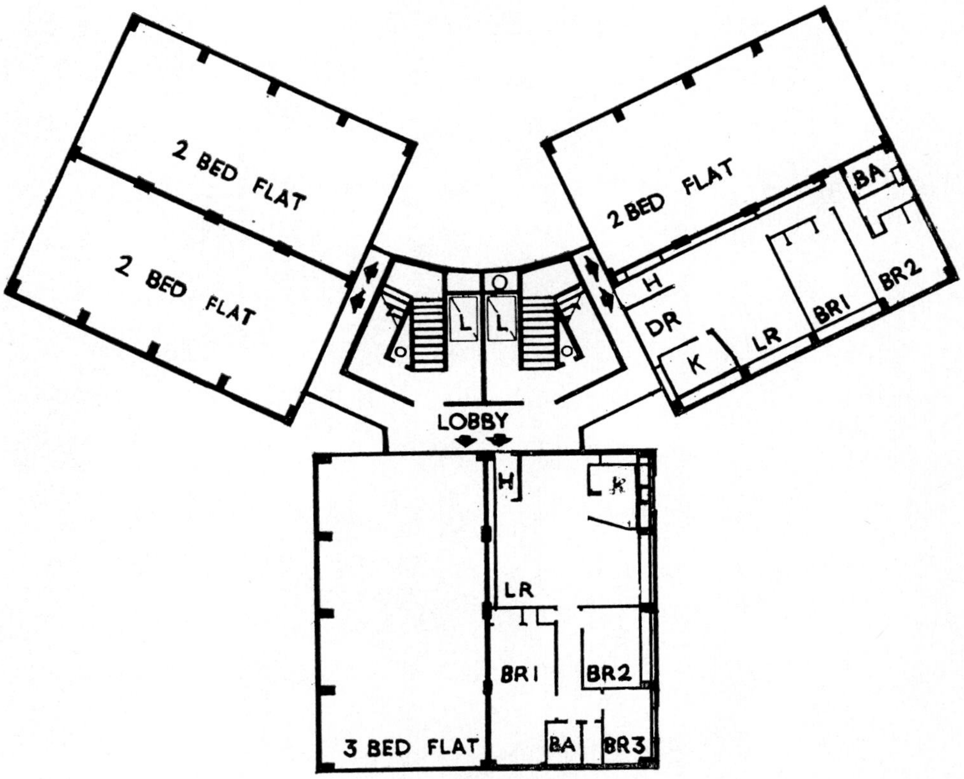

Typical Floor Plans

11 The Lawn, Harlow, Essex

Architect: F. Gibberd

A single butterfly type block of nine storeys, the first true point block to be erected in England, forming part of the development of Harlow New Town.

There are a total of 36 flats in the block, four flats to the typical floor—two bedsittingroom flats and two one-bedroom units with four bedsitters on the ground floor. As this block forms a part of a group in which the remaining housing is mainly in the form of two-storey terraces, the overall density is only 60 persons per acre.

The system of construction is reinforced concrete frame with concrete floors and cavity brickwork infill forming the external walls.

The block is served by twin staircases and a single lift. Bathrooms and kitchens are all planned on external walls and compactly grouped together. These have been clearly expressed in the exterior of the building as are also the private balconies to each of the flats.

The architecture is typified by the well organized fenestration and by the unusual but pleasing form of the building as a whole with the sympathetic use of materials which are particularly appropriate to the well landscaped area with fine forest trees.

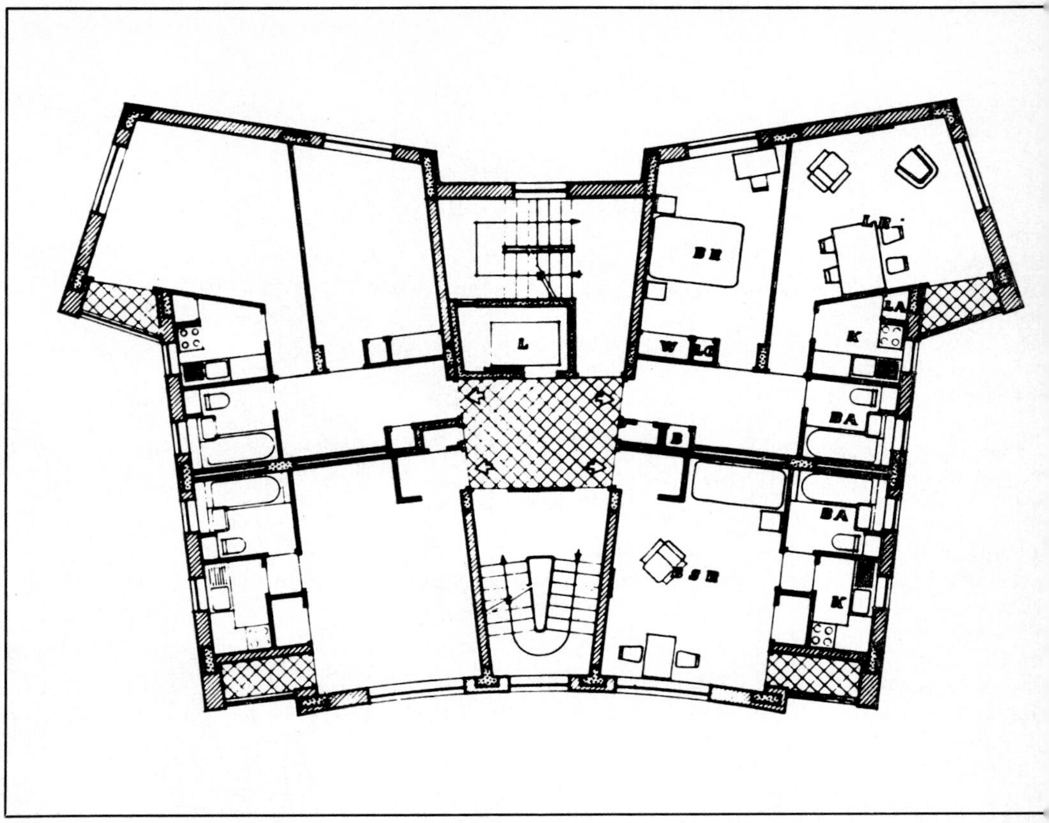

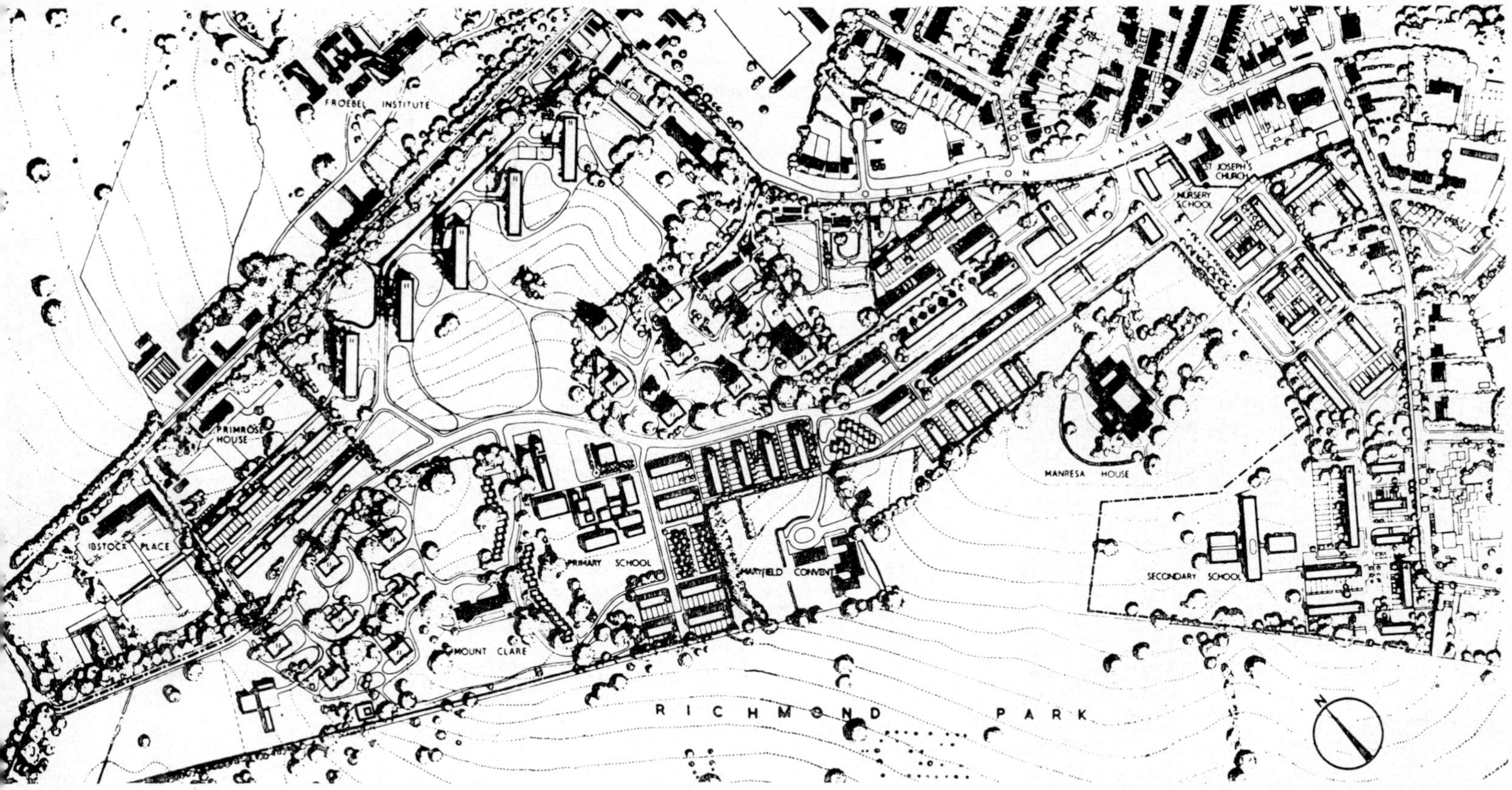

Alton Estate West, London (1955-59)

Architect to the London County Council

00-acre development on the fringe of the ropolitan area and adjoining a large park. :h of the site was already well treed and dscaped having earlier formed the gardens of e Victorian houses. A total of 1867 dwellings provided at an overall density of 100 persons ne acre with the smaller family units in high :ks; two groups totalling 15 12-storey point :ks containing two- and one-bedroom flats, one group of five 11-storey slab blocks taining two-bedroom maisonettes. Larger ily units are placed in low buildings; four-ey maisonettes and two- and three-storey ses.

he maisonettes have three bedrooms, and houses four bedrooms.

number of old people's homes are also uded in the scheme, as well as a local pping centre, two primary schools, a second-school, three nursery schools, health centre, ommunity centre, two churches, and a 'pub'. onstruction of the point blocks is reinforced crete frame, with precast cladding floors and ms. Slab maisonettes have alternate rein-:ed concrete frames and load-bearing rein-:ed concrete cross walls, with precast dding beams and stairs. Other low buildings in brick cross wall construction with panelled s.

n Estate East (1952–55)

earlier stage of this general development, acres in extent, contains 744 dwellings of ch roughly 60 per cent are in the 11-storey nt blocks. These are of the swastika type plan 1 four flats to the typical floor served by two rcases and two lifts; three of these flats being the three-bedroom type and one a one-room unit.

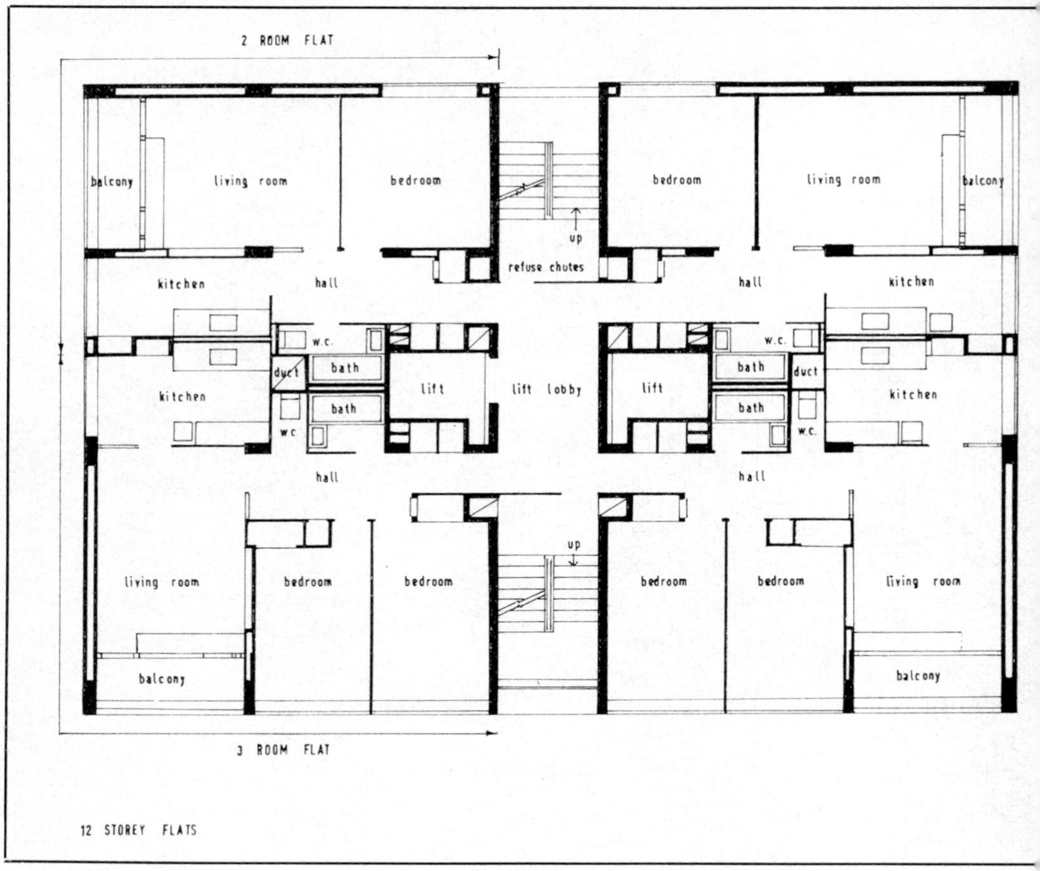

The ground floor includes three bedsitting-room units, together with tenants' storage and a laundry. The kitchens are naturally lit and ventilated but all bathrooms are planned internally.

The system of construction is poured *in situ* reinforced concrete for internal walls with external reinforced concrete frame and cavity brickwork cladding. Floors are of solid reinforced concrete; foundations are piled. All the dwellings are supplied with central heating and hot water, made economically possible by the compact grouping, although the maisonettes and houses have open fires with independent back boilers.

An interesting example of the application of a mixed development policy utilizing point blocks in which the low blocks are not always happily related to the architecturally superior multi-storey blocks.

Another site, the Fitzhugh Estate in Wandsworth, was developed by the same authority with 213 flats at a density of 105 persons per acre on approximately a seven acre site in five identical 11-storey blocks similar to Alton East. In that case, however, a good deal of the external concrete work was precast due to the arrival of the tower crane in England.

The somewhat uneconomical arrangement of the twin staircases with external lighting and ventilation was, however, still persisted in, although the developer was also the Building Act authority. The layout of this second site was also greatly enhanced by large well grown existing trees as a basis for parklike landscaping.

At a later date a very similar swastika plan was used as a part of the London County Council Lytton Grove Estate development, but in this case in five-storey blocks and these were planned with a single staircase and single lift only.

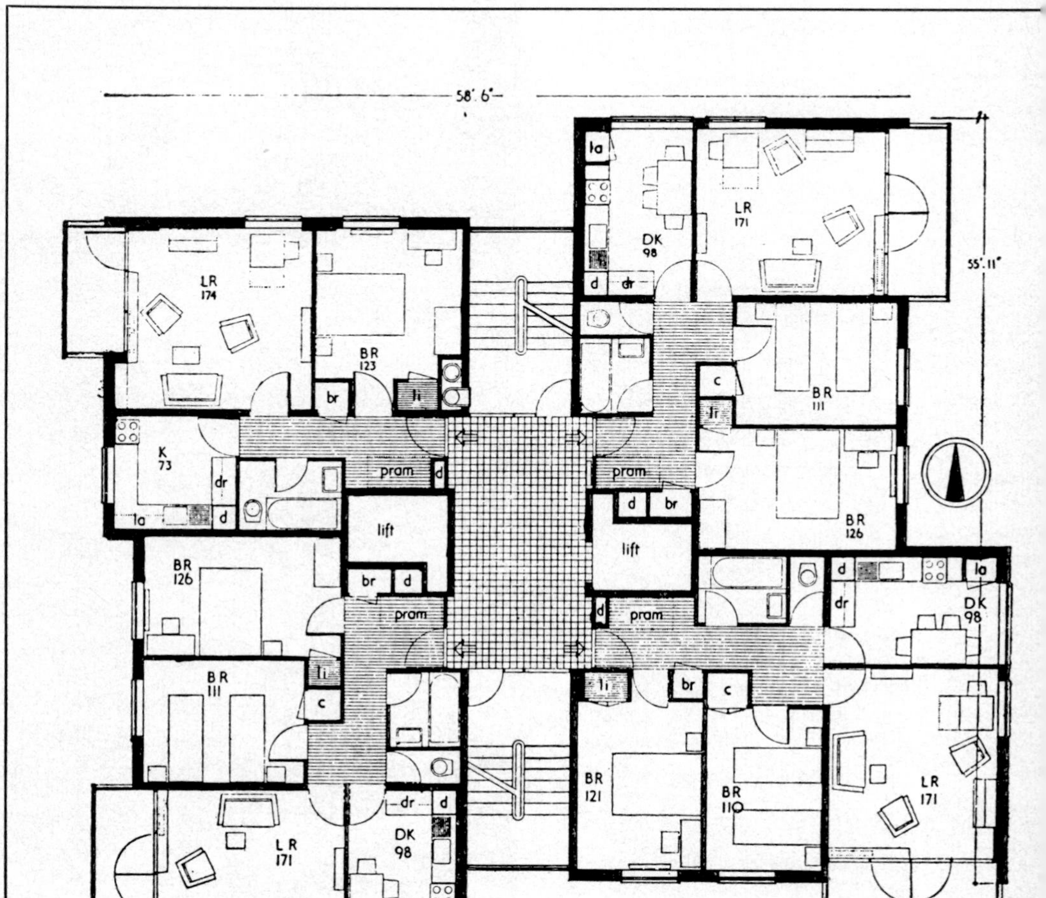

8 Claremont Estate, West Ham, London

rchitect: T. North

mixed development including 123 flats,) maisonettes and 18 garages and forming a art of an area of comprehensive renewal with ost office, church, multiple store, shops, orary, and day nursery. The residential area cludes a single 11-storey point block with ree-storey blocks of flats, and four-storey aisonettes. Private gardens are provided to any of the dwellings in the low blocks.

The point block contains 22 three-room and two-room flats planned in the swastika rangement with two two-bedroom and two one-edroom units to each typical floor. These are erved by two lifts and two staircases which are oth naturally lit and ventilated. All living rooms ave a private balcony adjoining.

The system of construction is reinforced oncrete frame and floors with brick cavity nd clinker block external walls. Central heating provided and two refuse chutes. There are undries and drying cabinets in all of the tchens.

The density of the whole development is 35 persons per acre. Site coverage, primarily ecause of the comparatively large number of w blocks, is rather high.

Total cost of dwellings: £300,000.

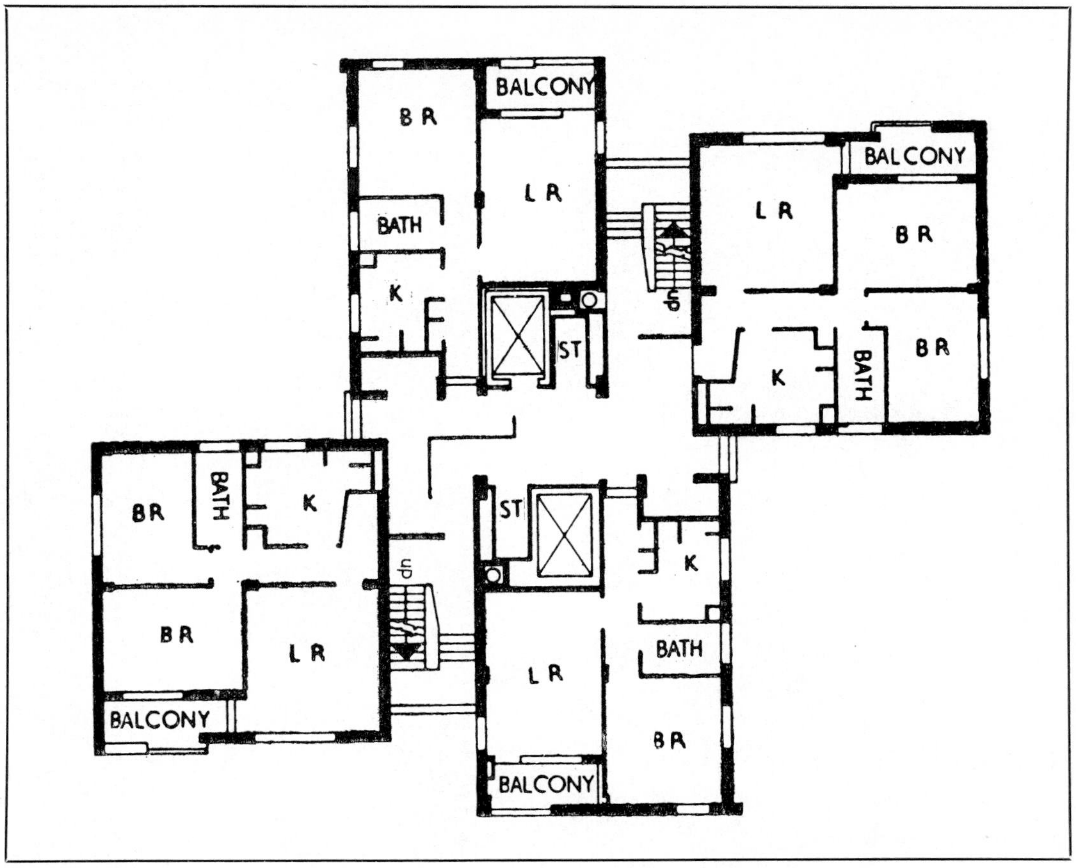

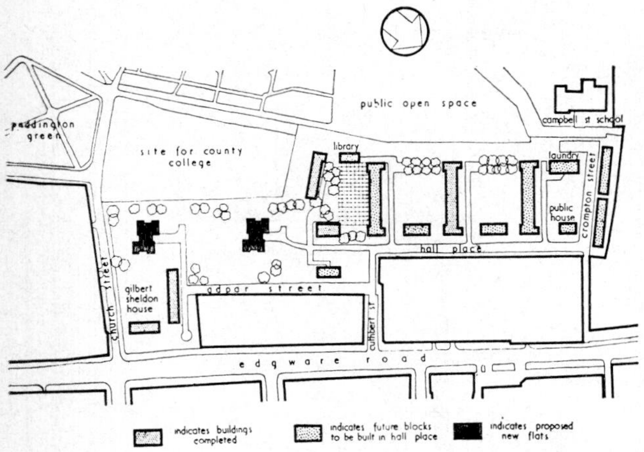

14 Paddington Towers, London

Architect: R. Jensen

In 1956 this scheme was developed as a proposal forming part of a large comprehensive redevelopment area. Although no precedent existed at the time, 16-storey point blocks formed the basis of this scheme in order to take far better advantage of the vertical repetition. The simplest form of planning was also adopted to produce even further constructional economies, and the two halves of the building staggered in order to reduce unnecessary circulation space and further to increase privacy as between adjoining flats. Aspect, orientation, and overshadowing were also carefully studied in conjunction with the spacing, the height, and the siting of the blocks; as also daylighting on the basis of the British Code of Practice.

Each typical floor contains two three-bedroom flats and two two-bedroom flats which are served by a single staircase and twin lifts, a reasonably economical arrangement within the circumscribed density maximum of 136 persons per acre.

The ground floor contains four one-bedroom units as well as an entrance hall containing tenants' delivery lockers.

The cost of construction and/or the sacrifice of space involved in the provision of individual balconies was not considered to be warranted but instead french doors are provided to each of the living rooms so that in suitable weather many of the benefits of the balcony may be obtained.

The dining/kitchens and bathrooms have been compactly planned on a back-to-back basis with grouped plumbing. Drying cupboards have been provided for every flat and also box rooms. Refuse disposal is by dry chute.

The system of construction is reinforced concrete frame utilizing patent precast concrete beam linings with prestressed flooring planks and an *in situ* concrete topping. The external cladding is in precast concrete slab with an internal skin as well as internal partitions in cellular plaster board. Electrical floor heating is used, using cheap current, at off-peak periods.

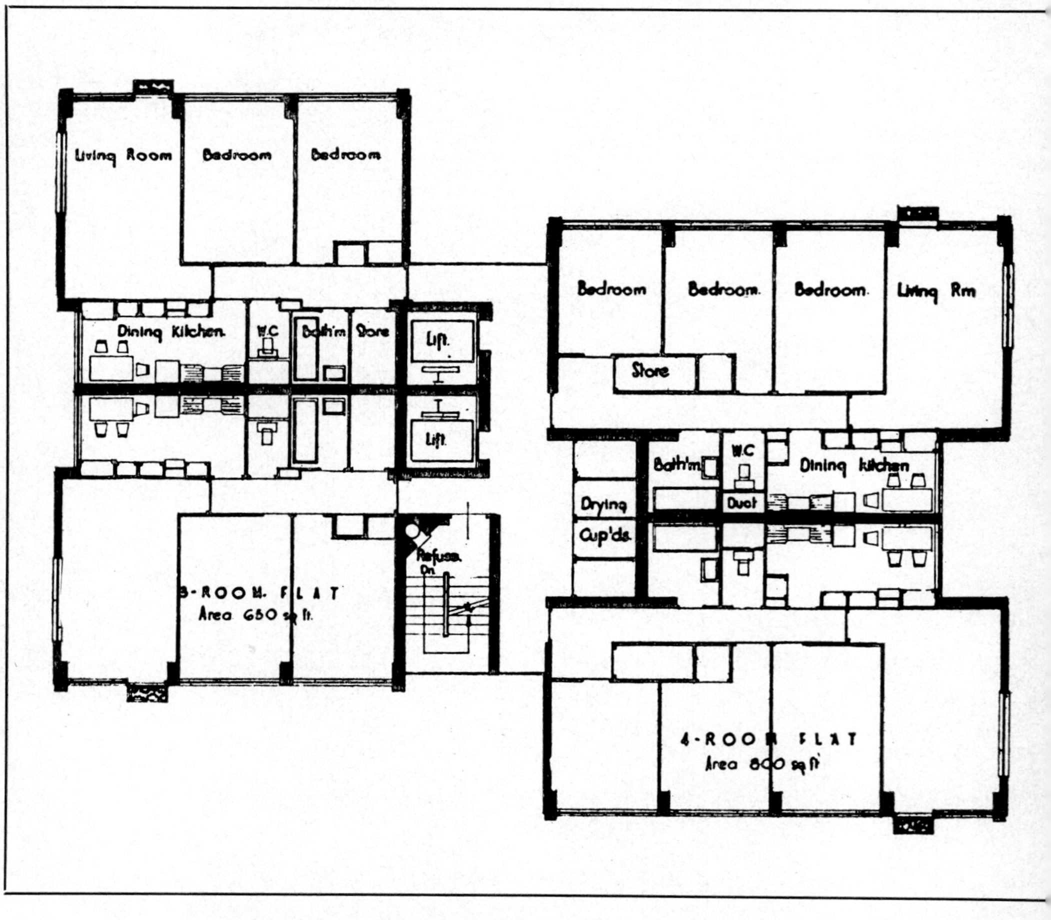

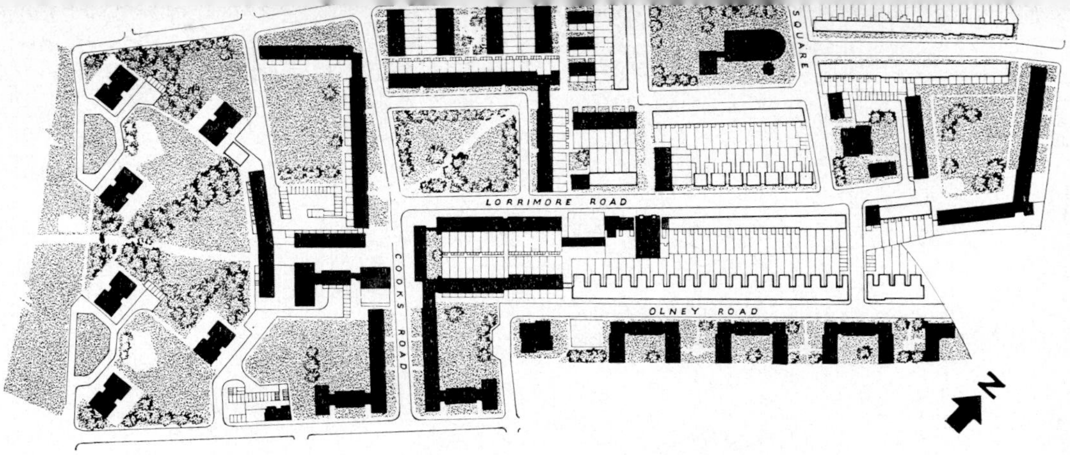

Brandon Estate, London

e Architect to the London County Council

36 acre area of Victorian London in which a ge number of the slum and war damaged perties have been rehabilitated where these re structurally sound. In order to facilitate velopment decanting was carried out into six storey point blocks which were first erected a cleared section of the area. This form of velopment, together with existing street uares, has provided the open space and land- ping needed for the whole development.

Some new four- and six-storey maisonette slab cks were also erected to complete the scheme. 9 dwellings were provided in all, of which are in the 18-storey blocks, and 321 in nversions. The overall density is 137 persons acre.

The tower blocks are of rectangular shape in n and the typical floor contains four similar s, all two-bedroom units, accessible from a gle staircase and pair of lifts which stop at ernate floors. The flats are planned back-to- ck, but only the kitchens receive light at the ends of the building, otherwise all the flats are of single aspect type. Kitchens and bathrooms are grouped together for economy in plumbing layout, and a secondary balcony is provided adjoining the kitchens which can also be used for secondary escape purposes. All the flats have their own large private balconies, and, in addition, maintenance balconies extend over the whole of the remaining external walls of the flats.

Building Act requirements have necessitated rather lengthy internal access corridors and some cross traffic occurs between bedrooms and bathrooms adjacent to front doors to the flats—almost inevitable if bathrooms and kitchens are to be grouped together. On the whole an economical form of planning, however, at the density prevailing.

The construction is reinforced concrete frame with timber framed cladding behind the continuous balconies and precast concrete cladding to gable walls.

The remaining blocks, up to six storeys in height, are of load-bearing brick cross wall construction.

All dwellings have individual heated drying cabinets and provision for laundry machines. Four refuse chutes are provided for each of the 18-storey blocks. A substantial number of dwellings are centrally heated. A library and club room, and shopping centre containing 12 shops, as well as 88 garages, and equipped playground and play spaces are also included in the scheme, as well as doctor's surgery, tenants' store and off-street parking.

Architecturally, and in the planning, the scheme forms an interesting comparison with the Alton Estate point blocks. In this case the architectural treatment is largely influenced by the continuous balconies as also by the heavy dividing bands at every fourth floor level with the object of breaking up what would otherwise be a monotonous fenestration pattern. The somewhat formalistic treatment of the roof penthouses containing lift machinery and ventilation plant rather tends to detract from the otherwise clean lines of the buildings.

These penthouses also include four bedsitter flats.

Total cost: £3½ million.

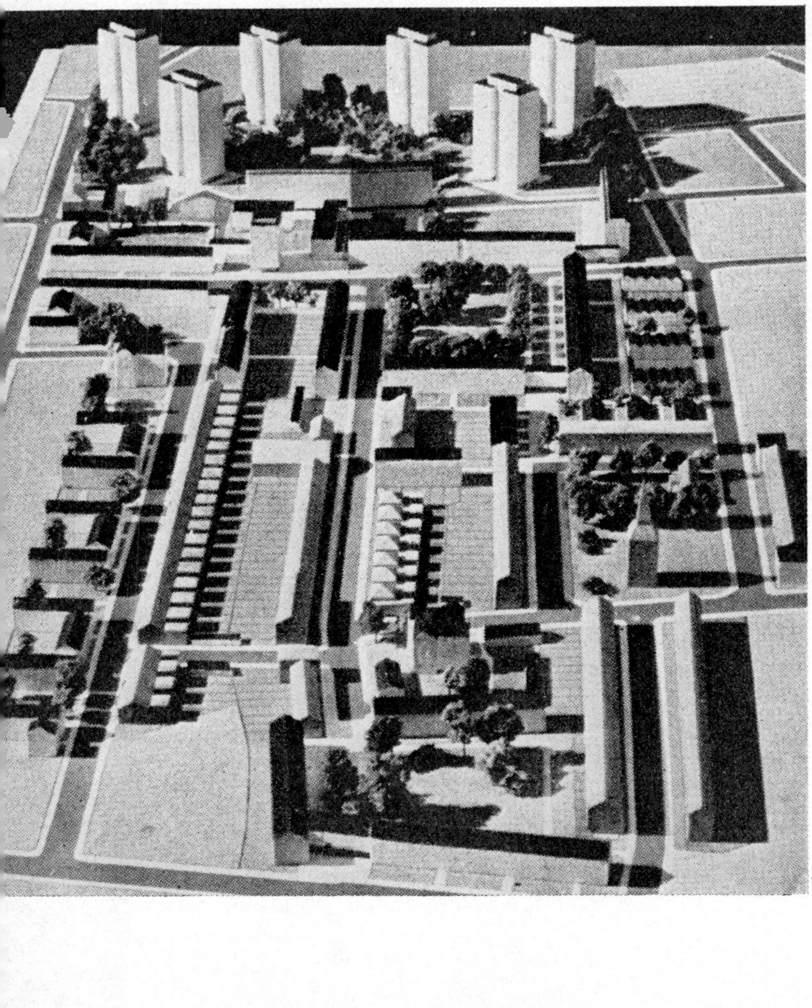

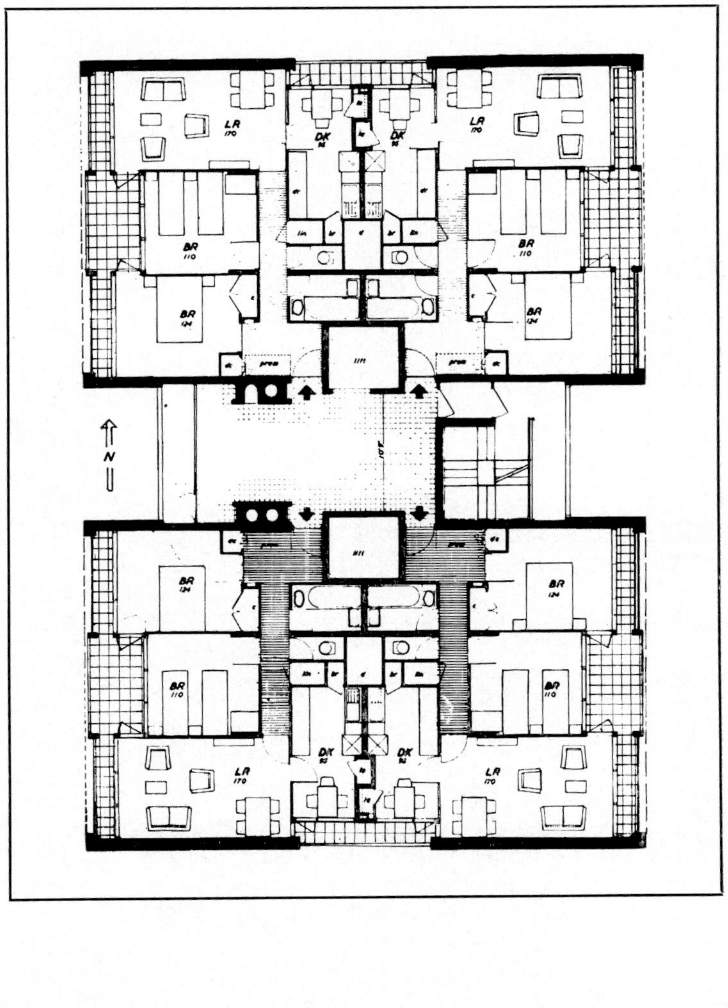

Warwick Crescent Area, Paddington

Architect to the London County Council

ther mixed redevelopment scheme on a site ome 44 acres including both new buildings rehabilitated 19th century terrace type town ses. Progressive decanting and limitation of spill are greatly assisted by the inclusion in scheme of three compact point blocks toreys in height. Otherwise, most of the new elopment scheme consists of four-storey case access flats designed to maintain the ting character of the terraces and to pre- e something of the open space pattern. rches and schools are also included in the eme, as well as considerable additional open lic space.

he point blocks are planned with access a single staircase and twin lifts, the typical r containing eight two-bedroom maisonettes essible from the central corridor, and two -bedroom flats. Secondary escape is nged for the maisonette units into the idor at the next upper level by means of a cat ler from the bedroom landing. Otherwise the or portion of the access corridor occurs only lternate floor levels.

onstruction is reinforced concrete cross wall pile foundations.

ectric floor heating at off-peak periods is vided to all the flats.

round floors to the blocks contain tenants' es, transformer chamber and caretaker's

simple and well proportioned scheme. hitectural expression is achieved in the nt blocks consistent with the use of the parti- ar structural system and reflecting the rnal planningawith the different types of elling unit.

hree similar point blocks, 17 storeys in height, e been used as a part of the Clive Street elopment by the same authority, and one 19 ey block at Mountmorres Road. The overall sity of development in each case is 136 sons per acre.

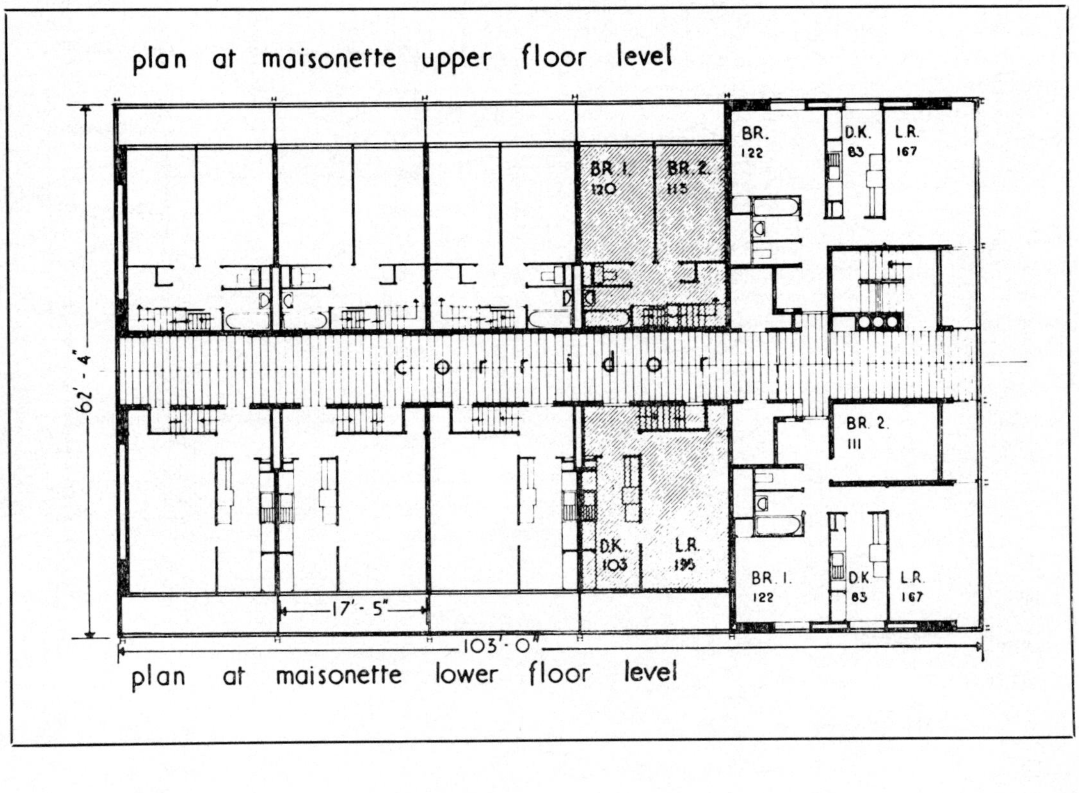

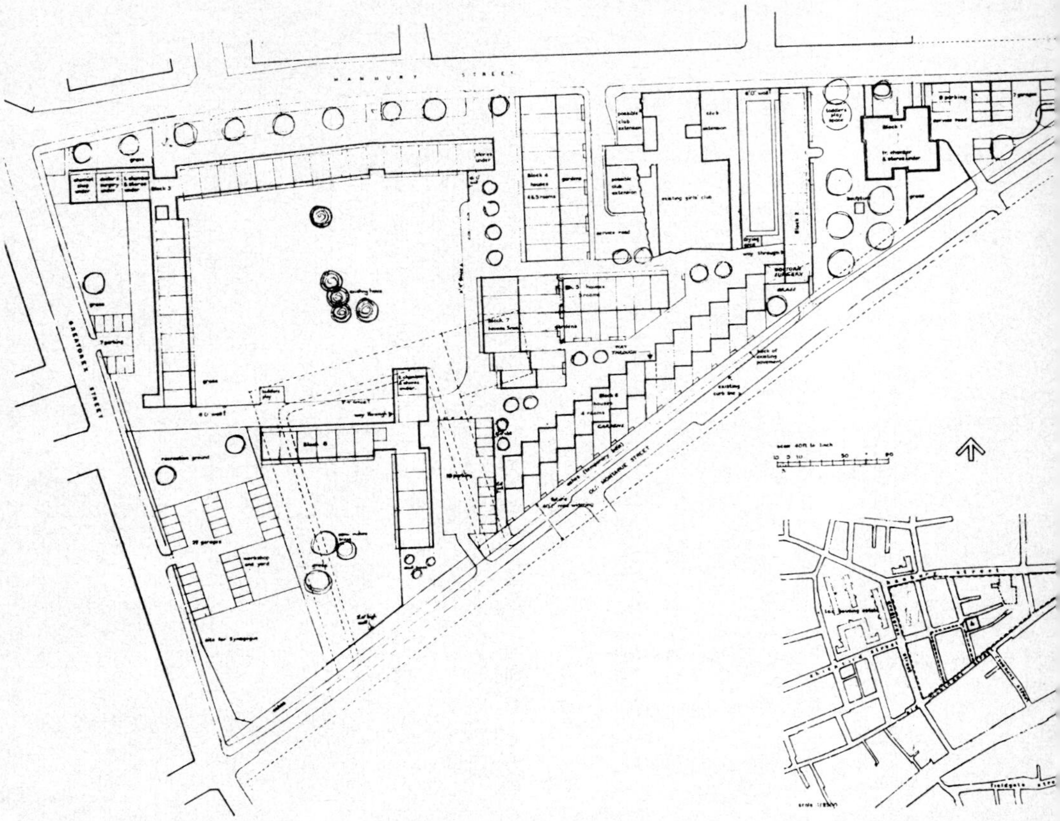

17 Chicksand Estate, Stepney, London

The Architect to the London County Council

A mixed development of two-storey old people's flats, houses, six-storey slab blocks, and a 19-storey point block containing 73 flats with a total of 210 dwellings for the whole development on a 5½ acre site. Twenty-seven garages are also included as well as parking space and a play area for children, and a club is located nearby.

Efforts have also been made in this scheme to provide attractive landscaping including the replanting of mature trees.

The planning of the multi-storey block is of interest inasmuch as it represents a revival of an earlier type of swastika plan used by the same authority but in this case served by a single staircase and pair of lifts.

Three two-bedroom units and one one-bedroom unit are included in each typical floor, and all bathrooms planned internally but kitchens with external natural light and ventilation.

The system of construction is load-bearing cross wall with external reinforced concrete frames with precast and prefabricated cladding in the form of panels.

Hugh's Tower, Harlow, Essex

ɪtects: F. Gibberd and V. Hamnett

second point block included in the Harlow Town development in this case forming a of a central group. The block is orthodox in ɪanning and contains in the 11 typical floors ɪdentical one-bedroom flats served by two cases and a single lift from a somewhat ɟested circulation lobby. Bathrooms and ɪens are all planned on external walls.
ɪe ground floor to the block contains two sitter flats and caretaker's rooms as well as ance hall and staircase access.
ɪe system of construction is mainly *in situ* forced concrete load-bearing walls of the no s type which is given a rendered finish rnally. This tends to produce a somewhat vy architectural quality but proportions and stration are well disciplined, and the roof is n a clean line by means of the terraces and g beams connecting the solid corner panels. round floor level the load-bearing walls are plemented by free standing reinforced crete columns to create a floating effect.

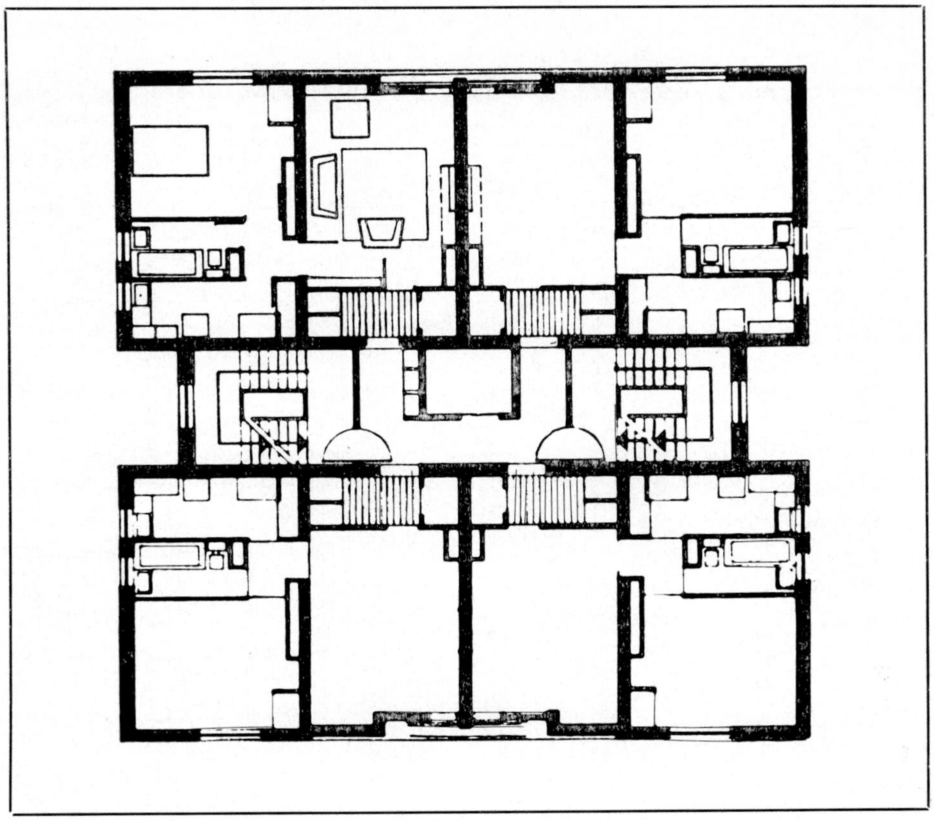

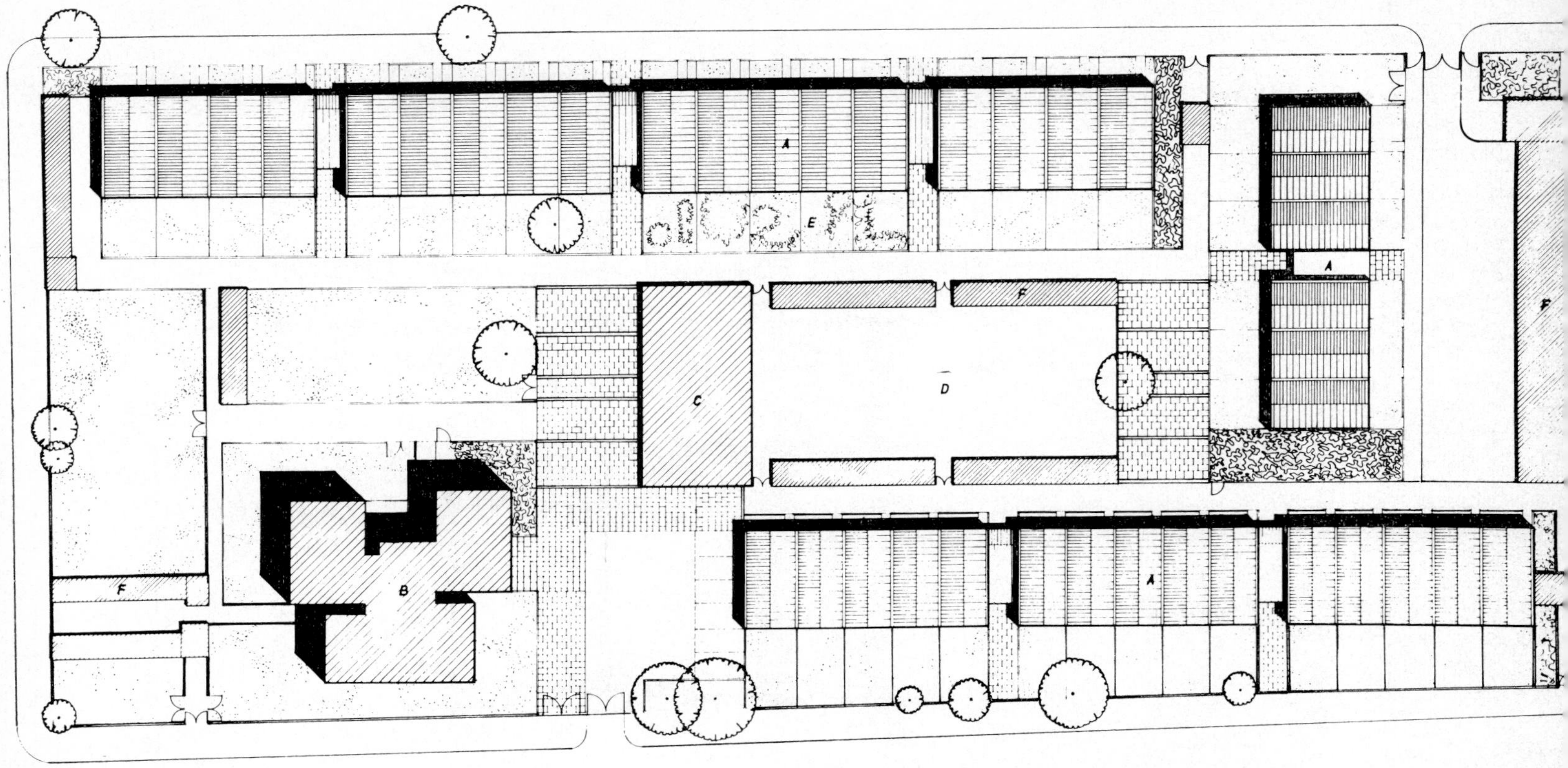

A 4 storey maisonettes
D Children's Playground
B 11-storey flats
E Private Gardens
C Community Hall
F Garages & Stores

SCALE IN FEET

19 Kingsgate Estate, Hackney, London

Architects: F. Gibberd with W. Downing

A mixed development surrounding a central pedestrian square with maisonettes on three sides and a tall block at one corner. The central space consists of children's play area and tenant terraces with tenants' common room and laundry adjoining, as well as pram and cycle stores.

The 11-storey block contains 44 dwellings with four flats to the typical floor—two two-bedroom units, one one-bedroom, and one bedsitter—grouped round the access core consisting of two lifts and a single staircase.

The construction is *in situ* reinforced concrete frame with flat concrete slab; infill panels are brick and 2in clay tile.

The planning system adopted in the core is largely influenced by the desire to obtain natural cross ventilation to the staircase and lift lobby, a Building Act requirement. This produces two very narrow light wells and a duplication of external wall adjoining the lift well.

The remainder of the development includes 78 dwellings of the gallery access type with two or three dwellings on each side of the staircase, construction being 9in brick cross wall with reinforced concrete floor slabs and timber intermediate floors to the maisonettes.

An interesting roof pattern is given to the maisonette blocks, rather at variance however with the treatment of the multi-storey block.

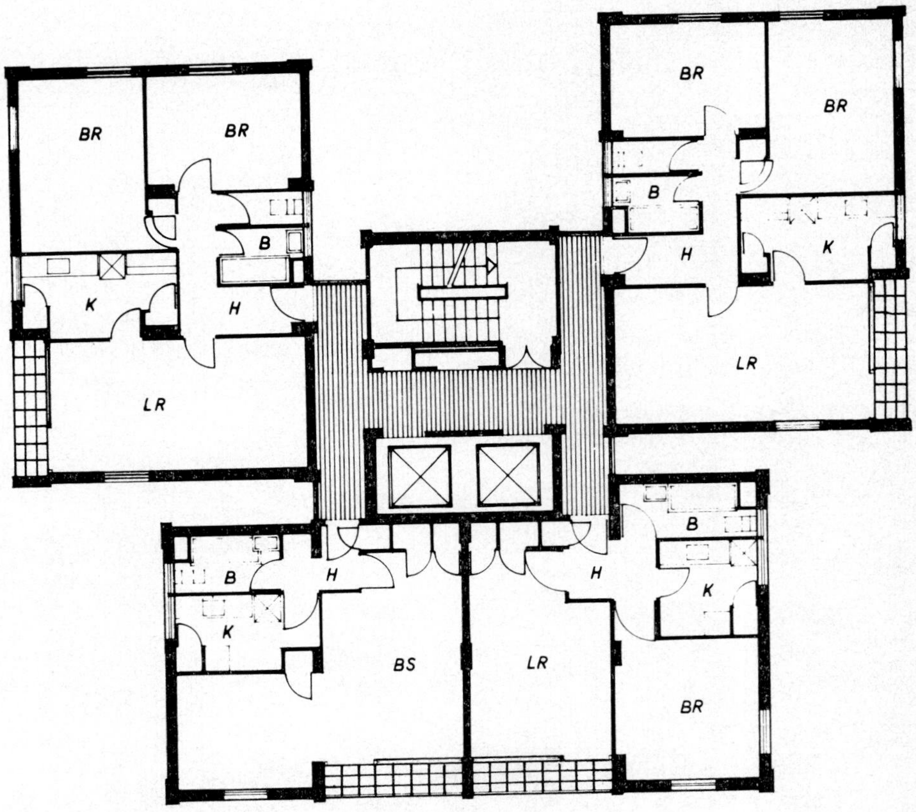

TYPICAL UPPER FLOOR PLAN

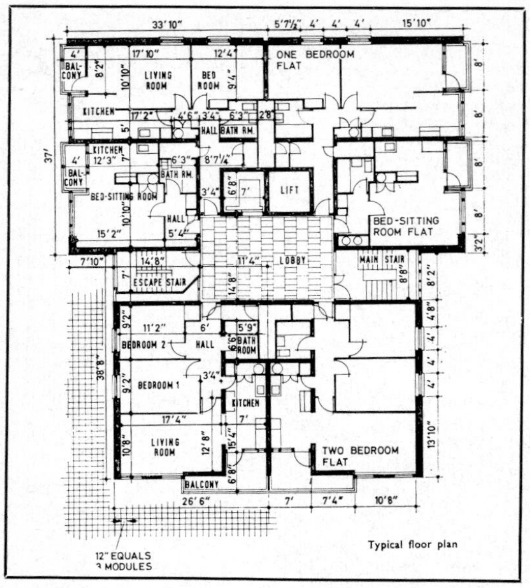

Typical floor plan

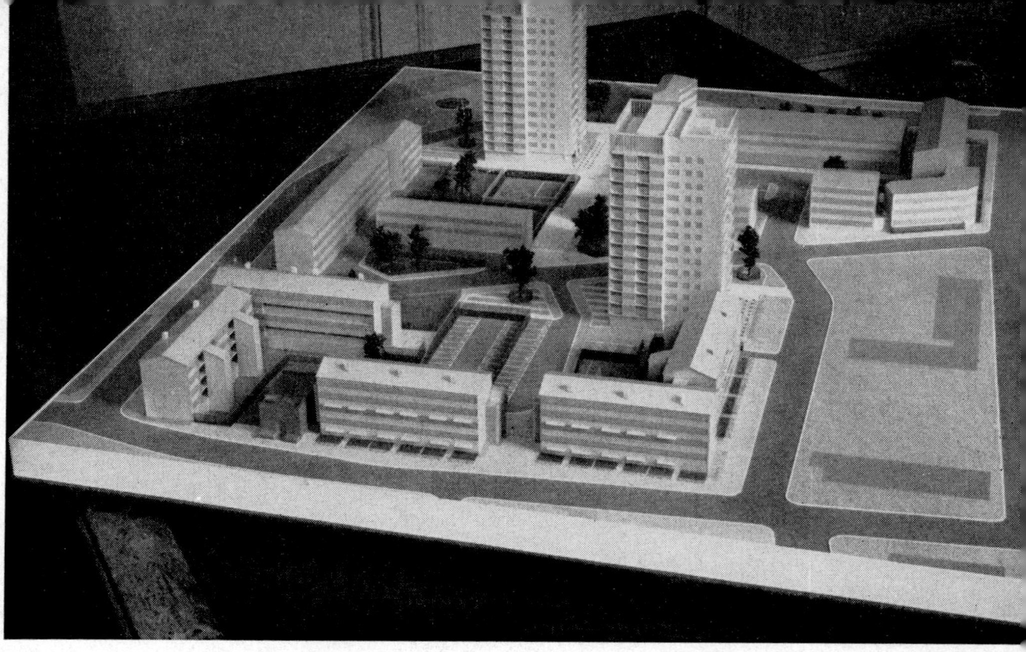

20 Kensal New Town, London

Architect: W. Holford

A large redevelopment area of some 21 acres containing slum dwellings to be replaced by 661 new dwellings at a density of 100 persons to the acre. The most important elements are two 14-storey point blocks sited among two three- and four-storey blocks of flats, shops, and community buildings. This is one of the first examples of its type using modular co-ordination in the design.

Ninety-eight flats are planned in each of the two similar 13-storey blocks with six flats to the floor planned round a central lift lobby containing two skip-stop lifts and two staircases. Two of the flats are two-bedroom units, two bedsitters, and two one-bedroom units.

Construction is in a patent reinforced concrete type frame providing for constant column size and simplification of shuttering with considerable structural stiffness. External cladding is mainly in brick but with vitreous enamel spandrel panels under the windows.

New Southgate, London

hitect: D. Aberdeen

nixed development on a 5-acre site at 116 sons to the acre in the form of single storey people's flats; four three-storey blocks having -bedroom or bedsitting room flats over three- room maisonettes, and three four-storey cks of maisonettes, together with 31 garages, two tower blocks containing 78 two-bedroom s and 24 one-bedroom flats. These blocks are storeys in height with four flats to the typical r of which three are two-bedroom units, and one-bedroom unit. Access is by means of a gle staircase and two lifts. Each flat is pro- ed with a private balcony, but this however is he expense of the area of the living room.

ccommodation at ground floor level, apart n entrance hall, consists of three two-bed- m flats together with plant room, switch and nsformer rooms, refuse chambers. Lifts serve rnate floors.

The motor room is accommodated in a neatly designed penthouse.

Excellent privacy has been secured for the individual flats by the staggered arrangement in plan, although the location of the living rooms in the corners of the building produces internal cross traffic, particularly between bedrooms and bathrooms.

The structure is in monolithic reinforced concrete with pile foundations and slab walls and floors. External cladding is in the form of an inner skin of 6in reinforced concrete or blocks, a $4\frac{1}{2}$in outer skin of bricks, and spandrels to the bay windows being finished with asbestos cement panels. Electric floor heating on off-peak current is provided to the flats.

The relationship between the blocks of various heights, the treatment of the intervening spaces, landscaping, and the architectural quality of the point blocks are particularly well conceived in this development.

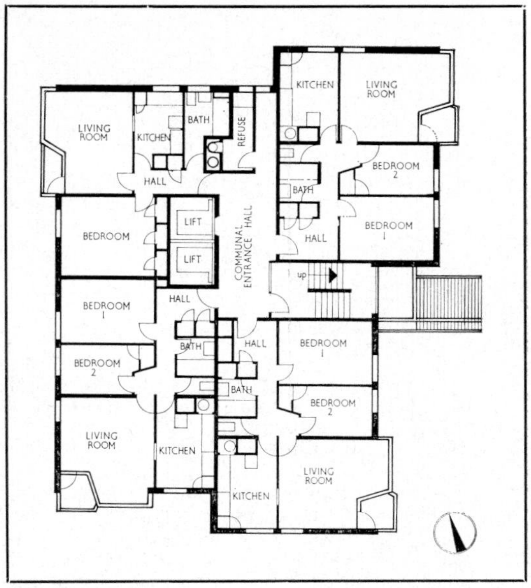

22 Bracknell Tower, Easthampstead

Engineer: O. Arup and Partners

This 19-storey block is the focal point in the central area of Easthampstead district in Bracknell New Town, and is sited in a pedestrian area. The unusual hexagonal plan has been ingeniously handled to give usable and yet compact spaces with a minimum circulation area loss.

The typical floor contains six flats accessible from single staircase and pair of skip-stop lifts. These are four one-bedroom units, one two-bedroom; and a bedsitter. All bathrooms are planned internally round the central access core and kitchens are on external walls. All rooms with standard equipment—bedrooms, bathrooms and kitchens are rectangular in plan. The living rooms are tapered but these are the more flexible spaces, and the shape has the real advantage of embracing the view through large panoramic windows.

Due to lack of suitable firefighting equipment in the area, an external escape gallery is provided at all floor levels round the perimeter of the block. This gallery also however provides useful additional outdoor space, and solar shading. Car parking under the entrance terrace is on the basis of one space to each flat.

Access for furniture vans, refuse carts, etc. is to the base of the flats.

Ground floor contains entrance hall and caretaker's flat.

Construction is in *in situ* concrete to internal structural walls, with precast columns and edge beams forming the external frame. Mullions are also in concrete.

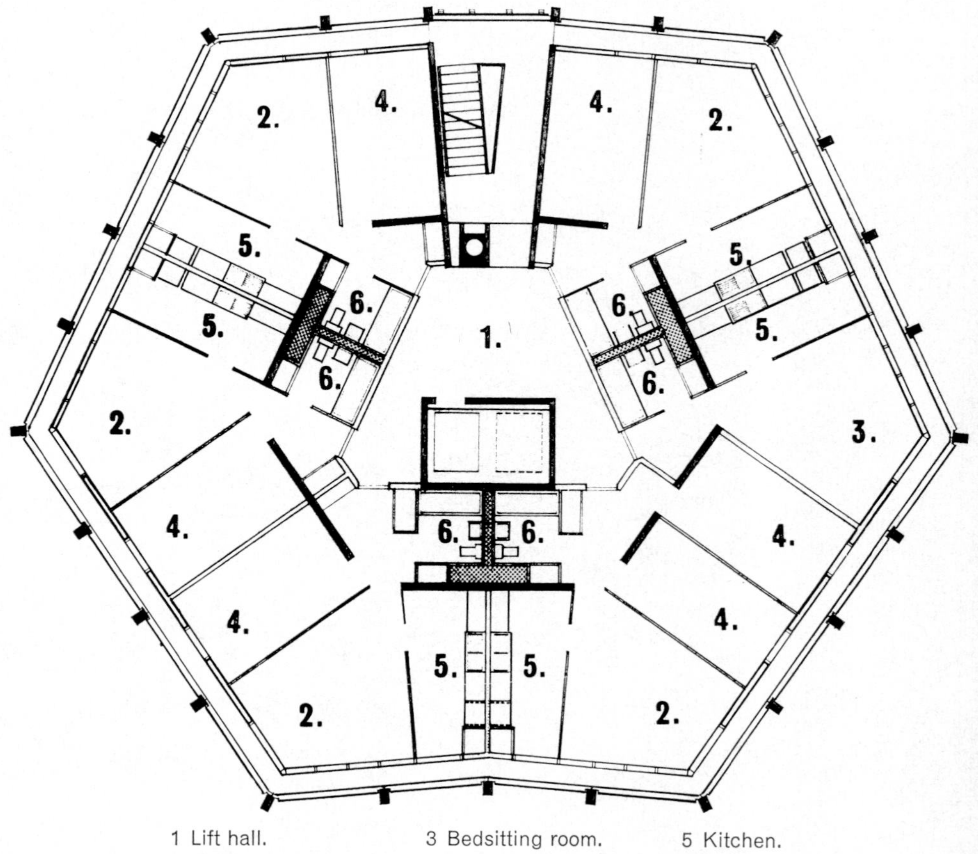

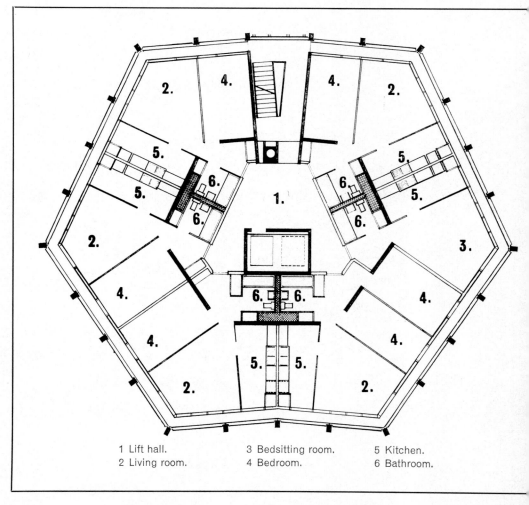

1 Lift hall.
2 Living room.
3 Bedsitting room.
4 Bedroom.
5 Kitchen.
6 Bathroom.

Samuel Street Redevelopment, Woolwich

chitect: Norman and Dawbarn

iis mixed redevelopment scheme provides 9 dwellings at 141 persons per acre. The site, iich is part of a comprehensive development ea and lies to the south-west of Woolwich ockyard Station, covers an area of about six res.

Most of the accommodation is in four 14-storey wer blocks which are 138ft high and contain a tal of 219 one-bedroom and two-bedroom flats. ie scheme also includes five four-storey blocks containing between them 37 three-bedroom aisonettes, 13 bedsittingroom flats, and a op—and one two-storey block containing ght bedsittingroom flats for old people. There also a four-bedroom doctor's house with rgery. A central spine walk links all these ildings. Private gardens are provided for the wer maisonettes, the old people's flats, and e doctor's house; the rest of the site has been d out as a communal open space with grass d trees; including children's play areas (with lets) and communal laundries.

The multi-storey blocks of flats are butterfly-aped in plan, giving the flats the maximum nount of natural ventilation. The two-bedroom ts have a floor area of 673 square feet; that of e one-bedroom flats is 533 square feet. These int blocks stand on 17-in diameter bored pile undations. The frames are reinforced concrete t plate construction, fair-faced where exposed d with a panel infill of flint lime brick and ncrete block cavity walls with aluminium foil in e cavity. Windows are metal and designed so at all cleaning and glazing can be undertaken m inside the building. Cast concrete panels ve been placed under the windows and the lconies have concrete floors and roofs, with bestos sides and wired glass panel balus-ading. The roof structure, which houses the motor and tank rooms, is faced with glass nelling.

The four-storey blocks are of cross-wall nstruction on a reinforced concrete raft with ick and precast concrete infill panels. Division ors and access stairs and balconies are of nforced concrete and the roofs have concrete es. The maisonettes have a floor area of 7 square feet and include an open plan dining d living room. The old people's flats are of nilar construction to the maisonettes but have de strip foundations.

All dwellings except the doctor's house have s-fired instantaneous water heating; back-ound heating to the living rooms and adjoining drooms is provided in the point blocks by ectric floor cables fed by off-peak current. In e maisonettes the living rooms have open fires th floor ducts for fresh-air feed.

Each point block is served by two refuse chutes livering into bins for collection and disposal the local authority. The lower blocks have a mbination of refuse chutes and household stbins.

Special care has been taken in landscaping e site including the planting of a number of ft high mature trees.

Total cost: approximately £618,000.

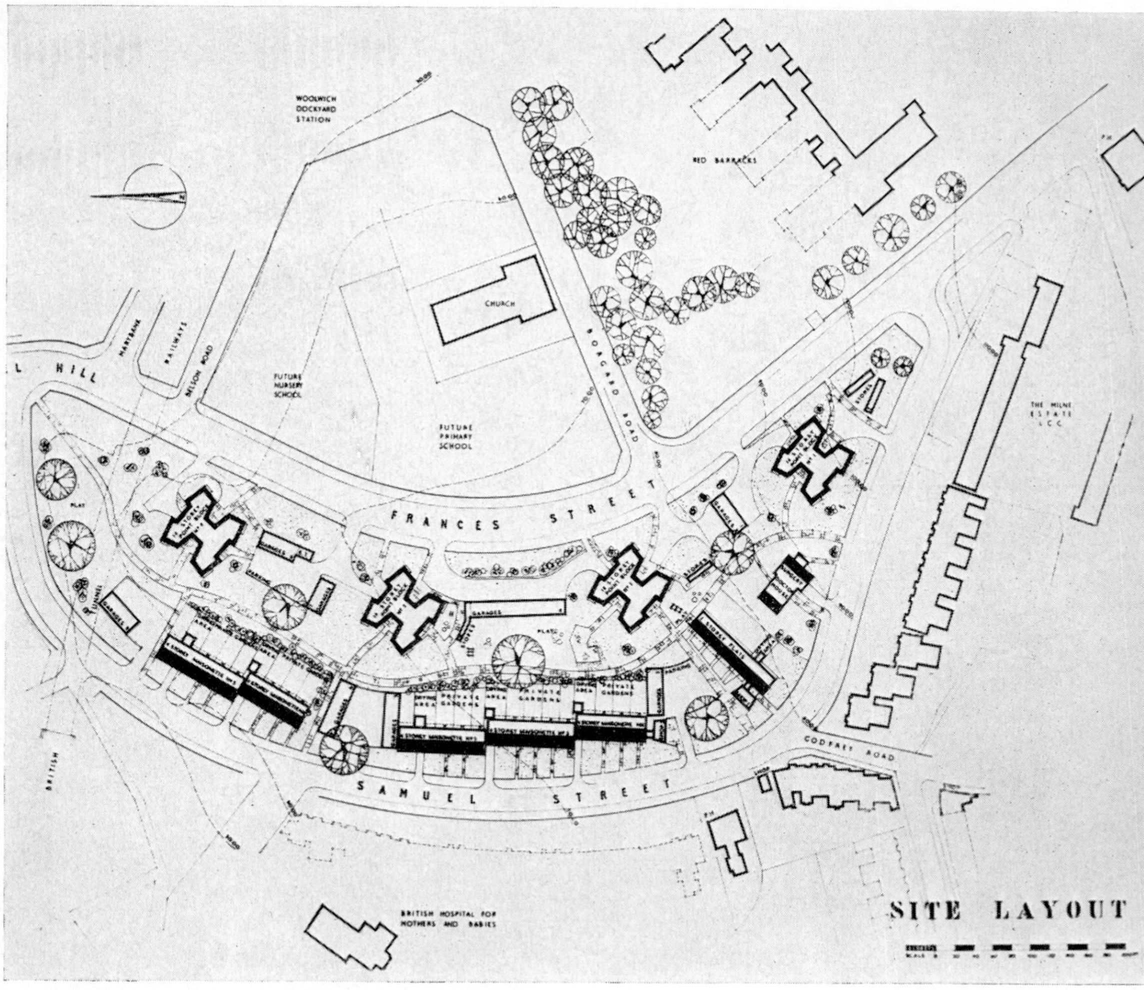

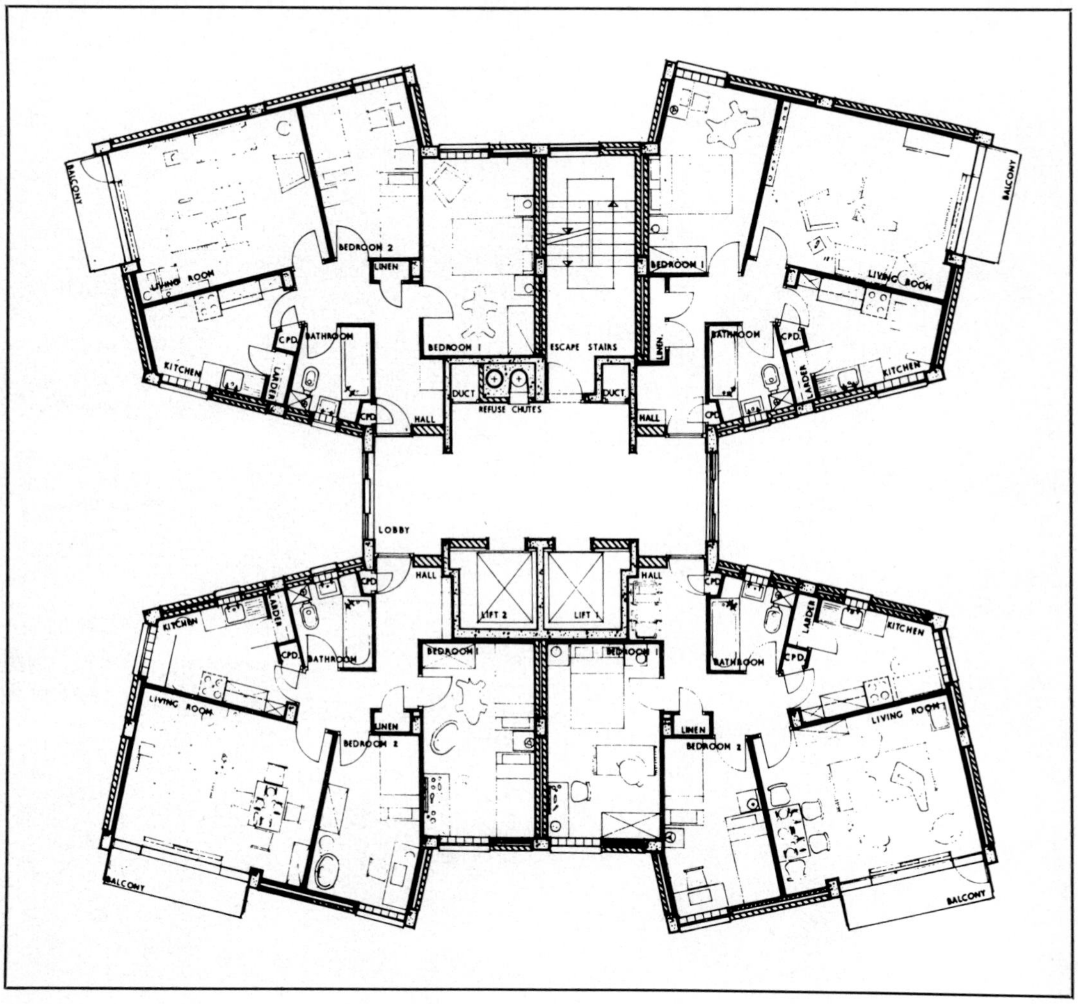

24 Hide Place, Westminster, London

Director of Housing: E. J. Edwards

Architects: Stillman and Eastwick-Field (Associates: R. Smorezewski and D. Stollar)

A single 23-storey tower block in a closely built-up and largely decaying area of London; on a site $1\frac{1}{2}$ acres in extent—and intended mainly for elderly people. Density of development is just over 200 persons per acre; and there are 160 dwellings provided—60 one-room, 80 two-room, and 20 four-room units. In addition there is car parking for 37 cars; a clubroom, communal laundry, tenants' stores, caretaker's workshop.

The building especially when judged in conjunction with nearby open space, has great architectural merit; and the internal planning is excellent. Two stairs and two lifts give access to eight flats on the typical floor. All kitchens are on external walls; bathrooms are located internally and mechanically ventilated. Electric floor warming is installed.

The building contains many technical innovations including new prefabrication techniques in the reinforced concrete, structure and cladding.

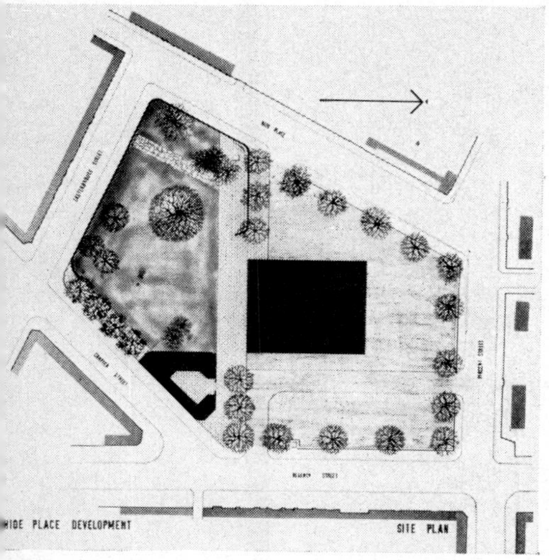

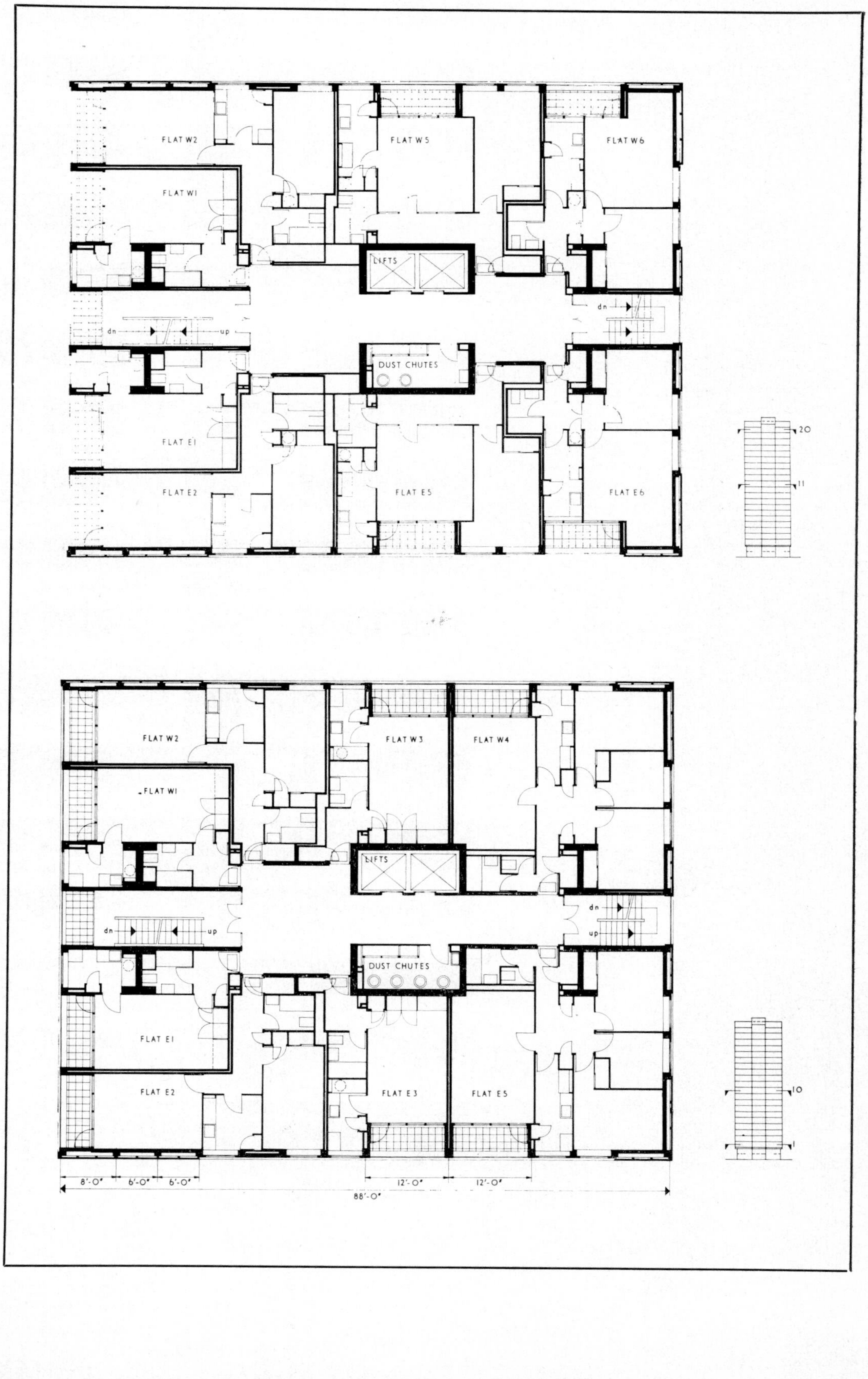

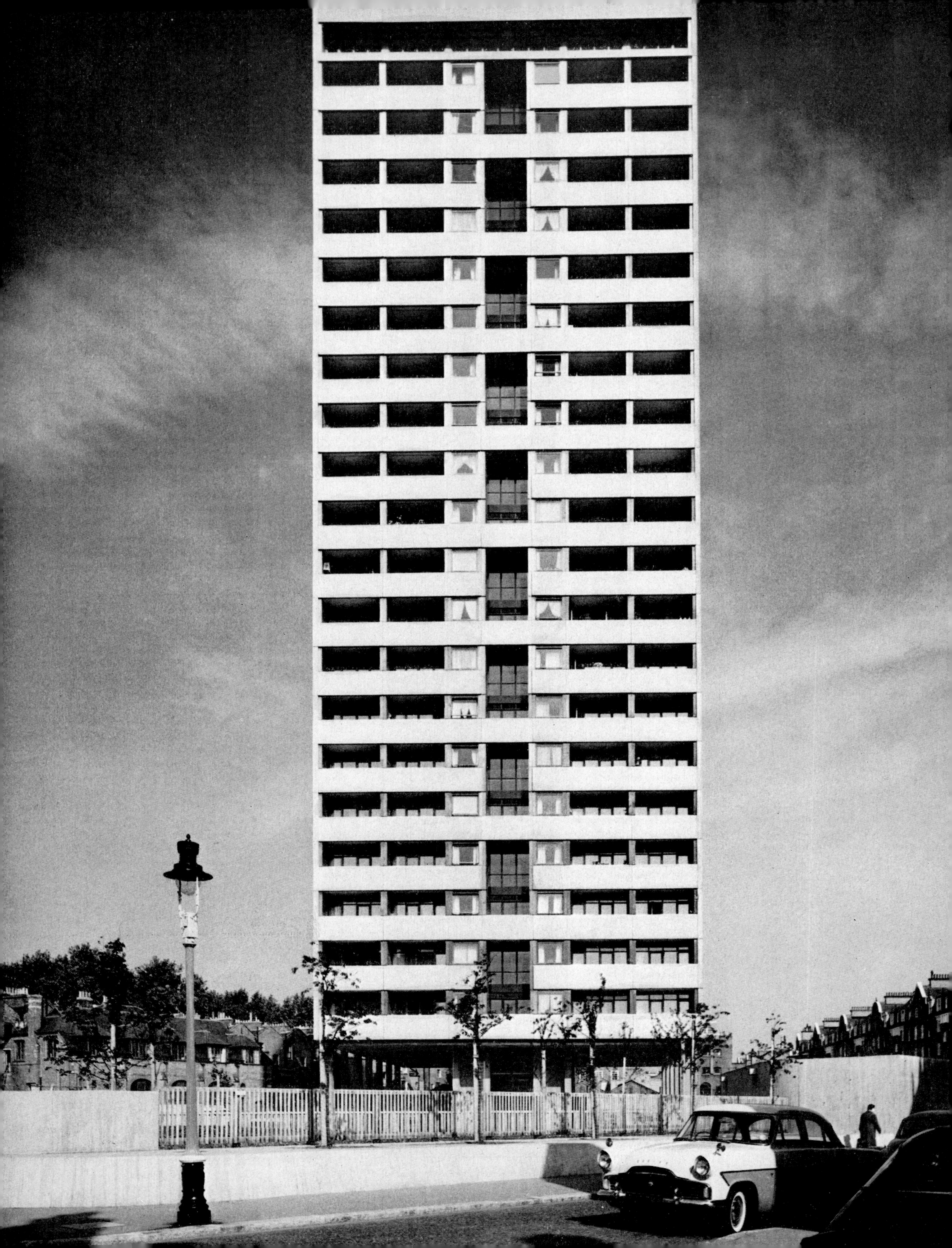

Eastwood Road Development, West Ham

hitects: Stillman and Eastwick-Field

enewal project in a blighted area of 5½ acres xtent; and including housing at a density of persons per acre, a community centre, ps, a surgery, children's and toddler's /grounds, garages and parking areas.

he main elements are two 19-storey resi- tial blocks linked by a raised podium with es under. The other accommodation is tained mainly within two crescent shaped gle-storey blocks forming part of the overall uping. One of the multi-storey blocks contains three-bedroom flats and 76 one-bedroom s. The other has 76 two-bedroom units and vith one bedroom.

oth blocks are raised on columns above und level which will help ensure privacy and estricted view for even the lowest level of ellings.

ccess is by two lifts and single staircase in ordance with the British Standard Code of ctice (C.P.3. Chapter IV—1962).

ll flats are heated by electric floor coils; and water is through local immersion heaters. bathrooms and W.C's are mechanically tilated but kitchens have natural light and tilation.

he structure is in reinforced concrete with slabs, columns and spine walls. External dding is in precast concrete slabs.

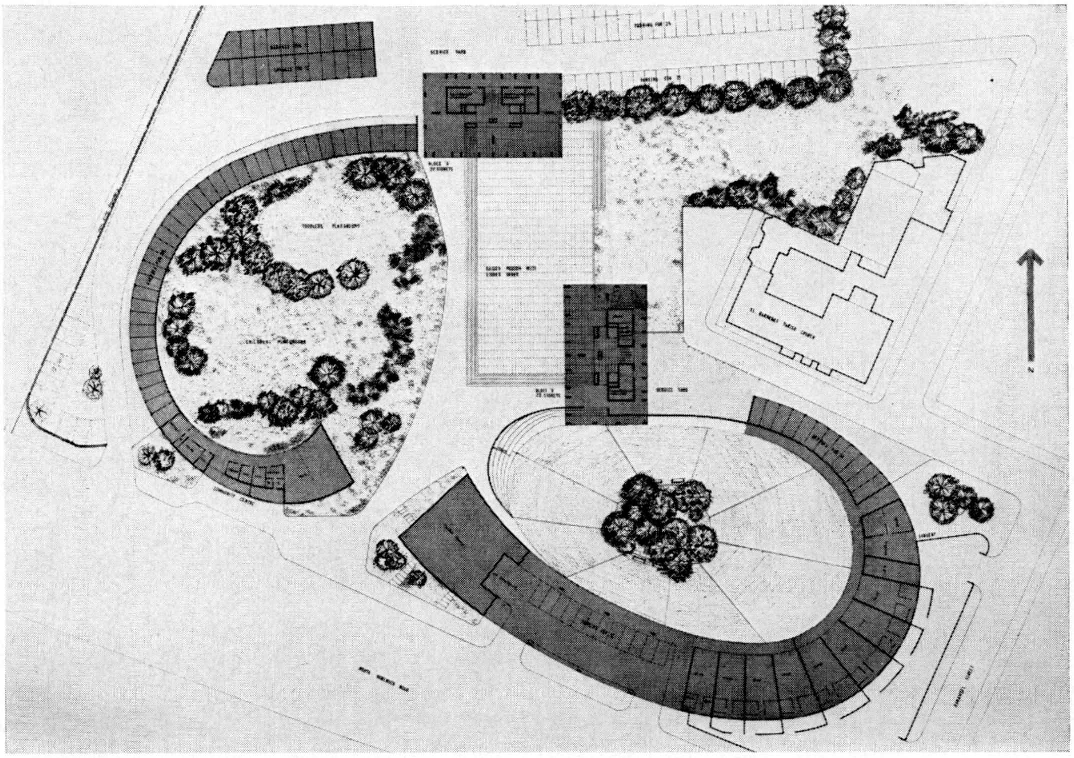

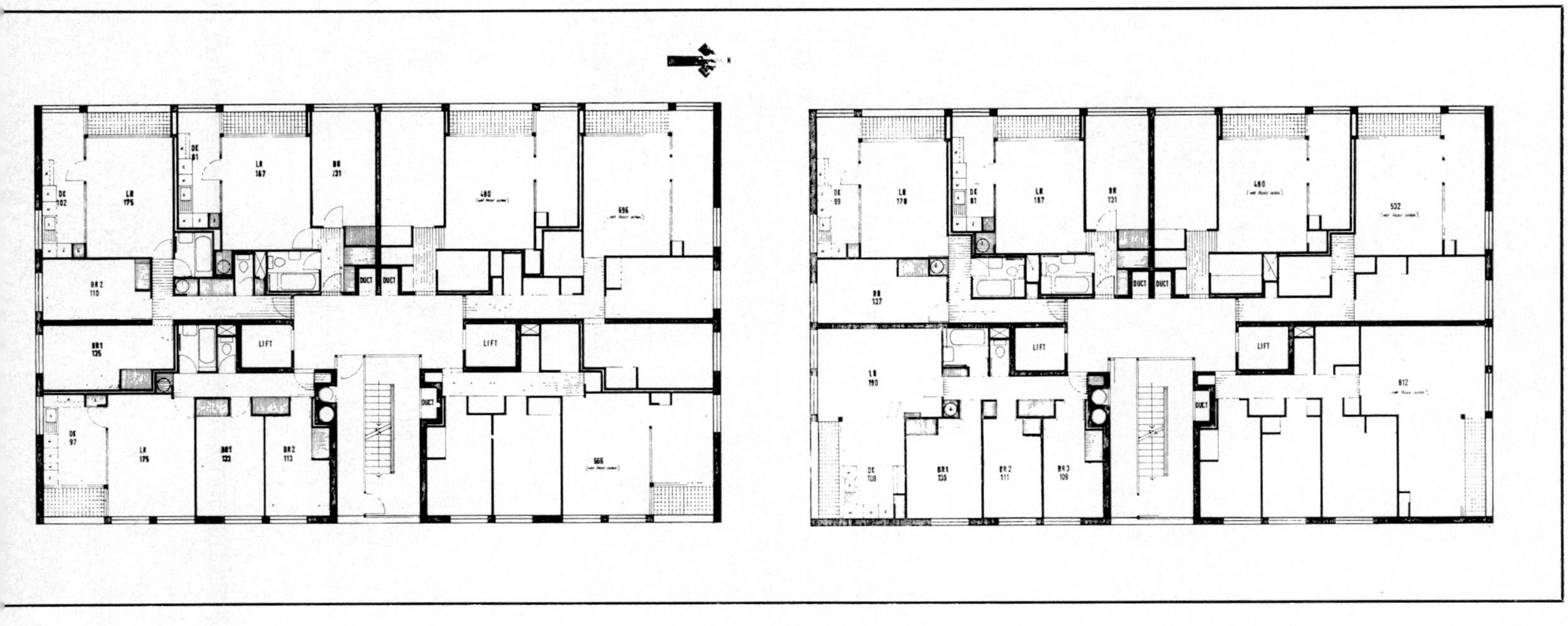

26 Langlands Road, Glasgow

Architects: Scottish Special Housing Association

A development including four-storey terraces and fifteen-storey tower blocks planned with four similar flats to the typical floor, each with two bedrooms. A rational back-to-back grouping arrangement of kitchens and bathrooms has been used but this results in traffic passing through the night zone to reach the day area, in order to provide kitchens with natural light and ventilation. Each flat has its own private balcony which though pleasing in their overall effect may perhaps be construed as a loss of possible normal living areas.

Vertical access is by twin skip-lifts and staircases, with escape balconies forming a link between flats across the stair bay. Electric floor warming is installed throughout. There are two refuse chutes to each block with access in a separate lobby which also contains service risers and fire mains. The ground floors contain tenants' storage and laundries.

Construction is reinforced concrete cross wall and core with brick facings.

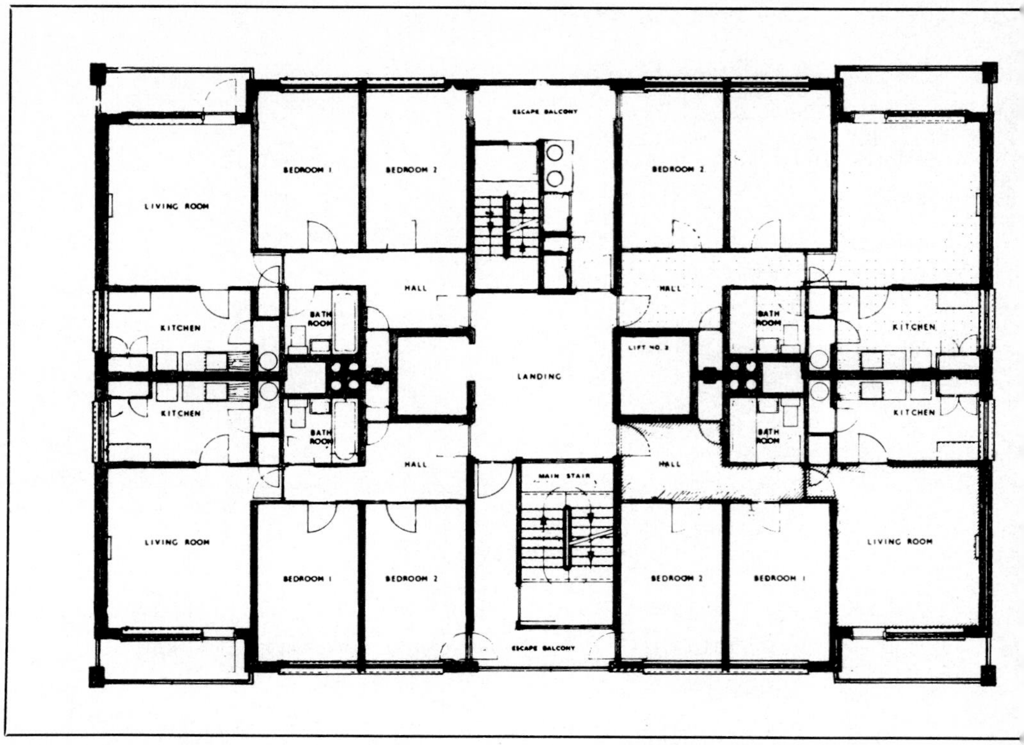

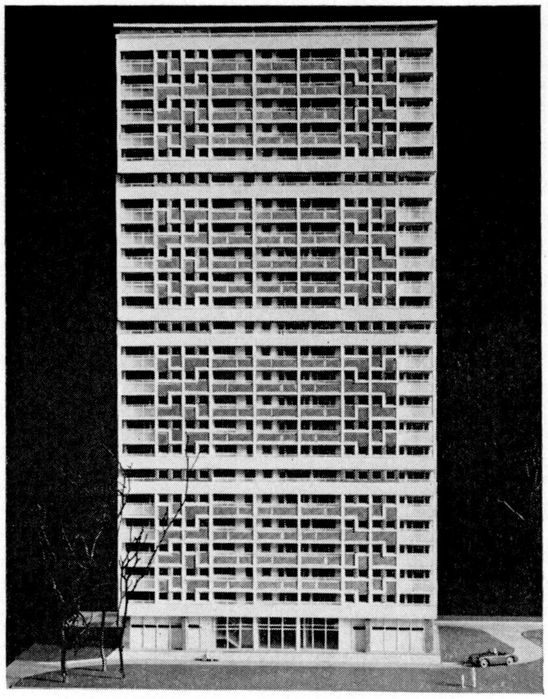

27 Hutchesontown, Gorbals, Glasgow

Architects: Scottish Special Housing Association

A comprehensive slum redevelopment area providing 1369 new homes at a density of 166 persons per acre overall, on a site of 25 acres.

Six hundred and fifty-six of the dwellings are provided in four multi-storey blocks and of which 455 are for households without children and only 122 for those with children.

The 25-storey tower blocks were decided on as a means of taking better advantage of very deep piled foundations found to be necessary.

The whole area as redeveloped allows ample open space and play areas; a total of $10\frac{1}{2}$ acres or four acres per 1000 population. Most parking and garaging is underground with landscaped terraces over shops, pubs and schools are also included in the scheme.

The scheme below is also at Hutchesontown, but is not the same as 27.
Architects: Prof. Sir Robert Matthew and Partners.

United States of America

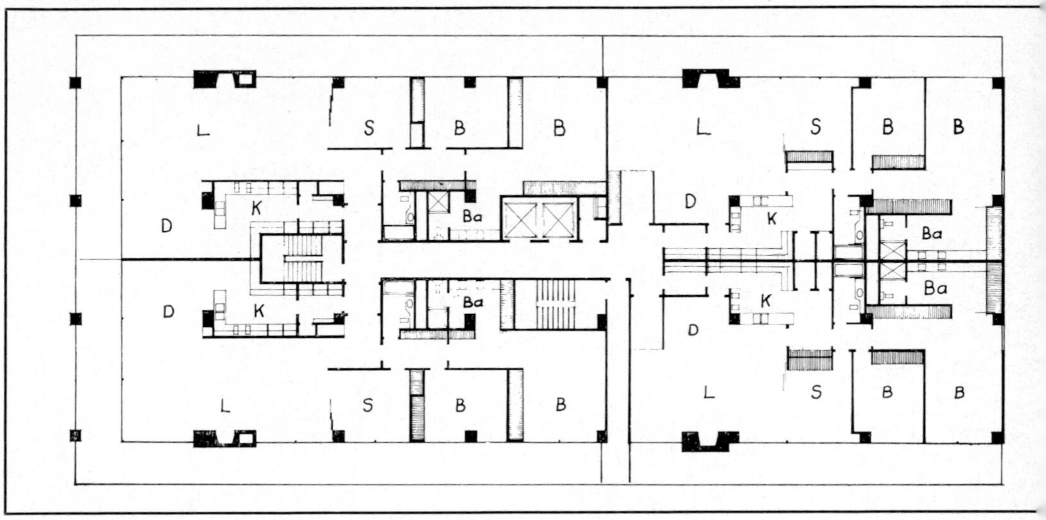

1 Co-operative Apartments, Long Beach, California

Architects: Killingsworth, Brady and Smith

An elongated type of point block with internal staircase and lift access to a typical floor containing four large flats; the building being 13 storeys in height. Orientation provides for panoramic views of harbour and coastline from every flat.

The flats are large, ranging from 1900 to 2100 square feet each plus large terrace areas, and the block is clearly intended for luxury living. Garages are provided on three levels giving two-car storage for each apartment as a further indication of the standard of accommodation intended. A two-storey lobby opens into the entrance court and a private court with swimming pool.

Bathrooms and kitchens are all planned internally. The system of construction is reinforced concrete frame which is very simply and clearly expressed in the facades. An interesting feature is the use of open fireplaces in all of the flats which of course raises the problems of fuel deliveries and ash disposal; not by any means simple problems in a multi-storey building of this type. *Cost: $3 million.*

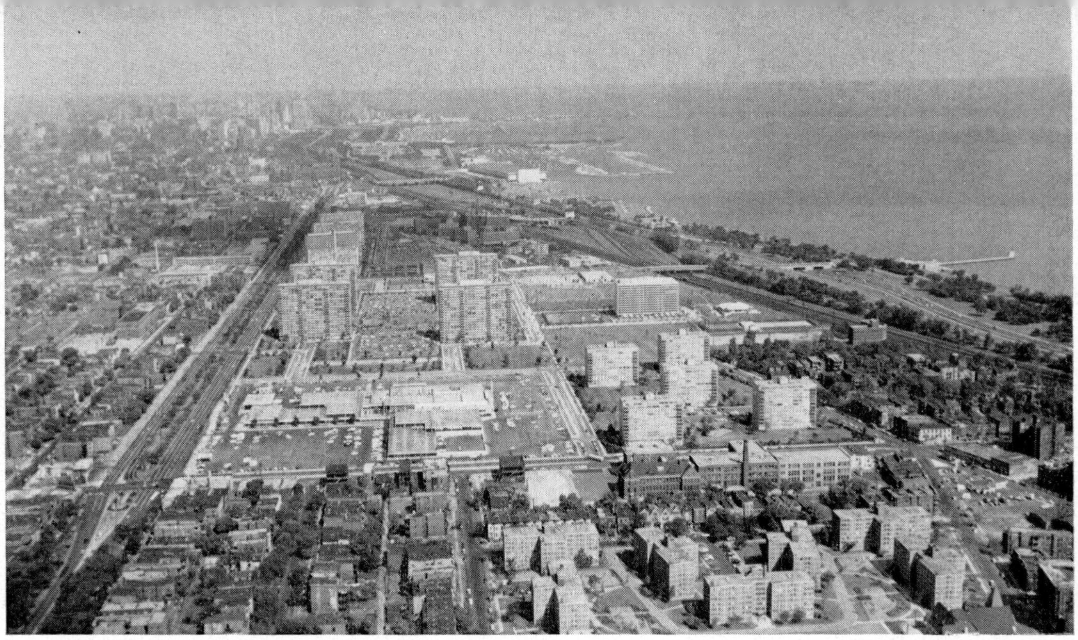

Lake Meadows Development, Chicago

hitects: Skidmore, Owings and Merrill

s is a scheme extending over 100 acres of aimed or redeveloped slum area in Chicago's thside. There are 2015 dwellings in 12- and storey and 21-storey blocks, all planned on the rnal corridor principle with the typical floor he 12-storey blocks containing 10 flats all of ch are either one bedroom or bedsittingroom ts, with the smaller units having internal hrooms and kitchens. The kitchens and hrooms are similarly planned in the 21-storey cks but in the 13-storey blocks are all internal. 21-storey blocks have 16 flats to the typical r and the 13-storey blocks 12.

ccess is from a double scissor type staircase he centre of the block and twin lifts in the storey blocks. In other blocks stairs are nned in separate wells but still do not entirely iate 'dead ends'.

he system of construction of the flat blocks is einforced concrete frame and flat slab with tain wall on the main facades with solid k end walls in the smaller blocks. The whole ject also includes its own shopping centre, king space for 1300 cars, and an overall sity of 32 families per acre in the area zoned residential use. There is also an elementary ool and park, club building, and professional ding.

acilities in the individual blocks for the ants also include coin-operated clothes shers and dryers in laundry rooms, as well as chanical ventilation to halls, bathrooms and hens. A central boiler plant supplies steam ll buildings.

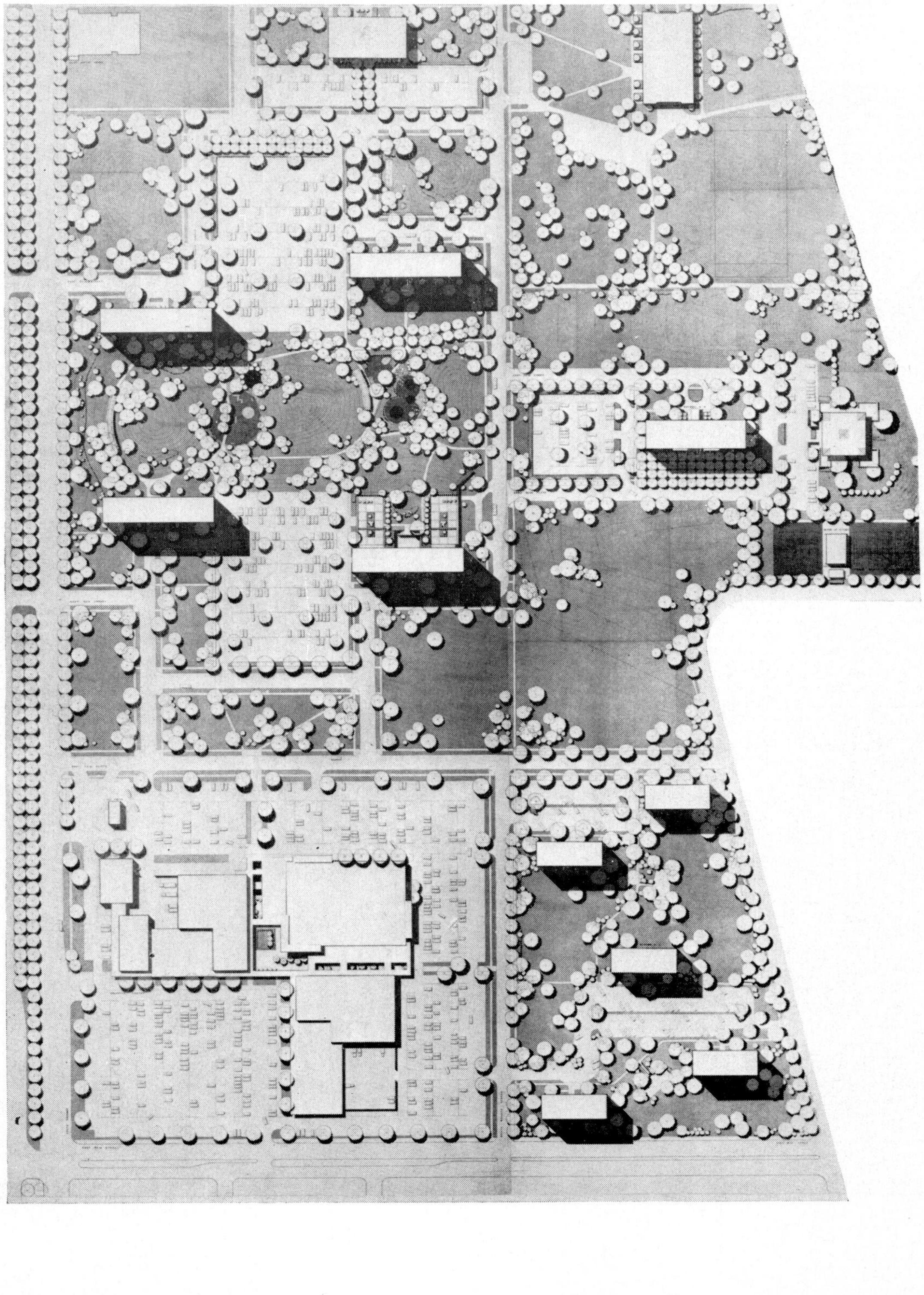

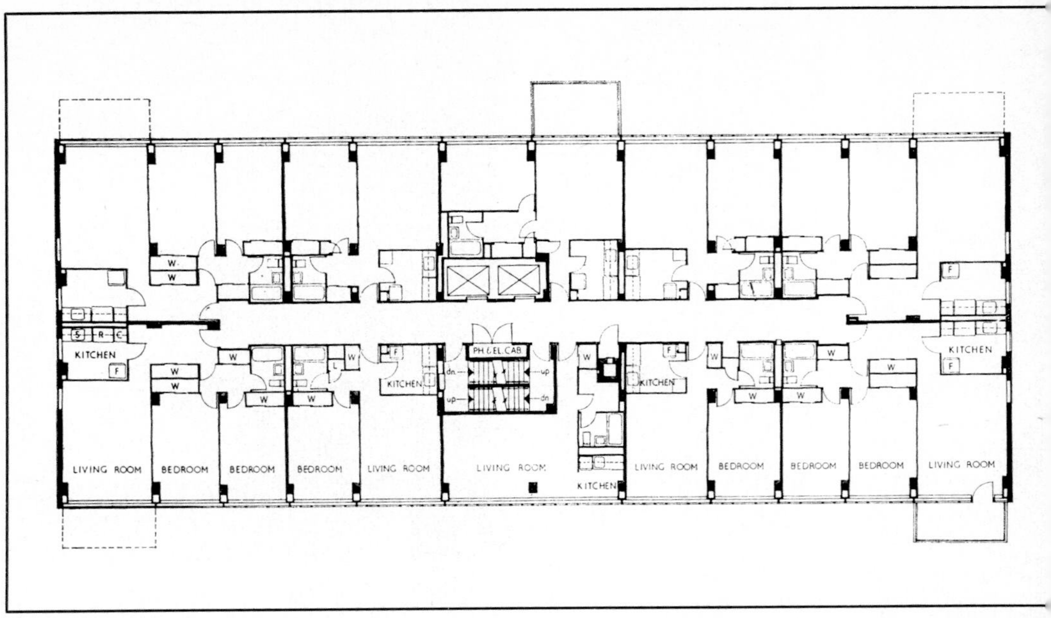
KITCHEN
PH & EL CAB
LIVING ROOM
BEDROOM

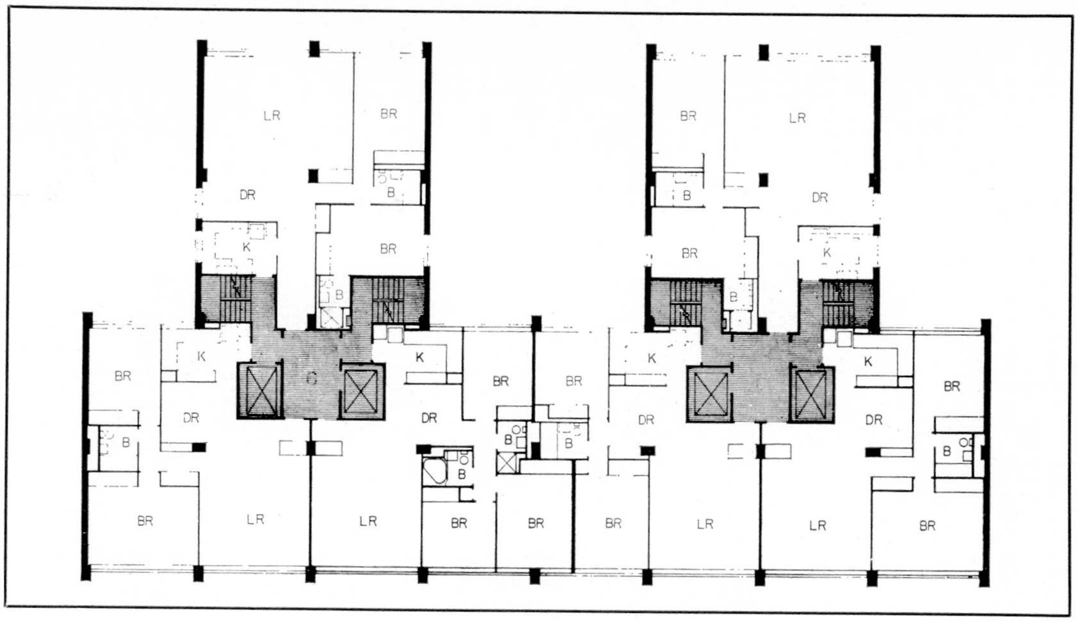

Promontory Apartments, Chicago

ıitect: Mies van der Rohe (1950)

planning consists of linked tees giving a of six flats to the typical floor, but with four and four staircases for vertical access. All have two bedrooms. Some of the bathrooms on external walls, some internal. Kitchens in ases receive natural light.

ıe form of structure is a reinforced concrete ıe based on an entirely regular grid. The only mpt that has been made by the architect to the somewhat monotonous appearance of strictly regular structural grid and window ern externally is that of stepping back the mn facing at every fifth storey.

ıe scheme includes 20 floors of flats and a ınd floor which consists solely of entrance s and tenants facilities. An outdoor play area ovided for on the site as well as car parking he basis of two car spaces to every three .

Cost: $8.55/*square foot.*

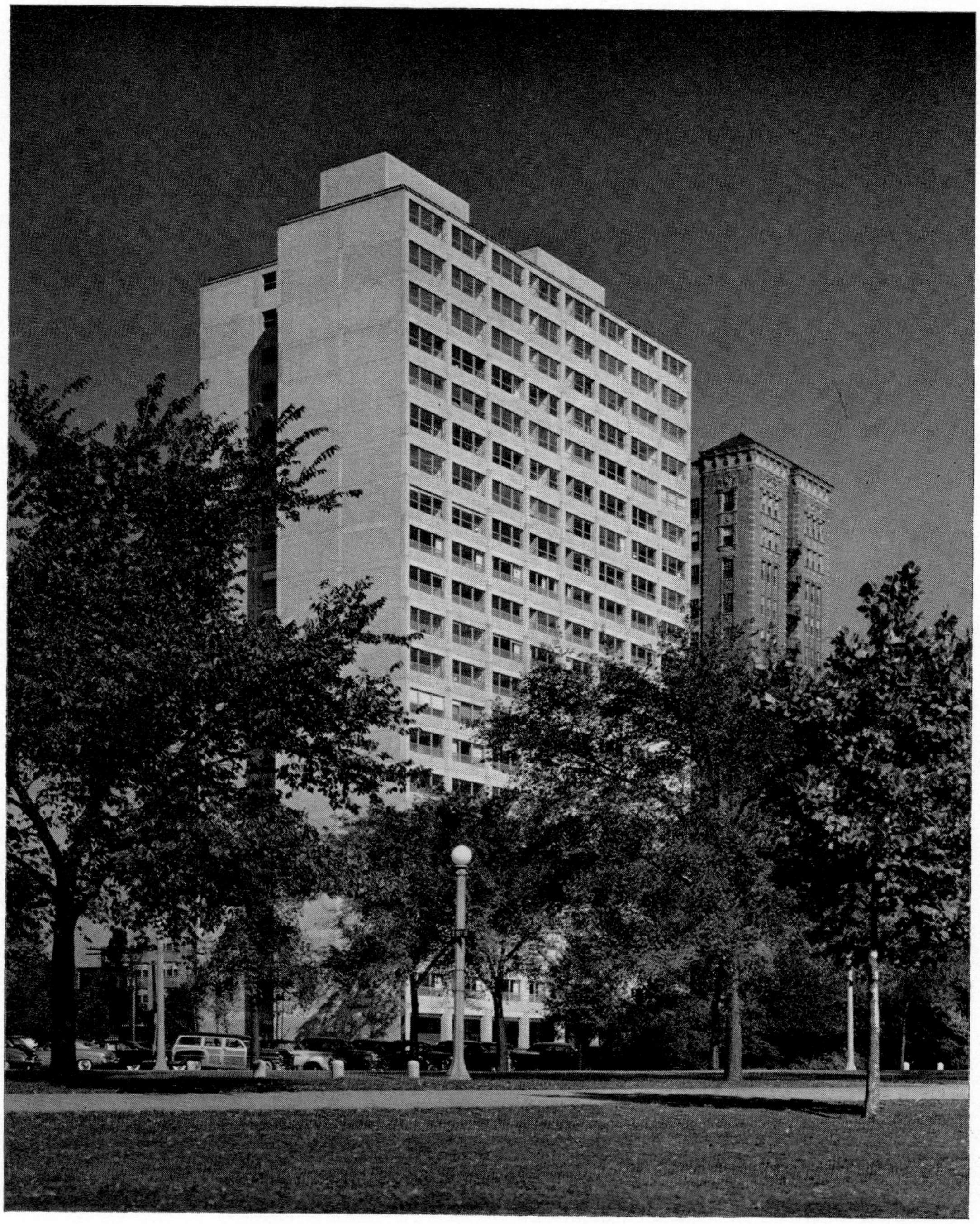

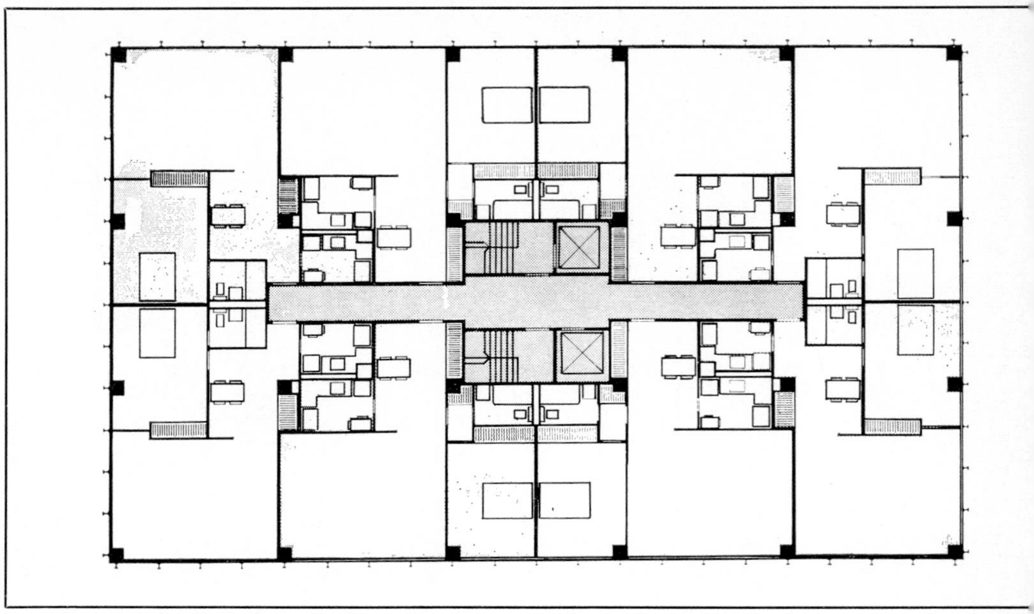

4 Lake Shore Drive, Chicago

Architect: Mies van der Rohe (1951)

This dramatic scheme consists of two separate but identical rectangular towers placed at right angles to one another, and each 26 storeys in height. Both blocks have their own entrance lobbies but these are connected by a covered way. Beneath the whole complex is a garage space for 116 cars, while the first floors are devoted to communal laundries, deep freeze and other service rooms. Above this level each floor contains identical flats of three-and-a-half room type in the north block, and six-room type in the south block.

The system of planning is with internal corridors, in each case with two lifts and two staircases.

The typical floor to the north block contains eight flats and the south block four flats. All bathrooms and kitchens have internal locations.

The construction is steel frame, and the whole of the exterior of both buildings is in the form of curtain wall. The extensive glass areas have been fitted with external roller blinds in order to reduce solar radiation impact.

The development of the site includes garden area to the extent of about 50 per cent of the total site.

Financing of the scheme was on a co-operative basis by which means intending tenants were enabled to purchase their flats with the additional payment of a rent to cover maintenance, running costs, taxes, etc.

5 Lafayette Park, Detroit

Architect: Mies van der Rohe (1957)

This is a mixed development including a variety of types of dwelling of which a number are concentrated into 20-storey blocks. These blocks, which are of the Lamella type, consist of a typical floor with seven flats ranging from a bedsitter to two-bedroom type.

The planning is with central corridor access and vertical circulation by means of two internal staircases and three lifts. As in a number of other American schemes bathrooms and kitchens are planned internally alongside the corridor wall. This arrangement helps in one sense to provide a buffer against noise transmission from the access corridor but it also involves mechanical ventilation not only for the bathrooms but for the kitchens too, which are by the same token deprived of any natural light or view.

The 20-storey blocks are of frame construction with a strongly expressed fenestration and structural pattern carried all the way round the building in order to gain the advantage of the addition of light to the larger flats which are again in this instance located at the ends of the building. The result is, however, to give a lack of contrast in the external architectural expression as well as a somewhat excessive use of glass for most climates.

Perhaps the most interesting thing about the whole development is the way in which different types of accommodation have been planned together at fairly high densities but yet preserving very ample open space which has been landscaped and planned in an informal way as an excellent foil to the general layout of the scheme with its strong rectilinear character.

Very ample car parking space has been allowed as well as additional facilities including retail shopping, a school, and a club building.

6 New Brunswick

Architect: Turano

This scheme for an 11-storey point block has a number of unique and interesting features both in the planning of the typical floor and in the general treatment and overall architectural expression.

The typical floors are divided up in such a way as to provide six precisely similar units which will include living-room dining space, kitchen, bedroom and bathing facilities with the sanitary and kitchen facilities forming a single combined core in the centre of each of the units which they serve. Arrangements are also made to combine two of the units together to form larger units.

A central service core is provided to the whole block containing two lifts which serve alternate floors, and a double scissor type of staircase. The core also contains the refuse chutes.

While this block was primarily designed for elderly people it could just as well serve the needs of single young people or young married couples without children. The system of planning provides a very interesting departure indeed from the normal more stereotyped plan forms, and with the very economical basis of six flats to the floor still manages to overcome entirely the problem of overlooking as between one flat and another.

The system of construction is reinforced concrete with flat slabs cantilevered from a two-column form of support, the columns being located in each case either in a party dividing wall or in the sanitary core to the flat.

The ground floor to the block is provided with a community room, space for a welfare officer, and the mail room as well as lift and staircase access. External treatment allows for pivoting sashes for easy cleaning and for the introduction of colour in the form of porcelain enamel spandrel panels.

Site cover is to the extent of only about 20 per cent, the remainder of the area being planned as park for amenity and recreation purposes.

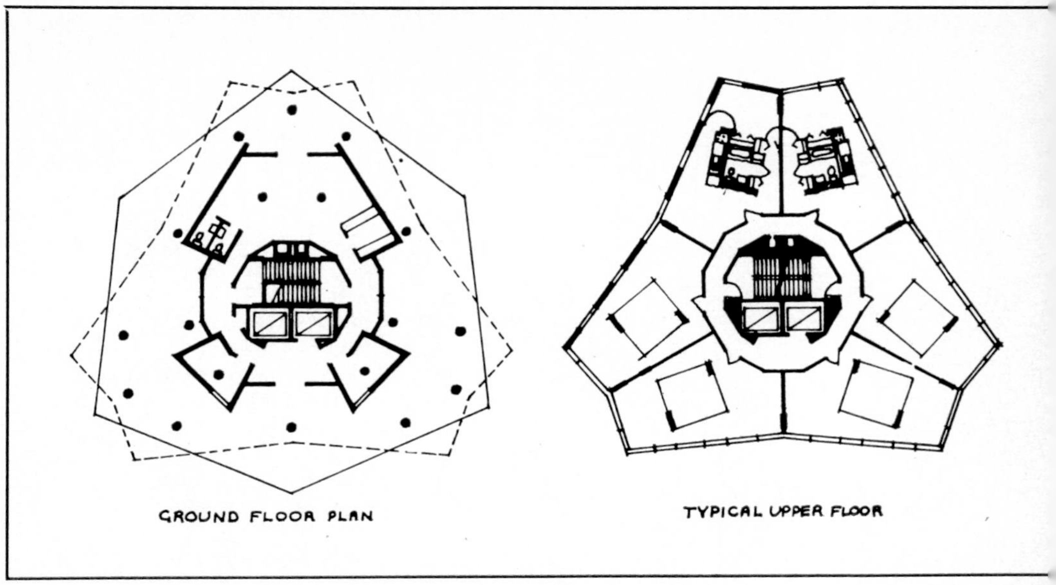

East Orange

chitect: Turano

is is basically a somewhat similar scheme to at in New Brunswick designed by the same chitect, except that in this case eight flats to e typical floor are provided, with the conse- ence that there is not the same degree of munity from overlooking mutually, as in the her scheme. Nevertheless the planning is genious and extremely economical, and for e small one-bedroom type of unit provided, s a great deal to commend it.

n this case seven habitable floors with eight ts per floor served by the two lifts and the two aircases are proposed, but there is no reason all why a similar form of planning could not be tended to 15, 20 or more storeys.

The system of construction in this case would identical with that of the New Brunswick heme and entirely in reinforced concrete with interesting visual checkerboard panel of ernating window positions as between adjoin- g floors.

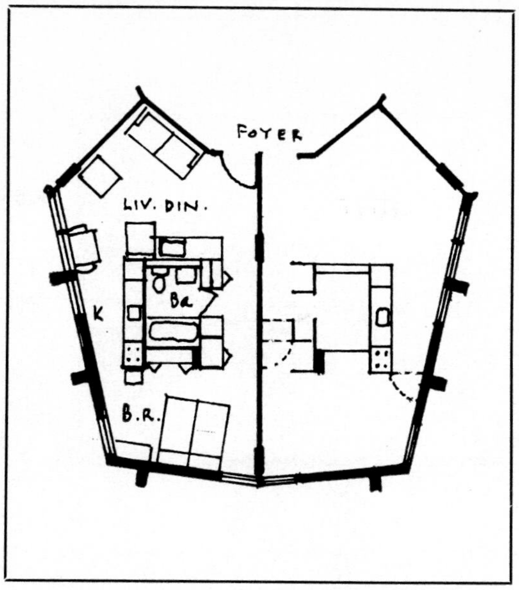

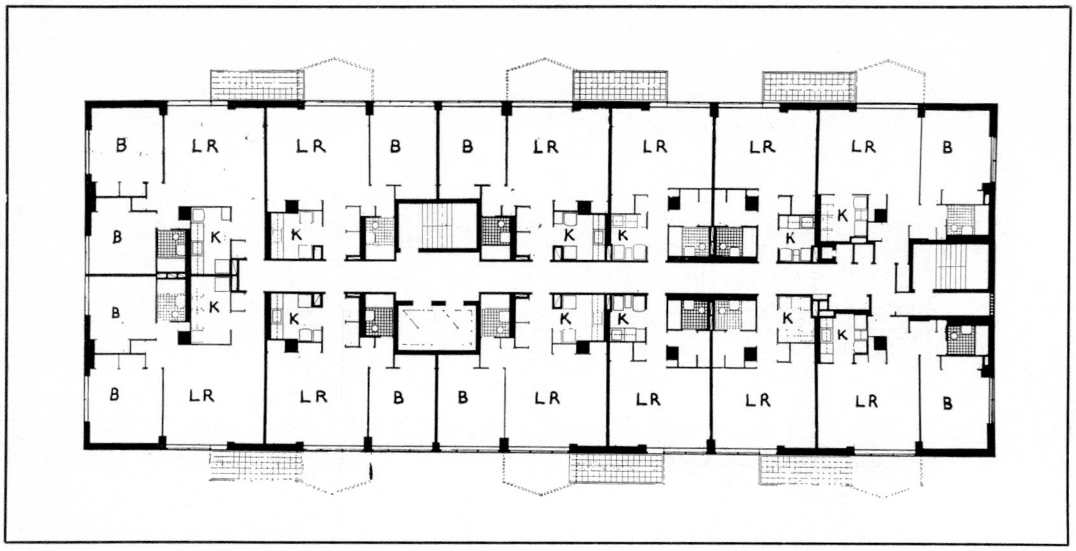

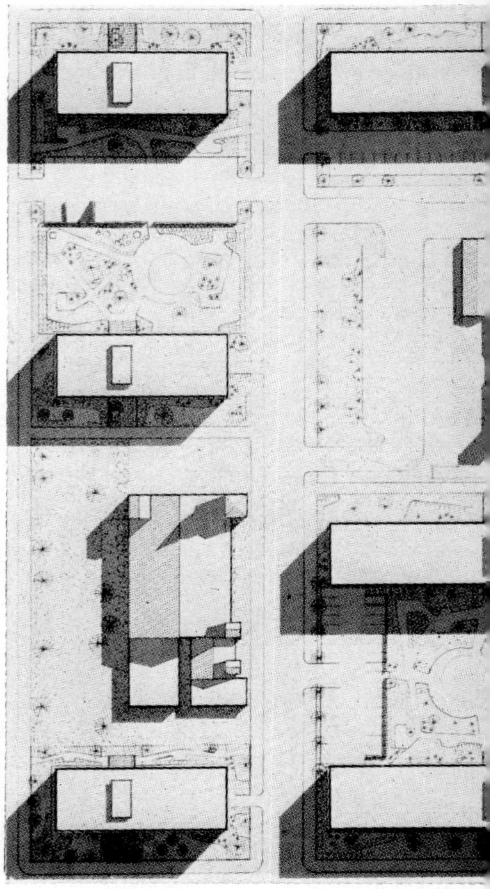

8 Plaza Square, St. Louis

Architect: Hellmuth Obata and Kassabaum

A central development area of 5 acres including six, 13-storey lamella blocks containing in all 1090 flats. The system of planning is on the basis of the central access corridor, with the typical floor containing 12 flats including one bedroom, two bedrooms and efficiency units. Internal bathrooms and kitchens are mechanically ventilated. Provision is also made for room air-conditioners, and telephone service between flats and entrance lobbies.

The whole development has a clean and well-co-ordinated appearance with a simplicity and directness of architectural expression. The layout is good with 45 per cent landscaped open area, 27 per cent for parking and 28 per cent building average. Construction is flat plate concrete. *Total cost:* $15 *million.*

Astoria Houses, Queens, New York

iitects: Harrison and Abramovitz (1951)

; is one of the large developments under-
n under the auspices of the New York City
sing Authority and containing in all over
; flats in 23 similar blocks, each six and seven
eys in height, and containing eight flats of
ing sizes to the typical floor. The site, which
2 acres in extent, has an East River frontage
a magnificent outlook for most of the tenants.
he building coverage is approximately
per cent, the remainder of the site being
oted largely to playground and park amenity
as.

ach block has a central circulation core
taining two internal staircases and one lift
well as refuse disposal chutes. Two large
s are located in each of the wings on what
/ be termed a 'back-to-back' system of
nning with the living rooms located at the
les of the arms in such a way as to prevent
tual overlooking between adjoining flats.
art from the somewhat awkward shapes which
ult from this method of planning, particularly
iving rooms and kitchens, the other main
ection is in the rather lengthy circulation
as giving access to the bedroom wings.
vision is included for children's indoor play-
ms, classrooms, child health centres, social
l craft rooms. *Total cost: nearly* $14 *million.*

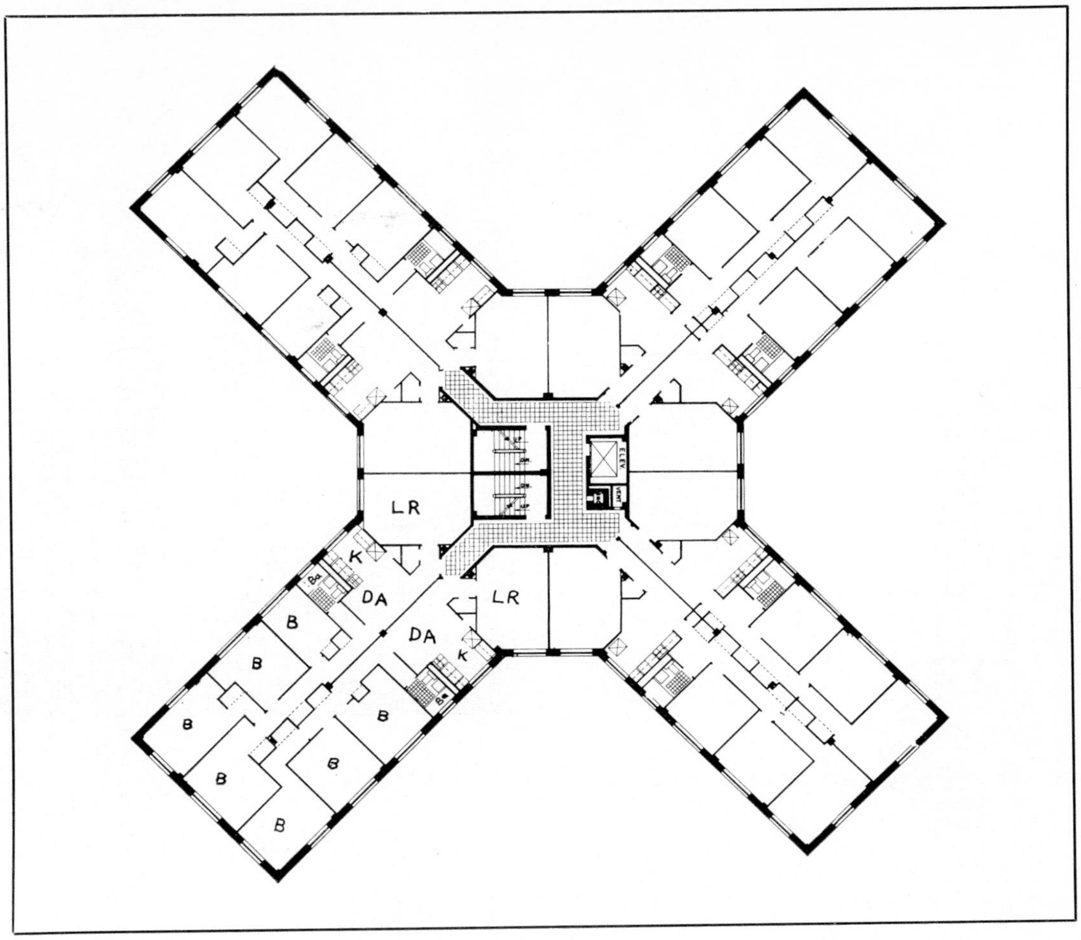

10 Albany Houses, Brooklyn, New York

Architects: Fellheimer, Wagner and Vollmer (1950–57)

This is another of the New York City Housing Authority developments on a site of about 13 acres, containing 1229 flats, and developed to a density of 350 persons per acre, and just over 15 per cent site coverage.

The flats are arranged in nine identical blocks 13 to 14 storeys in height with ten apartments to the typical floor and a central service core with twin skip stop lifts and twin scissor type staircases. As in a number of the New York schemes a central boiler house has been planned to supply the whole area, and central laundries, craft rooms and children's rooms are also provided.

The remaining parts of the site are available for landscaping and garden development for recreation and amenity purposes.

The two flats in each of the projecting wings have the living rooms planned at the points of intersection. The individual units are either of the three-bedroom or the two-bedroom type with the bedrooms placed at the extremities of the wings where there is likely to be least annoyance from overlooking and where they get angle cross ventilation. The bedrooms and kitchens are all planned with natural light and ventilation on external walls. The public hall at each floor level is very tightly planned, depending on artificial light and ventilation.

The disadvantages of this type of planning are that living rooms cannot be provided with cross ventilation and only certain of the bedrooms receive cross ventilation. Rather lengthy and wasteful internal corridor communication is also necessary.

Total cost: approximately $13½ *million.*

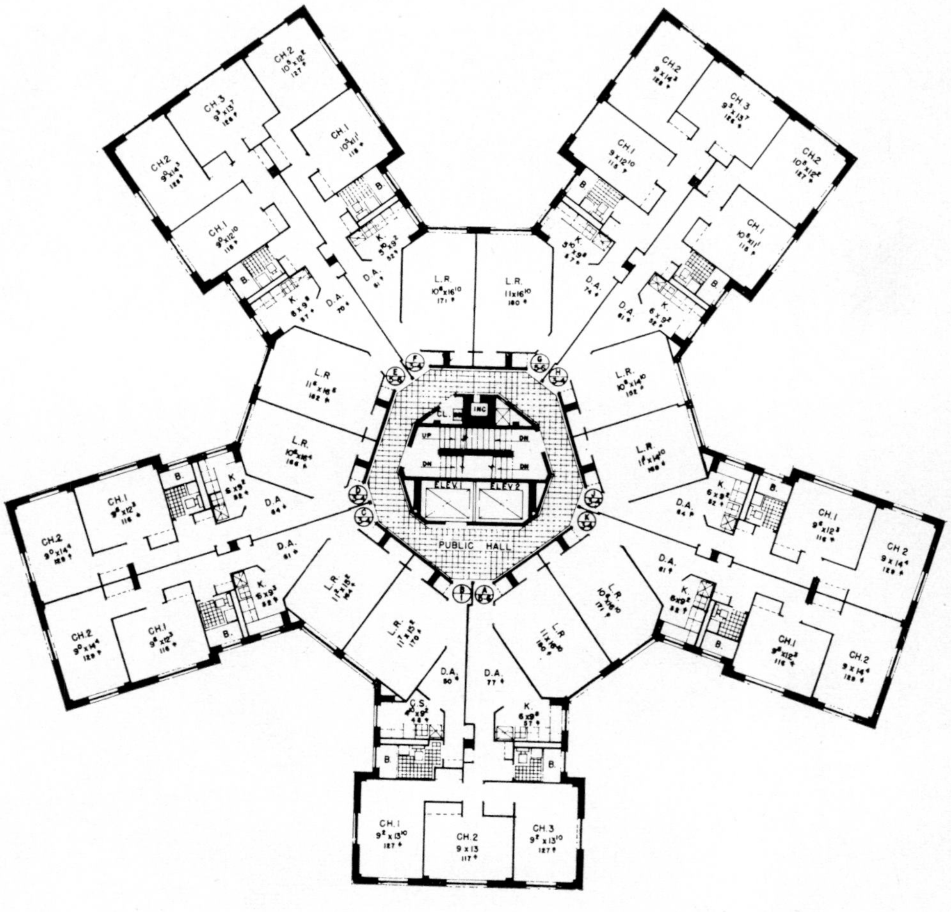

Bronx River Houses, New York

:hitect: William I. Hohauser (1951)

New York City Housing Authority develop-
ınt on a site of some 14 acres of which less
ın 14 per cent is built upon, the remaining
per cent being available for landscape garden
d amenity areas. In addition, a large city park
mediately adjoins the site. The design density
n this instance just over 350 persons per acre.
The development consisting of nine similar
ocks 14 storeys in height, containing a total of
l6 flats. The planning of the individual block
the form of a somewhat unusual double Y
:h central corridor access in the centre portion,
ovides at each typical floor 10 flats served by
staircases and two lifts. The planning
nbines the features of a number of the other
es of scheme including the star type and the
rmal rectangular slab block and central
rridor access. The scheme also includes
rks, playgrounds, a health studio, a children's
ntre and social rooms.

Total cost: about $12½ million.

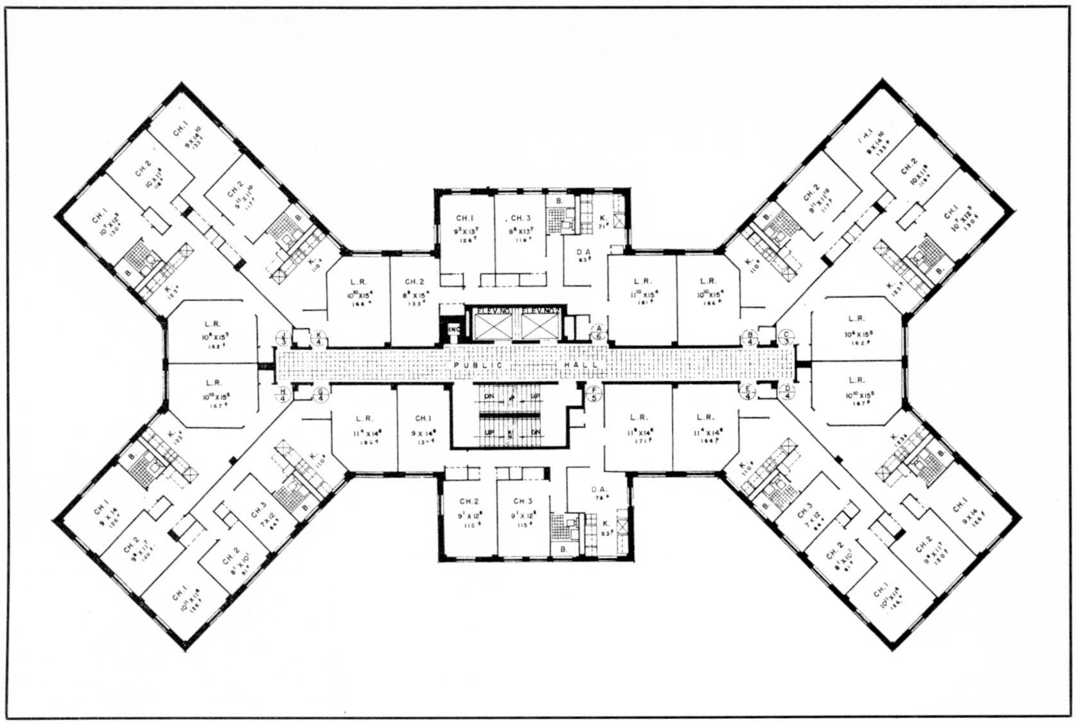

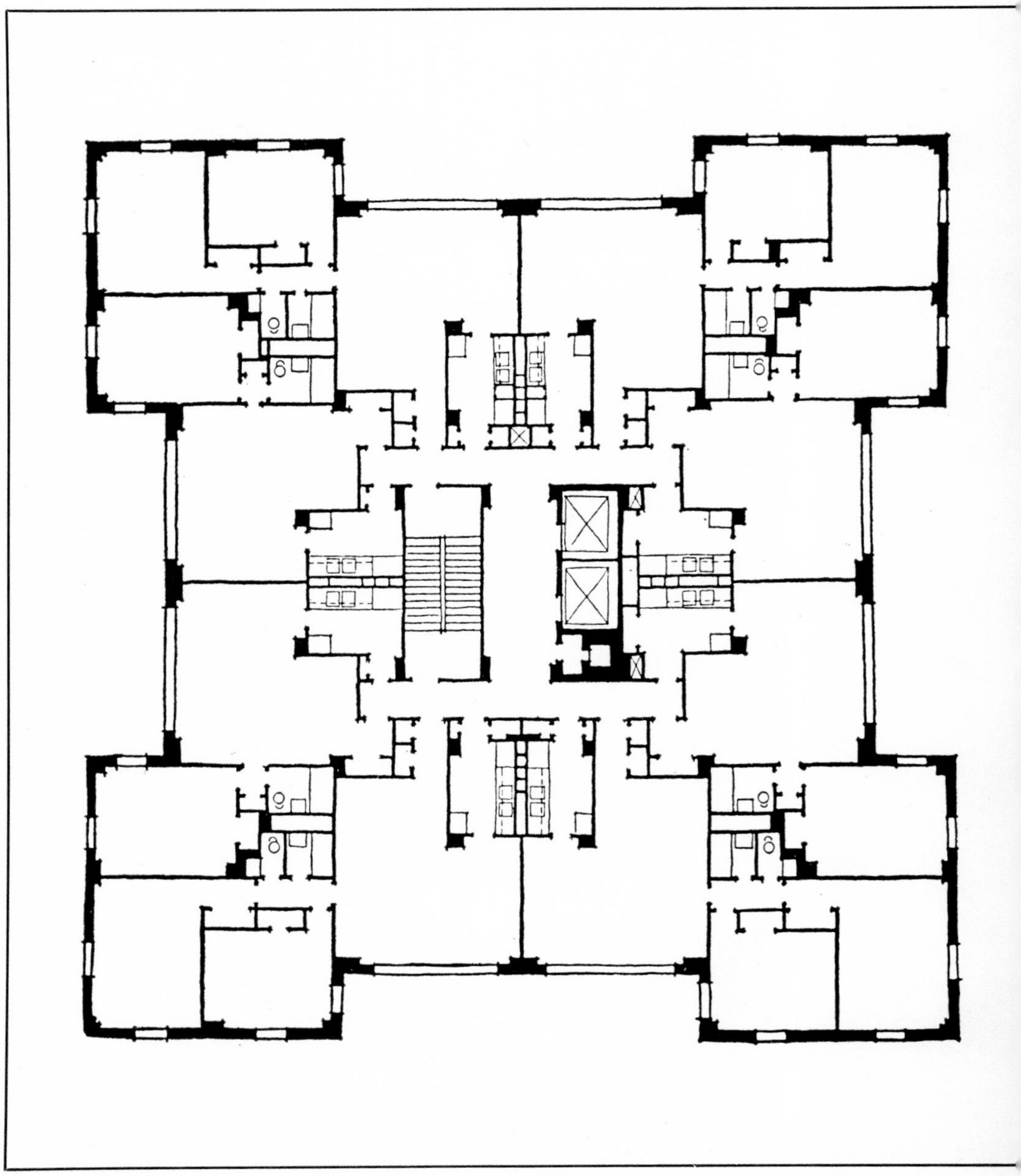

12 Fordham Hill, New York

Architect: Leonard Schultze and Associates

A development which much more closely conforms to the recent Scandinavian and Continental practice and to some of the earlier American schemes. The development is in the form of nine rectangular tower blocks of 14 to 16 storeys in height and the extremely economical arrangement in the individual block with eight flats to the typical floor, served by a single staircase and a pair of lifts.

The flat units are either one-bedroom or two-bedroom in equal numbers. Although compact planning of small units such as this is by no means as difficult as in the case of planning large family flats, the planning arrangement in this instance is extremely ingenious and apart from the questionable feature of the internal kitchens with indirect lighting and mechanical ventilation the flats are conveniently arranged in a way that provides the maximum privacy.

It will also be observed that in all the flats access to bedrooms is through the living room, an arrangement similar to that permitted in many Continental countries and one that entirely eliminates the need for wasteful internal circulation areas and lobbies.

99 Commonwealth Avenue, Boston, U.S.

:hitects: S. Glaser Associates

single slab block planned for a limited site in inner urban area, 17 floors in height, and with flats—each typical floor containing 7 flats, cessible from linked lifts and staircases. :chens as well as bathrooms depend on chanical ventilation. An underground garage floors) for 124 cars and four medical offices also included.

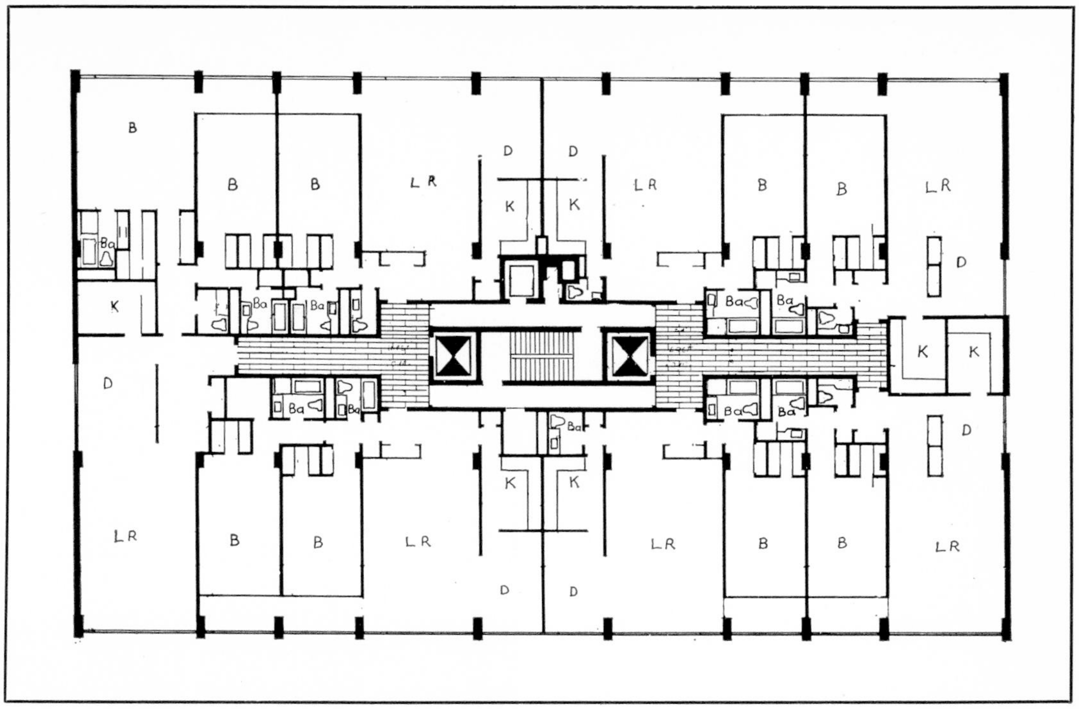

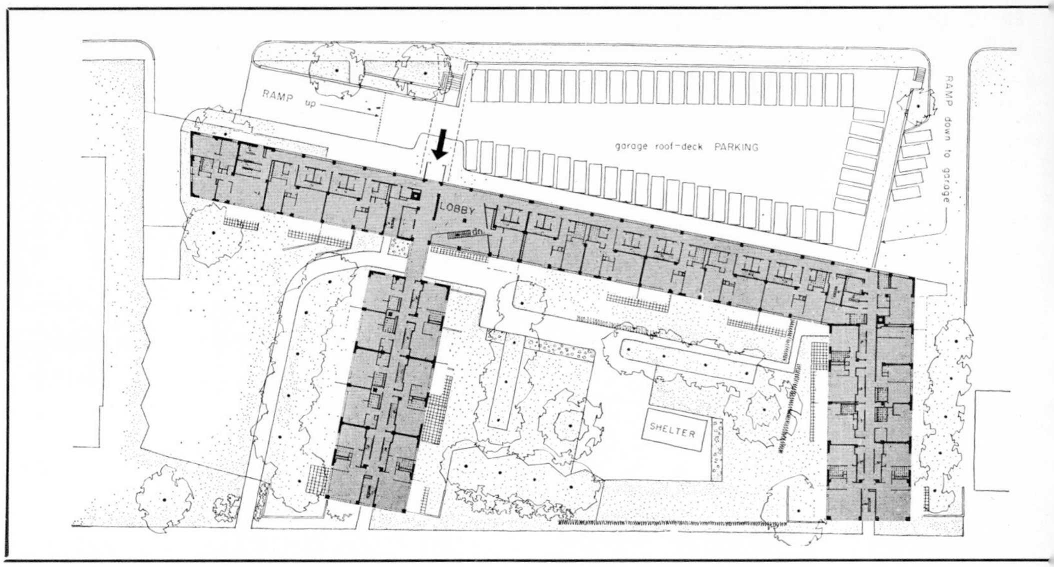

14 Eastgate, Boston, U.S.

Architects: W. H. Brown, C. Koch, Kennedy, de Mars, and Rapson

This unusual scheme containing 261 flats has been planned on a magnificent Charles River frontage and has a series of linked slab blocks utilizing the skip stop principle. Access corridor and lift stops occur at every third floor level and a full flight of stairs within each flat gives access to the upper and lower level from the access balcony which is incidentally fully enclosed, thereby eliminating any possibility of cross ventilation at the access levels.

This form of planning has another defect in that the access corridor passes over the bedrooms in the floor below in each case, which even with first-class standards of insulation cannot ever be a really satisfactory arrangement.

The blocks contain 12 habitable floors with 10 flats to the floor in the main block and five flats per floor in each of the projecting blocks. Some economies will result from the limitation of access from the lifts but additional costs occur with private staircase to two-thirds of the flats as well as having the main access staircase running the full height of the building.

An attractive scheme visually, with much of the character depending on the use of projecting balconies, which however in a number of cases have only a light dividing screen. Overshadowing the living rooms by these balconies also appears to be a problem.

The planning of the individual flats is good, with a minimum of waste circulation area, and with naturally lit and ventilated kitchens with splendid outlook. Unfortunately, however, there is bound to be some overlooking between the flats in the main block and those located in the wings in close proximity to them.

Beaumont Towers, Detroit

rchitects: Begrow and Brown Associates, with ickel and Moody

nree 30-, 17- and 12-storey tower blocks in a owntown area, providing a total of 680 dwell-gs; including one and two bedrooms and ficiency units. The typical floor contains flats with central corridor access, served by oor lifts and two staircases. All kitchens and athrooms are planned internally.

Balconies are glazed in with sliding panels nd form an all-weather room extension.

Flats are included at groundfloor level, as ell as a separate large shopping centre, araging for 692 cars, professional offices, staurant, children's pool, gardens, tennis and andball courts on a raised mall.

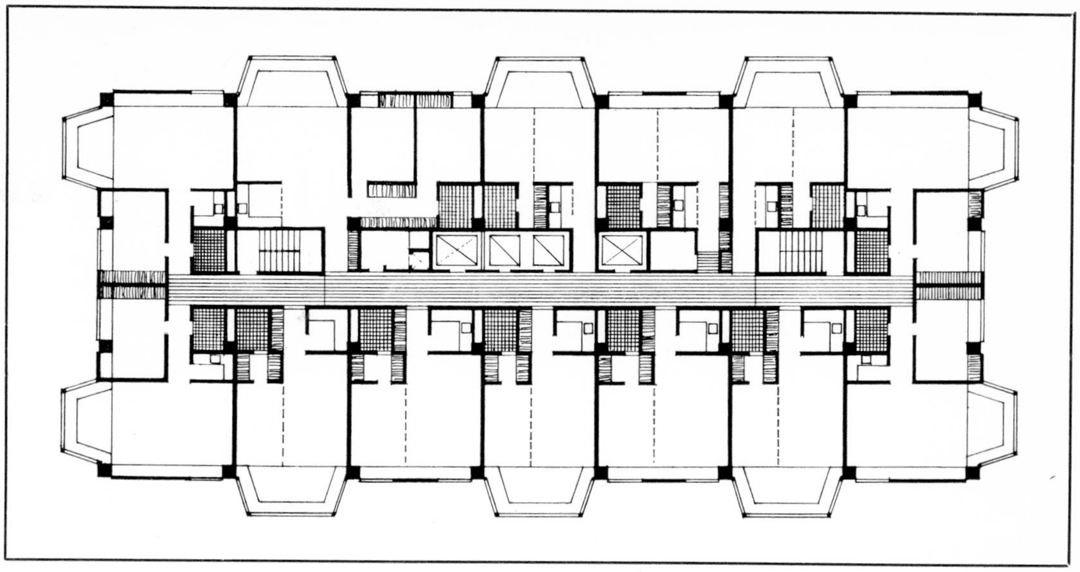

16 'The James Whitcomb Riley Centre', Indianapolis

Architects: Perkins and Will

A central city site of 20 acres developed with a total of 1842 dwellings of various sizes in the form of five 'Crown' towers, eight 'Twin' towers, ten twin house units, and in addition a restaurant, a theatre on Riley Plaza, two Clubs, an outdoor concert arena, swimming pool and tennis courts.

In each cluster a parking garage is also provided and all these are carefully landscaped. The Crown Towers have six flats to the typical floor served by twin lifts and stairs, two of these being studio flats. All have private balconies. The Twin Towers served by central corridor access, three lifts and internal staircases have 16 flats to the typical floor.

This is a very fine example of comprehensively integrated civic design of the most imaginative variety.

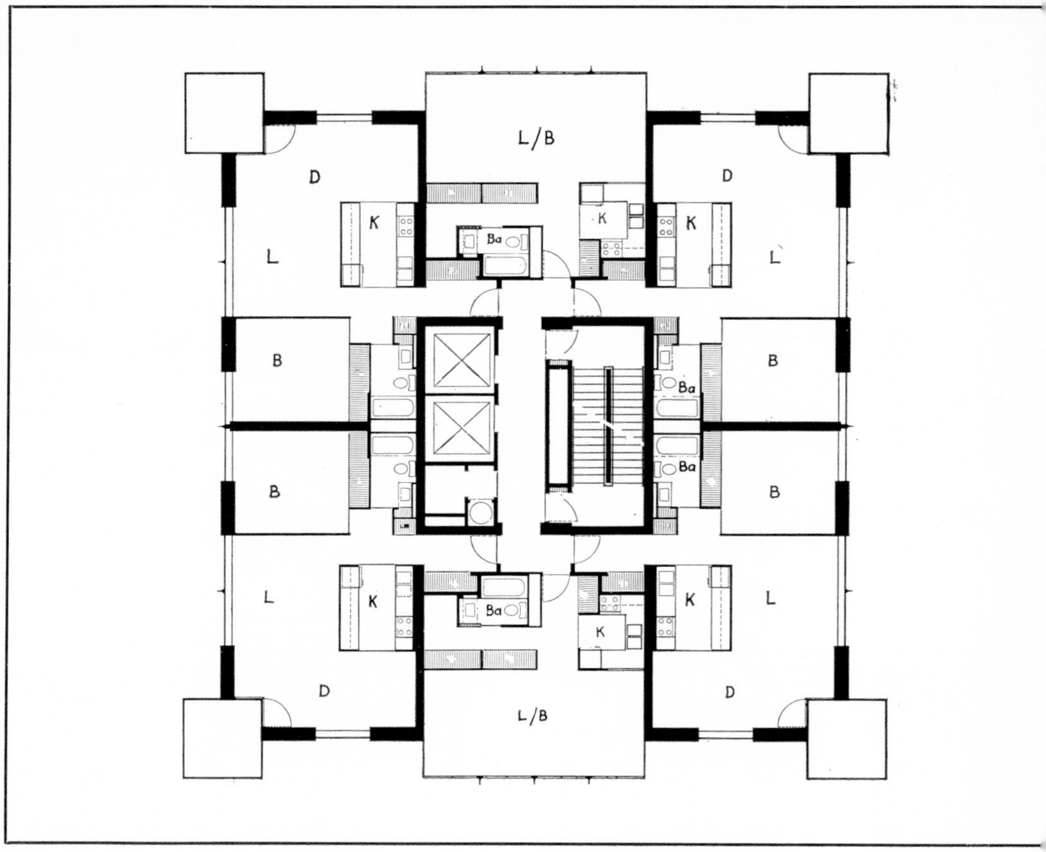

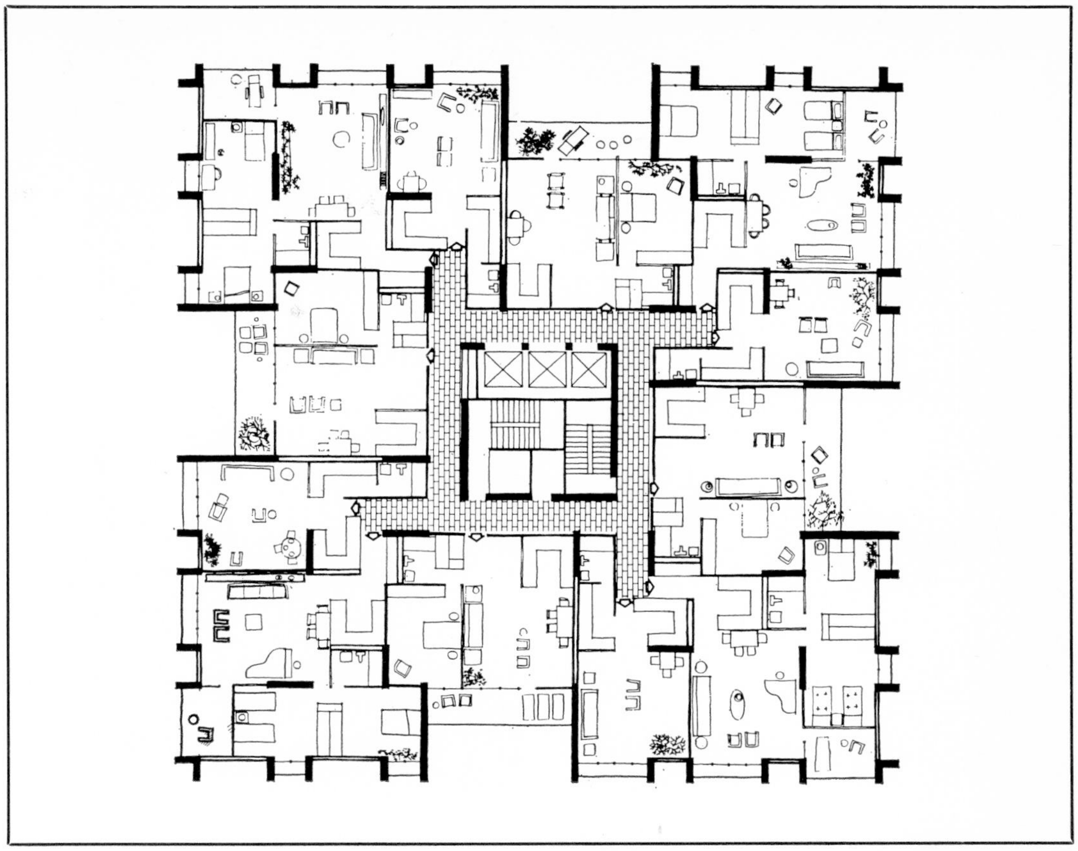

St. Louis Hills' Towers

ʳchitects: Hellmuth, Obata and Kassabaum

ɔur 20-storey flat tower blocks on a 13-acre site the heart of a residential and shopping area, cost $16 million.

The individual towers constructed in re-forced concrete are very compactly and geniously planned with 12 flats to the typical ɔor and almost direct access from central aircases and triple lift core, which also contains ı open 'smoke tower'. Planning is based on a ft module and structure suited to a variety of youts.

Intended as upper middle-means dwellings. ost kitchens are open-planned and with inter-al bathrooms mechanically ventilated. One-ɹndred per cent car parking is provided—rgely on surface.

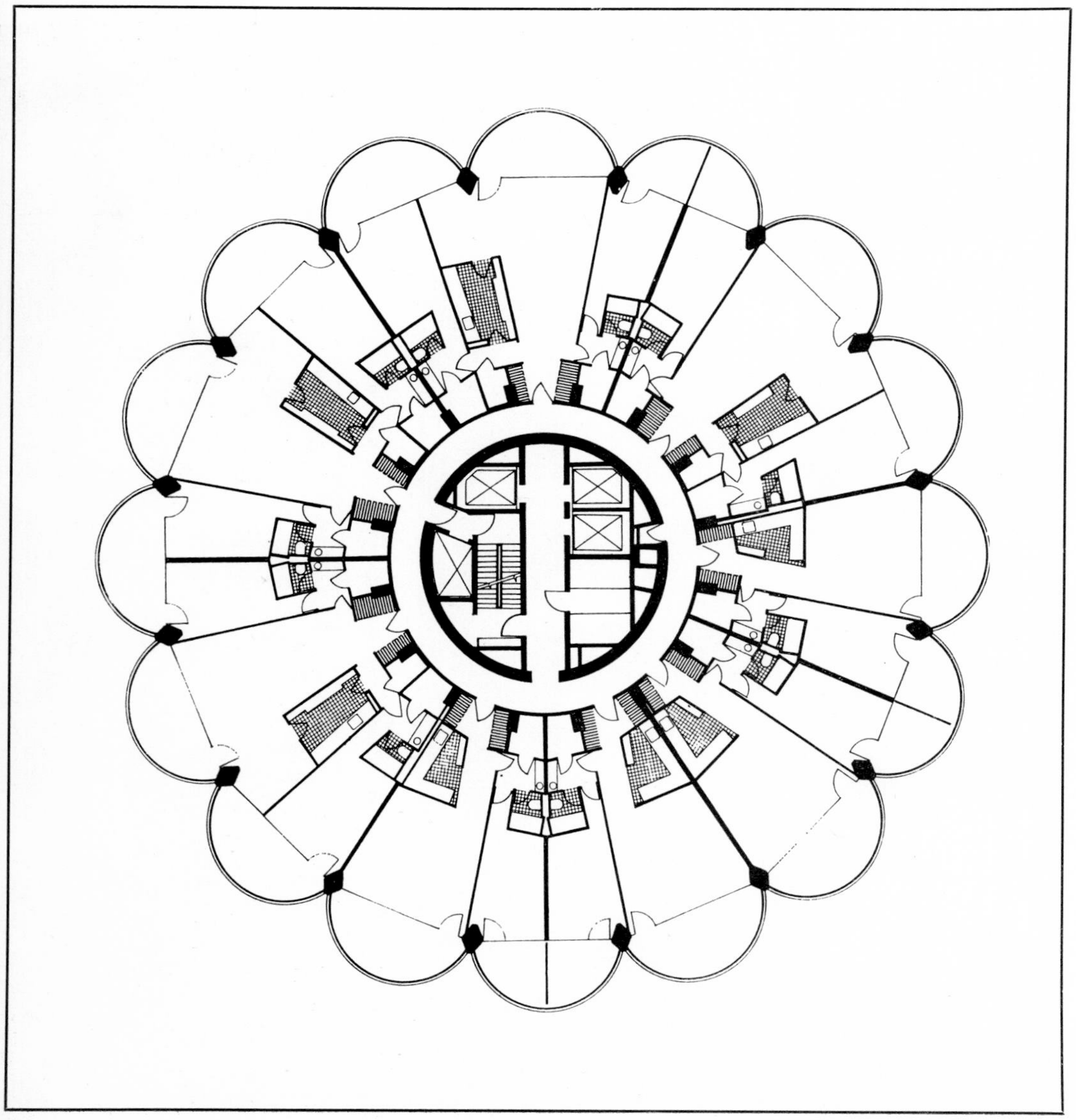

18 Marina City, Chicago

Architects: Bertrand Goldberg

The twin 60-storey towers in this scheme are tl highest apartment buildings in the world. The contain 19 storeys of parking and abov 40 storeys of flats.

Each of the flats, segmental in shape, served by five lifts and twin staircases in th central core and has its own large curved ba cony with a view over Lake Michigan or dow town; although perhaps there is some loss privacy where balconies adjoin. Construction of reinforced concrete with the core carrie out with sliding formwork.

Located on a site of just over three acres th self-contained community constitutes a comple renewal project in a run-down congested centr area; probably the most ambitious ever co ceived.

It includes a 10-floor office building, a 700-bo marina, swimming pool, ice-rink, gymnasiur bowling alley, 1250-seat theatre, a large aud torium and a shopping precinct.

These are all additional to the living spac provided in the two large circular tower buil ings, and the car parking, laundries, and tenan storage.

There are 256 single room flats; 576 on bedroom and 64 two-bedroom units; a total 896.

The circular service core contains in additio to the five lifts—two of which serve the lower 4 floors, staircases, smoke duct and rubbis chute as well as electrical and plumbin services. Construction generally is in reinforce concrete.

Overall cost: $36 *millior*

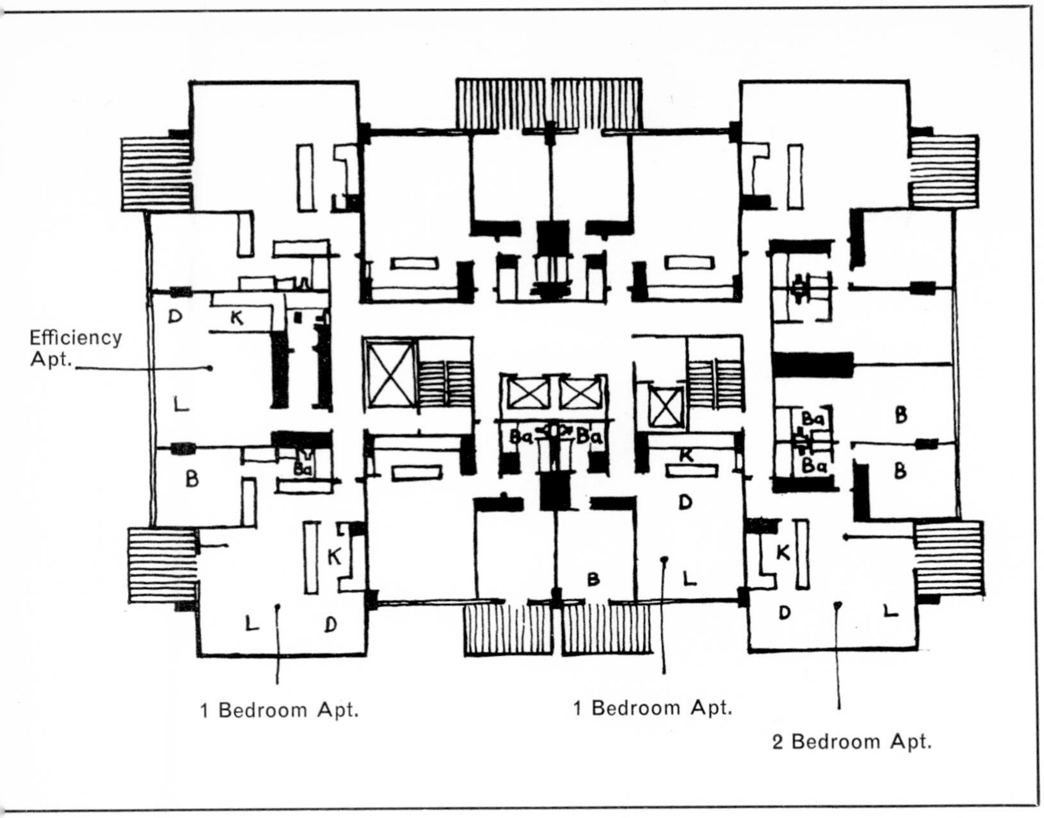

19 Ocean Park, Santa Monica

Architects: Welton Becket and Associates.
Kern County Land Co., Del E. Webb Corporation, Developers

Redevelopment of a downtown blighted area to provide 2000 dwellings, in four 21-storey and four 13-storey blocks. Surrounding these are clustered garden apartments with a large central park on the site of 18 acres.

Cars are mainly garaged underground preserving site area for garden layouts, swimming pools, tennis courts, library, nursery, shopping centre, restaurant and boat marina. Adjoining is another site of 18 acres with old people's flats, office and professional buildings and garages, one of the best examples of current high density comprehensive development planning techniques in the United States, showing a most sympathetic relationship of building groups and spaces with aesthetic refinement.

20 Tower East, New York City

Architects: Emery Roth and Sons

A luxury 35-storey point block with 25 per ce[nt] site coverage; and planned with four flats to th[e] typical floor.

The structural system is flat slab reinforce[d] concrete with exposed concrete columns a[nd] shear walls. On the east and west facad[es] aluminium duranodic panels have been used.

The whole building is air-conditioned.

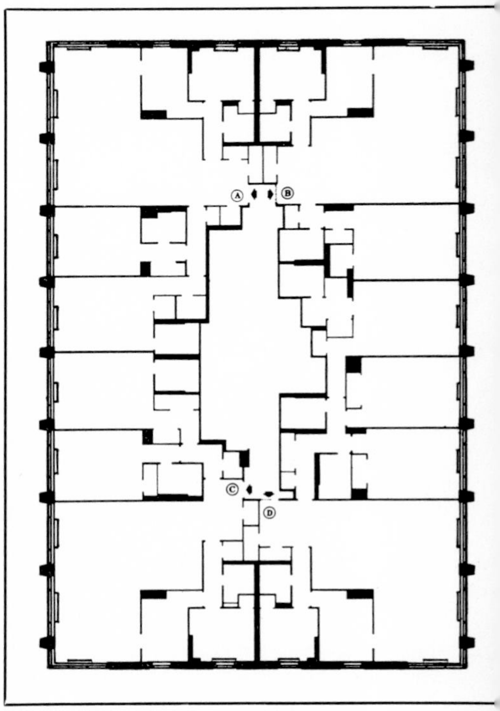

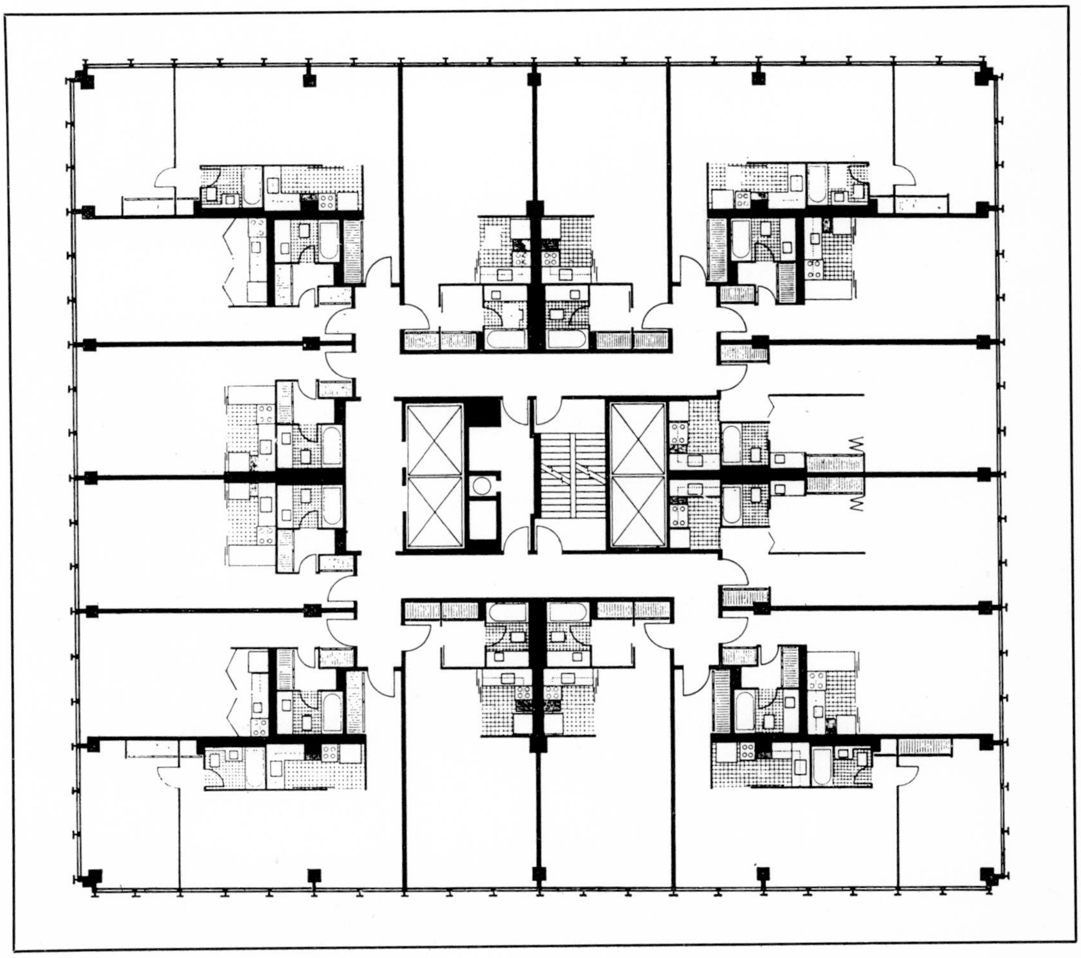

Lake View, Chicago

chitect: Mies van der Rohe

29-storey luxury block of flats overlooking ke Michigan. Its authorship is clearly recog-able and the building has in fact much in mmon with others by the same architect.

Ground floor level is occupied solely by a azed entrance hall and lift lobby as at Lake-ore Drive.

Four lifts are justified in this instance by the be of accommodation and the building height. nly two of these however serve each floor vel. From the 3rd to the 11th floors flats have e or two rooms with 16 units to the typical or accessible from the compact service re and circulation corridor. All dwellings ve both internal kitchens and bathrooms.

From the 12th to the 18th floor are 3-room flats; ght to the typical floor. Again in this instance ternal kitchens are adopted. From the 19th to e 30th floor there are 12 flats to the typical oor each with four rooms.

22 River Park, S.W. Washington

Architect: C. N. Goodman & Assoc. M.

This project consists of 518 dwellings including 134 town houses all built for sale, in the majority of cases to meet the needs of low and middle income groups, at an overall cost of $\$10\frac{1}{2}$ mill. An outstanding development it is part of an even bigger clearance and renewal operation being undertaken on a site that was once covered with slum property and will ultimately cost \$500 mill. Other parts of the development are being designed by other architects and undertaken by a number of different developers.

23 Golden Gateway Development, San Francisco

Architects: Wurster, Bernardi and Emmons, De Mars and Reay, Anshen and Allen, Belluschi, Warnecke, Skidmore Owings and Merrill.

$100 mill. development now under construction near the well-known Telegraph Hill and built on the site of a run down city market. This project which when completed will include 5 tower blocks 25 storeys in height and 3, 22-storey slab blocks with groups of town and patio houses, landscaped plazas, shopping arcades and parking garages, has been well described as a thoughtfully designed town community with an atmosphere of sophisticated urbanity.

24 Carl Sandburg Village, near Chicago

Architects: Cordwell and Partners

This fine development only five minutes from downtown Chicago located on bus and subway routes is the first big stage of an area renewal operation. In addition to the 6 multi-storey tower blocks of apartments a number of town houses and patio house groups are attractively linked together with formal courts and plazas. An underground garage extends over most of the site area and has permitted a spacious quality in the layout even at the high densities prevailing.

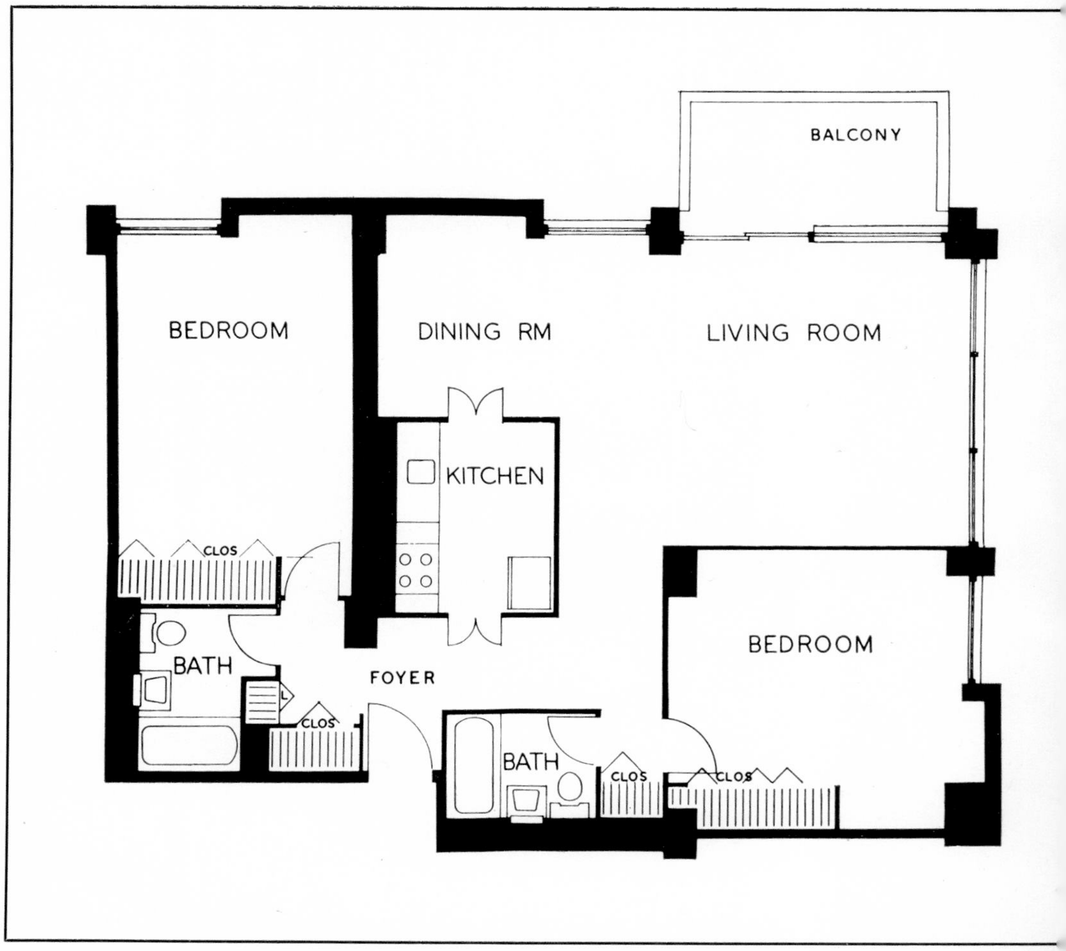

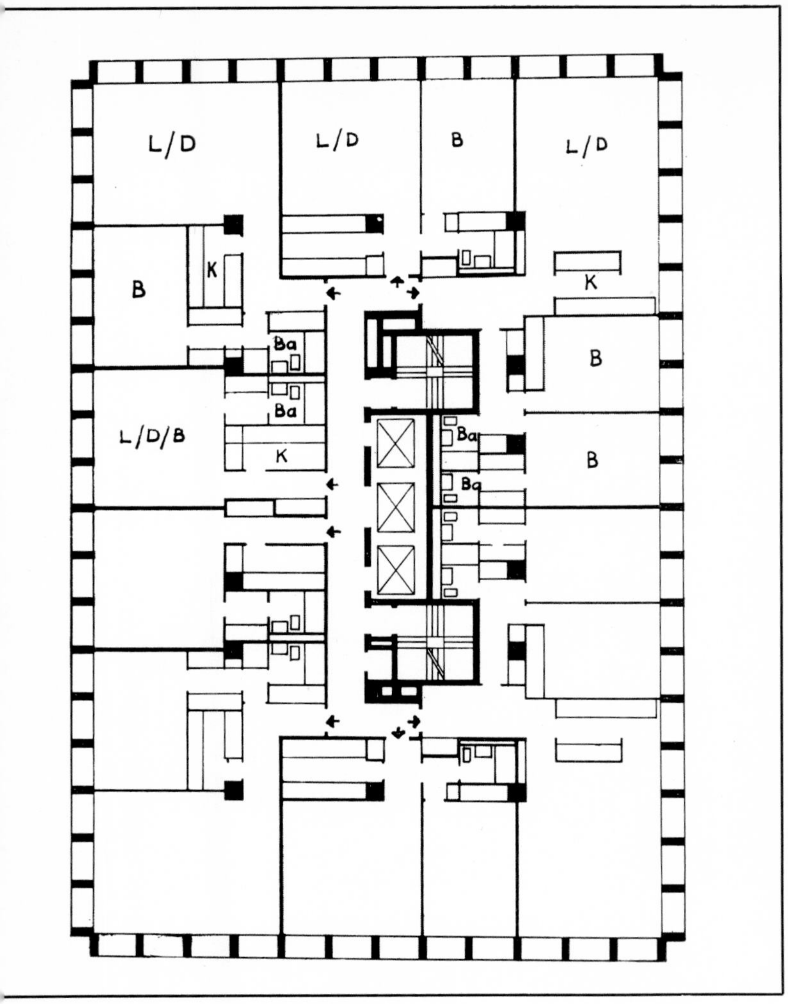

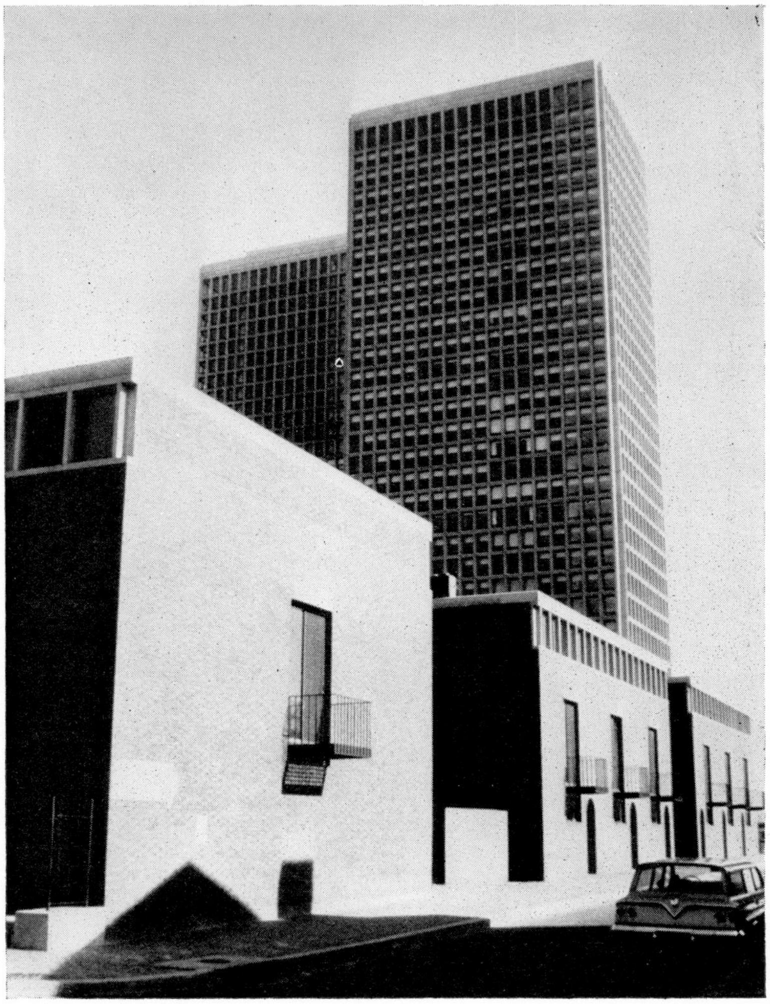

Society Hill, Philadelphia

hitect: I. M. Pei

important early stage in a large area renewal gramme on the site of an old city market nting the Delaware river. This stage consists , 32-storey tower blocks and a group of town uses closely linked with a conservation area older rehabilitated properties. Each tower ck contains 240 dwellings.

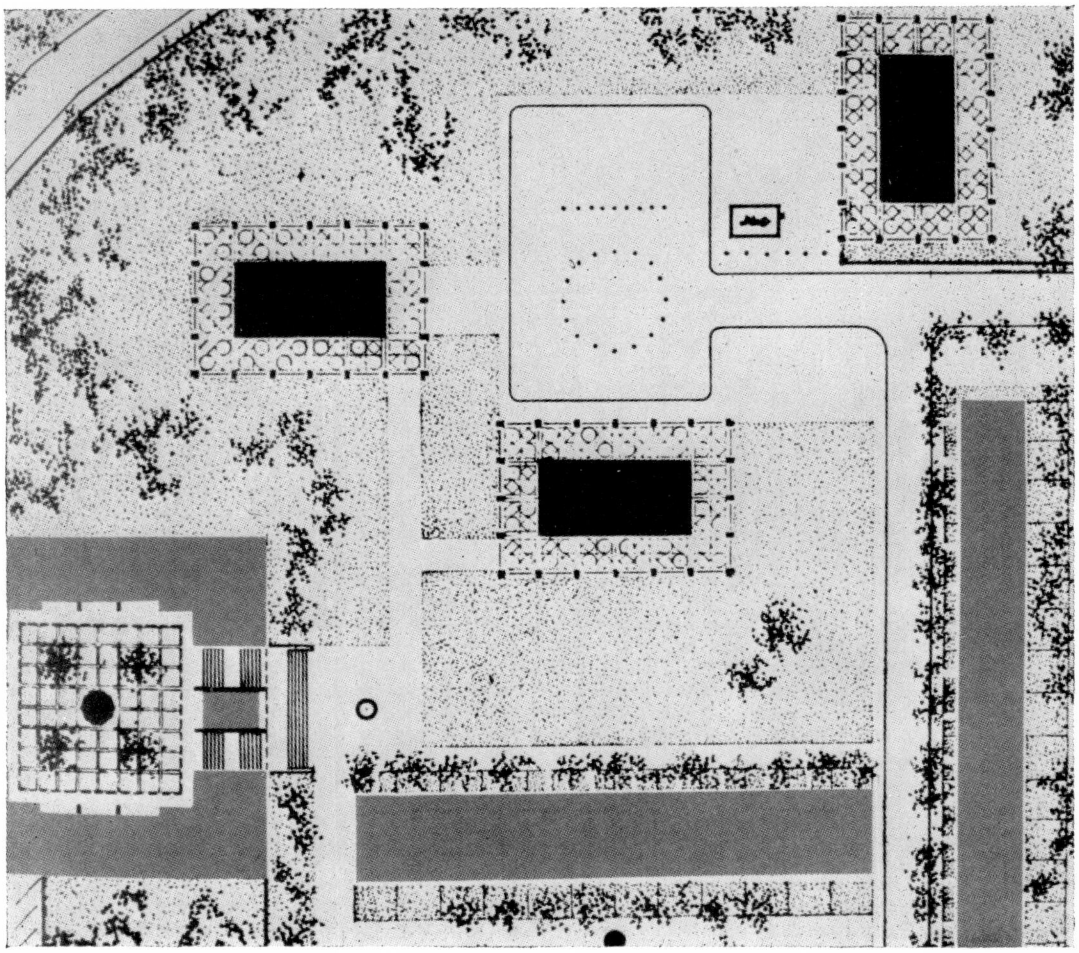

26 Hopkinson House, Washington Square Philadelphia

Architects: Stonorov and Haws

Also part of the Philadelphia South renewal area adjoining Independence Hall and the Mall area. Includes a 33-storey block containing 596 apartments and 18 family apartments on 3-storey blocks adjoining.

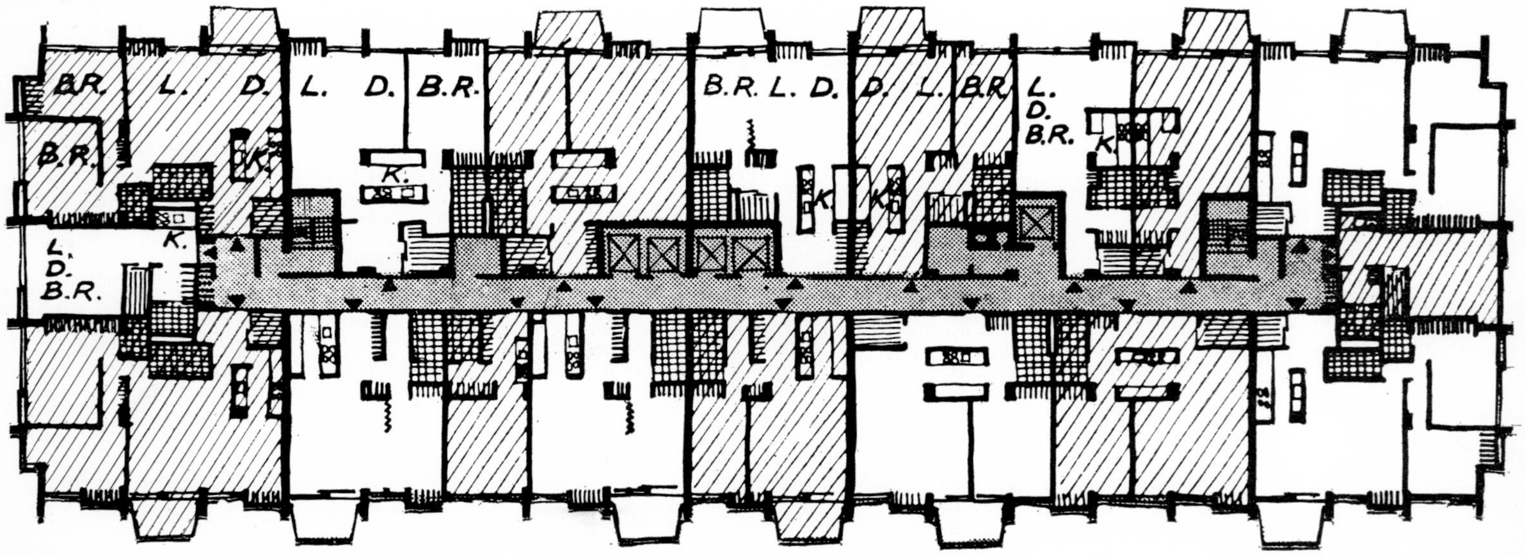

St. Francis Square, San Francisco

lso known as the Western Addition Develop-
ent.)
ll include when completed 1400 moderately
ced dwellings as well as a group of apartments
elderly people and a substantial number of
habilitated properties all constructed on a
ce badly blighted area. A fine example of the
ouping together of dwellings of different types.

Index

[redacted]